TURNING PAGES

The Extraordinary Autobiography
of
Ron Ramdin

VOLUME TWO

Compass

CONTENTS

PART FOUR: TURNING PAGES: LITERARY QUESTS, MEANINGFUL THOUGHTS

Library Building, St Pancras: My Shock! -
Ends and Beginnings

POSTSCRIPT

Acknowledgements

EIGHTEEN

SEVILLE, AT LAST - FILM AND BOOKS

By the turn of 1990, and ever since my arrival, I continued to hear talk at work and elsewhere about holidays in Spain for British people. 'Viva Espana' was a common expression and, for some who had experience of the Spanish sunshine, such breaks were treats. Although I'd been in England for some 28 years, only now was my interest in Spain enlivened. I was, at the time, researching a novel about Bartolome de Las Casas, the 'humanitarian,' Priest and Scholar, who was born in Seville, the home town of my friend Marisa. From the books and pictures of Seville which she had showed to me, I was quickly sold on the idea of visiting the city. Seville struck me as a pretty name ever since I'd first read and heard about it in my schooldays when I learned that Trinidad became a Spanish possession following its discovery by Christopher Columbus in 1498.

Eventually, with Marisa, I made my first visit to Spain in 1990. After landing in Torremolinos in the late afternoon, the evening was a magical experience. Compared with England, everything was so different: It was warm, almost tropical and I felt strangely elated; a sense of being at one with the place. In the deepening darkness as dusk fell, from the Sixth Floor window of the Hotel Al-Andalus looking down at the lit aquamarine pool below, I heard the strum of a guitar, a sound which for some reason both excited and disturbed me. Later, Marisa and I went out and spent a marvellous night in the Feria (Fair).

Early the next morning, we went to the beach before travelling to Malaga where we took the train to Seville. The journey and approach to the city was, to say the least, memorable.

When the train stopped at Seville Station, I was thrilled to be there and to meet Margarita, Marisa's elder sister, who took us to her Seventh floor flat.

In Seville, I witnessed the *Holy Week* processions and enjoyed my friends' warm hospitality. The newness of the surroundings, the squares, gardens and churches, the cafes and bars, the fine weather, the people and gaiety of life day and night were intoxicating. I was introduced to Brian and Mike of the University of Seville and had donated three books to the University's Library. Before I left the beautiful, historic city, Brian invited me to come back and deliver a Lecture to students in the University's English Department. I agreed. In the days that followed, I was happy to be in Seville for here though acutely conscious of the present, I was also powerfully drawn to the past. Certain thoughts were insistent. For example, Trinidad, Columbus and his introduction of the sugar cane plant from which the plantation system of sugar production in the New World was derived. I considered the connectedness of the island, the Explorer, India, the 'New world' he thought he'd reached, the 'plant' and why I had migrated to England.

In all, being in Seville and Spain was an eye-opener: With a freshness that surprised me, it generated a new and greater awareness of my personal history. In this relaxed environment (my first proper holiday!) far away from London I was able to gain a clearer perspective of my life. If Britain was important, so too was its imperial predecessor Spain. As if everything was on hold, now I thought also of the many and quick decisions that I had had to make since leaving Trinidad; indeed the relentlesss activity that had characterised my life. Then one morning as I sipped a 'Seville (Sevilleanos) coffee' (which I enjoyed very much) suddenly, as if it was for the first time, I dwelt on the fact that I was a *'driven man.'* This characteristic of my life's journey thus far, engendered positive feelings. With my thoughts never far away from writing (note-taking wherever I went), I warmed to the fact that my new book *The World in View: West Indies* was due to be published a few months hence. And while I continued to work on the 'Monograph' on East Indians in the Caribbean for the publisher Macmillan, I was thrilled by the prospects of returning to Seville in the New Year.

On my return to London, a letter informed me that Mervyn Assam, the High Commissioner of Trinidad and Tobago, initiator of the 'Annual Awards,' was leaving London. My relations with him were good and, during his tenure, I was selected to sit on a 'Think-Tank' that he'd set up to promote investment and business in relation to Trinidad and Tobago.

'Obviously I had not received your letter of 13 March when we had met at the Foreign Office Reception on Thursday,' I wrote. *'Your term of Office at the High Commission has clearly been a period of exceptional activity; a time when your guidance and foresight in sum, your leadership, reflecting certain qualities unique to Trinidadians and Tobagonians evoked an instantaneous warmth, camaraderie and sense of pride which made a significant impression on me. I am very pleased to have been associated with you and I feel confident that you will receive the unflagging support that had, on balance, attended you here in London, on your next appointment.*

I extend to you and Mrs Assam my warmest best wishes for the future.'

In relation to affairs in Trinidad, following my letter to Mr Assam, I received one from Pa. He apologized for not writing earlier and informed me: *'…we are having a hard time with the new Value Added Tax (VAT) the government introduced…it is very distressing to us, sometimes when I get my Pension, by the time I pay the Telephone and Light Bill very little remains…somehow we trying to survive, only time will tell what they will introduce next…'*

Such news, 28 years on, underlined why every Easter and Christmas I continued to send Pa and Ma money to help with household matters which, I felt even now, justified my migration.

Taken together, thus far I'd been drawn deeper into the literary world and its various publications, including compilations. As the author of a few titles, by April 1990, I was again informed of my entries in at least two Directories: *The International Authors Who's Who* and *Contemporary Authors.* These listings with my peers were a mark of my standing as an author. As if to confirm my inclusion in these Directories, after pressing and hoping for a reprint of *The Making of the Black Working Class in Britain,* I received a letter from

Scolar Press, now part of Gower Publishing Company: *'Some time ago you were informed that The Making of the Black Working Class in Britain was to be put "out of print." As a result of some changes within the company we have been looking again at various titles, including yours. As a result, we have decided to bind the remaining 250 copies which we have in sheet stock and place the book under the Scolar Press imprint of Gower for Sales purposes.*

I am sure you will agree that this news is good and I look forward to seeing this valuable book being made available once more'.

Good, I thought. The decision by Scolar Press to issue 'this valuable book' was a vote of confidence which, for a short while at least, would keep the book in print.

Meanwhile, doubts about my 'Black Odyssey' film project nagged me. In particular, I felt the need to make clear my position. In the summer of 1990, I wrote to Eric Davidson:

'Thanks for your call on Friday. Here is my present position which you said you need to know. After working on my original idea for a TV Series based on The Making of the Black Working Class in Britain for at least two years, through Nick Ardizzone, you were introduced to me and my project. Since then I have produced an enormous amount of time-consuming work to develop the Series "BLACK ODYSSEY" (significantly entirely on a voluntary, part-time basis - for love of the project!) and given the... pressure of work and the lack of Funding, I now feel that I cannot continue my work on the Series any further! I may, however, wish to reactivate it within a few months to a year, when I may consider approaching you.

I want to take the opportunity of thanking you for the practical assistance you have afforded me. I am grateful for the interest you have shown in my project and I regret that due to circumstances beyond my control I would not be able to take it any further...'

A few days later, I informed Jocelyn Barrow about my decision relating to BLACK ODYSSEY: *'Since our initial funding meeting, over a year ago, Eric Davidson (who had recently been introduced to me and my project) had been in touch with you... directly. Given the changed circumstances in my relationship with Mr Davidson, I shall be grateful if you would deal with me directly sending all communications on the funding of BLACK ODYSSEY at the above address.*

I hope by now you would have secured the additional £5000 (Funding) and I look forward to hearing from you.'

These two letters cleared the air for me and I felt the film proposal should, for the time being, remain on hold. There was more going on in my life than the 'Black Odyssey' project.

Having passed my forty-eighth birthday, Professor Hennessy, Director of the Centre for Caribbean Studies at Warwick University wrote: *'Congratulations on your Award - I tried to find you last night but to no avail. I wanted to see how the book "The History of the Indo-Caribbean People" was coming on. We are keen to get it into the 1991 Indo-Caribbean series - together with the collection of Essays rising out of the symposium. Steve Vertovec's and possibly one other - to coincide with the launching of the new Centre for Research in Asian Migration at Warwick!*

The exam period is just about finishing so I will try and phone you in the next few days or you could try me.'

I responded immediately to this letter. The 'History' referred to was in fact the 'Monograph.' which I'd titled : 'Survivors of Another Crossing.' I duly posted a copy of the manuscript to Professor Hennessy.

Soon after, I had heard from Curtis Brown about my idea for a book on C.L.R James. Literary Agent Anne McDermid wrote: *'I've been trying to contact you for a little while. I wanted to talk to you about the possibility of your doing a biography of CLR James. I think this could be a superb project for you. I am away until the 25th of June, could you please ring me then? Anne McDermid.'*

As I had said to C.L.R James when we last met in Brixton: 'After Paul Robeson, a biography of you is a book that I'd like to write.' James was very pleased about my interest in writing about him.

Apart from my fifth and twenty-first birthdays, I very rarely celebrated. Now that day had come again and I received a very unusual present; a copy of *The Sunday Times* (Est 1822) for June 21 1942. This was not exactly the date of my birth, but it was close enough. The sender was Nisa Khan whose accompanying note read: *'THIS IS THE LAST AVAILABLE COPY IN THE COUNTRY!*

MANY HAPPY RETURNS.'
As an historian, I valued this archival copy highly. I also marvelled about that day in 1942 when I was hardly able to open my eyes, never mind being able to read. Now after the intervening years of reading and study, I was able to appraise and add new meaning to the headlines:

'TOBRUK FACING NEW SIEGE, Strong Garrison of British Troops.
AXIS COLUMNS TURN BACK NEAR BARDIA
Harassed On flank By Ritchie's Mobile Forces
From Leonard Mosley, 'Sunday Times' Special War Correspondent.'
NAZIS START NEW PURGE, 'Elements of Unrest,'
MASS ARRESTS IN AUSTRIA
RUSSIANS STILL HOLD ON AT SEVASTOPOL,
Battle In a "Captured" Town.
U.S TROOPS IN ENGLAND,
In Camps All Over the Country
Political notes
SHIPPING AND LIBYA
MPs ANXIOUS FOR INFORMATION
By Our Political Correspondent.
BRITAIN JOINS IN BLOWS AT JAPAN
Our Submarine Sink Three Big Supply Ships
HEAVY RAID ON RABOUL
From William Courtenay, 'Sunday Times' Special Correspondent.'

Reading these lines, and between them, I was reminded of John Watson's favourite subject: The Second World War, in particular, his role in 'Bomber Command,' the effects of which had damaged him psychologically; and once more, I remembered the very first words he'd spoken to me: 'Young man, have you ever faced a bullet?' Although I was not a uniformed or direct participant in the War, I think it is worth saying that in the far-flung outpost of Empire, I and my family were not immune from the effects of war-time 'rationing' and price rises that had so adversely affected my childhood.

On matters historical and contemporary, my thoughts were very much on the Caribbean. My book *The West Indies* which I dedicated to my son was published by Heinemann's Children Educational Books and distributed worldwide. With 12 chapters, 50 photographs (colour and black and white) and an Index, it was an attractively produced book. Under the heading 'Islands in the Sun', the book opens thus:

'The group of islands called the West Indies lies in an arc more than 2,700 kilometres (1700 miles) long, between North and South America. The islands run from Florida in the United States to the Venezuelan coast of South America. To the east and north east of the islands lie the Atlantic Ocean with the Caribbean Sea to the west and south. The waters of the Caribbean are warm and its currents are affected by the Trade Winds...

All the islands, except the Bahamas, fall into two main groups–the Greater Antilles and the Lesser Antilles...Another way of grouping the islands is by the main languages spoken. This can be English, Spanish, French or Dutch.'

After this Introduction, I informed school children in at least 20 countries about various aspects of the region through the following themes: 'The First West Indians; The Europeans Arrive; The Move to Independence; West Indian People Today; Agriculture; Industry, Trade and Transport; A Mixture of Religions; Education, Health and Welfare; Leisure and Sport; Music, Dance and Carnival.' Concluding with 'The Way forward,' I wrote:

'The West Indies has many problems but the growth of tourism as a major industry has brought the possibility of much greater prosperity. Well over a million tourists visit Jamaica each year, the Dominican Republic has about 800,000 and even the tiny island of Barbados has over 400,000. The islands... cannot depend entirely on tourism and so many are building up their industries. The Cayman Islands have nearly half a million visitors, but they and the Turk and Caicos Islands have become tax havens which encourages many wealthy people and companies to the islands.

Although the islands have achieved nationhood, they still have deep-seated economic and social problems. For example, there are loans to be repaid to foreign countries, and high unemployment.

Emigration has helped to ease unemployment, but the problem persists. The islands are under-developed, and this has attracted the superpowers, the United States of America and the Soviet Union to the region. In spite of this interest, the people of the West Indies still have to earn a living. The United States has strongly influenced some West Indian countries, while Soviet influence in Cuba has aroused feelings against the island. However, most West Indians would like to be completely independent. CARICOM and CARIFTA are attempts to bring people of the islands together to deal with their economic problems, and the future may see a much more united West Indies in every respect.'

As a passionate contributor to a better understanding of immigrants and immigration in relation to Britain, my profile was endorsed by a Hansib (*Caribbean Times)* Community Award during a lavish ceremony held at the London Hilton Hotel in Park Lane on Saturday 6 June 1990. This was a pleasant surprise on a glitzy London night when other Awardees included Lord David Pitt, Commonwealth Secretary-General Sir Sonny Ramphal, Lady Aileen Thomas and television newsreader Zainab Badawi. I was riding the crest of an ever-rising wave of popularity and the Awards that I'd received so far did me no harm.

Against this background, in furtherance of the C.L.R James biography, I wrote to Andrew Best, the high-ranking person at the Curtis Brown Literary Agency: '*I was very pleased to speak to you about the possibility of my writing the authorised biography of CLR James. As you requested, I attach a sketch of the main aspects of my background and work which I hope will provide the information you require to introduce me to Mr Robert Hill (Literary Executor of James's Estate)*

I hope we can meet with Anne (McDermid) to discuss further details of this exciting project soon.'

After sending this letter, while anticipating a response, I was in an up-beat frame of mind not only about the prospects of writing this book but also for a while at least, with life in general.

Juggling with projects at different stages of development, I travelled to Belgium to visit the European Parliament in Brussels with renewed hopes of securing funds for my proposed 'Black Odyssey' Television Series. Being in Brussels was a new and enjoyable experience: I breathed-in the cool air and was observant of the streets, the architecture, the people and language. As it was, the 'Black Odyssey' project was revived when Sharon Atkin and I went to the Parliament to lobby Mike Hindley, the British Member of the European Parliament. Sharon knew of the Parliament's funding bodies and, it was fortuitous that we had already submitted an 'Application' before arriving in Brussels. We were optimistic as we queued for our 'Passes' to enter the Parliament building. Sharon had secured her Pass, and it was my turn to stand on the marked spot facing a camera to have my photograph taken. After two flashes in quick succession, my Pass was made and handed to me. When I turned, I was facing the glass doors of the Entrance to the Parliament. At that moment, I was aware of a tall, slim gentleman walking straight towards me. He extended his hand: 'Hello! I'm Kenneth Galbraith,' he said.

'Hello!' I said, 'I am Ron Ramdin,' not betraying even a hint of awkwardness or surprise. To the right of the place where I and Mr Galbraith (whom I recognised as the eminent Professor of Economics and former American Ambassador to India) stood, was a crimson cordon, behind which several well-dressed Officials stood. One of the Officials rushed forward and greeted Mr Galbraith with a hand-shake.

They chatted and moved away. So did I, but in a different direction: I rejoined Sharon and we made our way to Mike Hindley's office. While we waited for one of the lifts to arrive, Professor Galbraith and the European Parliament's entourage drew closer. When the lift doors opened, Mr Galbraith walked in, I followed and found myself standing next to him when the doors closed. Recognising me, he said: 'And where might you be from?'

'I'm from London,' I answered, adding 'but I was born in Trinidad.' This seemed to matter little for he'd already identified me as 'Indian' and spoke about his time in India as United States Ambassador when John F. Kennedy was President. I told him I very much enjoyed his book *The Affluent Society.* (Indeed the readability of the book was pivotal in getting me interested in the subject of Economics!) By now, the European Parliament Officials who were standing nearest to Mr Galbraith, looked exasperated, but could do nothing to end the conversation until the lift stopped and the door opened.

The meeting with Mr Hindley was most interesting and positive. Afterwards, Sharon and I made our way into the inner sanctum of the European Parliament to hear Professor Galbraith's 'Keynote Address:' I listened with great interest to what was an elegantly presented 'Overview' of 'Europe and the World Economy.' Most economists, though very knowledgeable and clever, are often incapable of communicating what they know; in this respect Professor Galbraith was head and shoulders above them, so to speak.

Later, in relaxed mood, I strolled through the cobbled streets of the city, including the fish market area and ate in one of the fine restaurants. I tasted a few beers including 'Framoise' (strawberry-flavoured) and had coffee in the plush, very impressive Metropole Hotel where I tasted and enjoyed chocolate, both black and white, as never before. Happy to be in this great old city, I departed in an optimistic mood. Sharon and I felt we had made as persuasive a case for funding the Black Odyssey, as was possible.

Given my knowledge of Blacks, Asians and 'minorities' in Britain, I received a written request from Rozina Visram, the author of *Ayahs, Lascars and Princes.*

'Dear Ron,

This is a cry for help! I've been appointed as a part-time Researcher by the Museum of London's major project PEOPLING OF LONDON. The Project will comprise several elements, including an Exhibition in 1991.

One of the aims ...is to put the cultural and ethnic diversity of London's population in its historical context, to show that London's population has always been heterogenous and that all Londoners, old and new, are immigrants. The Exhibition would span the period from pre-history to the Present day and would look at all the different communities

*that have made up the cosmopolitan population of London through the
ages. I am to produce a brief by March 1992...*

*I wonder if I could draw on your expert knowledge to enable me to
locate relevant photographs, paintings, artefacts and objects, landmarks
around London (plaques, gravestones, buildings, street names, etc) and
other visual material that could be used in the Exhibition. I would,
of course acknowledge all help and guidance I receive! Community
contacts for oral history and other personal source material would also
be of great help. Any other help, guidance, suggestions too would be
very welcome. I hope I am not imposing on your time too much and
very much hope you can help me.'*

This 'cry for help' was understandable, because far too much had
been taken for granted about what was, and wasn't known about
the history of non-white newcomers in Britain. As an historian
and writer working in the British Library, I knew more than most
people about the Collections and unrivalled sources not only in
the Library, but also in other libraries and archives. So I responded
positively to Rozina's letter; and subsequently, time permitting, we
met whenever she visited the British Library.

A few months later, when the *Peopling of London* Exhibition had
eventually opened at the Museum of London, I was glad to attend;
and importantly to see how the long hidden aspects of the Black
and Asian presence in Britain were acknowledged and presented.
At the entrance to the Exhibition, writ large on a Panel, my name
was acknowledged as one of the Contributors. Ms Visram had
indeed recognised my overall work which spanned decades and I
thanked her for it.

Living and working in London, I had met a large number of people
from all walks of life. Among those with whom I socialised a great
deal at this time was Richard West, a well-known journalist who
wrote regularly for *The Spectator*. He was the author of many books,
including biographies of Tito of Yugoslavia and Daniel Defoe.

I was also pleased to be reacquainted with Alan Benns after a
three-year absence. He said he was still working at the New London
Theatre on Drury Lane. We discussed his 'film' of the Book
Launch in 1987 at the Trinidad and Tobago High Commission in

London and I congratulated him on the 'rough cut' edited half-hour programme entitled: *News From London*. Importantly, this version included my Interview with Hugh Lynch, the London Correspondent of the *Trinidad Express*. I quite liked the film which, to this day, is still unknown because I have never shown it either to the British or Trinidad television networks. If Alan's film was a revelation, when I viewed it again, I was struck by it as being good historical footage for a documentary. For the moment, it remains integral to my steadily expanding multi-media archive.

Through the medium of film and film-making, there was much going on. Some months earlier in August 1990 I received news from Terence Baker who contacted me on behalf of United Artists and Yorkshire Television about the pending production of the Hollywood-HBO film on Paul Robeson, based on my book. The excitement that I'd felt before, returned instantly. He wrote:

'Citadel Entertainment in America have done a development deal with Turner Television and at the moment they are trying to agree upon a screen writer. Everybody in Los Angeles still seem very keen on the project and I hope that when we have the Script, Turner will put it into production.
I shall keep you informed.
Best Wishes,
Yours sincerely,
Terence Baker.'

To say this was good news would be an under-statement. Recruiting a Screen Writer suggested that the film project had progressed.

After reading Mr Baker's letter (and bearing in mind the earlier 18 July 1989 communication from the American Attorneys at Law) I felt a little more confident now, especially when I read about the film's backing by such big American media names as 'Ted Turner' and 'HBO.' I had always felt and continued to hope that a great movie of Robeson's life and work would one day be made.

While mulling over the news from Hollywood, a request made during my visit to the European Parliament for documents relating to 'Racism and Fascism' came to fruition with the arrival of a bundle of papers from Brussels. This was timely, providing valuable material for future reference.

A week later, in mid-September, I had heard from Shirley Hamber, Publishing Manager of Macmillan regarding my 'Monograph' on East Indians in the Caribbean. 'I was delighted to hear from Alistair Hennessy,' she wrote, 'that you have completed work on your manuscript. I look forward to reading it...' That month, Heinemann had published *The West Indies* and I was very pleased indeed when I received my free copies. At once, this prompted reconsideration of the fact that this attractive-looking book would be an integral part of schools curriculums world-wide for children between the ages of 11-14, and I was imbued with a sense of achievement. In turn, I remembered my own predicament when I was that age trying to learn as much as I could before leaving school at fourteen. Now I marvelled that this book as part of Heinemann's *World in View* Series would be found in schools and libraries from New Zealand to Canada; from China to Chile. My feeling that young minds would see the illustrations, read the text and learn for the first time about the West Indies was hard to describe. I felt deeply responsible, but also pleased to be associated with such an educational resource.

Appropriately, with my thoughts very much on the West Indies, news came from my sister Annette.

'Its been quite a long time since I've last written, but I do hope that all is fine with you,' she wrote. *'Well, things are beginning to get back to normal now since the Coup (the attempted violent take-over by a radical group). The curfew is still in effect from 11.00 p.m to 5.00 a.m. It is a good thing that the curfew is in effect because the crime has dropped. However quite a lot of people are disobeying the law and breaking the curfew hours. Anyway we are all hoping that everything here works out for the best. Everyone at home is fine. Pa is okay and as usual keeps himself busy with little odds and ends around the home. Ma is fine, she doesn't seem to be getting sick as often as she used to! She is resting some more now since Jimmy's wife has returned home (to New York). Jimmy and his family are all fine. He has gotten back his job (as a Groom) at the (Union) Park and things seems a little promising for him, but I think it's up to him to make it worthwhile. David and his family are fine too. Kaye is expecting a baby at the end of next month. (Oct, Susie)... Right now I am four months pregnant*

and I would like to think that I have started at the right time after two years of marriage!

Well, we were in for a surprise when Ronnie called us from Canada. It was really nice hearing from him. His voice sounds just like yours! Joey wrote to us and said that Irma was there also. It must have been great for Joey, Keno and Lydia to have them there! Ronnie said that you both will be home (Trinidad) next year. I do hope that you all could make it for our parents Anniversary which is in March. We are planning to have a little celebration for them, so it would be even grand if all the children could be there. So let us know soon.

How is your job and the writing doing? It is really great to think how hard you have worked to accomplish what you have and one thing for sure it's something no one could take away from you! We are very proud of you...'

There was much information in this relatively short letter. I always felt fully updated after reading Annette's rare correspondence. But sad to say, one of the Government Ministers caught up in the violent 'Coup' in Trinidad was Mervyn Assam, the likeable former London High Commissioner. Having been the victim of physical violence, thankfully he survived.

While I continued to research C.L.R James's life, I was hopeful that my Agent would eventually land a good publishing contract; in other words, nothing less than full clearance from the Literary Executors to do the *authorised* biography. At last, I heard from Curtis Brown's Andrew Best, who was also one of the Literary Executors of the C.L.R James Estate.

'Dear Ron,

I am so very sorry to have been out of touch for so long. You were prompt to respond to my thought that it would be marvellous if you were to be CLR James's biographer. And what you had to say about yourself and about him was very attractive and entirely relevant. However, I have had a very tricky time over literally months in trying to steer through contracts for two further CLR James volumes. Sad to say, the difficulty has been principally that of a disagreement between literary Executors and the rest of us here.

I know that until the climate has changed it could be fully for me to introduce you to the literary executor, though I have mentioned your enthusiasm to the Executors themselves. We simply have to bide our time.

All Best,

Andrew Best,'

To be frank, I was no less hopeful than I'd been before receiving Mr Best's letter.

Educationally, respect for my books was evident in the growing number of invitations that I had been receiving over the months to speak on various platforms: schools, universities, libraries, museums and town halls. On 14 November 1990, Madge Dresser, Principal Lecturer in History at Bristol Polytechnic contacted me:

'Dear Ron,

Since our telephone conversation last month, during which you kindly agreed to come to Bristol to give a talk to our Bed (Bachelor of Education degree) Students, I have been sorting out or next Term's schedule.

Would you be able to come for a 12.00-1.30 Session on either Thursday 14th February or Thursday 21 February. The theme would be "Sources and Approaches to Afro-Caribbean History" - with particular emphasis to sources for Black British Historians. These students are studying history as an academic subject but will also be interested in how they can translate their interest to Primary School history teaching.'

As I read Ms Dresser's words, I thought of the cross-fertilization of my work (*The West Indies* book being a fine example) for such Teachers in training as she had referred to. She continued:

' They (the student body) are mainly English and Welsh though there will be a few British students of Jamaican and Dominican origin. I also plan to invite interested members from various Afro-Caribbean organisations in the city...

Thanks again for agreeing to come. When you write to confirm the date we can then sort out train times etc.

Looking forward to meeting you, I remain,

Sincerely Yours,

Madge.'

Ms Dresser was conversant with my various books and writings which she spoke about when eventually we met at the British Library. Alas the proposed 'Talk' in Bristol never happened!

By now, however, Talks, Lectures and media Interviews had become inseparable from the other activities of my life. I did my best not to turn down any educational opportunity for who knows how long the demand for my work/services would last! My public appearances were only occasionally funded, but when this happened, of course, it was helpful. In spite of my need for money, I continued to speak regularly at various institutions free-of-charge. As with my staff representations, I thought that the knowledge imparted (much of it new to my audiences) was in itself a good thing. But the hard reality was that financial difficulties persisted. Fortunately just before Christmas 1990, I had received the second part of my Publisher's 'Advance' for *The West Indies;* and once more, though money was absolutely necessary, while still employed, *it was not the driving force of my writing ambition.* For better or worse, this ingrained attitude of altruism or sense of public service, underscored my motivation.

A fortnight later, another sibling made contact. A rare letter arrived from my brother Joel who lived in Canada:

'Hope you Irma and Ronnie are in good health... This note is to let you know that Keno and I may be going to Trinidad for Carnival. We have booked a flight leaving Toronto on January 31st 1991. We will be staying approximately 3 weeks. As you know next year will be Pa and Ma's 50th Wedding Anniversary. If we all meet there it would be nice... Ronnie had expressed his interest. Please convey this message to him.

I know you are a very busy man and your schedule is tight. But it would be nice to see you again...'

The warmth characteristic of this brother was always fully appreciated; and I too felt it would be a pleasure to see both brothers. My immediate problem was how to find enough money to make our meeting possible.

Gradually as Book Reviews of *The West Indies* appeared, once more I was honoured when Bloomsbury Rare Books on Museum Street used its shop front window to mount a major display of multiple copies of my new book *World in View: West Indies*, as well as *The Making of the Black Working Class in Britain, Paul Robeson: The Man and His Mission* and *From Chattel Slave to Wage Earner*. It was a most impressive display which lasted at least four weeks. Passing the shop window with the throng of tourists and others often during that period did not lessen the magnitude of such publicity in book-oriented Bloomsbury. In addition to the nick-name: 'The Lenin of Museum Street,' this second display (as the books' international themes suggest) not only justified, but also extended my authorial reputation far beyond Bloomsbury!

With the approach of Christmas, my thoughts were focused on seeing my son; and of course, I ensured (as I'd been doing for nearly three decades) that some Christmas money was sent to my parents. But however good I'd felt about some things, by the end of the year, the blanket of coldness, plus the stress and strain of life took its toll.

In the new year 1991, I pressed on with cautious optimism. On 27 January, the Trinidad-born academic Selwyn Cudjoe wrote to me from Cornell University:

'Dear Ron,
Greeting! It was good seeing you and sharing meals together while I was in London. I think our coming together was important and my dearest wish is that we keep in touch on a regular basis. I'm yet to read your book (The Making of the Black Working Class in Britain) that I will. Also please remember to send me the Constantine book Cricket... that you promised to send me... please knock 'em dead at the Paris Conference. Please remember to send me one of the brochures of the Conference.
Please let me hear from you.
With Warm Regards,
Sincerely,
Selwyn Cudjoe.'

In and around the Central London areas: Bloomsbury, Covent Garden, Fitzrovia and Soho, I had met and conversed with a circle of writers, locals and people generally who poured in from different parts of the world. London, the 'world in a city' was becoming more so. Among those who visited the capital regularly was Paul Brunswick, an American, who came to London often from Palma de Mallorca, where he lived. He was a regular visitor to the Round Reading Room and was friendly with some of the people that I knew in Bloomsbury, including Professor David Coombs, Fred Read and Peter Brewer, who was a rare book dealer, among other things. Almost everyone and, it seemed, everything that interested me were book-oriented.

Having not seen Paul for a while, I received a letter from him. 'Doubt if you'll remember me,' he wrote, 'and I don't even know if you're still in the BM, but I'll take a chance. I last saw you in 1980 around Bloomsbury. I was the friend of the late Fred Read.'

'Late?' I was glad to hear from Paul, but shocked to learn of Fred's death. If hitherto no news was good news, this was bad news. I remembered Fred well; a man who underplayed his knowledge and with whom I appear in a photograph taken by star London photographer Harry Diamond. Contact with Paul reminded me of two other users of the Reading Room: Mr Martinez (a studious-looking middle-aged Spaniard) and a younger man from Chile, with straight, shoulder-length black hair, whose name eludes me. Paul's letter kindled memories of these men and younger friends like John Henderson. My friendship with John was, of course, closer and special because of his involvement as CSU Branch Chairman which began in 1975.

Now, with a combination of excitement and worry I rehearsed the opening words of my forthcoming Lecture: 'Towards 1992: Discovery, the Black Experience in Britain and Ethnic Minorities in Europe' to be given at the University of Seville: *'Buenos dias Senoras y Senores.'* Again and again I practised speaking these words, plus a few more by way of introduction before giving the Lecture in English. Just a few weeks in advance of my visit and the event (given the newness of such a theme to Spanish audiences)

I had hoped to get some wider public exposure in Spain. On 7 February 1991 I wrote to the Editor of *El Pais:*

'I am writing to you in connection with a lecture I have been invited to give at the University of Seville on 20 March 1991. On the eve of the 500th Anniversary of the arrival of Cristobal Colon in the New World and implementation of the unified European Market next year, it is indeed timely that the theme of my lecture is: "Towards 1992: Discovery, the Black Experience in Britain and Ethnic Minorities in Europe." I am hoping to deliver similar lectures elsewhere in Spain (Madrid and Barcelona universities) before considering invitations… at the Spanish Institute in London and the European Parliament in Brussels in 1992.

I shall be glad if prior to my lecture (or indeed during my two-week stay in Spain) you would consider publication of a profile/book Review article in your Books Section. I enclose a copy of the acclaimed book The Making of the Black Working Class in Britain… and a biographical sketch. I hope to be in Seville on 18 March and will be available for interview.'

In the last ten years, experience had taught me many things about public appearances and, as a foreign land, I took my pending visit to Spain all the more seriously. Feeling that it was an opportunity not to be missed, some publicity for the Lecture seemed appropriate. As it was, I received no response from the Editor of *El Pais*, either in relation to receipt of the book that I'd sent or to my request for publication of a 'Profile.'

Having first met the brilliant musician Tunde Jegede when he was a prodigy, now my friendship with him and his mother Galina had become a warm and interesting one. The 'Tea Rooms' on Museum Street was a regular meeting place and it was there that they first spoke to me about an *Inaugural* musical event which they hoped to stage in London. I had seen Tunde perform before; memorably at the Africa Centre when Armet Francis had launched *The Black Triangle,* essentially a book of photographs to which, as mentioned, I'd contributed the *Introduction.* That night, I was fascinated by what were the relatively new sounds of the Kora; an African musical instrument. As I listened, I recalled the opening words of my *Introduction*:

'At the outset, it must be emphasized that before Europeans came into permanent contact with Africans, a survey of the scene showed that there was "considerable unevenness of development" in Africa. There were, for example, social formations representing hunting bands, communalism, feudalism and several positions between communalism and feudalism...

Thus Africa in the fifteenth century, far from constituting a jumble of different tribes, displayed a pattern of historical movement... The feudal societies of Ethiopia and Egypt were at the forefront of evolutionary development...'

From these far-off days, my mind flashed forward to the more recent and troubled 1970s and 1980s and the post-war settlement of immigrants and their children in Britain. Significantly, and interestingly, the closing words of my *Introduction* framed my evolving philosophy of **difference:**

'The British race relations industry assure them all will be well, but of course the reality of the black experience is quite another story...Not surprisingly (black youths) "ghettoised" lives have led them to see Britain as Babylon and to seek freedom from oppression and an understanding of their historical roots in Africa. To Britain's Black youth in crisis, the music of Bob Marley and other reggae artists has brought black culture and the African heritage nearer to a living reality. The presence of the black working class in Britain, they realise, is the legacy of the Black Triangle.

In effect, slavery, colonialism and neo-colonialism have taken our forebears and us from one part of the Black Triangle to another. Ultimately, our presence was demanded in the Mother Country...In Britain and the Triangle, black people struggle to retain their cultural identity...In a real sense, whether in the periphery or the centre... The quietly disturbing faces of those in The Black Triangle at once confirm their predicament and their determination.'

Since that performance, Tunde, Galina and I were now considering another. We spoke about the British Premiere of African Classical Music to be held in The Purcell Room on the South Bank in London. After informing me of their intention, to begin with, they said they would like me to appear on stage and introduce the musicians in the Ensemble; and before the start of the second half of the Performance, give a brief 'Introduction' that would place African Classical music in its wider context. I accepted.

As part of my background research in preparation for what I had hoped to say, on 23 February, I wrote to Pearl Connor-Mogotsi, a West Indian Theatrical Agent in London and former wife of Trinidadian actor Edric Connor.

'Ms Marigold Robertson-Saul of the Trinidad and Tobago High Commission gave me your address after I had explained the nature of my enquiry...I write to you in the hope that you, more than anyone else I can think of, will be able to provide the information which I urgently need concerning an African Kora player named M.A.Jobarteh with whom you appeared at the Royal Festival Hall in 1962. (Please see attached copy of the Programme). Jobarteh is said to have studied in England. Do you know where? And more importantly, I'll be grateful for any information on him that you can provide...'

The 'Programme' I referred to was provisional and the subject of continuing discussion with Tunde and Galina as details on the performance of African Classical Music were being finalised. Understandably, there was much excitement surrounding the event for it was not only going to be the 'premiere' of African Classical Music in Britain, but also a first for me walking out on the famous stage of the Purcell Room, at the start of the performance. In the world of Classical Music few concert halls were as prestigious as this. I'd often heard about 'breaking the ice,' and this is exactly what I have been asked to do.

Part of my preparation for the second half presentation was re-reading an article *Musical Neo-colonialism* that I'd written a decade before. Informed by this framing context, I also drew on what I'd learned during my forays in the world of Show Business, especially and memorably when I'd Produced and Directed the historic Charity Show at the British Museum. Although that was an amateur production; even then, I felt, as concerts go, it could not get any better than this. Or could it? Now with the Purcell Room Performance looming ever larger, there was no question of its potential as an extraordinary event. Not surprisngly, my anticipation grew.

738 · TURNING PAGES · RON RAMDIN · VOLUME TWO

Adding to the Spring-time levity was a Book Review of *The West Indies* which appeared in the *Trinidad Sunday Guardian* on 3 March. Under the heading: *'Handy Reference for Information on Region'* by Ron Ramdin, the newspaper stated:

'*Coinciding with the CARICOM Economic Regional Conference last week was the publication of this new book on the West Indies...it covers not only the countries who are members of Caricom, but extends to include the French-and Spanish-speaking territories such as Cuba and the Dominican Republic as well as Martinique.*

It is a tightly written book of information, a short guide to the various islands with the unusual facts and figures on population, climate, area, language and so forth.

But it offers more, such as short essays on some of the historical mileposts of the region. He writes of the first West Indians - the Caribs and Arawaks - who were eventually overwhelmed by the European settlers. He deals with the arrival of African slaves and East Indian indentured labourers.

There is something about the social unrest of the 1930s, the Grenada revolution, the attempt to form a political Federation and the move to Independence. There is information on agriculture, trade, industry and the colourful culture of these islands.

This book does not by any means provide a comprehensive account of the West Indies, nor was it intended to do so. It serves its purpose, however, in that it is a handy reference for information on the West Indies.'

But in spite of the considerable success of this attractively produced world-class textbook, one Indo-Trinidadian Lecturer felt that *only* Caribbean-based specialists (school teachers) should write and publish such books about the Caribbean. How stupid and short-sighted, I thought. But sadly, time and again, I would come up against this kind of narrow-mindedness camouflaged as academic professionalism. By extension, there are those who think that only people of a certain 'race' or background should write their particular histories. Given that New World slavery and indentureship constituted my heritage (as my long-standing exploration of 'difference' gained clarity with each day and each book that engaged me!) I could not disagree more with such thinking for surely knowledge should not be bounded by 'race,' class, colour, gender, religion, 'nation' or geographical location, but by less totalising, more meaningful ideas and arguments in furtherance of the social good. The civic responsibility of everyone should be paramount.

A few days after reading the Trinidad *Sunday Guardian's* Review, the title of my 'Monograph' manuscript on East Indians in the Caribbean 'Survivors of Another Crossing' became a matter of concern when I learned that it was also the title of another book on the same subject of which I had no prior knowledge. When informed of this duplication, Macmillan's Shirley Hamber replied saying she had written to the author of the other book. *'I do understand your concern,'* she wrote, *'but if her book is already in print this must be a consideration. It is indeed a very good title and hopefully the matter will be resolved satisfactorily...*

I understand your manuscript is now with Alistair so doubtless I will be receiving it in the near future. I look forward to reading it.'

By now, I had already been thinking of alternative titles which, for the time being, I reasoned was best kept to myself.

After I'd read the *Sunday Guardian's* Review of *The West Indies,* I thought well of it. Primarily because writing such a book was a challenge. While researching it, I had uncovered material which gave me tantalising glimmers that led to investigation and a deeper understanding of my roots! Against this background of developing knowledge of the Caribbean, I saw more clearly the connectedness of things: of places, people and cultures in the region. Indeed for quite some time and during this thorough-going process, I recognised the importance of a longer and broader study than the 'Monograph,' the need for a comprehensive work that would fill a major historical gap. Would that be stretching ambition too far? Certainly not in my view. Almost immediately, I jotted down the working title of the book that I planned: 'A History of the Indo-Caribbean People.'

The presence and contribution of Indians in Trinidad was, but one proposition. Guyana was another, but so too were Surinam, Jamaica, Martinique, Guadeloupe, Grenada and St Vincent. The more I thought of this greater project, both in scope and depth, the more I began to see the enormity of the research required because it would encompass not only the British territories, but also the French, Dutch and Spanish Caribbean. As if this was not complex enough, my interest was necessarily extended to deal with the history and cultures of the Indo-Caribbean people over a longer period than had previously been attempted: From their arrival in 1838 to the 'Present' which was 1991. Towards this end, it was fortuitous that I'd already done a preliminary historical 'Over-view of Indians in the Caribbean' in the form of the 'Opening Paper' at the University of Warwick's 150th Anniversary Conference in 1988 as well as research for the 'Monograph.'

With each day, my interest in this study not only of my ancestors but also of my contemporaries deepened for it was a long time coming; a primary task of enormous proportion which I hoped would break *new* ground at many levels. Fortunately, at this stage, I never stopped either to think too much or too objectively; I needed to get on with things because it was the *doing* that mattered. So as I waited to hear from Macmillan what they felt about the 'Monograph,' like a man re-born, I proceeded with the research and writing of the envisaged comprehensive history of Indians in the Caribbean.

From the outset, my interest was to write a book that would reveal the long-standing presence of the Indo-Caribbean people. I wanted to show the continuing need for *labour* in the Caribbean – in essence the evolution from African slavery to East Indian Indentureship and the inter-cultural relationships between both groups that had, in turn, developed and evolved into the cultural mosaic that is the modern Caribbean.

While thus immersed, Professor Hennessy and his advisors/editors, the 'experts' deliberated. Eventually they decided against publishing the 'Monograph' that I had submitted. This decision came as a surprise, but having been already engaged in gathering sources (inclusive of Indo-Caribbean research since 1970) I had accumulated an impressive amount of research material. Like most interested persons, for some 20 years, I had known that little had been published in relation to 'East Indians'; and that the few existing studies were confined largely to Trinidad and Guyana. Put simply, there was no published work of Indians in the wider Caribbean. Hitherto through unrelenting efforts over the years I had already gained a great deal of knowledge derived from wide-ranging research, including some new sources; and I wondered what sources of research and knowledge had informed the 'experts' judgement and authority on my 'Monograph.' Professor Hennessy had said they (the Caribbean academics) wanted a 'winner' for the Warwick/Macmillan Caribbean Series. I was convinced I had one; and so through pursuing the book that now preoccupied me, I hoped to change the perception of Indo-Caribbean history and culture by retrieving it from being further marginalised, from being just a 'footnote' to its central place in Caribbean historiography.

Since leaving the London School of Economics and more generally the University of London, my scholarly work had progressed a great deal. But it was abundantly clear from here on, given the gate-keepers' no entry signal that I would have to continue with my new research work as an *independent* scholar and writer. With my path effectively blocked in the Warwick academic direction, in terms of scholarship, I took a new and necessarily more challenging route. By so doing another leaf was turned, so to speak, towards realising a much-needed book.

My first task now was to *rethink* the scope and structure of the work which I titled 'Arising From Bondage: A History of the Indo-Caribbean People.' The title was crucial for I thought that the book should reflect both a retelling and, a first telling! As time passed, I found more new sources and steadily accumulated bundles of material. Setting all this down in note form, then writing drafts was a mammoth job; necessary stages in the process of realising the final manuscript. Having more or less a clear sight of what the book could or should be was all well and good, but completing it, was quite another matter. Even though I had no commitment from a publisher (as was the case with *From Chattel Slave to Wage Earner*), for better or worse, I had already embarked on a journey from which there would be no return.

Increasingly as work progressed, the book became more complex and valuable. For one thing (and this was of great significance) since Emancipation in the West Indies, there had been no serious reference book on the history and culture of the region. In fact, it was abundantly clear to me that writing the story of the Indo-Caribbean people necessarily meant also telling (to some extent) the post-Emancipation story of the mix of cultural influences of Africans and their descendants and of indentured and post-Indentureship Indians and their descendants who, together with Europeans, their descendants and others, made up the Caribbean's cultural mosaic. This was certainly a tall order. Nonetheless, I embraced the challenge knowing it was not a book that could be rushed. On the contrary, I'd come to terms with the fact that it would take some time.

RETURN TO SPAIN:
A RARE LECTURE ON EUROPEAN
MULTICULTURALISM

Meanwhile, having been to Spain for the first time some months before, my thoughts were now very much on writing about the country. This idea gained further credence because I knew I would be returning to give a Lecture at the University of Seville. For sometime prior to my first visit, a work that had engaged me was a novel entitled *Sword and Quill: A Spanish Tale* based on the life of Bartolome de Las Casas. It was composed of two parts and fifteen chapters. The synopsis read:

'... *This inspiring tale... is tempered by a contradiction (so common a part of the human condition) that in spite of his heroic, multifaceted activities and his unwavering concern for freedom of the individual (in this case the conquered Indians) he nevertheless justifies his cause celebre, the freedom of one "race" (the Indians) by substituting the enslavement of another (the Africans). The narrator therefore uses the device of his "journal" to voluntarily come to peace with himself, to make amends for his mistake (the tragic consequences which he may have foreseen) in an otherwise exemplary life. This becomes a confessional, because incredible as it seems, none of his contemporaries were aware of his blunder! Thus the "Bishop of Chiapas," a scribe and champion of the oppressed, the first European humanitarian in the New World, in this novel, makes the "Journal" his last testament, not only to free himself and the Spanish sovereigns, but also his beloved Spain from everlasting guilt and damnation.'*

After further thought I decided to put *Sword and Quill* on hold. Preference was given to a new book which I entitled 'Isabella's Legacy: My Discovery of Spain,' as I prepared my Lecture.

I returned to Spain in March 1991 to speak at the University of Seville. Given that the purpose of Christopher Columbus and the Spanish enterprise was to find India (and importantly the riches of the East) it seemed appropriate that I, a descendant of Indians, almost 500 years on should, via the New World, be the bearer of the message 'Towards 1992: Discovery, Black People in Britain and Ethnic Minorities in Europe.'

My audience was composed largely of students from the University's English Language and History Departments.

After weeks of practice, I prefaced my Lecture with these words in Spanish: '*Buenos dias Senoras y Senores. Estoy muy contento de estar aqui en Sevilla, y de tener el honor de hablarles. Me ponencia se titular: Hacia mil noveciento noventa y dos; el descubrimiento los experiencias de los Negros en la Gran Bretana, y las minorias ethnicas de Europe. Desgraciadamente, no hablo bien el Espanol, y asi tengo que hablarles en ingles.'*

I then spoke in English. I began by saying:

'Almost 500 years ago what had only months before seemed an unlikely event, actually took place in Seville. Through the cobbled streets, Cristobal Colon (Columbus) on his triumphant return after his first voyage to the "Indies," paraded seven exotic-looking Indians who were accompanied by equally strange looking green and yellow parrots. Imagine the confusion in the minds of those Indians as they walked through the city and the curiosity this spectacle may have aroused among the people of Seville for at this time, Europeans knew little about the people of Africa and Asia except through what they had read in the travel literature of the fifteenth century.

Although the Spaniards who actually saw the (New World) were naturally excited and aggressive, they tended to view the new lands from a Medieval standpoint, transferring to America certain attitudes and legends that were prevalent during the Middle Ages. This Medieval influence, especially evident during the early years of discovery and conquest was part of an ongoing process. For a thousand years Europeans had been developing a range of ideas on man and the existence of semi-men, even wild men which were freely drawn upon in the New World...

Fifteenth century Europeans had assumed their knowledge of the world to be exact and the appearance of a vast unknown Continent across the sea shook their confidence in themselves. Even more disconcerting was the fact that the people they encountered were from markedly different cultures. And because these people were seen as barbarians who should, in the first instance, be converted to Christianity (after all, this was one of the main objectives of Columbus's enterprise) war was waged against them. Somehow, it was felt, the natives had to be subdued and be made to surrender to the will of their conquerors. As it was, the poor state of the Spanish economy demanded the subjugation of such people; a matter on which all doubts had to be dispelled. Spain's Mission in the Indies was clarified in 1492 when Queen Isabella bluntly asked the Scholar Antonio de Nebrija, as he presented to her his Spanish Gramatica (the first grammar of a European modern language ever written): "What is it for?" the Queen asked. The Bishop of Avila, speaking on behalf of the scholar replied: "Your Majesty, language is the perfect instrument of empire." '

Fast forward to the twentieth century. I continued:

'*When post-war immigration to Western Europe started, the States concerned neither anticipated nor intended that it would result in large-scale settlements and the development of new ethnic minorities...*

At this point in time (1991), it is perhaps appropriate to ask: what in fact do Turks in Germany, Italians in Switzerland, Portuguese, Spanish North Africans and Blacks in Britain mean by equality of rights and opportunities? They certainly do not mean assimilation. Indeed if their equal rights and opportunities are to be won, they insist it must be done with no loss of identity! Today the citizens of Western Europe, reluctant as they are to accept the fact, must know that they already live in multi-ethnic societies, and that it is no longer a question of choice. For better or worse, Western Europe is an integral part of the Global village.

One of the fundamental connections linking the Spanish discoveries in the fifteenth century was the development of trade with foreign peoples upon whom the Spaniards unhesitatingly imposed their religion and culture. Other European nations also faced with the problem of alien cultures, imposed their own brands of cultural imperialism, the legacy of which is today evident in Europe in the manner in which black and other foreign people are victimised. On the eve of the historic implementation of the"Single (European) Market"(and the likelihood of closer economic and social intercourse between the Member States than ever before) the question remain: will 1992 mark a new chapter in European Enlightenment not only in trade within Europe, but essentially in human relations? Are some men really born to be slaves?'

After posing these questions, I concluded:

'In modern times and for some 500 years at least, Europe has been looking outward and had developed fabulously as a result. The Continent will no doubt continue to develop and consolidate its economic strength, but it must not lose sight of its less fortunate trading partners from the under-developed world. Indeed the opportunity of learning the lessons of the past, must not be missed! As we approach the opening of the World Trade Exhibition, Sevilla 1992, I would like to close with the words of an enlightened son of Seville, Bartolome de Las Casas who, more than 400 years ago (in his long, extraordinary defence of the indigenous American Indians against racism and xenophobia) during his Great Debate with the renowned Spanish scholar Sepulveda, proclaimed: "All human beings are born free and equal in dignity and rights. They are endowed with reason and conscience and should act towards one another in a spirit of brotherhood."
He dicho. Muchas Gracias.'

At the end of the Lecture which lasted about 50 minutes, the applause was long, loud and enthusiastic. The energy and warmth in the room touched me. Relieved and pleased, my fascination with, and appreciation of, Seville knew no bounds. Regarded as a triumph by the University's organisers, in the euphoria I decided to get on with the necessary research for my book on Spain: 'Isabella's

Legacy.' I had hoped that with my friend Marisa, I would visit certain key places and gather as much material as possible. Once this plan was laid, I moved irrevocably forward. In the remaining ten days or so, I took every opportunity of getting around in Andalusia (Southern Spain) hoping to meet and speak with people who would be of relevance to the embryonic book project. Time was of the essence.

First, I travelled to Palos (via Huelva another name from my childhood – relating to a piece of music) the place from where Columbus had set sail, journeying westwards in the hope of finding India. Then I moved on to the nearby monastery of La Rabida where Columbus, after crossing the Portuguese-Spanish border, sought refuge and eventually the ear of the King and Queen of Spain.

The next morning, I took a train from Seville to see Granada and its famous Alhambra Palace. Within this grand ediface and symbol of Moorish rule, I saw the room and the exact spot where Columbus is said to have knelt before Queen Isabella and King Ferdinand of Spain who had granted men and ships that would help the explorer to realize his quest.

On my return to Seville I interviewed a number of people and witnessed the great Easter spectacle of Holy Week (*Semana Santa*). What an incredible experience! Having delighted in seeing the Giralda and Cathedral on my previous visit, now I made my way to the Archivo General de Indias, the Archives of the Indies.

As a library and book-lover, I was very interested to see what was in store when I arrived. But first things first: I was especially pleased to receive my Reader's Ticket on which was a photograph of me. It was stamped as 'D.N.I o Pas. Britanico-296557-F' issued on 26 March 1991 and signed by El Director Rosario Palle. The back of the Ticket was also stamped and signed by the Secretary of the Archivo and myself.

I felt privileged on entering the reading room to see and touch the historic documents relating to King Ferdinand, Queen Isabella of Spain and Columbus that had led to the 'discovery' of the New World. Among these 'documents' were the famous two volume *Historia…*, by Bartolome de Las Casas: His *History of the Indies*.

All my life I'd been hearing about the 'discovery' of the New World; and if seeing is believing, on leaving the Archivo (as a man from Trinidad which was discovered by Columbus on his third voyage and as an historian) my imagination was fired and I felt thoroughly enriched.

This Spring-time experience in Seville was so marvellous that no place has ever taken such a hold of me as this city had done. 'Seville is a woman,' I recalled Marisa's words, and how enchanting it was to walk the ancient-modern streets, especially at midnight in moonlight, past orange trees with green and half-yellow fruit on branches, breathing deeply of the heady scent of jasmine and orange blossom.

So after my jam-packed and extraordinary experience of lecturing, travel, meeting and interviewing various people before leaving Spain, once more, I committed myself to return to Seville. This time, for another 'Special' occasion: The historic celebration of 'Expo Sevilla 1992' which would mark the 500th anniversary of the arrival of Columbus in the New World.

POST-LECTURE PREOCCUPATIONS

Having returned to the gloom and coolness of the London weather, sitting in the underground train travelling from Heathrow to Central London, I recalled sunny Seville. Uppermost in my mind was giving the lecture at the University, the warm reception of the audience and the thought that to my knowledge, it was the first time that anyone (especially a non-white person) had gone to Seville and given an *official Address* on 'Discovery and Ethnic Minorities in Europe' at the University. Indeed, it may well have been a first also for the rest of Spain!

As the train clattered on, further thoughts of Columbus going west to find India and my preoccupation with Indians in the Caribbean commingled; my mind aflame with shape-shifting ideas.

But soon I was confronted with the hard reality of living in London. In spite of being within walking distance of the British Museum, living in Central London came at a price. The significant compensatory fact was that being closer to the British Museum meant what I saved on travel was spent on rent and other essentials.

Nonetheless the expense of living at 44 Maple Street was a matter of concern: Just four months after occupancy, I was querying an electricity bill for £37.46. There were however compensations: For example, the rooms were spacious and I could write and type comfortably at the table near the window in the shadow of the iconic, cylindrical-shaped British Post Office Telecom Tower. The environment was unlike other more residential London areas that I'd lived in. The pub around the corner was quaint, its facade framed by hanging pots of flowers and plants. To the north lay Fitzroy Square and to the east was Tottenham Court Road. Oxford Street was just a few hundred yards in a southerly direction. Having long hoped for such a place of residence, now for better or worse I was installed.

From this more comfortable address, I wrote to my Literary Agent Anne McDermid:

'Dear Anne,

I recently went to Spain at the invitation of the University of Seville to give a Lecture... Fortunately for me the large audience... regarded my performance as a great success. Prior to this, however, I was asked to give a similar lecture at the European Parliament in Brussels in 1992, and later this year I hope to return to Spain to speak at the University of Madrid and at a meeting to be arranged by the Secretary of the Writers' Association in Spain.

While in Spain, I took copious notes for a book entitled: "ISABELLA's LEGACY - A Journey From Trinidad to Spain." This visit and meeting Gypsies intensified interest in my own identity and in the book that had engaged me: Arising From Bondage: A History of the Indo-Caribbean People. But even though immersed in this work, I could see the connectedness of it with Isabella's Legacy. Compared with the many academic books on various aspects of the Spanish conquest that are likely to be published next year, the prospects for my work looks good given its popular appeal in terms of its subject matter and readability. Indeed, its promotion is vital for success. As I write, I am fully aware of the fact that I will have to return to Spain before the book (Isabella's Legacy) is completed, hopefully by November. Of course, as ever, time is short and I need the commitment of a major publisher as soon as possible. Enclosed is a copy of the Synopsis and list of contents of the book.

I hope all is well... and I look forward to hearing from you. Please give my regards to Andrew (Best).

With Best Wishes,.

Ron Ramdin.'

The next day, as co-occupier of the flat, where I'd been spending more time (while, just managing to meet the cost of retaining the 30 Alexandra Grove room essentially as storage space for my books and accumulated papers) I queried another electricity bill. Feeling unsettled, a few days later, given my long standing residence in various London Boroughs, I wrote to the housing organisation known as The Peabody Trust.

'In the last two weeks, my flatmate - a low-paid employee...was told that she would become a part-time worker engaged for only four half days per week! Added to this unfortunate news is the fact that our occupation, as per contract, for the above Flat ends on 15 June 1991, only six weeks away. By then, there is no forseeable solution and we write to you in desperation because we will (if no acceptable accommodation is found) be homeless. We have turned to you, on the recommendation of one of your Peabody Housing Trust tenants of long standing. We shall be most grateful for whatever help you can offer us in our circumstances, and look forward to hearing from you as soon as possible.

Yours...

Ron Ramdin...'

All things considered, my need for affordable, better and more secure accommodation required urgent resolution. Surely, after 30 years of living and renting in London, I should have a very good chance of being housed in a flat. So not unreasonably, I was hopeful of a positive response from the Trust.

Meanwhile, hopes that through the Agency of Curtis Brown I would land a respectable book contract, remained high. When Anne McDermid's letter of 13 May 1991 arrived, with much anticipation, I opened it and read:

'Its good to hear from you again. It sounds as if you haven't heard that

Andrew Best retired in December last year, although he still pops into the office occasionally to tie up some loose ends. He gives you his best wishes.

Your project for a book called Isabella's Legacy sounds interesting, but I am afraid you are being hopelessly uncommercial about it...

Were there any developments on the question of you being the biographer of CLR James? Perhaps it is time for us to have a general chat. Would you like to come in to have a drink one evening?

Yours,

Anne.'

So with the focus of such big-hitters as Anne and Curtis Brown on the James biography, in June 1991 I travelled to Trinidad to do further research at the National Archives and at the Oilfield Workers Trade Union Library in San Fernando. Time was precious because my stay was for only three weeks, perhaps just long enough to scan documents relating to C.L.R James's life and work. During the time spent at the OWTU, I was engaged in an intense effort, something that I was no stranger to. And in this endeavour, Librarian Donna Coombs-Montrose was especially helpful.

I donated a copy of *The Making of the Black Working Class in Britain* to the OWTU Library and *The Vanguard* ('Voice of Labour') published a photograph of me making the formal presentation to OWTU's David Abdullah. The caption informed *Vanguard* readers: 'Ramdin wrote the labour history of Trinidad and Tobago called *From Chattel Slave To Wage Earner*, the most **sought after book of its kind in the OWTU Library.'**

So after all the London years of striving, the book found its place, elevated to being mentioned with the likes of C.L.R James's *Black Jacobins* and Eric Williams's *Capitalism and Slavery*. The last sentence of *The Vanguard's* article which stated that Ramdin 'has many books in the pipeline' including a book on C.L.James, revealed the true purpose of my visit to the Library.

Apart from autobiographical fragments, and boxes of James's unsorted papers, letters and books, I sought interviews with leading figures in the powerful OWTU and others in the wider Trinidad and Tobago Labour Movement with which James was closely associated. My hope was that taken together, they would be revealing of aspects of James's life and personality and thus be invaluable. So I contacted and interviewed the former OWTU Leader George Weekes. My Interview with this charismatic, hugely respected Labour Leader (who, while in office, had more power than his predecessor Uriah Butler) went extremely well. Afterwards, he kindly offered to drive me home. When I mentioned this to Pa who was sitting in the gallery, he was speechless. (Pa's area of employment before he'd retired was covered by Weekes's Union).

My other interviews included Errol McCloud, Weekes's successor as General Secretary of the OWTU; David Abdullah, a respected Executive Member and John La Rose, the well-known activist, publisher and founder of the popular New Beacon Bookshop in London. I recorded these four major Interviews at the OWTU's Paramount Building in San Fernando. Thereafter, I travelled to Port of Spain and managed to get a vitally important Interview with Lennox Pierre, a lawyer and close associate of James and the People's National Movement in its heyday.

Another significant Interviewee was David Rudder, the former Calypso King and role-model for Trinidadian youth, who was at the height of his fame. He had kindly invited me to his home in Port of Spain where I did the Interview. Rudder spoke appreciatively about James and related West Indian Independence (which James had championed) with his hit song *Rally Round the West Indies.* After the Interview, he asked what I was doing that evening. 'Nothing planned,' I said. David then drove to Bishop Anstey School. He left me in the car for a while and went inside. When he returned he asked me to join him. Musical Director/Conductor Pat Bishop was rehearsing the famous School Choir as we crossed the yard in the direction of the music. While David and I stood in the doorway, Ms Bishop turned to the large Choir and slowly lifting her arm she said: 'Let us sing for David and Ron!' I was overwhelmed by this gesture. 'It is my birthday and Pat's,' David said. 'We are having a party tonight and we would like to invite you.' Before this moment, it seemed Pat had already known about my books.

I accepted their generous invitation and together we travelled up the Port of Spain hills to a magnificent hotel where all was set for the double Birthday celebrations. We sang 'Happy Birthday' and other songs. Later, about midnight, David drove me down to Marine Square where I caught a taxi going south! So ended my visit to Port of Spain that day when, for the first time, I met, listened to, and had spent a wonderful time with the hugely popular David Rudder and highly-respected Pat Bishop. It was all the more satisfying because these two people were among Trinidad and Tobago's most outstanding role models. That day, and those impromptu musical moments, I fondly remember and will always treasure.

A few days later, David Rudder was due to appear in his well-publicised '*Spectakular.*' The Show drew massive crowds to Port of Spain and I must confess it was the first and only time that I'd been to anything resembling a rock concert in Trinidad. This Rudder *Spectakular,* a 'Calypso-Soca Concert' was like no other and made even more memorable by the mass of energetic people, dancing and swaying joyously; the young and old of both sexes. Being there, I recalled my often troubled teenage days when I would sneak away from home and go to Marabella to just stand and listen to the Southern Marines Steelband. Although that was a long time ago, today the unique sound of the steelband still evokes vivid Trinidad memories.

After the Show, I thought it might be a good idea to say thanks and goodbye to the Showman David Rudder before I left Trinidad. In the circumstances, this seemed impossible! Nonetheless, it was worth a try, I thought. Braving the crush of thousands of adoring, almost hysterical fans who had jammed the Entrance backstage, I pressed forward and managed to speak to a stern-looking Guard intent on blocking my path and that of anyone who tried to go beyond him. He was physically impressive, even intimidating. 'Hello!' I shouted. 'Hello! I'm from London. Please tell David, Ron Ramdin would like to see him. I'm leaving for London tomorrow!' Almost instantly, I was pushed backwards by those nearest to me.

'Wait a minute,' the Guard said before disappearing.

When he reappeared, he motioned to me with his index finger. 'Come!' he said. It was not easy getting through the crush which was about four or five deep. As I inched forward, people were staring at me, wondering: 'Who the hell is he?' Being Indian and thoroughly enjoying a Calypso/Soca/Rock Concert were not synonymous. But who knows one or two may have recognised my face which since 1975, had been appearing on Trinidad and Tobago television screens and in newspapers fairly regularly.

At last, free of the noisy melee, I approached the Star performer's inner sanctum. Then, as if reincarnated, the man who wowed us all on stage just minutes before, appeared: David Rudder was bare backed, his sweat-drenched skin glistened. With a white towel draped around his neck and shoulder, he looked like a prize-fighter. He'd put everything into the one and a half hour performance; and at the end of our brief exchange of greetings, he hugged me before I left.

As I made my way out, my already high regard for Calypso King David Rudder, both as an entertainer and a human being, increased dramatically. 'Rally! Rally Round the West Indies.' These words could (I felt then as now) equally apply to people from other parts of the world who were, quite rightly, asking searching questions about their own time and place.

Once again, the open spaces and warmth of the Caribbean had receded. I was back in London. The days, weeks and months that followed brought a renewed awareness of my time at the British Library: In particular, how, over the years, I'd been using my office and off-work time. I reaffirmed that I was a driven, 'multi-tasking' man, using time and, such talents as I possessed, as productively as possible. Work, writing, work. Yes, *Time* like the wind, goes hurrying by. And while I recognised there was nothing unusual about this familiar approach to life which was fairly well-known to many who had known me, I'd also become increasingly concerned about my job for two main reasons: first because my Post in the Bloomsbury office had been ear-marked for transfer to Boston Spa; and second, as a consequence, I would have to be redeployed to another area of the Library. The prospect of being dislodged was especially worrying for now I was much older and therefore more apprehensive: Being forty-nine was a significant milestone on my journey. I felt I'd reached a mid-way mark; a crossroads and was approaching an uncertain future. As with everything that I'd done in life, given my employment history, I took my job no less seriously than before.

For weeks the rumours spread; then finally the decision was taken to redeploy me to the Acquisitions Section in the Arched Room, which was located at the western end of the British Museum.

Some ten months later, I reflected that things could have been a lot worse. Why? Because I could, for example, have been placed in some other far less attractive department. How inappropriate such a move would have been for someone with my long (albeit unofficial) research-curatorial type work and Acquisitions background. What pleased me now was the fact that the Arched Room was *the* central point for all incoming books, magazines and electronic material to the British Library. What displeased me, however, was what Mr H, a work colleague in the Arched Room had waited several days to tell me. 'Be careful, brother,' he said, 'be careful.' I said there was nothing to worry about for I was, as always, 'careful.' Then one day a few months later, Mr H whispered confidentially: 'Just before you came here, I overheard a conversation between Mr P from another section of the Library and your manager, Ms S.' According to Mr H, it seemed that I was supposed to have gone to another office, but Mr P had objected. He is reported to have said 'He (Ron Ramdin) was supposed to come to me, but I could not entertain the proposition.'

'Why?' I asked. 'Because,' as Mr H put it, 'Mr P worried about you and himself being out of the office at the same time." '

'What do you mean? Ms S had asked Mr P,' Mr H added.

'I mean, Mr P said, he (Ramdin) goes walkabout. I need someone to stay in the office and do some work!'

Hearing this, I said to Mr H: 'But *I've always done my best* wherever I worked and especially now since they transferred me here!'

'I know that Ron,' Mr H said. 'I'm just telling you what I overheard.'

'Thank you man.'

Mr H was a fellow-West Indian from one of the smaller Caribbean islands where there were few people of Indian descent. Occasionally he made anti-curry jokes and I wondered if he knew where I was from and how much I liked curry which was an integral part of my West Indian upbringing. His anti-Indian-Asian remarks were unfortunate, but although he was a West Indian with 'conservative' tendencies, I liked, trusted and remained appreciative of him, especially after he'd told me what he 'overheard.'

By now, after twenty-two years in the British Library (having worked in about thirteen different 'sections') I had gained, not only the necessary experience and a good understanding of the Collections, but also something few (if any) members of staff of my Grade, past or present, could have boasted. But the way my superiors moved me around on the grounds that it would help me to gain *more experience* was spurious; something that had an *unhealthy whiff.* Clearly, this was prejudicial treatment and I was never happy with any of these moves which, on each occasion, I strongly opposed. In the main, I thought of this as a strategy designed to disrupt my life and disorient me to the extent that it would lead to my resignation. If this was indeed the great hoped-for goal of my detractors, it was a far-fetched one for I had no intention of leaving the Library. Why? Put simply, because I was not only a serious scholar and writer (matters on which some managers showed absolutely no interest) but also a lover of literature and books with a backstory steeped in more than mere interest in the British Library's Collections. What could not be ignored, however, was the fact that the job I did was not only low-paid; it was my *only* steady source of income.

NINETEEN

STAFF RELATIONS AND THE BRITISH LIBRARY REGULAR READERS' GROUP

Against the background of insecurity, and in the relatively new surroundings of the unusual iron, wood and glass structure of my new office known as the Arched Room, I was unusully careful for I saw this as a new beginning. But in spite of my feelings, there were surprises in store. Early one morning, line Manager Ms S passed my desk, stopped, then back-tracked and moved close behind me. Peering over my shoulder at the computer screen, she said: 'I hope you are not using *our* computer to type *your* letters?' I was appalled by her assumption. Then I recalled what Mr H had said about the negative talk between her and a fellow-manager before I came to the Arched Room. Not surprisingly, when Ms S eventually wrote her first Annual Report on my work performance, she felt that I 'could do more' or words to that effect! After this downright, inaccurate statement from her, I felt as if I was walking a tight-rope between her and her boss, Ms D.

Thereafter, there was an uneasy tension between myself and Ms S. Though she was soft-spoken, her voice always carried a hint of suspicion, a feeling that I could do more! How much more given that I was confined to doing repetitive work, a long way down from the exalted Chief Executive or his equivalent grades? Indeed, my years of dealing with the first Chief Executive and his staff was long past. And unfortunately for me, Ms S was like Ms D, a relative newcomer to the Library who knew absolutely nothing about my earlier roles: my Whitley Council meetings, copious minuting and regular correspondence with the Chief Executive, the Head of Central Administration and other high-ranking officials in the crucial first months and years of the British Library's history.

Now, in her first Annual Report, on a scale of 1-4 for 'Written Communication,' Ms S graded me as low down as Box 3. To compound my problem, her immediate superior, was none other than my detractor and chief antagonist, the power behind my removal from the Room T1 office to the Arched Room. Not content with her privileged position and casual abuse of power, Ms D was now determined to do more damage: I remember well her very first and unusually early morning visit to the Arched Room soon after I'd moved there. 'Are you happy in your new job?' she asked.

'Yes,' I said. 'Quite happy actually,' a comment intended to show my willingness to embrace the job.

A thinly-disguised professional expression, less a smile and more of a sneer, spread across Ms D's face. 'So you're "happy" are you?' she said. 'Well, we'll have to see about that!' True to her word, from that moment, her behind-the-scenes machinations did make me unhappy. Fortunately, I had experience on my side; and with the passage of time, familiarity with and focus on my job eased the pressure upon me.

Because I was an early morning starter and innately industrious, none of the job's extra demands bothered me. I took all that was thrown at me in my stride. But soon working in the Arched Room became like a game of musical chairs. Of the five separate jobs in that office (including mine) unlike my colleagues, I was placed in each for several months. Why? Because I was told I *needed more* experience of work in the Section!

Naturally, I reflected: Of the other four employees, no one else was moved about as much as I was, even though I was a member of staff for much longer than anyone else! Did these managers really feel I could do more? Plainly *I could not.* And yet, these comedic goings-on could not be more serious.

Heightened awareness had driven me to perform to the limit, as I'd been doing for years. Now I was unsure who were for, and who against, me in that work environment. Relying largely on instinct (while pursuing my 'part-time' writing) I remained uncomfortably conscious of the few managers who blatantly monitored my normal daily routine, especially my movements to and from the Round Reading Room; one of them going as far as pursuing his witch-hunt by being present in the Room during my tea and lunch breaks.

Surely, they must know that I was a respected author; that writing was not a pretense or ruse for me to skive-off work and engage in a useless 'hobby' above my station! This perceived over-simplification of my presence in the Reading Room could not be further from the truth for the discipline of writing had, over the years, seeped into the very fibre of my being. Therefore, in the face of the pitiful onslaught, I reminded myself that there must be no weakening of resolve. The challenge I faced was a tough one: I was pressed to practice what I preached which was essentially my own increasingly clear view of *respect for difference* and *inclusiveness* (both in the workplace and communities) which my books were concerned with. More and more, I began to wonder what motivated certain managers' games and attitude. Their disrespect was obvious and therefore could not be discounted. With jobs hard to find in the Trinidad of my youth, embracing opportunities in England, meant hard work; not the insistent suspicion of 'laziness' that was casually foisted upon me. Nonetheless, I held a steady course, determined to do the best job.

The counterpoise to the continuing workplace tension, was the success of *The Making of the Black Working Class in Britain* that had become a major source book. Where there was nothing, now there was something: *this British history.* Acknowledging this, a letter from David Heywood, Assistant Secretary of the National Union of Civil and Professional Servants (NUCPS)informed me that he was 'in the process of ordering copies.' A better and more opportune endorsement of me and my writings, I could not have hoped for.

My preoccupation with books intensified as I pursued research for my James biography. Waiting and hoping, I was glad to hear from Literary Agent, Anne McDermid who wrote:

'I was trying to return your several calls to say that the two publishers that I have so far been able to interest in the project namely Faber and Faber and Radius, an imprint of Random House, both say that they would be perfectly happy to contemplate a biography of the great man without it being authorised provided that you can prove access to a

sufficiently substantial bunch of material that you will not be seriously hampered by whatever the Executors are holding back; and provided that your general all-round knowledge of him and his work and his background, combined with access to papers and people, mean that you will be able to write a truly authoritative book. In other words, would you be hampered if they choose to prevent family members and former colleagues from speaking to you?

In short, what you need to do now I'm afraid is to produce a description of this book you propose to write and quite a dramatic and serious and persuasive one. I want it to contain as much information about him and his writing and his affairs as you can... and a very powerful and passionate argument for your intellectual interest in the case. Anything that will help persuade the publishers that you will write a lively, interesting and committed book on the subject which will help to introduce people to James's work.

We will have one shot with these people... I'm afraid... We are going to be up against the Executors and we don't therefore want a situation where the publishers will be tempted to ask the Executors their opinion of you!

I know you can do this, but it may take you a little time and I very much hope you will be able to let me have something by the end of the summer...In any case I think I'd like to see from you a first draft of such a document so that we can discuss it together...'

So there was some hope. At my own expense, in terms of time and money, I pressed on with what the Agent asked of me concerning the C.L.R. James project.

Meanwhile, at work I was informed that my Annual Leave entitlement after 21 years of service had increased from 27 to 30 days. This was very good news not because I wanted a longer holiday or rest. On the contrary, my immediate thought was that by taking 'half-days' leave on a regular basis, I could better manage my officially approved 'flexi-time' office job and thus strike a less pressurized *work-writing* balance.

It was just past mid-year in 1991 and, as the great new structure in St Pancras began to take shape, there was much talk about the future of the British Library. Among those members of the public most interested was the 'Regular Readers Group' which acted as the unofficial mouthpiece of the British public. On their behalf, in July 1991, Brian Lake wrote a covering letter which accompanied a nine-page document: *Is the British Museum Falling Down?* that was sent to Tim Renton, Secretary of State for the Office of Arts and Libraries. Mr Lake stated:

'As Regular Readers we write to express our deep concern about the future of the British Library.

We believe that it is essential for the Minister with ultimate responsibility for the Library to either undertake a personal review, or commission an independent report, on the present state and projected development of the Library before it is too late to change what is happening.

We attach the Memorandum which details our concerns, and suggest a practical, pragmatic and cost-effective plan for the future of the British Library.

In the face of limited funding, the most important measure we would urge you to consider is the retention of the Round Reading Room and the other British Library facilities in Bloomsbury at least until such time as all phases of St Pancras are completed. With the initial phase of St Pancras "operationally full" at the time of its completion in 1996 and with Readers seats only slightly higher than current provision (in the Round Reading Room), retaining facilities in Bloomsbury in space for which the British Museum has no specific plans, is a cheap and practical option... We would appreciate an early meeting to discuss these urgent matters.'

Keen to know more, I was able to see a copy of the 'document.' In its Memorandum the 'Group' had set out its essential aims, proposals and conclusions. The 'Aims' were:

' To draw the attention of the Minister and Government to a number of matters of serious concern relating to the move of the British Library to St Pancras.

To request the intervention of the Minister in order to undertake a personal review of the situation, or commission an independent report.

To suggest the practical benefits of retaining in continued use the Round Reading Room and North Library, and the associated storage facilities in Bloomsbury in light of the limited provision of both Reader and storage space at St Pancras.'

The Group also identified themes which included: Background; Areas of Concern, Reduced Storage Space, Readers Facilities, Conservation, New Technology, Reduction of Funding for St Pancras and Lack of Consultation with Readers. It summarised its 'Concerns' as follows:

'That the new building will not fulfill the function for which it was built - to unify the collections under one roof.

That Readers' facilities will be only slightly higher in terms of number of seats than at present.

That the Conservation priorities for St Pancras are wrong, and that priority should be given to post-1850 books printed on wood-pulp paper.

That there are serious and unresolved problems with crucial aspects of the new technology on which the St Pancras building is based.

That underfunding will mean St Pancras will not be completed, and that at present there is no clear plan of how the British Library will operate in the future if completion is not to go ahead.

*That there has been, and continues to be, **no real consultation with Readers which has led to lack of confidence in British Library management**.'*

On these matters, especially the last 'no real consultation with Readers,' I had been privy to sustained grumblings from a cross-section of people. Displaying the scope and depth of their knowledge, the Regular Readers' Group proposed:

'Retention of the British Library's facilities at Bloomsbury, including the RRR (Round Reading Room), the North Library, the Library Galleries (including the Grenville and King's Libraries) and associated storage to accommodate the books and Readers that will not now be accommodated at St Pancras.

That spare facilities at Bloomsbury be used to house all printed books published before 1850. The current situation was never envisaged by the planners of the new British Library. The central purpose of a new building was to house all the Library's holdings under one roof. This is no longer the case - unless Government provides funding for the completion stages which now seems unlikely, and would in any event

762 · TURNING PAGES · RON RAMDIN · VOLUME TWO

take another 10 years to build.

Therefore, outhouse storage and the problems of moving books between buildings will continue. Library management are already planning for continued out-housing in London and Boston Spa. Our argument is a simple one: that if out-housing is still required, and St Pancras only provides a handful of extra Reader spaces, the most economic means of providing the missing facilities is by retaining use of the Bloomsbury reading rooms and storage areas...

With the acceptance that out-housing is necessary, but while rearrangement of facilities is still under discussion, it is essential that further thought should be given to the distribution of the Library's holdings of books. Management promises of "25 minutes" delivery time for books at St Pancras will appear rather unrealistic when the book in question is housed in Boston Spa.

We therefore propose that the present storage facilities at Bloomsbury continue to be used for all books published before 1850.'

With completion of the new building now in sight, the Readers' Group argued that: *'A known cut-off date would enable Readers to know exactly where they can consult the books they require, and avoid the arbitrariness of present plans.'*

Given their understanding that the movement of books to St Pancras would now go ahead until 1992, they stressed that there was time to consider 'an alternative approach.'

And so, very much forward-looking, the Group concluded:

'With St Pancras nearing completion of its first, and apparently only phase we believe that: There must be a swift review by the Minister of the Arts of all aspects of the move, in the light of budgetry restrictions, the failure to complete St Pancras and serious concerns about the management of the BL.

There should be full funding for the satisfactory operation of the first stage at St Pancras, and that further funding be made available for completion of the new BL rather than selling off the land.'

They urged a commitment to the retention of British Library facilities in Bloomsbury until such time as St Pancras is completed. In particular, they were keen to keep in use the Reading Rooms which provide 'the finest space for learning in Europe.'

Hitherto having been at certain levels either involved or well-informed of most of the negotiations and meetings pre-and post-British Library, I was very pleased to read the RRG's 'Document' and the vital concerns raised therein. The hard-core of this 'Group' were academics, journalists and distinguished authors; men and women who cared deeply about the nation's heritage and, of course, the future of the British Library when the St Pancras showpiece was eventually occupied. Indeed the Group's concern was such that their 'Memorandum' was followed by another: *Bloomsbury and St Pancras: A Future for the British Library.* And once more Brian Lake wrote to Tim Renton, the Government Minister.

'We are responding by enclosing a report on developments since the publication of the Memorandum: **Is the British Museum Falling Down***?*

Having met with Commander Saunders Watson and Brian Lang and discussed the issues we believe that there is the real possibility of the future British Library incorporating the new facilities at St Pancras and the Reading Rooms & Storage at Bloomsbury, but that the direction must come from Government.

Brian Lang, in response to our request for comparative costings for the Library to retain Bloomsbury set beside the costings for Boston Spa and other outhousing currently envisaged, claimed that to do so would "play into the Treasury's hands" ... If the option of keeping Bloomsbury in the interim period from 1996 until the completion of St Pancras is cheaper and better than alternative accommodation, then surely it must be seriously considered by your department and the Treasury? The BL has failed to provide the information to counter our case.'

Incensed by the Government's position, Mr Lake added:

'Mr Kendall, writing in **The Author** *(the Society of Authors journal) and quoted in the* **Daily Telegraph***, described the abandonment of the Round Reading Room as an act of "cultural vandalism." At the time when the Library of Congress has just completed renovating its imitation of the Reading Room, and a new library has just been opened in Kyoto based on the Reading Room, it is an act of supreme folly to remove the books and readers from a room that has inspired and*

continues to inspire - and at the same time is a practical working space fulfilling the function for which it was designed.

Despite the confident tone of the BL management, reflected in your letters, there is something rotten in the state of our National Library that cannot be sweetened for long by honeyed phrases. We note your announcement of an Inquiry into public libraries; we hope that such an independent review can include the BL within its remit.

We look forward to positive movement on these matters. Books will not be moved to St Pancras until late 1992 at the earliest because of further serious problems with the mobile shelves so that there is time for further discussions. We stand ready to meet with you at any time.

Yours sincerely,

Brian Lake.'

The Regular Readers Group was thorough in its deliberations as reflected in *Bloomsbury and St Pancras: A future for the British Library*, which was duly presented to Prime Minister John Major.

In this second document, the Group stressed that it stood by the 'Conclusions' of its first Memorandum. And, at this crucial transition stage in the British Library's history, the Group reiterated a few of its earlier concerns that were genuine and urgent. While continuing to draw attention to serious matters relating to the management and funding of the Library, the Group also emphasized the desperate position into which *'our National Library is being allowed to slide, and believes that the Minister, and the Government will be failing in their duty by simply following the BL management, which seems willing to accept mediocrity and the second rate.'*

Thus, the Group advocated *'an approach with vision, combined with the down-to-earth realism of cost-effectiveness. **Retaining Bloomsbury alongside St Pancras** will provide a future for the BL- and leave options open for the time when management and government coincide in the view that the BL should be maintained as the best in the World.'* (Authors' emphasis.)

Having experienced three decades of employment in libraries, I fully appreciated the RRG's concerns as detailed in *The British Museum is Falling Down* and *Bloomsbury and St. Pancras: A Future for the British Library*. For me, both as a member of Staff and as the ***most regular*** of all 'Regular' Readers (having sat in the same seat for

27 years) the Group's comprehensive representations and insistence that the Round Reading Room in Bloomsbury be retained, were reassuring.

ONSTAGE IN THE PURCELL ROOM

At this time, my books were much in demand; and buoyed by what seemed like a tide of good feeling on 17 November, I was invited to speak on aspects of African-Caribbean and 'Black British' heritage at the Kilburn Public Library. I'd been giving such 'Public Talks' annually at various venues across Britain since 1973, a period of almost two decades. In effect, I'd been engaged in a 'one man crusade' as an American friend Willa Woolston had described my relentless writing, lecturing and broadcasting. Imparting knowledge of the 'hidden' aspects of British, colonial and post-colonial histories and cultures was never a 'career move' and certainly not a casual matter for me. In fact, speaking in public about what were seen as 'marginal' subjects were nothing less than intense experiences as was the Kilburn Library event. But, as previously, 'respect for difference' and *inclusiveness* were the fundamental ideas about which I wrote and spoke.

Five days later, I was approached to step into the broader cultural arena and reach out to the great British public. Some weeks before, over cups of coffee, Tunde and Galina had told me about their exciting plan: a unique presentation of African Classical Music, the Griot Tradition, featuring the Tunde Jegede Ensemble. Having invited me to participate, I was ready to play my part.

A few weeks later, publicity Leaflets for the performance of the Concert were widely issued. It read: '*This is the first ever presentation of African classical Music in Britain. These young composer-musicians have defined the legacy of the Griot Tradition – a journey spanning history from ancient empires to the popular music of today.*
Composition of brilliance and verve unite the rich contrast of dazzling Marimba and haunting melodies of the African harp, taking them far beyond their traditional uses. Theirs is a music of invention, stylish and light, sparkling ingenuity – a frieze of sound unfolding through the spectrum of the diaspora. This is the new music of the millennium.'
The Leaflet also stated: 'THERE WILL BE A SHORT TALK BY

RON RAMDIN OF THE BRITISH LIBRARY.'

And so on the evening of Tuesday 22 October 1991, around 6.30 p.m I made my way to the venue. From Drury Lane and Covent Garden I crossed The Strand and walked along Waterloo Bridge towards the South Bank.

Just before 8.00 p.m, from backstage, I heard the expectant buzz of the 'Full House.' This was the moment of truth and the performers were attuned for this British Premiere of African Classical music. The auditorium lights dimmed and faded to total darkness. Backstage, a man who had spoken to me earlier, hurried towards me. 'You're on now, Ron!' he said. 'Go!'

I walked onstage towards the spotlight directed at a bulbous microphone atop its stand. 'Good evening Ladies and Gentlemen, my name is Ron Ramdin. The Purcell Room has over the years been the venue of many memorable musical performances. With due respect to all those great performers and performances of the past, tonight's concert is very special: Why? Because it is about a musical form and tradition that is unique. This event has been a long time in the making: Ladies and Gentlemen, it is my great pleasure and honour to introduce to you The Tunde Jegede Ensemble, featuring Tunde Jegede, Orphy Robinson, Juwon Ogunbe, Jan Hendrickse and Maya Jobarteh.'

The first half of the performance received rapturous applause and, as stated in the Programme, after the Interval, I was again onstage speaking about African Classical music and its context: 'In the oral tradition, poetry, history, philosophy and music were integral and the poet-musician was the voice of the people...This Ensemble of young musicians meet under the umbrella of the Griot Tradition, as the new Africans. Here the new emerges from the old for both the Marimba and the harp, Griot instruments, which have been extended far beyond their traditional uses. For the first time the baroque harpsichord comes together with its predecessors, and with the voice of the melancholy flute African memory finds new foundations on the circular path of a journey.'

In my 'Talk' reference was also made to aspects of Griot's music such as improvisation and polyphony that were employed by the great European composers Bach and Beethoven.

Afterwards, amidst the euphoria, I noticed the colourful posters placed at strategic points in the Festival Hall, as well as around the Purcell Room; publicity that worked well for this premiere which was a sell-out. If earlier on my way across the Thames I had reviewed my lines for the performance, having delivered them, now as I headed home along Waterloo Bridge, I was filled with pride for Tunde and the young musicians' historic performance for the achievement of a 'sell-out' Concert which was hailed as a great success.

Appearing on such a prestigious, hallowed South Bank stage was, for me, not only a wonderful and pleasurable experience, but also an occasion on which, I felt quite comfortable presenting the brilliant Ensemble. In various ways, this appearance was a logical extension or progression of my journey from the New Lecture Theatre stage at the British Museum to other platforms.

Having worked for so long to reveal 'hidden' aspects of British history, for example, through *The Making of the Black Working Class in Britain,* after its second short-run reissue, it was now a matter of concern to me that the book was still out of print. After the positive reviews and the book's popularity, I tried again to get it back in circulation. On 9 December 1991 I wrote to the publishers Verso and received the following reply from Robin Blackburn:

'Many thanks for your letter of 6th and for the accompanying copy of The Making of the Black Working Class in Britain. I think that the idea of republishing this book would be attractive to us. However in order to consider this it would be a great help if you were able to furnish us with the sales history of the book.

As you may imagine it would be a rather large and expensive undertaking to reprint a book of this size, especially if there is to be some additional material as I think might well be desirable.

Our next editorial meeting will be at the beginning of January...'

On this theme of republication, before the end of the year, I also heard from Literary Agent Anne McDermid who said she had passed the book to Neil Belton, a man whose judgement she respected. On this matter, it seemed, there was hope.

As the year ended, my thoughts were of course on my job in

the British Library fundamentally because of its centrality to my well-being. Without it, I would be on the streets looking for work and penniless again. Such a scenario was depressing but, as we've seen thus far, for me workplace matters were never free of worry. In fact, at this juncture, it had become a very serious matter for once more, I was confronted with the yearly merry-go-round of management's performance-promotion exercise. The 'kindergarten games' is how one colleague described the annual 'exercise.' The comments made this time round were, I thought, more interesting than previously. For the Reporting period ending in December 1991, the Counter-Signing Officer Ms D flatly contradicted the view of the new Reporting Officer Ms N who had absolutely no doubt about my ability to work at a higher grade. Indeed she thought that I would be *most suitable* for a Curatorial post! She recognised that I possessed '*an extremely wide knowledge of the Collections, which can only benefit the Library,*' and added that my expertise in my '*personal interests is sought continuously by staff as well as Scholars outside the British Library. Ron is asked to Lecture here and Overseas on his knowledge of his personal interests.* **This could be used to promote the valuable material available at the Library.**' (Author's emphasis)

The fact that my 'expertise,' so regularly called upon for many years in the service of the British Library, had yet again been ignored by Counter-Signing Officer Ms D, did not augur well as the new year beckoned.

My son who had several months before left Walthamstow for St Vincent to supervise and physically help to build his mother's house, wrote:

'Dear Dad,
My deepest apologies for not putting pen to paper. I did not wish to appear selfish, but I am sure that you will appreciate my situation.
I hope you are well, happy and in good spirits. You are my dad and as old as I am, I miss you! Thank you for your letters and your gifts. It's nice to know that not everyone has forgotten about me.
I am sure you will be anxious to find out how far the house has

progressed. Well, I have painted all of the interior of the house; fitted kitchen cupboards, tiled the two bathrooms etc. I think it looks very passable. Unfortunately my Ma does not think so... I am a person who can take any criticism, but constant bone-picking and fault finding is unnecessary and uncalled for... So you can imagine how upset I felt. Dad I worked so hard on this house only I would know... I almost came home before Christmas...

Well that is water off a ducks back now...Life is for living and learning; I'm surely doing that.

To swiftly change the course of my thought, the weather is very wet and cloudy. All I do is work, work and work. Well its better than being on the dole queue eh!

I am supposed to return to London on February 28th... I will try and contact you A.S.A.P...

Enough!! How are you? I know you will be working hard. Please don't leave it too late to find out that life is so very short and that happiness is our only ambition...I want you to be happy.

My life feels like I have full grasp of it now (maybe not control). Thank you for everything dad you have done a lot for me without probably being conscious of it. Right now I feel "rich."

Try to conserve as much energy as possible. Keep good health and I will look forward to seeing you in the near future.

Take good care.

Much love.

Ronnie.'

I have read this letter a few times and on every occasion it affects me (as it does now) deeply. Why? Because this was my son's first written communication to me and I was impressed not only by his maturity and ability to express himself, but also his great courage at such a young age (nineteen) to go to a foreign country and start from scratch with no experience as a builder. With the help of local people and labourers, eventually Ronnie was able to complete the building and decorating of the house, two years later. I was very proud of him.

In the first half of 1992 the harsh day-to-day reality of earning my living struck me hard. The wear and tear, mental and physical, of an essentially driven and unsettled life was visibly taking its toll. I was approaching my fiftieth year and found it stressful to be earning just enough to cover my basic expenses: rent, food and travel.

Nonetheless, given my nomadic, ever-changing existence as if mimicking the hustle and bustle of London, I continued to hope for a more stable pattern to my life. In furtherance of this, I hoped for better, cheaper accommodation. When? When? When? I questioned. Several months earlier I'd written to the Peabody Trust, but had yet to hear from them.

As the tense months passed with no news from the Trust, eventually my flatmate at 44 Maple Street moved out. I had no choice but to move back to the Alexandra Grove premises where, once more all my belongings were stored; and where each day I anticipated the landlord's next move: the expected final date for vacating the room. Amidst the clutter, not surprisingly, looming eviction played on my mind.

NINETEEN NINTY-TWO: SPEAKING AT THE SORBONNE AND NOTES ON C.L.R JAMES

Macmillan's editor Shirley Hamber contacted me about the rejected Monograph manuscript. She hoped that I would 'find another publisher for this' and expressed the possibility that we may be able 'to work together some time in the future.' I remained hopeful, but more immediately, there was much to do.

On the recommendation of Dr Robert Fraser of Cambridge University, I was invited by Professor Michel Fabre of the Sorbonne, to present a Paper at the African-Americans and Europe Conference to be held in Paris at the Sorbonne University between February 5-9, 1992.

Some months before, having spoken to students at the University of Seville; now, at the turn of 1992, as I prepared my presentation I looked forward to travelling to France. From the advance publicity, correspondence and the themes of Papers, this 500th Anniversary Conference promised much. The night before the opening day of the five-day gathering, I attended a champagne Reception at the Hotel de Ville (the Town Hall) in Paris where, among others, I met Professor Henry Louis Gates Jr, Director of the W.E.B Du Bois

Institute for Afro-American Research at Harvard University. He was one of the leading black American academics present.

In the days that followed, I attended many Sessions at various venues in the Sorbonne. I also made the most of my time meeting people, having coffee in the cafes and dinner in one or two nice restaurants. In the evenings I strolled along the River Seine and certain Parisian locations, rode on the Metro (underground train system) and visited the Louvre where I saw Leonardo Da Vinci's masterpiece the *Mona Lisa*. I was surprised how small the painting was. Art and culture abounded; Paris was delightful in the Springtime and I did as much as I could. After meeting Rabida Chbihi, Robert Fraser's Parisian friend, she kindly showed me around the Sorbonne. We took photographs at various popular places in and around the famous university and at the Pantheon.

After attending several sessions, it was my turn to speak at the Conference. Under the general theme: 'The Realities of Racism in Europe,' my Paper 'Blacks in Britain, Paul Robeson and Ethnic Minorities in Europe' was the last to be delivered on the final day, Saturday 8 February 1992. I gave my presentation in the Institut Du Monde Anglophone Amphitheatre where, it was said the dead body of the French revolutionary Marat was laid out. My fellow-panellists included Professors Lydia Lindsay of Central University, North Carolina and Carlton Wilson of the University of North Carolina, Chapel Hill. In the Chair was Professor Katrine Dalsgard (Professor of English at Odense University, Denmark) and the moderator was Professor Tylor Stoval of the University of California, Santa Cruz.

As the last to speak, and conscious of the new and distinguished audience that I was addressing, I opened by reiterating these words from *The Making of the Black Working Class in Britain:*

'*The long standing black presence in Britain dates back to Roman times; and although this presence was small, it would later become significant with trade and economic expansion. A significant consequence of the commerce and trade in slaves, cotton and sugar was the fact that black people began to appear in England in increasing numbers; and throughout the period of slavery and thereafter, black labour has remained a crucial factor in the development of the British economy.*'

I continued:

'Since the arrival of the first group of West Africans in England in 1555, many slaves, former slaves and the descendants of slaves from the West Indies and America found their way to Britain, and by the mid-nineteenth century many Black Radicals had emerged to play leading roles in British working class struggles. Later, the African-American Frederick Douglass was followed by W.E.B DuBois and Booker T. Washington, among others, who visited Britain towards the end of the nineteenth century as a Pan African brotherhood was being forged. It was around this time that Paul Robeson was born, an African-American destined to make his mark in Europe, especially in Britain.'

As I spoke, I glanced at many thoughtful faces in the audience. I closed by saying:

'... Since the Berlin Wall came down, there has been a disturbing escalation of racial violence in Germany, of racism, not only in Germany, but elsewhere in Europe which prompts the question: Will the 500th Anniversary of the arrival of Columbus in the New World mark the beginning of a new barbarism in Europe?

Today in Paris, we would do well to recall the courageous, uncompromising stand that the internationally famous African-American Paul Robeson took at the time of the Spanish Civil War: "I, as an artist," he said, "was drawn into that Movement and I came to see that the struggle against Fascism must take first place over every other interest."

Ultimately, this was Robeson's song of freedom, the deep, dark echoes of which is as timely as ever in Europe in 1992.'

Once again, I'd taken the *long view* within which I delineated conquest, imperialism and racism.

The applause that followed filled every nook and cranny of the jam-packed Amphitheatre.

During the discussions which followed, I responded to many questions, one of which was put by Marika Sherwood, the Hungarian-born, London-based educator-activist in the field of 'Black history.' What surprised me, however, was the comment of a white American Professor, who was based in Uppsala in Sweden. At the end of the Session, he came up to the platform and congratulated me on my Paper especially on the Robeson bit.

'Listening to you,' he said, 'I was wondering where you were taking us, but it all came right at the end.' Then he added: 'When I was a star,' and went on to confide details of his past glories as a popular lecturer. It was a surprising comment from the Professor, a total stranger who, at that moment, seemed very pleased to be there. Alas, I could not allow myself the luxury of wallowing in compliments, but in addition to the Professor, others came near the podium. Looking around the Amphitheatre, I breathed in the atmosphere. These were heady moments: a fitting conclusion to the Session which ended formalities of the historic five-day Conference at the Sorbonne. As delegates and participants, our next engagement was the finale: A Conference Banquet, due to begin three hours later.

As planned, I met Lydia and Carlton, who returned the borrowed copy of my biography of Paul Robeson. Together we made our way to the Banquetting Hall which was abuzz with chattering people; a gathering not only of Conference delegates, but also of high-profile African-Americans who were in Europe at the time. After taking a few photographs with Lydia, Carlton, Tylor and Jeffrey Green (a London-based historian), I carried around the Robeson book which caught the attention of a few people.

Later, before the New York Jazz Band had begun to play, someone said 'Danny Glover is here.' Glover was a big international star, best known for his role in the successful Hollywood film *Lethal Weapon* which also starred Mel Gibson. Knowing that my Robeson biography was being Scripted in Hollywood for a Citadel HBO film, having a copy of the book in my hand, this was a fine opportunity to meet the actor. Carlton was happy to introduce me to his fellow-American.

As we approached, to my surprise, Danny Glover, immediately recognised me. How was this possible? I wondered. Like that other occasion when Jeremy Paxman had recognised me in the British Library, because he'd seen my photograph on the inside flap of the Paul Robeson book jacket, now Danny Glover responded: his eyes were on the book in my hand. I told him about the prospect of the HBO film and he said he was approached to play the part of

Paul Robeson. This unusual conjunction of factors: led to another surprise: Danny Glover was happy to pose for photographs with him holding my book and I wearing his baseball cap!

While the New York Jazz Band played, a noisy party atmosphere had overlaid the earlier whispered formalities in the Hall. The audience was informed that the Banquet's entertainment was being bounced 'Live by Satellite' to the United States. After a while, the Master of Ceremonies, an attractive fair-skinned 'black' woman asked if anyone would like to sing a song. By now, enjoying a sense of general upliftment and the good company of Tylor, Lydia and Carlton, amidst the merriment, I moved closer to the Jazz Band and soon I was facing the distinguished audience.

'What is your name?' the MC asked. 'Ron Ramdin,' I said. Then: 'What key?' I said I did not wish to be accompanied. I took the microphone off its stand and conscious of the 'African-American' theme of the Conference, I said: 'Ladies and Gentlemen, after delivering a prosaic presentation earlier today, I would now like to sing sixteen bars of a song by that well-known African-American Nat 'King' Cole.' And so, as the cameras rolled and the audience waited. I sang: '*This, is a lovely way, to spend an evening. Can't think of anything I'd rather do…*' I may have sung more than the sixteen bars which really did not matter. Afterwards, as I made my way to the Gents Room, my path was blocked by people, a few whom I'd seen over the last five days in the various halls, rooms and corridors of the Sorbonne University. Then, they had looked at me with an air of formal academic distance. Now they saw me with new eyes, so to speak. Many agreed: 'You *can* sing!' One woman said: 'You should come to Los Angeles and try for a recording Contract'. Another said: 'You're as good as Johnny Mathis.' I took it all in my stride.

When I eventually returned to my seat which was located directly behind Professor Michel Fabre's, the Conference's Chief Organiser, he turned around and said: 'You are a man of many talents, Ron Ramdin.' I responded: 'Well Michel, after rehearsing for many years, the time comes when you have to *perform*! Today in Paris, is that time!' In effect, that day intellectually and musically I'd given a double performance at the Sorbonne.

On my way out of the Banquetting Hall, an impressive-looking African-American woman who was also leaving said: 'That was a very brave thing to do!' The 'thing' she referred to was my rendition of the song.

'Was it?' I responded.

The woman then introduced herself: 'My name is Gloria,' she said. 'I'd like to invite you to join me.' I accepted her invitation and visited the Parisian night spot, Club Saint Germain. It is said this was the place where American Jazz Great Miles Davis had met the French singer Juliet Greco and fell in love. Gloria said she was a United Nations' employee stationed in Germany. I thoroughly enjoyed her company during this unexpected, sensuous taste of Parisian night-life.

After leaving the famous Night Club, when I eventually got back to the Grand Hotel in the Latin Quarter, dawn had broken, but I was not sleepy. A couple of hours later, I packed my bags and made my way out of the hotel. Thus my eventful visit to the Sorbonne ended with a most extraordinary final Conference day and night; the climax of six days amidst the magic of spring-time in Paris!

Soon I was back in London looking through the glass panel of the tube at drizzling rain and overcast weather. As the packed train travelled from above ground into the dark tunnel, my Paris triumphs were very much on my mind: in particular, being on the Sorbonne's Amphitheatre platform from where I related how Robeson, one of the most famous singing stars of his day, had used the Concert stage to get across his message, namely the struggle of African-Americans for recognition and upliftment. By the time that I'd reached the front door of my home, London had already reclaimed me!

For those who were absent, but interested, at the request of *History Workshop Journal*, I wrote and submitted my 'Sorbonne Conference Report' for publication. It read:

'The African Americans and Europe Conference, an unparalleled event, held at the Universitie de la Sorbonne Nouvelle in Paris from 5-9 February, was organised by the Centre d'Etudes Afro-Americaines (Sorbonne Nouvelle), the W.E.B. DuBois Institute for Afro-American Research (Harvard University), the Centre for African Culture Studies

(Columbia University) and the Centre for the Study of Southern Culture (University of Mississippi).

A constant trickle of the 158 participants and those invited, from 10.00 a.m on Registration day, had by about 1.30 p.m swollen into a dense cluster of people in the small space – the Hall de la Bibliotheque, where there was also a book display. Here, there was an excited buzz as many old friends and acquaintances from various parts of the United States (the main focus of the Conference) and elsewhere in the world met again while others met for the first time.

A few hours later, we had all assembled for the grand Opening… (and) listened almost reverentially to the Welcome Address by Madame le President de l'Universitie de la Sorbonne Nouvelle…

The first Conference sessions, held in various historic halls of contrasting sizes and décor, notably the Salle de Bourjac and the Salle Liard, marked the beginning of a number of Papers on Richard Wright, James Baldwin, Chester Himes, Langston Hughes, Claude McKay, the Harlem Renaissance, Creole Louisiana, Women Writers in the Harlem Renaissance, African-American Musicians in Europe, Negritude, African American Cinema, Ideology, Music and Performance, Contemporary Poets, Visual Performing Arts, African-Americans Seen from Europe, Europe as a Haven for African Americans: Fact or Fiction? And the Realities of Racism in Europe. At all times, the well-produced Conference Booklet, a 'collector's item,' guided delegates to everything that was on offer.

The Conference organiser, Professor Michel Fabre responded sharply to those academics opposed to multiculturalism. Commenting on the fact that many African-American writers now have an international audience, he said, "it should make some of these people think twice."…

Multiculturalism was a recurrent theme at the Conference. But although the main focus was on the life and experience of African Americans in Europe, the last Session "The Realities of Racism in Europe" placed the Conference proceedings in a larger context…'

Prior to, and after the Conference, even while delivering my Paper, I was acutely aware of the juxtaposition of 'Ethnic Minorities' in Europe and Robeson's pronouncements on the 'Oneness of Mankind.' Increasingly, I felt something about this was not quite right. It needed to be examined; to be unpacked. Such thoughts were timely in terms of the evolution of my own ideas as addressed in my writings thus far.

Less than two weeks after the Paris Conference, the net-working moved apace. I received a letter from Jeffrey C. Stewart of George Mason University, Virginia. He congratulated me on my 'excellent presentation' and said he was working on a biography of Alain Leroy Locke (1885-1954), the first African-American Rhodes Scholar to enrol at Oxford University as well as a leading critic of the Harlem Renaissance. Mr Stewart was not only interested in discovering information in the British Library relating to persons that Locke had associated with during his years as a Rhodes Scholar in England (1907-1910) but also on the nature of 'Race Relations' in England at that time. Once again, my 'expertise,' arising from years of research work in the British Library was recognised. Mr Stewart added: '*I was encouraged by your remarks at your session… if you do not have ready answers you might be able to point me in the right direction…Let me say that I was impressed by your remarks…and I hope my request is not too much of a bother or a distraction from your own valuable research.*'

Given this call upon my knowledge, happily I duly responded.

A few days later Jinty Nelson wrote to me from the History Department at King's College, London, to say that my Conference Report for *History Workshop Journal* was now with the Open University Press. With much satisfaction, for a while I reflected on the excitement that I'd felt over the jam-packed days in Paris. 'Sounds like a jolly interesting Conference,' Jinty added.

While advances were being made on literary matters, I felt the time had come to put to rest a pressing matter on the home front. With my final move from 30 Alexandra Grove pending, I wrote to the Landlord:

'*I returned from Paris over the weekend to receive your letter dated 7 February and hasten to write to you, after consultation with my fellow tenants.*

I accept your offer… but, of course, as you say this offer is conditional on me vacating the premises. Given that I have, so far, been finding

it difficult to find alternative accommodation, like my fellow tenants,
I feel that vacant possession of the whole property would only be
realistically achieved if we are given more time – let's say an end of the
April deadline. I look forward to hearing from you.
Yours sincerely.'
    And so I waited.

After requesting and receiving confirmation from Peter Owen
that *Paul Robeson: The Man and His Mission* was out of print and
therefore the Publication Rights had now reverted to me, I wrote
to Penguin books:
    'Dear Mr Whitfield,
I am writing to you by way of a conversation I had recently… concerning
my biography of Paul Robeson which was published by Peter Owen
in 1987. Within months, the book was sold out and has been out
of print for about two years now. I own the publication rights for
this work, a film option of which has been bought and renewed three
times by United Artists, Yorkshire Television, Citadel Entertainment
(Hollywood) and Ted Turner. Mr Owen felt unable to republish the
book because of the…pages which Paul Robeson Jr found contentious.
    Given that the book has been widely reviewed in the United States,
Britain and the Caribbean; and judging from the PLR (Public Lending
Rights) borrowings, the indications are that a Penguin paperback would
fill a demand. I…hope we would reach an agreement on publication
(and) I shall be glad to pass on my copy of the book for your attention.
I do look forward to hearing from you.
    With Best Wishes,
    Yours sincerely.
    Ron Ramdin.'

With the matter of vacating the Alexandra Grove premises still
unresolved, at last I received a letter from Solicitors Richard Peat
stating that my Landlady *'is very anxious indeed to sell the property*
and cannot cope with the idea of waiting until June… Owning
the property now worries her to such a degree that she wants to sell
immediately. I must carry out my instructions. I regret to say therefore

that it would appear that the brief window of opportunity for each of you has closed. It is possible that I could ask Mrs Powell to agree to a payment of £1,500 to each of you provided that vacant possession was given by the time that contracts are exchanged but I can promise nothing. I do not know when contracts will be exchanged but a draft Contract has been submitted to the purchaser's solicitors and so I would expect exchange to take place within the next 2-4 weeks.
Yours sincerely,...'

This reduction in the original sum offered £2,000 provoked a quick response. Fearing a further reduction, three days later, the other tenants were unanimous in their decision and, in my absence, one of them had informed the Solicitors that:

'Subject to Contract
Further to our conversation yesterday, I am writing to you on behalf of C. Graham and M. Fillery to confirm the points we discussed.

As you can appreciate, I cannot write on Mr Ramdin's behalf. I have not spoken to him since our call. However, C. Graham and M. Fillery having spoken to him (Mr Ramdin) on Wednesday night, I understand that he is happy to agree to whatever the rest of us decide. Mr Ramdin will no doubt confirm as much should you be able to contact him.

We agree therefore, providing that your offer of £1,500 still stands and bearing in mind points B and C of our letter to you 10.2.92 to leave no later than Monday 23 March.
Yours sincerely...'

Faced with this 'decision,' I had no choice but to follow suit: accept the payment and move out. But where to? The thought of homelessness made me anxious as once more I looked for accommodation. My former flatmate Marisa said there was a nice room in the house in Northwest London where she now lived. I was, of course, interested and went to see the Landlord and Landlady, Brian and Bridie Cunningham. When I viewed the first floor bay-windowed room at 22 Plympton Road, I liked it very much. This was fortuitous for at this time of stress and strain, I craved peace and quiet. Soon after moving in, I realised the appropriateness of the room in that it afforded me the much-desired privacy for writing.

Having found this better and more secure space for my steadily accumulating precious manuscripts and books, I was also pleased to have completed what I regarded as the penultimate draft of my new book *Arising From Bondage: A History of East Indians in the Caribbean*; the result of several years of painstaking research and writing. Holding the bulky, more or less completed manuscript, I regarded it as an achievement. And so it was with some confidence that I wrote to Robert Molteno, editor of Zed Books. '*This is the first history of its kind (covering not only the former British, but also the French, Dutch and Spanish territories in the region) a timely work that fills a major gap in Caribbean historiography.*

Given my hope of an early publication of this book, please let me know of your interest in publishing it, should it meet your approval...

I do look forward to hearing from you.'

Mr Molteno replied that the book sounds 'an interesting project that we should consider,' and asked if I could send to him a Curriculum Vitae, the Table of Contents, a two or three page Synopsis and one sample Chapter. I did as requested and, hoping for the best, I stated: 'There is growing interest in this book in the Caribbean and I would like to promote it on my visit to Trinidad later this year 1992.'

Unlike his promising quick response to my first letter, with the passage of time, having heard nothing more from Mr Molteno, I sought other avenues.

At this time, I received confirmation of my biographical entry in the Fifteenth Edition of *Men of Achievement* published by the Cambridge Biographical Centre in Cambridge, England, a copy of which was in the British Library. Such a listing was all well and good, but other matters were still unresolved.

My pursuit of the C.L.R James biography was not lacking in enthusiasm, though I was concerned about not having a firm deal with a publisher which I'd hoped Curtis Brown would have brokered by now. Nonetheless, the dialogue between myself and my Agent continued.

'*Dear Ron,*

I'm sorry that you are never able to get me, I am always on the telephone, with somebody, or out of the office, so my only hope is to ring people back. It is not easy to get you! But obviously I haven't yet been able to find a buyer for your project or I would have told you so…I'm still submitting of course and will let you know the moment I get any positive news.'

After reading this, I thought about James's literary strengths and weaknesses as compared with his preponderant political bent. The news from Ms McDermid was, however, not what I was hoping for. I felt I'd been patient and, to be honest, I had begun to think of alternatives.

In the meantime, my friend Robert Fraser in his distinctive, upright hand-writing, contacted me from Trinity College, Cambridge, regarding the Sorbonne Conference

'Dear Ron,

Many and sincere thanks for your note. I am sure that you acquitted yourself - and all of us - in Paris marvellously. Indeed, I had already heard from Rabida to that effect. Fabre is a great man, and Rabida a sunny and plucky spirit. Was Paris big enough to contain the three of you?

Teaching in Cambridge is absorbing more energy than I expected, but I hope to be down in the smoke (London) again very soon, and will be sure to look you up. I have a long standing arrangement to meet Sebastian (Barker, Editor of the Poetry Society) to discuss some reading which we hope to mount jointly up here. Might I suggest that, on one occasion at least, to turn it into a threesome, and revive the honours of friendship in the French (the French House, Soho). Since you are doubtless more fluent in the language, this seems the best venue.

Until then, may your courage sustain you, and your pen never be still. Robert'.

The last eleven words were kind, generous and wise, which I heeded.

Dr Fraser's commendation triggered my reply to a letter that I'd received from the OWTU Librarian in Trinidad after my last visit there:

'Dear Donna,

Since I received your letter in September last year, my reply has been

pending as I felt with each passing week that agreement would be reached on the CLR James project…I am engaged in.

Anyway please accept my apology for the delay in responding to the permission you have granted to me of researching the James "Papers." Although I am not sure exactly when I will be arriving in Trinidad, I can say with some confidence that it will be sooner rather than later. In any case, once I have decided on a date, I shall write to you immediately. I am, of course, keen to begin work and to this end I am most grateful for the facilities you have offered. Given that time will be a pressing factor, I welcome your assistance.

Many thanks for the two copies of The Vanguard and the photocopied photos (one of which we thought was James's 'father'). If he's not James's father, who could he be? Perhaps Selma James (James's third wife) will tell me!

I look forward to meeting you again. Until then, I hope all goes well with you.'
Yours sincerely,
Ron Ramdin.'

ARISING FROM BONDAGE

By now, while work on the manuscript of *Arising from Bondage* continued, as I buckled down to my daily tasks, I was again approached by Tunde Jegede and Galina to introduce a second performance of African Classical Music on Tuesday 17 March 1992 in the Lillian Baylis Theatre, Sadler's Wells. The Purcell Room's one-night only concert had generated great interest and I was, of course, happy to support Tunde and the Ensemble in whatever way I could. So almost twenty- five years after I had sung in the Town Hall on Upper Street, now on 17 March 1992, though not as a singer, I was invited to appear once again on a stage in Islington; albeit a far bigger and more illustrious one!

As day-to-day Library office work took precedence, Robin Blackburn of Verso Press wrote expressing 'regret' that he could not republish *The Making of the Black Working Class in Britain*. If there was such a thing as an 'appropriate' publisher for the book, I thought Verso would have been the most likely to fit the description. I too regretted Mr Blackburn's decision. But life goes on and I pressed ahead with research on the James biography. In March 1992, I wrote to Mr Buhle, the American expert on Jamesiana.

'Dear Mr Buhle,

I enclose a copy of my first book which you may not have heard of and to which CLR James had written an Introduction. I had met James on a few occasions while he was engaged in doing the Introduction and subsequently we had… discussions at his Railton Road (Brixton) residence while I was researching and writing my biography Paul Robeson: The Man and His Mission and The Making of the Black Working Class in Britain.

I have, of course, read your books and other writings on James and recently received a letter from Mr Jim Danky, Newspaper Librarian at the Wisconsin State Historical Society, in which he said he had met and spoken to you about my work on a biography of James. He gave me your address in the hope that contact between us would eventually be made… Your contribution to my biography on James is, in a word, necessary; and whatever assistance you can give me would be deeply appreciated.

I will be returning to Trinidad in the next few weeks… I hope to come to the United States to do the rest of my research sometime later this year; a visit which will focus on gaining access on the relevant James Collections but primarily on your views, reminiscences, your work and papers on James.

I do look forward to hearing from you,
With Warmest Best Wishes,'
Ron Ramdin.'

In pursuit of more information, in the summer of 1992, while in Trinidad on a research mission, the well-known local journalist Harry Partap came to my father's home and interviewed me. True to his word, before I left the island, his article, a full page 2 spread under the title 'Ramdin Researches Bio of CLR James,' had appeared in The Sunday Express on 24 May 1992:

'Research for the first biography of the late writer and political thinker CLR James is now being done and the book should be on the shelves in

London, the United States and the Caribbean by the end of next year.

Trinidad-born reseacher/author Ron Ramdin, now resident in Britain, had been in the country for the past four weeks doing research and interviews for the new book. Ramdin had special permission to (access) five boxes of James's personal papers now at the Oilfields Workers Trade Union (OWTU) Quintin O'Connor Library in San Fernando.

James had bequeathed his papers to the OWTU before he died two years ago. Ramdin, in an interview last week…said he discovered information in James' correspondence that had never been made public before. He said the material is significant in understanding James's thoughts and actions.

From these papers Ramdin said, one can really assess James's impact on the intellectual community. Ramdin said the project was made "all the more exciting because of the information uncovered…correspondence left to the OWTU by James." The book will trace James's ideological and political thought and will take the author to the US where James spent some time lecturing. Ramdin interviewed a number of people in Trinidad, including calypsonian David Rudder, trade unionists George Weekes, Errol McLeod and David Abdullah as well as Attorney Lennox Pierre.

Ramdin, a researcher in his own right, has three major works to his credit. His first book, From Chattel Slave to Wage Earner with an Introduction by James was published in 1982 and is believed to be the first serious attempt at writing the history of the trade union movement in the Caribbean. The book was written after five years of research and is today required reading at most universities.

Ramdin is also the author of The Making of the Black Working Class in Britain. This monumental study of minorities in Britain was written after ten years of research. Ramdin refers to this volume as a "labour of love." The book is considered the most comprehensive analysis of the black working class in Britain and forms part of the orientation package for those who wish to understand the black communities in Britain.

His other major work is a biography of the late black singer, actor and political activist, Paul Robeson. Ira Aldridge distinguished himself as the first black man to play major roles in Shakespearean plays in the 19th century. Robeson…played similar roles in the 20th century…

Also to Ramdin's credit is a glossy book introducing the West Indies published by Heinemann. The book is titled simply West Indies and part of a series... introducing various countries to 11-14 year olds. The book gives snippets of information on social, political and economic activities in the region with special reference to the contribution of women, the East Indians, Africans and other ethnic groups as well as the religious-cultural mix...

Apart from the James biography, Ramdin is working on two other large works. He is currently researching material for a historical volume entitled "Isabella's Legacy - A Journey from Trinidad to Spain." And he is completing a comprehensive study of East Indians in the Caribbean. Ramdin said this will be the first comprehensive history of East Indians in the Caribbean diaspora. Ramdin had been discussing with interested firms in Trinidad, the funding of the publication of the book...

Armed at first only with a primary education from the Harmony Hall Presbyterian School, Ramdin studied Industrial Relations at Middlesex Polytechnic and Economics at the London School of Economics and Political Science. He is now employed with the British Library... Commenting on race relations in Britain, he said "it is like a time bomb waiting to explode." He said successive Conservative British Governments have done little to solve the problems of unemployment, lack of social amenities and educational opportunities for the black community in urban Britain. "Unless positive action is taken to address these social problems," he warned, "a Los Angeles situation can very well develop at the slightest provocation."...

The lessons of Los Angeles should be taken quite seriously... he said, adding that the black communities are crying out for more attention. "Race relations in Britain are like a time bomb waiting to explode," Ramdin says.'

Many in Trinidad who should know better thought I was scare-mongering. As well-informed and engaged as I was in fighting racism, why should I exaggerate or lie? Given the recent events of rioting in Britain, sadly my words of warning had been prophetic!

Following the maximum exposure that I'd been receiving as an author of valuable books, I was approached by Lennox 'Bobby'

Mohammed, a local Indo-Trinidadian musician whom I hardly knew. He was a friendly person and unusual in that he was a gifted steelbandsman at a time when few Indians were involved in this form of music-making. I soon learned that this man had been in the doldrums; the victim of a devastating nervous breakdown and for twenty years he was unable to take his place at centre stage, where he had been. In its 'Tribute to Pan Great' *The Sunday Guardian* stated: Lennox "Bobby" Mohammed was 'a great influence on the pan movement in the 1960s. As a teenager attending Presentation College, he and his younger brother Selvon joined the Gondoliers Band in 1958.'

A year after Bobby had started arranging for the Band, during our meeting, he told me most of the rest of his story and suggested that I write a biography of him. Apart from being flattered, Bobby's approach gave added significance to the attention I was receiving in Trinidad and elsewhere in the Caribbean.

While I encouraged him to rekindle his career he, in turn, was insistent that I should *write* about him. He said he would post some documents to me about his life and work. He kept his word; and when I returned to London, I received several newspaper clippings. Alas the pressure of other projects on my limited time meant that taking on Bobby's biography was a near impossible task. Nonetheless, having learned as much as I had, it was clear that he deserved the plaudits he'd received in recognition of his trail-blazing musicianship as arranger and composer, which predated such greats like Jit Samaroo in the pan genre.

The fact that someone as prominent as Bobby Mohammed should seek me out was a true reflection of my example as an 'achiever' to a few aspiring people in Trinidad, not just the young, but also those who were older.

On my return to England, after the high profile publicity received in Trinidad, with renewed vigour I maintained my research on the James biography for which no publishing commitment had as yet been secured. There were, of course, many other balls in the air, so to speak, and I tried to keep them in motion. I had no option and fortuitously the knock-on effect of one thing on the other was energising. It was the time of year when my Library work was once again assessed and recorded in an Annual Report. According to the Counter-Signing officer, I had the ability to work at a higher grade, but still she felt I did not show 'enough commitment' in my duties to take on the 'responsibilities for staff or resources at a higher grade.' True or false? By now, I'd come to believe these annual assessments had nothing to do with telling the truth; or about work!

So rather than pursue this hoary old chestnut as to the pros and cons of my 'fitness' for promotion, I thought it was best, in so far as I could, to let the matter lie. This attitude confirmed the fact that what really mattered was my love for the British Library and my multifaceted work therein which continued to grow.

Fortunately my reputation now as an *author* was recognised by a few distinguished British Library scholars who, as Senior Curators, time and again, introduced me to Visiting Scholars. One notable visitor was the American James Danky, the State Librarian of Wisconsin. Mr Danky rated my research, my books and knowledge of the British Library's Collections very highly; and as I continued to work on the James book without a publishing commitment, on 7 April 1992, from Providence, Rhode Island, Paul Buhle, the leading C.L.R James authority, wrote:

'*Dear Ron Ramdin,*

My good friend Jim Danky passed on news of your call, but I wasn't quite sure how I could help. Now I have somewhat more idea and... more important to me...some strong suggestions of a meaningful collaboration toward the fullest possible effort on James. Unfortunately, I am rarely in New York or even Boston, which may rule out any visit to me: almost no one actually gets to Providence. If however, you do wish to make the trip, I will be happy to sit down with you for a few hours...I dimly recall a conversation with Nello (CLR James) about your Robeson book, but foolishly I hadn't known of the volume you sent (From Chattel Slave to Wage Earner) or, I would have used it and commented on it in the James bio. At any rate, my chief concern here is that each new bio which appears best compliments the others. Kent Worcester is working on a political-intellectual biography and I've urged him to focus on James the 'New York intellectual" because a great deal of footwork remains to be done in that area. (Anna Grimshaw's focus of interest on the American Civilization manuscript helped to make some breakthrough along those lines).

The most immediately important work you can do...if I may be so bold...is to find some old-timers in Trinidad who remember the younger (pre-1932) James and others who can talk about his 1950s-70s visits in more detail than I could manage. Nieces, nephews, etc might be persuaded to talk...Also, if you can find correspondence in Trinidad it would be great. The legal complications relating to the James Papers guarantees, I think, that these will not be seriously collected for some years, and many will simply be gone by that time. Please try to do these things! **There may not be anyone else in the near future. Ron, it is up to you**! *Also as a lesser priority, scan the Labour Leader for any articles by him in the 1920s...*

In a more general sense, the West Indian James, and the Pan African James, remain the most "missing." In June, a volume I coedited with Paget Henry "CLR James Caribbean" will be published by Duke and fill in many gaps. But there is still no sustained critique of Black Jacobins. Nor is there an in-depth discussion of the 1930s London Movement, its personalities and its publications (including James own editing role, some materials, esp. International African Opinion) are at the Schomburg Library. In Black Jacobins...I wrote about James the way he thought about himself, Marxist foremost and the US period as his most creative one. Now we need to move to a wider framework... P.S...wait till we meet.'

Reading **'There may not be anyone else...Ron, it's up to you!'** reminded me of what the lawyer Lennox Pierre had said to me when I interviewed him in Trinidad: 'Nello (James) once said to me: "Who will write my biography?" ' I never forgot Pierre's words which were most encouraging as I pressed on, seeking every opportunity to meet and talk with those who knew James. So far, ever-hopeful of a publishing contract, I'd already spent quite a lot of my own money and time going to places of research far and wide.

Later, I met George Lamming, the West Indian novelist in London.

He knew James well and interestingly over a long period of time. The constraint of a tight schedule confined my meeting with Lamming to sharing a bench near a lawn adjoining Golders Green Bus Garage. During this hard-won Interview, as with others, I had to maximize limited time. What Lamming had said, was quite revealing; grist for my slowly, but steadily turning research mill. In his opinion, James would have stayed in the Caribbean (indeed there were attempts by intellectuals and artists at the University of the West Indies to keep James there in some capacity) but, it seemed, when it was put to the University's Vice-Chancellor, the proposition was rejected.

Lamming impressed upon me, his suggestion that James should write his autobiography. And it seemed that he had persuaded James to begin to do so. This work was all the more necessary because people in the Caribbean knew very little, for example, about James being in the United States, where during his fifteen year stay, he had immersed himself in political theory and organising small movements.

On the women in James's life, Lamming said 'Nello' was upset by the pressure his second wife (the American-born Constance Webb) had placed upon him. And although it was 'difficult to think of James without Selma' (his third wife) they too had parted company.

'When did you first come in contact with James?' I asked Lamming.

'We met in a peculiar way,' he said. It was sometime in 1956, a meeting which he recalled as 'memorable.' James had recognised him, having seen a picture on the book jacket of his 1953 publication *In the Castle of My Skin*. Even then, as Lamming pointed out, James's hands were 'shaky,' he could not hold a cup with one hand because he suffered from Parkinson's disease. As an admirer, Lamming was concerned with James's 'general possibilities' and had often visited him and Selma in Hampstead, London, at their flat which he had occupied when James returned to Trinidad in 1958.

In the hot-house that was Trinidad politics at the time, James broke-off with his former pupil Eric Williams; a breach which became acrimonious. Why? I pressed Lamming to tell me more. James, he said, was received in a 'humiliating way' when, after a long absence, he went back to Trinidad. All things considered, there was little or no hope that the relationship between them could have survived. The way the People's National Movement was organised was not the kind of group that James could have been party to. For James, the difference between him and Williams was a 'personal matter' not simply a policy issue.

Lamming was, however, unhappy with the manner in which James dealt with 'race' in Trinidad. His approach, said Lamming, had to do with his Victorian upbringing, his concept of 'coming out of good stock.' James was a romantic, who 'universalized' issues. He was essentially an intellectual who articulated ideas on cricket, politics and novels, a Thinker looking for connection. He possessed a sympathetic vision, hitherto in Lamming's opinion, the only Caribbean person to have that unique vision. James's mind was influenced by the imperative of philosophy. Unlike Williams, James had a philosophical mind; and in this respect, he was a bit of a 'freak' more to be found in French colonials. British imperialists, Lamming said, were not interested in ideas.

Lamming commented on other aspects of James's life: On money, he told me that James was 'a maroon, marooning all the time' and indulging in the non-academic thing, namely cricket. He also pointed out that James had over-stayed in the United States and that the last chapter of *Mariners, Renegades and Castaways* and the Ellis Island chapter does not belong to the book: It should be a separate monograph; and were it not for the McCarthy period, James would not have left the United States.

Listening to Lamming, I thought about Robeson and how McCarthyism had devalued, defamed and destroyed his great career.

Always, more or less political, not surprisingly, James went underground in America. Lamming, like many others, was impressed with James's lectures on Herman Melville. 'Those who encountered CLR never forgot him,' he said. Hearing this from the accomplished and highly-regarded novelist, I was reminded of what James himself had told me about Robeson: 'He was the greatest man I've ever met. And I've met a few!'

On food, Lamming said James enjoyed 'very good cooking.' He was especially fond of 'Buljowl,' a salt fish dish.

When James had left the United States in 1958, he was under 'heavy medication' for his Parkinson's disease, though Lamming suspected that a lot of his unsteadiness may have been 'psychological.' Lamming said Selma had told him that within two days of being in London, James had stopped 'shaking.' But having returned after his long absence to a 'very different England' where he had little or no connection on arrival, few people at the time would have known him.

Until he went to the Caribbean, James and Selma lived in Parliament Hill at the Staverton Road flat and, according to Lamming, it was a difficult period for them. James had become used to the world of 'small movements' supported by the 'Detroit Groups,' but as that world was being lost, on arrival in Trinidad, the People's National Movement entered his life and provided him with a platform.

Fascinated by Lamming's answers to my questions, I extended the bounds of my interview to include thoughts on Richard Wright, the American writer whom James had known, but had not seen for a long time. The mutual respect between James and 'Dick' Wright was well known. By now the scope and depth of my knowledge of James was such, so nuanced, that I was able to understand very well all that Lamming was saying.

After leaving the Golders Green Bus Garage while travelling on the underground train I was struck by Lamming's shock of white hair, a reminder of James's snowy crown. Both men had other things in common: their ancestral home was 'Little England' (as Barbados was known); both were advancing in age, and remarkably they both had hair as bushy as if they were youths. Clearly, Lamming appreciated James's intellectual legacy, and because he was not afraid to criticise his hero, I was all the more impressed. Before we parted company, George gave me his London telephone number; and should I need to follow up what turned out to be a wide-ranging and candid Interview, he added his home address in Barbados. This was my first and last meeting with one of the Caribbean's most celebrated literary men.

Before I got home that evening, I remembered what Sam Selvon had told me about the high regard in which he held Lamming as a Caribbean writer. In turn, I was reminded of Lamming's words about persuading James to begin writing his autobiography, sections of which I had uncovered in the OWTU Library. So, with a burgeoning cache of new research material for my James biography, but still without a publishing commitment, I proceeded.

By now, life and literature were intensely intertwined, one flowing daily into the other in such a way as to be almost indistinguishable. I was never without pen and paper. I vividly recalled certain events prior to my move to the Arched Room; a testing time when there was still no resolution to my job relocation from the Overseas English Language Section. The impending change was distracting; nonetheless, I maintained my work-rate on the Kardex Files which contained indices of listed periodicals and monographs that were in the process of being transferred online to a new computerised system. Aiding and abetting my worry were the attitude and comments of a few managers who were intent on seeing me leave the British Library voluntarily. Once more I recalled the Head of Department saying: 'We've been trying to get rid of you for years!' Then as now, I knew those words were a clear admission of his **true** thoughts; an utterance made at a time when Mr S basked in his omnipotence while I clung to my subordinate, ever-weakening position. And so the casual brutality that I'd hitherto attributed to one or two lower-ranked people, was really not the full picture. In this 'top-down' culture (a marked shift from the earlier years of management-staff side collaboration towards corporate well-being) any show of personality or evidence of a lively spirit (far from being rudeness or truculent opposition) were deemed threatening and unacceptable. Given my growing local and international reputation as an historian and writer, it was therefore not difficult to see me as a pariah. '*A square peg in a round hole,*' is how Mr S had subsequently described me. This description was the clearest indication that I'd ever heard of intolerance from a Senior figure in the British Library.

Rather than wait while the long drawn-out situation regarding my posting to another department dragged on, several weeks earlier, before my Paris visit, I had decided to bring forward the issue;

to reach some resolution. How? Every manager knew (or should have known) that my research and writings were, as we have seen, connected to my 'office work;' and so for the first time, I formally disclosed my 'research interest.' Time was pressing on all fronts and while I had no control of the job situation, it was, of course, entirely in my hands how to proceed with my writings. So, at the time, I wrote to Ms N (my new manager) who was refreshingly and to my great relief, a reasonable person:

'Given that we are now at the end of the "Sachet Conversion" of the Kardexes, the imminent relocation of my job to Boston Spa and the fact that I have not yet been able to get a job placement within the Bloomsbury book collections, it is with a sense of urgency that I submit my application for two weeks unpaid leave to facilitate important research… I have spoken to the "North American Section" Curator… about this and he has offered his full support.

If possible, I would like this Leave to spread over two months, July-August 1992.'

Alas, another request was denied. The fact that this 'Leave' was not granted, compounded the disgruntlement over my impending redeployment. Against this background, again I was feeling hemmed-in from all sides. As it was, I tried with some desperation to keep things in perspective, determined that my employment problems should not interfere with my much-valued work as a scholar and writer. If I was enthusiastic about my writing prior to December 1972 when I was first published, with my multi-dimensional writings reaching an increasing international readership, during my second visit to the OWTU Library in Trinidad, I decided to contact Margaret Sinclair, Commissioning Editor of Heinemann Educational Books and publisher of *The West Indies.*

'Dear Margaret, I wrote, *I have just returned from Trinidad where (a)… knowledgeable Librarian…was astonished when I showed her a copy of World in View:West Indies. Given her interest in children's educational books, she confessed she had never seen or heard of the book before, although it was published in great haste to meet a deadline in 1990.*

Subsequently, I was appalled to learn that your Agent in Port of

*Spain, following the Librarian's enquiry, knew nothing of the book…
except that she saw something about it in a catalogue. The view of
several teachers and a Headmaster that I had shown my copy to, is that
it is a much-needed general reference textbook for schools and libraries,
especially at this time when Curricula changes are being made. With
such a recommendation, for the first time, the book needs the best
publicity possible…it is now imperative, as I have been advised by
local educators, that the book should immediately be brought to the
notice of the "Education Committee" of the Ministry of Education. I
have been reliably informed that a Fund has been recently allocated to
buy such books.*

*If this necessary book is so little known in Trinidad it would be
interesting to know if the same is true in Jamaica and in the rest of the
West Indies. I did speak to Ms Lam Pow, your Trinidad Agent and she
said she would be in touch with your office. But ordering one copy is
hardly what is evidently necessary to meet an urgent demand. Indeed,
a more aggressive sales technique is crucial. I will be returning to
Trinidad early next year in the hope that by then all schools, libraries
and bookshops will be well-stocked with World in View: West Indies.*

*I shall of course be most grateful for your full support in dealing with
this matter.'*

To underline the international success of the book which was
quickly sold out in Britain (and copies distributed in schools as
far away as New Zealand), after another edition was published
in North America by Steck-Vaughan, that too had fully satisfied
demand. Altogether, through this engaging book tens of thousands
of children around the world would have, for the first time, learned
about the West Indies. The thought of this, made me proud.

In addition to the highly respected persons of Trinidad and Tobago
mentioned earlier in *The Trinidad Express* article, I also interviewed
Hulsie Bhagan, an Indian woman who had been making a name
for herself by standing up for women's rights and other local issues.

So involved had I become with the James project that I felt I was
increasingly crossing boundaries. In research terms, this visit was
clearly one of the most intensive and ambitious. I met Literary
Critic Chris Laird of the Banyan Film Company for the first time.

It was a good meeting; and recognising my unrelenting schedule, the devotional way in which I approached my use of Banyan's archive, he described me as 'The man who does not eat.' Why? Because ever-concerned with *time* and its fleetingness, bearing in mind that my stay in Trinidad was limited, I never took a break for lunch!

So it was that over three weeks, each morning after breakfast, I travelled from the Sand Road to San Fernando, then on to Port of Spain and the offices of Banyan, where I went through a number of unedited videos to get copies of the audio-tape recordings of filmed C.L.R James 'Interviews.' This little known material was, of course, invaluable. On my return to London, I contacted Chris to thank him. He replied: '*Great to hear from you! Happy New Year! As you write of the work you have been doing on CLR James's biography I have images of you in the midst of winter in the British Library researching – far from the fresh air of the Caribbean.*

I am pleased we were able to forward your work in some way with our material. I look forward to the East Indians in the Caribbean book – Arising From Bondage. Yes, Yes, Yes! I would be thrilled to work with you on a television version of that story.

How do we proceed? When can I see a copy of the book?'

Knowing the importance and dearth of a filmed story of East Indians in the Caribbean, the next day I wrote thanking Chris for his 'positive response.'

Following the correspondence with Chris Laird, Toni Morrison, the celebrated African-American novelist, had come to London to promote her latest novel. Having enjoyed *The Song of Solomon* and *The Bluest Eye,* now I looked forward to her latest offering. Unable to attend one of her personal appearances, through her London publisher, I sent a copy of my book *The Making of the Black Working Class in Britain* to her. A few weeks later, I received her personal Postcard embossed with her name. I was struck by her penmanship. Her handwriting in black ink was impressive; strong and distinctive:

'*Dear Ron Ramdin,*
Your gift of The Making of the Black Working Class in Britain lessens

*my disappointment in missing you while I was in London. I am eager
to read it and hope when you are in the States that we can meet.
Warmest Regards,
Toni Morrison.'*

Meanwhile, my authorial reputation, widely respected in Britain
and abroad, led to an invitation from the new High Commissioner
of Trinidad and Tobago in London, Mr P.L.U Cross, a war-time
hero in the British Air Force. Mr Cross had contacted me about the
High Commission's Awards Ceremony to celebrate the Thirtieth
Anniversary of the Independence of Trinidad and Tobago which
he would be hosting at the High Commissioner's Residence on 5
September, 1992. 'This year's event takes the form of a Garden Party,'
the Invitation stated and 'as one of our distinguished awardees your
presence at this event would be very much appreciated...'

I accepted the invitation and at this essentially Trinidad-Caribbean
Event when asked what new project engaged me, I was happy to
say that I was writing the first comprehensive biography of C.L.R
James. In this connection, just a few days later, James Danky, the
American scholar and Librarian (whom I'd met earlier when he was
a Visiting Fellow at the British Library) was in touch.

*'Dear Ron,
Please drop Paul Buhle a line as soon as possible. He wrote to me and
is confused that he has not heard from you. I am sure you are busy but
he wants to be helpful to your project... I will call sometime to catch
up in a more immediate way.
Sincerely,
James Danky.'*

I was very pleased to know the Buhle connection was still alive for
thus far I had exerted enormous energy and time, as well as money,
on the James project. I did write to Mr Buhle and the research was
shaping up nicely, but as yet, *no publisher* was willing to commit to
publishing my book. Nonetheless, as I kept up the momentum of
travel and research, Paul Buhle eventually replied to my last letter:

'*Dear Ron,*

... I don't have use of an institutional phone and so can't call you. I should be contacted here by phone only in the day times (as early as you like). See if you can delay your trip (to the US) till April '93. I say so because we are having a Conference at Brown University: "CLR James's America" the most extensive treatments by far of the 1938-53 and 1970-... periods!! There are no travel funds and so forth, but it will be lively and informative. More details later (we have to set the weekend!). That's my best advice! Meanwhile I have a foot out of town, I'm travelling over the weekend but I will try to get to the Post Office with an airmail copy of the Journal issue...I suspect you won't find much new anyway. Now as I think James Danky suggested, the best way to win my time and interest is through reviewing CLR's Caribbean for some English publication. We need help, but it is surely the best way of knowing that your intention is good... in the collective or cooperative sense that a wide circle of us have managed to establish with each other! Not that criticisms of the book should be absent, its an oddly mixed text which began as things left over from the bio and then evolved in Paget's (Paget Henry, a West Indian academic) hands. But material in it will prove valuable I am sure, to anyone deeply interested in James. And it is in danger of simply disappearing.'

There could be no doubt, as to how 'deeply interested' I was in the James biography as my continuing self-financed travel, research and writing commitment had shown. But as with *From Chattel Slave to Wage Earner*, I was equally determined to proceed without a publisher's Contract. Borne by sheer commitment, founded on a strong belief in the value of the work, I was carried forward.

PART FOUR

TURNING PAGES:
LITERARY QUESTS,
MEANINGFUL THOUGHTS

TWENTY

ISABELLA'S LEGACY:
OLD WORLD, NEW WORLD

Over the years, prior to, and especially since I'd left the London School of Economics, increasingly as research led to deeper study and I became more knowledgeable, I began to appreciate even more the relationship between subjects such as history, travel, memoir, culture and identities. And so in October 1992, with the approach of autumn, as planned, once more I was on my way to Spain; to Seville in particular. I was returning for the great *Expo: Sevilla 1992* which marked the 500th Anniversary of the arrival of Christopher Columbus in the New World.

In the last weeks of the quincentenary celebrations on 8 October 1992 I was back in the city for the third successive year. As before, I stayed with my friends Marisa and Margarita. The next morning after opening my *Short History of Seville*, I reiterated my interest in pressing on with writing my book on Spain in which the sisters were very interested. After reading a few pages of the *Short History of Seville*, we left for the Expo.

Immediately inside the massive complex, there were an assortment of shops or stalls selling a wide range of memorabilia: magazines, postcards, caps, T-shirts etcetera. We turned left onto one of the many impressive bridges spanning the Guadalquivir River, which took us into the main Expo area. As we approached the various pavilions, to my left, was one of the largest: The gigantic US Spacecraft *Discovery* with its familiar NASA insignia in large blue letters; and, as we had expected, long queues snaked their way along the main and subsidiary pathways leading to the first pavilion, appropriately entitled: 'Discovery.'

From the Exposition's Bookshop, at the end of this section, we stepped down an incline which led to the water's edge, where replicas of Columbus's three caravels (the *Nina*, *Pinta* and *Santa Maria*) all sailing ships of the period of 'discovery' were moored. These were magnificent models. Swaying gently, proudly, they were the focus of the curious, admiring gaze of hundreds of thousands of visitors who had come from far and wide: from different parts of the 'Old World' and the 'New World,' as well as from the East and the West to pay homage.

I did not go aboard all three vessels. My focus was on Columbus's flagship the *Santa Maria*. While on deck, leaning against a fixture, I imagined what it must have been like for Columbus and his intrepid men cocooned inside as this small vessel rode the gigantic swells of the forbidding 'Ocean Sea' (the Atlantic) during their fearful journey to the then 'unknown' world from where almost 500 years on, I had come! Given my wide reading and understanding of history, being an integral part of this historical moment and mindful of the immensity of the *SS Canberra,* it was with a sense of wonder that I toured the small caravel. I peered through the port-holes, examined the cramped cabins and climbed up to the Captain's room. All this gave me some idea of the confined spaces as my imagination came into play: I considered the battering that the wooden structure, the ropes and sails would have taken during the voyage in 1492. One brochure informed me that the ship I was in had travelled thousands of miles around the world as part of a publicity exercise for *Sevilla '92*. Moored on this famous River, these sailing vessels facing seaward (westwards) were juxtaposed just a few yards from the 'Discovery' Space capsule which pointed skywards, the direction of mankind's future exploration. Both modes of travel (evocative of human inventiveness) spanned the half-millennium of man's quest to reach out and discover new worlds.

Being on the *Santa Maria*, I realised it would be impossible to see all the magnificent pavilions, or at best, most of them. I therefore decided to be selective: from my Guide, I targeted the pavilions that I could realistically visit and collected leaflets, pamphlets and the like relating to those exhibits that I regarded as being of low priority.

Fortunately, I was able to spend some time at the Trinidad

and Tobago booth. Symbolically and physically, I derived great satisfaction from the time spent there. My next move was to the India, Dominican Republic and Spanish pavilions, including the 'Parbellon Andalucia.' The many pathways through the entire Exhibition area was covered by a green canopy of vines and flowers; an environmentally friendly, pleasant and effective way not only of keeping cool in the heat, but also of affording shelter from possible showers of rain. By the end of our long and winding walk through the Exhibition, I had been the subject of several photographs taken at key junctions, including one or two along the new spectacular bridge, so emblematic of the event.

Overall, the visit was an extraordinary experience, which I was determined to capture through writing, complemented by photographic images. I was especially conscious of the connectedness of places and people, notably between India, Trinidad and the Spanish pavilions. Given the conjunction of so many factors, I was overwhelmed to be present for the Anniversary; and, of course, to have seen Palos, the very place where it all began! By 'it' I mean my historic connection, identification and 'identity' in relation to Spain. So, with great satisfaction and arms full of commemorative material, I walked with my companions across the vibrating, high-tech suspension bridge; a symbolic spanning of East and West that afforded me a route away from the milling, feverish Expo crowds to the less congested space that was the Calle Alameda.

Having anticipated the Expo since 1990, now I was looking back at it. My continued reading of the *Short History of Seville* made the prospect of visiting the Roman settlement of Italica, a real possibility. Conscious that this was more than likely the last visit before getting down to writing my book on Spain, I was keen to take every opportunity of meeting and interviewing Flamenco artists: singers, dancers and musicians; and generally to take a fresh look at things that had earlier caught my attention. Vigilance was the key for by my reckoning especially now, the 'interesting thing' was the 'important' thing.

The sound of El Camaron was everywhere: in life and now after his death, he was regarded by those in the know as the 'King of Flamenco' singers: an icon. His legend and spirit lived on;

everywhere I went there was evidence of this. Interestingly, he was highly appreciated by singers and musicians in Seville. Among them was Fernanda de Utrera, the famous and enduring Flamenco diva.

In Camaron's absence she was the singer that I most wanted to meet. Eventually (with the help of Marisa and her friends) Fernanda agreed to meet me. With her entourage in tow, our meeting took place in a café. Through an interpreter, she told me about her life and work: about singing and clapping and the main centres of the Gypsy art of Flamenco. She had stood the test of time; and to many experts, she was also 'iconic.' I felt deeply honoured to have met and interviewed her.

Later, in the flat, while leafing through a copy of the magazine *Encounters*, I stopped suddenly when I came across a full page advertisement which provoked deeper thoughts. As a child and teenager, the Texaco Oil Refinery (formerly TLL) at Pointe a Pierre dominated the lives of thousands of people in the surrounding villages and towns of south Trinidad. My father had worked there, as I had done temporarily. But Texaco was especially significant because it was there on the beautiful Guaracara Park that I'd made my debut as a top League footballer wearing the Texaco jersey with its red star and green T logo. Now I considered the 'advertisement' which was published several months before: Under the heading 'Texaco is proud to sponsor the Rediscovery of the New world,' the company stated:

'As the 500th anniversary of Columbus's historic voyage draws near… Texaco is proud to be the first corporate sponsor to work in concert with the US and Spanish Quincentenary Commission in planning the…Western Hemisphere tour of the official replicas of Columbus's three ships. By helping to make this historic event a reality, we are pledging our continuing commitment to the same ideals personified by Columbus: leadership, determination and vision. Join all of us in this grand celebration as the Nina, Pinta and Santa Maria sail to their ports of call in the New World. We are constantly exploring to find new sources…and better ways to make high quality petroleum products.'

Thus, from sugar cane (the plant that Columbus had originally introduced to the New World) production to Texaco oil exploration in Trinidad and various other parts of the Americas and elsewhere, the spirit of multinational enterprise was alive and well.

Over coffee, I considered what one Sevillean had said to me about the Pope's forgiveness in relation to the infamous decimation of the Indians that Columbus had found in the newly discovered lands. At the time of Spain's colonisation, views on the ill-treatment of the indigenous people were polarized. The 'good' Bishop Bartolome de Las Casas, for example, himself a former slave-owner, had devoted over sixty years of his life exposing the massacre of the Indians. He had tried tirelessly to get the Spanish government to adopt a more humane attitude toward their charges and fought against Spanish officials who were blinded by greed for the spoils of the New World. If indeed there was a time for prayer and 'forgiveness,' whatever the Pope may or may not have done, 'the time is now,' I thought. 'Better late than never.' Thereafter I reflected on Mac Shapin's article on these Indians which places them in historical context:

'In recent years, scientists have been telling us about the necessity of maintaining the planter's biological diversity. Cultural diversity is no less important. As it diminishes, the lives of all of us become more impoverished. As the forests disappear across the tropics, so do cultural groups that reside within them. We are thus losing both biological and cultural diversity simultaneously.

The first step in the reflection process should be consideration of the long overdue task of discovering who these people are and what they think about the world we inhabit together. They need to be given both a voice and a vote. They need support in their efforts to organise and protect their lands and their resources. They need to be given the freedom to determine the course of their own lives and to maintain their own cultural configurations. Above all, they need to be accorded the status of equals. It will only be when some of these things come to pass that the Indian peoples of the Americas will perhaps be able to view the "encounter of two worlds" in a less tragic light.'

An interesting piece. Later, the city that had hosted a massive show of human ingenuity was treated to a spectacular display of fireworks that lit up the night sky for some time before the final flickering lights of *Expo Sevilla '92* went out. For eight months, an estimated 20,000 people had gained employment. What would they do now that work was no longer available? How do Sevilleans feel about the Expo anyway? A man named Ilario gave me his views:

'I am not sure this Expo was a good thing for Seville,' he said in almost perfect English. 'Many people had employment, but now they are unemployed again.'

As he spoke, I was prepared to ask what he thought the cost of mounting the Expo might be, but instead I listened: 'No one knows for sure,' he said. 'It must have cost billions.'

Ilario was thirty-four years old and I asked him why he was not sure about the benefits of the Expo. 'Well, do you know that we have only recently finished paying the debt of the last Expo held in Seville in 1929?'

I admitted my ignorance of the particulars of that event of the late Twenties.

'Officials said that this Expo was not running at a loss,' he added, 'but we don't know that. Not yet, anyway.'

In all the conversations that I had had with Spaniards and non-Spaniards during the months leading up to the Expo (and for its duration) I had heard talk of the 1929 Ibero-American Expo debt which fell on the people of Seville. Now Ilario had aroused my curiosity and talked a great deal about his job prospects. 'The market is for younger people,' he stressed in a weary whisper. 'And this *is* a problem not only in Spain.'

'I agree with you', I said. 'It is not the same, but similar in London.'

Ilario leaned forward and reached for his glass of lager. 'What part of London are you from?' he enquired.

'I work in Central London, in Bloomsbury, where I spend most of my time after work researching and writing,' I said. 'I recently moved to North West London to live near Hampstead in the area known as Kilburn.'

'I don't know Kilburn,' he said. 'But I lived in London for two years, and for five years in Germany. What kind of books you write?'

'So far, I've written history, a biography and a school textbook.

My historical writings focus much on Britain's pre- and post-colonial history, as well as on the problems of migrants in Britain and Europe.'

Ilario talked about life in Germany; and as he did so, I felt he was answering the questions I would have asked. Thus he gave me ample information about himself: for example, as a young Spaniard working in northern Europe that he had experienced exploitation and discrimination against Spaniards. 'You might well write about black people in Britain,' he laughed, 'but I also had problems in Germany. There I was "less white" than other whites!'

I was moved and most sympathetic to what Ilario had said. In fact, it was the very problem of race and colour and national boundaries in Europe that I'd addressed when I spoke at the University of Seville; a Lecture which, in large part, was also given some months later at the University of the Sorbonne in Paris in 1992. With no encouragement or direction from any organisation or institution, I was spreading the word. To my knowledge, no one had previously given a Lecture entitled: 'Towards 1992: Discovery and Ethnic Minorities in Europe' in Spain and to have done so also in France during this Quincentenary year was significant.

'Anyway, the longer I stayed in Germany,' Ilario continued, 'I realised that the problem of being "less white" was not a great problem because as more and more black people arrived, after a while I was treated *as white!*' Among migrants and minorities, this privileging of one group over another was an ongoing and integral part of my own experience.

In spite of this acceptance in northern Europe, Ilario chose to come back to Spain to live and, at the time of our meeting, he was studying for a higher degree at the University of Seville. If he was unhappy about encroaching change in the city, others were less concerned, at least on the surface. On the whole, however, from the many people of all ages with whom I'd spoken, among the young in particular, there was little about Sevilla '92 to get worked up about. And so I reflected that in its long history of survival, it seemed Seville had seen and absorbed the changes of many conquerors and remained an Andalusian conjuction of many cultures: an evolving rich mix, with a capacity to transform itself.

The former capital of the New World, as we approached the end of the century and the end of the millennium, was still a most exhilarating and wonderful city.

While some Expo commentators regarded the encounter between the Old and New Worlds as 'tragic,' others saw it as less so. As the debate continued, until his dying day, the Genoese sailor believed that on his first landfall in the West, he had indeed reached India in the East. And now 'Here I am,' I noted, 'not only a descendant of people from India, but also born in Trinidad (one of the Explorer's "discoveries") and unable to speak either Hindi or Spanish. Nonetheless as I moved around the city, I was perceived as 'Gitano,' a Gypsy. Columbus mentioned India often in his writings and incredibly I had survived to make the reverse voyage from West to East. Thus, if 'historical moment' is an over-used term, I hope the reader will forgive my indulgence in stating that being in Seville on the Quicentennial Columbus Day, I felt rather special for I was not only part of the celebrations, but also a maker of history.

To say that I wasted no time in Seville was an understatement; all the more so because arrangements had been made for me to meet an 'important person.' It was the day after Columbus Day when I met Emilio Acosta, a Gypsy at Albero's Bar. He was distinctive-looking: slim, handsome, his tousled hair turning silver, his dark-brown eyes intense, a man in his late Forties, perhaps fifty. He was with a girl-friend, who doted on him. He said he'd heard much about me. From whom? I wondered, but did not ask. It could only have been my friend Marisa.

Very soon I felt the presence and energy of Emilio the 'Maestro' Flamenco dancer *extraordinaire.* He struck me as a 'man of substance' and, as such, I felt his views on certain questions relating to Gypsies in Spain would be invaluable.

Emilio's command of English, though limited, was spoken with due deliberation and with remarkable authority; his words clearly pronounced. He understood a great deal more than he was able to articulate in English. Nonetheless whatever he said, given the prodigious store of experience and knowledge he possessed, would be well received. Thus far, there were many gaps in my understanding; and knowing little or nothing about this man, I adopted a direct approach: as it were, I took him at face value.

'What kind of dancing do you do?' I asked.

'Flamenco,' he said as he stepped off his stool and raised his slim arms above his head in an elegant gesture. Holding that position, he then clicked his fingers and moved one step sideways. Then he said: 'Flamenco music is a mixture of both Indian and Arabic influences.' This statement, to some extent, echoed the thoughts of another Spaniard I had met.

'Flamenco music is identified all over the world with being Spanish,' I said. 'Why aren't Gypsies, the main performers of this music, given a higher profile, especially in this year of unprecedented international attention on Spain.'

Suddenly Emilio's brown face assumed a darker shade. 'We Gitanos are at the bottom. The whole society is against us.' Hearing this, I recalled Kiko's words: 'Flamenco will remain a specialist music, for a specialist audience, because Gypsies are *outside* the mainstream of society. This is their own choosing.'

'But why?' I asked Emilio, 'after so many years, centuries, is this still so?'

'Because Gypsies do not want to be controlled,' Emilio answered. At this juncture, remembering my earlier hopes of interviewing Camaron who had extended the boundaries as a Flamenco artist, I asked: 'What do you think of Camaron?'

'Camaron was the *King*,' Emilio said, 'not only with his expressive face, but also with his whole body. He is a hero among the Gitanos. He expressed their fears and joys. He was also *very proud* to be Gitano.'

Last year while I was in Seville,' I said, 'I heard a recording of Camaron singing with the London Philharmonic Orchestra. A wonderful 'idea' and what a superb performance! What is your opinion of this shift away from what some call "pure Flamenco?"'

'It shows what an artist he is,' Emilio was quick to say. Then after a long pause, which gave due weight to his words, he added in a firm voice: 'But *that* is not Flamenco!'

More than once, Emilio had invited me to be present in his studio in Seville to see him at work: conducting a Master Class. On the appointed day, I watched as the Maestro of Flamenco Dance put his students through their paces. The lightning speed of his booted feet and the elegance of his carriage, his arms and torso, was breathtaking. How fortunate his students were, I thought. And how fortunate I was to have met him, at this time, in this place. He inspired trust and confidence in him. There was no one in Spain (indeed in the world) better placed than Emilio to inform me about the things I needed to know. I hung on the words of the Maestro and almost as a passing reference, he told me he had danced in the Sistine Chapel in Rome for Pope John Paul. What? I thought I'd heard him incorrectly; a statement which I quickly came to terms with for what he'd confided in me confirmed my initial positive impression of him.

Later, Emilio kindly invited me to his home where he went through numerous documents, including newspaper cuttings, concert programmes and photographs. He put aside some of the material and placed them in a large grey folder which he said I could take back to London for use in my book. I was deeply touched by this magnanimous act; most grateful to have precious documents which helped me to gain further insights into Emilio's background and importantly on his life and greatness as a performer.

I learned that he was born in Seville where he grew up and from the age of eleven he was drawn to the art of Flamenco. He was not 'trained' as such, but studied every movement with characteristic Gypsy passion. Gradually, with growing confidence, he had practised and mastered the pattern of steps and movement required: blindingly quick footwork, whirling, stamping and emotional engagement with the inimitable rhythms of Flamenco. Flamenco, the Gypsies say, is 'in the blood,' and thus the boy became the young man with flashing eyes and the cat-like walk, as he emerged into a beautiful dancer.

Having joined Lusillo's Company in Madrid, young Emilio toured all over Spain, Europe, Australia, New Zealand, Japan, the Far East and North and South America. So brilliant a dancer had he become that Lusillo created the role of *Don Quixote*, especially for him.

Reading through Emilio's papers from the grey folder, I was

impressed by a corrected, typewritten draft of an unsigned Review (or statement) entitled 'SPANISH FESTIVAL' written after a performance in South Africa, which read:

'On a good festival there is always something for everyone; for those who desire only the best and want to be entertained, no matter what the cost. A Spanish Festival is no exception to this rule...

The best dance and...I speak of the best dance in the full sense of the word. Technical graceful movement and true emotional content without which the paces cannot be called dancing, was performed by Emilio Acosta. The man has the ability to DANCE which is equally enviable...

*The height of his performance in this programme is his zapateado in the Flamenco section of the program. His feeling for rhythm and his complete muscle control and his musicality makes this dance **something a person will not easily forget**...'*

A fitting tribute, I thought, to a man who, at this stage of his life, was obviously at the top of his game and thus a worthy ambassador of dance.

In spite of his success and great acclaim in South Africa, Emilio returned home to Seville to recharge the Spanish spirit. Seventeen years later, after his South African sojourn, I had the good fortune, the privilege of not only meeting this great Dancer, but also of enjoying his companionable company, his 'friendship' and, to some extent, his confidence of which I have ever since been respectful.

Both Emilio and Fernanda de Utrera, Gypsy artists of the highest rank, have on separate occasions, and independent of each other, honoured me by giving of their time and answering my questions. Interestingly, Emilio and Fernanda both recognised my 'Gypsy likeness.' Although I'm not a Gypsy I am proud to put on record my meetings with these fascinating human beings who (while belonging to a group that had been – and is - abused and oppressed in various parts of Europe) are among the greatest of Spain's exponents of Flamenco art.

In my imagination, another part of Spain interested me. Before I thought of visiting Cordoba, I had read of it as 'a place of learning,' a place of Muslim enlightenment. The names Averroes and Maimonides came to mind as we travelled by road. Our stop for lunch at a hotel was brief for the simple reason that I wanted to spend as much time as possible to see the much-praised Mosque in Cordoba.

The Mezquita was at the centre of the city and, at the time of my visit, I had entered through the Puerta del Perdon. Having no pre-conceptions, I was overwhelmed by the architecture: most strikingly, by the forest of columns; the impressive arches and windows. I tried to make sense of the maze-like complexity and huge size of the structure and, as I moved about inside, I became more and more appreciative.

Coming out of the Mezquita, I was greeted by the brilliant glare of Spanish daylight, the hubbub of crowds of tourists milling around and passing in and out of souvenir shops and cafes that encircled the Mosque-cum-Church. Just beyond this huddle of colourful sights were white-washed pathways, patios and the Calle de los Flores, or the Street of Flowers. Leaving Cordoba, after this short stay, I turned to take one last look; and once again, my eyes followed the Guadalquivir River and the nearby bridge which spanned it. How emblematic was that cross-over both culturally and socially for the people of Cordoba, all the more so because the River was, for centuries, the crucial link between Cordoba and the great city down-stream: Seville, to which I was now returning.

In Seville, I was hoping against hope to meet a bullfighter. After several attempts, I was eventually guided towards a spacious flat off Calle Alameda where I was introduced to Manuel, a gangling fresh-faced youth, not the sort of person I'd expected to meet. Why? Because he was a boy in training to become a professional bullfighter. Seeing him, I was overwhelmed by a strange feeling: a combination of excitement and sadness too.

Manuel talked to me about the importance of the bull. 'It is the symbol of Spain,' he said. 'You see the map of Spain,' he added, 'If you spread the skin of a bull, it is the same shape as the map of Spain!' I'd not heard this before. His respect for bulls took me aback.

'Rong,' he said. He could not pronounce my name as Ron. The bulls for the bullring are spess-sial. They are prepared for the bull fight. They live a good life. They eat very well so when they are killed in the fight, no part of them is wasted. Bull meat is very expensive and all parts of the bull are eaten.'

As I digested this mouthful of clearly pronounced words, Manuel got up from his chair and pointed to the side of his upper leg. 'This is the *best* part of the bull for eating,' he said.

He then spoke about the bull fighters 'hat,' an image which provoked thoughts about a passage written by Ernest Hemingway in *Deaths in the Afternoon* in which he informs the unwary reader:

'*The bullfight is not a Sport in the Anglo-Saxon sense of the word, that is, it is not an equal contest or an attempt at an equal contest between a bull and a man. Rather it is a tragedy; the death of the bull, which is played, more or less well, by the bull and the man involved and in which there is danger for the man that can be increased by the bullfighter at will in the measure in which he works close to the bull's horns... This danger of goring which the man creates voluntarily can be changed to certainty of being caught and tossed by the bull if the man, through ignorance, slowness, torpidness, blind folly or momentary grogginess breaks any of these fundamental rules for the execution of the different suertes (acts)...*'

As these words played on my mind, young Manuel explained that in the bullring, the bullfight is in three parts. As he talked, I recalled what I'd read about the beginning and subsequent events in the lives of two other boys who were eventually ranked among Spain's most renowned bullfighters: Belmonte and Manolete.

Belmonte was regarded by many bullfight enthusiasts as 'the face of Spain.' Born in 1872, he was the eldest of 11 children and was brought up amidst the debilitating poverty and hopelessness of the slums of Triana in Seville. His formal schooling ended when he was eight. Thereafter, he fell prey to a life of stealing and generally getting into trouble with a gang who imitated bullfighters by practising passes using their jackets as capes. In this tough neighbourhood by the time he was 16 (about Manuel's age) he entertained the grand ambition (or was it delusion) of becoming a professional Torero. Did he have the wherewithal: The physical and mental attributes to make it? On the face of it, that seemed quite unlikely for he was 'sickly' and 'bandy-legged.' Taken together, the disadvantages of being poor and ill-educated were enormous. But he worked hard to turn liabilities into assets, as time and again, he was cheered in Seville's Maestranza by fans who were the most knowledgeable in Spain. In time, Belmonte not only had fame, but also wealth and beautiful women.

Manolete was also a poor boy. He grew up in Cordoba and remembering that his real name was Manuel, I wondered if the aspiring boy before me (Manuel) was named after the great man. Manolete was, by all accounts, a frail child, having suffered from pneumonia when he was a baby. Like Belmonte, he was not modest in his ambition. He aimed to become nothing less than the greatest bullfighter who ever lived. A tall order, to say the least, because he was an unlikely candidate: malnourished, skinny, awkward and 'ugly.'

Many laughed, seeing him as a weak, pathetic figure pitted against raging bulls. Then as his apprenticeship passed and he came to public notice, according to one bullfight enthusiast, it seemed as if Spain was 'waiting for this kind of fighting.' His subsequent rise was meteoric; and by 1946, he reigned supremely as 'King' of the bullfighters. At the height of his fame crowds imbued with ever-growing adoration followed their hero to Linares where he was scheduled to fight a Muira bull. As the fight proceeded, unexpectedly, he was gored. Of this tragic incident, Kenneth Tynan, the British writer and critic wrote: 'The cheers pursued Manolete to the Infirmary, but he was already insensible and did not hear the last ovation of his life.'

Manolete and Belmonte were motivated not simply by money, but by a desire to be someone respected, as well as hoping to achieve something great.

Listening now to young Manuel, my thoughts on the great bygone fighters Belmonte and Manolete, persisted. Before Manuel's parents had served dinner, we were all in the dining room where the conversation was centred upon, and dominated by, Manuel. I remained fully engaged, spell-bound: listening attentively, aiding, encouraging him every now and then when he hesitated to find the right English word.

'Are you afraid of facing a bull?' I asked.

'All Torero are afraid,' he said.

Later that night, I marvelled that hours earlier I had no idea what Manuel would turn out to be.

As it was, he showed great respect for the training he was undergoing and, looking forward, he invited me to come back to Spain to see him fight his first bull. Touched by his invitation, I embraced him; and as I walked away from his father's flat, I thought about his future, mostly his respect for bulls and of that moment to come when he would have to kill a bull. Nonetheless, such a killing would, of course, only be credited with all due respect by aficionados if it was done *artistically!*

The finer points of the blood sport of bull-fighting were all very new to me and now I was close to being overwhelmed by all that I'd heard.

As ever on my visits to Spain thus far, time was of the essence; and, once more, it was against me. I had only two days left and yet again, I had to forego an 'Italica' outing. I had pinned reasonable hopes on doing an Interview with Kiko, a Composer, singer and recording artist. Some months before, by chance, I had seen him in a café on Museum Street in London. Now in Seville, I was on my way to Interview him.

Kiko was close to the singer Camaron. This was fortuitous. Over coffee, Kiko revealed his knowledge of the legendary Gypsy. Without doubt, Camaron was 'the Number one Gypsy singer,' he said. 'And Paco de Lucia (the famed guitarist) was Camaron's close friend and accompanist.' I had already known something about the connection between the guitarist and the singer, but not much more. Music had cemented the relationship between the Gitano and non-Gitano in an extraordinary, even unique way and Kiko spoke about the two men easily and with authority. I was most encouraged; and for the rest of the Interview Kiko was happy to speak his mind.

As on previous visits, I'd seen posters along the streets about the Gypsy bullfighter, Curro Romero and wanted to know what Kiko felt was the link between Flamenco music and bullfighting. 'Why do you like bullfighting?' I asked.

'Because it is more than theatre,' he said. 'It is real life tragedy.'

The closest I'd ever got to a bullfight was walking around in the yellowish sand near the Maestranza. I'd read Hemingway's descriptions, seen photographs and films and had followed the debate about the pros and cons of the dramatic spectacle that is bullfighting, but I'd never been in a bullring. I became increasingly curious and interested in being inside one. For now, however, I was content to settle for hearsay and Kiko did not duck the questions. He gave full-blooded answers as to where he stood. I wanted to learn about the Gypsies and Kiko was an authentic source. He was forthright in his comments on Gypsy brotherhood, a community which 'expressed their feeling in music.' While he stirred his coffee, he said: 'They cannot *write!*' And, as if to underline the quincentenary celebrations, he said, 'But the Gypsies have no protection. They have no documents, no buildings, no archaeology, no monuments, no cemeteries!' I'd seen references to what he had said in books, but when I confessed the extent of my ignorance, Kiko took responsibility for my tutelage.

'The Gypsies have a sense of life,' he said, 'a sense of mystery.' He spoke about the connection between Gypsies and drugs which some of them sold. 'But what they sold,' he said, 'is not for accumulation, *only* for ready money to spend.' This statement left me in no doubt that as Kiko understood it, the *present* is what really mattered in the thinking of Gypsies 'not the future.' The Gypsies were survivors in a tough world and their continued presence in Spain, in Andalucia (Seville in particular) attested to this. As Kiko enlightened me, I was reminded of passages from Federico Garcia Lorca's powerful poems: *Village* and *As Time Pass By.*

'VILLAGE
On the bare hill
Calvary
Clear water
And ancient olive trees

Along the narrow streets
Men with faces covered,

And on the watch-towers.

Everlastingly
Turning
Oh village lost
In Andalucia lamenting'.

AS TIME PASS BY
Children look
Into the distance
Oil lamps go out
Blind girls
Question the moon, and spirals of weeping
Rise in the air.
The mountains look
Into the distance.'

After visiting Sevilla '92 and exploring the various pavilions during the celebrations, I was further enlightened and the contours of my book began to emerge. By now, I had done a great deal of thinking, note-taking and preliminary work, but there was more research to do in relation to southern Spain.

On my return to London, from the notes and all that I'd gathered, I began to write, identifying important links from all that I had seen and heard. For example, while travelling by coach towards Palos, it was difficult not to think again about the historical connection between myself, India and Spain: The powerful realisation that I was an Indian descendant from that India to which Columbus had travelled west to find. In turn, I had travelled from the west eastwards. And so I decided to call my book *Isabella's Legacy: My Discovery of Spain.*

From the outset, I knew that no writer from the New World (or anywhere else) had gone to Spain, covered as much of the same ground as I'd done and attempted an account such as the one that I'd envisaged. Now, I proceeded to explore further.

Given my seemingly strong resemblance to Gitanos (Gypsies) as some had said, their lowly status in Spanish society made me think a little more: By now I'd become aware and curious about Spaniards' perception of me and my identity. I could not help reflecting on the journey from Trinidad to Spain which was made via my long residence in Britain. Was I a misplaced person? In my birthplace Trinidad, I have often been called a 'Coolie;' in Britain, a 'Paki' and perceived now as Gitano in Spain. Gazing at the skyline of Seville, I considered the presence of myself (and members of other groups) who were integral to 'ethnic communities' across Europe.

On Saturday 17 October 1992, with my Spanish friends Marisa, Margarita and Manuel (the trainee Bullfighter) and his father, I attended a Bullfight in the afternoon in Seville's famous Maestranza bull-ring. It was a splendid arena.

In the ritual before the combatants appeared, one, then two trumpets sounded. A thin, lithe figure, beautifully dressed in tight-fitting trouser, jacket and cap (or hat) appeared. He walked slowly into the ring. Seeing this man, my immediate thoughts were on Manuel, the boy who was sitting beside me. I tried to imagine his first bull fight and his possible entrance here one day. What were his thoughts now, I wondered. The packed terraces greeted the bull-fighter with loud applause and when it died down, the ensuing mild hum of expectation was punctuated by occasional shouts from the crowd. Here and there, elegantly dressed ladies waved white handkerchiefs. Overall, it was quite a scene. But I was aware of a contradiction: while there was something unsentimental and worldly about this assembly, there was also a strong, pervasive sense of the solemn and religious as well as an element of a festive spirit. Hence, whenever I heard 'Ole!' it seemed to contain more than a mere shout.

From my position, which afforded a very good view of everything before and around me, with biro in hand and enough blank paper placed on my lap, I scribbled furiously, trying to record everything that interested me.

Soon all eyes were turned towards the door just below, to my right. Up to this point, the excitement had built up to a pitch of great expectation as everyone anticipated the appearance of the first of the afternoon's bulls. For a few tense moments, as we waited,

I looked around with heightened interest at people in the stands and the men on horseback as if to confirm that all eyes were indeed turned in one direction: Towards the door through which the bull would appear. As we waited, I was aware of the noise from the crowd which was unlike that at a football match. I would liken it to an air of controlled expectancy. Just then, another trumpet blast heralded a bounding black bull which trotted onto the sandy arena and stopped some distance from the centre of the ring.

A man on horseback attended to the bull in a circling and provocative way. The Torero watched grimly, expectantly; and instead of moving forward, for the moment, he stood his ground. Although the scene before me seemed surreal, I could do nothing now, but bear witness to the life and death drama that had begun to unfold before me. With the Muleta, the Torero moved closer and closer to the bull which, by now, had become more agitated as it moved about more energetically after being prodded time and again by the man on horse-back.

Now the combatants: man and beast were engaged in a 'sport' in which for one or the other, death would be the outcome; an engagement which, it should be remembered, was for the delight and appreciation of the fans who were reputedly among the most knowledgeable in Spain and the world. So here I was, I reminded myself, and before me were the bull, the man, the capacity crowd; in all a grand spectacle, unlike anything I'd ever seen and was unlikely to ever see again.

As expected, after many twists and turns of the man with his Muleta (at times graceful, I must admit) and the frantic bull, eventually there was death. The bull before me met his inevitable end to the delight of the spectators. 'Ole! Ole! Ole!' This was the first bull killed that day and I watched with amazement as before me on the blood-stained sand were the victor and vanquished. The Torero bowed graciously as he received the applause and then left the scene. His triumph was followed by other Toreros, including the star performer that afternoon Curro Romero, whom the spectators loved, showering upon him repeated, appreciative Oles!

Later, I learned that 'Ole,' a Moorish word, meant 'For God's sake.'

That evening I was invited by my companions to dine at the El Cordobes Restaurante, conveniently located near the Maestranza where, after eating some of the tastiest food in Seville, I was presented with a 'Speciality' of the house: 'bull's balls.' I must admit, it tasted no different from other cuts of beef that I'd eaten. We stayed in the Restaurante for quite sometime before this long and extraordinary day with its many surprises ended with champagne at Manuel's home, where he displayed his Muleta with pride. The boy was deliriously happy with the 'Spectacular' at the Maestranza and made a point of saying: 'I will dream of being a Torero!' As I was about to leave, he said he would like me to take a photograph with him and his Muleta. He was in euphoric mood and even said he would accompany me the next day to the airport.

And so after many days and weeks of travel, I bade goodbye to the young Torero to be. It was well past midnight, my memory bank was full to overflowing and that night, among the things that commanded my attention, I considered the significance of my earlier meetings with the artist Dalia Daza.

That same month in 1992, I had the opportunity of viewing an Exhibition of Ms Daza's paintings at an Art Gallery in Seville. On seeing these large canvasses on the walls, I was stunned by the effectiveness of the painter's impressionist technique. Having previously exhibited in Madrid, her Seville Exhibition featured portraits of the greatest Flamenco performers of all time: Artists such as Paco, Chico, Chocolate and El Camaron, among others.

Later that evening, as if to confirm at least my physical likeness to the greatest Gypsies she'd honoured, Dalia spoke to Marisa about the possibility of painting me. She thought a British writer was a good subject. When we met again to discuss the project, I was flattered and agreed.

So while I was in Seville, between spending wonderful times at cultural in-places like the Carbonaria, true to her word, Dalia got started on her painting. I remember well my visits to her studio where I sat for her while she moved around, talked, studied my face and did several charcoal sketches before working on the canvass. Her dark eyes and overall expression was a study in concentration.

The objective was to commit my image to paint in the same artistic form: her distinctive impressionist style as demonstrated in the brilliant portraits of her 'Exhibition.' Dalia requested, and I promised to send a few photographs which she said she would look at. Thus the process initiated by a unique Spanish artist immortalising me in paint, was set in motion. Before going to Spain, this was an unlikely development. And so with thoughts of the possibilities of the Impressionist's impression of me in mind, I left Seville for London.

A ROOM OF MY OWN

With the approach of Christmas, as rumours of the impending move from Bloomsbury to the new British Library premises in St Pancras gained urgency, I accomplished something that I'd long thought of doing; a matter which I felt could no longer be postponed: the writing of something meaningful about the Round Reading Room. Over the years, I had seen many references and short articles relating to the Room but, as yet (certainly in recent times) there was no sustained piece of writing about it. Sitting at my regular Seat M7, at last, I began to write down my thoughts on the most uplifting place I had ever known. I intended that it should be a personal appreciation which, at first, I had titled: *Marx, Shaw and Me.* But, in the hope that it would evolve into a book, I retitled it *A ROOM OF MY OWN: Inside the Round Reading Room* and structured it thus:

'CONTENTS
Prologue
From Trinidad To Bloomsbury
Panizzi's Reading Room
Radical Causes
An Author Against the Odds
Disenchantment
Epilogue.'

With more than a dose of nostalgia, I wrote a lengthy account about the Room which I reduced to the following Synopsis:
'*The world famous British Library Round Reading Room in*

Bloomsbury as we know it today will in the near future, cease to serve the purpose for which it was designed since it was opened in 1857. For many years now, and especially during the last two, the nation and the world have been regularly informed through journals, newspapers, pamphlets, books and the media of the imminent removal of invaluable books and manuscripts from the British Museum site occupied by the Reading Room; and in the coming months, the fanfares will be sounded with increasing loudness for the Grand Opening in the "controversial" building at St Pancras.

The change in function of the Reading Room will mark the end of an era of a Library which can be dated back to 1753 when the Library of the British Museum was established. The history of this institution is as fascinating as it is glorious; and as if to pay homage to the shrine it had become for many, each day members of the public queue to get a glimpse of the circular room, the focus of a collection of over nine million volumes on site. This, however, is only a part of the British Library's overall collection which has, in the last twenty years increased to over 250 million separate items housed in nineteen buildings in London and Yorkshire. "The facilities and services which will be provided," as one senior official enthused, "are without parallel in any national library... The magnitude of the collections is a source of great pride which has to be matched with determination to achieve solutions to problems which libraries have never hitherto faced." It is this challenge,... that has created in the last two decades, and with each passing day, among members of staff and readers, real fears about the future in terms of jobs and a better service, respectively.

If, as a former Chief Executive of the British Library believed, "books are eloquent, but rarely shout," there are many... who feel the need to speak out, as I have always done and propose to do. While the historical background of the Room will be reviewed, the focus of the book will be my story as it relates to this Room and the Library generally. Apart from my election as the first Elected Secretary of the Whitley Council when the British Library was formed in 1973, how I came to write and my herculean struggle to continue to do so, is the main theme of the book which will also incorporate lively anecdotes of readers, how members of staff had, over the years, viewed them and vice-versa. It is through this approach that I intend to reveal the human face of this great institution.

The Round Reading Room has been, since I first saw it in 1969, a magnetic space, especially for me now as a writer, the mecca of literary research workers. Since the publication of my first paid feature article in 1972, I have written six books (five have been published, the sixth is expected to be published in 1993); and two half-completed manuscripts (new book projects), mainly on history and biography. So it is with the understanding of the Reading Room both as writer and as a member of staff, that I will write this timely memoir in a style that would reach the widest audience, to coincide with the departure of the facilities and services from the ambience of Bloomsbury to the St Pancras building.

Over the years, the presence of great writers and thinkers in this Room (Karl Marx, Charles Dickens Thackeray and George Bernard Shaw, for example) have been well-known. But although the lives of millions of people have been affected (in many cases transformed) by the private thoughts and ideas of these men translated into book-form as they sat in this giant cranium, the wealth of knowledge contained in the Library as a whole and its evolving significance is still largely unknown to the mass of people here in Britain and abroad. The true mark of the Room's value can be measured, to some degree, by the steady stream of visitors, from generation to generation of scholars and writers from many countries. It is to this Room's great credit that it has generated among its users' continuing interest, love and affection.

Marx was first granted a Ticket to read here in June 1850 and although he worked in the "Sixth Reading Room" (one of the British Museum's earlier reading rooms) it is in connection with the present circular Reading Room that he is best remembered. Ironically, the Room, is the "creation" of the remarkable Antonio Panizzi, who was, like Marx, a political refugee; and with time, both Marx and the Reading Room became synonymous, symbolising free and radical thought.   More recently, I myself as another emigre, have become forever closely linked with the Reading Room as employee, Organiser, Staff leader and writer.

It was during the late Victorian period that the Reading Room enjoyed its greatest fame amongst the general public, and during the 1880s the distinctive figure of George Bernard Shaw, a regular reader, attracted the attention of William Archer, the drama critic, who was intrigued by the odd combination of authors whom Shaw studied. "I saw him day after day," the critic wrote, "poring over Karl Marx's *Das Kapital* and the orchestral score of Wagner's *Tristan and Isolde.*" Shaw appreciated the Reading Room so greatly that when he died he left a third of his residuary estate to the British Museum, which has since benefitted hugely in consequence (as has the British Library) largely as a result of the royalties accruing to the success of *My Fair Lady.*

Marx and Shaw were closely identified with the Room and their achievements were well beyond the reach of the vast majority of users of the Room. Like both men, however, though of a different kind, I too have written challenging books, articles and given lectures but, with no where near (and unlikely ever to have) the great success that Marx and Shaw had achieved over their lifetimes.

Of necessity, my regime has been, and is, strict. But unlike both men, I have turned what to most people who work here consider as just a job into a privilege affording me the opportunity to make use of the Room at various times each day, both before and after it opens to the reading public. I also have an invaluable working knowledge of what goes on behind the scenes! If anything, the common interest that I share with Marx and Shaw had been the regular use of the Room as our "literary workshop."

The publication of my acclaimed book *The Making of the Black Working Class in Britain* has been likened inaccurately by a few prejudiced readers as being Marxist! Though I am not a 'Marxist,' I am an admirer of Marx's great contribution. But even before I'd read anything written by the great man, I was encouraged by the fact that he had written *Das Kapital* right here and felt compelled to read it in the Room that had so overwhelmed me when I had first walked through it. Since then, I have sat in seat M7 every day, six days a week, except on public holidays and during the annual "Closed Weeks" for the last 24 years. For what its worth, no other reader or member of staff, alive or dead, can claim this! As a consequence, it seems only natural that I would have developed a special affinity with the exciting intellectual atmosphere of this unique place.

Coping with over half a million readers' visits each year (which is more than 1,600 each day) it cannot be entirely a haven of peace. But each day after the rustle and bustle, I am often there alone with the ghosts of William Thackeray, Thomas Carlyle, Charles Dickens,

Marx and Shaw, among others; a time when I have a very special view of, and feeling for, the Room. It is particularly impressive on summer evenings when the sun streams through the great windows high above, and all is quiet. Yet, the proper view of the Reading Room is when it is full of life, thought and movement; and until the sun slowly sets on this incomparable "paradise," it will remain for me and the ages what it has recently become in mankind's continuing quest for knowledge: the best known workshop for writers in the world.
Ron Ramdin
Copyright 2 December 1992.'

After writing this, more and more I was drawn to expanding it. But with time, the book idea of 'A Room of My Own' lapsed and was never written. After typing the biro-written 'Synopsis' of about1,500 words, I decided to keep it as but one reader's deeply felt respect and appreciation.

By now an eventful twelve months was drawing to a close. Nineteen Ninety two had yielded and signified so much that was extraordinarily good; indeed it was hard to think of a scenario that would be better.

IDENTITY, AMERICA, CORRESPONDENCE

Early in the new year, since my return from Spain, I came to recognise and gain a clearer perspective of myself and that country which I had loved being in. Meeting people and seeing new places touched and deepened my thoughts, thus underlining an essential connection made with Spain. The themes of slavery, indentureship and matters relating to Europe, Africa, Asia and the New World, hitherto areas of relative darkness, became much clearer to me. Who was I? A West Indian? An Indian? A Caribbean person? 'Melting pot' and 'multiculturalism' were buzz words at this time; a consequence of the post-war influx, as hundreds of thousands of migrants came to Britain from outside the Commonwealth.

Amidst this state of flux and diversity, significantly, I continued to think about the 'Oneness of mankind' which I'd quoted six years before in my book on Paul Robeson. Prior to this, arising from my experience in colonial Trinidad, I'd often heard the negative name-calling by members of different groups who publicly traded nasty insults in terms of race, colour, gender, religion and so on. My puzzlement at first quickly gave way to concern, then anger. In my first piece of writing (published in *Race Today*) I saw all Trinidadians as *one people,* as working towards the *same goal of nationhood.* Ten years on, in my first book *From Chattel Slave to Wage Earner* I had already begun to deal with and identify the various groups in cosmopolitan Trinidad, *differently.* Five years later, in the book that followed *The Making of the Black Working Class in Britain,* my interest in identifying different groups became more pronounced. But within months of completing the Robeson biography, struck by the statement: the '*Oneness of mankind,*' I was unsure of what it really meant. I was uneasy, even troubled by this all-encompassing vision, which I felt needed to be explored and challenged. Why?

Because I could not make headway with the sweeping generalisation that is the 'Oneness of Mankind,' I was confronted by the question: How do I unpack that other totalising expression: the much-talked about 'commonality of beings?' Unlike the Robeson book, *The Making of the Black Working Class in Britain* did not compromise the *essential differences* between different social groups. Nonetheless, rooted in my childhood and youth, as my philosophy of 'difference' (and importantly '*respect for difference*') evolved, as social tensions and social injustice widened the fractures and scarred societies world-wide, I had already written and published *The World in View: The West Indies*, an exacting test of writing simply and logically for a younger age group about *differences* in relation to the history and cultures of the complex region known as the West Indies.

At this stage, having undergone the experience of writing about the big picture diasporically in relation to Africa, now a new wave of interest and excitement gripped me as I continued researching the Indian-Caribbean diaspora for my new book *Arising From Bondage*. As my ideas about the 'general' and the 'particular' gestated, by 1993 London and Britain at large had become increasingly concerned with identity and identification: Who was who or what? How they related to others? And interestingly, my former identity as a 'West Indian' had changed at a breathless pace when African-descended people from the West Indies recognised and identified themselves as 'Afro-Caribbean.' Thus by default, I was perceived as *Other* and, in turn, identified as 'Indo-Caribbean.' With this shift, my ideas about histories, cultures and identities became more compelling as a wider range of immigrants entered Britain. Furthermore, as migrations world-wide led to crossing national boundaries, more and more, my interest was centred on a better life for all (not in terms of groups, groupings or universals) but in essence, on the basis of *respect for difference* in relation to each individual. This, I felt, should be the starting point of co-existence, human rights and social evolution. I was searching for a more meaningful social approach for 'minorities' who felt alienated: in other words, an *inclusive* way forward that would engender among each person a greater and real sense of *home and belonging*.

After completing the second draft of *Arising From Bondage: A History of the Indo-Caribbean People,* as the *first* history of its kind, it was timely. Thus with the knowledge and insights gained so far, I wrote to Chris Laird of Banyan Film Company in Trinidad:

'Thanks for your positive response to our working together on a television version of my book Arising From Bondage, the story of the East Indians in the Caribbean which is unique, but its evocation through the medium of television was (still is)... long overdue. In fact, time is of the essence in that 30 May 1995 will mark the 150th Anniversary of the arrival of East Indians in Trinidad. All our efforts should be geared towards producing and screening this story to coincide with this very special occasion, which means that we have two years and three months to make the film. Bearing this in mind and given that the publishing process is time-consuming – rather than wait for the book's publication, I hasten to send a copy of the typescript for your attention. Although this material is copyrighted, please restrict its circulation to only those directly involved in the production of our film.

The format of the story, as I see it, is that it should be presented as a Drama/Documentary written and narrated by me, and produced and directed by you. What needs to be done, and I think very soon, is for us to reach a formal agreement, incorporating the funding of Script development so that I can begin to work without much delay.

Given that there are an estimated 12 million Indians in the Indian diaspora (and the growing emphasis on inter-cultural matters in today's global village) as a Banyan production, this first television presentation of Indians in the Caribbean will, no doubt, be of international interest.'

Soon after my visit to Trinidad to view Banyan's videos and get copies of the audio recordings of Interviews of C.L.R James, on my return to London, once again, I contacted Chris Laird.

'I am especially thankful to you for granting me permission to view the CLR James Interviews on video and for all the help you and your staff had given to me during the…(time) that I spent in your offices. Since I left Trinidad, I have done a great deal of work on my James biography and, of course, as we both agreed, you and Banyan will be acknowledged for any material used from the recordings.'

Meanwhile as routine British Library work necessarily preoccupied me, with some urgency, I wrote to Paul Buhle. Commenting on why he had not heard from me earlier, I explained: *'because I wanted to be sure that I could act upon your advice to attend the CLR James's America Conference at Brown University.*

Given the hectic work schedule and having already made some adjustments, it now seems more than likely that I will be able to attend. Indeed I feel I must! Please send me all the relevant details (the dates in April when and where the Conference will be held and the cost of accommodation for the duration) as soon as possible. Your prompt response in sending the CLR James Journal and your letters are deeply appreciated. Yes, I would be glad to review CLR James's Caribbean, as soon as I can get through, at least, some of the present workload.

Once again Paul thank you for all your help, and, of course, I look forward to meeting you!'

The Conference 'CLR James's America,' was finally announced. It was due to be held from 23-24 April 1993 at Brown University in Providence, Rhode Island. This promised to be a major event that could and should inform and give added nuance to my work thus far on the biography. So fifty-five years after James had gone to America as one of the leading Marxist/Trotskyist intellectuals in Britain, now, I was about to make my own first trip there (not as a

'Marxist') but as James's biographer to ascertain as much about his 'intellectual legacy' of that period as possible.

And so I flew to America. Soon after my arrival at Boston's Logan Airport on 23 April, I travelled by coach through the New England countryside to Providence, Rhode Island, where I checked in at the Holiday Inn Hotel for a six-day stay, as a 'Guest' of Brown University. Brown, it should be said, is one of the top 'Ivy League' universities in the United States of America. I was pleasantly surprised that my accommodation was in a plush Presidential Suite on the Hotel's Sixth Floor.

During the Conference, I met and spoke with many of James closest American associates, a few whose names were acquiring legendary status. They included Martin Glaberman and Grace Lee Boggs. I also had an in-depth Interview with Jan Carew, the Guyanese-born writer and activist, who gave the Conference's Opening Paper.

In the late evenings and early mornings, from the window of my sixth floor Suite, I looked out at the highway traffic following their lanes; and while watching television, boyhood memories of American culture abounded: I remembered sitting in the 'Pit Section' of the Embassy Cinema and looking up spellbound at the flickering screen (on which were moving images of the Great Film Stars and the place called America) as Bill Haley and the Comets performed 'Rock Around the Clock,' The Platters sang 'The Great Pretender' and Elvis Presley gyrated to 'Jail House Rock.' My thoughts of America then could not have been more romantic and idealised. Indeed throughout my teen years, America was the country to which my attention was largely directed: it was the place where black people spoke *differently*. Indeed, after seeing Sidney Poitier in a film, Black faces on the silver screen had a powerful effect on me. America offered magical things: pop music and film stars, great possibilities, I thought. Now, here I was in America, in the Presidential Suite looking out! Not as a musician or film star, but as an author of growing international prominence.

Knowing that James was a Marxist, a leading Trotskyist spokesman, a Thinker whose philosophy incorporated historical materialism, race and class, reappraising his work during and after the Conference, I saw his interests more clearly: *Aggregates,* rather than 'individual freedom' in society, was the focus. Gradually, I felt I was getting somewhere. I was deeply immersed in exploring the 'Oneness of mankind' as it related to *my own* evolving ideas. Once more, I was faced with the fact that Marxists, Socialists and other 'progressive' groupings were, it seemed, content with their totalising approaches of race, colour, class, gender, religion and so on. But in spite of rousing rhetoric, their universal calls for freedom, human rights, multiculturalism and diversity always seemed to end up in the cul-de-sac of other forms of human bondage.

Following my visit to America, as my writings reached wider audiences, I received a letter from V.T Verghese, Executive Director of the Indo-British Historical Society based in Madras, India. My connection with them arose because of an article that I'd written relating to the Society's journal *Indo-British Review*. The Journal was celebrating its 25th Anniversary and on this occasion, Mr Verghese took the opportunity of offering me membership of the Society at a discounted rate. I was flattered but did not join. Of course, I wished the Journal continued success.

Among the many things that were on my mind after my last 1992 visit to Spain was setting down further thoughts relating to the novel 'Sword and Quill' that I had put on hold. Mulling over the ideas therein, I did another take on this theme which I entitled: 'Columbus's "Children of God." '

Such preparatory research, changes and writings were a reflection of the depth of thinking that Spain had provoked in me, both prior to and during my visit there. Spain, the New World and myself were inextricably intertwined with history, writing and language; and not surprisingly I was reminded of what the Bishop of Avila is reputed to have said when he presented a 'Grammar' of Spanish to Queen Isabella of Spain: 'Your Majesty, language is the instrument of Empire.' Indeed!

At this time, I had also reached a literary juncture; a cross-roads at which while considering the novel, I was seriously inclined in the direction of writing *only fiction*. To this end, I listed sixty-five Themes for Short Stories under the general heading: 'TALES FROM THE SAND ROAD.' This was another indication of my growing desire to relate the connectedness of people (as individuals) as well as things; the particular with the general, and in literary terms, the relative importance of fact and fiction!

Then on 4 March 1993, such 'stories' as I'd planned to write necessarily had to be foregone. Why? In part, because I could not stop the flow of correspondence, not only from the publisher who was expected to publish *Arising From Bondage*, but also from others including a letter from the Banyan Film Company on whose behalf Chris Laird wrote:

'*I received your massive manuscript of Arising from Bondage. Yes, I know about 1995 and was thinking of some projects. This would of course be ideal. I won't be able to really get down to reading it for a month unfortunately because I'm writing a pilot for a Drama Series at the moment...*

That is something I expect we will have to work on (in relation to) Arising from Bondage... I can certainly produce it as far as the logistics and technical/creative side is concerned but do you mean also raising money and looking for markets? That end of things I can't do alone! Any way the first thing is a treatment and proposal to seek funding for "development" which is scriptwriting, fundraising etc. I will be much clearer when I have read the typescript. Are you planning a trip soon? I'm trying to get to the UK at the end of May if I can raise some funds as there is a festival in Bristol that one of my films has been selected for and I would like to make some headway on the film of Sonny Ladoo's book No Pain like This Body a script of which Channel Four is holding and it would be a good opportunity to also get Arising From Bondage started up! I will have read it by then.'

As it was, Chris's letter of promise had to be juxtaposed with the fact that all hope of my history of the Indo-Caribbean People (the first work of its kind) being published *to coincide with* the 150th Anniversary of the arrival of East Indians specifically *in Trinidad* was slowly *slipping away;* and, given any further delay, a golden opportunity would be a missed! Having begun the writing of this book way back in 1988, even now I was determined not to let this happen.

Travel had become an unavoidable feature of my life and my correspondence and telephone calls encompassed an ever-widening circle of prominent people. I received news from Willi Chen, the distinguished Trinidadian artist and writer.

'I hasten to answer because I am terribly impressed with your book,' he wrote, *'and feel proud that it was written by a man originally from Marabella.*

It is really amazing to recognise the scholarship, erudition, painstaking diligence and the microscopic details that went into your research!! For that alone - I am awed by the sheer weight and power of the book. And to know that you have written more books and now attempting another, expresses the magnitude of your capability and talent for doing a purposeful and precious service to humanity.

For all this you must be congratulated and here I express my sincere happiness for you and wish you continued success in all that is in store – which you will produce. But always remember that spreading the good word in distant parts of the world – you still belong to Marabella! Trinidad and Tobago now shines like a beacon with your illustrious contribution. I thank you for the nice letter and the book and don't forget to call on me whenever you visit Trinidad. It will be a privilege to have you for a special dinner.

Best Wishes Always,
Willi Chen.'

Reading this heart-felt letter was as good a greeting as I could have hoped for.

As an integral part of my research, while I was in Providence, Rhode Island, I had telephoned Constance Webb (now Pearlstein), C.L.R James's second wife. We spoke about 'Nello' and just over a month after returning from America, she had sent me a postcard. Dated 26 May 1993, from her home at 195 Alhambra, San Francisco, California, she wrote:

'Dear Ron,
Thank you for the book and copy of Robeson. I'm delighted to have them. As soon as I complete editing… I'll make copies of material and

photos to send to you.

Just before you wrote, I came across an acknowledgement from (the British Museum Library) for The Tale*, thanking me for the little grey book on Dick (Richard Wright). Glad you found it useful.

Sincerely,

Constance'.

*'The Tale' refers to a small volume that she had written.

This connection with Constance Webb whom James had so adored and to whom he had written many 'Love Letters,' reinforced my feeling that I was on the right track and highly likely to get a publisher's commitment for *C.L.R James: A Life* sooner, rather than later.

Meanwhile, demand for my services as speaker and Lecturer which had grown annually in the last ten years remained high. One invitation requested that I give a one-hour Lecture at the Teachers Centre, Queen's Road, Walthamstow, London E17. As always, I was glad to oblige. And while commenting on certain problems associated with particular groups in relation to society as a whole, I tried always to orientate my lectures and Talks towards inclusiveness.

At this time, in spite of student demand, *The Making of the Black Working Class in Britain* was still out of print. After approaching various publishers, at last on 18 August 1993, I received a Contract from Sally Davidson of Lawrence and Wishart Ltd to which I responded. '*Your approach to publishing it (The Making of the Black Working Class in Britain) as one of your "Classic" texts, will indeed not only be appropriate, but will also, as you said (on the phone), help enormously in the kind of promotion that is necessary for the forthcoming second edition. The book... had been out of print much earlier than I had been told and it seems that the real reason for Mr Simpson (Managing Director) using the "uneconomic" argument was the fact that Gower Publishing Company was about to be bought by Ashgate Publishing Company who, recently sent me a Contract in the hope that I will agree to do a new Edition of my book for them.*

Subsequent letters show how desperate they are for this work, but I'm more concerned with the agreement that we are about to sign.'

Following this letter, given that an updated edition of *The Making of the Black Working Class in Britain* would have been both time-consuming and expensive, I requested an advance of £1,500. Alas, my request was not granted, nor was my book published by Lawrence and Wishart.

In the meantime, a formidable personality, the black politician Sharon Atkin had been in touch. Reading her postcard, I recalled my first meeting with her at a Reception in the Durbar Room at the Foreign Office. She was then one of the leading Black spokespersons in Britain: certainly the most outspoken black woman, who was on course to become the first Black woman MP.

'*Just a quick note to thank you,*' she wrote before leaving for Washington. '*Having experienced a difficult and miserable time when nothing was going right, I suppose I was almost suicidal. Seeing you and meeting Eric (Davidson, the Film Director) was such a joy, real caring people with positive ideas lifted my spirits.*

Perhaps I spend too much time working and alone so I forget that there is life and decent people around…

America needs hard work and little opportunity to relax and take in some music. I am not even able to be anonymous there. Washington is a small city and I know too many people. Well, I guess you understand what I am saying…it would be nice to see you when I return. I'm back on April 26th. You know that I am very anxious to help raise the funds in order that you and Eric can make this wonderful Series….

Thanks again for your generosity and kindness. I do appreciate you and the very excellent work that you do…'

Enclosed was a continuation of the postcard:

'*I am sitting in my armchair… reading your book (The Making of the Black Working Class in Britain). This time (her first reading of it was in Oxford over a weekend soon after the Neil Kinnock-Labour Party decision not to endorse her Candidacy for a Seat in the Parliamentary General Elections) I shall do it justice! I don't think that I ever told you that when 'The Making…' was first published I was at a very low ebb and I started to read your book feeling that I had no anchor for my views and politics. However you, through your book made me remember first how much we have suffered and contributed to many societies and political movements.*

Now I read your tremendous book fired with enthusiasm because I know how much we still have to do.

I cannot ever produce a work such as yours. I don't have the skills but I do have a lifetime of commitment to our people and all the pain, sacrifices and achievements that you so magnificently documented.

I do at least feel that in a very small way I can contribute something, at any rate I have tried to be an honest advocate on behalf of working class interests. You have a great talent, please keep on doing it and don't be discouraged because people like me need you. Looking at your book again reminds me that I really have not done much at all but I do strive to write and do something of value. If I can get you the money for the TV Series then maybe I can say that I have done something worthwhile, you deserve that...

I need your encouragement and friendship. Thanks again for making me see how much more I need to do. Much love and appreciation. Sharon...'

Sharon's note was, to say the least, uplifting; and I was reminded of another meeting. That same evening at the Foreign Office, after being among the 'great and the good,' I also met a charming, bearded man who gave me his card and kindly invited me to join him for a pint in the pub 'over the road' in Whitehall. The affable gentleman-raconteur was none other than Robin Knox Johnston, the first man to sail single-handed non-stop around the world; a feat which he had performed between 14 June and 22 April 1969.

Within the frosted glass and varnished wood décor of the pub, Mr Johnston regaled me with wonderful and scary adventures of the high seas that only he could tell. He also talked much about his need to be alone; something which, as a writer, I understood only too well. After almost two hours of conversation, during which he was never boastful of his great achievement, I parted company with the 'lone,' but wonderfully sociable, sailor, feeling honoured and even more appreciative of his extraordinary courage, endurance and tenacity, the requisite qualities demanded of attempts to explore and thus extend the bounds of human endurance and knowledge.

Space and time was never far from my mind. Unlike the three decades past, now at fifty, though I was not excited by the thought of having just fifteen years before retirement, I felt I should remain in the British Library so that I would qualify for a pension. This was a compelling case for not leaving; but thoughts of being in a new office (the Arched Room) and the negative thinking behind the decision to move me rankled, as I pounded new paths to and from this workplace located at the north end of the Egyptian Gallery in the British Museum. An incidental, but wonderful bonus was that six times a day, I passed the historic *Rosetta Stone*! This incredible discovery, a tablet of perhaps man's earliest attempt at WRITING, enriched my daily strivings. Although I had to get used to the new office, one thing was much clearer: If I'd been vigilant before, now I felt even more so in order to keep my job, such as it was.

Following Ms Atkin's de-selection as a Labour Party Candidate to fight the Parliamentary Elections for a 'safe' Nottingham seat, having given much of her time and talent to 'Black politics,' I remember well the editor of *Race Today's* comment that Ms Atkin was better off 'out' of Parliament than 'in.' She was a persuasive speaker and I was struck by her understanding of the issues surrounding the presence of migrants and their descendants in Britain. She and I often discussed the 'Independence' of the former British Commonwealth countries and the European Economic Community as the 'Rich Man's Club!'

While mulling over Sharon's talent and contribution, I received news of E. P Thompson's death. He would be remembered for having worked tirelessly for the Campaign Against Nuclear Disarmament (CND). And for those who appreciated history, Thompson was an historian *par excellence* whose 'history from below,' *The Making of the English Working Class* was, quite rightly, highly praised. Although he did not mention the present and past contribution of black working class radicals in his book, his passing deepened my appreciation of having had the privilege and honour of meeting and talking with him about a few of the great and vexed issues of our time.

Some months following Toni Morrison's London book tour and after receiving her special Postcard, I arrived back in Spain. While travelling from Seville Airport to the city centre, over the car radio, it was announced that Toni Morrison had won the Nobel Prize for Literature. As if I'd known her better, I felt pleased that she had won. Later, I read her 'Acceptance Speech' as Nobel Laureate.

'I entered this hall pleasantly haunted by those who have entered it before me,' she had said. *'That company of Laureates is both daunting and welcoming. For among its lists are names of persons whose work has made whole worlds available to me. The sweep and specificity of their art have sometimes broken my heart with the courage and clarity of its vision. The astonishing brilliance with which they practised their craft has challenged and nurtured my own. My debt to them rivals the profound one I owe to the Swedish Academy for having selected me to join that distinguished alumni...*

I will leave this hall...with a new and much delightful haunting than the one I felt upon entering: that is the company of the laureates yet to come. Those who, even as I speak, are mining, sifting and polishing languages for illuminations none of us here dreamed of. But whether or not any one of them, secures a place in this pantheon, the gathering of these writers is unmistakeable and mounting. Their voices bespeak civilizations gone and yet to be; the precipice from which their imagination will rivet us; they do not blink or turn away...'

Through Ms Morrison's books and through her personal message to me, I felt a certain literary kinship which informed my delight in her elevation; all the more so as I continued along the pathway of a slow, but growing clarity of vision of my own long-standing literary endeavours: ever-questioning myself as to what I should and shouldn't write and speak about. In this process, I have continued my dedicated struggle for social justice *vitally* through championing and fostering *'respect for difference'* and thus social inclusiveness.

TWENTY- ONE

THE BRITISH LIBRARY: 'THE FUTURE'

In the wake of my move to the Arched Room office, there was little time to settle. A 'Time and Motion' study became daily practice; and having been at the centre of proceedings at its inception, unlike most people in the institution, I had thought a great deal about the British Library's future. What may have seemed like too grand a statement when I'd first read it, now made perfect sense. I refer to the booklet *The British Library: Past, Present and Future* which stated:

'*...given its resources for an understanding of the past, the present and what we choose to make of the future, has no parallel in any country... It nourishes invention and curiosity; it provides for the needs of industry and commerce, without which national prosperity withers; it sustains research, without which there can be no progress; it possesses the documentary sources for the evolution of thought in all countries at all times, without which we would be deprived of history! Before the invention of writing when history was an oral record, handed down from generation to generation, its custodians were honoured above all. Millennia later, libraries preserve that tradition. Among the many thousands of libraries throughout the world, the British Library is pre-eminent in its determination to serve those institutions and individuals for whom information is an imperative, to preserve the heritage of knowledge and to demonstrate its belief in the unity of knowledge and the benefits which flow from such a belief.*'

This idea or vision of the 'unity of knowledge' and bringing the collections together on one site was no longer a distant goal, but one that drew nearer with each passing day.

In November 1993, Sam Selvon made another visit to England and was due to speak on the 12th at London's South Bank Centre on the theme 'Out of the Margins.' That morning an Interview with him by Naseem Khan appeared in *The Independent* newspaper. Glad to know that Sam was back in Britain, I fondly recalled our meetings, including my 'Interview' with him at his home in London some ten years earlier. So it was with more than mere interest that I read what Ms Khan had written: '*Selvon could hardly have picked a better time to come to Britain. He had stepped into a renaissance and was to help shape it. For the Fifties marked the steady arrival of many Caribbean artists whose work has now been recognised for its true stature. George Lamming had been Selvon's companion on the same boat in the voyage over. V.S Naipaul and Edward Kamau Braithwaite came to take up scholarships, one at Oxford and the other at Cambridge. Andrew Salkey and Aubrey Williams followed two years later. The tide of West Indian creativity was running high, profiting from the stimulus that a shift of place brings - new horizons, new forms of expression, new and challenging definitions of roots. It was says Selvon a wonderful time, "a period which marked the beginning of our future." An informal federation of writers and artists met frequently in the corridors of Bush House. Later, in the 1960s, they came together in an extraordinary grouping called The Caribbean Artist Movement. Behind today's Black arts developments stand these sterling days.*'

Revising Sam's life and his book *The Lonely Londoners*, Ms Khan concluded:

'*His forte is the compassion of his view, involving a distance that he had always instinctively maintained. "I've always been pretty much of a loner. I've felt that my creativity should as much as possible come out of my own experiences. And I have this fear that if I analyse the innocence you discover in A Brighter Sun and the exuberance in The Lonely Londoners I'll lose their originality. It's good to be a little ignorant about your processes and work out of that, creating something that is coming out of you, not something that can be seen as being part of a school of writers. To me that is the firing force that keeps me going, and I have to guard it very preciously"….*

Forty years and more have gone by since Selvon first left his island (Trinidad), thoughts full of Piccadilly Circus and the wider world. No he says he has no regrets; in a sense, he has never left! "I have always remained a Caribbean. I don't want to lose that girl, because that is all I have."'

THE OTHER MIDDLE PASSAGE

I did not see Sam on this last visit, but I recalled his warm and amusing performance, a reading at the Africa Centre during which he had his audience in stitches; and his encouragement that I should write fiction! His words about isolating a theme or topic and writing about it as a novel echoed my own long-held feelings. Indeed for some time while researching my latest historical work, I'd been thinking about moving on from the short stories that had thus far engaged me to writing more fiction - a novel! And as indicated earlier, it was a question of when I would finally begin doing so. Deep inside, I always knew it was just a matter of time. For the moment, however, I turned my attention to completing a new kind of book.

The Other Middle Passage, based on my discovery in the British Library of a Diary kept by the Captain of a 'Coolie' ship relating to his journey on *The Salsette* from Calcutta to Port of Spain, Trinidad. This was a fortuitous, rare and most exciting discovery, especially by a descendant of indentured 'Coolies!' For one thing, it was well hidden, virtually buried within a volume of nineteenth century pamphlets housed in the 'Iron Works' area of the British Library. But I found it! Importantly it related to my own *Indo-Trinidadian story*. Thrilled by this find, a researcher's dream, I wrote an 'Introduction' to the 'Diary' which several months earlier, I had submitted for publication by the Company that was then in the process of printing my manuscript *Arising From Bondage* as page proofs. At the time, with some financial help, this printed form augured well for its publication *on time for* the 150th anniversary of the Indians' arrival in Trinidad.

Meanwhile, the core of *The Other Middle Passage* (the document that had excited my interest in a novel) was that rarest of things - the *Journal* of the ship's Captain written in 1858. I knew of no other such document of that early date and wondered: how significant was this? Put simply, its appearance was especially timely for it came to notice not only just two years **before** the 150th Anniversary of the arrival of Indians in Trinidad, but also because it was coincident with the completion of *Arising From Bondage*.

With so few documents of its kind (to my knowledge this was

the first to be found) my great hope was that publication of both books on Indians in the Caribbean would fill a major gap in Caribbean historiography! Clearly they would add up to another 'pioneering' contribution. So my expectation was understandably high. *The Other Middle Passage* was eventually published and my Dedication read: 'To all those who ventured across the kala pani.' The 'Publisher's Note' stated:

'Ron Ramdin first uncovered Captain Swinton's Journal 15 years ago. The publication of this Facsimile now 135 years after it was first printed, is an invaluable and timely document given that until very recently, few (if any) Caribbean scholars had actually seen it.

It is possible that only one other living historian (from Britain) has seen it and used part of this material. Be that as it may, we are indebted to Ron Ramdin for retrieving this primary source material from obscurity and making it available not only for scholars and students but also for the enlightenment of the general reading public.'

On publication, *The Other Middle Passage* had roused a great deal of interest and the Journal was *primary source material!* My twenty one page *Introduction* (with 12 illustrations) placed the voyage of the 'Coolie ship' *The Salsette* in its context. I wrote:

'European economic expansion in the fifteenth century generated great interest among enterprising explorers who sought a sea route to the riches of the East (to India)…This quest which led Christopher Columbus to travel westwards across the Atlantic Ocean brought him instead to the islands of the West Indies on his first landfall in the New World.

Soon after his arrival in the West Indies, the uncommonly ambitious and wealth-seeking explorer had carried an item on his ships that would have profound implications not only on the indigenous peoples (the Caribs and Arawaks) but also for generations unborn from far-off lands, thus changing the course of European, African and Asian history.

Columbus introduced the sugar cane plant on his second voyage to the West Indies and thereafter the enforced labour endemic in the production of sugar for European consumption…led to the destruction of the native West Indians, the first of the Caribbean peoples to resist their European oppressors. This decimation led, over a period of time, to a repeopling of the plantations first, by unsatisfactory white indentured labour before African slaves were brought in to satisfy the insatiable European demand for sugar.

Consequently, African slavery and the Slave Trade reached new and barbaric heights…The times were brutish and memorably evoked in the writings of Fielding and Smollett…Merchants plied their trade with the aim of making large profits from their ships' voyages during the "Middle Passage"…often mentioned in relation to the African Slave Trade and slavery…Once the Slave Trade and African slavery were abolished and the Apprenticeship system ended… the labour resources of the East remained a possibility, moreso from India than elsewhere. Eventually, the introduction of East Indian indentured labourers effectively filled the colonial plantations' labour vacuum.'

On the 'Coolie ships', I stated:

No sooner had slavery been abolished…the idea of introducing "Coolie labour" from India to the Caribbean was finally translated into action. And so in 1838, while slavers and cruisers (ships) were still employed on the high seas, "coolie ships" engaged in the trade of carrying indentured Indians from far beyond the Eastern shores of the Atlantic. The arrival of the Whitby and Hesperus (Coolie ships)…in Guyana in 1838 heralded a new enterprise and controlled plantation labour to the Caribbean through the institution of the East Indian Indentureship System which fed it…'

Closing my Introduction, I wrote:

'Throughout this traffic, Officialdom remained largely unmoved… And to expect more from a privileged and foreign elite was perhaps expecting too much. Whether or not the Indians were of "inferior" quality as potential labourers, it is clear that they were all (regardless of caste, class, colour or religion) perceived by European administrators as being of an inferior and heathen race. The fact that the official literature of the time is littered with references to the Indians only as "Coolies" confirmed this high-handed attitude, one lacking in basic

human decency, as pointed out by Jane Swinton (the Captain's wife).
Indeed this was reflected in the fact that after all was said and done,
throughout the 108 days of the voyage the Indian emigrants had
experienced untold anguish, despair, suffering and ultimately death,
yet as far as the records are concerned, they remain voiceless; a mute
statistic in both the Captain's Journal and the inquiry that followed.
The echo of this loud silence leaves a void of speculation. But the fact
remains that the selective use of the Indian Interpreters who were well-
versed in the emigrants' languages, has left much to be desired.

Nevertheless, the insights gained from the Journal opens a window
through which we could view with greater clarity, and thus apply better
judgement to a relatively unknown aspect of the East Indian indentured
emigration experience – the epic voyage of an uncommon quest, deeply
ingrained in the very being of a remarkably tenacious people. Whether
or not "push" or "pull" factors took precedence (more than likely it was
a mixture of both) it cannot be assumed that the emigrants on the
Salsette were, in toto, a tabula rasa. On the contrary, many among
them were, as individuals, highly sensitive to the implications of their
actions. So that for 124 of them, the hope and dream of coming to
the dreaded and (for the high castes) tabooed "kala pani" (dark water)
for a better life was a risk worth taking. They had, indeed, gambled
everything and lost.

For those who were fortunate enough to land barely alive and
profoundly shaken, the hard struggle that would, in the years to come,
be their essential experience on plantations was only momentarily
obscured by the more immediate concern of preserving life and limb.
And to compound their problem, the fragile-looking though dignified
Indians were not welcomed with open arms by the local Creole society
who viewed them with intense hostility.

Having left the confines of the ship, who knows what relief and mixture
of emotions they may have felt as they made their way for the first time
in over three months on the firm ground of the lush island which until
now (they only knew by name as "Chinedad") to the various sugar
estates where they were to be bound as replacement labour. And so in the
process of repeopling the Caribbean 366 years after Columbus thought
he had reached India, the indentured Indians had come voluntarily
via a tortuous and tragic passage (a transforming experience which

brought them together as Jahaji bhai – the brotherhood of the ship) to occupy…, the renovated but still cramped, unsatisfactory barrack dwellings and labour on the same land vacated by the African slaves, who had themselves survived the horrors of their "Middle Passage."

In the aftermath of the Salsette's voyage, Captain Swinton's call for an inquiry and his wife's safe keeping and publication of his Journal, led in subsequent years, to improvements in the facilities available on the "Coolie" emigrant ships, including a hospital on deck, a nurse, purified water, improved diet and more Indian assistants. The overall effect was a marked decline in the number of deaths on the Indian emigrants' long and unforgettable journey…which would, with each day, remain ever-present in their collective memory, even though they would gradually be released (at times, powerfully) from their ancient Indian roots and become increasingly anchored to their modern Caribbean moorings.'

Importantly, the blurb of this well-received book states:

'In the wake of the African slavers there followed the "Coolie ships" from India, carrying Indian indentured labourers, to replace African slaves on the colonial plantations after Emancipation. With the first shipment of indentured Indians to Guyana in 1838, a new system of slavery was introduced and between then and 1917, more than half a million Indians were transported to the Caribbean. This traffic formed part of the wider dispersal of Indian labour to an ever-expanding Indian diaspora, which included Malaysia, Mauritius, Fiji, Natal (South Africa), Kenya, Uganda (East Africa) and Seychelles.'

Diaspora. Yes, a new word about Indians who had left India. At this time of major migrations world-wide, the Indian labour migrants were victims of much injustice and double standards. Race, colour and religion were deeply divisive factors. In the words of the Captain's wife, Jane Swinton, 'Why have one law for our Indian emigrants to the West Indian colonies, and another for our English emigrants to Australia?'

Though on publication *The Other Middle Passage* was an attractively produced and well-received book, there was no money in it for me. Through advertisements in the *Caribbean Times* newspaper it had reached a wide audience which knew little or nothing about the Indo-Caribbean people. Thus, beyond the confines of the academies, my years of relentless research and travel far and wide had produced a growing body of work which I'd hoped would add to or complement the existing material available for students from elementary and primary to university levels.

But significant a contribution though this book was, I was propelled by the insistent need to move on from the short stories and write a novel; the genre that would better allow me to engage with, and explore certain ideas and issues about, indentured migrants from British India to the Caribbean. Once this was achieved, my hope was to follow the novel envisaged with another fictive work that would deal with aspects of the Indian labourers' early arrival, settlement and experience.

NINETEEN NINETY FOUR:
RESPONSES TO *THE OTHER MIDDLE PASSAGE*

Gradually, following my move, I came to love my new office space in the Arched Room. It was hidden from public view by a tall wooden door that opened immediately into the magnificent Egyptian Gallery of the British Museum, which was always crowded, the most popular exhibits being the *Rosetta Stone* and the gigantic bust of Rameses. Though potentially traumatic, I did not allow the quick successive changes of office and home relocations to either check or diminish my energy and enthusiasm for my work and life.

On 10 May, Michael Rolfe, the film director had contacted me after a long gap since our last communication. *'Just a brief line to reassure you that I am still in existence,'* he wrote, *'and to apologise for not being in a position to keep in touch. I have had to be out and about so much these last couple of weeks that I have not had the chance to phone (you during your office hours) and am all too conscious of the fact that time marches on. Anyway, do not be dismayed.., I am getting there... I most certainly want to contact Peter Ansorge...while Saeed (Jaffrey, the well-known Indian actor) is in town, and will not let these deadlines slip away...Yours in haste.'*

Thus the hope of working with Mr Rolfe on the Documentary film was revived.

By now, I had come to know a few more things about the hard realities of life: that often good news was succeeded by bad news. Having corresponded with and met Sam Selvon, whom I liked, I was saddened to hear that he had died while on a visit to Trinidad. At once, I remembered our two meetings and reflected that by dying in his homeland, he had fulfilled his own prophecy about his beloved Trinidad and those who eat the Cascadura (fish). In his novel *Those Who Eat the Cascadura*, he used a quotation from Allister Macmillan's *History of the West Indies*: 'Anyone who eats the cascadura, wheresoever they may wander, shall end their days in Trinidad.' Sam Selvon certainly did.

As the 'idea' of writing the novel matured in my mind, I pondered the short stories that I'd written and measured them against the fact that I had no book length fiction. So I pressed on with greater urgency to write the novel which I entitled *Rama's Voyage*.

A few days later on 25 May I found a letter on my desk in the Arched Room. The postage on the envelope revealed its origin. Willi Chen, the multi-talented artist, writer, painter, playwright and businessman was moved to write:

'Your book (The Other Middle Passage) was a pleasant surprise (received today). You are the unsung genius of Trinidad literary and historical oeuvre. I marvel at the scholarship, the depth and the energy.

I have gotten a piece on Selvon which I read at his funeral in Trinidad, accepted by London Mag. today. And a story to appear in the Malahat Review, Canada. But I am yet to do a grand project like any of yours. For this I have neither patience, skill, will nor ability.

So I leave this to you. Keep up the good work. When you come we must have a chat...

Cheers and let's keep in touch and say when is your arrival date, so that I shall begin to unroll the red carpet.

Peace.

Willi Chen.'

How fortunate I was to have had these warm words from Willi who, following Sam Selvon's death, had written 'An Appreciation' which he read at his friend's funeral on 26 May 1994:

'Sam Selvon stood tall and indefatigable in his winter coat and read like a hero...as soon as he gained momentum into the reading... Sam spoke authoritatively to reveal the latent cohesiveness of voice and diction melded so expertly in his distinctive personal style... of his

words and phrases.'

After these opening words, my imagination was enlivened as I read the rest of Willi's tribute, especially the closing paragraph:

'It was the local landscape presented with such evocative and intrepid panache that captivated the audience who found themselves spell bound by a simple reading done by a simple man. We shall never forget him for the passion, warmth and beauty of human life he has given us as a writer, much of it immeasurable entrenched in Sam Selvon himself as an artist of intense courage and simplicity.'

After reading this, I recalled something else that Sam had said about Trinidad: 'This island is my shadow and I carry it with me wherever I go.'

Another Trinidadian, Nisa Khan, a lawyer and friend resident in London, on receiving *The Other Middle Passage* wrote: *'...Upon receipt of your book and letter from Afzal (Nisa's brother) I wrote to you in haste yesterday. Congratulations on yet another achievement.*

I read parts of it last night and it is so concise - in fact a journal of one voyage and it would appear that you are really a brilliant researcher as I have never heard of Captain Swinton before and this is a remarkable "discovery"...

I have read Ramphal's book ('Inseparable Humanity') and just about to read (Hugh) Tinker's ('A New System of Slavery') I thought I should catch up on my Caribbean history!

I personally think your new (forthcoming) book Arising From Bondage will be greatly appreciated by Indians in Trinidad in view of the current situation at home. Perhaps Afzal can try to approach schools as he suggested but the recession is so great in Trinidad at present that I cannot guarantee "profits" as such, so if you have someone who can act as your agent and "push" it that may be a better idea....

The High Commission cannot even afford a function!...

..Please drop me a line and once again I wish you all the very best. I think ...Afzal should ask Mrs Brereton whom he knows quite well to review this as a review by her will be beyond dispute, the best you can hope for in Trinidad. She is well respected as you know. Can you send Afzal an "autographed" copy and he can lend his copy ... I think he feels proud whenever he receives his own from you personally...'

Here, I would especially like to formally thank Afzal very warmly for his belief in my books, as well as his valuable assistance in their wide distribution in Trinidad.

Ms Brereton had reviewed the book in the *Trinidad Guardian* as did Professor Birbalsingh of York University in Canada. In the *South Asian Review* he wrote: '*Ramdin's presentation of Captain Swinton's Journal, along with his well-researched and lucid Introduction is therefore an invaluable addition to works that illuminate dark areas of Caribbean history.*'

And, on the same theme, a Postcard from the Sorbonne University in Paris from my friend, Bissera Gorgatchev, a Linguistics expert and teacher read:

'*Thanks a lot for the most delicious surprise! Your book is more than perfect: it is profound and emotional. I learned a lot and I love your style too.*

It has been a long time that I wanted to read you and now you really surpassed my expectations.

Reading your work was breath-taking, you know I am subjective but I have to tell you it is a fascinating experience.

Congratulations!

I am happy for you because I am sure you feel good having written something as wonderful as that.'

'Subjective' or otherwise, overall, such comments on *The Other Middle Passage* had a pleasing effect on me.

After the successful Paris Conference on 'African-Americans in Europe,' once again, I met Professor Henry Gates Jr. of Harvard University. He was in London to deliver the Chadwyck Healey Lecture at the British Library; and that evening he introduced me to Wole Soyinka, the first African writer to win the Nobel Prize for Literature. After the Lecture, I spoke with Mr Soyinka about his work and my research on C.L.R James whom he knew well and respected. Showing a willingness to help, Mr Soyinka gave me his card and said I should get in touch with him. Before we left the post-Lecture Reception, a young cameraman took a photograph of Professor Gates, myself, Wole Soyinka and Armet Francis, which I kept as a memento of my meeting and connectedness with these three brilliant men.

As I juggled with all that was going on in my life, I became more familiar with the new environment of Kilburn's Plympton Road, particularly the first floor bay-windowed Room facing south. The light here was as good as I could have hoped for. Realising this, one morning I drew the heavy curtains back and they have stayed that way ever since!

Following my six-day stay in Providence, still with no publisher, as I considered my commitment to the James biography, news from America reached me.

'*Dear Ron*', Paul Buhle wrote, '*Hello again. Just come across your address…*

Things seemed to have collapsed at the James Society and apart from the continuing level of discussion in the journals… there's regrettably little to report. I guess the Conference volume will be out this fall for the U-Mass Press. Please let me know about the stage of your work. Several people are contemplating a "James Cultural Studies Reader" and perhaps an essay on CLR and Trinidad by you might bring a breath of fresh air into the subject. All Best Wishes, Paul Buhle.'

After reading Paul's letter, how interesting, I thought, that prior to the James Conference, no approach was made to me: either to write or present a paper! Why? I had so many things to say that the James 'experts' did not say or know. I thought about the factions and 'cliques' which I was told were engaged in Jamesiana (James Studies) and, for the first time, I wondered if they (bearing in mind their cliquishness) would either block my progress or encourage my work.

Before the end of 1994, I had spoken to Dr Vincent Thompson, who after teaching in England, had gained a Professorship in the United States. He was on one of his frequent visits to London, which included the British Museum's Round Reading Room. After congratulating me on the publication of *The Making of the Black Working Class in Britain*, Dr Thompson and I discussed the pioneering qualities of both *From Chattel Slave to Wage Earner* and

The Making of the Black Working Class in Britain which, he insisted, could earn me a PhD.

'How?' I enquired. He explained the academic process.

Thereafter, I consulted those in the know at the University of London's Senate House and after further consideration, I thought: Why not? And so I read through the University's 'Rules and Regulations' for Higher Degrees. This was a very tall order – a list of requirements that demanded a great deal from Candidates. Nonetheless, I considered myself eligible and duly applied for the PhD, submitting five of my published books.

A few weeks later, the University of London's Board of Examiners informed me that instead of a PhD, my work should be submitted for a *'Higher Doctorate.'* A 'Higher Doctorate?' Yes, the Doctor of Literature, the Board of Examiners confirmed. I followed their advice and instructions and duly applied for this Higher Degree. After three months, I received another letter from the Board which conveyed the good news that they were passing on my work to two 'Independent Examiners,' one of whom, they were pleased to inform me, had already been contacted. In the summer of 1996, the Board again wrote to me to say that the second of the 'Independent' Examiners was found and that they were now ready to proceed. I noted that they had announced the recruitment of one of the Independent Examiners' as if it was an achievement. How rare was this Doctor of Literature process? I wondered.

For the rest of the Summer and in the months that followed, all I could do was wait as the quality of my published work was rigorously tested.

GLASGOW: SPEAKING AT THE
KELVINGROVE ART GALLERY

As I pursued my literary work, necessarily a certain pattern and direction began to appear more clearly: In effect, my wide-ranging interests were concerned not only with European Colonisation, African slavery and Blacks and Asians in Britain, but also on aspects of the relationship between India and Indians in the Caribbean. This was all the more evident when, at last, my work on *Arising From Bondage* was completed. It was a cathartic moment, to say the least. Soon my greater knowledge was in demand by students, especially those engaged in research for PhD and MA degrees. Early in 1995 a student at the University of Warwick had contacted me about her Thesis: 'Voices From the Boundary: The Indo-Caribbean Experience in Britain.' As always in my relations with students, I was only too glad to be of help to the Warwick-based Researcher on her visits to London. I had no doubt that her work was valuable and would eventually be successful.

By this time, I'd carved a niche of sorts as an author and writer of the Black and Asian experience in both Britain and the Caribbean. From the book reviews and comments, it seemed the scope and depth of my books were unsurpassed. Spring had come again and each morning from northwest London, I continued to traverse the relatively new pathway along the busy Kilburn High Road northwards to the tube station. Having travelled for years on buses and on the underground system from various addresses in north, northeast, southwest and west London to get to work at the British Museum, the difference now was this: For the first time, my way in was on Jubilee and Central or Metropolitan Line trains. What did not change were my hours and the routine of office work.

By now however I'd become more familiar with the Acquisitions job and the chair and desk that I had occupied in the unusually spacious and well-lit Arched Room. As previously (when I was in the T1 office) while publicity and commitments accumulated, my hectic life as writer and lecturer became even more so. Few things were planned; I dealt with engagements as they arose, borne along on a wave of feverish activity and always with a sense of ever-renewing anticipation of what was next.

Having first met Nat Edwards in the British Museum, now as Senior Curator at the Open Museum in Glasgow, on one of his visits to London, we discussed the possibility of me doing a Lecture at the famous Kelvingrove Art Gallery and Museum. Later, Nat wrote:

'*It was good to see you. I really enjoyed The Other Middle Passage and I think we should be able to arrange a review in The Asian Voice (Glasgow). I have checked out our facilities, and the best place for a Talk, the Conference Room at the Art Gallery and Museum is free on*

Friday 7 April...Would this be a good date for you? Can you let me know what kind of figure we should think about for fees and expenses, so I can balance my books, and before you become too famous for us to afford.'

Pleased to hear from Nat, and with the prospect of earning a 'fee' I responded positively. In turn, Nat confirmed that my Lecture would indeed take place in Glasgow's Art Gallery and Museum in Kelvingrove. He wrote:

'Dear Ron,

Thanks for your letter of 6 March, I am hoping that the event will start at 6.30pm. If this is too late please let me know. I have arranged to have plane tickets sent to you at the Library by our travel section. The arrangements are for Friday 7 April the 11am flight up from Heathrow arriving in Glasgow approx 12.15 p.m and I have booked you back on the 5pm on Sunday 9th April but this can be changed to Saturday 8th April if you wish to go back on the Saturday. You should receive an official Order from the Council for your fee... We can arrange accommodation for you if you want. Otherwise you can arrange your own and we can reimburse you. Please let me know what kind of accommodation you would prefer.

Looking forward to seeing you,

Yours sincerely

Nat Edwards

Senior Curator

The Open Museum (Art Gallery and Museum, Kelvingrove).'

Having never been north of the border before, now I looked forward to being in Scotland. While I prepared for my visit, I remembered the photographs of Edinburgh Castle and Holyrood House that I'd seen stuck on walls of the classroom when I was a schoolboy. On the morning of Friday 7 April, I flew from Heathrow Airport to Glasgow and was met on arrival by Nat Edwards at around 12.15 p.m. A taxi took us straight to the BBC Radio Studio where I was interviewed live about my Lecture that evening. Afterwards, Nat and I had lunch before I booked into a plush Hotel in Kelvingrove. I lay on the fluffy tartan-covered bed awhile thinking of my presence there. A couple of hours later,

I made my way over to the Venue. With some time to spare, I looked around and realised what an incredible treasure house the Art Gallery and Museum was: paintings, artefacts and a range of exhibits.

Then, at the appointed place and time, Curator Nat Edwards arrived and we entered the hall where I met local dignitaries before the formal proceedings began. After Nat's Introduction, I began my Lecture by saying:

'*Mr Chairman, Ladies and Gentlemen, 27 years ago I arrived in England as a young immigrant with great expectations. It was not long before I realised that there was a pattern of which my experience in the workplace, in the community and the wider society, formed an integral part. Almost at once, it seemed my youthful ambition or imaginings had ended and a long period of continuous study, committed organisational work in the Trade Union movement and multifaceted writings began.*

To date, I have written six books, including history, biography, a textbook for schools, short stories and I am presently working on a novel. A fundamental theme in my historical works is the connection between black and Afro-Asian labour, the two largest non-white groups, and the British economy. In my opinion, an understanding of this relationship is crucial to an understanding of some of the problems facing Afro-Asian people in Britain today. Therefore, the topic I have chosen for my talk tonight is: "From Colonial to British Labour"...'

I went on to consider racial discrimination and the lack of *inclusiveness* in society, a theme which would continue to preoccupy me as part of my exploration of what were to me the essential social ideas: 'respect for difference,' and 'home and belonging.'

At the Reception afterwards, many people were keen to talk with me; among them were those who had long settled in Glasgow from the Indian subcontinent – Scottish Asians. The editor of the *Asian Voice* said he would like to do an article on my 'Talk.' I agreed and provided him with a copy of what I'd said. An hour later, guided by Nat, I had a sense of what it was to be in Glasgow on a Friday Night: As it was, that year Glasgow was the European 'City of Culture.' Predictably, there was much gaiety, camaraderie and boisterousness and I was happy to be there. It was a very enjoyable Glasgow night out!

The next day, after a full breakfast, I strolled through the streets and took in the sights. It was a rare, leisurely Saturday which I enjoyed very much. Then on Sunday morning, I walked across the park, past the cemetery with its great mausoleums to my right before ascending the hill up to the University of Glasgow, which overlooked the city.

Standing at various points around the buildings, I took in the architecture; what a wonderful university precinct, I thought. It was cold, but crystal clear; the glittering sun cast a brilliant glow on the buildings and park below. There were benches where I stood. I sat down on the nearest one and conscious of the moment and Nat's generous invitation, on an A4 sheet of paper, I wrote a few lines. I reflected on my Talk in the Art Gallery below, its red brick exterior bathed in sunshine glowed and I was warmed by thoughts of the way the full house had responded; a mixed audience of middling age and older, as well as many young Asian and white Glaswegians. And reminding myself that this was the furthest north of the British Isles that I had been, I felt I'd broken new ground in Scotland. Historically, my connection with this place was clear: I was baptised with the Scottish name 'Andrew' in a Canadian Presbyterian Church in Trinidad which had its origin in Scotland.

After a while, I looked in the distance towards the horizon in the direction where I imagined Paisley to be. From several tall chimney stacks, I could see wisps of smoke rising; a sign of industrial activity, I thought. Nearer still was the River Clyde. Why was I here? The question was timely: Because I'd been invited to impart knowledge; to educate my audiences - both the wider community through BBC Glasgow radio and those in the lecture hall about hidden, but linked British histories. Given my understanding of Scotland"s legendary manufactures, its industrial life and this experience of being in Glasgow, home of the great ship builders (including of course, those 'Coolie ships' one of which had taken my grandfather from India to Trinidad) I was profoundly moved. At that moment, I considered another connection: Just across the water, in a westerly direction was Belfast where the *S.S. Canberra* that had brought me from Trinidad to England was built and launched. So Glasgow was central to two voyages: One of my Indian Grandfather Ratnam; the other of myself that had led to this journey across the Scottish border. As emotion got the better of me, I stood up, steadied myself and walked around the University buildings.

With some time to spare, unhurriedly, I walked down the hill, then along the grounds of the Kelvingrove Art Gallery and Museum before returning to the hotel. Refreshed and relaxed, now I appreciated the room even much more: it was spacious and tastefully furnished with things Scottish. It felt more homely than merely functional. I lay on the bed and, for a while, I wallowed in a sense of place. As if I'd come full circle, being in Glasgow had revealed much more that I'd expected. Then with time pressing, I made my way to the airport and flew back to London feeling richer for the experience and the bonus of a £150.00 fee.

For the rest of the summer months that followed, at times, I wondered about the progress of my University of London 'Higher Doctorate' Application. The tendency of publishers to hype their books was one thing, but now, the quality of my published works faced the ultimate test by being placed under the academic microscope. In sum, twenty-four years of research and writing was subjected to the rigour of the University of London's highest standards. What at times became a compelling, tense and exciting wait for the outcome, was tempered by my daily routine of office work and the demands of writing.

LOSS AND HOPE: A RETROSPECTIVE

Overall, the years from 1992-1995 were jam-packed and revealing. After the Warwick 'Monograph' set-back, and for almost all of the previous year and thereafter, I'd been working very closely financially and editorially with a publisher. As it was, we had got as far as the printed page proofs of *Arising from Bondage: A History of the Indo-Caribbean People.* It was wonderful to see the entire manuscript in a bundle, but working through the proofs, I became increasingly concerned about meeting the May 1995 deadline. In fact as the early months of 1995 passed it was clear that the hoped-for 150th Anniversary publication would not happen. In a word, I felt cheated, which did relations between myself and the publisher concerned no good. There was no point in waiting around. I began thinking about my options.

Hitherto, having done everything in my power to publish *Arising From Bondage* this was one of the most regrettable things that had happened thus far in my writing-publishing career; all the more so, because I felt I'd let down many people. For one thing, I felt that I could not compensate for the goodwill and work of my friend, the designer Wendy Greenbury who, to her credit, had done three excellent book jacket designs. Put simply, in spite of all our efforts, the historic opportunity was missed. Why? Surely, there had to be *very good* and *strong reasons* for this. When I questioned the publisher, in essence, his casual remark was: because it is history, it would not date! So once more (following the Warwick 'Monograph') my comprehensive 'History' of the East Indians in the Caribbean was rejected and, interestingly, in both cases, Indo-Caribbean people were instrumental in the final decisions. This made the disappointment all the more difficult to understand!

Having made the proof corrections of *Arising From Bondage* on the master file in my computer, now I needed a printed copy from which I would make photocopies to be sent out to other publishers. To this end, I proceeded to use the printer in my friend John Henderson's office. Printing from my computer, after the first 100 pages, John said he would do me the favour of printing the remaining pages the following day. Good idea. While closing down the printing operation, I mistakenly pressed the wrong key and the entire file containing the manuscript of *Arising From Bondage* was deleted from my computer. For a while, I could not believe that this had happened. Then the full impact of the shock hit me. Although John was supportive, I was devastated.

After the most uncomfortable of nights, I woke up the next morning feeling dreadful, thoroughly miserable. It was cold, dull and raining as I stood on the platform at Finchley Road Station staring at the wet railway-track. It was difficult to get the loss of the book, the accumulation of almost ten years of work, out of my mind. Later that day, John had tried to retrieve what was left of the file from my computer's hard drive. What eventually came out was largely indecipherable; more like hieroglyphics than a printed text in English. At that moment, I felt the only sensible course was to make a fresh start. In other words: to proceed immediately with *rewriting* the book.

So I began again. With all the energy and enthusiasm that I could muster, I worked towards another version of the book. Then one day, quite by chance, through John Crabb (an employee of the publishers I.B Tauris) I was introduced to Dr Lester Crook, the history Editor of I.B Tauris, one of the few Englishmen that I'd met who was very knowledgeable about the Indo-Caribbean people. He expressed an interest in seeing a synopsis and sample chapters of the manuscript of *Arising From Bondage* once it was ready. But although I was not holding my breath, I was encouraged and worked hard to finish the new manuscript. As I went over familiar research, I also explored further. In the process, I found and incorporated new sources, and given the scope and depth of my understanding of the subject and its importance, gradually my undimmed faith in the book was reinforced. Eventually, I was able to submit a synopsis, list of contents and sample chapters to Dr Crook.

Against this background of relentless, meticulous research, as the bulk of the writing and rewriting of *Arising From Bondage* neared its end, as if the 'crisis' of loss had generated a new vision, with the benefit of new and richly-nuanced knowledge and various stories, I also pressed on with the earlier work that I'd done on my first novel *Rama's Voyage*. Thus immersed in my busy schedule, during May 1995, I took a much-needed break. At the invitation of Clive Lloyd (former West Indian Test Cricketer) and Trevor McDonald, I attended a Special Event: The official Launch of the 'Sonny Ramadhin and Alfred Valentine BENEFIT '95' in the Long Room at Lord's Cricket Ground. This venue in St John's Wood, London is internationally known and respected the world over as the 'home' or 'shrine' of cricket. Having spent many years in Trinidad listening to ball by ball BBC radio commentaries of matches featuring these two West Indian 'greats,' being aware of Ramadhin's and Valentine's exalted reputations for most of my life, the invitation to *meet them* was a wonderful opportunity. When at last they appeared amidst a crush of people in the famous Long Room at Lord's, unlike the photographs of them in action, they were now, but a shadow of their former sporting selves. Nonetheless, the spirit of what they had achieved was palpable, and naturally I conjured up a sense of that time when 'Ram and Val' were the toast of cricket-lovers as they helped the West Indies Cricket Team to victory against mighty England.

After I'd met and shook hands with both men, I found myself standing before the urn containing the 'Ashes;' a surprisingly small trophy over which so many tense, exciting battles (Test Series) were fought between the England and Australian Cricket Teams. When I turned away from the urn, I was greeted by another extraordinary sight: from the perspective of the Long Room, I looked out at the green carpet that was Lord's Cricket Ground; and, as if it was bursting to get through, I was reminded of the popular calypso: *'Ramadhin and Valentine…'* It was late Spring in London and being in The Long Room, I also reflected on the hummable strains of the song *Cricket, Lovely Cricket* as the cricket season approached.

After that pleasant evening in St. John's Wood, refreshed and having gained some new insights, I alternated between writing fact and fiction: *Arising From Bondage* and *Rama's Voyage*. This twinning of genres opened a window through which I had a much clearer vision of my concerns and responsibilities as a writer.

'LETTER TO A CLOSE RELATIVE…'

With the approach of the 150th anniversary of the arrival of Indians in Trinidad, though hugely disappointed that *Arising From Bondage* was still unpublished, before leaving London, I thought of doing something worthy of this historical moment. And so I wrote a special *Open Letter* entitled: *Letter to a Close Relative on the 150th Anniversary of the Arrival of East Indians in Trinidad*. This was a rare, indeed a bold approach. To my knowledge, hitherto no Caribbean writer had ever attempted such a thing.

From London, I had sent copies of the '*Letter*' to one of India's leading newspapers *The Hindu*, as well as to journals in Britain, Canada and, of course, to *all* the newspapers in Trinidad and Tobago. I also did a BBC Radio 4 'In Living Colour' programme and two BBC World Service broadcasts from Bush House in

London: one for the Caribbean Service, the other for BBC South Asia.

On arrival in Trinidad, just before the Anniversary, at the invitation of Hans Hanoomansingh, a leading Indo-Trinidadian radio personality, I read the *'Letter'* which was broadcast in its entirety on Radio 103 FM on Indian Arrival Day 30 May 1995. In part, the 'Letter' read:

'Dear Les,

Your photograph is before me on the table where it has been on view since it arrived with your letter two days ago and, as I write, I am reminded of your great-Grandfather, Nattan, (a former East Indian indentured labourer of legendary physical strength, independent-minded and outspoken) whom I vaguely remember. I was but a child, not much older than about five or six, when he died. And for some reason, perhaps because of whispers I had heard long ago, I have continued to believe that he did not die peacefully in his bed, but through a dark and cowardly act of violence. What was his crime? My curiosity was met with conspiratorial silence so intimidating and of such finality that it inhibited further enquiry and, instead of clarifying such questions as I posed it had the effect of deepening the mystery and mystique of the man. From what my mother told me, and I believed implicitly in what she said, he was an industrious and generous man, who loved children and young people generally...He would have been proud of you and it is likely that you, in turn, would have looked up to him...And though you bear striking resemblance to your parents... your eyes flash the fire of your great Grandmother Rajindi, the wife of Nattan, and like her, your face evokes an animation that is tempered by mysterious calmness...

On the eve of your admission to University, I feel proud of your achievement. And I congratulate you on your exceptional letter. It has generated a rare excitement in me, especially the manner in which you communicate, expressly your experimental handling of the language, changing, evolving, growing (an audacious departure from the rigid, oppressive, policing language, so neat, so final, so life-sapping, so prevalent) used to good effect by your imaginative, inventive and altogether refreshing use of words that suggest boundless possibilities...

I am very pleased with your choice of English, history and philosophy, a trilogy that will, in time, aid your understanding of the world you live in. But be mindful also of the importance of hard experience, a precious asset that tests the most noble of ideas. More than a decade before you were born, a feverish zeal had gripped the people of this country, who were for a while, deeply moved by the motto: "Together we Aspire, Together We Achieve." Alas, much time has elapsed since then and the desired togetherness remains largely unachieved. Our failure to respect racial difference shows how little we have learned since that renowned Genoese Explorer imposed his standard on these islands, and of other exploiters who followed with their refinements of oppression, instituting differences in race, colour and class...

You will, of course, be 18 years old on 30 May 1995, the day on which the country, more particularly sections of it, will be commemorating the 150th anniversary of the arrival of the first indentured Indians in Trinidad...

Such conscious seeking of knowledge as you engage in, can have beneficial results and will, I hope guide you in your pursuit of excellence as we approach the end of the century and enter the uncharted waters of the third millennium. All things considered, this is a unique historical moment for you, proud bearer of an inheritance that spans the generations of courageous Indians who crossed the "kala pani" (dark water). I feel confident that as you grow in self-knowledge and come to know and rise above the more obvious "man-made" differences, you will reach out for that essential fellowship with your brothers and sisters who comprise the cultural mosaic that mirror the marvellous capability of human creativity in this extraordinary land, for knowing oneself is the best preparation for knowing and respecting others...

I thank you for the photograph and the letter, for your concern about the mass of poor, dispossessed descendants of the East Indian field hands, who through the spirit of Jahaji bhai (brotherhood of the "Coolie" ships) rose from the ravages of their plantation bondage. You inspire in me, dear Lesley (determined representative that you are of a generation of Indo-Trinidadian womanhood) renewed, justifiable hope that more meaningful "togetherness" will indeed be achieved and for this, and much more, you have my everlasting gratitude. But most of all, at this time of reflection, of meditation on history, I thank you for being you. Godspeed and Happy Birthday, Affectionately,

Your uncle,
Ron'

So it was that by Indian Arrival Day 1995 in Trinidad and Tobago, through my interviews and messages, I had informed many people who may not have heard of the long-standing presence of Indians and their descendants there!

But it was significant that no Trinidadian newspaper bothered to publish the *Letter* or even a part of it. Outside Trinidad, however, through the vast circulation of *The Hindu* newspaper, Indians in India (and the Indian diaspora) were able to read about Indians in Trinidad and Tobago. Lest I forget what a 'race-conscious' country Trinidad could, at times be, this was a sobering reminder of its social short-comings. Yet, I remained hopeful of a time to come when recognition of the divide would be acted upon.

In addition to India's *Hindu* newspaper, the *Letter* I was told would also be published in the *Indo-Caribbean Review* in Canada; and it was heartening to learn that the BBC Caribbean Service and Trinidad radio Broadcasts were great triumphs. So over the world's airwaves, both in the East and West, having written my own lines and spoken them on the BBC at the time of the 150th Anniversary, I'd reached millions of people.

With my father sitting on his chair beside me in the gallery on Arrival Day 1995, we listened to the entire sixteen- minute reading that I'd recorded the previous day. Afterwards, he responded: 'It sound just like you talking to me now!' This was the effect I had hoped to achieve. And later, when we had tuned into the BBC World Service, together with Ma (who had joined Pa and myself in the gallery) we listened to my recorded Interview being broadcast from London. At that moment, I was reminded of space and time; of my boyhood when, with a sense of wonder I had pressed my ear close to the Mullard radio and heard the English announcer speak the words: 'The is the BBC World News...' which then sounded like the voice of God. Now I was back in the small wooden house hearing myself speak on the BBC; and doing so with some authority, I might add. How extraordinary, I thought.

In Trinidad, the Indians were not backward in coming forward to mark this Arrival Day. Among the many celebratory events was a Special Service held at Susamachar Church in San Fernando. In attendance were an impressive array of representatives from all religious faiths in Trinidad and Tobago. The Reverend Cyril Paul, one of the leading Indo-Trinidadian Presbyterians and Pastor at Susamachar (the pre-eminent Presbyterian Church in the country), welcomed the largest gathering of its kind there: The assembly was such that it had overspilled and spread out at the front and sides of the Church.

Inside, as proceedings began: 'Ladies and Gentlemen,' Reverend Paul said, 'we have in our midst a Special Visitor from abroad. He is a local boy, the Historian Dr Ron Ramdin.' I was caught unawares. It was as if the Reverend was speaking about someone else. Then he said: 'Ron, would you please stand.' When I stood up in response to the Reverend's request, he added: 'You look good!' Overwhelmed by the surprise announcement, after this very public recognition of how 'good' I looked, though used to large audiences, I was glad to sit down.

Taken together, this pre-and post-Anniversary visit to Trinidad turned out to be more memorable than I'd expected; and on my return to London, Lynette Lithgow, the Trinidad-born Presenter of the BBC 'Arrival Day' Programme for the Caribbean Service broadcast, wrote to me:

'Dear Ron,

This is just to say thank you for so kindly helping with the programme on Indian-Arrival Day. I was pleased with the result. Your contribution was especially appreciated because of your particular knowledge in this area. I hope you had a good time in Trinidad and Tobago and that the English summer eventually arrives so that the contrast in weather is not too painful.'

Tragically, not long after this communication, Lynette was brutally murdered in Trinidad.

On 4 July I wrote to my parents: *'Life's been hectic since I arrived back in London which delayed the writing of this note. I had a busy, but quite wonderful time with you all. Each time I visit, the pleasure of being with you both becomes ever greater. The memories I've brought back are precious.'*

I was happy to inform them too of what I'd learned since my return to London. I confirmed that:

'While... in Trinidad, my "Letter..." was published in The Hindu, one of India's largest newspapers (half a million copies sold each day) in its Sunday Magazine - that same Sunday when I went to Susamachar! I am still awaiting publication of my book "Arising From Bondage."

I will be writing to Keno and Joey soon and will shortly be sending you about £100 to help towards the cost of reflooring the house.'

Reference to the unpublished *Arising From Bondage* was surprisingly still hard to take. But I could not be happier knowing that gradually, the old wooden house through periodic incremental additions and repairs had become more sound and accommodating; and with a new kitchen in-house, it had assumed an altogether different shape. To cap it all, a water pipe was laid to reach the house. Thinking of this last facility, given that my entire childhood and teen years were indelibly marked by the continuous daily fetching of buckets of water, now I was filled with deep satisfaction that finally water could be had in the house at the turn of a tap!

ANOTHER PROFILE, FILM PURSUITS
AND BOOK RESPONSES

My fairly well-established reputation in Trinidad and the Caribbean was complemented on my return to London when I was approached by *The Caribbean Times* to be the subject of their next 'Profile' in a series of Who's Who in the black community in Britain. This was written by Sharon Atkin, then at the top of her game as activist and leading black politician. Her 'Profile' of me appeared in *The Caribbean Times* on 5 August, 1995. In this full page spread highlighting community achievement under the title 'MAKING THE PAST SERVE THE PRESENT,' Ms Atkin wrote:

'The pursuit of excellence is what he (Ron Ramdin) constantly strives for, and the deepening of understanding of shared history and destiny among the African-Caribbean and Asian communities is his Mission.'

To this opening paragraph, she added:

'Ron Ramdin is a prolific writer and historian, who has dedicated his life to documenting black history both in Britain and the Caribbean... He was born in Trinidad and Tobago to Asian parents. His grandfather was an indentured labourer, so Ron's anti-imperialist politics were formed at an early age.'

Here I would add that hitherto, all that I had said and written were propelled by my willingness to redress the balance between rich and poor, the haves and the have-nots. I was not a man who conformed to some perceived ideology. But, on the whole, I found Ms Atkin's 'Profile' agreeable:

'Ron grew up in a small house which was home to 12 people, seven of whom were children,' she continued. *'... Ron says by the age of 14 he knew that he had to leave Trinidad in order to find himself...*

Like many newly-arrived immigrants, he saw the value and importance of education. Not being independently wealthy, he worked first...in the University of London Library, and then paid his way through Drama school, studying at the New Era Academy of Drama and Music...

But his education was still not complete. He went on to study Industrial Relations at Middlesex University and thereafter Economics and History at the London School of Economics and Political Science (LSE)...

Ron had a burning ambition to start writing the histories (to fill the gap) of working class black struggle...

One of the things that motivated him to write was his view that black youth of today do not understand much about the black presence over the last hundred years. They exist in ignorance, and therefore also deny their own parents' experience.

He is critical of the way history is both written and taught. So rather than simply remain a critic, he set about documenting the Asian, African and Caribbean contributions to British society...

The pursuit of excellence is what he constantly strives for, and the deepening understanding of **shared** *history and destiny among the African, Caribbean and Asian communities (in relation to Britons/ Europeans) is his mission.*

Ron Ramdin's career to date is a reflection of the man. He is passionate about... and...concerned that the (Black and Asian) communities' needs and aspirations are unlikely to be met by the election of Tony Blair as PM, although he believes it is imperative that the present Government be turned out of office. Meanwhile, Ron Ramdin continues to research and document that which is most dear to his heart...he hopes that more black publishers will be established...'

This Profile in the leading newspaper of the Black Press in Britain underlined my reputation as a writer and spokesman on behalf of Blacks and Asians in Britain. By implication, every other marginalized person or group fell within the ambit of my social concern.

The 'pursuit of excellence,' always at the foreground of my mind was now much more in evidence, as increasingly my attention turned to writing fiction. Hitherto, I'd been preoccupied with histories and related stories; now the constraints of evidence-based writing gave way to my imagination, to works of greater creativity. Thus *Rama's Voyage* became an insistent, compelling project.

As the written word became increasingly adaptable to the medium of film and television, on 9 August 1995, I wrote to the Film Director Michael Rolfe about translating some of my writings to the medium of television. After a few meetings, as I got to know Mr Rolfe better, I also became more critical of a few things regarding his approach to the two Projects that were already in hand: 'The Sand Road' and 'Reluctant Voyagers,' the latter based on my manuscript of *Arising From Bondage*. The fact that I'd pursued publication of this book even though I did not have a publishing contract was a reflection of the degree to which I had trusted those concerned. Sadly, they did not trust themselves.

As talks about the 'Reluctant Voyagers' continued, I wrote to Mr Rolfe:

'As always, it was a delight to see you again... And I was pleased to meet Dinesh and Chris. The one-page structure which you showed to me was good, but I was very surprised to see it copyrighted with Dinesh's name at the bottom of the document. I strongly object to him claiming a document derived from our work before we even get started! He has also said that he needs to do some research, which you said you would fund. Dinesh is not from India, as I thought, and my understanding

is that the research for the project has already been done by me. To be frank, at this moment, it is unlikely (unless I can get a firm guarantee in writing, as to my role and input in this project) that I will be able to trust or work with a person who already believes he knows best!

Sorry, but I feel it is only fair that I should confide this in you.'

Mr Rolfe took note and I never saw either Dinesh or Chris again.

At the age of fifty-three my health was still quite good. My son Ronnie (after his time in St. Vincent, where he'd built his mother's house) was back in London with his girl-friend Melissa, who was from Auckland, New Zealand. Young and seemingly sure enough about each other, like every proud parent, I wished them very happy days together.

Meanwhile, materially, financial constraints forced me to continue to live frugally. By now I'd known this kind of austerity for more years than I care to remember; and it is just as well that I continued to apply myself at work in the British Library with no less self-application than at any time before. The Bloomsbury and wider London environment that had shaped, and continued to shape me, were crucial in sustaining and keeping my appetite for work keen. After all, in essence, it was my general desire for a job and self-improvement that were the *raison d'etre* for me leaving my parents, siblings and the home on the Sand Road.

Michael Rolfe, the well-connected film director, invited me to attend a party at the home of Saeed Jaffrey in Stratford- upon-Avon. I had seen many films including *Gandhi* in which this well-known Indian actor had appeared. Michael had said that Saeed's wife (a film and theatre Agent whom I'd previously met at BAFTA) was influential; and that Saeed could play an integral part in our project 'The Reluctant Voyagers.' This was an interesting stage in our film-making journey. My first meeting with Saeed in his Stratford home was a memorable occasion. I remember well my immediate liking of him not just for his acting, but also his warm and engaging personality. Interestingly, our conversation was quite prolonged; and when he suggested that I should write a story for him to perform, I was flattered and hoped that this would indeed happen.

About this time, in October 1995, some six years into my research and writing of the C.L.R James biography Anne McDermid left Curtis Brown. Now, I turned to Literary Agent Faith Evans for help in placing the 'biography' with a publisher. To this end, Ms Evans suggested that I write a chapter by chapter break-down of the book and a Synopsis which I proceeded to do. As it turned out, Ms Evans's clients included not only Saeed Jaffrey, but also Helena Kennedy, whom I liked and respected.

Since my first visit to Seville five years earlier, I was struck by the uniqueness of Flamenco song and the mesmeric dance of the Gypsies. Moved by their music, and knowing that often while in Spain I was seen as 'Gitano' both by Gypsies and non-Gypsies, as I'd said to my Spanish friends Marisa and Margarita, I was not uncomfortable with such a reference even though I realised that many Spaniards (in Andalusia and elsewhere in Spain) did not take too kindly to Gypsies and Gypsy culture. This matter made me pause for reflection on my own experience of identity and identification: in Trinidad, I was a 'Coolie;' in Britain, I was a 'Paki;' in Spain, I was perceived as 'Gitano.' And, as we have seen, hitherto I was given other names.

How extraordinary, I thought, as more and more, I grappled with my *difference* from others, whoever they happen to be and, wherever I happened to be! In my view, it was easy to argue, to shout and verbalize, but it took courage and commitment to act: to explore the issues that I had felt strongly about over many decades. Being in Spain, not only did I feel the need to understand, but also to write about Gypsies and their Flamenco culture, which gave greater credence and urgency to get on with writing *Isabella's Legacy: My Discovery of Spain*. But though Flamenco was integral, so fascinated was I by Gypsy-Spanish culture that I also set about researching a separate book entitled 'Flamenco.'

Overall my experience of Spain was becoming better understood and revealing, with almost every twist and turn: on one of my visits to Seville, while sitting outside a Café, I was joined by an Argentinian painter/artist named Molina. He knew my companions, Marisa and Margarita, who had introduced me as a writer from Gran Bretagna. Fascinated by my appearance, Senor Molina took a sheet of A4 paper from my folder, and using my black biro pen, he drew a sketch of me. I was interested in the artist's technique: in particular, the squiggles and lines he used to compose a likeness of me. Fascinating stuff.

Back in London, I received a copy of the *Indo Caribbean Review,* a Canadian publication which was issued by the University of Windsor. In it, my *Letter to a Close Relative on the 150th Anniversary of the Arrival of East Indians in Trinidad* was published in full. Taken together, with its publication in India and multiple BBC broadcasts in Britain and the Caribbean, this special literary composition had reached a massive audience.

Warmed by thoughts of the *Letter's* success, at this time of greater familiarity with the Arched Room and its interesting location, I received more news from Canada: This time it came in the shape of a post-card with a picture: an alluring autumnal scene with the gold and green colours of trees and vegetation through which a meandering pathway passes beside a blue lake. The sender was Lynda Harrysingh, a white Canadian who was my brother Kenrick's good friend.

'*Ken shared your wonderful news with me,*' she wrote, '*and I wanted to acknowledge your achievements. Congratulations!*

As the road in the picture on the front winds and turns through the changing landscape of the countryside it passes through, so has your life and your literary career. What an achievement!

It is a great honour to be able to say that I met you and that you are the brother of a friend of mine. I have enjoyed reading your books that Ken has lent me and I am eagerly awaiting your new publication with Penguin books.

As the road continues off into the unknown in the picture, so does your journey continue. I pray that God will bless you with good health and the continued ambitious drive to search out and write about the truth and in so doing honour your father and mother and fellow Trinidadians. They must be so very proud of you.

Once again Congratulations.'

Such appreciation, from a stranger, amidst the festive songs and overall merriment, was perhaps an appropriate note on which to end the year. During the Christmas holidays, I took full advantage of the days off work, going to bed at a reasonable time and, as usual, rising early to fill a blank page each day, with either pen or typewriter. As I'd been doing since 1962, I continued to motivate myself, often seeing opportunity where others saw nothing! But while I maintained a steady course, the disciplined approach was habitually broken by time spent reading from either a text book or a novel. Necessarily my literary work was done in solitude. Occasionally, I was overcome by melancholy feelings; and at such times, as a counterpoise, I tended to think in relative terms of loneliness and aloneness; especially the aloneness and near-starvation endured during my first three months in England. But, I was thankful too that in spite of everything, my son was growing up well: he was now 25 years old and I took great pride that he'd become a fine young man. Though of a quiet disposition, he was strong-willed, bright and busy, making his own way in life. In the main, as before I felt it best to let him be, rather than impose any of my standards upon him.

It was nineteen ninety-five. Ever-conscious of time, I hoped this would be an auspicious year: all the more important for me because it was not just another historical marker. In effect, it had the contemporary significance of moments that were deeply personal: for example, the combination of having been to Trinidad and writing the *Letter to a Close Relative*...was cathartic. It brought greater clarity to my earlier colonial confusion. Elements of this 'clarity' began to emerge and were articulated when appropriately enough, the English-born Simon Lee, an academic, came to my father's house on the Sand Road to Interview me for the *Trinidad Guardian*.

By now, my research on C.L.R. James had become extensive, thanks to regular self-funded visits and determined efforts to glean as much material as possible in Trinidad, the United States and across Britain. Lee, in his article 'Indian Synthesis,' stated:

'*Although he (Ron Ramdin) admits to having "invested so much of my time in England, my roots lie here. There are things that I can never forget." He is grateful for his "two homes" and the "two perspectives" they offer him. Now working on two sample chapters of his CLR biography to send to a New York publisher,*' Lee concluded:
'*The "parachutist" from Marabella should be spending more time in the gallery of his Union Park home in the future. The James biography will require much research under the mountains.*'

My use of the word 'parachutist' (as well as 'truffle hunters') referring to the general and the particular (in terms of Indo-Caribbean research) as stated in *Arising From Bondage* seemed to have touched a nerve in a few academics.

TWENTY-TWO

LEARNING EXCELLENCE:
A HIGHER DOCTORATE!

A few weeks before the end of 1995, after a routine morning's work, very much concerned about my future in the British Library while I'd been out of the office on my morning tea break, a brown envelope was placed on my desk. It was addressed to 'Dr Ron Ramdin. The Arched Room, The British Museum.' That morning of the many other letters addressed to me in the Arched Room, none had the prefix 'Dr.' Seconds later, as I opened the tightly sealed envelope, I remembered my Application and the correspondence that I had had with the University of London's Board of Examiners.

In the envelope were enclosures and a letter informing and congratulating me on my success: I had gained the rare honour of being awarded the Higher Doctorate, namely the Doctor of Literature by the University of London. The letter dated 27 November 1995 was from the University of London's 'Academic Registrar' and marked 'PERSONAL.' It read:

'Dear Dr. Ramdin,
I have pleasure in writing to inform you that the Examiners for the Degree of Doctor of Literature for which you are a candidate have reported that you have satisfied them with regard to your work in the field of history, race relations... You will receive a Diploma bearing the Award (29 December 1995) after its formal conferment on the authority of the Senate.
Mrs. S.F. Roberts.'

Among the enclosures, was a request that I should contact the Registrar's Office, which I did during my lunch-break. Once inside the University's Senate House, I walked past the Reception Desk, turned right and entered Room 16 at the far end of the corridor. Behind a counter at which I stood, a woman was busy at her typewriter. I interrupted her by asking to see the Registrar. Moments after leaving her desk, a tall, elegant middle-aged woman approached the counter.

'Ah!' she said. 'You must be *Doctor* Ramdin.'

'Yes, I am,' I said. After hearing 'Doctor' so officially pronounced and, for the first time *voiced* by anyone, the woman disappeared. Soon, she reappeared with a bundle. This contained the second of the two sets of five books that I had submitted to the Board of Examiners. Seeing this, I said: 'Please don't tell me there is a problem with the D.Lit!'

'Oh, don't worry Dr Ramdin,' she said, now with a touch of informality which instantly reassured me. Then, in a more formal tone, she said: 'We do not divulge the names of our Examiners nor do we show any part of the Examiners' Report. But because successful candidates for the D.Lit from the University of London are *so rare*, on this occasion, I have decided that you might like to have *this*.' She handed me an oblong-shaped piece of paper about eight inches long and four inches wide, a photocopy. As she did so, she added: 'It is the *last paragraph* of the Examiners' Report.'

I read the paragraph, my eyes skimming the print. Then I read it again, less hurriedly taking in each word. When I'd finished reading, overwhelmed and not knowing what else to do, I extended my hand towards the Registrar. 'Thank you,' I said. 'Thank you *very much*!' At that moment, the tall and dignified-looking woman personified the University of London and I was grateful for the human contact. Removing the books from the counter, I cradled them and said: 'Happy Christmas!'

Walking back along the ground floor corridor of the Senate House, I checked my pace and thought of the thirty-four years that had passed since I was tasked with my first job there: cleaning the University Library's toilets with no realistic prospect of ever gaining an O Level or a first degree, never mind a Doctor of Literature.

Further along the brown-carpeted corridor, I also recalled those days when I came down the lift from the Sixth floor to collect each day's post from the Post Room which was just about six yards away from the dark-brown door of the Registrar's Office. If the physical distance between these two rooms was short, the intellectual (inner)

journey that had resulted in this call to visit the Registrar's Office
was a very long and troubled one. The years of striving and struggle
had eventually brought its immeasurable reward. At one point, I
stopped in the corridor and, being alone, instead of skimming, now
very slowly, I re-read the four sentences of the closing paragraph of
the Examiners' Report:

'*We should like to add that Mr. Ramdin's work represents a
remarkable scholarly odyssey of an individual working in his
own time and without the benefit of supervision. Far from
cutting corners he has been truly adventurous and ingenious
in discovering new sources and adding new dimensions to his
chosen subject matter. He has shown great patience in rounding
out and finishing off his research. His writing has commendably
used a form of address which because of its openness, its lucidity
and its grace, should generate the envy of professional historians
because of its accessibility for the more general reader.*'

With these words in mind, a tear fell on the back of my right
hand which clutched the books. I placed the piece of paper in
my breast pocket and, after composing myself, I approached the
revolving door at the entrance of the Senate House. Turning left
and walking through the familiar west courtyard, as I made my way
across Montague Place to the British Museum, I remembered the
first time that I saw the magnificent University building, which was
also my first visit to Bloomsbury.

Some weeks later, I showed the University Examiners' final
paragraph to a respected fellow-writer Mr M who, given his
characteristic scepticism, surprised me. After reading it, he said:
'Seamus Heaney got the Nobel Prize for linguistic brilliance and
lyrical beauty. I would prefer to have *this citation*,' he said. I
searched his face for dishonesty and/or sarcasm. But for once, I
could find no such trace. I think he really meant what he said.
How odd, I thought, that such complimentary words should
come from Mr M, of all people, the sceptic *extraordinaire*. And
how satisfying it was that as the year ended, seemingly impossible
dreams and seeds sown over decades, projects that had at every turn
pushed and challenged me, now began to bear fruit. Many matters
were still outstanding and, as usual, I was determined to press on.

But, common sense prevailed. I paused for a short break.

By the turn of another new year, I was reminded of, and marvelled at, the coverage that the *Letter to a Close Relative…* had received; a personal message which became truly public, informing a global audience. The effect of the *Letter* was incalculable.

Six months later, I had reached the mini-milestone of having been in the Arched Room for over three years.

If, at times, the job in my previous office was demanding and trying, the Arched Room, especially in the last 2-3 years, was proving to be no less so; and now there were rumours that this 'Acquisitions Section' would also be restructured.

Ms D was overall in charge and Consultants were employed to interview staff, take evidence and do their 'hatchet job' as one trade union official described it, for both the Arched Room Acquisitions and the Binding Sections.

To my astonishment, Ms D who earlier oversaw my last job-transfer, now brazenly proposed that I move again! This time to, of all places, the Accounts Department. Was this provocation or an intelligent and serious managerial decision? I wondered. Ms D did not ask if I had a preference, or if I would indeed like to work there, as was more or less custom and practice pre-Margaret Thatcher. Having spent all my working life in England in Libraries, deeply respectful of, and fully engaged with the Collections, I was not in the least interested in the accounting aspect of the Library's operations. What an awful mismatch of my interest, proven experience and talent such a placement would be, I thought. A square peg in a round hole, indeed. Thus I was being pushed further and further away from my curatorial potential. Could Ms D not offer me an alternative? Clearly it was in her power to do so. Was this another shifting of the goal posts?

In the weeks that followed, no decision was taken. But with the looming threat of another move as the decision-makers dragged their feet, worry took its toll. My see-sawing weight at this time, bothered me as never before; and routine visits to the Reading Room was so obviously monitored by a Mr S that for a while I cut short the time spent there during my legitimate tea and lunch breaks. This was a very unhappy period and to compound my problems, after weeks of unbearable physical pain, I was told by Professor Boulous, a Surgeon at University College Hospital that I must have an operation to remove a fistula. This was the second time that I had to have surgery; news which increased, rather than lessened my anxiety and worry. When I informed my line manager of my medical predicament, she looked surprised, even sceptical. Thereafter, absences from the office specifically to attend *necessary* doctor's appointments before I was eventually admitted to hospital for the operation were closely monitored.

My immediate post-surgery circumstances was not helped by the fact that I was living alone. The unusually deep wound of my operation had to be dressed daily for about two weeks by a visiting Nurse. In an otherwise busy life, being laid-up was an uncomfortable and rare lull. Stopped in my tracks, it was a very unhappy time for me.

Idleness was foreign to my nature. Predictably I made every effort to get out of my sick bed. Just moving about however was not enough. Eventually, in spite of some pain and discomfort, I decided to show willing and return to work earlier than expected. But being back on my feet, so to speak, on the second day following my return, I was informed that our Section would be losing at least two members of Staff whose jobs would be transferred. Where to? I wondered. The answer: Once again, to Boston Spa! Irony of ironies, I thought.

Then Ms L, the person with overall responsibility in the Department, said she would be having a word with *all* members of staff in the Arched Room.

'When will you be free?' she asked me.

'Oh sometime tomorrow or perhaps the day after,' I said.

We agreed on a date and time; and I duly went up to her office 'to have a chat.' She set out the gloomy position that whoever was not selected to stay in the Arched Room, would be redeployed.

'Oh no!' I thought. My stomach churned and the still raw wound of my operation ached: It was an insistent, throbbing pain.

Confronted with an attitude that I'd experienced before, now Ms L put it to me that there were two posts vacant in 'Book Moves,' a recently formed section. She spoke well about the 'posts.'

'What are Book Moves?' I asked.

She explained that it was a new Section; and the persons redeployed would be part of a 'Team' engaged in what would be perhaps the greatest book moves of all time; a mammoth transfer from the British Museum's Collections to the new St Pancras building. An estimated nine million books (plus maps, manuscripts and so on) were to be moved and Ms L assured me that recruiting for this operation was a very careful process. This was, she elaborated, the job to which the two surplus Arched Room members of staff would be redeployed.

'But this job means climbing ladders and long periods of standing,' I said.

'Oh that would be at a minimum,' she assured me.

'But I've just come out of hospital,' I said. And just in case she did not fully understand, I added: 'I also have trouble with prolonged standing because of varicose veins on my left leg.'

Ms L was not sympathetic. In turn, I was more disappointed than I thought I'd be by her response which added insult to injury. When I left Ms L's office, I was pretty close to being the unhappiest that I'd ever been since I came to the British Museum Library, now the British Library.

With a final decision pending as to which two members of staff were to be selected, in the days that followed, walking in and out of the Arched Room I reappraised and fully appreciated it architecturally; in some respects I thought of it as a mini-version of the 'Ironworks' book-stacks that were at the south-eastern end of the British Museum. Importantly, the Arched Room also housed 'Incunables' in large glass and wood cases on the Ground Floor as well as rare early fourteenth and fifteenth century Manuscripts and books. It was an unusual and attractive Room as any book-lover would wish to find! But regardless of its merits, this was the hard fact: once more, I was engaged in a potentially lingering office departure. As if this was not bad enough, on 7 February 1996 a 'Message from the Chief Executive to All Staff' made me seriously think about my future in the British Library. Why? Because in spite of my best efforts, my situation had not improved at all in the

14 years since I had returned from the LSE with my degree.

Clearly the overriding aim of the British Library was reducing cost which, in essence, meant lowering staff levels before the fast-approaching move to St Pancras. Now, at last, as the rumours persisted something was put in writing in the form of an *Office Notice*. Under the heading: 'PRE-REDUNDANCY MEASURES' the Chief Executive stated that the Library was putting in place '*pre-redundancy measures*, in accordance with the British Library Redundancy Agreement.' It went on to explain how the 'Agreement' would be implemented, and declared that where cuts were necessary, staff in the affected Departments would be redeployed. The *Notice* concluded: 'The reduction of posts and subsequent matching of staff to posts will take time to arrange, and will create a period of further uncertainty. Every effort will be made to minimise this. Staff should feel free to contact the Personnel department or their Welfare Officer for advice...'

With 'redundancy' no longer just a rumour or a remote prospect and with my almost certain redeployment to the 'Book Moves Team,' in my delicate post-surgery state, I was certainly in need of some welfare and all the 'advice' I could get. Thus far, in my twenty-six years in the British Museum and British Library I had never sought welfare or advice. But now that both were options, incredibly they seemed almost impossible to access.

Being of infirm health, I was nonetheless steady in my resolve to get on with my long-pending novel; and now I did so much more confidently as I developed the story of a boy who, recruited as an 'indentured Indian labourer' makes the voyage to the Caribbean. Thus the emerging novel *Rama's Voyage* became the story line for both the novel and a film for which I had submitted seven of a ten-page 'Outline' to Michael Rolfe. The last sentence read: 'The resolution of *Rama's Voyage* is therefore not so much one of belonging or unbelonging, as it is of displacement (arising from inevitable change) and adaptation to the changed circumstances which constitutes the very *essence* of *all* human life.' Stating this, I was, for the first time, consciously linking certain strands of my work to larger evolving themes: migration, home and belonging. And I confirmed my belief that the appropriate genre for expressing myself on these crucial issues was through fiction: in the form of the novel. Thus I felt a new freedom as I worked on the story through which I expressed a hitherto unrealised creativity and inventiveness. Coincident with this 'freedom,' on Sunday 25 February 1996, I read an article in *The Observer Review* entitled 'DEATH OF THE NOVEL.' The writer V.S. Naipaul, aged 63 was asked in an interview why he had given up writing novels: 'I hate the word novel,' he said. 'I can no longer understand why it is important to write or read invented stories. I don't need those extravaganzas. There is so much reading, so much understanding of the world to do...'

I could not agree more that there was 'so much... understanding of the world to do.' But I was at a loss to understand why as writers engaged with the task of '*understanding*' we should restrict our exploration of the world by excluding the novel! Such grand pronouncements by a fellow-Caribbean-British writer, though interesting, was inconsequential for my unbounded mind which now carried me forward with great enthusiasm to write my novel *Rama's Voyage*.

Over the months while my son was still in St Vincent, I had been hearing a great deal about the foundation and construction of the house. Now, at last, I was able to see an image of it. From a photograph which I received in March 1996 it looked very attractive, alluring. Not surprisingly, after selling the house in Walthamstow, Irma returned to her native St. Vincent. Once she was installed in her brand new home, a dream fulfilled, she wrote to me: 'Mr Cato the builder, gave Ronnie a good standard of work, everyone likes the house.' After her 'criticism,' this was praise indeed for all the hard work Ronnie had done. The little boy, whom I had worried so much about while he was growing up in Hackney, had become strong and more confident. I was very pleased about his wonderful achievement. While there was always the possibility that I would visit the island, alas, my personal circumstances were such that it looked most unlikely that I would be able to inhabit the house.

My 'home' was now in North-West London where I had tried

to make myself comfortable. The Landlord and Landlady Brian and Bridie Cunningham and family lived in the house next door. They were aware of my work as a writer; and since my occupancy we have had warm and friendly relations. Given that my fellow-tenants were mainly students, quite reasonably, I requested that I be left alone. Except on the few occasions, there was enough peace and quiet so that I could write. As time passed, gradually I warmed to the new, but modest accommodation (nothing was ever going to be as spacious as the St John's Mansions flat and the three bedroom Walthamstow house) and redoubled my efforts as a writer hoping, as always, for the best outcome. Thereafter my good relations with Brian and Bridie became friendlier and warmer with each passing year.

But while literary pursuits remained my focus, I tried to incorporate related activities: most immediately, Michael Rolfe's idea for the documentary film entitled: 'The Sand Road.'

'I shall try to spend… Thursday on the Document THE SAND ROAD,' he faxed, 'integrating your comments as discussed and formatting it more as a presentation... It was a splendid evening on Thursday, always good to see you and talk, let us hope that the next time the discussion topic is related to dates for meetings with investors.'

'Investors' – an interesting word. Very promising, I thought, feeling encouraged by Mr Rolfe's business-like attitude at the end of his message.

Although I lived within my means, the need for money remained a part of everyday reality; a familiar pattern which I tried to turn to my advantage. In tandem with low-income, being mobile, both mentally and physically was the key in the sense that researching my books did not simply mean sitting around in one of the comfortable leather seats in the Round Reading Room. On the contrary, it meant a great deal of leg-work; incorporating travel, making telephone calls, writing letters, and so on.

Furthermore, living in London was becoming increasingly more expensive: not only did rents rise, so did many other prices. As costs rose, I sought funds by applying for a Wingate Scholarship. Nothing ventured, nothing gained, I thought, as I waited. A few weeks later, the Wingate Administrator wrote requesting an example of my published work and 'a copy of or extracts from a recent book whose content and approach would be similar to those of your proposed biography of C.L.R. James?'

I complied and soon after, Professor Michel Fabre of the University of the Sorbonne, invited me to attend another Conference: 'African American Music and Europe' to be held between April 24-27, 1996. Clearly I had made a good impression when I last spoke there, but alas, I could not go to Paris because of a hectic schedule.

Among my concerns and interest now was further consideration and work on the film of my backstory: THE SAND ROAD. Recognising the point that Michael Rolfe and I had reached in our meetings and correspondence over many months, I was confident that such a documentary was well worth our efforts. I felt the time had come for us to commit ourselves to a 'Document' that, on signature, would be legally binding. We discussed a six-page 'Draft' of THE SAND ROAD; a documentary 'Proposal' presented in four Sections as follows:

1. RON RAMDIN
2. BIOGRAPHICAL SKETCH
3. CONTENT AND STRUCTURE
4. PROGRAMME OUTLINE.

So far, Michael and I had collaborated well. Now we turned our attention to formalising all we'd done. We reiterated the need, and agreed, that a 'legal document' should be drawn up. This was the clearest indication yet of how far we had come in the making of a dramatized film of my life; and all things considered, the momentum was with us.

Having met Professor Vincent Caretta of the University of Maryland some months earlier in the British Library, he wrote first to thank me for my 'generous comments' on his Penguin edition of Olaudah Equiano's *The Interesting Narrative and Other Writings...* and to say that he would 'love to hear more' about my work in progress; the book *Black Britain*.

The Editor who had contracted me to write *Black Britain* was also the person for whom Vin Caretta had edited the Equiano book. There was an air of general expectation and excitement as I worked on the commissioned Penguin book; and at this time, it seemed my reputation appreciated with each passing day.

BBC RECOGNITION AND THE ARTS COUNCIL

Writing in advance on 13 May 1996, Horace Lashley, Book Fair Organising Tutor at the University of Reading invited me to give the Opening Address: 'The Black Contribution to Social and Political Life in Eighteenth and Nineteenth Century England' during 'Freshers' Week in October 1996. The expectation was that I would speak for about 30-35 minutes with an additional 10 minutes for questions and discussion. Unlike so many presentations, Lectures and Talks that I'd given over the years (before and since 'Black History Month' was instituted) it was proposed that a fee of £50 plus travelling expenses would be paid. This was most welcome given the many occasions when no payment was forthcoming for Lectures/Talks and travel. As it was, illness got the better of me and I could not attend the proposed Reading University engagement.

Following this lapse, by the Summer of 1996 demand for me to speak as an historian rose to new heights. I received a phone call from Linda Mitchell the BBC's Community Affairs Editor, who invited me to give the 'Opening Address' of the *first* ever BBC National 'Community Affairs' Conference to be held in Marylebone, London. The focus of this gathering would be to appraise and chart the way forward for black and Asian programming at the BBC. Soon after our telephone conversation, I met Ms Mitchell.

'All expenses will be paid,' she assured me. *'Shall I send a car to pick you up.'*

For a moment, thinking that I'd heard her incorrectly, I observed her more closely to be sure she was not kidding. She wasn't.

'Yes,' I said.

Why did I hesitate? In part, because in spite of all the years of giving speeches and interviews on radio and television, as mentioned earlier, payment was not always received. I never grumbled because such high-profile activities were, as I saw it, an extension of the decade-long *voluntary service* that had earlier engaged me as Organiser and workers' leader. So the lack of payment for my public appearances, I attributed, in large part, to the fact that the organisers did not have the money. More funding was needed, I was told more often than not. As it was, for over 26 years, all my public work was motivated by an innate desire and commitment, not what payment I received. Linda Mitchell's approach and offer was, however, of a different order altogether; unusual, but of course, most welcome.

On the morning of Monday 10th June 1996, I woke up anticipating the Inaugural BBC Conference. Soon after I got dressed, there was a knock. When I opened the door, standing before me was a man wearing a navy-blue uniform and a black cap.

'Mr Ramdin,' he said. 'I'm your Chauffeur. I have come to take you to the BBC Conference Centre.'

'Thank you,' I said matter-of-factly as if having a Chauffeur knocking on my door was a regular thing. 'Just give me a moment,' I added. I walked back inside and from the bay-windowed front room, I peeped through the curtains. To my surprise, parked in front of number twenty-two Plympton Road was a large white limousine. None of the cars parked on the street and its environs could match it. Wow! I thought.

When I appeared outside the house, the Chauffeur was already standing beside the opened back door of the limousine. 'Please sir,' he said. I stepped inside and sat down. Plush and posh it was; and I felt at ease! As this unusual vehicle moved silently, smoothly away, though very pleased, I was not overwhelmed. Why was I 'at ease?' Because I'd always been under one kind of pressure or other and though this situation was relatively pressured, let me be clear: it *was* as exciting as it gets. This was really the *big time*; London celebrity stuff, I thought, as the conspicuous car, a cut above everything else on Kilburn High Road that morning, weaved its way through the heavy morning rush-hour traffic towards the BBC Centre in Marylebone.

After a few anxious glances at my watch, I relaxed, then became more confident that we would arrive on time. At our destination, the English Chauffeur opened the limousine's door and stood dutifully as I got out. I thanked him. For a while, I stood on the pavement and breathed deeply.

It was a bright summer's morning. In the foyer of the Centre, there was lively chatter. Many well-known faces milled about. While sipping a cup of coffee, I was introduced to a number of people, surprised that many of them already knew who I was. My task that day was to put in historical perspective, the presence of Blacks and Asians in Britain in relation to the BBC's responsibility of serving these communities in Britain. How much did the assembled delegates and broadcasters know about these 'communities' and therefore the wider context of their jobs? I wondered.

My 'Opening Address' which lasted half an hour was therefore timely and, I'm glad to say, well received! Delegates came from all over Britain, including BBC Wales, Belfast, Scotland and the Southwest; and the networking that had begun in the foyer before the Conference opened continued during the coffee interval, at lunchtime and for the rest of the day.

When I left in the late afternoon, I could have insisted on using the limousine, but I opted instead to travel home by underground train. Amidst the London crowds, I reflected that for such a day, my presentation was worthy of a Chauffeur-driven limousine; another indication of how far I'd come, a clear acknowledgement of how I was perceived as an *Historian* of the little known and little understood, but burgeoning 'ethnic' communities in Britain.

Status was nice, but my real concern were the *ideas and philosophy* that had already been evolving at a pace that was taking me to the margins and beyond the confines of such sensitive and contentious themes as immigration, race, class, colour, gender, religion and culture. Against this background, as I worked towards completion of *Black Britain*, my thoughts centred not so much on the philosophy of the 'Oneness of Mankind,' but more on the idea of *'difference,'* in particular, *'respect for difference.'*

Two days after the historic BBC initiative, Linda Mitchell wrote: *'Just a quick note to thank you for your Lecture at the Conference on Monday. Many people said how interesting they found the historical perspective. I'm sure they'll make good use of the reading list!'*

The cheque she enclosed was very helpful.

Later, after meetings with Sharon Atkin, knowing her better, she introduced me to her fiancée Bill Louther, the gifted Dancer who was one of the original members of the American-based Alvin Ailey Dance Group. Their wedding was a wonderful event, attended by many celebrities. During the Reception in Covent Garden, Sharon introduced me to 'Sinitta,' a pop sensation at the time. Then on the day after my birthday, Sharon wrote:

'Dear Ron,

Bill and I should like to express our gratitude for your very generous wedding gift which have already been used and admired by our guests this week. Belated birthday greetings and many happy returns.'

I had no idea how she knew it was my birthday, except to say that I may have told her during one of our meetings. She continued:

'We sincerely hope that you enjoyed the wedding celebrations, almost as much as we did! Our honeymoon in the beautiful 16th century house in (the English countryside) was restful and enjoyable, sadly all too short… life goes on and we remain positive and very happy looking forward to seeing you soon. Thanks again.

Sharon and Bill.'

Just over a month after midsummer's day 1996, I experienced another major moment in life. My roots in Britain were sunk even deeper when on 27 July my first grand-child was born. She was named Georgia by my son and his partner Melissa. Moira, Melissa's mother, had flown from Auckland, New Zealand to be in London for the child's birth. At the time, my son and Melissa lived in Islington and I visited them often. It was a strange, yet real pleasure getting used to being a grandfather, to knowing Melissa better and indeed meeting the warm and delightful person that was Moira. She was the personification of my new extended family, the Slaters, who lived very far away, near the edge of the South Pole, which made me aware for the first time that with my brothers in Canada, not far from the North Pole, my family links now spanned both ends of the globe.

By now, as a seasoned participant and observer in educational matters (having sat on one of the Greater London Council's earliest post-war forums on Education) Ian Reid, Director of Combined Arts at the Arts Council of England, wrote to me:

'The Arts Council has been approached steadily over time by individuals' he stated, 'wanting to know how to gain access to, or information on, various sets of Black Cultural Archives. We are conscious that the answers we have been able to give indicate a situation where information is fragmented and, at times, inaccessible.'

The word 'fragmented' was significant and, of course, many years before when I had begun researching my 'histories' I also recognised the need for comprehensiveness and accessibility. Mr Reid continued:

'Consequently, it has seemed useful to us to assemble a group of people with a particular interest in this field to have a brainstorming session around the subject and issues involved. We would like to invite you to a discussion at the Arts Council…'

Clearly this was 'pioneering' work. I was curious and warmed to the idea. Mr Reid then identified four themes with accompanying questions that could usefully be addressed. They were:

'*DEMAND*

Is there a significant demand for archives? If so…From which sections of the Community – scholars, students, cultural historians, funding bodies, researchers, ordinary individuals, etc. (e.g where should the focus of a Collection lie?)

NATURE

What would constitute an archive – e.g. print (books/reports/papers and/or ephemera such as programmes)? Sound video, film material?

Should an archive be responsive or proactive (e.g. should it commission "living history" or a repository? Should it undertake research?

Is there a similar need for archives across racial groupings? Would one collection contain all (e.g. Ukraine to Caribbean?)

LOCATION

Should an archive be located in one place, or have specialist areas sited in various places? If the focus is academic, is there a university department that would be particularly suitable? Should the location be in this country, or - as been suggested - in institutions such as the University of the West Indies?

Should the community be Curators or Collectors?
What is the possible role of new technology in creating a homogenous online Collection.
   PROBLEM
What are the potential problems? Are they solvable?'

I appreciated this initiative all the more because of my long-standing engagement with libraries and archives, not only in my role as employee, but also (and significantly) as researcher, historian and writer. I did not hesitate to accept Mr Reid's invitation.

It is true to say about the British weather the one thing that is constant is its variability. Over thirty-four years of being out and about on the London streets from as early as 6.30 a.m, six days a week, I had witnessed the weather's capriciousness; and if, at first, I had often commented on British people's tendency to talk about little else, now I was as guilty as they were. British summers, it seemed, were cooler than they were in the Seventies and Eighties; and as I'd said often enough, the warm, bright, golden days of summer were fewer and fewer. Though I was not a sun-worshipper, I could not get too much of the summer weather for all too soon, the long days became shorter.

As heavy autumn winds blasted the windows one afternoon around 4.00 p.m, while at my desk in the Arched Room, I received a telephone call from Professor David Skilton, Head of the Literature, Philosophy and Communications Department at the University of Cardiff, where he was also Pro-Vice Chancellor.

'Would you be free on 20 March next year?' he asked.

'Yes, I can be,' I replied.' Why?'

'I am thinking of nominating you as a candidate to give next year's Cardiff Whitbread Lecture,' he said. I knew about the annual 'Whitbread Prize for Literature;' and the suggestion took my breath away. 'Nomination' as a candidate was in itself an achievement, I thought. Flattered by the prospect of being nominated, I listened as the Professor explained the procedure and selection process.

'When would I know?' I queried.

'In a few weeks,' he said confidently. 'As soon as the candidates have been assessed by the Selection Committee.'

As promised, a couple of weeks later, Professor Skilton rang again. He said that I was selected as the Candidate to give the 1997 Whitbread Cardiff Lecture. Elation was not too strong a word to express my delight. But I also felt a sense of responsibility. As a writer, giving this highest of literary lectures was a big break: a great opportunity to demonstrate, more humbly, to submit whatever learning and literary skills I possessed. While I was very pleased, my selection prompted questions: who were the other candidates? I wondered. Did the Whitbread/Cardiff University Committee approach writers like V.S Naipaul or Salman Rushdie? Or perhaps Ben Okri? Clearly, none of them fitted the profile of the selectors. But none of this mattered now. After the Professor's call, I felt that something very special had happened. After leaving the office that evening while walking down the steps of the British Museum in the brilliant silvery autumn sunshine that lit the courtyard, I decided to stroll over to the French House where writers and artists, many of the highest calibre, tended to meet. While conversing with Mr M, himself a writer, I casually mentioned that I was selected to give the 1997 Cardiff Whitbread Lecture.

'Have you no shame?' Mr M's acid response was immediate. He totally ignored the fact that what I'd said was true. Although he was well-known for his sarcasm, cutting wit and a sense of his intellectual superiority over others, I must admit I was taken aback by his short, sharp words: *'Have you no shame?'* But after he'd spoken, like a flash of lightning, I recalled what he'd said to me some years before when as a newcomer to Bloomsbury, I was a brand new face to him. 'Well, you can't complain,' he'd said to me. 'At least, they *tolerate* you.' By 'they' he meant Tim, Martin and Brian, my first publishers, as well as other members of the Bloomsbury literary circle.

Now after reconsidering Mr M's comment, I responded positively to his use of the word *'shame.'*

'Is that a Christian thing?' I asked, my voice firm and even-tempered.

If at this point, Mr M had had second thoughts that maybe the

Lecture news was true, neither he nor his admiring friends took it seriously.

A few days later, I received a formal letter from the Whitbread Company confirming that I was their Committee's choice to give the 1997 Lecture! I also learned that the previous Lecturers were a constellation of distinguished star writers: Barry Unsworth (Booker Prize-winner), Michele Roberts (novelist and broadcaster), Victoria Glendinning (Whitbread Prize Winner) and P.D. James (Prize-winning Crime Writer). I would be the Fifth Whitbread lecturer and in the days that followed, I considered possible themes for my Lecture, which I learned would be published *for the occasion*.

I thought long and hard about the importance of history upon which literature was based; the fact that story is driven by time and, given my own view that art is a symbolisation of the experience or being, I considered approaching literature from an historical perspective. Just before Christmas, with three months left before delivering the Lecture, I stopped taking notes and began composing a draft with the working title: 'Homelessness and the Novel.' How this would evolve was, as yet, unclear. I would only get one shot at this, I thought. I hoped therefore to do something unusual, even original, not only because it was my exposure to the glitterati in Britain, but also to make the occasion one on which I would, in the glare of the British and world public, present the best piece of writing I was capable of.

So amidst the newfound excitement of being the Cardiff Whitbread Lecturer for 1997, driven as ever, I continued to play several roles, one of which was very dear to me: my willingness to help all students: from primary school level to those in Higher Education. A typical request was the following letter:

'Dear Dr Ramdin,

I am a post graduate research student at Southampton University and am interested in the impact that the black struggle for Civil Rights in the United States had in British Race Relations during the 1950s and 1960s. I am currently trying to identify primary sources for this work and wondered if you might be able to offer me some advice. I have spent the last two years working on a study of responses in the press and would now be very interested to see any papers and publications produced by black groups in Britain. Much of the documentation that I have found relates to the period after 1970 when, it seems, interested groups began to collect and I would be very grateful if you could help me identify earlier sources. I noted that you listed the journal of the West African Students Union in the bibliography of your book The Making of the Black Working Class in Britain amongst other journals. I would appreciate it if you could spare me some time to let me have your thoughts and suggestions that you might be able to make.'

I was happy to oblige and duly met the student with whom I discussed 'primary sources' and the wider literature with which the Black and Asian experience in Britain was intertwined.

By now, two things that had been a source of worry were almost resolved: first, my post-surgery recovery and the possibility of having, yet again, to change jobs. As it was, while still in delicate health, of the four people in the office, I was selected and told about my work relocation. Thus from the Arched Room I was inducted into the newly-appointed Book Moves Team, which would be responsible for supervising and ensuring the safe transfer of millions of books and other items from Bloomsbury to St. Pancras.

To begin with, I attended regular 'briefings' and had to be at my post by 7.00 a.m. deep inside the new building: four floors down in Basement 4, Compartment 4, which was located south of Euston Road. Here, amidst miles of empty buff-coloured metal book shelves, the rumble of passing underground trains to and from St. Pancras Station could be heard. So having viewed the architect's model of the new British Library structure almost a quarter of a century before, here I was in the depths of its fortress-like bowels.

On Christmas morning 1996, my son had picked me up as usual in Kilburn and on reaching his flat in Islington, I did the honours of opening a bottle of champagne. Ronnie and Melissa seemed more of a couple; indeed they were now parents, after the birth of their daughter named Georgia. We drank toasts: to the child, to Ronnie and Melissa, to me becoming a grandfather and to Christmas. Time passed quickly and soon that memorable Christmas Day was over.

Lazily, I woke up early on Boxing Day, knowing only too well what I had to do. On my way to St. Pancras to work on the Book Moves Team, London was almost deserted: what a contrast to the day before. The job entailed working in pairs; my colleague that morning was Jane Fowler. While waiting at 7.00 a.m amidst the eerie silence and the smell of newness at the lowest level of the building in Basement 4 for the Harrow Green haulage workers to arrive with the crates of books to be placed on the shelves of Compartment 4, I said to Jane: 'What the hell are we doing here at this hour on Boxing Day?' We were there, of course, to supervise the placement of a steady stream of books because deadlines had to be met. Jane and I had to be vigilant and on our feet. This was the reality of the job which I was assured would not require much standing. With so many untruths, I found it difficult to know who to believe.

As the year ended, I considered the highs and lows: for example, the self-appointed Warwick University Caribbean 'experts' and the publisher who had rejected my work on Indo-Caribbean history. Taking a long view, given rejections and the attitude and actions of various people since childhood, I now saw very clearly a through line of negativity, along which, at every stage, I had responded *positively*. But with the great literary opportunity of giving the Whitbread Cardiff Lecture just weeks away, as I jotted down ideas, made copious notes and worked on a 'structure,' like a beacon in a sea of darkness, I was refreshed and spurred on by the closing sentence of the University of London Examiners' Report for the degree of Doctor of Literature: '*His writing has commendably used a form of address which because of its openness, its lucidity and grace should generate the envy of professional historians because of its accessibility for the more general reader.*'

MEETING ZAC: AND THE GREAT MACAULAY FAMILY MANUSCRIPT

As the days passed, I sometimes thought about my distinguished predecessors who had given the Cardiff-Whitbread Lecture. I felt it was a challenge big enough to justify being awarded the D.Lit. Now I had to prove it.

I felt that such a literary 'challenge' should have originality and certain qualities that would be compelling enough to lift the audience and all those who read it afterwards. So having set down my thoughts and ideas, soon after I'd completed the first draft, I felt the title of the Lecture should be: *Homelessness and the Novel.* While working on subsequent drafts I decided not to show it to anyone. Then after completing the final copy of the Lecture, I sent it to Professor Skilton at the University of Cardiff.

Afterwards, things moved quickly: I had a foretaste of just how high-profile this Whitbread-Cardiff event would be. Early in 1997, I received a phone call from the Whitbread administrators based at Cardiff University. The Secretary rang to say that as the 1997 Lecturer, I would need to attend a Photoshoot! This, she said, was being arranged by Lowe Bell Good Relations, the organisation that would provide the publicity including photographs for the occasion. I was told that the name of the photographer was 'Zac Macaulee,' which I duly noted while listening carefully as the Secretary spoke in her Welsh accent. Eventually, 'Zac Macaulee,' an Englishman rang me and we agreed to meet one Saturday morning on the Colonnade of the British Museum. Zac was a fresh-faced young man who was perhaps in his early Thirties. He was aristocratic-looking, enthusiastic, easy-going and professional which helped me to relax a bit before engaging in a photographic exercise which hitherto was like no other.

After we'd met, instead of going through the Round Reading Room, I guided Zac past the British Museum Bookshop then turned right and walked the length of the Egyptian Gallery towards the door that led to the Arched Room which I felt should be one of the locations for the 'Shoot.' In the Room, I briefly explained some of its history and its relevance to that other Room in the Museum - the famous Round Reading Room.

'Yes, I have heard a lot about the Reading Room,' Zac said, 'but I've never seen it!'

On hearing this, knowing as much as I did, I felt bound to oblige. 'Please leave your equipment here,' I said. After placing his cameras and rolls of film in a cupboard drawer, I added: 'Let's go.' I took Zac back along the way we had come so that he would approach the Round Reading Room properly: from its main entrance. Soon we were inside, dwarfed by the high ceiling. 'This is my favourite Room,' I said. 'It is where some of the greatest writers Thackeray, Dickens, Carlyle, Marx, Lenin and Shaw, among others have, at different times of course, sat. To my surprise, Zac interposed.

'My great, great, great...grandfather used this Room.' I can't remember how many 'greats' he used, but he was certain of his ancestral line.

I stopped to take in what he'd said and immediately realised his name was not 'Macaulee' as the woman on the telephone had said, but Macaulay. There and then, I told him about research that I'd begun for a biography of Thomas Babington Macaulay (the famous historian of England) and how much I had learned about Thomas's father Zachary Macaulay, the first British Administrator of Sierra Leone in West Africa and a 'Humanitarian' at the time of the Campaign to abolish the African Slave Trade.

'I am named after Zachary,' the photographer said. 'Hence Zac.' He smiled as he spoke.

Having read several books and imagined the lives of the great Macaulays (father and son) here I was in the Reading Room with a descendant! As readers attended to their work, Zac and I walked slowly around the quiet circular space with a sense of the moment. I observed Zac looking here and there and, at intervals, upwards at the ceiling, the beautiful dome with its arching glass panels through which brilliant sunlight streamed in. He was visibly moved.

When we returned to the Arched Room, Zac chose his places for the 'Shoot.' Afterwards, he said: 'It went well!' He was easy to work with; a true professional.

I invited him to join me for coffee in a Museum Street café, where, given my keenness to eventually write the biography of one or other (or both) Macaulays, I elaborated on the reading and research that I'd done thus far. Zac seemed impressed by my detailed knowledge of his ancestors. To enable me to advance my biographical work, he invited me to his home in Walton-on-Thames. The purpose of my visit was to see certain papers, including a rare family portrait written by a concerned and caring member. When I saw this document, as a respecter of historical manuscripts and the private papers of influential persons, I immediately recognised it as primary source material which few (if any) Macaulay biographers would have seen. I felt honoured and privileged to have visited Zac; and before I left the house, in furtherance of my interest and work on the biography of his ancestors, Zac kindly, generously lent me the only copy of that precious type-written manuscript. This was a wonderful gift for which I felt hugely responsible and, of course, I promised to return it at the earliest opportunity. The document titled: *MACAULAYS, GRIMWOODS AND OTHERS* (For Private Circulation Only)' was dated 7/7/85 and its author was 'Marcus.' Fifty four pages long, it includes a 'SYNOPSIS OF PARTS.'

Soon after I'd visited Zac, he spoke to Rose Macaulay, a relative, about my research and biographical intention. Although I'd spoken to several people and had sent my synopses to various publishers, as yet, I had been unable to get a publishing contract.

While pursuing these significant biographies, as an historian deeply immersed in the history of England, Africa and India, I was excited by my 'discoveries.' Now I was fascinated to learn new things about the *Macaulays, Grimwoods and Others*. Here, I include two of Marcus's unpublished, intimate portraits of his most illustrious forebears: Zachary Macaulay and Thomas Babington Macaulay. Macaulay's *History of England*, the most famous book of its time was written by the man who through the 'Indian Education Minute' had introduced English as the language of instruction in India; a significant, pivotal moment when language, in effect, became (as Spanish had been for Spain) the instrument of Empire!

For me, as a Caribbean-born historian immersed in colonial and British history, it seemed that fate had brought me to England to explore and better understand the lives of the Macaulays. Marcus's manuscript was indeed grist for the mill; and as I pondered the past and the present, I was fascinated, enthralled by how thoroughly my life was entwined with English history and British culture. I gained invaluable insights and felt it was absolutely necessary to include in my autobiography the following revealing paragraphs relating to two towering figures in English (British) history: Zachary Macaulay and Thomas Babington Macaulay.

Marcus wrote of Zachary Macaulay as: '*my great great grandfather, who was born in 1768 in the Manse at Inverary (in western Scotland, on the shores of Loch Fyne) where his father the Rev. John Macaulay was then minister. Those were the days of big families - for churchmen at any rate - and Zachary was one of a family of at least twelve brothers and sisters by their father's second marriage (to Margaret Campbell of Inveresregan, Argyllshire) plus one by their father's first marriage.*

Zachary's father, the Rev. John, was the first of the Hebridean branch of the family to break away from the outer islands...Zachary's grandfather, Aulay Macaulay, had been Minister at Tarbert in Harris, so that Zachary was born of two succeeding generations of Churchmen which is probably what gives him his strong sense of duty and of dedication to good causes.

Not that these qualities showed in Zachary's early youth. The family, because so large, was poor, so young Zachary was sent at the age of fourteen to be a clerk in a merchant's office in Glasgow, where his colleagues were all older than him. He quickly learned to imitate their ways, and took pride in being able to drink his seniors under the table. In his own words he pursued "a career of vice and folly," and finally got into such a fix that the only way out was to go abroad.'

I had already known about Zachary Macaulay's early family history as outlined above and his involvement with slavery, but reading Marcus's version of events was very interesting indeed.

'So, at age sixteen rising seventeen go abroad he did - to Jamaica to become an under-manager on a sugar plantation, in charge of Negro slaves. At first appalled by the duties of a slave overseer, Zachary quickly adapted to them and himself became, to use his own words "the slave and the sport of the basest of passions...and to feel the utmost reluctance to be freed from them." '

Strong echoes here of John Newton, the former Slave Trader who wrote *Amazing Grace* and became the Reverend John Newton. Marcus continued:

'However…in 1789 after four years in Jamaica he returned to England and went to stay at Rothley Temple, a country house in Leicestershire, the home of Thomas Babington who had married Zachary's sister Jean. The Babingtons provided a sort of country home for the leaders of the Anti-slavery movement, headed by two brilliant members of Parliament, Wilberforce and Thornton, who were frequent visitors at

Rothley. Zachary at once became a fervent and valuable supporter of the movement - and the only one who knew just exactly what slavery meant **in practice.**

By 1792 Zachary, *at the age of twenty four, found himself a director of the newly formed Sierre Leone Company, and was out in West Africa, grappling with the settlement of over 1,100 freed slaves who had escaped to Canada during the American War of Independence, and now wanted to go home. Zachary was at Freetown, in fact, which he and his colleagues virtually built with their own hands in a climate still thought of as "the white man's grave." Freetown was built on a peninsular with, as neighbours, no less than five slave depots or "factories" headed up by powerful European slave dealers. That Zachary managed to get on good terms with the slave dealers must be, if not some kind of miracle, at least a wonderful tribute to his personality. But he did so, and at times relied on the slave-masters for food and supplies. At least one, a Mr Aspinwell, became a close friend.*

In truth Zachary's earliest difficulty came from his own settlers, the freed slaves, who in June 1794 revolted and sacked his office. In the same year, September 1794, his work was nearly destroyed - not by the slave masters but by men dedicated to liberty, equality and fraternity. A squadron of seven French (Revolutionary) ships sailed in, shelled Freetown, and then their crews came ashore and sacked and looted the town and burned down part of it, continuing thus for two weeks, during which time Zachary had to spend his nights on board the ship of the French Commodore.

The result was a ruined settlement, and if it had not been for the help and supplies given by the local slave traders it might have been impossible to get things going again. But it was impossible, and Zachary did it.

The next year, 1795, Zachary was ill with recurring fever and due for home leave. By then he knew a good deal about slavery - at both ends - and about human nature too. But he had not seen for himself the actual slave trade in action - that is, conditions on a slave ship. So he chose an unusual route home. He sailed on a slave ship bound for Barbados! The ship had no passenger cabin, and it seems that Zachary travelled pretty close to the slaves, and perhaps in the slave hold.

After his English holiday Zachary remained in Sierre Leone,

*strengthening and enlarging the Freetown settlement, until 1799
when, aged 30, he gave up the Governorship, returned to England for
good, married Selina Mills of Bristol, and started a family.'*

I was fascinated to read this nuanced account by a descendant
of Zachary Macaulay. But what perhaps Marcus did not know
was the fact that the 'settlement' (or, as I had written about it in
Reimaging Britain as the Sierre Leone 'Experiment') peopled by the
London Poor, had included a number of prostitutes and that the
'settlement' (opposed by the former black slave and anti-slavery
campaigner Olaudah Equiano) was a failure. But to his credit,
Zachary Macaulay was also a Humanitarian and member of the
'Clapham Sect' which had zealously campaigned for the abolition
of the African Slave Trade and slavery. Nonetheless, I was keen to
follow what next Marcus had to say. Zachary, he added,

*'also pursued, for the rest of his life, so many Good Causes that his wife
saw too little of him. Suffice it to say that his years in a nice house on
the south side of Clapham Common have left a legacy of a "Macaulay
Road" and (until recently), a Macaulay telephone exchange.*

*With such a father it is small wonder that his eldest son, Thomas
Babington, later Lord Macaulay (my great great uncle) was an unusual
man. And some of the other eight children were not bad value either.
After all, No. 5, Henry William, my great grandfather, became a
Judge in Sierra Leone, while No. 7, Hannah, married a young Indian
Civil servant, Charles Trevelyan, and founded the famous Trevelyans -
successive Masters of Trinity College Cambridge and leading historians.*

*As sometimes happens with great men, Zachary's declining years
were in fact a decline. Due to an unwise appointment the finances
of the Sierre Leone Company took a disastrous plunge, and with them
Zachary's finances too. The children had to help out with money; the
Clapham Common house was sold, and what remained of the family
moved to a much smaller home in Great Ormond Street. Zachary's
eyesight failed, and his general health too, and, truth to tell, he became
rather an exacting and tyrannical father. His wife Selina died in
1831, and seven years later, in 1838, Zachary followed her at the age
of seventy. He is buried in Mecklenberg Square, Bloomsbury. But, for
one who was not a politician or a statesman, he was granted a most
unusual honour - a rather splendid statue in Westminster Abbey.'*

Of another of his ancestors, a remarkable character named Colonel James Skinner ('Sikander Sahib' - 1778-1841), Marcus wrote:

'While Zachary Macaulay was wrestling with his various difficulties in West Africa a half-caste youth, James Skinner, was, in another dark continent, setting out on a career which was to make him one of the most spectacular military figures of his time - or, so far as India was concerned, of all time.

Like Zachary (ten years his senior) James Skinner started young. Apprenticed to a Calcutta printer at age 16 he ran away after three days. Set to work for a lawyer he lasted three months. On being asked what he did want to be, Skinner replied briefly "A Soldier."

But Skinner was a 'country born,' the son of a Scots soldier and an Indian girl, and the East India Company had, just a year or two earlier, decreed that half-castes could not join their armed forces. So he joined instead the Army of a great Mahratta Chief, Sindhia, commanded by a French General de Boigne...

Skinner, a very young Ensign..., a hardened soldier at age 25 offered himself again to the British Army, this time successfully. He remained with them virtually the rest of his life, becoming eventually the confidant and adviser of successive Governors General...He was also an exceptional soldier... utterly fearless... In short Skinner was a commander of light cavalry unsurpassed since the days of Alexander the Great, and so came to be known by that legendary name - except that Iskander...was modified slightly to Sikander. Sikander Sahib, in fact...

Skinner was not un-rewarded financially either...'

At this point, I stopped reading. I was much surprised to learn that Skinner was part Indian. This connection added to my interest in the Marcus manuscript which continued:

'By the time of his (Skinner's) death in 1841 he was the owner of 194 villages, valued later at 300 lakhs of rupees...his third son Hercules (b.1814) who, in 1847, married Rose Ann, eldest daughter of Samuel Cardozo of Redruth, Cornwall. And one of Rose Ann's children was my dear Auntie Queenie of such happy memory. Which is why I have been telling you about Sikander Sahib.'

Marcus then says this about the kind Aunt Queenie: *'Every family should have a fairy godmother, and Auntie Queenie was the undoubted fairy godmother of ours.* **A lovely and loving person with glowing dark Indian eyes, a dusky complexion and nature I ever knew…'**

Reading thus far, I had gained a few insights into Imperial history and my interest hitherto in race, colour, class, gender and religion in relation to my ongoing exploration of the concept of *difference*; and more particularly in social terms *'respect for difference'* which, in my mind, loomed larger. Now through Marcus's eyes (having explicitly integrated the concept of difference in my recently completed attempt at a first *inclusive* history of Britain), as a writer of history, I was especially interested to read about one of England's greatest historians Thomas Babington, the only Macaulay to become a Lord. He was, Marcus wrote, *'short, fat and ugly…also an insufferable know-all and a compulsive and non-stop talker. Small wonder that nobody loved him…(except)… his sisters, Margaret and Hannah.'*

Then Marcus gave this personal view:

'You feel this to be an unfair and a really rather nasty problem? Well yes, maybe. But then I have a grudge against TBM. For if he had had less affection for his sisters and more for his brothers then my brother would be the present Lord Macaulay and I should be the Honourable Marcus - which does have rather a nice ring to it! Now that I have got that off my chest shall we start again in a more dispassionate and kindly vein?

Today people think of Lord Macaulay…as an essayist, or a poet, or an historian. And indeed he was all of these. But in the days when he lived (the first half of the 1800s) lots of people wrote essays and poems and Macaulay's history, written late in life, covered little more than a fragment of time, say about seventy five years. It is less well remembered that Macaulay was, at intervals, a Member of Parliament, a statesman, and a cabinet minister and that, for some years, he was one of the five men who governed British India and re-shaped the course of its history, giving it a common language (English) and a brand-new code of criminal law which is still largely in force to this day….'

Here, I paused to reconsider a salient and powerful fact: That I am a descendant of indentured labourers ('helots of the Empire,' as Mahandas K. Gandhi had described them) who had been transported by the British from India to the Caribbean and now as an Historian who had earned his professional status in Britain, I appraised Marcus's 'Private' manuscript, more and more as providing an invaluable historical perspective:

'*Today, thanks to television,*' he wrote, '*India is thought of as having been "The Jewel in The Crown." If that is right then Macaulay, in a few short years, **helped to make it so**. Oddly enough, he started on this process not from any high-flown motives but because he needed money.*'

So here it was, the unadorned truth.

'*His father Zachary (of anti-slavery fame) had fallen on hard times and (Thomas Babington) Macaulay faced the need to support him. The chance to do so came by reason of the extraordinary way in which British India was then governed. That is, by a weird sort of dual control system which had been instituted in 1784.*

In Macaulay's time the East India Company still held sway, governing through four men - the Governor General and the Governors of the three Presidencies of Calcutta, Madras and Bombay, all servants of the Company...at a salary of £1,500 a year. He thus became, in a sense, one of the "masters" of the Supreme Council of India...'

Thus far, Thomas Babington Macaulay had *made* history in India. Then, on his return to England in 1838, he had started to *write* his famous *History of England*, a 'task' which Marcus stated, was 'to occupy him for every spare hour of the remaining twenty one years of his life as recounted by Marcus - in fact he was still at his desk, hard at it, when he died on 28th December, 1859.'

But, how does any man become the pre-eminent Historian of his day? was the question that Marcus posed. I paused again so that, in turn, I could consider this question: How did I an Indian descendant of indentured labourers from colonial Trinidad become an historian? Hopefully this book of my life will go some way towards explaining that. For now, however, I was eager to learn more about Thomas Babington Macaulay's place in British history. And so, both as a writer and author of histories, I was thrilled to read this insider's view as to how Macaulay became an historian:

'*A private income, though certainly useful, is not enough. And having a famous father could actually have been a handicap. The fact is that TBM was born with a sense of history. With an enormous appetite for facts, he had been an avid reader since the age of three, and had a freakish memory (inherited from his father) which enabled him to hold in his mind just about everything he read or heard... his family, though of modest origins, found themselves surrounded by men who were, at least in part, the giants of their age. At Rothley Temple, where TBM was born and where his aunt Jean lived with her husband Thomas Babington, Wilberforce was a frequent visitor. And Wilberforce was not only the founder of the Anti-slavery movement: He was also the friend, the close colleague of William Pitt, the man who had become Prime Minister at the age of twenty four and who, until his death in 1806, had seemingly fought almost single handed the battle to keep Napoleon away from the shores of England. Invasion had seemed a real possibility in 1804 and was, arguably, only frustrated by Nelson's victory at Trafalgar the following year...*

Lord Brougham, a strong ally of the Clapham Common "Saints" and their Anti-slavery Movement, was a brilliant Parliamentary speaker, and in 1820 he had, as Attorney General, joined with Thomas Denman (then Solicitor General) in the famous defence of Queen Caroline against King George 1V. It was Brougham who gave the young TBM some useful tips on how to become an effective orator... Incidentally, Lord Brougham was to become Lord Chancellor in 1830, at about the same time that Denman became Lord Chief Justice...

(So) ...the young TBM, despite his "lack of pedigree" (as Lady Holland put it) rubbed shoulders with some of the most influential men of his day, watched history being made, and, in the case of the famous Reform Bills of 1831 and 1832, took a leading part in making it. It was said (and by an enemy at that) that when TBM spoke on the third and final Reform Bill in March 1832 "you might have heard a pin drop in the House." His sister Margaret commented that the House "was entranced, almost breathless" and that he had been "Holding the House of Commons absorbed as the Opera House is by a first rate singer." It seems as if Brougham's hints on oratory may have been useful...'

Once more, I was able to situate certain aspects of Thomas's life from my voluminous readings, especially of certain events and dates.

1838, for example, the year when the period of 'Apprenticeship' of Africans in the West Indies had ended and the first indentured Indians had arrived on the sugar plantations in British Guiana. I marvelled at how intertwined were the lives of the Macaulays with Africa, India and the West Indies as I read further, bearing in mind that a year later in 1839 Macaulay had set about writing his famous *History of England.* But, as Marcus wrote: *'it was not truly a history of England at all. Look inside on the flyleaf and you will see the magic sub-title "From the Accession of James 11."*

Only the first of the seven volumes deals with England prior to the Accession of James II, and only the last deals with the arrival and subsequent doings of William and Mary. If you wanted to be unkind you could say that Macaulay's "History of England" covered the period 1685 to 1697 - a total of twelve years!

I think the reason is that Macaulay studied and wrote with, as it were, a microscope in his hand. He was not content to discover and record what happened - he wanted to know why it happened. And if someone took - or did not take - a particular course of action he wanted to know what pressures were on him and how he actually felt at the time. For he believed that the actions of all men grow out of their "circumstances," and he was determined to discover and disclose what these circumstances were.

Now that Macaulay is hardly read...one wonders how he came to be a best seller at the time. I think the secret may be that he wrote with prejudice - the prejudice of a convinced Whig - and without confusing impartiality. He knew who and what he like or disliked, and his readers were thus easily able to distinguish the "goodies" from the "baddies" - rather as with the Hollywood films of a later age.

The result was a fame which in the 1850's outshone that of his literary contemporaries - including (hard as it may be to believe now) Dickens, Thackeray and Tennyson. Another result was un-expected wealth. The first two volumes were published in 1848 and in 1849 a cheque for £6,000 arrived from Longmans the publishers. The next two volumes appeared in 1855, when a print order for 25,000 copies had to be increased to 30,000 before publication and a few months later Macaulay received a cheque for £20,000.

The sales of the complete history came to over 140,000 in England

*and, rather surprisingly, to more than that in America. I am sure Macaulay enjoyed the fame, but the money did not turn his head at all - he just found it amusing, invested the capital and gave away most of the resulting income. I guess that for him the best moment came at Lunch time on 28th August 1857, when a letter arrived from Lord Palmerston offering him a peerage. Since Queen Victoria had already agreed, Macaulay could hardly refuse, even if he had wished to. But he accepted on ter*ms *which assured that the title would die with him - which it did a little more than two years later.'*

So enlightened, once more, my historical sense generated a desire to pause again because of the significance of another date 1857. This was a dark period in British-Indian history when the Indian Uprising or 'Mutiny' occurred with atrocities committed on both the British and Indian sides. One escape route for a few mutinous sepoys was to make their way overseas as indentured labourers! Be that as it may, Marcus concludes his portrait of Thomas Babington (Lord) Macaulay (the man whom Queen Victoria had described as a ' book in breeches') thus:

'Macaulay must also have been greatly pleased, in the Autumn of 1857, when he was elected High Steward of the Borough of Cambridge. It was after all, Trinity College Cambridge which had seen the first full flowering of his talents - and it is nice that he is still held in remembrance in the Chapel at Trinity as well as in Westminster Abbey. Zachary would, despite all his grouchy criticism, have been proud of him.'

All's well that ends well, one could say.

But for such a powerful and illustrious family as the Macaulays who were participants in the great events and movements of their times (closely associated with the East India Company, the contradictions of banking Humanitarianism and anti-slavery campaigns and, as a consequence, the post-slavery world of Indian indentureship in the Caribbean and elsewhere in the British Empire) being privy to Marcus's manuscript handed to me personally in the home of a descendant of the Macaulay family had struck me then, as now, as a most significant and quite extraordinary coming together.

After I'd read Marcus's account, I expressed warm and grateful thanks to Zac (Zachary II). Among other things, the year 1857 stands out powerfully and all the more so because it was the year that saw the opening of the British Museum's Round Reading Room; a studious place which Thomas Babington Macaulay recognised and had frequented. Incredibly 112 years later, this is where I, a former child of Empire came to work each day and had written five histories.

It is interesting too that while writing these books, as if the ghost of Macaulay was in the Room, I came across many references to his great nephew, the historian George Macaulay Trevelyan, who was regarded as one of the last historians in the 'Whig tradition.' Alas, my 'tradition' was far removed from these Whigs. I was not, as Marcus had described Lord Macaulay, 'born with a sense of history.' I arose from a less one-sided, quite diverse set of circumstances and perspectives that were incorporated both in the pre-and post-Empire periods.

Of the many photographs that Zac took that Saturday morning of the Shoot in the British Museum, the one selected to publicise the Cardiff Whitbread Lecture was sent to me. It was taken on the first floor at the north-western end of the Arched Room, where the spines of various-sized rare books on the shelves formed an impressive, colourful backdrop. Zac's trained eye led him to choose this spot; and I remember well that moment when the camera clicked. I am glad to say that the outcome and selection was a presentable image; **the** photograph (emblematic of the art of Zac Macaulay) that would forever give meaning to our connection and identify me with the Cardiff Whitbread Lecture for posterity.

Early in 1997, I received a note from the Commissioning Editor of Penguin Books, who said he was 'looking forward to reading the finished manuscript' of *Black Britain*. I welcomed this prospect. For the time being, with my Lecture just a few short months away, I thought it would be helpful to inform Professor Skilton of my success in being awarded the 'Higher Doctorate,' the Doctor of Literature, by the University of London. Recognising my selection as Whitbread Lecturer, he commented that my 'double triumph' could only add to the big occasion at Cardiff University on 20 March 1997.

As if indirectly arousing public interest for my Lecture, *The Observer* newspaper published an article under the heading: 'The Slave Boy Who Wowed Literary London.' It related to Ignatius Sancho, the slave whom journalist Roger Tredre described as a 'Black Dr Johnson.' This piece coincided with an Exhibition about Sancho at the National Portrait Gallery in London. Although Sancho's achievements, his story was still relatively unknown quite rightly the newspaper felt there was 'a need to get him into the public eye.' But for at least 15 years before this 'Exhibition,' I'd been writing and talking about the early Black presence and literary figures in Britain, including Sancho, Equiano, Gronniosaw, et al. Now in 1997, no less interested in what I'd known and had written about as integral parts of 'British history,' with no less enthusiasm, I continued to explore roots and routes!

As an author, increasingly my work was drawn to the attention of others. A number of academics across the Atlantic were aware of, and interested in my books and other writings. Among them was my friend Dr Johanna Smith who, following a research visit to England had returned to the University of Texas from where she wrote that she was sorry we didn't get the chance to meet before she left London and 'As soon as you're able to send me your CV Carolyn (a fellow-academic) and I will get to work on a possible Texas visit for you…I hope the last touches on the Penguin book (Black Britain) are going well and I look forward to seeing the Whitbread Lecture and hearing of your triumphs.'

By now, following my surgery at University College Hospital, London, the earlier raw pain became a dull, but present ache. Still sore, but now very much a part of the Book Moves Team, I ambled along trying to keep up with the scheduled pace demanded by the regularly reviewed work deadlines. If I had not been unwell, this job would have been less troublesome. But instead of matters improving, they got worse.

Eventually I wrote to Ms F, Head of the Collections, but for an unusually long while there was no response. This was not like her, I thought. While wondering whether or not I should write again, the following letter arrived:

'Dear Ron,

Today I found inside a file on my desk your unopened letter dated 30 December...I am very sorry...that I did not receive it sooner... First of all, I would like to congratulate you warmly on your D.Lit and on your Fellowship of the Royal Society. These are both splendid achievements and I am very pleased for you. I am very sorry indeed that you are unhappy with your job in the Book Moves Team. I would obviously have to discuss this with (Ms. D) and I will also raise the possibility of a transfer with Personnel. I hope you will understand that transfers are not always easy to arrange...I will pursue the matter and I will get back to you as soon as I can.'

Thirteen days later, I received another letter from Ms F:

'Further to the note I wrote you earlier this month, I have now made enquiries... I have not yet heard from Personnel. However, there is a short term project within C&P which seems to me you could do very well... The project is part of the preservation aspect of the Legal Deposit...Your work would have to start in mid-February and would take up to one month...'

An opportunity at last! I replied immediately expressing my appreciation of her assistance in placing me in a more 'appropriate job.'

Soon after, a 'Health Declaration' about working in the basements of the new building at St Pancras was issued to me by Mr JS of the Personnel office. Among other things, he warned: 'If it is decided in consultation with the OHSA Medical Advisor that you should not work in the St Pancras basements, we expect you to undertake equitable work in an alternative area.'

My ailments at the time were identified as follows: that I took pain killers; that I had an operation in June 1996; that I was diagnosed with arthritis of the upper spine and giddiness as a result of prolonged standing or physical activity; and that I'd been operated on for varicosed veins on my left leg which reappeared with attendant pain. It was against the background of this clear evidence and Ms F's recommendation that I duly undertook the new temporary post.

A few weeks earlier, while nursing my infirmities in Compartment

4, Basement 4 of the St Pancras building, having questioned myself repeatedly about the progress, pitch, tone, pace and texture of *Homelessness and the Novel*, now my thoughts were never far away from it since submission to the Whitbread-Cardiff University Committee. Hoping for a positive response, I waited anxiously.

Meanwhile, I received another Draft outline for the Television film entitled: 'THE SAND ROAD' from Director Michael Rolfe. We had at an earlier stage, considered three working titles: 'Struggling Off the Streets;' 'Dr Ron' and 'The Sand Road.' At the outset, I'd suggested 'THE SAND ROAD,' which was my preference. Mr Rolfe ended the new three-page Draft saying: 'More biographical concrete visuals are needed…Yes we must keep it brief and punchy, but it is a selling document.' He added: '*We hardly need to sell you*, we need to sell *the idea* of the program to potential investors – big names help to raise big cash.'

Yes, indeed. So, inevitably, without money nothing could be set in motion.

With just five weeks to go, I made final adjustments to my Lecture (all the while wondering how it was received by Professor Skilton and publisher Andy McKillop at Random House) as I prepared to go to Cardiff for what I expected to be one of the biggest days of my literary life.

As the days passed and life in all its variety ebbed and flowed, I tried to maintain a steady course in relation to my literary work. Since my visit to the Sorbonne in 1992 I'd kept in touch with my friend Bissera, a teacher in Linguistics at the Sorbonne. In her latest Postcard from Paris, which shows a painting of Renoir's 'The Luncheon Party,' she wrote:

'Dear Ron,
Thank you so much for your warmest wishes… since I haven't written to you for such a long time and you've been so busy (as you always are).
I would absolutely love to attend your lecture, to see you and talk to you…
P.S. I have to tell you that although I haven't written to you I've been… in touch with you through your books…Your books are fascinating and

906 · TURNING PAGES · RON RAMDIN · VOLUME TWO

instructive…and I am extremely proud of having you as my friend.

Please write to me about your History of Black Britain. It sounds an ambitious project…

Here, in Paris, things are coming back to normal. Yours forever, Bissera.'

I had first met the Bulgarian-born Bissera some years before she went to Paris. She was introduced to me by Margaret Duff, who was a high-ranking Officer in UNISON, one of Britain's largest public sector unions. Since then, corresponding with Bissera had been a most pleasant and rewarding experience.

With my Cardiff Whitbread Lecture much closer now, I had, at last, heard from Penguin's Commissioning Editor who noted: 'The good news of progress' in his reading of my manuscript *Black Britain.* I could hardly have expected better news.

Looking back, I realised that I'd spent thirty years researching and writing 'Black and Asian' histories in Britain and the retrospective 'Exhibition' of Sancho at the National Portrait Gallery was but part of a continuing wider campaign to challenge the erroneous perception that Black history in Britain began with migration from the Caribbean in the twentieth century. As I'd written nearly ten years before, the one thing that was fundamental to the Black presence in Britain whether it was in the fifteenth or the twentieth centuries, was *labour;* both in the pre-and post-colonial periods. This aspect of my work as it relates to Britain had been crucial. In this sense, as I'd consistently argued, no history of the Black and Asian experience in Britain was ***as comprehensive*** as *The Making of the Black Working Class in Britain.* While Fryer's *Staying Power* peters out, so to speak, in the post-war years, *The Making of the Black Working Class in Britain* tells the essential story of labour and thus the presence and contribution of the largest non-white British population well into the last-third of the twentieth century. But now, as part of that continuum, in the twenty-first century low-paid workers not only from Asia, Africa and the Caribbean, but increasingly from the European Union and other countries are recruited to work in fields, factories, offices, businesses and service industries.

In spite of the centrality of the matter of wage-earning and struggle in relation to migrants and migration, until recent years (even as late as the early 1980s) 'mainstream' British historians had been remarkably disinterested in the Black and Asian presence in Britain. But even when they did show some interest, they displayed a lack of awareness of the works of certain authors. Against this background, the organisers of the Cardiff Whitbread Lecture had, as I later learned, sought a writer who approached literature from an historical perspective. Thus I was chosen; and having sent *Homelessness and the Novel* to the Lecture Committee, the passage of time added a keen edge to my need to know how it was received. This was the big test. My wait ended when, early in February, Professor Skilton wrote:

'Dear Ron,

I've had trouble contacting you by telephone…

Andy (Editor at Random House) and I are both delighted with the text of the Lecture, and Andy will come back to you - probably early next week - with any queries.

Meanwhile Whitbread's PR Consultants (Lowe Bell Good Relations) would like from you photocopies of any sections of your work mentioning Cardiff or South Wales. (We can't get copies of your books at the moment. Let's hope that changes!) Send them direct, if you have the address, or via Deborah Williams at Whitbread, or via me.

The High Commissioner (of Trinidad and Tobago) has accepted. This is going to be a good event – unless (John) Major (Prime Minister) calls the election then. He'd be mad to.

With Best Wishes,

David.'

Wow! This was, as I thought, not going to be an ordinary occasion: 'The High Commissioner has accepted.' Yes, this was something very special! In many ways, the event had the makings of an ambassadorial occasion; and bearing in mind the positive response from Professor Skilton, the relief and excitement I felt was mingled with a sense of satisfaction not only for the originality of the title, but also my boldness of approach to the content and structure of the Lecture.

With just a few days to go, I received blue-tinted Leaflets and

Posters as designed and printed by the publicity company Lowe Bell Good Relations, featuring their choice of Zac's photograph of me, with the date and venue of the Event. The poster also offered the following information:

'Whitbread's Cardiff Lecture has become an important part of the capital's literary scene. To celebrate its fifth year, the 1997 Lecture reflects Cardiff's history as a multi-cultural city and features the well-known historian of racial minorities Ron Ramdin.

On Thursday 20 March 1997 Ron Ramdin, novelist, biographer of Paul Robeson and author of the forthcoming Penguin History of Black Britain will give Whitbread's fifth Cardiff Lecture.

His subject will be HOMELESSNESS AND THE NOVEL.'

While reading this, I realised the 'Lecture' was now in the public domain and suddenly everything about it and the occasion took on a new urgency: telephone calls and correspondence between myself and the organisers became more frequent and intense. I stepped-up to meet the challenge.

TWENTY-THREE

TOWARDS LITERARY EMINENCE: PRINCESS ANNE CONFERS D.LIT AT BARBICAN CEREMONY

With so much going on, my head was aswim. But even this headiness as I prepared for the Whitbread Cardiff Lecture could not dampen my enthusiasm for another pending engagement due to take place on 13 February. When I woke up that morning I tried to slow down my thoughts and my stride as I moved around purposefully. Why? Because it was the day when I would officially receive my Higher Doctorate during the Barbican Hall Ceremony for University of London Graduates. Given the magnitude of the achievement and the Ceremony's importance, I had invited my son Ronnie to come with me.

When I approached the Administrator Ms Brown at the Information Desk in the Barbican Hall and told her my name, she said: 'Ah, *Doctor* Ramdin!' Like the Registrar at Senate House, she emphasized the prefix. 'Your gown is russet brown. It is unlike all the others you will see today.' Why would it be so? I wondered, but said nothing. Then, as if reading my mind, Ms Brown answered my silent question: 'You are the ***only*** recipient of the Doctor of Literature for 1997. You will be presented **last** and will receive the ***loudest applause***.' My son was standing beside me and hearing what was said how he felt he did not say. Ms Brown then directed me to the 'Robing Room.' After donning my Gown, with the accompanying Cap in hand, I walked out. On our way to the cafeteria, my son said: 'Dad many people are looking at you.' Why the looks? Of the hundreds of Graduates appearing at this Ceremony, I was the only wearer of the D.Lit russet brown gown, hence my conspicuousness of which I was forewarned. On leaving the cafeteria for the Auditorium, I was conscious of the stares which added to the surrounding hum of chatter and excitement arising from the thousands who had come from many parts of the world to be in the Barbican Hall.

Soon after taking our seats, formal proceedings began. The Opening Address of Welcome was given by Professor Andrew Rutherford, Vice Chancellor who pointed out: 'Study for a University of London Degree is not an easy option. We have an international reputation for higher standards and you can be proud that you (as graduates) have achieved those standards.'

I smiled on hearing 'Study for a University of London Degree is not an easy option.' No kidding. He could say that again.

Then Princess Anne, as Chancellor of the University of London, began to present Graduates with their degrees. After all the BAs, BScs, MAs, MScs, MPhils and PhDs came the 'Special' category of the *Higher Doctors* and, among the few, I was indeed the last to be called. After the University's administrators had read out the D. Lit citation, I walked forward and knelt: Princess Anne then placed the sash over my shoulder, thus investing me with the Doctor of Literature. This formal act was especially poignant for it was a very long and incredible journey which led to that moment. I stood up and the Princess and I shook hands. After congratulating me, she enquired.

'Where did you do all that work?'

'In various archives and libraries in Britain,' I replied, 'but also in the Caribbean.'

'The Caribbean is surely a better option,' she said. 'Where are you from?'

'I was born in Trinidad,' I replied proudly. 'I grew up there, but I'd been living in Britain for many years. I am British.'

Our conversation lasted a few minutes; much longer than the brief silent moments allowed to all the preceding graduates. My talk with the Princess seemed to have stalled proceedings for a while, but when it eventually ended, as I moved away along the bright red carpet in full regalia, the applause which burst like a thunderclap, seemed to lift me off my feet. Those great and memorable moments marked the climax of the Graduation Ceremony. I was centre-stage receiving the plaudits of an audience of 4,000 well-informed, happy people: proud parents, family and friends in the Barbican Hall, London.

Administrator, Margaret Brown was right about the merits of being the 'only D. Lit recipient this year.' The applause for me was indeed the *loudest* and *longest!* It had *real meaning*.

My exit off stage marked the end of the grandest ceremony that I had ever attended or participated in. On the way back to my seat next to my son, with a spring in my step now, I smiled as once more I thought of Professor Rutherford's words, *'study for a University of London degree is not an easy option.'*

Attending the Ceremony were graduates and students from many of the University's different institutions, including King's College London, the Royal Academy of Music, University College, the London School of Economics and Political Science and those graduates who had studied as 'External Students.' More than thirty-four countries were represented that day.

Over the years in Bloomsbury, I had learned much about the University of London which had its origins in the 1820s and 1830s with the creation of University College on Gower Street and King's College in the Strand. As one of England's newer universities, it had received its Royal Charter in 1836. The only other English universities in existence at the time were Oxford and Cambridge. The University of London had, of course, expanded and changed over the last 160 years, but it had, according to its officials, always maintained the principles of its founders: to provide an institution open to all, irrespective of race, creed or political beliefs. Consequently, hundreds of Commonwealth students, mainly from well-to-do families and scholarship winners had enrolled, studied and graduated from the University. But, from this year's showing, it was clear that there was an alarming absence of graduates from the African, Caribbean, Indian, Pakistani and Bangladeshi communities; as well as from the lower ranks of white and non-white British society.

For my work on history, biography, race relations and industrial relations, I received the University's highest literature honour, which was, of course, not won in a day! It was in all likelihood the *first* D. Lit ever conferred upon a candidate for *'Black' history and biography*: themes that were not only new and diverse, but also a timely reflection of contemporary Britain. Changing attitudes in academic institutions at this time was rare if not nearly impossible. Taken together, thus far, my literary work had indeed brought about a shift in the University of London's thinking. But this was, in my experience, *one more* example of how through sheer determination I'd helped to *change attitudes*: for example, conceiving and bringing about the first Charity Concert in the British Museum; helping to foster better Staff-Management relations in the British Museum as CSU Branch Secretary and importantly as Whitley Council Staff Side Secretary in the British Library as with other representatives we tried to establish a workable Industrial Relations System in the first crucial years of its history! Against this background, having extended the boundaries, I accepted the D.Lit with humility and wonder; the outcome of decades of determination as I wrestled with making the most of the few opportunities that were available to me. In effect, at every step of the uncertain way in my intellectual, artistic and literary sojourn, I'd been **making my own luck**. *What you put in, is what you get out.* How often had I whispered this to myself. And so having practised what I preached, at this juncture in the Barbican, I hoped my example would indeed have encouraged and activated the desire for self-discovery in others.

Soon after the Ceremonial programme, with the Degree Certificate, the Cap and Gown that I'd rented from Ede and Ravenscroft, I posed with my son Ronnie for photographs taken by Gillman & Soame. My orders for images of that memorable day included several photographs, as well as a tastefully done University of London video of the occasion.

Overall, it was quite a heady day and when I left the Barbican Centre about 5.30 p.m, it was with mixed feelings of tiredness and excitement. My son made his way back to his flat in Islington, and I took a bus travelling towards the West End. My destination was that venue of writers and artists, the French House, where the week before the Barbican Ceremony I had informed Lesley (the Manager-Proprietor) of my meeting with Princess Anne and the presentation of my D.Lit. As Royalists, both Lesley and husband

Noel Botham (Princess Margaret's biographer) were intrigued.

Lesley was in conversation with someone when I walked in. Nearby, was the actor, Struan Rodger, whom I'd known since he'd been a player with the Royal Shakespeare Company. In my hand was a copy of the 'List of Graduates' and my D. Lit scroll. Struan and I chatted briefly and while he was looking through the oblong-shaped, maroon-coloured Graduation booklet, I commented: 'As you can see, I have the honour of being the *only* person to graduate with the University's D. Lit this year.' Just then, Lesley noticed me and motioned to the girl behind the bar who reached for a bottle of champagne already in a bucket which she placed on the counter in front of Lesley.

'Where is your cap and gown?' Lesley asked.

'In the end,' I said, 'I decided not to *buy* the outfit. Instead I rented it just for the day!'

Disabled by a fall, Lesley had a stick in her hand which she put aside. She filled two glasses with champagne, one for her, the other for me, and a third for Struan. She then banged her walking stick three times on the counter. I'd never seen or heard this behaviour in the French before; and not surprisingly there was a hush, a difficult thing to achieve in that place. Customers in the packed House looked in Lesley's direction. 'Ladies and Gentlemen,' she said, 'would you please raise your glasses to toast Dr Ron Ramdin. Today he received the degree of Doctor of Literature from Princess Anne!' A loud high-spirited sound – applause rose above the lively chatter of the clientele, many of them high-achievers (writers, artists, lawyers, business men, celebrities, sceptics, blase revellers, hardened socialites and tourists) and my thoughts flashed back to my first encounter with, and subsequent early visits to, that famous West End social space. Then, as a stranger and 'green-horn' I was viewed with suspicion by 'regulars' and, at times, with downright rudeness. Now with champagne 'on the House,' I was riding high in London! Like it or not, I was now the toast of The French House, from where it was said Charles De Gaulle had conducted the 'French Resistance' during the Second World War.

As a favourite meeting place for stars of stage, screen and radio, appropriately this Establishment was also fast becoming an 'Art

Gallery.' It was here that 'Harris' told me about Paul Newman being God-father to one of his children. Adorning the walls were photographs of the great and the good, including Rex Harrison and the painter Francis Bacon, whom I'd seen there on many occasions with his friend and fellow-painter Lucien Freud. Standing cheek by jowl, as I talked with their friend Harry Diamond often I observed that Bacon and Freud were a self-contained duo, always absorbed in conversation. The one thing about them that had the strongest resonance with me was their attitude which had to do with work: an intense commitment to their art.

At the time, another person that I'd seen in the Bacon, Freud, Diamond company was Dan Farson, a writer, who had previously informed me that his family was related to Bram Stoker, the author of 'Dracula.' When he'd mentioned this, as always, I listened with great interest, but I was never able to verify the Bram Stoker connection. What was never in doubt, however, was Dan's qualification to write the biography of his good friend Francis Bacon.

Another interesting French encounter was with a bespectacled man who spoke English 'properly' in a clipped school-masterly accent. He wore a suit and looked the epitome of a respectable, bookish gentleman. While talking with him about literature, our attention shifted to history. I was, of course, glad to discuss what my research and findings had led me to believe in relation to British history. He strongly disagreed with my interpretation of certain events, as well as much of what I had to say about British history and the black and Asian presence in Britain. Rather quickly the man became combative (which surprised me) and then he left. He did not give me his name or profession. One evening while watching television the man appeared on the screen. Interestingly the programme opened with a shot of the man getting into a taxi just outside the French House. Then he began his presentation of what would become the popular television history of King Henry VIII. The man was the historian David Starkey.

Over the years, I'd met and enjoyed the company and goodwill of many people from a range of backgrounds in various parts of the great city, including Soho and the West End. Now on this night of my Doctorate celebration initiated by Lesley, I was reminded of the decades of hopes, dreams and hard work. And given the many great writers, artists and intellectuals who were associated with the Bloomsbury Group, my dogged aspiration had brought me thus far to achieve 'excellence' in literature. Having dreamed, the reality was this: I had received the University's D. Lit which was undoubtedly the *highest literary* accolade that Bloomsbury, London, Britain and the world of learning could have bestowed upon me.

Towards the end of February 1997, Andy McKillop informed me that Random House was publishing *Homelessness and the Novel,* copies of which would be distributed after I had given the Lecture as a 'Memento' of the annual Cardiff Whitbread Event. Such a publication was a mark of literary distinction which underlined the prestige associated with this Lecture.

Among the few people who knew that I was preparing to give the Lecture, predictably there was much interest in the fact that I had been chosen instead of others. Film Director Michael Rolfe saw the Whitbread Cardiff Lecture as a dramatic opportunity that would boost the chances of a documentary of my life. And so with due haste he sent me another version, a refinement of THE SAND ROAD proposal on which we had both collaborated. It included three main components: Biographical Background, Content and Structure and Programme Outline.

In part, the 'Biographical Background' read:

'Ron has lived and worked and has dedicated his life to telling the story of Blacks and Asians in Britain and the Caribbean. His work has gained him International recognition as an Historian, Biographer and Novelist. On March 20 1997 he will give the Whitbread Cardiff Lecture at the University of Cardiff joining an illustrious coterie of contemporary literary figures – Barry Unsworth, PD James, Victoria Glendinning and Michele Roberts…But Doctor Ramdin is no dry, ivory-tower academic. He carries his learning lightly. He's street wise, loves life and is a great bloke…

Under 'Content and Structure' the Document continues:

'The programme will address the question: How Did He Do That? How did a relatively "unschooled" Indo-Caribbean boy from an impoverished family ... find his way into the streets of London and not only survive the pitfalls of life in a foreign capital but also make his way through the Establishment jungle of English academic and publishing worlds, gaining en route, one of the highest Doctorates in the world of learning and presently to give what is perhaps the most prestigious literary Lecture in Britain.

The Programme is not intended as mere hagiography. The intention is that the telling of the story of Ron's journey will encourage other young people: Blacks, Asians and Whites to engage in their journey of self-discovery, to realise their own potential and to find their own place in life.

The Programme will intercut real and remembered time, the juxtaposition serving to highlight the similarities and the differences between Ron's past and present.

The Framework will derive from filming Ron's actual journey from London to Cardiff and from covering the various events surrounding the giving of the Whitbread Lecture. Within this framework, Ron will be prompted to recall details of his physical and spiritual journey through life – the core of the Program. Incidents, places, events viewed from the train or taxi window remind him of key points in his life. His recollections will be supported visually, as appropriate, by archive footage and interviews with family, friends and colleagues.'

Thus far, this represented a good summary of my life. Finally, the 'Programme Outline' read:

'Ron travels by taxi from the British Museum in Bloomsbury to Paddington Station...Shots of the streets (in the Swinging Sixties) and now remind us of the Cosmopolitan nature of those still on the streets... While purchasing a ticket and boarding the train, Ron recalls his first experience of arriving at Waterloo Station (on the "Boat train.")

No one has promised Ron anything, but he has promised himself that he will survive! As Ron boards the Cardiff train, images of his Grandmother and Grandfather laid out in the living room returns to haunt him...Although part of a large family, Ron recognised at an early age that life's journey, as with any other journey, has a beginning, middle and end…

The train moves from dreary rain swept suburbs into open country as the weather brightens up…seeing a game of cricket or football from the train window, he's reminded of his own boyhood prowess in both sports in Trinidad. Denied the proper education, sporting prowess offered the possibility of fame and fortune, or at least some social recognition and a sense of self-worth…(Horse-racing was an annual Event. Thus sports, hoofbeats and footsteps coloured his life)

Approaching Cardiff Station, Ron hears again the tune that had echoed in his mind during that first train journey from Southampton to Waterloo. 'Stranger on the Shore' had been played constantly on the Canberra's juke box by Ron's fellow-passengers, who were all strangers: In 1962 the title was apt. Now, no longer a stranger to this shore, Ron is met on the platform by the University's VIP Reception Committee and a whole scrum of reporters and photographers…His immediate tasks completed, Ron stands alone on the docks at (Cardiff's) Tiger Bay and reflects on the journey that he has undertaken. Reminded of T.S Eliot's lines: "In my end is my beginning and in my beginning is my end," the sounds and images of the applause following his Lecture mix in his mind with the most extraordinary remembered moment on his sea voyage: on the Captain's Night this hitherto shy, young teenage traveller had stood up in front of some 3000 people, more white people (than he'd seen and been among)… and sang "Diana." After taking a bow, again to tumultuous applause, he slipped quietly away to his cabin, there to lie down and dream his dream of the land he would see for the first time when he awoke, the following day – the land where he would seek to fulfil his promise to himself – a promised land where that seemingly impossible fulfilment awaited him.'

So as a consequence of being invested with the D.Lit and invited to give the Whitbread Cardiff Lecture which was now just a week away, director Rolfe's interest in doing a 'role model' documentary of me became keener.

In the count-down, as final arrangements for me to travel and deliver the Lecture were made, Deborah Williams, on behalf of the Whitbread Company wrote: 'I am pleased to enclose your rail tickets for your journey to Cardiff later this month.' My seat reservation was on the 8.30 a.m train from Paddington on the 20th March. The ticket was an 'open ended return;' and also enclosed was the 'Programme' for my visit. *'As already explained,'* Ms Williams continued, *'the afternoon of the 21st March is entirely flexible and can change as the day goes on. No formal arrangements have been made and I can confirm that you have a room booked at the Cardiff Marriott for that evening as well. Obviously, you will be introduced to Jeremy Badcock (Whitbread's Personnel Manager) who will be taking you around Cardiff, earlier in the day.*

The only change that has been made is that David Skilton will meet you at Cardiff Central rail station and when you arrive at the Butetown History and Arts Centre, Allan Owen, Whitbread's Regional Community Affairs Director will greet you. Unfortunately, Chris (Hughes) has been called to a management meeting and gives his apologies. However, Chris will collect you from the hotel later that day and take you to the Lecture Theatre.

Any problems or queries, please call me. I will phone you a couple of days before the lecture just to make sure that you are happy with the arrangements.
Yours sincerely,
Deborah'.

THE 1997 WHITBREAD CARDIFF LECTURE

A few hours after daybreak on the morning of 20 March, 1997, at last, I was on my way to deliver the Whitbread Cardiff Lecture. Leaving 22 Plympton Road, as I walked along Kilburn High Road towards Kilburn Park Station, I recalled the chauffeur-driven car that had taken me to give my BBC 'Opening Address' in Marylebone. Now, in many ways, I was going much further. After a short underground journey, I was at Paddington Station scanning the Departures schedules. While trying to identify the train that would take me to Cardiff Central, I thought about the two-day jam-packed Itinerary: a procedure which my distinguished predecessors would also have had to follow.

Dressed in a dark suit, my best clothes for the big occasion, while waiting for my train in the busy concourse of Paddington Station, a passenger who had arrived from one of the incoming trains walked directly towards me. As I tried to get out of the way, I heard my name: 'Ron!' It was John Sheldon, my former fellow Trade Unionist and good friend whom I had not seen for many years. He was now joint General Secretary of the Public and Commercial Services Union, an amalgamation of the former CSU and CPSA unions. At last, John had achieved his cherished goal: becoming the top man in his profession! I could not be happier for him.

In all the years we'd known each other, John had never seen me (with the exception of my attendance at the CSU Blackpool Conference dinner) as well-dressed as I was that morning. He'd come to regard 'blue jeans and sneakers,' my normal dress which, in truth, arose from economic necessity rather than a style of choice, as my trade mark. Now, like him, I was wearing a suit. We had not seen each other for 15 years; the last time being that memorable day in 1982 when he headed the CSU Panel that had interviewed me and eventually decided against appointing me as the CSU's 'London Organiser.'

'Where are you off to?' he asked.

'I am travelling to Cardiff,' I said.

'Cardiff?' he questioned.

'Yes,' I said. 'Tonight I will be delivering the 1997 Whitbread Lecture at the University of Cardiff.' John's pleasant expression changed somewhat as I spoke.

'Your heart was never really in the Union,' he said. His words and their tone were entirely unexpected. Was this comment meant to justify his decision not to appoint me all those years ago? I was stunned; *very* surprised indeed to hear what he'd said. How could he, of all people, a 'brother' (and in all the time we'd known each other, I'd treated him as such in the 'Brotherhood of Man' Movement) who knew better than anyone else what was widely-recognised as my *dedicated* and *voluntary* role as Organiser and workers' leader, think of me as he did!

Being far removed from the trade union movement now, I responded warmly, as I'd always done in my relations with John Sheldon. But sensing his discomfort and readiness to move on, I thought it best to help him. 'Have you got a card?' I asked breezily. He handed me his card and moved towards the fast-moving crowd. When he was gone, I realised that he did not say anything about the lecture that I was going to Cardiff to give, nor did he say goodbye. Walking away in this manner did not entirely sever the link between us. As an employee of the British Library, I was still a member of the PCS Union of which John Sheldon was Joint General Secretary. As his back receded and disappeared, I remembered our first meetings in the British Museum: Appearance-wise, beneath the donkey jacket that he sometimes wore, he was always well-dressed in a suit and tie, and I regarded him as a capable and ambitious negotiator. But now that he'd achieved what he desired most, somehow he did not seem happy. That he'd doubted my commitment to the Trade Union movement was both a shock and a revelation: a grievous, unfounded and disrespectful opinion. In short, a lie. As it was, he was the 'career Trade Unionist,' *par excellence*, not me! I was the man on-the-ground who faced ever-demanding bosses and often disgruntled members, every moment of every day, year in year out and, because of my diligence in doing the best I could, I paid the heavy price of being tarred by managements (not only in the British Museum and British Library, but also by my own side at CSU headquarters) as having been perhaps too zealous a practitioner of Trade Unionism. So this was my dilemma: while doing my best to effect good Industrial Relations in the British Library, managers and Union officials were both unhappy! As a direct consequence of their perceptions, I was destined never to be promoted either by my employers or within the union.

In the intervening years since we last saw each other, I posed this question to myself: was John surprised to learn what I'd turned out to be – an author (a very rare thing for a working class leader to be doing) and furthermore one who had the depth of knowledge and intellectual capability worthy of giving the Cardiff Whitbread Lecture? Maybe. Nonetheless, I resented what he'd said that morning; accusatory words that recalled his emphatic rejection in 1982, which forced me to seek new pathways. Now, through the efforts of my pen, my direction of travel was to Cardiff Central to meet high-profile people and fulfil my demanding Two-Day Itinerary, which included media Interviews before delivering the biggest Public Lecture of my life, significantly not as a delegate at a union Conference, but as a writer before a highly critical literary audience at the top-rated University of Cardiff.

This trip to Cardiff (and Wales) was heightened as I walked along the Paddington Station platform. After boarding the train, the journey through the English countryside was pleasant. With stops at Reading and Bristol, it was full of expectation and significance. Often, as I looked out from the window myriad thoughts flooded my mind; images of the past: for example, on arrival at Southampton while the 'Boat Train' sped towards Waterloo Station, my worry had increased as to whether or not my correspondent would be there to meet me. Thirty-five years later, I was no longer that worried-looking teenage 'Stranger.' How extraordinary, I thought, that having taken so many twists and turns in the intervening years, I should now be heading in this direction. Even the cows that I'd seen from the 'Boat Train' were somewhat idealised; now they appeared more realistic: I could almost smell them. And if on arrival at Waterloo I was a labourer, a destitute immigrant in a state of combined excitement and confusion, now, I was travelling in a Reserved Seat, more confident having become a distinctive name in the world of learning, books and literature.

As the journey progressed, at times, John Sheldon's words echoed with a negative effect: I became reflective, saddened that he should so off-handedly devalue my dedication. But with no less determination I had also set out on the lonely quest of one day becoming not simply an author, but a writer who was now just hours away from speaking to the most testing of audiences: the glitterati of the world of Literature, symbolised by the glamour and the aura of excellence associated with the Whitbread Cardiff Lecture.

For writers, giving such a Lecture was regarded as the mark of high achievement, as a glance at my predecessors confirmed. To justify and maintain the standards they had set was the challenge and prospect before me. Film Director Michael Rolfe, well-versed in life's dramas, realised the true significance of the occasion and was committed, come hell or high water, to being there to record it for posterity. Having considered these aspects of my life that had enabled me to be on the Cardiff-bound train, as we passed the Severn Bridge and entered Wales, feeling strangely aware of my fast-approaching destination, I refocused on the task ahead.

On arrival at Cardiff Central station, I was met by Allan Owen, Whitbread's Director of Regional Community Affairs. From the platform, he helped me with my luggage which we deposited at the Marriott Hotel. Mr Owen then drove me to my first assignment: A visit to the Bute Town Community Centre on Bute Street. At the entrance to the building there were a few officials, next to whom was Michael Rolfe. For the first time, I saw him at work with his hand-held camera; and in close attendance was a Sound-man who held his furry microphone aloft. Their focus was on me and on every move that I made. In the lobby of the Community Centre I signed the Visitors Book, then guided by Allan Owen, I did the pre-arranged 'Photo Call.' All of Cardiff's media men and women were there and I obeyed their requests to pose here and there in the Museum Annexe of the Butetown History and Arts Centre. Afterwards, I was led into a spacious room where I met the leading members of the Butetown Community; a few of them Founding members. We all sat at a large Round Table.

The 'veterans' and others told me about the foundation of the Community and its activities. Many of their concerns sounded familiar and could have been applied to parts of London. Among other things, the footballer Ryan Giggs' lineage was mentioned, a connection between him and legendary black local sportsman Billy Boston. Much was also said about Shirley Bassey (not all complimentary, I must add) who was, of course, born in the neighbourhood. After this very informative meeting, I was escorted by Allan Owen and two Founder members of the Butetown Community Centre down Bute Street to Cardiff's famous Tiger Bay.

On the way, I could not help thinking of this renowned port city and the early twentieth century riots that had occurred here; and the enduring black and white images in the movie of the same name starring Host Bucholz, John Mills and his young daughter Hayley. I'd seen *Tiger Bay* the film a long time before, and a very long way from Bute Street, in the Embassy Cinema when I was a youth in Trinidad. How incredible, I thought that I was now the centre of attraction and being filmed on Bute Street that led to Tiger Bay! While Mr Owen explained certain aspects of this area of Cardiff to me, all along the way, with his hand-held camera, just a few feet before me, Michael Rolfe filmed every step that I took, while his Sound-man did his best to keep the microphone above my head.

At the waterfront overlooking Tiger Bay, Mr Owen suggested that we should pose for another Official photograph. I did so with him and two of the Butetown Community Elders - Gerald Ernest and Vera Johnson. The spot chosen for this 'Special photograph' was next to two sculpted figures by John Clinch, appropriately titled 'People Like Us.'

While we were there, Michael Rolfe covered every angle, moving this way, then that, his lens focused as he filmed. From the Bay, I could see the Scandinavian Church and in the distance to the right, there were ships moving in and out. I took in as much of the scene as I could, and felt greatly privileged to be the city's Guest of Honour. Then, consulting his watch, Mr Owen indicated, it was time to move on to my next engagement.

Soon after returning to the Marriott Hotel, I was taxied to the BBC Cardiff Studios where I did a live Radio Interview showcasing the forthcoming Lecture that evening at the University. Afterwards, from my Hotel room, I did another Interview: 'down-the-line' (over the telephone) with a local Cardiff Radio station. Then around 2.30 p.m with just about five hours before the Lecture, I relaxed a while, collected my thoughts and got dressed. Before leaving the room, I glanced at my Itinerary which stated that at 6.00 p.m Chris Hughes, Whitbread's Regional Director would meet me in the foyer of the Marriott and take me to the Trevithick Lecture Theatre at the University of Cardiff.

On the way, Mr Hughes said he'd just finished reading my Lecture: *Homelessness and the Novel.* I waited expectantly. He said he liked it and I thought his positive comments were well-timed. As the car came slowly towards the entrance of the Lecture Theatre, I could see that a number of photographers, as well as Michael Rolfe were already there. When the car stopped, the media crowded round. As I made my way up the steps of the building, with Michael

Rolfe's camera and Sound-man ahead of me, to my right, someone in the crowd extended a hand and said: 'Hello Ron Ramdin.' I raised my head slightly and turned in the direction from which the voice came. 'I am Labby Siffre,' the man said. 'I look forward to your lecture!'

Carried by the momentum of movement up the steps, I had just enough time to glance at Labby Siffre, the once very popular singer, a former Pop Celebrity whose performances on television Shows I had enjoyed.

Professor Skilton, Pro-Vice Chancellor of the University of Cardiff was in the foyer to meet me. With Chris Hughes, we posed before large publicity posters for the pre-Cardiff Whitbread Lecture 'Official photographs'. As more people arrived and milled about, amidst the growing buzz of expectation, I was taken aside and wired-up, so to speak: a microphone was attached to my lapel. Like an ear-piece, Michael picked up everything that I said and for a while with his ever-present Sound-man, he continued to film and Interview a few people. In the fast-growing crowd, I recognised the High Commissioner of Trinidad and Tobago, Ms Sandra McIntyre Trotman, who came forward to greet me. With the National (red, black and white) flag at the front of her Diplomat's limousine, she was driven from Belgrave Square in London all the way across the West of England to Wales. 'I am here in Cardiff to fly the flag!' she said. This was incredible! Although I was told that she had accepted the Invitation, this level of Diplomatic support took a while to sink in. I was most impressed and grateful to be so respected as a 'Son of the soil.'

Soon, the crowd began to file into the Theatre; and when the audience was seated, I followed Professor Skilton inside. An enlarged image of the front-cover of the published Whitbread Cardiff Lecture was projected onto a big screen behind the Lectern to which Professor Skilton made his way. In his fine 'Introduction' he spoke about my body of work and, among other things, he said I was good with titles. While he was speaking, from the corner of my eye, I saw a familiar face: it was that of my British Library colleague, Senior Curator Dr David Paisey, who was seated just ahead to the right. Because he was someone whom I respected and the fact that he was Welsh-born, were two reasons why I had told him about the Lecture. Seeing him there, was a pleasant surprise. Moments later, around 8.15 p.m, Professor Skilton invited me to give the 1997 Whitbread Cardiff Lecture: *Homelessness and the Novel.*

I opened with the following words:

'From the quayside a young man in his late teens looked out in the distance at the shimmering bay and there, at anchor, the gleaming white ship rose majestically above the silvery sequined water, silhouetted against the orange glow of the dying sunlight before sudden darkness enveloped him and the massive vessel as it cleared the Dragon's Mouth on its way to England. This is a vivid and lasting image, which remains with him to this day. But he had another haunting memory. Or perhaps it was a jumble of people and events, a story stitched together by wish-fulfilment, personified in Christina, the religious, kindly and, at times, fiery old black woman, who would often sing quietly, almost trance-like and oblivious of everyone around her: "Coming for to carry me home." The word home was especially resonant. It seemed to comfort her.

Her death marked a new beginning for him, as if his leaving the island was in itself not enough...'

Just over ten minutes into the Lecture, I said:

'The sponsors of the...Lecture, in their Foreword to the published lectures, declare that their aim is "to broaden our understanding of modern literature." Distinguished Guests, Ladies and Gentlemen, I hope my contribution tonight, "Homelessness and the Novel" will foster this aim. My subject is concerned with the issues at the very heart of twentieth century literature. And where better to give this Lecture than in your capital city. The Cardiff of my imagination during my research as historian, and of Wales in my capacity as biographer, the Welsh Valleys, the Eisteddfod of Paul Robeson's time, and all my Welsh friends, are positive images that I've harboured for years. My presence here tonight, though real, is but part of the ongoing process of knowing more about this city where so many have sought and found refuge over

the years.'

How has *"home"* been invoked in modern English Literature? *The idea of "home" and a sense of homelessness have been major themes in recent decades, one that has preoccupied many distinguished novelists. Albert Camus has written of a "universe that is suddenly deprived of illusion and of light (in which) man feels a stranger. His is an unremediable exile," and V.S. Naipaul has identified in his novel In a Free State that "Everything in it was far from home," before going on to make the larger point:"In the aftermath of the political, cultural, economic and geographical dislocations that our century has generated as well as inherited – all of us are exiles…"*

To the question *"Where is home?"* some experts direct our attention to a place in the past full of childhood memories while others regard home as being *"neither here nor there."* But if the poet John Donne's idea of *"God as our home"* has *"tailed off into pallid cliche"…* the concept and sense of home remains potent, fulfilling a need, symbolising a powerful source of identity in the 20th century, a sensibility that is the raison d'etre of *"voyages of self-discovery"* that have so characterised modern literature…'

If through migration, the expatriate is consigned to a state of homelessness, Joyce nevertheless continued to create a *"Dublin-Paris"* in his novels, while Henry James constructed an America-Europe to overcome his feeling of homelessness. On the other hand, the Third World expatriate novelists, Naipaul, Lamming, Rao and Rushdie, also express nostalgia for their homelands in their novels… (And when asked why all his fiction took place in Czechoslovakia, even though he emigrated from his country a decade before, Milan Kundera responded positively:

"This is something really quite mysterious, Gombrowicz left Poland when he was thirty-five. That is to say, he lived the most adventurous years of life in Argentina. In spite of his rather violent relationship to Poland, he could not write about anything else but Poland. It is very interesting to see just how rooted we are in the first half of our lives. We are fatally rooted in the first half of life, even if life's second half is filled with intense and moving experiences. Not only is there the question of experience…but of obsessions, of traumatisms which are inextricably

tied to the first half of life - which includes childhood, adolescence and adulthood. To answer your question: No, I don't believe I could situate a novel (should I go on to write another) in France, for example. But the "How to situate the novel geographically is one of many major aesthetic dilemmas and is something I am trying to resolve..."

Moving on, I added:

'If expatriate novelists feel compelled to write self-consciously, it should not surprise us if the need to transform reality into a creative art form becomes less urgent. Indeed Naipaul, as Rushdie points out, "feels that the novel has outlived its historical moment, no longer fulfils any useful role, and will be replaced by factual writing." Rushdie then adds that it comes as no surprise to learn that Naipaul "is presently to be found at the leading edge of history creating his new post-fictional literature." But this raises the question: does this amount to propagandist writing? Few would doubt that the positive contribution of the expatriate sensibility has generated new art forms and techniques bringing together writers from different places to write creatively in a different country and in a different language. The danger with the novelist's prolonged expatriation is that he loses his edge, rising brilliantly in the early years, then fading, his language becoming insubstantial! But paradoxically, migration has its pleasures, mainly of detachment that accompanies being away from home. But as a literary phenomenon the expatriate sensibility has permanence, reflected in the bleak finality of exile as evoked in A Bend in the River and The Enigma of Arrival for there can be no return.' "

At this point, just a paragraph away from the end of my Lecture, I observed that the audience was in a state of quiet expectation. And so I proceeded at a slower pace with my closing words:

'It is now thirty-five years since I stood looking out at the shimmering bay for the last time as I waited to depart. Since then, and in spite of the Professor's comments, I have been engaged in the fictive process, most recently in creating Rama's Voyage (the story of a homeless waif from the streets of Calcutta in search of a home oceans away in the new and hostile world of the Caribbean plantations) an historical, inextricable dimension of my own imaginary homeland. But whatever it is that I may long to go back to, the landscape of my childhood or the

land of my ancestors, I am only too aware that there is no ship waiting at the quayside to take me back, for all journeys are final.'

In all, I had spoken for about 50 minutes. Enthusiastic applause rang out. As the audience filed-out, two young women standing opposite each other at the entrance of the Lecture Theatre handed out copies of *Homelessness and the Novel* published by Random House. In the foyer, as he'd done earlier, Michael Rolfe continued filming: he approached a number of people for 'On-Camera' post-Lecture interviews and/or comments. He was not disappointed.

About half an hour later, I was guided in accordance with the next part of my Itinerary: The VIP Dinner in my honour. In the University's Dining Hall, on a long table, name tags were placed before each seat: a grand-looking arrangement. Extraordinary. I sat down and opened the Menu which read:

'**Dinner Menu**
Homelessness and the Novel,
Ron Ramdin, 20 March 1997'.

The following and succeeding pages informed the diners (among them bon vivants) that the white wine to be served was '*Meursault 1995 (Michelot), the Red Wine – Casa Lapostolle 1995 (Merlot) and Brandy and Port.'*

The mains were: Smoked Fish Platter, sliced Duck Breast followed by warm Apple flan, a Welsh Cheese Selection, Coffee and Petit Fours. So soon after delivering the Lecture, I was less hungry than excited to be seated at the beautifully laid out table on this wonderful occasion; and in such distinguished company.

Among the Dinner Guests were the Chancellor of the University of Cardiff and many local dignitaries plus the Trinidad and Tobago High Commissioner, Sandra McIntyre-Trotman. Soon after we had taken our seats, a woman approached. 'Mr Ramdin,' she said, 'Alan sends his apologies.' She was the wife of the prolific English playwright Alan Ayckbourn. I was, of course, flattered to receive Mr Ayckbourn's apology and thanked her. Before Dinner was served, Michael Rolfe informed me that the singer Labby Siffre had joined the Dinner Party. 'Oh good,' I said. Having anticipated my Lecture, Mr Siffre may have enjoyed it, I thought.

After a short speech by Chris Hughes on behalf of the Whitbread Company, I responded with a few words expressing my delight, the very great honour and unforgettable pleasure of having given the Cardiff Whitbread Lecture! This was a proud moment: one to savour and celebrate. Though not a connoisseur, by now the taste of the wines (the red in particular) was excellent; and the food presented was quite special: delicate and delicious. Overall, it was an amazingly heady and memorable day and night.

Early the next morning, I re-read and reflected on the 'FOREWORD' of the published Lecture:

'As sponsors of the Cardiff Lecture, Whitbread and Random House UK Limited we are delighted to provide you with this memento of the 1997 Lecture by Ron Ramdin.

This is the fifth annual Cardiff Lecture, an event which has developed and grown in stature since the idea was first mooted in 1992. At that time, those of us with an interest in Cardiff and its status as a European Capital were conscious that whilst its reputation for music was widespread, its literary scene was relatively unknown.

A literary lecture was seen as a way of raising awareness of the Welsh Capital's reputation as a thriving literary centre. The first Lecture was given by Booker Prize-winning novelist Barry Unsworth, and in the following years the writer and broadcaster Michele Roberts, the acclaimed novelist and crime-writer P.D. James and the Whitbread Award-winning biographer and novelist Victoria Glendinning were the guest speakers.

By offering free public access to authors of this standing, our aim is to broaden the understanding of modern literature. The response from audiences has confirmed the demand for such an annual initiative.

We hope you have enjoyed this year's Lecture and that you will continue to support Cardiff's growing literary scene.'

The following morning, I had breakfast and a long chat with the Trinidad and Tobago High Commissioner who had spent the night in the Marriott Hotel. Before leaving Cardiff, she said she was 'very proud' to be there to listen to my Lecture.

Later that morning, my next assignment was to meet the A Level English Language and History students from Cathays and Fitzalan schools. Professional that Mr Rolfe was, as usual, he was on hand to film the entire Session. Before this, he told me he had already done some filming outside the University of Cardiff's main buildings as well as taking shots of certain prominent Cardiff landmarks and street scenes.

After Lunch (originally scheduled at the Welsh National Opera) Jeremy Badcock, Whitbread's Personnel Services Manager, who was my Guide, showed me around the city. He took me to a few historic sites and other places of interest, including a tour through some replicas of depressingly austere Miner's Cottages: stark, bare habitations, evocative of harder times which I found deeply moving.

On the morning of my last day in Cardiff when I visited a Bookshop in the city, a Professor from the University approached me. 'Do you sing?' she asked.

'Why?'

'Because,' she said, 'I enjoyed the musicality of your voice!' In her hand was a copy of my published Lecture!

Later on, filming continued at the Scandinavian Church and elsewhere in Tiger Bay where, against the background of ships entering and leaving the famous harbour, under Michael Rolfe's direction, I did 'some acting!'

Over the three days, the experience was truly wonderful and, looking out from the window of the train as it pulled away from Cardiff Central, I felt on this my first visit to the Welsh city, something *quite special* had happened, and all of it was filmed! I was overwhelmed by a sense that having done my best, something worthwhile had been achieved. But trying to relive those great moments so soon were frustrated by an insistent drowsiness as I sat in the train. I closed my tired eyes and, at last, I felt a shudder - the first movement, then the familiar sounds of the speeding train that was bringing me back to London.

Having worked on a few drafts, after articulating the final version of *Homelessness and the Novel,* posing the question: Where is home? was especially timely and significant. 'Home?' The question remained with me as the train pulled in and eventually halted at Paddington Station. On leaving the train and platform a certain familiarity of place, like a cloak warmed me and I embraced the fact that in a strangely nomadic and unconventional way, for me as a writer and a person, London was home!

A few days later, *The Western Mail* published the following article:

> ## 'RESIDENTS GO BACK TO THEIR ROOTS
>
> *A group of Butetown residents had the chance to meet the UK's leading historian of black and ethnic communities. Whitbread Cardiff Lecturer Dr Ron Ramdin visited the Butetown History and Arts Centre last week. The Centre's Founder members were asked to tell Dr. Ramdin about their various cultural backgrounds, with grandparents coming from far afield as Nepal and the Bahamas.*
>
> *He also met residents of the area to discuss their roots. They left Dr Ramdin in no doubt that the famous spirit of the old Tiger Bay has not been forgotten.'*

Accompanying this report was the 'Special photograph' taken in Tiger Bay with the caption: 'Dr Ron Ramdin and Allan Owen of Whitbread with Butetown residents Gerald Ernest and Vera Johnson.'

Reading this Welsh newspaper report and seeing the photograph, I felt deeply satisfied and considered my Cardiff sojourn as a literary triumph; an engagement that would never be forgotten.

Undeterred by the let-down that I'd suffered at the hands of the Publishing company with whom I had hoped to publish *Arising From Bondage*, now I looked forward to hearing from Dr Crook, the editor of I.B. Tauris. After posting copies of the Synopsis, List of Contents and sample chapters to him, propelled by ten years of unflagging belief in the book, I allowed myself to think that perhaps something good would come out of this new approach. Why? Because significantly this time the history Editor was a well-informed Englishman. In fact my hopes were now higher than average. As it was, soon after my extraordinary literary journey to Cardiff, a letter from Dr Crook had arrived.

'*Dear Dr Ramdin,*

Arising From Bondage: A History of East Indians in the Caribbean 1838-1996

Thank you for your letter of 4 March and for sending the blurb about your book and some details of your own academic and writing experience. Thank you also for the detailed list of contents and chapter one "From Slavery to East Indian Indentureship".

This look extremely interesting material and it covers a very long historical span. I shall read this chapter in detail in the next day or two and will be pleased to have a meeting with you if at all possible before you go to Trinidad in April. This subject has long been of interest to me and I at one stage tried to get Professor Hugh Tinker to produce a new study of indentured labour. Of course I understand that his book does not only deal with indentured labour in the Caribbean. I also came across this particular subject during my own researches many years ago.

May I therefore read this material in the next day or so and perhaps you could give me a ring either at the office in London or at my home address where I work for two or three days a week...'

This was wonderfully positive news. At last, I felt someone would seriously appraise what I had done and perhaps justify my expectations. Yet it must be said that past experience in relation to this subject matter and this particular book necessarily tempered my temptation to be too hopeful.

Two days later, I received a Postcard from Senior British Library Curator Dr David Paisey:

'*London 22/3/97*

Dear Ron,

Many congratulations on your beautiful Cardiff Lecture. It was unusual and poetic, and struck many chords in me. The last words brought a tear to my eye. I felt very proud to know someone so talented.

Yours,

David.'

How unlike those managers who regarded my work with great suspicion, David was! How considerate, I thought, that this distinguished scholar of international renown not only took the time to travel from London to be in Cardiff for my Lecture, but was also moved enough to write to me. As a Curator at the British Library, his well-chosen words reminded me of that memorable day when I'd first spoken to him in the Round Reading Room.

Having gained some knowledge about the Room where so many great writers had sat, thought and written, I had put the question to him: 'Dr Paisey: Who is Karl Marx? What is he famous for?' Many years later, Dr Paisey invited me to his retirement leaving party. In his Farewell speech he told the audience (most of whom knew of my British Museum and British Library Staff representations and writings) about my 'question' to him about Karl Marx. It was remarkable how little I then knew about revolution and revolutionary politics. But ironically just four years after I'd put the question to Dr Paisey, being an émigré employed in the very Room where Marx, another émigré had written *Capital* or *Das Kapital* (a place also visited by Marx's disciple V.I. Lenin) I reflected on Tim O'Keeffe's dubbing of me as 'The Lenin of Museum Street.' Did Tim mean by this that I had the courage of my conviction to explore ideas and express what I truly believed? It is in this spirit that my 'unusual and poetic' Lecture as Dr Paisey had put it in his postcard must be read for like Mr O'Keeffe he too had been a close observer of my activities and development over many years.

Given my publishing woes and preoccupation hitherto, I regarded the news from I.B Tauris publishers as promising. Coincident with this, for the first time, I felt that many Indo-Caribbean people's understanding of, and attitude to, my work was far-off the mark. So following Dr Crook's letter, I sensed that perhaps he was the only one who would truly understand the scope, depth, gravity and importance of *Arising From Bondage*. Thus encouraged, I anticipated Dr Crook's assessment of chapters of the manuscript that I'd sent to him.

Giving prestigious lectures was one thing, but feedback to them was crucial. Eight days after my Lecture, Cardiff University itself had issued the following Press Release:
"'Homelessness and the Novel:" 1997
Whitbread Cardiff Lecture delivered by
Trinidad writer Ron Ramdin at the
University of Wales on March 20, 1997
  Ron Ramdin, a Trinidadian historian and writer who has lived in

England since 1962, delivered the 1997 Whitbread Cardiff Lecture at the University of Wales at Cardiff on 20 March 1997.

The Whitbread Cardiff Lecture, prestigious literary occasion now in its fifth year, is sponsored by the Whitbread group of companies and the Random House Publishers. It is organised by the School of English Studies, Communications and Philosophy at the University of Wales at Cardiff.

The appreciative audience at the 1997 Lecture included members of the Cardiff academic, literary and business community.

In this year's lecture entitled "Homelessness and the Novel" Ron Ramdin explored the phenomenon of the twentieth century novelist as exile, expatriate and world citizen, a condition illustrated most sharply, in his view, by Third World expatriate writers of fiction.

The city of Cardiff, capital of the principality of Wales, was the site of one of the earliest settlements of black people in Britain and a focus of much internal migration within Britain itself.

There is also an apt coincidence between the history of the city and the themes of migration, identity and the struggle of the dispossessed explored in much of the previous work of the lecturer...

He has lectured extensively in Britain, Europe and the West Indies.

A documentary of his life and work is currently being made by the BBC?'

The fact that the University of Cardiff and Whitbread were happy with my performance and fulfilling all my obligations was a relief for me. But how would this most public of high-profile performances measure up against other distinguished attendees' comments, I wondered.

By now, in addition to what she had said, the High Commissioner of Trinidad and Tobago put pen to paper:

'Dear Ron,

I enjoyed the Whitbread Cardiff Lecture immensely.

I was happy to "Fly the Flag" at this important event in the literary calendar and appreciated the opportunity to discuss ideas and literature if only for an evening.

I enclose a copy of the Press Release issued to the Editors of the following Sunday newspapers in Trinidad: Trinidad Guardian, Trinidad

Express, The Independent and Newsday.

Please let me know if you would like the Press Release (complete or abbreviated) to be issued to the British press.

Sincerely, Sandra.'

A more appreciative endorsement and from the highest Diplomatic level in relation to Trinidad and Tobago, I could not have wished for.

And there was more: Dorothea Hodge, President of the Cardiff University Students, wrote to Professor Skilton offering her 'apologies for being unable to make the dinner appointment with Ron Ramdin...this dinner engagement...I would have thoroughly enjoyed. Please could you convey my thanks to Ron Ramdin for a truly evocative Lecture.'

Overall, the written responses to my Lecture as 'beautiful,' 'truly evocative' and being enjoyed 'immensely' were satisfying and humbling. It engendered a positive effect and now my focus on I. B. Tauris being the publisher of *Arising from Bondage* became more concentrated. What did Dr Crook really think about my manuscript? I wondered. Then his letter arrived. He wrote:

'Dear Dr. Ramdin,

Thank you for calling at the office on the 1 April. I much enjoyed our very interesting discussion. May I set down some of the points?

*I have read your script and it is a very impressive piece of work. I am afraid I had to read it at some speed but will of course read with more attention and leisure at a later stage. We shall also be considering the academic assessments. **I thought that the book was a splendid narrative history with the analysis being worked effectively into the text. I think that in many ways this is how history should be written. The text is lively, clear and frequently striking and graphic. I am sure that this is a book which would be read not only by scholars and students but also by the general reader.** You seem to cover a very wide range of subject matter including politics, sociology, religion, culture, education, the economic reasons for Indian emigration and the subsequent economic activity and advancement. You also deal with health and the gender aspect is always there. Running through the text is the question of ethnicity and the development of a* *pluralistic society in the Caribbean.* **The history involves the entire or most of the region and is within the framework of the history of the British Empire and the colonial experience including slavery and the ex-slave owning society.**

I think that this would be a book of interest to academics and students and the general reader in the UK, the USA, the traditional Commonwealth market and of course in the Caribbean. It would interest students of history, black studies, ethnic studies and also the rather more specialised aspect of...Afro-Caribbean studies and also Asian-Caribbean studies. The whole question of great movements of populations and diaspora will be a most important element of study.'
(Author's emphasis)

I was very pleased indeed; impressed by the academic rigour that Dr Crook had brought to bear on my manuscript which I felt was far more serious, honest and perceptive than some of the dismissive (even derisory) comments that I'd received from other Indo-Caribbean history 'experts.' Dr Crook, who knew well the leading British historians of the day, revealed his editorial hallmark - thoroughness. His letter continued:

'I will be in touch with Professor Robin Cohen and also Professor Henry Louis Gates at Harvard. I would also like the script to be at least looked at, by say, Professor Peter Marshall. I will also take advice from our historical advisors in the USA especially Professor Roger Louis.

The text I have read is very near the camera-ready copy stage and we are very grateful indeed for this. It will have to be proof ready but I do not expect the scholarly assessors to recommend much in the way of revision.

I will now include the book on the Agenda at our Editorial meeting on 10 April.

I look forward to working with you on this book and I am also very grateful to you for the Cardiff Lecture 1997. I shall reserve an hour to read this very interesting looking piece this evening.'

Though encouraged and optimistic about all that Dr Crook had said about the manuscript, it was not as yet, a done deal. Fortunately, however, thoughts on my earlier disappointments were occasional and fleeting.

Now that the big literary challenge was behind me, I wrote to Professor Skilton, who had championed my candidacy, to formally thank him for inviting me to give the Whitbread Cardiff Lecture and 'for your incomparable Introduction. That was a wonderful moment... And, as I said very briefly at the dinner, I shall always cherish the memory of all those who helped to make my visit such an enjoyable occasion.'

Financially, at this time in my mid-Fifties, I was prone to feel more insecure than in previous years. I dwelt on the fact that never again would I be able to buy a Flat; and felt condemned to remain in rented 'affordable' accommodation. I still dressed casually, modestly; and being more often than not, out of pocket, nonetheless I was very pleased when I learned that a cheque for my Lecture was on its way. In her letter informing me of this, Wendy Lewis, the University of Cardiff's Finance Administrator added: '*I would just like to say thank you for giving everyone who attended, such a wonderful evening.*' Ms Lewis's comment had a special resonance: the value of her words mattered as greatly as did the £500 which alas, in my circumstances, was already 'spoken for,' so to speak.

FLAMENCO DANCE

Ever driven, it seemed there was always something else to do. When I lectured at the University of Seville in 1990 my interest in Andalusian culture (Flamenco, in particular) and in Spain generally, had grown. Having taken copious notes on my visits since 1990, now in 1997, I approached and submitted the following Synopsis on 'Flamenco Dance' to Mr X, Editor of a popular art history publisher, whom I thought well of as a friend.

'FLAMENCO DANCE

Flamenco embraces song (cante), dance (baile) and guitar playing (toque). The main focus of Flamenco is well known, but little understood. Each year hundreds of thousands of holiday-makers and "culture vultures" from various parts of the world (especially from

938 · TURNING PAGES · RON RAMDIN · VOLUME TWO

northern Europe, the Americas and Japan) jet off to sun-drenched Spain and should the word Flamenco be mentioned, the vast majority of these visitors more often than not, respond with a click of fingers, mimicking the sound of castanets and an "ole!" But Flamenco has little or nothing to do with this popular misunderstanding. And what is more, Spain and Flamenco are identified as being synonymous in a way which gives the impression that the vast majority of Spaniards proudly engage in and practice one or other aspect of this artform. As Spaniards, both at home and abroad, will tell you, this is a popular misconception, for the great artists, the practitioners of Flamenco have in the past, and are today still drawn essentially from among the Gypsy minority in Spain. What remains abundantly clear, however, is the emotional impact of this exciting, life affirming dance and music, evoking pain, life and death, the essence of the human dilemma, which is readily recognised by peoples from very different, or indeed similar, cultures. In other words, it touches at once, all those who witness these performances, and it is a mark of its power that few (if any) are left indifferent.

The proposed book FLAMENCO DANCE will therefore necessarily open with an Introduction, giving due weight to the historical background in approximately five to ten thousand words, which will, as it were, frame the striking photographs and images that will follow. This narrative will be primarily concerned with identifying the origin of Flamenco and the evolution of the dance. First there was the music and then the dance; performances within the family and extended family groups and later by professional singers and dancers. Given that certain parts of Spain have become famous in the development of Flamenco, emphasis will be placed on the "Gilded Triangle" of Andalusia, where the main centres of Flamenco are to be found, namely Seville, Cordoba, Jerez, Granada and Madrid. For as one writer put it: "Flamenco is Andalusia and no Catalan, Galician, Aragonese or even Castilian, all of whom call themselves Spaniards, could nearly claim to know anything about, let alone how to perform, Flamenco. Some learn and often know a great deal or perform very well. But to be born with it, you have to be from Andalusia, the South."

It can, in fact, be argued that Spain's tortuous history over the last thousand years is reflected in Flamenco. The contribution of some of *the outstanding artists of today and from the past, their peculiarities, dramatic flair and, in some cases, genius, will constitute an integral part of the Introduction. It is significant that the connections I have made in Spain are invaluable to the project. For example, the sample photographs that I have so far been able to collect during my last two visits to Spain are from people who have been (and, in some cases, still are) at the very centre of Flamenco, either as performers or administrators, whose lives have been immersed in Flamenco and for whom Flamenco is a way of life. Moreover, my advisers include the film-maker and record producer, Ricardo Pachon; the classical Flamenco dancer and teacher of Master classes in Seville, Emilio Acosta; and Jacinta Delgado, the photographer from Madrid, among others.*

I have been informed, and it seems to be a widely held view among knowledgeable Spaniards, that black and white photographs work powerfully to evoke the beauty, intensity of feeling and passion that form the essence of Flamenco dance...

Taken together then the Introduction and striking images in a well-produced book will effectively carry the essential message of this art-form to a vast international audience which, in my opinion, will be very appreciative of it. My research (which involves checking through various bibliographical files in the British Library and elsewhere) has revealed that there is no book along the lines that I propose which, in itself, makes a powerful case for publication. I have no doubt that my book FLAMENCO DANCE will also add another dimension to Carlos Saura's film "Flamenco" (hailed as a "masterpiece" in Spain and here in Britain) and his earlier and famous film "Carmen." In this sense, the filmed performances of FLAMENCO will complement the book admirably, significantly because Saura's narrated introduction to his film is, to say the least, brief.'

A few weeks later, Mr X returned my Synopsis and book proposal with no mention of a publishing commitment. He had instead commissioned someone else to do a book on Flamenco! Of this 'commission' to publish someone else's book, Mr X said nothing to me when we met subsequently. It was only by chance that I learned what he had done. After one of our post-'Flamenco' proposal meetings, he wrote to me: '...I hope all is well with you– we must meet again soon.' Why? Fortunately, I was far too preoccupied to be unduly concerned with his brass-faced pretense and deception.

Now, no less than at previous times, money was a preoccupation. After the first advance on signature of the *Black Britain* book Contract many months before, after submitting the final manuscript to Penguin Books, I wrote requesting the second payment. But because of a fundamental disagreement between the editor and myself on the kind of book *Black Britain* should be, Penguin and I parted company. I paused for a while to consider my options.

How strange I thought that time (some thirty-six years in London) had passed so quickly. I realised that unlike so many migrants who had come primarily to work and settle, I was not simply a resident: I'd become devotedly engaged in British society in terms of thought and action (especially as writer, spokesman and Educator) with ongoing economic, social, political and cultural issues. As I'd done ever since my arrival, in various ways, I have lived *a very public life*. Reflecting on this, I recalled characters I'd met from the Sixties, Seventies, Eighties and now in the Nineties as I moved around in many places, including Hornsey, Finsbury Park, Holloway Road, Turnpike Lane, Tottenham, Edmonton, Brixton, Hackney, Clapton, Walthamstow, Bloomsbury, Soho, Covent Garden, Fitzrovia, Chelsea and Kilburn, among other districts. I had a capacious curiosity to learn more about London.

I particularly remember meeting the eccentric, but very talented Brian Behan in the Seventies and Eighties. When I told him about the book I'd been writing at the time, he remarked: 'You know, writing is a sign of degeneration.' Brian's brother was Brendan Behan, the Irish playwright who had written *Borstal Boy:* Legend has it that as a Guinness-stained manuscript, the play was rescued from the bar of *The Plough* in Bloomsbury and eventually found its way into the hands of Tim O'Keeffe, who edited and published it.

At this point in my life, I began to develop an interest in biography. Why? Good question. I was struck by the thought: Why read or write about another man's life unless it illumines an aspect of yours. So began a growing interest in this literary genre, which I understood only too well for thus far, my whole life (clearly of an altruistic orientation) had been coloured by the lives of others.

It was at this time that I first met Sebastian Barker in Bloomsbury. His father, the poet George Barker (whom T.S. Eliot had described as a 'genius') was a friend of Martin Green. I had often seen both men in and around Bloomsbury in the Seventies. Through Sebastian, I met his mother Elizabeth Smart, author of the well-known book *By Grand Central Station I Sat Down and Wept*. Poets like Martin and George were surrounded by literary people, including Patrick Kavanagh, Hugh McDiarmid, Colin MacInnes, Seamus Heaney and David Lodge, among others, who came and went.

By now, willy-nilly as the hectic days, months and years passed, I marvelled at my ability and desire to meet and speak with people from all walks of life; and such prodigious and responsible public engagements as I'd undertaken hitherto had transformed me to the extent that my early shyness was now a thing of the past: something that most people who knew me (or thought they did) could not imagine. Of necessity, I'd become one of the most gregarious persons in Bloomsbury and London. Saying this, I must however make the distinction that my hard-won confidence should not be mistaken for arrogance, as was so often the case.

On the essential matter of 'Education' by which I mean both lecturing and writing, as I'd been doing for decades, I continued as a provider of resources in the form of textbooks and research information. In fact, I had always made myself available to researchers and scholars. This readiness to help, honed by the years of voluntary staff organisational work in the British Library, now came naturally and my weekly telephone calls, correspondence and meetings increased markedly. Many students who had read my books and knew of my presence in the British Library, did not hesitate to 'pick my brain.' Those who had seen the growing number of references to my books in various texts and bibliographies wrote to me seeking whatever guidance I could give. One letter from Ms S from the University of Southampton thanked me for my 'time and interest' when she had visited London.

'It was good to meet you and kind of you to look up those references for me which I shall certainly follow up.

You have really set me thinking now of the implications for groups such as Indo-Caribbean and those Asians that came here via Africa... By the way, I had a letter yesterday from Anna Grimshaw who directed me to the Director of the James Institute in New York and said she had "retired from James studies." Thought you might be interested.

Hope you enjoyed the Whitbread Lecture and all goes well and that your holiday in Trinidad isn't too interesting!

Thanks again and next time we meet I owe you a coffee. You can put it down to me being slightly overawed.

Yours.'

Southampton! It occurred to me that I'd never been back to the port city since I'd landed there as a worried teenager. Then I was entirely lacking in experience and knowledge: I was a *tabula rasa*. Decades later, I'd been thoroughly worked on by what I was working on. So much so, that I'd accumulated a body of knowledge which I could pass on to others. What a wonderful connection it was, I thought, for having travelled on, so to speak, now a PhD student from the University of Southampton was seeking my professional advice and I was gladly delivering it to her satisfaction.

In spite of the challenges of time and money, I maintained a relentless pace of life and work. Ten years spent writing a book is a very long time, and the least I could have expected was that it would be published reasonably quickly. On 16 April 1997, I heard from I.B. Tauris:

'Dear Dr Ramdin,

*I discussed your proposed book Arising From Bondage: A History of the East Indians in the Caribbean 1838-1996 at the editorial meeting on the 10 April. The meeting received the proposal **extremely well and with enthusiasm and we would like to go ahead with the book**.*

A number of points were raised and it was suggested that the title might be "Out of Bondage: History of Asians in the Caribbean 1838 to the Present." This was a suggestion from our sales and marketing department but obviously I would want to obtain your view on this. We envisaged a hardback with a good jacket to be followed as soon as possible by a paperback! I must now obtain reader's reports on the text and I have written to Professors Louis and Henry Louis Gates at Harvard. I have also got in touch with Professor Peter Marshall for a general imperial history view.

*I look forward to working with you on this book and the meeting agreed strongly with the argument that here was **a splendid and major history** which involved all of the elements which go to make up a history of the pluralistic Caribbean society and set within the context of slavery and the end of slavery and the history of the European Empires. The book will of course be of **great interest to historians** of the European Empire, the students of slavery, black studies, ethnicity studies, Diaspora studies and Afro-Caribbean and Indo-Caribbean studies. The book should have a very strong impact in the UK and in North America and also in the region...I look forward to receiving the specialist scholarly assessments and also to meeting you again on your return from the Caribbean and of course to working with you on **this major book**...'* (Author's emphasis)

Dr Crook's understanding of the subject matter had fully justified my expectations: It is what I had intended and hoped the book would be; and so the response touched me deeply. Why did the 'experts' at Warwick University's Caribbean Studies Department not understand this? I wondered. To cap Dr Crooks's perceptive and comprehensive assessment on *Arising From Bondage*, he added:

'I read with very great interest your Cardiff Lecture. It is so good to have a person on the history list who has such a deep knowledge of the relevant literature and not only historical literature. Of course, I could see how the themes of home and exile and their effect on creative writing lead directly into your major book which is in many ways a life work and a life statement.'

The scope and depth of Dr Crook's knowledge and wisdom confirmed his editorial eminence. I took in all that was said in his thoughtful letter and replied:

'Dear Dr. Crook,
I was delighted to receive both your letters of 4 and 16 April on my return from Trinidad and was also very pleased to meet you again briefly in the company of John Crabb (a member of the Tauris publishing team).
Given your strong recommendation and the enthusiastic endorsement

at the Editorial meeting of 10 April 1997 (as we await Robin Cohen's assessment) I too anticipate working with you on Arising From Bondage. In the last week, I've been going through the material with a view to incorporating the section 'Culture and Caste' (now as Appendix 1) into the main text.

As I see it, "Out of Bondage: History of Asians in the Caribbean 1838 to the Present" is inappropriate for two main reasons: first, it is not as evocative of the complexity of the book and, second, it is not as saleable as the original title. Furthermore, 'Asians' as defined in North America does not include Indians! I shall however be happy with either of the alternative titles: "Arising from Bondage: A History of East Indians in the Caribbean 1838 to the Present" or "Arising From Bondage: A History of the Indo-Caribbean People 1838 to the Present."

I enclose a copy of a rare, nineteenth century photograph of Indian women who have arisen to become the 'keepers' of Indian culture, so necessary to their communities' survival. I therefore suggest that because of Indo-Caribbean women's lowly status, this compelling historical black and white photograph should be used on the book jacket…'

As mentioned, my good friend Wendy Greenbury had already done a few designs for the book jacket of *Arising From Bondage* while it was with the last publisher. They were all attractive and I'd hoped to use one of them. A while later, however, publisher I. B. Tauris presented me with a copy of their version of the book jacket which featured an impressive, colourful painting of Indian indentured labourers arriving at their destination. The title of the painting was: *Arrival.* Seeing it, at once, I felt it was the appropriate jacket for my book. But while my cherished dream of getting *Arising From Bondage* published moved apace, other matters intervened.

At work in my office, things were not at all well. A few weeks after being transferred to the Book Moves Team, leg-pains prompted me to write to Dr F, Head of the Department concerned. But although she had been instrumental in finding me an alternative job placement on a new Project within the Department, it was temporary. Having reached the end of my time on the 'Project,' I received the following letter from Ms H of the Book Moves Team.

'Dear Ron,

Thank you for attending the meeting with me yesterday. I am now writing to you to confirm details of our discussion...

We... discussed the effects of book moving duties on your health... If you wish to discuss any aspect of this letter or your position in Book Moves Team please let me know.

Welcome back to the Team!'

Within a week, I replied:

'As I have repeatedly indicated to you the effect of prolonged standing is not conducive to my health and the prospect of returning to a Book Moves rota on 26 May and other related jobs (which necessarily means prolonged standing!) is indeed cause for concern on my part.'

Just over a month after the dust of toing and froing, inclusive of preparing and giving the Whitbread Cardiff Lecture had begun to settle, my 'Tour Guide,' Jeremy Badcock had kindly sent me a Post-Card with an interesting accompanying note. I was pleasantly surprised to learn that apart from his day-job, Mr Badcock was a dancer. *'The twenty four hours encompassing your lecture and our time in Cardiff,'* he wrote, *'were a highlight of my year and I enjoyed your company...since I last saw you I have danced in two London shows and both seemed to go down well. This weekend there is a full costume ball in the Guildhall in Bath and then after that I can give my legs a rest for a bit...the invitation to you to visit Cardiff again stands indefinitely...I thought you might like the enclosed Card as you did a photo call at the point shown. (Note that the picture is taken pre-barrage.')*

'Pre-barrage' was the period before Tiger Bay was redeveloped into the harbour and complex of buildings (including the Welsh Assembly) and other facilities that we see today.

The 'photo' Mr Badcock referred to was the one which was published in *The Western Mail*.

Having listened to me speak, and as a mark of the seriousness with which he regarded the message contained in *Homelessness and the Novel,* his well thought-through note read:

'Thoughts on the 1997 Cardiff Lecture
The other day I fed my cat, a habit both she and I have come quietly

accustomed to and I observed what I now perceive as recognised behaviour. She ate her meal then left the dining area and placed herself on the rug in front of the fireplace. Here she diligently cleansed her paws and promptly lay before the fire. It occurred to me that she exhibited this form of behaviour every time I fed her and I wondered if indeed we are creatures of habit. For when I considered my own circumstances I began to recognise there was a distinct pattern in terms of my own activities.

I then thought of how the cat would react if I was to place her in a different environment. I must admit I had my doubts but why? Reflecting on my own life I considered the consequence of a misdemeanour some years ago whereby I was legally placed in a culture which was totally alien to me; its culture was totally antagonistic to my presence! There was no escaping the hostility or hatred that fellow companions expressed.

A few years later I sat and thought of my experience and came to the conclusion that as human beings we are all travelling our own lives journey in whichever shape or form. I remembered a young man from India once saying to me "You are a gift to God. What you become is a gift to God." At the time I found it to be a poignant statement and drastically affected my outlook on life.

In a sense it really homed in on the point we, as human beings, are all in the same boat! Yet for whatever reason we, at times, ostracise ourselves from each other. Possibly, the reason for this may lie in the spatial framework in which we exist? It seems there are three dimensions to our lives the past, the present and the future. Each one integrates with each other enabling us to formulate the judgements we make.

The past seems to have an enormous bearing on our decisions; the culture in which we are indoctrinated immense influence. Yet the future grips us with anxiety. In terms of the cultural difference that exist within the world I wonder if relinquishing the past, nurturing the present and looking forward to the future might usefully assist us?

That *Homelessness and the Novel* should provoke such serious 'Thoughts' was most gratifying. Mr Badcock had taken the time to carefully set down his innermost feelings which were significant because they related to my intellectual-philosophical development as I refined and incorporated different strands of thought into various aspects of my writings. Given my continuing exploration of ideas of 'Home and Belonging,' as well as 'respect for difference,' Mr Badcock's question: 'In terms of the cultural difference that exist within the world I wonder if relinquishing the past, nurturing the present and looking forward to the future might usefully assist us?' seemed too general and simplistic.

After the Lecture, I kept in touch with members of the Bute Town History Group and had met the key organisers of the Lecture Chris Hughes, Andy McKillop and David Skilton in London. Beyond professional roles, their convivial company pleased me enormously and we agreed to meet again socially.

In this post-*Homelessness and the Novel* period, as historian, biographer, writer and thinker I felt I'd entered a new phase on my journey of developing certain ideas in my writings that were becoming clearer and thus more meaningful.

TWENTY-FOUR

A FAREWELL NOTE TO THE BELOVED ROUND READING ROOM

Life and living, never straightforward, was no less so now. Even as late as 17 May 1997, I was still trying to resolve an outstanding issue connected with the publisher who had decided not to publish *Arising From Bondage*. Although this was an unsatisfactory end, it was but one more thing to affect me personally. Approaching mid-year (like the great British reading public and many in the intellectual/book world) I was about to witness the greatest change to the Round Reading Room since it was erected in 1857.

After months and years of planning, at last, the vast collections of books, manuscripts, maps, sound archive and other items were about to be moved from the fortress-like British Museum and other out-houses to the new St Pancras building. What had seemed so distant and unrealisable in 1973 (at the British Library's inception and the time of my election as first Staff Side Secretary) had become a reality. And now once more, I found myself at the forefront of things; this time as part of the Book Moves Team engaged in one of the biggest operations of its kind - the removal of millions of books, manuscripts and maps from one location to another. Though it was hard to believe, the message struck home: the world renowned Round Reading Room in Bloomsbury was, as we had known it, to be no more! Soon it would be closed to the public and all the wonderful volumes, including the thousands of rare books that lined the walls of this majestic Room from Ground level up to the first and second floor tiers were to be taken away to St. Pancras.

A date was set for the Room's closure; and the count-down moved incredibly fast. When that day came, I was strangely, but not surprisingly very sad for I had sat in that Room for decades and written my first as well as several other books at Seat M7. In a sense, over the years, I'd made this public Room my own special 'private' space. Within the closing hour on the last day before the first books were removed from the Room, I entered and for a while I stood and scanned the familiar and beautiful sight of all the books still in place where I'd always seen them. Then with due haste, I made my way to Seat M7 before the Room's closing time at 5.00 p.m. As the minutes passed, with my ever-present black biro, I hurriedly scribbled my final thoughts:

'*Monday 19 May 1997 (4.16pm)*
THE ROUND READING ROOM
Here at seat M7 (and its environs) in this famous Room, I began in the summer of 1969, positively, energetically to pursue my ambition to write, to become a writer! Since then (and after many years of study, research and writing) I have achieved the status of author and "writer" having been invited to give…the 1997 Whitbread Cardiff Lecture!

I used this seat regularly, religiously from early morn till late evening, Mondays through Saturdays before the Room opened to the public and after. Indeed, legitimate claim could be laid to the fact that no person alive or dead has used this room as much as I have in the past 27 years. But after publication of my books The Making of the Black Working Class in Britain & Paul Robeson: The Man and His Mission (the proofs of which were corrected right here) I changed the location of my hours of research & writing by occupying Seat B8 for two reasons: first, it was further away from the historical reference books (where there was increasingly a noisy thoroughfare) and second, because the B8 seat was… more convenient in terms of the volumes I had to carry during my research on Arising From Bondage, a work which entailed ten years of research and writing. Of course (I'd published) other books such as The World in View: West Indies and The Other Middle Passage.

Over this 27 year period, I have been a constant user and frequenter of this marvellous Room and working here has given me a privilege that I value very highly. I have thought much about the closure of this Room as the transition is made to the new high-tech building at St. Pancras; and yet, I (having spent more time here than at home) feel a deep sense of loss. In less than an hour, the present look of the Room will be transformed as the first books lining the walls of the first floor balcony (with multi-dimensional, multi-coloured spines) will be removed from the shelves, packed in crates and transported to the St. Pancras site; an operation which will last until 11.00 pm tonight and recommence on Friday evening from 5.00-11.00 pm.

Tomorrow, the (visiting) public will behold a Room denuded of its former adornment and progressively so in the coming weeks and months until the first week in October, when the Room (as we know it) will close forever.

Its reopening will have a new orientation, though it will, of course, retain its structure as Panizzi's Room (but) not with the same orientation for which it was designed.

The Library Assistants are now busy clearing away the unattended books and putting the lights out, reminding readers that they must leave. And interestingly, as the readers next to me and around me vacate their seats, I realize that I too must leave! I do so, however, knowing that tomorrow, this (my) favourite Room... would have been changed forever! And perhaps the closing Bell which just sounded is heralding not only a new chapter in the history of this Room, but also a new future for me!

(4.43 pm).'

Exactly at 4.43 p.m I stopped writing. I stood up and took a last lingering look before walking out of the Room that had been so integral a part of my life. Five years before when I was still only vaguely aware of the impending loss of this meditative space, I was moved to write the above-mentioned *A Room of My Own*. Looking back now, I am glad that I'd done so.

A week after writing my 'final thoughts,' when I dared to walk through the Room, there were yards of gaps - empty brown wooden shelves: it was depressing to see the once book-filled architecture made so unattractive by ugly bareness, thus changing the aesthetic of the Room. For a long while I reflected on the place where I had sat for thousands of hours thinking what were, at times, the unthinkable; the place where I dreamed the seemingly impossible and had achieved extraordinary things, including authorship. Put simply, for twenty-seven years, this Round Reading Room had been my *Spiritual Home*.

Prior to, and coincident with, my Lecture, the Whitbread Company had agreed to grant some funds to Michael Rolfe for filming the event and activities surrounding it. His ubiquitous presence in Cardiff during my two-day visit had engendered great expectations of the documentary film of my life: *The Sand Road*. Like the Whitbread Company, I too looked forward to further developments; and to this end, Mr Rolfe as Producer-Director wrote to Chris Hughes, Regional Director of Whitbread.

'As you may know, Ron visited Trinidad in late April and was able to initiate contact with a number of potential investors. These contacts have subsequently been developed and discussions are taking place about the details of facilities or moneys that might be provided from this source.

We have also been in contact with a distributor who has shown a positive interest in the finished documentary for distribution in both the India and the Caribbean markets. At the moment the proposal is being considered by Chris Blackwell at Island Films and we are hopeful that this may lead to us securing the balance of the funding required to complete the filming.

The Island Films operation, which includes a distribution arm, is such that they may wish to invest in 100% of the remaining budget required in order to maximise the potential profit share from the expected world-wide sales of the finished program. Rest assured that as an initial investor in the project, Whitbread will retain the right to a screen credit and a pro rata percentage share of any profits accruing from program sales as previously agreed.

Should you require any further information on the progress of the project do give me a call at any time.'

This was, I thought, fair and clear enough, for at this stage in making the film, it seemed that much depended upon Chris Blackwell and Island Films.

To maintain momentum in relation to the Documentary, a few days later, I wrote to a Ms Hocking:

'On the suggestion of my friend, David Pritchard-Jones, I enclose a proposal for a documentary film on which I have been working with Michael Rolfe in the hope that it might be of interest to Island film

*division. I think that the proposal and Michael's covering letter to
David are self-explanatory...*

*A short sequence of film on the Cardiff Lecture, funded by Whitbread,
has already been shot, and, provided that they receive recognition for
this funding, it is understood that Whitbread are happy for this to be
incorporated in the documentary. If there is any further information
which you require, please do not hesitate to call me.'*

All was well and I was more hopeful than ever. I even thought
that with much material already 'shot,' the talented Mr Rolfe had
enough footage of me on film (plus footage previously filmed
by others in my possession) to be able to put together a good
documentary.

Three months had passed since my first meeting with Zac Macaulay;
and having rekindled my interest in biography, to follow up on
a few lines of enquiry and research, I had written to Ms Wendy
Macaulay, asking for permission to view more of the family papers.
From her Surrey home, in a letter dated 20 May 1997, she wrote:

'*Dear Dr. Ramdin.*

*Thank you for your very interesting letter with regards to your intention
to write a biography of Lord Macaulay. Zachary (Zac) probably told
you that a very good biography by John Clive was published in 1973.
However I am sending a copy of your letter to a Cousin in Scotland
who is an expert and holds quite an amount of material to get her
comments. I shall be in touch with you again when I hear from her.*

Yours sincerely,

Wendy Macaulay'

This was indeed a positive response, but I heard no more from
Ms Macaulay and with a succession of projects to deal with, the
Macaulay project lapsed.

Thankfully, it was summer; August was hot and many days were
bathed in golden light; but a pall of gloom had descended and
hovered over Britain when it was announced that Princess Diana
had died in a road accident in Paris. Her death stunned the British
nation and millions of people around the world. Like many
people, I watched the funeral procession and service on television;

and for sometime, there was an outpouring of grief in Britain that would have previously been unimaginable. A. N Wilson, author and journalist was moved to appraise the Princess's life in an article in *The Evening Standard*. He wrote:

'If God or the Fates who rule our destiny had been writing the screenplay of the House of Windsor it could not have been possible to contrive an ending of greater cruelty or distress...

She was neither the complete saint...nor the scheming witch portrayed by her stuffier enemies. But she had elements of both in her nature, and we all responded to both...It is probably because Diana aroused mixed feelings in so many people and because these mixed feelings were so intense that the shock and grief will be...widespread and enduring... She was never quite the two dimensional media princess. She was that supremely rare being, a person who could project a real personality to millions and actually affect their lives. Indiscreet, modern, emotional - she was on one level everything which a royal personage trained in the stiff upper lip school of the Queen and Prince Philip, should not be. Yet by her peculiar genius for affecting multitudes, she demonstrated in the best moments of her life, what a royal family could be. And those moments were very good indeed.'

Not everyone agreed that the Diana phenomenon was a good or desirable thing. Nonetheless, the country as a whole was affected. Everyone had a view and I too was caught up in it. I was no Royalist, but I tried to fathom the so-called un-British outpouring of grief. Commentators and commentaries filled the media. Among the newspaper 'Tributes' one stated: 'Flowers at Palace Say What Words Cannot.' With Princess Diana's passing, there was a palpable sense that the British Monarchy would have to change. This was left to be seen, but for many days what remained an enduring image were the brothers Princes William and Harry walking behind the hearse at their mother's funeral. Death is no respecter of persons; and whether high-born or low-born, pain and grief were deeply etched, almost disfiguring the boys' faces.

Given that *Paul Robeson: The Man and His Mission* had been out of print, I approached Pluto Press in the hope that they would consider publishing a new edition. Anne Beech, Editorial Director, responded positively and my general optimism was enhanced when I met Andy McKillop for dinner in London. Having mentioned my first novel *Rama's Voyage* in the closing lines of my Lecture, I spoke to Andy, who was Editorial Director of Arrow Books, about it. A few days later, I received a card from him: '*You're going to send me some pages from Rama's Voyage which I look forward to reading. If it's not something that Arrow could publish, I'll pass it on to someone else here at Random House who might be able to publish it on their list.*

I hope to see you soon.'

The hard-nosed calculations of the publishing world I knew only too well, but I thought, it was worth a try. So I posted a section of the novel to Andy.

Meanwhile my good friend, Ms S, a teacher in Pimlico, had called me from her school. She was the *Times Higher Educational Supplement's* Book Reviewer of *The Making of the Black Working Class in Britain*. I enjoyed her company enormously and remember well our weekend visits to Lyme Regis in the South Coast and to Dieppe in France. These pleasant interludes, alas, ended too soon. But given that in life all good things must end, soon I was back on my relentless path. Alternating between office work and writing, I was contacted by John Thompson, Presenter of the BBC 'Omnibus' Programme.

As Robeson's biographer, Mr Thompson was interested in interviewing me for the 100th anniversary of Paul Robeson's birth. I accepted his invitation and recorded the Interview at Bush House in London, after which John said he was very happy with the result. When the Programme was eventually broadcast, so was I. The BBC World Service had repeated the broadcast and, taken together, millions of people world-wide had heard it. Another broadcasting triumph. Wow!

Almost by way of Introduction, I had sent a copy of *Homelessness and the Novel* to the newly-installed High Commissioner of Trinidad and Tobago, Sheelagh de Osuna. In turn, she wrote:

'*Thank you so much for sending me a copy of your Lecture - indeed this year's Whitbread Lecture at the University of Wales. I read it with great*

interest and can only say that I am proud to claim such a distinguished and erudite thinker as a fellow Trinidad and Tobago national.
  I very much regret that I was not able to attend the lecture in person...'

Following her predecessor Ms Trotman-McIntyre, given such remarks from Trinidad and Tobago's top diplomats in Britain, my sense of being, both as a writer and man, was enriched.

So my multidimensional-life aimed at achieving great and onderful things, persisted. Thus far, I had managed to cope fairly ell with the unusual situation of combining 'celebrity' with my y-job. So far, while much had happened, hopefully more was in e offing. One of the few things that happened with regularity, is news from my friend in the United States, Louise Floyd. She is ageing gracefully, but the last time that I saw her in London, ysically she looked smaller and more frail. In her letter dated 8 ctober 1997 she wrote:

Dear Ron,

sterday I visited the Swarthmore Borough Public library to check in ? current Books in Print...I'll secure the volume (World in View-st Indies, American Edition, published by Raintree Steck-Vaughan) you as soon as possible and mail them to you or arrange for the book ler to send them...

  Tentative arrival of your friend, Louise (back in London) will be anuary at Terminal 3...'

entative arrival of your friend' was an expression that I'd come to ow well. As if she couldn't bear to be away from England, she'd ady booked her flight and thinking of touch-down at Heathrow ort. She told me about her flights across the Atlantic for over ty years (twice each year) to visit the venerated Round Reading om. Like many other readers, she was deeply attached to the om. In a sense, she had become a regular fixture there. Thinking ut the impending change from Bloomsbury to St Pancras was thema, an awful prospect for her. For several months she'd n muttering her disapproval of using the much-talked about v 'high-tech' British Library building. She was distinctly uneasy out going there. Now in her Eighties, she was not only set in her ways, but also (in spite of a healthy 'walks'-oriented life-style) becoming less fit. She walked with difficulty because of swollen ankles; and sad to say, she presented a sorry sight. Nonetheless, carrying her ever-hopeful and forward was the prospect not only of once more being in the Round Reading Room, but also of walking in her beloved Lake District where she always stayed close to Dove Cottage, former home of the renowned poet William Wordsworth and his wife Dorothy.

Unlike Louise, though not a regular correspondent, it was good to hear again from my younger sister Annette.

'*The last time you called,*' she wrote on 13 October 1997, '*I think Pa said you went to the States. If you had gone already, I do hope that it was quite successful. We always like to hear about your trips and lectures. You always continue to make us very proud'...*

Six months had passed since the first books were removed from the Round Reading Room's first and second floor bookshelves. Now the 'gaps' had become extended rows of empty shelves which looked very odd indeed. The Room was transformed into something less than itself; it took some getting used to. As more books were removed, the cathedral-like Room seemed desecrated, and more clearly now the ever-lengthening empty spaces detracted from its symmetry and beauty. Now in October a significant juncture had been reached: having dreaded it, I watched as the very last volume was taken off the shelf in the Room.

Soon after, the *Yorkshire Post* under the headline: 'A VOLUME OF HISTORY CLOSES AS HOME OF FAMOUS WRITERS IS MOVED AWAY,' stated: '*This Saturday the Reading Room will close its doors and be moved to St Pancras. The British Library is expecting a flood of visitors in the next few days...Events to mark the end of the Reading Room housed in the British Museum in Bloomsbury, central London, include a Choir performance on Sunday, but in the meantime staff expect it will be crowded with those eager to catch a final glimpse of the room...*

Only those with official passes are allowed in, but a British Library spokesman said it was expected that many readers who had not visited for a long time would be there this week... "I'm sure it will be very emotional for some to come back for the last time."...'

For the first time, just before they were moved to the new site at St Pancras, I learned that the Reading Room had held 100,000 books. This statistic provoked thoughts of the first two years of the British Library's existence when I had organised and attended a continuous round of meetings as we all (Management and Staff) took tentative, but exciting steps forward. Now, as the rest of the mammoth Book Moves operation moved apace, press coverage of this historic moment reached every part of the civilised world. Many who had, at one time or another, used the Room felt bound to speak.

The novelist David Lodge, author of *The British Museum is Falling Down* was one such person. In relation to the *Daily Telegraph's* headline: 'UNDER THE DOME OF LEARNING,' he mourned the closing of the British Museum's Reading Room which he described as a 'refuge of indigent writers.' In this extended piece, Lodge revealed his feelings for the place: '*There is an amusing short story by Max Beerbohm called Enoch Soames about a neglected minor poet-author... whose title the narrator has forgotten who, in 1897, sells his soul to the Devil in return for a time-travel trip to the Reading Room of the British Museum 100 years later. He begins to bask in the posthumous fame he is confident of achieving by consulting the secondary sources listed under his name in the library's catalogue.*

A high price to pay, you might think: but the vanity of authors is notoriously insatiable. Entering the Reading Room on June 3, 1997, Soames eagerly opens the... volume of the catalogue at the appropriate page to find...only titles of his three slim volumes, with not a single work of criticism or biography appended to them.

If Soames had made his visit a few months later, he would have been spared this humiliation and perhaps got out of his bargain with the devil. He would have found the Reading Room closed, deserted by readers and stripped of its catalogue. For next Saturday the Reading Room will cease its operations, and those who wish to use the incomparable resource of the British Library must do so in its brave new home next to St Pancras Station.

This is not the time or place to rehearse the sorry saga of the new library's inception, design and construction...and it is too late to question the wisdom of the whole enterprise. We have the new British Library at last; we may as well make the best of it. But the closing of the Round Reading Room is a solemn moment in British cultural history, which deserves some elegiac notice...a unique place, frequented by some of the greatest minds of the era...but also by countless obscure, ordinary people, united by a common interest in the knowledge that can be found in books. It was Britain's Open University long before that admirable institution was founded or even dreamed of.

It has been the refuge of political exiles, a place of pilgrimage for foreign scholars, a resource centre for researchers of every kind, and a free, warm workplace for indigent writers...No other library in the world is mentioned so frequently in literature. And in no other library that I have visited is the physical space so imaginatively appropriate to its function. The new redbrick pile in the Euston Road will have superior facilities, more electronic gadgetry and should serve its readers more quickly and efficiently. But it is unlikely to inspire the same intensity and variety of emotions as its parent building in Bloomsbury: awe, affection, nostalgia, amusement and sometimes (human nature and intellectual life being what they are) ennui and despair...

Pictures can give some idea of...the Reading Room's design, but hardly of its astonishing scale... Sitting there was like having a cosy little room all to yourself.'

Unlike the desks in the Round Reading Room, by comparison, those in the new library at St. Pancras, I was told, had no partitions which many readers felt would be a loss of 'privacy.'

More newspaper headlines appeared in *The Guardian* and the *Daily Telegraph*: For example, 'Bibliophile's Temple,' 'Last Orders for Tearful British Librarians'; 'Readers tell tales of lust between the covers' and 'Reading Room slips into history books.' On the Room's very last day of opening, *The Times* article 'QUIET END FOR READING ROOM' which appeared on 25 October 1997, took a more muted tone: '*The 140 year history of the Round Reading Room at the British Museum is ending not with a bang, nor even a whisper,*' wrote Robin Young. '*As befits a space devoted to the pursuit of silent study, the room is reaching the end of an era almost soundlessly. The Reading Room closes today, but few readers are expected to be there for the final hours...'*

The closure had further consequences as Young added:

'The move is also regarded with some concern by the coffee bars, restaurants and bookshops surrounding the British Museum. "We had the most learned dining tables in London," said a manager of Pizza Express. "Our singles tables were regularly occupied by great scholars from all over the world and now we will not be seeing them again." '

But Young was wrong. On that last day, the Reading Room was almost full of people, the mood among them was unmistakeably sombre. Everyone had their own special memories; and many shared some of them. For me, the effect of the closure was, in a word, profound! In the strange atmosphere that pervaded the place that afternoon, following Chief Executive Brian Lang's poignant speech, for the first time in that environment, I drank what tasted like champagne (sparkling wine, I was told); and having consumed more than I had intended, later that evening with another member of staff, I found myself in the Museum Tavern reflecting on the end of almost thirty years of an extraordinary and full-on way of living and learning!

The next day in the *Sunday Telegraph*, Christy Campbell wrote:

'It was closing time in the BL yesterday. Assistants swept up books and whispered to readers as they had done for decades – "the Reading Room closes in 15 minutes." But this time it was different. At 4.30 pm Brian Lang the Library's Chief Executive addressed assembled readers: "I have never before been allowed to use my voice loudly in this space... This is the end of an era," he said, standing on the central desk under the middle of the dome..."

In the final hours, many among the 300 Readers who had turned up were 'dewey eyed.' Campbell continued: *'Emotion had been building all day...one elderly reader could not be appeased as he shuffled off. "Something of me has died today," he said.'*

Campbell's article caught the mood which I recognised, because I was there taking in the last moments.

JUGGLING WITH MANY BALLS;
CORRESPONDENCE WITH MARTIN GREEN

The day after the Reading Room's closure, still in a state of mild depression, having had my daily routine for so many decades disrupted, I received news from Anne Beech of Pluto Press about my out-of-print book *Paul Robeson: The Man and His Mission*. She wrote:

'Because I think its rude to give people less than positive news over the phone, I'm writing to let you know the outcome of our deliberations on the Robeson reprint. I'm very sorry to say that I don't think we can take it on...

This will be a disappointment, I know, but I hope you will understand that we're turning the book down not because we have any reservations about the quality of your work. Rather we just don't think we have the resources to handle and promote it properly and to greatest advantage...'

Anne kindly suggested other publishers including Jamie Byng's *Payback Press;* and, having earlier submitted a copy of the completed manuscript of *Black Britain* to her at Pluto Press, she concluded: 'Can we still talk about your Black History? I am very keen indeed to encourage you on that score...I think I should propose Lunch. It would be a pleasure - although I know it won't make up for our failure of nerve on the Robeson I'll hope to hear from you.'

I did not admit it to her, but at this time, the Robeson disappointment was more than offset by the potential publication of my 'Black History.' Following my fundamental difference of opinion with Penguin about *Black Britain*, disappointed though I was, given the tone and texture of the book, I regarded this parting of the ways as an opportunity and, as such, I'd been quick off the mark: I'd sent a copy of the manuscript to Pluto Press.

After they had had a chance to read the manuscript of *Black Britain*, Pluto Press's owner Roger Van Zwanenberg and editor Anne Beech invited me to discuss its publication. After our meeting in north London, as the underground train hurtled southwards, I marvelled how quickly things had changed: Penguin's loss, I thought, became Pluto's gain. Thus Ms Beech's interest allowed me to maintain my core orientation of *Black Britain* and proceed to write a timely and more meaningful book.

In the meantime, as my health see-sawed, a Senior Physician for the Occupational Health Department informed my employer that having seen me, he was now better able to assess my fitness to work in the basement at St Pancras.

'He has suffered from neck and back pain in the past,' the Physician wrote, 'but at present he is much better, and there are no major restrictions on him working in the basements. However…I believe his own doctor has already written to you and I feel that it is advisable that he should avoid prolonged standing for more than one hour at a time in one place. Walking around or climbing stairs is perfectly acceptable, but a largely sedentary job would be ideal.'

There I hoped the matter would end as I waited for a response. Feeling sorry for myself was not an option for regardless of health, I had much to do.

Makeda Coaston, an African-American whom I'd previously met and had discussions with while she was researching a Television Series on the African Slave Trade, sent me a Complimentary Ticket to attend 'AFRICA AT 40:' An International Conference to be held on 28-29 October 1997 to discuss 'African Independence: Past, Present and Future' at Westminster Central Hall.

'Dear Ron,' she wrote, 'Thanks so much for your input regarding the slavery TV series, no funding decision has been reached by Channel 4 to date. I'm sure you can make a contribution of value to this (Conference) initiative if you have time to attend. Stay well and keep writing.'

'Keep writing' indeed. This was an opportunity to re-visit Central Hall, but unfortunately I could not attend the Conference. Nonetheless, I was reminded of speaking in that grand Hall; the scene of my triumph twenty-two years before when I had addressed the 5000 who had gathered in protest against Government Pay Policy as it affected the low-paid in London and across Britain. Such an appearance in Westminster was all the more remarkable because so few black and Asian people were to be seen, especially at this time, addressing audiences in such great, even hallowed forums in Britain. Since then, in relative terms, in spite of incremental pay rises over the years, economically, the job in the British Library was still my only source of regular income. And so on 11 November 1997, while doing my best (in spite of persistent provocation!) to stay in work, given ill-health, Mr J of the Personnel Department, wrote to me on the matter of 'STAFF WORKING IN BASEMENTS AT ST PANCRAS.' Having accused me of writing 'Epistles' to him, Mr. J said Dr C had advised Personnel that I 'should avoid prolonged standing for more than one hour at a time in one place.'

Six days later, amidst the feverish activities and various problems encountered during the transportation and sequential placement of millions of books from Bloomsbury to the St Pancras building, a familiar blue aerogramme letter arrived on my desk. From Swarthmore, Philadelphia, Louise Floyd wrote:

'Dear Ron,

I have not heard from you since I sent word that your West Indies is out of print, but my grand daughter Kei had offered to make copies for you...

On 12 November I went to Pittsburg primarily to enjoy hearing a paper Edwin (Louise's son) was giving for the Classics Department (excellent). On Friday evening we went to a performance of Hamlet which was not entirely in the vein. The ghostly white rags of the murdered K. Hamlet dangled and danced behind the screen every few minutes. There was a Polonius of sorts but had no listing on the program...

My train arrived back at 30 Street Station, Philadelphia on Saturday evening with Ted and Kei at the Station to meet me...She (Kei) had presented me with the copies of West Indies on Saturday evening...

I hope you have an enjoyable Christmas...'

This was, more or less, a typical Louise letter. Importantly she was fit, well and as busy as ever.

Before the Whitbread Cardiff Lecture, Michael Rolfe thought he had knowledge enough to place, even categorize, me. But after the Lecture, he thought differently: he was now perhaps more respectful and forthcoming about progressing what he'd done so far on the film THE SAND ROAD. Listening to him, I was reminded of Alan Benns and his half-hour documentary NEWS FROM LONDON, which was filmed ten years earlier.

Though Michael Rolfe was also interested in my proposed Three

Part Television series 'The Reluctant Voyagers' about Indians in the Caribbean, with time his initial interest in filming THE SAND ROAD continued to grow. He liked the ideas we discussed and we proceeded to seek funding to develop both film propositions.

I was all for getting these new projects off the ground and, as part of refreshing my memory, I perused various autobiographical writings, among which was my 20,000 word Essay *Carnival in Trinidad* which I'd completed eighteen years earlier. At this time, not only did I *think* about writing a book-version of my autobiography, I began to *write* it! From the outset, I had thought about titling the crucial period of my childhood, boyhood and teenage years 'HOOFBEATS AND FOOTSTEPS.' And although the first words of the opening section of 'Hoofbeats' were not as free-flowing as I had hoped, I kept going.

By now, my years of research on C.L.R James's life and work continued to expand and, as previously, I took every opportunity to approach publishers, the latest being Publishing Director Tim Farmiloe at Macmillan. 'Yes, I recall with pleasure our meeting,' he wrote, 'I confirm that I would be keenly interested to consider your proposed biography of C.L.R James and perhaps you would kindly answer the relevant questions in the enclosed proposal form and return to me together with the two draft chapters. I will then try and let you have a reasonably quick decision.'

Predictably, I pursued this perceived opportunity.

Then, before the end of the year, I had the rare pleasure of receiving a letter from my first publisher and friend, the poet Martin Green, whom I'd not seen for many years. From his home in Newlyn, Penzance, on 10 December 1997, he wrote to thank me for sending a copy of *Homelessness and the Novel* which he said 'looks extremely interesting' and was looking forward to reading it. Like Tim O'Keeffe, Martin was on warm, friendly terms with a few of the big literary names of the Sixties, Seventies and Eighties. After his divorce from Fiona Green, a well-known personality in Fitzrovia and Bloomsbury, he had remarried and was now the husband of Judy Cook, a journalist and writer employed by *The Guardian*. Martin enclosed 'a couple of things' which he hoped 'would be of interest to me.' He wrote: *'Firstly, my own view of the Salman Rushdie affair, which was published in an obscure literary magazine down in Plymouth and hasn't been seen elsewhere. I sent a copy of this to John le Carre, and he has thanked me for it.*

Secondly, some lines I wrote after a trip to Mauritius (now a Republic) late this year. My sister is married to a French Mauritian and I found the visit very disappointing, which is why I wrote the lines, hoping to expunge the memory.

My own Gandesa Elegy is not really a poem to be read, but I'm hoping to have a public reading of this next year in February probably at the Conway Hall and I'll hope to keep you posted of this. And I will indeed give you a ring next time I'm up and hope perhaps we can have... a lengthier chat than we had.

Salud,

Martin G.

PS. And by the way, do get hold of a copy of Knut Hamsun's Hunger - a man exiled by starvation in his own city! I'm looking for an actor for my dramatization.'

Also enclosed was a surprise: A Poem by Martin Green dedicated to me:

'For Ron Ramdin

MAURITIUS
A volcanic fissure threw up
This island in the sea, a cup
Of blacknened rock which nature blessed
With tropic shrubbery; it dressed
An outcrop giving sustenance
To bats and birds and toiling ants.
Portuguese sailors were the first
To set foot here and slake their thirst;
It was a useful port of call
Between the East and West landfall.
Then came the Dutch who settled here
killed the dodo and brought deer.
The French were next who crossed the waves

With regal blessings and with slaves;
The Republic briefly made its mark
(The only sacrificial victim topped.
Was a goat whose head was lopped.)
Thanks to Napoleon next came
A British fleet to stake a claim
For George the Third, a monarchy
Thousands of miles across the sea.
The slaves were freed and in their stead
Indentured labourers were bred.
The island's now self-governing
Owing allegiance to no king.
The language and law of France remain
From England now is little stain.
Tourist hotels the repository
Of five hundred years of history.

from Martin Green
December 1997.'

A week later, on 17 December 1997, he was again in touch, and in the envelope was another of his poems relating to Colin MacInnes the celebrated white author of the novels *City of Spades* and *Absolute Beginners,* who had recently died. Martin said he'd written it 'when he (Colin) was still with us, but never dared to show it to him.' I was intrigued.

The Poem revealed much both about its subject and author:

'HEY WHITEY!
(A gentle corrective addressed to a well-known writer on class and race,
now dead. Alas!)
Hey, Whitey
Walkin' down the street
You and my black ass
will never meet!

Hey, Whitey
You nigger-lovin' boy
You ain't gonna share
My black-assed joy!

Hey, Whitey
Just 'cos you's queer
doesn't mean the black man
gonna kiss your ear!

Hey, Whitey
Why you so 'fraid
Of lovin' the white boys
Who've got ass to trade?

Hey, Whitey
Two blacks don't make a white
Why you so liberal
In broad daylight?

Hey, Whitey
You want some advice?
Just cut yourself a piece
Of poor-white vice?

Hey, Whitey
Why yo' hair so grey,
Too many black boys
Done passed yo' way?

Hey, Whitey
I'se gwine to fill you in
Lovin' don't take heed of
The colour of skin!

Hey, Whitey
Dey ain't no more

I got my problems
Don't give me Your!

Goodbye, Whitey
Don't bring me yo' care
I don't wanna love
De kinks in my hair!'

Looking back, after reading these lines I felt that Martin Green never quite fulfilled his potential as a poet and writer. Nonetheless he was one of Bloomsbury's best known, well-liked and liveliest literary figures. He was most encouraging of my efforts, especially while I was writing *From Chattel Slave to Wage Earner*, which eventually bore the imprint of his name in the publishing Company – Martin, Brian & O'Keeffe Ltd.

Now that Bloomsbury was no longer what it had been, reading Martin's letter and poems, I had hoped it would be possible to meet him. Some things had, of course, not changed since we last met: for instance, I was still writing feverishly and chasing publishers. And recalling times past in that most intellectual of places – Bloomsbury, now I looked forward to hearing from him again.

Then, as the year drew to a close, I heard from Dr Crook about *Arising From Bondage*. It was the news that I'd been waiting and hoping for.

'*Dear Ron,*
…I am very pleased indeed that you will be able to submit the final Script by about the second week in January.

Thank you for the copy of the letter from the Centre for the Study of the Indian Diaspora. We will obviously have to discuss the best means of ensuring that all interested readers and areas of interest are reached…'

Now at last, more than at any time, I felt at ease that the book was finally about to be published.

My correspondence with Martin Green continued in the New Year. *'Dear Ron,'* he wrote, *'I pass on the enclosed because I think it could well be that the organisers would think you might be a good person to run one of their Tobago courses (see Skyros in the Caribbean).*

Judy's been invited to do one on Skyros in October and the organisers seem to be very delightful people. I think the Cardiff Lecture might well be a good idea for the subject, and you might send them a copy, if it's something that would interest you.

Salud,

Martin G

PS I hope you got that Harry Diamond photo that I sent.'

The photograph referred to was of Martin Green and George Barker and in the background was John Henderson and myself. Being one of the best-connected men in the London-British literary scene, it was, of course, Martin who had introduced me to Harry Diamond. At the time, Harry was already a highly regarded photographer and, as the years passed, the quality of his work became even more distinguished.

NECESSARY ADJUSTMENTS AND VARIOUS ENCOUNTERS

With the Whitbread Cardiff Lecture still a resounding echo, the copies of Zac Macaulay's photographs that I'd ordered arrived. On the contact sheet it was good to see the range of Zac's 'Shoot' spread over two rolls of film; and underscoring our memorable meeting was a friendly fellow-feeling. While looking at the images, I marvelled at the set of circumstances through which I had acquired added insights and meaning because of my research into the lives of the Macaulays and indeed my visit to Zac's home. I thought about the sequence of extraordinary events that had led me to Walton-on-Thames and, all over again, I appreciated and felt the connectedness between Britain, India, the *History of England*, Caribbean slavery, indentureship, migration and the Whitbread Cardiff Lecture. As descendants of opposite sides of the social spectrum who had been drawn to work together on one of Britain's most prestigious literary Lectures, Zac and I (and before us Zachary Senior, Thomas Babington Macaulay and Abraham Ratnam) were proof of that historical continuity.

As always, the consequence of past events demanded attention. Linda Mitchell, BBC Editor of Community Affairs, had been in touch once more:

'I gather from my colleagues that you have recently written a book on the history of Asians. I may have the resources to produce an hour long radio documentary on the history of Black and Asian people in this country as part of the 'Windrush' celebrations. However, I would like to stress that the programme should cover the period preceding 1948, possibly going as far back as Roman times.

If this is a project you'd like to be involved in, perhaps you could call my office ...anytime next week.

I look forward to hearing from you.'

I was, of course, interested in Ms Mitchell's proposition and noted her recognition of the scope and depth of my knowledge of Blacks and Asians. In this respect, Ms Mitchell was like film directors Eric Davidson and Michael Rolfe; and it should be said here that long before the Phillips brothers (Mike and Trevor) had written their 'Windrush' book, I had already written voluminously on the pre-and post - *SS Empire Windrush* West Indians in Britain. It was therefore fortuitous that as Ms Mitchell had suggested the 'programme' would take a long view of this integral aspect of 'British history.' I could not agree more because I was a strong advocate of the 'long view' of history, combining at every stage, the general with the particular. Interpretations of history, underscored by such a perspective is, I think, far more informative and perceptive than only knowing more and more about less and less, valuable though such approaches and foci are.

Since meeting with Professor Henry Louis Gates Jr. at the Paris Conference in 1992, I'd been considering giving a lecture, at the appropriate time, in the United States. The 'appropriate time' because, no less driven than before, to say I was busy would be an understatement. But almost a year after I'd delivered the Whitbread Cardiff Lecture, feeling that the time was right, I wrote to Professor Gates, enclosing a copy of *Homelessness and the Novel* and suggested the possibility of giving a Lecture either at the New York Public Library or at Harvard University. On this matter, a date between October and December looked best. Why? Because significantly my commitment was to the imminent publication of two long-gestated and, in my estimation, important books: *Arising From Bondage* and *Reimaging Britain*.

At this time, things American were much in the air: for example, it was the year of the 100th anniversary of Paul Robeson's Birthday on 9 April 1998, for which, as Robeson's biographer, as mentioned I'd done a special Interview for the BBC. With the pleasant congratulations that came from many people who had heard the BBC World Service programme ringing in my ears, the day after the broadcast, as I entered the Tube at Tottenham Court Road Station, I found myself standing next to a well-dressed, distinguished-looking woman. In the carriage, jam-packed with other important-looking people, she stood out; a remarkable achievement, to say the least. A glance confirmed that it was Helena Kennedy, who had for years been much in the news as a leading Human Rights lawyer - a Queens Counsel and recently, a titled Lady known as Baroness Kennedy of the Shaws. We had not met for twenty years; and during our brief chat on the train we recalled our younger radical Bloomsbury days and years. I promised to drop her a line and later, I sent her a copy of the Cardiff Whitbread Lecture. From the House of Lords, on 11 May 1998, using light blue ink on buff-coloured House of Lords paper, she responded.

'*Dear Ron,*
It was so great to hear from you and wonderful not only to have news of your own success but also to receive your lecture - which is terrific.

I still remember our evenings, solving the world's problems in Bloomsbury!

It would be good to see you again. At the moment I am bogged down in a long trial but when its over I'll get in touch

Yours ever,
Helena.'

Those were the days, my friend, I thought. Our many conversations while Bloomsbury was being 'radicalised,' were not a reflection of mere youthful idealism. Remembering that time, Helena's words were all the more poignant because we were not kidding ourselves about 'solving the world's problems:' we had acted; indeed moved on, and in our different ways had made real and sustained contributions for the betterment of British society. As so often happens with people who are too busy to meet, should our paths cross, wherever and whenever that may be, I am certain that such a meeting would be no less warm and convivial than our chance encounter in the crowded carriage which interestingly occurred underground.

Being busy each day did not preclude evening activities. After all, as the world's greatest Theatreland, London boasted an exciting Night Life. The capital was a magnet for the arts and artists. On 19 May, I was invited to attend an Exhibition in Belgravia by the artist Cazabon, whose work relating to Trinidad encompassed a number of themes grouped as follows: 'Cazabon; Folklore; the Country Portrayed; Social History, Faces, Figures and Personalities; Images of Carnival, a compelling illustration of the well-spring for so much of the cultural expression of the Trinidad and Tobago visual idiom; Sculpture; and Glimpses of the Future.' Included in the accompanying illustrated book were 'pioneers' of the Trinidad and Tobago 'visual idiom,' among whom were M.P. Alladin, Boscoe Holder, Maguerite Wyke, Carlisle Chang, Sybil Atteck, Hugh Stollmeyer, Dermot Louison, Isaiah Boodhoo, Sonnylal Ramkissoon, Leroi Clarke, Althea McNish, Ralph Baney, Hetty de Gannes, Joseph Cromwell Assee, Horace de Bourg and Ainsley Yearwood.'

Having championed Trinidad and Tobago's causes and cultures since I came to Britain, such art was a source of cultural updating and great pride for me. Hearing the steelband and seeing the images in the book that evening in the High Commission, touched off essential memories that tended to generate nostalgia.

Towards mid-summer in 1998, I was reminded of my meeting with a Ms Hermer who had informed me that as a Film Director she was making a documentary on Paul Robeson and, knowing of my work as the biographer of *Paul Robeson: The Man and His Mission* she was interested in speaking to me. We eventually met in Bloomsbury and I was quizzed during a long and exhaustive chat-Interview. Because I trusted Ms Hermer and was under the impression that she would indeed call on me again so that we would proceed further to do an 'On Camera' interview, I co-operated fully. Weeks, then months passed with no word from Ms Hermer. Then her film was advertised as a forthcoming broadcast on British television. I watched the film with a sense of rising disgust. Why? As it turned out, much of what I'd said to the Director and had written about Robeson in my biography were integral to the Narration of the film. Of course, I was not credited. Why not? I thought. As a last resort, I wrote to Ms Hermer:

'I watched with interest your BBC documentary "Take Me As I Am" and was very disappointed that you chose not to acknowledge me (either for my writings or for the lengthy conversation we had during which I clarified some points you raised and offered advice and whatever guidance I could because I care a great deal about the contemporary significance of the life and work of Paul Robeson. Your omission of my name from the credits has not gone unnoticed by many people who continue to draw my attention to the programme, even now, several days on! To say the least, your response to my genuine openness and interest in the documentary, was shabby and unprofessional...'

I copied the letter to the Comptroller of the BBC. The matter rankled not only because of what Ms Hermer had done, but also because a few Black and Asian figures who were in key broadcasting (commissioning) positions (thanks to Equal Opportunities' campaigns!) did not think that I had the 'experience' on television, even though I was one of the few persons that the 'experts' were calling upon and consulting more and more. Once again, I was confronted with opportunist 'experts' masquerading as knowledgeable people, both in educational institutions and in the media. With such 'Gate-keepers,' I could well have done without Ms Hermer's attitude.

At this juncture, I'd like to make it clear that while the focus of my books was on 'Blacks and Asians' (and migrants generally) at no stage in my essential writings are White Britons and other Europeans excluded. While exile, homelessness, home and belonging are key themes, *respect for difference* and *inclusiveness* have been the hallmark of my literary endeavours which deals with the lives, identities and cultures of various groups and individuals.

At work, my physical discomfort showed no sign of lessening. Dr C, a Senior Occupational Physician, wrote to the British Library Personnel Department saying 'Medical retirement' was not an issue with which he would concur. While coping with my health problems, I requested a meeting with Ms M, Director of the Department which was still at Russell Square. After we had met, I sent her the following email:

'Thank you very much for your crisp and clear introduction to the Office's aims and objectives. Since our meeting yesterday, I have perused two folders of material, a booklet and the Job Description Profile of the Grade D post offered.

Now that I am better informed, I must emphasize the fact that this is a job for which I am entirely unqualified, the type of work in which I have no interest and one, the occupancy of which I was never likely to seek! This is neither what I expected when I spoke to Dr F… several days ago, nor what I had been in discussions with (Mr) S… about these past six to ten months. It is therefore fair to say that this is not a job I can accept,

Ron.'

Soon after, I also wrote to Dr F who was overall in charge of the Department.

*'I have never done any sales/Finance/Management work in all the 29 years I had been in the Library and, to be frank, I am not now interested in this area of British Library work. I am deeply concerned about being caught up in discussions about a position of such great disadvantage. **This is certainly not the direction in which Mr. S… was leading me these past months**.*

I truly believe that there is some other type of work that I can do to the best of my ability for the Library and I continue to hope that this will indeed be found.

Ron.'

Given that a final decision on my posting had yet to be made, I informed my line manager that

'… The offer you made yesterday assumes that after being taken off the Book Moves Rota over a year ago (on the recommendation of both my GP and the OHS doctor) I am healthier than previously. In truth, the opposite is my preoccupation… The idea of placing me once again

on a Rota (which had initially led to my doctor's recommendation!) is indeed cause for serious concern

In the light of this I hope you and Personnel will reconsider this particular posting.'

I copied this letter to my Union representative as well as to the British Library's 'Equal Opportunity Officer.'

A NEW ERA BEGINS:
OPENING DAY AT ST. PANCRAS: MY SHOCK!

For several days, I thought about the presence of an ***Equal Opportunities Officer*** in the British Library. This was, of course, a step in the right direction. All the more so, I felt, because eight days hence, the Head of the Nation, Her Majesty Queen Elizabeth 11 was due to grace the new redbrick St Pancras building with her presence. As expected, on 25 June 1998, she had formally declared the building open by unveiling a plaque in the foyer. The much talked about Reading Rooms were however not yet open to the public. Naturally my anticipation of Opening Day for Readers and writers grew. As the author of five published books, and having achieved some local and international prominence, after hoping and *waiting for quarter of a century*, I looked forward with much eagerness to seeing and using the much talked about Reading Rooms. For many days, I imagined this scenario: walking into the brand new Reading Room in the knowledge that my published books were indeed part of the Collections and hopefully they would be used by readers. This thought was pleasing; and in turn, my anticipation was heightened. Then, when Opening Day dawned, being the only member of British Library Staff still occupying the Room T2 Office in Bloomsbury, given that it was my special day-off work (Leave that I'd been careful to book well in advance) that morning from Bloomsbury I strolled across Russell Square and made my way northwards to St. Pancras. From the Euston Road entrance, I crossed the piazza and entered the building. Before me was the 'plaque' and just a few steps up, high above on the left wall, was the huge Kitaj Tapestry. Lower down, to the right, attached to the brick wall were busts of the Founders of the British Library. With an acute sense of this historic day and moments, I walked further up the marble steps towards the Humanities 1 Reading Room. It felt excitingly good as I pulled the door open. Just as I was about to enter, someone called my name: 'Ron!' The voice was not familiar. I turned sharply. Before me was Patricia Chapman, the Reading Rooms' Manager. 'As a member of staff,' she said officiously, 'you must allow members of the *public* first preference to use the Reading Room.' I was astonished to hear this and replied: 'Today, *I am* not a member of staff,' I said. 'Today, I am a member of the reading *public*. I am on *a day's annual Leave!*'

Ms Chapman was unimpressed, adamant. Though I was shocked by what she'd said, I tried to calm myself. My immediate thought was: perhaps, I should wait a while. So for a few minutes, I stood aside and watched as members of the 'public' (not an eager crush, but a thin, steady trickle) entered the Reading Room. Then, I walked over to the canteen area where Dr Brian Lang, Chief Executive of the British Library was attending a Reception with a group of people. They were sipping Opening Day celebratory drinks near the Cafeteria. Eventually I told Dr Lang what had happened. 'They won't let me into the Reading Room!' My words were, in the circumstances, as calmly spoken as I could manage. Alas, Dr Lang erred on the side of impartiality; in short, he could give me no good reason as to why I was being shut out.

As more time passed, still hopeful, I stood around and after about thirty minutes which I thought was long enough to have waited, I moved slowly back towards the Reading Room door and pulled it open. Once again, there was that voice: 'Ron!' I turned and there she was: Ms Chapman's order was that I should stand aside, remain *outside* the Reading Room. So repeating more or less what she'd said earlier, now I felt its full impact. In effect, I was **banned** from using the British Library Reading Room on Opening Day! I could not believe it. Why this unreasonable and disrespectful attitude towards me? Was her **ban**, her own doing? Or was it sanctioned from above? And anyway, was not such a ban a misuse, indeed an abuse of power? And to what purpose? Did this Reading Room manager not know that I was a recognised and respected author? Could she not free herself from her attitude towards me? And was that 'attitude' founded on Gradist prejudice? Or official policy?

Many regular readers, among them scholars and writers who knew of my daily presence in the Bloomsbury Reading Room were very surprised to see me standing around *outside* the Reading Room for as long as I had. At one stage, I felt a sudden rush of blood to my already inflamed head: in fact after Ms Chapman had spoken for the second time, I struggled desperately to summon all my inner strength to remain composed and silent as I walked away from her towards the exit! On my way out, a few members of staff who were greeting members of the public in the piazza, were most surprised to see me leaving so soon. 'You are going the wrong way,' a Senior Manager who was also a lover of literature commented.

'They won't allow me in,' I said. 'You should write a letter of protest,' she said. Protest?

'To whom?' I asked. 'I am a writer of books and yes, a man of letters, but not one who is prone to writing *protest* letters if I could avoid doing so.' These were the best words that I could utter as I tried desperately to contain my disappointment.

Thoroughly sickened by this refusal to let me use the British Library after my quarter of a century long wait for Opening Day simply *because* I was a *member of staff*, beggars belief. It made no sense whatsoever, I thought as I walked back to Bloomsbury. Approaching the familiar façade of the British Museum, I vivdly recalled what the former Chief Librarian, Sir Anthony Panizzi had said about the Museum's Round Reading Room: '*I want a poor student to have the same means of indulging his learned curiosity, of following his rational pursuits, of consulting the same authorities, of fathoming the most intricate enquiry, as the richest man in the Kingdom.*' With these words in mind, in a deeply reflective mood which lasted for a long while, I sat alone at my desk in the office, not feeling sorry for myself but saddened, aggrieved, overwhelmed by a sense of having been betrayed by a Senior member of the institution that I'd served well, for so long, and for which I had the greatest love and respect.

Thus amidst all the public anticipation and excitement, the grand Opening Day of the St. Pancras building was, for me, unforgettably sad. I have repeatedly asked myself then, as I do to this day: What good did this 'official' denial of my entry to this place of learning achieve? And once more I asked myself: Why? In effect Ms Chapman or whoever had instructed her to ban me, had indeed achieved their goal of denying me the legitimate right of entering the Reading Room. But there was nothing sinister about my desire to be in the room. My motivation was, as it had been for years before Ms Chapman came to the British Library, simply to use this wonderful, free public facility; and by satisfying my curiosity, learn a little more. What was Ms Chapman's?

ENDS AND BEGINNINGS

The announcement of the death of Rudy Narayan, the campaigning lawyer, came as a surprise. I immediately recalled my first meeting and chat with him. Since then I had seen him at various gatherings and had heard him being interviewed on BBC Radio Four, commenting on the law and aspects of policing *vis-a-vis* the Black communities in Britain. To my knowledge, he was the first professional lawyer to publicly criticise the British police and accuse them of being 'institutionally racist.' He was, without doubt, one of the cleverest non-white lawyers in Britain. At a time when there was so much intimidation, he was most courageous in speaking his mind, based of course, on the evidence before him. In this sense, his life and work had been invaluable.

At a time when racism was a 'disease' at the heart of English Society, Rudy fearlessly exposed its every manifestation, both in his chosen profession and in the wider society.

Only a few people from the African, Asian and Caribbean communities had made it through the obstacle course and the glass ceiling to a legal career in Britain, especially when Rudy Narayan became a well-known name. He had prevented many cases of miscarriage of justice, and took the lead in high-profile political trials such as the Thornton Heath 10, Cricklewood 11 and Bradford 12. Sadly, he was disbarred for professional misconduct from the profession he loved. His advocacy of the law in defence of the oppressed made him a highly respected figure; and not surprisingly in 1985 he published a book *Barrister For the Defence*. This was just three years after my own first Book Launch in Knightsbridge which the busy Rudy had found time to attend; an occasion when we had talked about our mutual interest in fighting injustice. Our conversation that night was fully engaged, animated; and I was pleased to see him enjoying himself to the point of getting tipsy. I felt at one with him for we were clearly 'brothers in the struggle.'

At Rudy's funeral in Brixton, I witnessed an unusual outpouring of respect from people of different backgrounds who had packed into the Church near the Town Hall. As the coffin was lifted and slowly passed between the pews and taken out of the Church, the steelband struck up an up-tempo calypso version of the Hymn *How Great Thou Art*. Near the church steps, while speaking to Herman Ouseley of the Commission for Racial Equality, I paused briefly to look as the hearse left the churchyard and carried Rudy's body up Streatham Hill on his last journey.

My commitment in the field of education could not be separated from that vital lifeline - my income. Therefore given my unfortunate health problems, maintaining my job was a constant preoccupation: On 2 July 1998, for example, the Personnel Department informed me that Dr C had given them the green light to employ me in an environment that was more conducive to my health. While this news was, for both myself and colleagues in management, most welcome, one thing was abundantly clear: I could not afford to be sick or infirm for very long.

After I'd submitted the manuscript of *Black Britain* to Pluto Press, I realised that a number of my other writings merited publication. On 8 July 1998, I contacted Anne Beech about a new book proposal entitled 'COMMUTER IMMIGRANT' which, as I stated, was the 'unifying theme of writings and lectures (given at various universities in Britain, France and Spain, in libraries and at conferences including the BBC Conference Centre) spanning the years from 1962 to 1997. Taken together, these writings would, I thought, constitute a timely and unique selection that was both historical and contemporary. After all, with few exceptions, given that every country in the Global Village had its 'minorities' increasingly people were becoming *Commuter-Immigrants*! By implication, this refers to the deep questions that preoccupied me: *home* and *belonging*; where and what is Home? as well as the evolutionary essence of social life - *respect for difference* and *inclusiveness.*

As often as I could, I tried to maintain a social life. Having got through the deadening effect of the loneliness and aloneness of the early months in England, more and more I grew to respect and enjoy the company of others; in particular those with learning, especially writers, actors and artists. Where they congregated there was always a lively discussion. As it was, time's arrow had the sobering effect of bringing Gaston Berlemont to face retirement from his beloved establishment the French House with which he'd become synonymous. He was born in the premises on Dean Street where he'd met the good and the great. With his distinctive handle-bar moustache, he fitted the role of Proprietor-Manager well and had become a respected figure.

Not surprisingly, the 14 July, Bastille Day was the day on which Gaston finally decided to celebrate his departure. Where was he going? was hardly the question. More importantly, the general feeling among those who knew him well was the fact that he would be greatly missed, not just as one of the West End's and Soho's most recognised characters, but also as a decent man.

The opportunity for a short break presented itself and I travelled to see my parents and family in Trinidad. To my utter amazement, the Union Park Race Course was no more: it was demolished. In its place, a Stadium had risen and named after a local athlete, Manny Ramjohn. What I had thought of as an iconic fixture, and taken so much for granted, was destroyed. It was a painful realisation. So complete was the destruction that there was no physical evidence that a Race Course had ever existed there. But though saddened, I had the richest of memories of hoofbeats and footsteps; the place of my childhood and youth that had so powerfully challenged and helped to shape me. I made the most of the 'break' for soon I was back in England.

Among the many people for whom the loss of the British Museum's Round Reading Room was felt most, was my old friend Louise

Floyd. For a while, she had been somewhat withdrawn: a certain look of sadness etched on her deeply-lined pale face. Still a regular Reader and keen Lake District walker, when I last saw her in the foyer of her favourite residence in London, the Tavistock Hotel in Bloomsbury, her feet were badly swollen. It looked painful as she sat, hardly able to move, much less walk up the marble steps of the new St Pancras building which she disliked. How ironic and sad I thought, that this woman who so loved walking (always briskly) was now hardly able to move. Naturally, I was concerned, but also pleased when, from her Swarthmore, Philadelphia home, on 31 July 1998, her trademark blue aerogramme letter arrived:

'*Alas, I've not recovered enough strength to permit me to move naturally,*' she wrote. '*I still use the walker in my apartment and more often than not have difficulty in getting to my feet.* **I have cancelled my plane ticket.**'

If reading this last sentence and reference to a 'walker' took me aback, what followed was even more surprising:

'**I much regret that I shall not see you and talk with you in the near future.** *May all go well with you and I look forward to some letters.*'

The general tone of Louise's message was of her facing up to the reality of her predicament. This was the shortest letter that she had written to me; and for the first time, there was no hope of better times. Her words reverberated and for a long while, I thought: How sad. As time passed, I felt a deepening sense of the finality of her words about the cancellation of her plane ticket and 'regret' that she would not see me in the 'near future.' How near? After reading the letter, though my mood was sombre and reflective, knowing how resilient Louise was, I hoped for the best.

TWENTY-FIVE

NEW YORK FILM TEAM ARRIVES IN LONDON TO SHOOT NEW ROBESON FILM

Some weeks earlier a film crew from New York had come to London to do a number of Interviews for a documentary film on Paul Robeson. Yes, another film project on Robeson and, as a potential contributor, once more, I was approached. Interestingly, this time I was invited to appear On-Camera. A special set was constructed at the Commonwealth Institute in Kensington and my filmed session lasted over 50 minutes! My Interviewer was none other than the distinguished film's Director Mr St Clair who, I was told, had worked with actor Wesley Snipes, among others.

After my lengthy, in-depth Interview, I felt reasonably pleased that I had not wasted words. What I'd said was clear, strong and relevant; and both the Director and Producer expressed their satisfaction! Afterwards with his small camera, Producer Chiz Shultz took a photograph of me and promised to post a copy. Before we parted company, he asked me about the 'Black Communist' that I'd mentioned. In turn, I undertook to find this man before the film crew flew back to New York. Later, I wrote to Mr St. Clair and Producer Shultz, offering any further help they might need.

My links with America were getting stronger which I felt was a good thing. On the morning after my filmed Robeson Interview, going through the letters that came in the morning's post, I opened one dated 24 August 1998. It was from 'SOCHI & FLOYD,' a combination of names that I'd not seen or heard of before. With due curiosity, I opened the envelope and read the following hand-written letter:

'Dear Mr Ramdin,
My name is Kei Sochi, grandaughter-in-law of Louise Floyd. I'm writing to let you know the very sad news of my grandmother's death on the 14th of August. She had very often spoken of you with great

fondness and respect, and I know that she was very much looking forward to seeing you at her beloved British Library. As she had no doubt told you, she was experiencing mobility difficulties in March and April, and soon after that she had problems with her digestion. We took her to the hospital in August, and when it became clear that she wasn't improving, we made arrangements for her to come home and to be with the books she had carefully and lovingly gathered over the years.

It was her last wish to be cremated and scattered in England (White Moss Common, the Lake District, to be exact). My husband Ted and I are making arrangements to bring her ashes to England the week of October 11th and tentatively to scatter those ashes on the following Wednesday. I hope I might be able to meet you during that week. My Grandmother **held you in the highest regard, and it would gratify me to meet the friend who had so many 10.30 am teas with her. (She kept all the notes you left for her on those British Library bookslips for tea).'** At this point, I paused, then resumed reading.

'I've written to many of her friends from Japan, Cyprus and Sweden, and to the Tavistock, but if you know of any other old friends who might be alarmed by her absence at her usual places in London, I would appreciate it if you'd let them know the news.

Again, I hope to meet you when we come in October. And a million Thank Yous for the wonderful Friendship you extended to my grandmother.

Sincerely,

Kei Sochi…'

Reading about Louise's death, the regard in which she had held me, as well as the 'Thank Yous' and extraordinary words from Kei Sochi touched me. I realised that Louise had lived just fourteen days after she'd written about her 'regret that I shall not see you and talk with you in the near future.' These last penned words provoked memories: I recalled first meeting her in the Readers' queue at the British Museum as we waited to enter the Reading Room; her unwavering respect for books, especially the Classics; her appreciation of Greek civilisation and culture, enjoyment of plays, concerts and her great love for England, her walks in the Lake District and being near Wordsworth's Dove Cottage. For almost twenty years, she wrote to me (often planning the next trip before she left England) and I believe those letters helped to keep her going. Indeed towards the end, they helped to keep her in good spirits and alive! A few days after receiving the news of Louise's passing, her grandaughter wrote:

'*Dear Ron,*

As I promised, I'm sending news of my husband Ted and my plans for our trip to bring Grandmother's ashes to England. We're still finalizing parts of it – but we do know that we'll be in London on the 10th…(on) 13th… we head off to the Lake District. 4 of her close friends from the U.S. will also be joining us for the ash scattering on the 14th. We'll be returning to London soon thereafter before our departure on the 18th. I hope we'll be able to visit with you, perhaps for tea?… Looking forward to meeting the Legendary Ron Ramdin! Sincerely, Kei.'

Kei, Ted and I met fittingly at the Tavistock Hotel in Bloomsbury where Louise had stayed for several weeks (at least 3 months) each year for about forty years. I felt honoured to have met this wonderful young couple. I spoke to them about the learned and fine person that Louise was. When I left Kei and Ted, walking south towards Russell Square, I remembered the time when I'd called Louise the 'female Michaelangelo;' and with much confidence, I can say that I have met few people who loved the Round Reading Room and Bloomsbury as much as Louise did.

Soon after the new St. Pancras building was opened, one by one, my colleagues in the Book Moves Team were relocated to offices in the various British Library departments. As the only one whose position had yet to be decided, each day for nine weeks I was left alone in the Room T2 office in Bloomsbury. This was quite a new and unnerving experience.

'They are trying to break you,' one of my former work colleagues remarked. Who were 'they'? Regardless of what the intention was, dutifully I came into the office and held my nerve. For someone as driven as me, doing 'nothing' was very hard work! So there was absolutely no chance of me remaining idle.

Then at last, I received a communication from Personnel. 'As you are aware, your case has been referred to the Human Resources

Placement Panel for a decision on your future posting.' These were ominous words: they had an air of unflattering specialness, as if I was deliberately set up and targeted.

'The Panel has considered your case carefully and has now decided that you should be posted on a temporary basis to the National Preservation Office for a period of 6 months, at the end of which your position will be reviewed formally and it is expected that you will transfer to a permanent post.

I am therefore writing to inform you that you will transfer to the National Preservation Office... with effect from Monday 5 October 1998...

I am aware that you feel that you are unsuited to this posting. However, I regret that there are no other suitable vacancies...'

By this time, the St. Pancras building was more or less fully staffed. Among the last employees to move in were those in the National Preservation Office (NPO) and the Book Moves Team. All members of the 'Team' who were offered 'placements' (usually after giving their preferences) were now installed. Initially, I had been offered a post in the NPO which I had turned down; now, they re-offered it with the threat that it was my *last* placement. This was hardly a career move; and after much thought, given the real possibility of losing my job, I decided to accept the NPO post which, at the time was located at offices near Russell Square. In my letter of acceptance, I stressed the importance of *reviewing the post after six months.*

Coupled with news of this new job, was a letter from my friend John Henderson and his partner Marlane who had announced their wedding. For the occasion, I travelled down to West Sussex and had an enjoyable time socialising with John, Marlane, their family and friends in the back garden of their house which was separated by a far from fortress-like fence from Ford Open Prison where John worked, appropriately in the library. The weather was glorious; and during the celebration I could not help remembering John's first marriage. On that occasion, I was his 'Best Man;' and after the wedding ceremony which took place in the Registry at

Finsbury Town Hall on Roseberry Avenue, Islington, we adjourned to a Reception Party in the Museum Tavern. To my knowledge that was the *first* wedding Reception-celebration to be held in that famous Bloomsbury venue. Unlike this 'Do,' John and Marlane's marriage and Reception were, of course, a very different affair and occasion.

John had been a good friend and an ever-engaging conversationalist. By now, we had known each other for 24 years and my brotherly feelings for John over that time were consistently warm during those demanding, hyperactive years in Bloomsbury and its environs. My sense of brotherhood and brotherly hope for John was that his union with Marlane would indeed grow ever stronger as time passed.

REIMAGING BRITAIN:
ANOTHER FIRST - EXPLORING DIFFERENCE

The final manuscript of *Black Britain* was now accepted for publication by Pluto Press and I was thinking of a title change. In essence, the book provided something rare in British historiography: in 349 pages of text (402 pages altogether, including Bibliography and Index), it took a long view - 500 years of Black and Asian history. Continuing with my theme of *inclusiveness,* my intention was to present in a major book, the Black and Asian presence in Britain in relation to the Scots, the Welsh, the Irish and the English. A large undertaking? Yes. And to what purpose? Britain had been a melting pot for centuries: a 'multicultural' Britain, long before Post-war immigration in the twentieth century. Considering that since the 1950s, the face of Britain had changed markedly, I continued my search to find the *appropriate title* for the book. Given my evolving ideas about social relations and society, somehow I felt that 'Black' in *Black Britain* was too general, too totalising for the emerging central idea of the new enlarged manuscript that I'd presented to Pluto Press. So if *Black Britain* was not the title, what should it be?

One evening while waiting for my son at the front gates of the British Museum, I thought long and hard about various themes and titles including 'Images of Britain' and 'Imagining Britain.'

I was getting close, but not quite there yet. Then it came with stunning clarity: *Reimaging Britain*! My son's arrival was about fifteen minutes overdue, time enough for me to find the elusive name of the book. So pleased was I that I felt it appropriate to celebrate the new title with my son that evening.

Apart from the title, something else had become much clearer: The idea and philosophy of 'difference' that I'd been slowly developing in my writings hitherto. With requisite courage and confidence, I had made *difference* (and importantly *respect for difference*) the central, recurring theme of *Reimaging Britain: 500 Years of Black and Asian History*. In principle and historically 'Blacks and Asians' were a major component of what constituted 'Minorities' in Britain. The book starts: 'Difference has always been a feature of humankind…' and ends with the words 'we should celebrate human difference.' What was of great significance is that my years of day-to-day practical concerns and my study of groups in societies had led to attempts to unpack the 'Oneness of Mankind' which I had referred to in my book on Paul Robeson. A related matter was why, in spite of the ten years of sustained pressure from Socialists of every kind, did I not become a Marxist or Trotskyist? Now in 1998 I'd begun to see more clearly that the Marxist tendency to totalise social relations (and thus human relations) was, and is, indeed problematic. Why? Because concepts such as class, race, colour, gender, religion and so on deals with *aggregates,* not with the individual. Thus more and more, I began to relate 'Freedom' and 'Human Rights' as meaningless expressions if, in essence, they did not apply to the *individual* which I felt was the acid test of any 'ism' or social theory. In other words, 'Freedom' and 'Human rights' should and must ultimately relate to 'individual freedom' which reduces it most meaningfully to one-to-one relationships based on 'respect for difference.' From this starting point, we get a grounded, clearer and more practical perspective of what 'freedom' really means.

On reflection, as long ago as 1972 when I began my first book *From Chattel Slave to Wage Earner,* even then I had been writing *inclusively* juxtaposing different groups and identifying the historical moments when they joined forces in Trinidad and the

Caribbean, though it must be said that 'difference' and, to a large extent, the lack of 'respect for difference' were endemic in that book. Bearing in mind that man is essentially a social being, this approach of **difference and inclusiveness** has been adopted in one way or another in most, if not all my other books and writings thus far.

Identifying difference and applying 'respect for difference' as integral to my writings was, in earlier years (and even more so now) a new approach; one that I've consistently followed for I believed that difference is the DNA of social relations and thus I coined the phrase: *'What is common to us is our difference.'* So, at this juncture in the evolution and application of my idea of respect for difference, I thought long and hard about the final pages of *Reimaging Britain*. In fact, the closing paragraphs of this challenging book are crucial to respect for difference, a reflection of how far we in Britain have come; and how far we have yet to go! They (Black and Asian people in particular) as I wrote: '...*like their forebears have struggled for the right to demonstrate their sense of identity in the heart of the former Empire. Today's youth demonstrate a strong sense of belonging: they want to win for Britain. And when they do, they proudly parade their Union Jacks. They do not want to be misrepresented like a Norman Tebitt pastiche. They are engaged in a massive pop culture that is seemingly everywhere in Britain...the popular contemporary trend now is "Cool Britannia," a phenomenon that can be found all over Europe. British identity is flagged up time and again in the debate over Europe, as though it is something specific (a sameness) common to everyone. The absurdity of this is emphasized when one considers that pluralistic Britain is considering whether or not to become more fully involved with pluralistic Europe. In making a decision as to Britain's future and the (European) Community, those in power should not forget the groundswell of feeling reflective of the "new" Britain of British youths and Black and Asian people generally. For their part, the actions they take proclaim that they too are integral to the historical flux, by inscribing as a corrective to the Western versions, their own histories; participants in the act of cultural renewal, of making and remaking themselves, of enforcing the crucial connection between anti-racism and culture, thus giving meaning to life as lived and creatively expressed in their own hybridised art forms which defy, redefine and transform "Englishness" and "Britishness" through a regenerative and liberating accommodation of multiple British identities. Thus Blacks and Asians vis-a-vis other groups have been making positive contributions to the process of reimaging Britain.'*

These paragraphs are followed by the concluding passages of this attempt at a *first inclusive history* of Britain in which the *main text* is about Blacks, Asians and other ethnic minorities and the *context* is about the peoples of the British Isles.

By this time in 1998, no one had attempted to write an *inclusive history* of Britain foregrounding Blacks and Asians and explicitly beginning and ending with the underlying and *essential* evolutionary catalyst that is 'difference.'

Against this background, in social terms, the insistent quest for 'Agreement,' the glue or binding element of communities presupposes 'disagreement' and therefore no 'Agreement' is (or should never be) permanent. On the contrary, every 'Agreement' has to (or should be) *reviewed and renegotiated*, as and when its subscribers deem it necessary.

Implicit in 'respect for difference' is, of course, 'Otherness' and, as I had said to my son about my new-found book title *Reimaging Britain*: 'For as long as there are human beings on the planet, the message in this book would apply.'

In November 1998, I was invited to attend a Reception for the first elected Indo-Trinidadian Prime Minister Basdeo Panday. I had, of course, first met Mr Panday some years before when he was both Leader of the Opposition and Leader of the All Trinidad Sugar Estates and Factory Workers Trade Union. On that visit to London, I'd invited him to join me for lunch, after which I took him on a tour of the British Museum's Reading Room where I presented to him a signed copy of my first book *From Chattel Slave to Wage Earner*. Before we parted company at Tottenham Court Road, Mr Panday had held the book close to his chest and said: 'I will always cherish the book. Thank you!'

Later, on one of my subsequent trips to Trinidad, when we spoke on the telephone, he said my book was helpful to him in relation to speeches he'd been giving in the 'House,' meaning the House of Representatives in Trinidad. Since then, the former Trade Unionist and Opposition Leader had become Prime Minister. Now on his official visit to London, I accepted the London High Commissioner's invitation to attend a Reception for Mr Panday who looked and behaved markedly different since our last meeting. Elevation to high office had taken its toll and intuitively, I thought it best to keep my distance.

A NEW JOB AND IMMORTALISED IN BRONZE!

On my first day of work in the Preservation Office, its Director took me aside and assured me that she would not prejudge, but deal with me as she found me. I welcomed this refreshing approach; a clear departure from all that I had hitherto experienced and especially now while rumours circulated that Personnel were wary of recruiting members of staff with 'reputations' for St. Pancras. Why? No one explained. Whatever 'reputations' meant or represented, it is worth noting that the Department I was then in was the last to move into the new St. Pancras premises and I was part of its Team.

Eventually, before the end of 1997, I did all that I could to effect a smooth entry and settlement of my new Preservation department into its designated space on the fifth floor. Once we were in the new premises, as I'd done whenever I was moved, I wasted no time in focusing on the task before me. For six months at least, I thought my job would be safe. After that, who knows? For now, I made myself as useful as possible; and, being naturally sociable, I got on well with members of staff, in particular with the Director. I learned a great deal about the vital Preservation-Conservation process of books and manuscripts; an area of knowledge and expertise, the centrality of which I warmed to for what is a great library without the means to conserve and preserve its irreplaceable printed and manuscript treasures. But conscious of my written request that this posting should be temporary, before Christmas 1998, after reminding my line manager, she in turn, informed Personnel of the pending situation.

Sorting through the Office post one morning, it dawned on me that I would no longer receive the familiar blue aerogrammes from Philadelphia. For a while, I dwelt on this fact; and, though I was invited to be present for the scattering of Louise's ashes, during this period of disorienting transition at work and in my personal life, I was unable to attend.

Some weeks later, Kei wrote to me enclosing three photographs of those final moments of 'scattering' amidst the beautiful, dramatic scenery of the Lake District. And so the morning queue of regular British Library readers was shortened by one, but I took the positive view that Louise's life was fully lived.

With hardly time for reflection, now, the accumulation of work: writing books, giving lectures, talks, radio and TV interviews, had brought 'popularity' (not celebrity) which I had coped with for almost 30 years. Along the way, thus far, among those whose respect I was honoured to have were a core group of writers, publishers and artists, including the internationally respected Interior Designer and Sculptor Alan Henderson. His creations were many and impressive. He was particularly proud of his work on the Palace of Brunei. Ten years before, Alan had attended my Book Signing Session at *Quevedo's Bookshop* in Cecil Court off St. Martin's Lane in London. He had bought a copy of my Paul Robeson biography and some months later when we met socially he said he liked my book. He told me he had retired as a Designer and was now fully engaged with Sculpture: his first love and the subject that had concerned him most when he was at Art School in Liverpool. He spoke for a while about his work as a Sculptor. Then he showed me a few miniature bronzes that he had done. 'I am doing writers,' he said. 'I would like you to sit for me.' I was flattered and listened: 'Could you get me some photos of yourself?' he asked.

'Yes,' I replied.

A few weeks after I'd sent several photographs to him, he invited me to visit his Studio in Greenwich. He needed me to 'sit' for him. When I entered the Studio, he untied a canvass draped over an object and removed it. It is difficult to say exactly what I felt at that moment. I was stunned to see a likeness of my head in clay!

'Would you take a seat here?' he said pointing at the stool near the image. For about an hour and a half he used a knife to take off bits and reshape areas of the clay bust. When he was through, he sprayed the object with water, replaced the covering and said: 'Let's go for lunch.'

We got into his car and as we drove away, he said, 'I'm going to cast your head *in bronze.*'

'*I do not have any money,*' I declared.

'I am not asking you for money,' he said. 'I will cast it at my own expense.'

I was astonished to hear this. After parking the car, we went into a posh-looking Italian restaurant. For a while, I was speechless, allowing Alan to hold forth about his work as a Sculptor. After a few sips of wine, as he explained more about his work, I found both my voice and appetite.

Since I had known Alan, I was always impressed by his easy style; a ladies man whose friends were largely a refined lot: busy, knowledgeable people engaged in all-consuming creative work. Among them were Allen Synge, 'Allan Allan,' Bobby Hunt and Ashley Brown. Alan had always struck me as an upright man, business-like and passionate about his artistic work, a true professional I'd say; and now in his role as Sculptor, so it proved to be. 'I'll give you a call soon,' he said as I took leave of him that Saturday afternoon in Greenwich.

Walking away from the restaurant, all over again, I could hardly believe what I'd seen of the clay head, then the experience of sitting for about an hour as he worked on the clay and my amazement that he was going to cast it in bronze!

When he eventually got in touch, he invited me to visit his home in South London. From a shelf in his living room, he lifted a greenish-gold object and placed it on the coffee table. Now I stood face to face with an image of me in bronze: it was the finished sculpture, a bust of me staring ahead. For a while, once more I was speechless. My feelings were imprecise, difficult to describe. Alan's dark, piercing eyes were fixed on me. 'It is yours!' he exclaimed. It was the first time that I'd seen him in a mood so relaxed, quite unlike his normal hard-working, business-like self. 'I have the cast,' he said. At that moment, a photograph that I'd seen of the death-mask of Abraham Lincoln came to mind. And looking intently at the bronze face and head suddenly I was drawn into a new realm; the surreal sphere of being immortalised.

Later, I placed the bronze in a bag. It was heavy, but not cumbersome. Travelling by bus from South to North London, through the traffic and ever-present bustle of crowds of people, especially at the tourist zone that is Trafalgar Square, as I passed the National Gallery and National Portrait Gallery, I was overwhelmed to be holding a genuine work of art, conceived and created in London; a bronze likeness of me. How odd, I thought, to be carrying my own image, which made this the strangest of journeys. Then I remembered what Alan had said about the intention behind his work of art, in particular, the slight tilt of the upraised gaze.

'If anyone ask you about the bust, tell them it is my interpretation of you!' he declared, unabashedly proud of his creation. 'I decided that you should be looking up and ahead,' he added. 'You have that positive look about you.'

Amazed and deeply moved by what I was carrying home, I could not argue with the artist's interpretation of my persona.

By now, I was more attuned to my Northwest London neighbourhood, in the main, the direction of travel to and from work, as each day I trod the High Road towards Kilburn Underground Station which ironically was on ground level. To reach my Central London destination, bearing in mind it was rush-hour and allowing for cancellations, if I was lucky I would board two trains: first, the Jubilee Line then change at Finchley Road for the Metropolitan Line to Euston or King's Cross.

In the absence of the familiar Bloomsbury Cafes where, for so many years habitually I had tea and toast, now, I had to find new breakfast places in St Pancras. Alas there were fewer cafes around than I'd expected and, in many ways, I was reminded of the stark difference between Bloomsbury and St Pancras, which was regarded at this time, as a disreputable area. But, I hasten to add, it was this difference of mood, architecture and the feel from district to district that was, and is, so wonderful and fascinating about being in this great sprawling city. And I should know; for having lived in many places and travelled from so many directions, I had seen a variety of streets at 6.00 a.m and at night for almost four decades. Yet my curiosity remained undimmed; renewed at every turn by London's mesmeric immensity.

After all the years of research for my C.L.R James biography, my concern that no publisher had so far been found, now took a new and hopeful turn when I met Caryl Phillips. The West Indian novelist, who was an Editor at Faber and Faber had reviewed my 'pioneering' book *The Making of the Black Working Class in Britain* and, had also written a book about James and Cricket. Taken together, this augured well and, at Mr Phillips's request, I sent him a Synopsis and List of Contents relating to '*C.L.R James: A Life.*' A few weeks later, on 26 December 1998, he wrote:

'*Dear Ron Ramdin,*
Good to meet you at Robert Antoni's book launch and to hear of your on-going C.L.R James biography. I recently received your material, and read through it with great interest. While I think the proposed shape of the biography is fine and stimulating, even as I read your outline I suspected that Faber would be unable to commit to a major biographical work at this stage. Having now discussed the proposed book with some colleagues, the disappointing conclusion is that Faber won't be able to support the James biography .
I think the idea of a major biography is a wonderful one, having both met James and written on him, but the logistics of publishing at Faber means that we're reluctantly going to have to pass this time. I wish you all the best placing this book, and I hope that 1999 is a successful and productive year for you. We'll no doubt run into each other during the course of the year, and be able to catch up.
All the Best...(signed)'

My feeling that the Caryl Phillips-Faber connection was perhaps the best opportunity yet of getting a Commission for the book was proved wrong; and if hitherto I'd been too optimistic, now I was prone to reconsider the journey I'd taken on this long-standing, demanding project. But disappointing as the trend was, always a believer in what I do, I remained positive.

Once more, it was Christmas Day. I visited my son at his Islington flat as a grandfather and enjoyed being with my grand-daughter Georgia who was now just over one year old. That morning I learned that Georgia was going to be joined by a brother, due in July of the new year. Wow! In celebratory mood this news of another grand-child was wonderful; and all the more so because I did not have to be at work in the St. Pancras Basement the following morning. Between grand-children, so to speak, one born and the announcement of one to come, this Yuletide celebration was enhanced beyond measure.

On matters to do with archives and libraries about which I had knowledge gained over 36 years, just before the end of 1998, I received a letter from the Arts Council of England. It was written by the Senior Policy and Planning Officer responsible for Cultural Diversity, Naseem Khan:

'Dear Ron,

You may remember being invited to the meeting of an ad hoc Black Archive Working Group in 1996.

The discussion which took place at that meeting guided a programme of research which was subsequently undertaken by Jacob R(oss) and Valery Small... on behalf of the Arts Council of England. Their draft report Archiving the Arts of England's Culturally Diverse Communities – A Mapping Survey has now been delivered, and we would like to discuss it with you before proceeding further.

I hope you will be available to consider the issues and recommendations raised by the report...I am enclosing a copy of the notes from that first meeting for your information.

An early indication of your interest and availability would be greatly appreciated...

I look forward to hearing from you.'

Such a policy-oriented meeting was invaluable in mapping the way forward. So who were the other Invitees? They were Catherine Ugwu (ICA), John La Rose (New Beacon Books), Margaret Busby (Publisher), Gilane Tawadros (Director of International Visual

Arts), Jatinder Verma (Tara Arts Centre), Zig Layton-Henry (Centre for Ethnic Relations, University of Warwick) and Sam Walker (Director of Black Cultural Archives).

These were pioneering meetings and having attended an earlier Arts Council Meeting a few weeks earlier on 17 October, I assured Ms Khan of my attendance at the meeting to be held on 15 February 1999. Now (and as I'd been arguing for years) *inclusiveness* in most local and national institutions was still not integral to policy-making. There was a great deal of work to be done. Thus my readiness to serve was not motivated by a sectarian Agenda, but by my acute sense of the narrowness of 'British' history which, in multicultural Britain needed to be broadened.

At the turn of the New Year, outside my library office hours, I pressed ahead with conception and execution of the literary work in hand. By so doing, as usual I was making my own luck, for as I had learned only too well: *nothing ventured, nothing gained!*

Fortuitously in January, Professor Skilton was approached by Dr David Walton of the University of Murcia about potential participants (lecturers) for a week of British Culture in Spain. This promised to be a significant Event and, as one of the Speakers, Professor Skilton suggested that I should join him and the two other participants that made up the quartet of British Speakers. Following my Lecture at the University of Seville in 1991 and subsequent travels in Andalusia, giving a Lecture in Murcia eight years later was an attractive proposition. So I accepted the invitation of returning to Spain, albeit it to another region, to give one of the four high-profile Public Lectures in April.

Meanwhile, I remained steadfast in my habit of being punctual at work each day, arriving in the office around 7.00 a.m and finishing early at 4.00 p.m. Within these hours, given the circumstances of the new job, I did all that was asked of me and over the weeks, gradually I got to know one or two members of staff much better, including Jane Fowler, who had previously worked with me on the Book Moves Team.

'What do you think of Tony Blair?' Jane had asked me during a conversation one morning.

'He's a clever politician,' I said. 'But, perhaps too young to be Prime Minister.'

'What do you mean?'

'Well, I mean he's *clever,* but perhaps not wise,' I added. 'One day he may make a misjudgement (which is only human) that could undo him.' No more was said about Mr Blair, though Jane and I continued our talk about aspects of the Department for which we worked and its vital objective of conservation and preservation of invaluable books and manuscripts in the British Library.

Still finding my way in the new building and around the Euston-St Pancras area, on Valentine's Day, I visited the Euston Flyer for a get together with other members of Library Staff. Many were in high spirits and inevitably we reminisced about the old days in Bloomsbury. Soon the talk moved on to prospects for the future. Struck by how few among us were optimistic, I was determined that this pessimism should not infect me, even though my 'temporary' position in the new office was still unresolved.

It had been a while since my On Camera participation as biographer in the making of the American-Produced and Directed Paul Robeson film *Here I Stand* and I'd been wondering about its outcome when, at last on 18 February 1999, I received news. Peter Williams from 'PWTV International,' the Company that had invited me to be filmed, wrote:

'Dear Ron,

Re: "PAUL ROBESON: HERE I STAND" documentary for American network television.

I am writing to tell you that the programme for which you were interviewed last year will be broadcast on the 24th February (9-11pm Eastern Standard Time) on WNET in the United States. In the event of it being screened in the UK, we will let you know as soon as possible. In any case, the American production company, Menair Media will send you a video of the completed programme.

Menair Media have explained to us that because they wanted to include footage of Robeson himself in concert and his speeches around the world, they were forced to sacrifice many of the interviews (which totalled some 60 hours). Unfortunately, yours was one of those...'

These words had a familiar ring in that once again, my contribution and participation in a Robeson film was denied. To sugar the pill of bitter disappointment, Peter Williams added:

'Let me assure you that the exclusions had nothing to do with the quality of the interview, but rather with those aspects of Robeson's public and private life that were felt should be included...'

Soon after, Chiz Schultz, the film's Producer, also wrote to me:

'Dear Ron,

...I hasten to add that a much longer version of the documentary will be produced after the broadcast. This version will be available for schools, universities and archival purposes for generations to come. This version will, of course, include practically all the interviews we videotaped.

Again, I'm sorry that the restrictions of broadcast time made such tough choices unavoidable. But I want to assure you that your contribution meant and will mean a great deal to the project in its future, ancillary uses.'

For 'ancillary uses' but not for the full public, international broadcast. Was the final decision down to Paul Robeson Jr? I pose this question because he had done his best to side-line my book of his father and the Hollywood Movie based on it? Or did the film's Director and Producer (for whom I'd signed a contract in relation to the Interview) have another agenda? Who knows?

Whatever the truth, the stark fact remained that in spite of my best efforts of preparation and performing before the cameras for some 50 minutes, I did not appear in the final cut!

All things considered, my thoughts were positive. Having agreed with the organisers, looking ahead to my Lecture in Murcia, I contacted Dr David Walton of the University of Murcia. 'Please confirm,' I wrote, 'the date on which I'm scheduled to give my lecture and send all other relevant information about the Lectures.'

After decades of exploration, of serious thought, reading and study on the much bandied about words and calls for 'freedom' and 'human rights,' time and again I had revisited such expressions and now I was confident enough to be more explicit about what I felt to be the way forward towards more meaningful social relations. Important as 'groups' were, the more I thought about them, I began to see that they needed to be unpacked in a similar way as I'd been doing since I'd written about, and became deeply interested in the 'Oneness of Mankind.' What did this statement really mean? Surely this '*Oneness*' was too much of an *aggregate* to make practical sense to each person of whom it could fairly be said: one size does not fit all. And so more and more I came to see difference and recognition of the individual as increasingly significant; indeed as the *key* when talking about 'freedom.' I came to understand that without 'respect for difference' in society, all else was that bit more problematic, taking us further away from the essence of what should constitute the 'Common Good,' good-will and therefore democratic and more meaningful social relations. Thus on the eve of the publication of *Reimaging Britain* I was reminded of the opening words: '*Difference* has always been a feature of humankind…' and what I had stated at the end of this inclusive, multi-group story: '…we should *celebrate human difference*.' For me, these words were especially resonant and germane whatever changes there were in social *composition*.

And so, applying *difference* in an *inclusive way* to a work of history, as set out in *Reimaging Britain* (and either implied or explicit, in varying degrees in all my other books) marked a shift away from the approach of other British historians. It was with such clear thoughts that I anticipated the eventual publication of *Reimaging Britain*.

Meanwhile publishing procedures on my other and long gestating book *Arising From Bondage* moved apace. The publisher I.B. Tauris and I were, at last, in the final stages and, according to the editor, things were going to plan. In the circumstances, it occurred to me that I was about to repeat a very rare feat: Ten years before, in 1987, within six months of each other, I had the great honour of having two major books: *The Making of the Black Working Class in Britain* and *Paul Robeson: The Man and His Mission* published. Now in late 1999-2000, a double-publication was about to happen again! Given that such an recurrence verged on the stuff of dreams, authorial levity apart, my feet rested firmly beneath my desk in the St. Pancras office as I awaited news of my temporary job review and a decision on my pending new placement. To this end, I emailed Personnel: 'I now have about two weeks left of my six month employment in the Department, I am looking forward to leaving here and to a permanent posting elsewhere.'

The reply was prompt.

'Negotiations are still going on and at this stage I regret that I am unable to give you any further information.' The communication ended with the statement: *'individuals not redeployed are to be retained in their existing Directorate until arrangements can be made to post them.'*

To avoid the real danger of being left in 'Preservation,' I responded on 25 March 1999:

'I am writing to thank you for your email of 16 March in which you said you could not as yet, give me any information about my pending transfer from the (Preservation Department) because "negotiations are still going on."

While you deliberate, I would like to briefly review what has been communicated to your office over the past five months... After Ms. H wrote to me on 18 September 1998 stating that my posting to the (Department) was only on a 'temporary basis' (for 6 months at the end of which I will be transferred to another post) in November last year I informed you of my strong feeling about the inappropriateness of the job, but assured you that I would do my best for the remaining months until the end of March 1999 ...as I approach the end of my contractual obligations which I have honoured fully, I look forward to my transfer.'

Having copied this to all relevant Senior managers in the British Library, on 13 April 1999 I replied to Dr F's earlier letter: 'over the last 6 months, no one in this office has been in any doubt that I was anxiously anticipating (especially these past few weeks) a transfer out to another post...'

This was followed by another letter to Personnel:

'I am writing in response to your letter of 1 April informing me that the Staff Planning Group has decided (without informing me of a change in the terms of reference) to "transfer" me to a permanent D Post in (the Department).

Throughout the six months of my "temporary" posting here... I was, at no stage, given to believe that I was not going to be transferred out of this (Department). I am very disappointed that I am still here in Preservation, a job in which I have said repeatedly I have no interest. I was not contracted to work in Preservation, and would have thought that until six months ago, with my D. Lit from the University of London and 30 years experience in library work (26 years of which has been in the British Library) surely I could better serve this institution in another capacity...

After all the correspondence that has passed between myself and Personnel these past months, given my deepening unhappiness here, I do hope that my appeal for a transfer to more appropriate employment will be effected very soon... Given my... history of illness, the present situation is placing me under a great deal of stress and is having an effect on my health.

I do look forward to hearing from you....'

Like the previous letter, this one was copied to all the relevant persons in authority. My appeal could not be clearer.

SPEAKING IN MURCIA, SPAIN: 'MULTICULTURAL BRITAIN'

I had known and socialised with the artist (of 'Inflatables') Maurice Agis for many years, and given his part-time residence in southern Spain, when we met in London, I had mentioned my forthcoming visit to Murcia. Just before travelling there, I emailed him to say 'Hello' and express the hope that he would be able attend my Lecture. I ended by saying: 'I'll be leaving this office in about 30 minutes and if I don't hear from you, I trust we'll meet in Spain!'

So, leaving my office with some work matters unresolved, on 20 April 1999 I arrived at Alicante Airport and took a taxi to Murcia. The Spanish driver sped so dangerously fast along the highway that at times, I was quite fearful for our safety. Eventually, we reached our destination: the Hotel Siete Coronas. On arrival, I was surprised to see that the 'Lectures' sponsored by Caja Murcia was advertised as clusters of large posters stuck on billboards in the city centre: they were designed with the colours of the Union Jack and *I Semana de Cultura Britanica* emblazoned across it.

The next day, at 7.30 p.m I made my way to the Conference Centre on Gran Via with an additional copy of my Lecture for the Spanish 'Translator,' who was expected to translate simultaneously as I spoke. Once again, as I stopped to cross a busy street, I saw another cluster of Posters on the side of a building. How weird is this, I thought: Seeing my name and the title of my 'Talk' up there.

When I entered the auditorium many people were already seated; and soon after I'd taken my place on stage, amidst the hush just before proceedings began, a man and woman made their way along the aisle towards the stage. As the man drew closer, he looked familiar: it was my friend from London - Maurice Agis. He was with his partner, Paloma. They had travelled from Alicante to be here and I was thrilled by this wonderful surprise. I felt it was to my credit that yet again, I was in a European country ready to speak about 'Multicultural Britain.' Unlike the University of Seville Lecture which was exclusively for students, this one was a *public* lecture; but no less controversial in its subject matter.

So taking the central concept and message forward, quoting from my book *Reimaging Britain*, I opened by saying:

'Difference has always been a feature of humankind, and differences were present and necessarily integral in human civilisations long before Britain became an expanding Empire... to begin with, it might be useful to consider the making of the "English Empire" which emerged in the British Isles during the sixteenth century, and crucial to this emerging entity was the element of difference in the relationship between England, Scotland, Ireland and Wales whose histories were intertwined rather than separated. Indeed much of the varied British Isles' interests became increasingly attracted to the growing commercial wealth of London and southern England as trade with Ireland, Scotland and Wales by 1500 connected the British Isles to the London markets.

The links between these regions have been more often than not, missing from histories of England, a distortion which tended to exclude the other cultures of the British Isles...'

In conclusion, I said:

'The repeated Government slogan that Britain must change if it is to survive, is true enough. But in saying this, it cannot for much longer continue to overlook the stark fact that multiculturalism has brought profound changes in "British culture" as new identities came into being, thus shifting to some degree, the stereotypical approaches to people in terms of their gender, ethnicity, sexuality, age and class… British civilisation and society has come a long way and we should not miss the opportunity at the millennium not merely of acknowledging, but also of celebrating the creative potential of human difference.'

Later that night I was treated to a sumptuous dinner by Professor Monroy and Dr Walton; and before leaving the city, Caja Murcia presented me with a special book on Murcia. This was a fitting gift, I thought, and given this airing of British 'multiculturalism' to the Spanish public, I left Murcia feeling as if I'd added something of value to our thinking on social matters in Europe.

Towards the end of my first week back in London, as if to consolidate what had taken place in Spain, I wrote to Dr Walton thanking him *'for the time you spent with us (the two other speakers: Sue Bradbury and David Skilton). All of it was most enjoyable, which emphasizes the necessity of such interludes in life! On the way back, David (Professor Skilton) spoke to me positively about the possibility of Caja Murcia's bilingual publication of the lectures. Please let me know when such a publication is likely to happen…'*

Eventually after my six-month employment had been completed, my work was assessed and an appointment was made for me to see my Reporting Officer. This was a crucial moment for me because a negative Report would clearly have had bad consequences. As it was, I received a very good 'Report' with the recommendation that the 'Temporary' post I was in be made *Permanent!* Reiterating that I was not interested in this particular job, once more I wrote to the Head of the Department, copying my letter to other Heads and to my local Union officials.

Early one morning, the Director of the Department approached me: 'No more letters Ron,' she said and promptly informed me of my transfer to the Oriental and India Office Collections. I was greatly relieved to hear this, even though I was laid low by a heavy cold.

She said that I should go and see David Blake, Head of European Manuscripts in the India Office Collections on the third floor. The Job Description of this new post, as explained to me, had a central Curatorial element to it with which I was happy. It entailed working with the 'Collections;' something that I had hoped for, especially now that I had greater knowledge of the Library. Reflecting on one Manager's earlier insistence that I be transferred to the Accounts Department, I asked myself: what was the point of experience and knowledge of the kind that I had, if it could not be implemented and imparted. It was (and is) after all, the very reason why I write! Put simply, I was pleased with a large proportion of the job and looked forward to learning all that I could about the India Office Records and European Manuscripts.

But before I had left the 'Temporary' Post on 30 April 1999, the Director of the Department Ms V sent me a personal, hand-written letter:

'Dear Ron,

This is to say "thank you" for your efforts on behalf of the office over the last 6 months. I have appreciated your positive attitude and have had good reports of enquiries of your helpful approach.

Good luck in the new post and keep up the good work on behalf of Preservation.

Best Wishes…'

In my 37 years of Library work, this was the most direct and honest appreciation of my job performance from any manager and unusually, in this case, it was from the Director herself! The warmth and genuineness of this message is evocative of the mutual respect that had underscored our work relations from the outset. If my arrival was questionable, now my departure was infused with enough good feelings to prepare and uplift me for the assignments that awaited me two floors below.

With the matter finally resolved, in a lighter mood now, I felt more than duty-bound to write to another very helpful British Library Director, Dr F, who also happened to be a woman:

'RE-TRANSFER...

Following our meeting on Tuesday, I met all the Managers concerned
with the... vacancy and I am writing to formally confirm my
acceptance of this post which, it was agreed, I shall begin on my return
from Annual Leave on Monday 7 June.'

Now, at last, seventeen years after I was recommended for
Curatorial promotion, I was placed in a job dealing directly with
British Library Manuscripts and Records. It was the closest that
I'd come to being employed to do 'Curatorial work' in the British
Library. From then on, notwithstanding the variations in conduct
between staff and management, I began a friendly and productive
working relationship with David Blake who was in charge of
European Manuscripts.

In spite of the physical aspects of the job, ranging from the
relatively straightforward foliating of European Manuscripts
(including a large number of letters!) to moving around files, boxes
of papers and large volumes, I felt it was a job well worth doing
which confirmed my insistence on moving on to work with the
Collections.

By September of that year, as my interest in, and knowledge
of, European Manuscripts grew, I came to know my new office
colleagues better and settled down to learn all that I could in yet
another department of the vast British Library. If a challenge
is what it could be called, I relished it: in other words, as with
everything else that I'd done thus far, I hoped to achieve nothing
less than mastering the job.

A TELEVISION FILM BREAKTHROUGH:
THE UNKNOWN SOLDIERS

On 28 September 1999, if I had any doubts (I didn't) now I
received proof positive of the importance of my recently published
book *Reimaging Britain*. This came from an influential and
informed reader, Jane Stanton, a Producer and Film Director at
Granada Television in Yorkshire, who contacted me following an
earlier telephone conversation.

'Dear Ron,
I am writing to confirm that we are very grateful that you have agreed

to be filmed for the Memorial Programme (The Unknown Soldiers) on
Thursday 30th September.

We will be at the Imperial War Museum's All Saints annexe to start
at 8.30 a.m. The annexe is on Austral Street. We will be interviewing
you regarding the role of black and Asian service personnel who fought
in the first and second world wars.

The Museum will have a collection of photographs for you to be looking
at during the interview.

I look forward to meeting you on Thursday morning.
Thank you again
Kind Regards
Jane Stanton, Granada Television.'

Delighted to receive this invitation, early that morning as I travelled
by taxi to the Imperial War Museum to be filmed, I was conscious
of the disappointments I had had with the makers of Paul Robeson
films and other projects.

Speaking with Jane Stanton on the phone and having read her letter,
she projected a friendly and very professional persona which I liked.
In turn, she trusted my knowledge and judgement. So for a while,
I paused to consider how over many years of painstaking research, I
had become conversant with the contribution of Indian, African and
West Indian soldiers in both the First and Second World Wars and
was reminded of the fact that 'The Unknown Soldiers' programme
in the making (scheduled to be broadcast on Remembrance Day
1999) was long overdue! Surrounding this relatively little-known
subject of the non-white soldiers' contribution to the Wars, many
contentious issues remained unaddressed and therefore needed to
be aired. As I wrote in *Reimaging Britain*:

'By the turn of the 20th century, the African-American scholar W.E.B
DuBois's prophetic remark that the problem of the 20th century was
"the problem of the colour line" had a depressingly true ring.

The huge profits that poured into Britain from the Empire, in large
part, helped the British nation to maintain the status quo, for the
"Imperial Question" was a "bread and butter question." In the face
of a rising challenge from British workers, this is what Cecil Rhodes

had said in 1895: "I was in the East End of London yesterday and I attended a meeting of the unemployed. I listened to the wild speeches which were just a cry for 'bread, bread, bread, and on my way home I pondered over the scene and I became more than ever convinced of the importance of imperialism...My cherished idea is the solution for the social problems. In order to save the 40 million inhabitants of the United Kingdom from a bloody civil war, we, colonial statesmen, must acquire new lands to settle the surplus population, to provide new markets for the goods produced by them in the factories and mines. The Empire, as I have said, is a bread and butter question. If you want to avoid civil war, you must become an imperialist."

But Imperialism means war and Britain had for centuries proved its military might. Following the Boer War, in the 20th century Britain was twice engaged in global conflict during which she called upon Indians, Africans and West Indians to fight against her enemies at a time when virtually every European concerned with Imperial theory and Imperial administration still believed that physical racial appearance was an outward sign of inborn propensities, inclinations and abilities.

In both the First and Second World Wars, thousands of Africans and West Indians served as did more than three and a half million Indians, among whom was one of the most unusual of the decorated Indians, Noor Inayat Khan, an extraordinary Indian woman of truly outstanding ability and courage. Taken together, the massive contribution of Blacks and Asians remain largely hidden and as we approach Remembrance Sunday 2000, we should not forget to target the shameful neglect of their ultimate sacrifices in the service of Britain.

Unlike the Second World War, the First World War had been a very different experience.

At its outbreak in 1914, France, Germany and Russia had vast armies mobilized through conscription, Britain however had only 100,000 men, reliant on voluntary enlistment.

This forced Britain to look to its Empire for desperately needed support. Hundreds of thousands of men and women from India, Africa and the West Indies played a vital role both at home (including the production of munitions on the land and in hospitals) and on the battlefields in Europe, the Middle East and North Africa.

Much of the action of the First World War took place in France and Belgium, on the Western Front and in the Somme Valley. It was the Indian soldiers who were amongst the First to be dispatched to the Front, being mobilised from their locations in north India and transported to Marseille (France) in October 1914. During 1914-15, some 150,000 Indian soldiers were at the Western Front, knowing little or nothing about the enemy, about Europe or the biting cold of European winters. As it was, this was one of the bitterest winters on record! When they first arrived the Indian soldiers were full of hope, optimism and loyalty to the British King Emperor. But soon, the reality set in...'

Prior to the publication of *Reimaging Britain*, few books had made the connection between imperialism, the wars and the long standing Indian, African and West India presence in Britain. So as an author, my journey to the Imperial War Museum on the morning of 28 September was timely and significant.

After meeting Jane Stanton and one of the Museum's Archivists, I was guided to a large desk upon which were documents and photographs. Around the desk were bright lights, props and cameras, the wherewithal of the Granada Television crew. This was the specially constructed set; and after receiving a few final words of instruction from Director Stanton, the cameras rolled as my Interview began. During and after the filming Session, I got the impression that Ms Stanton was satisfied with my role. But this counted for nothing because New York Director St. Clair had felt more or less the same way after I'd completed my long Interview for his Paul Robeson film. Nonetheless, on my way home, I was very critical, going over every word and nuance of my performance and yes, yet again, there was some hope even though I was doubtful about being included in the final film.

A few days later, I wrote to Jane Stanton: *'It was a pleasure meeting you! I hope the rest of your filming in London went well and I look forward to your Remembrance Day film "The Unknown soldiers"...'*

TOWARDS THE MILLENNIUM AND
REIMAGING BRITAIN

As I got on with living, alternating between office work, writing
and related activities, my busy life got busier. Yet, I never stopped
to worry about it! I continued to rise early and, in so far as I could,
I went to bed at a reasonable hour conscious of my energy level
as I coped with the many things in my fevered head. In spite of
the successes that I had had so far as a writer, my life lacked home
comforts: in particular regular conversation with family and close
friends. But paradoxically though it was essentially a lonely life, I
maintained a wide circle of social contacts. My socializing was,
however, largely focused on people and events relating to literature,
writing, ideas and publishing.

By now, Trinidad and Tobago High Commissioner Ms Sheelagh
de Osuna was fully installed at Belgravia, where I was introduced
to her by the Trinidad War Hero and former High Commissioner,
Mr P.L.U. Cross. To give some continuity to our meeting, I sent
Ms de Osuna a copy of my recently published *Reimaging Britain*.
In a hand-written letter she wrote:

'My Dear Ron,
Thank you very much for…your new book "Reimaging Britain - 500
Years of Black and Asian History." I have not had a chance to read
it yet but I am sure it fulfils the characterization "landmark book on
British history."

***It always gives us at the High Commission**, and indeed, the wider*
*community of Trinidad and Tobago in the United Kingdom, **great***
satisfaction when one of our nationals achieves acclaim in the
literary field.

We are proud of you, Ron! Very many congratulations.
Kindest Regards,
Sheelagh.'

Such ambassadorial appreciation was much appreciated, an
important aspect of the pay-off after years of effort. As it was,
Reimaging Britain not only reflected my ever-deepening thoughts,
it also filled an historical gap and thus informed students and
interested readers. Put simply, it was a bold attempt to bring into
being something tangible where there was little or nothing. The

Preface states:

'This book adopts an integrative approach to Black and Asian history in Britain which encompasses the period from Britain's early Empire aspirations to the 'Empire Within.' Its aim is to put Britain and its African and Asian descended settlers into historical perspective, a history of British domination which devalued the cultures and economic contribution of the peoples of Asia, Africa, the Caribbean, the Americas and the Middle East as "inferior."

Britain's imperial conquests were an astonishing, rapacious achievement. Vast regions of the world were colonised and – after initial private ventures – administered and controlled by government officials who, over the centuries, behaved autocratically...

Unlike my earlier book The Making of the Black Working Class in Britain which explored the industrial and related struggles of Blacks (Africans) and Asians, especially in the twentieth century, Reimaging Britain is a work of wider scope. Not only does it point to similarities and differences, it indicates and makes connections between the various indigenous and migrant groups. Blacks and Asians are considered significantly in the context of the British Isles with which these "subject" peoples were closely bound for centuries.

While much of what constitutes Black and Asian history in Britain focus largely on the period from the sixteenth to the eighteenth centuries, Reimaging Britain broadens the scope and brings the history up to date in the late twentieth century. Moreover, the book takes a new approach to "British" history, reconfiguring the images of Britain that arose from relations with its colonial and former colonial possessions – a perspective that contextually juxtaposes the Scots, Irish, Welsh and English (the British) with black and Asian peoples, whose histories until recently, have more often than not, been considered separately, rather than seen as reflecting the interdependence of their histories. Blacks, Asians and Whites in Britain have been influencing each other for centuries and this legacy is reflected in the hybridised lifestyles of Britain's Black and Asian youth. ***British history should no longer be written from the point of view of English nostalgia. Rather it needs to reflect multiculturalism for this has been Britain's identity for centuries****. It is my hope that this book will lead to a reappraisal of how we approach "British" history in the future. In this* *sense, Reimaging Britain makes an important and timely contribution to British historiography…'*

Significantly, Chapter One: 'Africans and Asians in the British Isles' begins with a word which denotes a key concept that either implicitly or explicitly, runs through the book:

'**Difference** *has always been a feature of humankind. Indeed difference was present and integral to human civilisation long before Britain became an expanding Empire in the sixteenth century. Historically, and crucial to the making of this "Empire" was the element of difference in the relationship between England, Scotland, Wales and Ireland whose histories were intertwined. With the passage of time, differences in colour, race, religion and culture would become central to the images and imagery in the history of Black and Asian people in Britain…'*

Through the course of eight chapters, I had reached a juncture where I stated:

'*In retrospect, the history of Britain's Imperial experience should teach some invaluable lessons. But in spite of the dispersal of British cultures to the United States, Canada, Australia, New Zealand and South Africa, tradition and xenophobia still haunt the British imagination. While class is still an issue in British politics, ethnicity (that other social construct) remains a factor of future political significance.*

Just prior to the 1990s no fewer than eight cultures co-existed in the British Isles and the long-standing presence, history and culture of Blacks and Asians in Britain which accrues a profound and incalculable contribution to Britain at every stage of its modern history must be added…

As we approach the end of the century and, as ethnic minorities increasingly define themselves as British and identify and see Britain as their home, Seamus Heaney has acknowledged this trend towards reimaging Britain. Indeed, the "frontier" is there for the crossing and having already considered the more pragmatic dimensions of ethnic minorities, let us finally turn to those among them who have sought to redress the balance of diversity and disadvantage, and of image and reality…'

In music, painting, photography and the dramatic arts (on stage, movies, radio and television) gradually Blacks and Asians have been making their marks. Commenting on the book *The Other Story*, and its contributions which depicts cultural difference, I wrote:

'The problem with creating such a synthesis is that it either "obscures difference by assimilating it, or makes it re-emerge as a sign of Otherness," though the cultural difference in its reassertion as Rasheed Araeen (one of the artists and curators of the "Other Story Exhibition) claims, have the merits of also being a "critique to the dominant forms."

Sonia Boyce, who integrates "material into the creation of a pictorial space tells stories" which address the black woman's experience in white society. She is intent on the recreation of self by using her own image not as a mirror, but as a metaphor, the means through which she emphasizes core issues relating to the "regeneration of a cultural identity within racist society." She deals with imagery which transcends stereotypes and, in form and subject matter, encourages broad-mindedness by demonstrating that drawing is (or can be) as expressive a medium and carry as much potential as painting. Thus the picture plane was seen 'as a space to be patterned in every sense of the word, in order not to imitate the world, but to create it.'

On a number of writers and their writings in relation to Britain, I continued:

'With the passage of time, the migrants' and migrant writers' experiences were expressed in many works of fiction and non-fiction such as George Lamming's The Emigrants (1954) and The Pleasures of Exile (1960), Andrew Salkey's Escape to an Autumn Pavement (1963) and V.S. Naipaul's The Mimic Men (1967). In The Emigrants, Lamming addresses the nature of the migratory experience: "The interpretation me give hist'ry is people the world over always searchin' and feelin,' from time immemorial, them keep searchin' and feelin." In the "postmodern" world, an ever-increasing body of literary texts are related to migration. "Writing Across Worlds," are among the major themes being expressed today. As citizens not just of one country, but many, one writer proclaims the "boundless kingdom of the imagination, the half-lost land of memory."

Migration has become an important subject of study for both social scientists and literary scholars, who together can advance our understanding. Of all the writers who came to London, Sam Selvon, *in his trilogy The Lonely Londoners, Moses Ascending and Moses Migrating, perhaps evokes best the black migrants' attempts to recreate "home" in a "city of words." The migrants' entry into Britain confronted Selvon with his own identity. It is just such a confrontation which inspired him to use language in his art to decolonise, both in style and content, the traditional imperialist novel. His black Londoners are rootless characters through whom he uses language to remake the city in their own image. He used the "oral calypsonian ballad" to good subversive effect, a striking departure from the strictures of "Queen's English" or "Standard English." Indeed his efforts at literary decolonisation both colonises England in reverse and looks forward to the later works of Caribbean poets and writers such as James Berry, Michael Smith, Jean Breeze and Linton Kwesi Johnson, who combined the literary with the oral.*

Michel Fabre has said of Selvon that he "does not assimilate into the mainstream (of writing "standard" English) he explodes it. And adding his subversive mix to the oral tradition, John Agard, like other Caribbean writers who use standard English, challenges its privileged status in the continuum of the language in Listen, Mr. Oxford Don:

"Me not no Oxford don
Me a simple immigrant
From Clapham Common
I didn't graduate
I immigrate.

But listen Mr Oxford don
I'm a man on de run
And a man on de run
is a dangerous one
I ent have no gun
I ent have no knife
But mugging de Queen's English
is the story of my life
I don't need no axe
To split/up yu syntax
I don't need no hammer
To mash/up yu grammar…

So mek dem sen one big word after me
I ent serving no jail sentence
I slashing suffix in self-defence
I bashing future wit past tense
And if necessary
I making de Queen's English accessory/ to my offence." '

Finally, given the great challenge of ending such a 'multicultural' book with literary inventiveness, I set down the crucial concluding paragraphs of *Reimaging Britain* as follows:

'Whether or not the novel is dead, these writings, creations by people from the former British Empire, whose British-born children are, in effect, redressing the balance by writing back in a new linguistic mixture; a vital and inescapable task at the heart of the post-colonial enterprise. Given that postcolonial literature is "essentially political," its creation and study necessitate serious questioning of the axioms upon which the whole discipline of English has been founded, for they are "not immutable 'truths,' but changeable social and political constructions."

Like Boyce, the generations of writers of postcolonial literature and other Afro-Asian artists before her, who had learned to draw and to "paint," the multitude of black and Asian British youths in the 1990s (who are among the majority of the "underclass," the long-term unemployed, with precious little space for manoeuvre) are engaged, through momentary configuration of images and attitudes, in reinventing themselves within the "Britannic melting pot"...

At the end of the bloodiest century in recorded human history, diversity and disadvantage have underscored this multifaceted black, Asian and "British" history of racialised interdependence which, in turn, has been characterised by black and Asian peoples' dignity, courage and self-belief. But although the "brothers" and "sisters" are still denied the "upper hand," they have learned much about the use of colour. Such an imposition subjected and consigned black and Asian people to the wretchedness and frustration of being at the margins of a racial divide along economic, social and political lines. From these unpromising circumstances, in the fast-changing technological world of recent decades, a new and proliferating multi-coloured, cross-cultural mosaic of cultural tolerance (reflecting more light and less shadow, subtle nuances giving perspective to a modernist version of an essentially primal story) has appeared to contradict certain prevailing norms and values, the legacy of white mythologies. This post-Empire counterpoise, has been converted into highly-charged creative "un-British" lifestyles, new and positive images of their humanity imprinted on a time-worn canvas; portrayals that are evocative of the art of living with difference in a society whose elites, contrary to political realities and incontrovertible evidence of a pervasive racist culture, still perceive themselves and British institutions, not as striving for, but as providing the ever-elusive equal opportunities for all.

Few would argue against the advances made, but the vision of cock-eyed power-brokers, architects of the economy and patrons of the arts continues to inspire in those they mislead a desire and urgency to add their individual and collective brushstrokes in the making of a truer, though less defined and unfinished picture of British life and living, which insists that the people in these "Sceptred Isles," far from being the "Lords of humankind," have been and are of many cultures, with a tendency to look outwards and more realistically at themselves and release the imagination from the Empire within.

Clearly, at least from the time of the Viking invasions, among the peoples of the British Isles the legacy of British traditions is integral to what has evolved in today's multicultural Britain. So in speaking about contemporary British cultural identity certain questions arise. For example: Whose Britain? Whose culture? And whose identity? We should therefore be concerned with Britain as a complex society, in terms of age, gender, sex and the family, ethnicity, language, youth, culture, class, politics, the environment and heritage; a diverse Britain with conflicting group interests. Not surprisingly, each of these groupings has its own interpretation of Britain and none can claim to be solely representative because each is influenced by region, religion, education and profession. We should therefore speak in the plural, of identities in terms of British culture, rather than identity. By so doing, in this post-Empire, devolutionary, pro-Europe period of British history, British civilisation and society – in the face of the uncertainties of a fast-changing world, in which the ugliness of racism looms large – we should not miss the opportunity at the new millennium not merely to acknowledge, but also to celebrate the creative potential of human difference.'

This call 'to celebrate the creative potential of human difference' is, of course, contrary to what the Elites tell us. As it was, prior to and at the millennium, the truth of my *Reimaging Britain* statement is no less germane today.

THE BOOK LAUNCH

Within and outside the British Library, my reputation and writing career was raised to a new level when Pluto Press published *Reimaging Britain: 500 Years of Black and Asian History*, a book which they had hoped would appeal especially to the young people of Britain. Why? Because a whole generation of Black, Asian and White youths knew little or nothing about the multicultural aspect of 'British' history. My task following *The Making of the Black Working Class in Britain* was not merely to update, but to tell the essential but hidden stories that were so relevant to our troubled times. Anne Beech and Roger Van Zwanenberg of Pluto Press were so pleased with the book that they launched it on 21 October 1999 at Waterstones Bookshop on Camden High Street, London. A large poster in the shop window proclaimed the Event; and just before the Launch, Waterstones manager had requested that I sign 100 copies for sale as gifts for Christmas! Taking pride of place, a copy of the book was displayed on a plinth in the bookshop window. Around the book was a paper band with the words: 'Signed by the author at Waterstones.' That evening, under the Chairmanship of Ms Beech, I spoke to a packed audience about the book and took questions. In effect, the Event was a reading and discussion session which lasted about two hours. Since then, the book has become a favourite with students and the general reading public in Britain and overseas.

After the successful Waterstones Launch, among the first Book Reviews was one from the Commission for Racial Equality which stated simply that this five-hundred years of Black and Asian History 'is a thorough history' that 'recounts the major historical episodes…' Though it was not a bad Review, my impression is that the Reviewer did not get into the book, so to speak.

By now, given my continuing exploration of the idea of 'difference' in relation to social groups, significantly, the book was much more than being another history. Before I wrote the closing paragraph, I thought long and hard as to how I should end the book, which necessarily contained many groupings and sub-groups, cultures, subcultures and identities. Was *Reimaging Britain* just about race and so on? Was it just about Blacks and Asians? No! was the simple, but resounding answer. My focus and preoccupation was to do with something other than the groupings of race, class, colour, gender and religion. Given such aggregations and after revisiting 'freedom' and 'human rights' (and, of course, Citizenship) I realised that what lay at the core of social dynamics was something deeper and more truthful, not the above-mentioned 'categorizations' because people (individuals) of the same race, colour, class, gender and religion, for example, do not always agree with each other. Why? Because categorizations (groupings), promoted the deadening, life-sapping effect of suppressing the energies and creativity of individuals through '*sameness*,' the opposite of what concerned me: namely that the heart of the matter was clearly not simply race, colour, class, gender and religion, but *difference!* Indeed it is difference which drives social evolution, hence my insistence on 'respect for difference.' And so I came to a clearer understanding, and firmly believed that *what is common to us is our difference.* Given that the truth, as I saw it, relates to all that I'd been writing about for almost 30 years (namely various social groupings which I termed 'Blacks,' Asians' and 'Europeans') this was a profound revelation. Indeed, it explains why for so long I'd been uneasy, in fact deeply concerned, about the 'Oneness of Mankind' which had to do with totalising and aggregations (for example the Marxist concept of 'class' and 'society') which overlooks the essential importance and value of the individual.

Apart from its scope and depth, and the various issues (historical and contemporary) raised therein, in essence, *Reimaging Britain* is about difference and, as such, to my knowledge, it is the **first text to apply 'difference'** (indeed 'respect for difference') **to an *inclusive history* of the Britain**! At this time, I had added a further refinement, the phrase that I'd coined: '*What is common to us is our difference.*' At last, it seemed that my writings as historian, biographer and novelist began to make sound sense. I felt for the first time that my intellectual odyssey had yielded something precious: a revelation which, in turn, affected my writings and thinking; not simply about Blacks, Asians or Europeans, or race, class, gender, religion and so on, but necessarily clarification and application of what the expressions 'freedom' and 'human rights' really mean. It is only through the *personal* that these pronouncements become practical and thus more meaningful in social relations. Hence, in my view, the quest for the 'Common Good' gives credence to, and underlines the crucial importance of 'respect for difference.'

The celebration of 'Black History Month' had come round again. Between 26-30 October, a special event: 'A Dance Alliance Festival of Theatre, Dance and Music' was held at the Cochrane Theatre (formerly home of *The Ballet Rambert*) in Central London and I was invited by Sharon Atkin, one of the principal organisers of the event, to do two readings before the Dance performances of the 'New Works' section of the Festival which was staged on two consecutive days: the 27th and 28th.

Coming so soon after the publication of a major book like *Reimaging Britain*, promotionally appearing on stage at the Cochrane Theatre was a timely and wonderful platform. My first reading was from *Paul Robeson: The Man and His Mission*, the second from *Reimaging Britain;* excellent examples of text and context.

Among the star dancers performing that week were Tina Tutkova, Janne, Dollie Henry, Paul Jenkins and Ray Schell. In keeping with this big occasion, the whole Programme was contained in an attractively produced silver-grey booklet entitled *Dance Alliance Festival*. Over the four days, copies of my books were on display in the Theatre's foyer and altogether the event was a great success.

Ms Atkin wrote thanking me for both my readings and support for BHM at the Cochrane. '*As you know it was a hard event to organise with so many artists and three different shows throughout the week but your input made it more rounded and bearable. All of the shows received very positive feedback from audiences and I was heartened that in the end we were able to pull it off…Once again my thanks and good luck with the sales of your book…*'

I hope that I shall see you soon under less fraught circumstances.'

After the Cochrane Theatre performances, my thoughts were on another performance that I'd given earlier at the Imperial War Museum. While she chased her Remembrance Day deadline, I wrote to Jane Stanton advising her on a particular document which she had hoped to use in her Film.

'Dear Jane,
Apologies for the delay in getting back to you. A copyright holder for "The Black Soldiers Lament" which is from a PRO (Home Office) source cannot be traced...So, applying the 50 year rule for official papers, this document should now be out of copyright and should therefore not incur any infringement.'

Eventually, I felt we should err on the safe side, so I advised that we should not use the material. Time was of the essence and with just a few days to go before Remembrance Sunday on 8 November 1999, I received a faxed six-page Draft of the Script of *The Unknown Soldiers* film which was sent by Director Stanton from Granada Television in Manchester with the message: '*As promised. Thanks very much. Regards, Jane.*' This job was important because it carried a big responsibility. Her specific request was that I should have a look at the Script and make my final corrections or additions before the voice-over was done by actor Andrew Sachs, star of the hit television comedy *Fawlty Towers*. With due urgency, during my lunch-hour I carefully read and corrected the Script. After a short discussion with Jane on the telephone, we agreed on the final version of the Script, which was structured in three parts.

Eventually, on Remembrance Sunday 1999, the Granada Television production *The Unknown Soldiers* was broadcast on Yorkshire Television, which meant that being in London I could not see it. The next day at around mid-morning, Jane Stanton telephoned me: 'You were brilliant!' she said. At last, I knew that my contribution was *included* in the film! It was good enough not to end up on the cutting room floor. Ms Stanton promised to send me a copy. After viewing the 50 minute documentary, I realised how relevant my contribution was: my On-Screen time amounted to quite a few minutes. In effect, having won the Director's respect, overall I had played a significant role in the film. A few weeks later, I learned that *The Unknown Soldiers* was nominated for a British Television Award. In itself, just a nomination was quite an achievement.

Among other things, from the early rushes that Jane Stanton had seen, she was confident of the authority of my role as Historian and thus recognition of my book *Reimaging Britain.* As I appeared on-screen, Narrator Sachs introductory words were: *'As one of only a few historians with a dedicated interest in Black and Asian history, Doctor Ron Ramdin has spent over 35 years researching and writing about black and Asian people in Britain; the wartime experiences being a major part.'* This was the first of my many appearances in *The Unknown Soldiers* film.

Around this time, I recalled that when I began to write the book for Penguin (formerly *Black Britain* now *Reimaging Britain*) I had felt that it was not only an important contribution to British historiography, but something more. I began to see a kernel of something profound emerging from my approach of juxtaposing social groups, which I'd been doing for many years. Apart from the film which contained much of *Reimaging Britain's* information and interpretation in relation to the World Wars, I felt the book's message needed to reach the widest audience. It was this conviction which led me to think that certain influential people should see, and, if possible, comment on the work. And so following the post-Remembrance Day screening I sent a copy to Max Hastings, editor of *The Evening Standard* hoping that he would accept an article based on excerpts from *Reimaging Britain.* Never before has so *inclusive* a history of Britain's largest minorities been attempted and published; and some people recognised this. Many others (sadly, including one or two minorities' leaders) did not know what to make of it. What would be Mr Hastings's response? I wondered as I waited.

A few weeks earlier Sue Bradbury, Editor-in-Chief at the Folio Society, had invited me as her Guest at a 'Books and Bookmen' Dinner at the Savile Club where Max Hastings was the after dinner Speaker. Ms Bradbury was an official and one of the first women members of that distinguished Club. Regardless of his political leanings, I must say, I was impressed by Max Hastings. Eventually, he did write to me about my 'inclusive' history:

'Dear Dr Ramdin.
...I don't know whether there will be an opportunity to commission a piece immediately but we will bear you in mind if an opportunity occurs.
Max Hastings.'

I'd heard the words 'bear you in mind' before, albeit in a different context, nonetheless I thought: was that a stock phrase in the vocabulary of literary editors, including the editorial gate-keepers of national newspapers?

Aware of the significance of the inclusive orientation of *Reimaging Britain,* as a Fellow of the Royal Historical Society, I knew and had met a number of respected historians of the day, including Peter Marshall and David Cannadine. After attending Linda Colley's Lecture at the British Library, I learned she was not only on the staff of my Alma Mater the London School of Economics, but was also author of the well-received book *Britons;* and so as fellow-historians, I sent her a copy of *Reimaging Britain.* On receiving it, Ms Colley wrote: 'I much look forward to reading it not least because it looks to be dealing with some issues which I'm trying to tackle at present.'

Another popular historian was Roy Foster, author of *Modern Ireland,* whom I'd met at a literary gathering. He expressed an interest in *Reimaging Britain.* After receiving a copy, he wrote to say he was looking forward to reading the book, but before doing so, he commented on the epigraph which he described as a 'master stroke.' Entitled 'Lion Beaten By a Man' the *Epigraph* read as follows:

'A picture was exhibited
In which the artist had depicted
A lion of immense stature
Floored by a single man

Those who were viewing were drawing pride from this.

A lion when passing, stopped their chatter
"I can see," he said, "that in fact
You are given the victory here;
But the artist has deceived you:
He had the freedom to invent.
More reasonably we should have the upper hand,
If my brothers knew how to paint."
        La Fontaine, *Fables*, Book 111, No.X1'

This sampling of responses was fortuitous for British history was enjoying unprecedented exposure on British television. The most high-profile exponent being Simon Schama, whose *History of Britain* was aired episodically each week. At the height of his popularity, Mr Schama was granted an additional accolade: centre stage at the Queen Elizabeth Hall, South Bank, where he gave the 'Voice of the Century' Lecture. Afterwards, I handed him a copy of *Reimaging Britain*. While looking at the book, he said he was leaving for the States soon and asked if I'd put a note inside. 'Yes,' I replied. Getting copies of *Reimaging Britain* to fellow historians was, I thought, important, not only for information, but also because of the inexplicable absence of any reference at all to the Black and Asian presence in their books!

Around this time, moves were afoot for my name to be submitted to the British Government for a National honour, a gong of some sort. And in this connection, the Trinidad and Tobago diplomat, High Commissioner Sheelagh de Osuna was glad to be of service. 'I would be happy,' she wrote, 'to support you for a British nomination. You are without doubt one of our most distinguished nationals living here…'

And while *Reimaging Britain* was receiving attention from the great historians and the British reading public, I felt the need to inform the man who would be King: His Highness, Prince Charles, about the diverse composition of his subjects both historical and contemporary. To his credit, instead of ignoring the book, the

Prince graciously acknowledged it. A *hand-written* letter from St James's Palace, dated 29 November 1999, was sent to me:

'Dear Dr Ramdin,
The Prince of Wales has asked me to thank you for your letter of 18 November and the copy of Reimaging Britain you so kindly enclosed. His Royal Highness very much looks forward to dipping into this when he has a moment, and was touched that you should have thought of him in this way.
Yours sincerely,
Nicholas Archer.'

I sincerely hoped that the Prince had been 'dipping' into the book; indeed since then, I had observed in him a distinct shift in attitude: More and more in his public pronouncements, he referred to a *more inclusive* approach in social relations: embracing 'all faiths' in Britain which I thought was interesting and encouraging. More recently, after the riots in Tottenham, he was not backward in coming forward. Indeed following post-Riots developments, he appeared in person in Tottenham; appearances that hitherto were unheard of. Rather than 'dipping,' perhaps the Prince may have read a little more of *Reimaging Britain*. Who knows?

Against this background, while *Reimaging Britain* became better known, after the disappointments and subsequent efforts, at last, my other book *Arising From Bondage: A History of the Indo-Caribbean People* was nearing publication. Given its extraordinary passage from idea to book, I now considered the fact that it was about to be released simultaneously not only by I.B. Tauris in London, but also in New York by New York University Press and in Trinidad by Lexicon Books. A more fantastic prospect I could not have imagined. But as happens so often in life, amidst the euphoria, I had to deal with a matter that I'd neither thought of previously nor had expected: my son had decided to emigrate.

For months he and his partner Melissa had been preparing to leave London with their two children and travel to New Zealand. I remember well the farewell scene: Standing outside the Pizza Express on Upper Street, near the Angel in Islington, I hugged my grandchildren Georgia and Josh and Melissa tight. Then

I embraced my son; my only child and said 'Goodbye.' These were difficult moments, but, of course, I understood my son's and Melissa's predicament in London: with the expense of child-care and other problems, they were between a rock and a hard place, so to speak. The prospects of a better life in New Zealand were, in many ways, far better. My hope that they would have great adventures ahead of them, somewhat tempered my sadness. That day marked the end of a chapter in my life; and the start of a new one.

Before the year had ended my good friend Wendy spoke to me about Richard Homewood, a Barrister who wished to contact me about giving a 'lecture.' Curious and interested, on 2 December 1999, Mr Homewood wrote:

'Dear Ron,

Thank you for the letter of 18th November enclosing your book Reimaging Britain: 500 Years of Black and Asian History which I have looked through with interest.

I am sorry that you were not able to go to the Kapila Lecture this year but I am sure that you will have a place reserved for next year! In that regard I have forwarded your book today to my friend Viru Kapila and you may wish to contact him at his home address...

I hope that we will have the opportunity to meet soon and perhaps we can arrange to get together with Viru so that he can introduce you to the organisers of the Kapila Lecture.'

As it was, the aforesaid meeting did not take place, therefore the 'Lecture' was not given. Being busy and happy enough I philosophized: you win some, you lose some.

But, towards the end of 1999, my earlier Lecture *Multicultural Britain* was published both in English and Spanish. It became an integral part of *Four Fragments of British Culture* (Cuatro Fragmentos de Cultura Britanica) edited by Dr David Walton of the Departamento de Filologia, University of Murcia. In his 'Introduction,' Dr Walton wrote:

'...between the twentieth and the twenty third of April 1999 Caja Murcia initiated the First Series of Seminars dedicated to the exploration of British culture, co-ordinated by Professor Rafael Monroy

1024 · TURNING PAGES - RON RAMDIN - VOLUME TWO

Casas and myself. Four speakers from distinct areas of British life were invited to present their thoughts and experiences to the general public. No attempt was made to feature any one particular area of life. For the first series of seminars an eclectic approach was adopted in the hope that the talks would appeal to a wide range of interests. The four texts delivered at these seminars are included in this modest volume which has been published in the belief that they are, indeed of sufficient interest to warrant distribution to a wider public.

Before readers proceed to the texts themselves they may wish to know something about the speakers and the subjects upon which they chose to speak.'

And so like my fellow-lecturers, my work was introduced to the reading public in Spain. More than that, its significance went far beyond Iberia for the Spanish language was fast becoming (indeed had already become) one of the top three languages in the world.

By this time, I'd been getting closer to another important literary juncture: the final Draft of my first novel *Rama's Voyage*. As a work in progress, I had submitted an excerpt from the novel to Richard Dyer, Managing Editor of *Wasafiri,* a highly regarded journal of international literature. Mr Dyer informed me that the 'excerpt' would be published and, after publication, he wrote to thank me for my contribution to Issue 30 of *Wasafiri* which he hoped I was happy with. I received a cheque and as an indication of our good relations, Mr Dyer added encouragingly: 'I hope you will submit future work for consideration by our Editorial Board.' This was, of course, always a possibility.

2000: MILLENNIUM YEAR!

Over the Christmas holidays of 1999, the few stretches of quiet moments provoked many thoughts, one of which was the sobering fact that I'd spent thirty-five Christmases and winters in England. Quite a tally, but somehow it didn't seem that long for try as I might, I could never forget my first winter, particularly the first sight of snow during the fantastic snowfall and freezing temperatures that I'd experienced in 1962-3. Neither could I forget the mistiness and swirling fog that had surrounded everyone and everything.

Looking back, since the early Sixties, one positive development was implementation of the Clean Air Act and thus removal of fossil-fuelled factories from London which helped enormously to lessen and eventually make of the 'silent killer' (the pea-soup smog) a thing of the past.

As the year neared its end, months of talk about entering the new millennium came to a head. Things millennium were here, there and everywhere: The Millennium Dome, the Millennium Bridge, the Millennium Wheel, memorabilia in various shapes and sizes, and so on. The celebrations were colourful, huge, spectacular and rightly so, for no one alive now would be around for the next such event! Many people made predictions and 'Nostradamus' was much quoted. Some consulted astrological charts, but I was more earth-bound for amidst the January weeks of the winter, my thoughts were on my two published books; each being of long and often difficult gestation, and each like two newly-minted gold coins.

Looking ahead, soon Spring my favourite season would come, I thought. With the passage of time, it seemed to arrive earlier with each year, while summers were not as reliable in terms of prolonged hot days as I think they were two decades before. There were, in fact, some years when people complained: you could count the sunny summer days on the fingers of both hands. Anyway, amidst the winter chill of the closing year, my thoughts were again on brilliant Spring days to come and gradually I was imbued with feelings of optimism.

On the 26 January 2000, I wrote to the Trinidad and Tobago High Commission in London on the pending matter of my nomination for a British National Award.

Meeting Sir Viv Richards, the great West Indian
Cricketer at a reception in London

Prestigious Honour at the Royal Garden Hotel in London. A first
recipient of the Scarlet Ibis Award from
The Trinidad and Tobago High Commission

My European Parliament Pass,
Brussels, Belgium

Onstage in the Purcell Room,
South Bank, London.
Before and after presentations of
Introducing the Tunde Jegede
Ensemble and giving the context
of African Classical Music

My Central London Address:
44 Maple Street, directly opposite the
British Telecom Post Office Tower

Front door

First Floor window:
My writing desk and typewriter

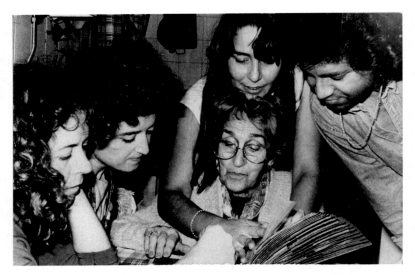

In Seville, Spain: L-R Margarita, Carmen, Marisa and Mother

On a replica of the *Santa Maria*, Columbus's flagship on his first voyage to the New World

On podium at the University of the Sorbonne, Paris,
following presentation of my Conference Paper

On my Birthday:
From Gillian with love

Kelvingrove Art Gallery and Museum,
Glasgow

Meeting Wole Soyinka: Winner of the Nobel Prize for Literature; and being reacquainted with Professor Henry Louis Gates Jr of Harvard University and Armet Francis

c Macaulay's publicity photograph for the 1997 Cardiff Whitbread Lecture.
Taken in The Arched Room, British Museum

Delivering the 'Lecture' at the University of Cardiff, Wales

Before the 'Lecture': L-R
Chris Hughes (Regional Director Whitbread Company) and
Professor David Skilton (University of Cardiff)

Overlooking Tiger Bay with Gerald Ernest and Vera Johnson, Founder
members of the Butetown Communtiy; and Allan Owen
of the Whitbread Company.
This image was published in *The Western Mail*

A lighter moment during my meeting with members of
the Butetown Community

After my 'Talk' a Question and Answer Session with Students

At the centre of a gathering of students from
17 countries studying in Cardiff

Princess Anne, Chancellor of the University of London, confers the Higher Doctorate: the Doctor of Literature degree at Barbican Hall, London

With Ronnie: A proud moment

The new British Library building,
St Pancras

IMPERIAL WAR MUSEUM: The Venue of my Granada
Television Interview for the Double Award-winning Film
THE UNKNOWN SOLDERS

Pride of place at Waterstones Bookshop, Camden Town.
Reimaging Britain On Plinth: 'Signed by Author at Waterstones'

The *'Talk of Trinidad'* Book launch.
Presenting President A.N.R Robinson, Head of State of Trinidad and Tobago with a copy of *Arising From Bondage* in the Savannah Gallery, the Trinidad Hilton Hotel, Port of Spain

Ronnie and Melissa's Wedding,
Waiheke Island, New Zealand

Ronnie and Melissa's Wedding,
Waiheke Island, New Zealand

Wearing a 500 year old Maori cloak. Auckland, New Zealand

After my appointment as a Commissioner by the Mayor of London here at City Hall meetings of the Commission on African and Asian Heritage were held

On the balcony at City Hall

Meeting President Max Richards of Trinidad and Tobago on his special visit to the High Commission in London

'You dominate the picture', Horace Ove commented.
Together with Horace (photographer and Film-maker) and
Mustapha Matura (playwright)

Speaking in the British Library Bookshop, St Pancras, during the Launch of *Martin Luther King Jr.* (Photograph by Richard Cullern)

On iconic Book Sculpture. The Front Hall, British Library.
Photograph by Stefan Cagnoni

On Show in London's West End. This impromptu photograph was taken
by John Claridge, framed and displayed in the
French House, Soho, London.
(Photos of east wall taken by Richard Cullern)

My British Library Departmental 'Leaving Card'

Delivering the Heritage & Legacy Lecture at Docklands
Museum, Canary Wharf, London

CANARY WHARF: The Barclays, TSB and other
buildings at night

Shakespeare's Globe Theatre, Bankside, London.
The first ever recording on this site was conducted by me
when I interviewed the Founder, Sam Wanamaker

The Globe Theatre CD:
Sam Wanamaker Talks To Ron Ramdin About Paul Robeson

The *Griot's Tale* Book Launch
at the Trinidad and Tobago High Commission

Presentation of *Isabella's Legacy: My Discovery of Spain*
in the Trinidad and Tobago High Commision

A copy of the Book Cover portait painted
by Dalia Daza in Seville, Spain

With distinguished actor Rudolph Walker at Book Launch

The Victoria and Albert Museum,
Kensington, London

The Houses of Parliament

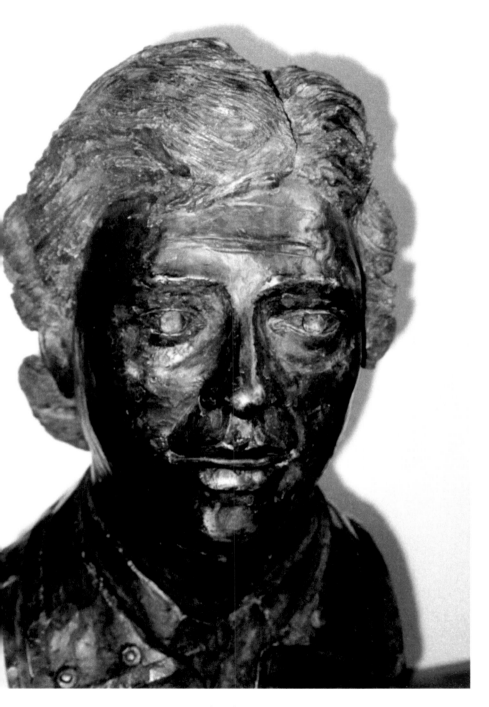

Immortalised in Bronze

TWENTY-SIX

PRELUDE TO THE PUBLICATION OF ARISING FROM BONDAGE

Following my correspondence with the High Commissioner, I had a much-appreciated chance to meet and talk with Dr Crook, editor of I.B. Tauris at his office in Bloomsbury. He spoke positively, as he'd always done, about *Arising From Bondage;* and, unlike the 'experts' at Warwick University, Dr Crook had recognised the merits of the book as a winner!

Just a few months apart *Reimaging Britain* and *Arising From Bondage: A History of the Indo-Caribbean People* were published. As she had done on receiving *Reimaging Britain*, High Commissioner Ms de Osuna wrote to say that my new book had arrived and pointed out that Isaiah Boodhoo's *Arrival* painting which was the image on the book jacket 'is a brilliant choice.' She reminded me of the submission of my 'Nomination' and five days later, she wrote to say that she had a letter from Professor D 'indicating his willingness to support your nomination.'

The prospect of being nominated for a British national award generated a warm feeling, but I hasten to add (in spite of encounters with negative perceptions from people, including certain work colleagues and managers) for my part, at no stage have I ever felt that I did not belong in Britain! Alienation is a common feeling among migrants (especially among writers, as we have seen in *Homelessness and the Novel*) but I never succumbed to it, even though my earlier trade union representations were seen by some as 'foreign' and 'radical,' and by others as anti-social behaviour and therefore a reflection of my 'alienation' from society. But let me be clear, though I concede to having been at the margins, I was deeply concerned and engaged in studious thought and struggles on behalf of the poorly-paid at multi-levels within British society.

With the publication of *Arising From Bondage*, increasingly I focused upon writing fiction: in particular, I proceeded to complete the final draft of my first novel *Rama's Voyage*. On completion, I experienced moments of deep satisfaction. Why? Because I felt that in this genre, I could say new and different things about the complex shadings of human nature; about life and my experiences which I could not engage with in my historical and biographical works. I felt a great sense of release from the years of evidence-based writing. Through my imagination and the medium of the novel, I was able to get closer to elusive 'truth' or reality. And if, as I believe, art is a symbolization of the experience of being, the process of composing and thus creating *Rama's Voyage* was a significant shift in my perception and practice of literary art. Buoyed up by this experience, I wrote a Synopsis which began:

'Rama's Voyage is a rare novel which is concerned with themes never before dealt with in British/Indian fiction. Its central characters are Rama (an orphan from a village in northern India) and Cathy (Caitlin) an English woman, the wife of Captain Timothy Fairweather. Both in content and style Rama's Voyage is a unique work of fiction... an uplifting story studded with vignettes, dramatic episodes featuring memorable characters...Ultimately, this novel is evocative of human endurance, love and loss, courage and hope as boundless as the sea...'

Thereafter, I sent the first two copies out to publishers.

As spring approached, Book Reviews of *Reimaging Britain* continued to pour in from far and wide. On 13 February I received interesting feedback from Trinidad. Dr Brinsley Samaroo, Head of the History Department at the University of the West Indies, commenting on the Black and Asian presence in Britain said: 'It is very useful and gives some good comparative insights in a field which is most often dealt with separately.' Dr Samaroo did not use the words 'diversity' or 'inclusiveness' but I think this is what he meant.

Three days later, I received a letter from the Prime Minister of Trinidad and Tobago, Basdeo Panday.

'Dear Ron,' he wrote, *'I was indeed pleased to receive the copy of your book "Reimaging Britain... I am sure it will be as interesting as your*

first book "From Chattel Slave to Wage Earner."
    Basdeo.'

Like me, Mr Panday never forgot that first meeting in London or the book which he said he found helpful in formulating some of his parliamentary speeches. And like the High Commissioner in London who used her first name, the Prime Minister also signed his letter to me using his first name: 'Basdeo.' These were heady days for the former Trade Union leader who was conscious of his roots. I was told that while on the General Election campaign trail, as Mr Panday passed our house on The Sand Road, through his loud-speaker, he said: 'Remember Ron Ramdin was born here!' If true (and why should my father and others lie?) those words from the Prime Minister (whom I'd met just once!) said something about the power of books: in this case, the power of *From Chattel Slave to Wage Earner*, which Mr Panday treasured. 'Basdeo' was therefore a nice touch reflecting a certain brotherly familiarity and perhaps a measure of genuine respect too?

So these positive responses from the UWI academic and the Prime Minister were well received. What I was also hoping for was a Book Review from someone in Britain who was engaged in this field of research, so I sent a copy to Rozina Visram, the British-based, African-Asian author of *Ayahs, Lascars and Princes* in the hope that she would review the book. A while later, I received not a book review, but a post-card from Rozina about *Reimaging Britain*. 'I shall not only treasure it,' she stated, 'but dip into it again and again as a valuable source. Congratulations on a splendid achievement.' And so the 'dippingness' of *Reimaging Britain* began to take greater hold.

I valued and welcomed Rozina's words. But after thirty-five years of relentless writing and publishing books on Britain and the Caribbean, now it was abundantly clear to me that, myself apart, few (if any) Africans and/or Asians (indeed Europeans) were inclined to write about anything but their 'own groups' or groupings. In other words: Asians wrote about Asians and Blacks (Africans and Afro-Caribbeans) wrote about themselves. I felt this tendency of knowing more and more about less and less could lapse dangerously close to too much narrowness and therefore 'special pleading.'

All things considered, I thought it would be more interesting to continue to write *inclusively* about Blacks and Asians and Europeans as I'd been doing thus far. This essential approach has been the hallmark of my books and other writings. Many writers and leaders representing particular groups were nonetheless advocating multiculturalism and the new brand of 'diversity' which someone knowledgeable in these matters referred to as 'Super Diversity.' Yet these writers and 'experts' in politically-charged and sponsored groupings, ignored connectedness and tended to remain imprisoned, but comfortable in their own aggregations. For me, such grand declarations made under the banner of 'diversity' amounted to unhelpful posturing. In my exploration of ideas, I was, of course, seeking to better understand *connectedness*, not entrenched groupings or totalisations. In other words, very seriously and importantly, I'd been trying to understand the meaning of an ever-increasing and bewildering array of social groups and yes, once again, the familiar, jargonised historical categorisations of race, class, colour, gender, religion and so on. These matters continued to preoccupy me because they fostered narrow thinking and insular groupings, rather than addressing the need for a more 'open' society. Mired in their neat and comfortable aggregations, it seemed that the core problem for leaders and followers was: how to free themselves (and us) from the devaluing constraints of such totalising categorizations. Too much generalization devalues the particular: striking a *balance* is a delicate matter, but a tendency towards this should, I think, always be the achievable social goal!

The millennium had come and gone. But my awareness of time's arrow could not be more acute and the desire to reach out and spread the messages of my books continued to grow. In the case of *Arising From Bondage*, I wrote to film-maker Christopher Laird of Banyan Film Company in Trinidad. My hope was that there would be some collaboration between Banyan and Michael Rolfe in relation to the proposed big Book Launch at the Trinidad Hilton Hotel.

Against the background of this exciting prospect, I attended to the immediate day-to-day concerns at the British Library: Within a year of being transferred to the St Pancras building, I reflected on having been in a job which, as it turned out, was more responsible and Curatorial than Administrative and therefore much to my liking. Dealing with European Manuscripts and India Office Records in the Oriental Collections was altogether interesting. With time, I warmed to the job. One aspect was especially revealing: the foliating (numbering each page) of bundles of manuscripts, which I untied, perhaps for the first time since they had arrived in London from the far flung parts of the Indian Empire. These documents included private letters and correspondence of the British who went to India. In one bundle, I read of the Lawrence family and other high-ranking British officials' who, for example, wrote distressing accounts sadly, in some cases, last words while they were under siege during the Indian Uprising or 'Mutiny.' In this Department, I began to feel a little more valued, certainly intellectually at ease; and with time, I got on very well with the Curatorial staff, most of whom were among the most knowledgeable in their field.

Several months later in July 2000, to add variety to my new post, I was given the responsibility of taking charge of a new project: The Microfilming of India Office Records which I welcomed; and for the year ending 31/3/2001, my work 'Performance' drew this comment from the Reporting Officer: 'Ron has carried out his work to a consistently high standard and is up to date with his output. His computer files are kept up to date and he is very familiar with - and able to utilise to an optimum - departmental procedures.' This was clearly an improvement from the previous year when the Reporting Officer wrote: 'Ron has achieved all his targets. He is a conscientious and careful worker...I've found Ron very pleasant and helpful to work with willing to adopt changes in the pattern of work and willing to take on new tasks... '

With the exception of the Preservation Office, I reflected on what a stark contrast with previous Reports the last RO's statement was. I was reminded of the salient fact that hitherto, my attitude and efforts in the workplace were no less focused than they had been since my employment in the Library began thirty years before.

'THE TALK OF TRINIDAD'

The rare, but good fortune of having two well-received books: *Reimaging Britain* and *Arising From Bondage* published within months of each other meant that now I had to work harder, dividing my time (though not equally) between their promotion. Both books could be seen as filling historical gaps and in terms of publicity they deserved the widest coverage; a view with which my publishers concurred. As alluded to, Pluto Press did their best at the Camden Town Waterstones Book Launch of *Reimaging Britain* which had a knock-on effect.

And now, at last, in book form, I was thrilled that *Arising From Bondage: A History of the Indo-Caribbean People* was available for all who wished to read what was a relatively little known epic. In my *Preface* I wrote:

'*This book is an attempt to fill a major gap in Caribbean historiography: the first comprehensive narrative which puts into historical perspective the struggles of the Indo-Caribbean people, a story based not only on official reports and papers, but also on unpublished material from disparate British, Indian and Caribbean sources....by the beginning of the 1970s, scholarship in the relatively neglected field of Indo-Caribbean history, tended to focus largely on the former British colonies, and even so there had been a paucity of material. Since then however, interest has grown, as manifested in academic papers presented at a number of symposia on East Indians in the Caribbean, including those held in 1988 at the University of Warwick in England and at the University of York in Canada, to mark the 150th Anniversary of the arrival of the Indians in the region.*

But in spite of the many theses, papers, monographs and articles (each emphasizing a specific aspect, or aspects, of the Indo-Caribbean experience) their limitations have highlighted the importance of a synthesis of the general and the particular, an alignment of the "truffle" hunter's view with that of the "parachutist." Apart from limited introductory background, until the 1970s, very little serious attention has been given to the evolution of Indian emigration to the Caribbean in relation to the geographical areas and complexities of the cultures and castes from which the Indians came; a theme which, due to the constraint of space, could not be further elaborated upon in this book… Nevertheless of special significance are the voices of the recruits themselves that are interwoven in this opening chapter and elsewhere.

The second crucial chapter examines the debilitating effects of the Indentureship system, the indentured labourers' responses (essentially their resistance) and the ensuing prolonged opposition and campaign which, headed by Mohandas K. Gandhi, among others, eventually led to abolition of the system in 1917.

Chapter three focuses upon the post-Indenture period of challenge, including the Indians' concerns and responses to integration and consolidation. No longer under the charge of plantation employers, colonial administrators and strict legal controls that had circumscribed their movements, the Indians faced the tough challenge of being a "free" people in direct competition for scarce resources with other better-favoured economic, religious, cultural and political groups in societies that had hitherto abused and treated them as aliens. As it was, hard experience had taught the Indians that effective religious and cultural organisations were vital in maintaining their sense of identity, vis-a-vis the impositions of the larger societies.

Finally, in the most recent phase of their history, the East Indians had set about establishing their identity. As the succeeding generations… became… more "Caribbean" people and less "Indian," historically, they have gradually gained in strength and confidence becoming less hide-bound to tradition and in some ways, better organised, so that today over one hundred and sixty years after their arrival …they are a force to be reckoned with: an estimated one million people of Indian descent live in the English-speaking Caribbean alone, forming a clear majority of the population in Guyana and is close to becoming …the majority of the population in Trinidad and Tobago. They constitute the backbone of the economy of Guyana, yet (especially in the period before the long-awaited voting system was re-established in Guyana) they were denied their share of political power. A consequence of discrimination against East Indians in some parts of the Caribbean, in education and employment, has resulted in the emigration and exile of thousands to North America and Europe…

Arising from Bondage is an epic story of extraordinary perseverance and courage of an enterprising people whose contribution to Caribbean societies has been (and is) enormously important, even though it has been little understood and much undervalued. It is hoped this book…

will not only help students interested in the rich mosaic of cultures in the Caribbean, but will also attract general readers and bring us closer to a more informed view and better understanding of the people and problems of the Caribbean.

Given that there is an estimated 10 million persons of South Asian descent living outside Asia (the bulk of whom are Indians and their descendants who constitute the Indian diaspora)...this work will complement existing and potential studies of Indian populations in other parts of the world, thus retrieving it from relative obscurity. It needs to be said that for too long the unrelenting struggle of the East Indians have been seen in certain circles as a footnote to Caribbean studies, a view which it is hoped this timely book will help to correct. If it is true that until recently Indians in the Caribbean have been ignored and therefore "written out" of history, then it would be appropriate to assert that the time has come to "write them in"...

Indo-Caribbean history and culture must be retrieved from the margins and placed at the centre as an integral part of discourse on Caribbean historiography, a direction in which there has been continuing movement, notably the 1995 Conference: "Challenge and Change: The Indian Diaspora in its Historical and Contemporary Contexts"... In the process of research, this was yet another historic opportunity for scholars from all over the world to direct their attention to neglected and emergent issues. Against the background of rapid global change, the events in Trinidad had attracted further attention to, and interest in, the Indian diaspora (a Centre for the Study of the Indian Diaspora was recently established in India) and Indo-Caribbean Studies...

Researching and writing Arising From Bondage has been a great challenge, an expensive and painstaking process of learning, a humbling and deeply rewarding experience that has taken me back, as it were, to my roots. Now after many years, at the end of this work, I reflect upon countless journeys (both physical and intellectual).'

It must be said that for the period between Emancipation and the achievement of political independence of various territories in the Caribbean, there had been no proper, comprehensive history of the Caribbean. I was especially aware of this in 1988, while researching and writing my school textbook *The West Indies.* In so far as *Arising From Bondage* tells of essential aspects of that post-Emancipation period, it is invaluable. One major aspect is that it tells the story in great detail of the recruitment, arrival, settlement and development of the Indo-Caribbean people. Furthermore, and of special significance, in terms of my own intellectual development and the refinement of certain ideas, in conclusion, I wrote:

'*While disparities between rich and poor in Caribbean societies bring sharply into focus the class distance that has long separated the privileged elites from the impoverished masses in Guyana (especially during the Burnham and Hoyte regimes) Trinidad and Surinam (larger countries with larger populations) ethnic group interests still, though relative, remains a lingering problem as the Indians continue their struggle for cultural, economic, social and political recognition. Given that they are no longer "immigrants" their history reflects an implacable engagement against oppressive forces that have done all in their power to keep them at the bottom rungs, largely separated from the rest of society. They have been used as a buffer between the European elites and Afro-Caribbean masses. At this time, following the Indo-Caribbean peoples 150th anniversary celebrations and reflection, especially during the last decade when serious attempts had been made at reappraising Caribbean historiography, we are reminded of generations who have been subjected to strict legal control affecting all aspects of their lives, an experience evoked through ancestral voices…and lists of emigrants' names that fill mouldy volumes of official colonial registers and records and the nameless unfortunate thousands, including those of more recent times, which echo the deplorable working and living conditions, social and cultural exclusion, violent physical attacks and abuse from Europeans and Creoles; and of the plight of unlettered, but intelligent and dignified men, women and children whose deeply ingrained scars (lacerations of both the body and sensibilities) were marked as in any ritual of sacrifice, by an outpouring (over a long period of time) of blood, sweat and bitter tears that have ironically nurtured tender succulent canes which, in turn, were finally converted into the sweetest of consumer goods, the source of fabulous wealth for complaining sugar Barons. Alas, this was a daily grind, a repetitive process which represented, in all its starkness, a demoralising "system" founded upon the sexual brutalisation of Indo-Caribbean women, as well as the unsparing exploitation of their menfolk. In all, the Indians have remained positive, making… invaluable contributions* to national and regional development nothwithstanding the current state of ferment in the Caribbean.

Though many Indians are proud of their heritage, with few exceptions, contemporary Indians are deeply attached to their New World environment, having continuously adjusted in varying degrees to changes imposed upon them and to their changing contexts and by adopting new concepts, they have helped to shape the circumstances of their children's lives and, in turn, the succeeding generation have influenced their descendants, who became increasingly integrated in their particular societies.

But even though they have for generations embraced their Caribbean homelands, they are nevertheless still stereotyped and their history and culture are largely misunderstood by other Caribbean ethnic groups, in the main, because of an Education system that was Eurocentric which tended to perceive and treat the "Indians" more as aliens, exotic groups (on the periphery of society) rather than as an integral part of "Caribbean studies" which should include in its curriculum aspects of African and Indian/South Asian history and culture. Race relations can benefit a great deal from the introduction of such an educational programme for schools where, for too long, prejudices based on ignorance have been given legitimation. More surprising perhaps is the fact that far too many Indo-Caribbean people (notably non-Hindus) are themselves lacking in knowledge of their own history and culture and are therefore confused about their identity. This is all the sadder because many of them either think they already know enough of their past or that knowing more is irrelevant. Of course, there are others, the few, who are well-versed in where they have come from, but for them and Indians generally…the question is: in which direction should they now turn?

For one thing, the hard-won lessons of the past, present in their collective memory, will be invoked in their autonomous struggles which reflect an integral part of the history of racism in the Caribbean: a story of restriction, rejection and political oppression with violent and tragic results in Guyana. So disenchanted had Indo-Caribbean people become that many have called for the creation of "Bharatiyadesh, an 'Indian' homeland in the Caribbean through political unification of Guyana, Surinam and Trinidad. But for thousands, the degree of alienation was so urgent and profound that the only alternative was exile (no easy option and yet another heart-searching uprooting of strong ties with the lands of their birth, socialization and settlement) to the US, Canada, Britain, France, Holland and elsewhere in Europe, where they now constitute part of an ever-widening Indian diaspora and where many of them, living as Commuter-Immigrants have given voice to their double-identity, their double-oppression (particularly in the case of Indo-Caribbean women) and in these colder climes their haunting Caribbean preoccupations. For many others, matters relating to the Caribbean are anachronistic and therefore of little value. Those of this persuasion, identify strongly with their adopted countries, where new generations have now come of age, ready to proclaim their Indo-Canadian, Indo-American and Indo-British presence.

But while local descendants of indentured immigrants in the various Caribbean communities cope with the sharp end of the continuing crossing: from their "Indianness" to their distinctive identities, they are likely to face the future perhaps with a greater sense of urgency than their forebears, against all forms of oppression to counteract the imperialist social and cultural stigma of indentureship, negative images of the despised '"Coolie" who had been so calculatingly used by the inheritors of post-Independence power; political actions often taken in the name of the people... which has in recent years inhibited the Indians' progress...

Diversity, so characteristic of this part of the world, must be cherished and until the elites can recognise "difference" and act in response to the popular appeal of the masses to bring about social change through genuine respect for the human rights of others, the contradictions endemic in Caribbean societies cited above, underscored by domination and control, will continue to be overemphasized at the expense of a more integrative approach to future policy-making. Politicians who so readily exploit human differences of one sort or another, do so often knowing well the essential similarities that bind people socially. But whether or not the elites recognise and respect difference for what, in essence, it represents, the Indians' massive contributions to their societies are incalculable. And historically (like the enslaved Africans before them) they have been resilient in adversity and after more than a century and a half of resistance and revolt endemic in the process of arising from their bonded status and its residual prejudices, both individually and *collectively, their lives movingly evoke an epic and exemplary story of human resourcefulness, dignity and self-determination, sustained by a deep spirituality invoked through imaginative interpretations of songs, dance, artforms, elaborate rituals and colourful, symbolic festivals of ancient tradition.*

But as we approach the end of the century, new identities and new world views are being forged from tensions arising from the underdeveloped world generally, particularly in the Caribbean in response to new technologies and possibilities of the richer world that are likely to test the human spirit in disturbing ways. But, for some time now, the peoples of this region have been creating a multi-hued, multi-faithed admixture of enriching cultures and indeed if this is to continue into the millennium, pondering (more than five centuries after the intrepid Genoese sailor mistakenly believed he had reached the East – and lest we forget the concern of one writer that the "struggle of man against power is the struggle of memory against forgetting") the history of the Indo-Caribbean people could well surprise us by yielding some invaluable lessons and some warnings; a legacy and compass melding elements of East and West which informs us of the Indo-Caribbean people and their descendants' odyssey towards new horizons.'

With fifty-four pages of *Notes* and, to date, the most comprehensive *Bibliography* on the subject, this work was (still is) unlike any other. On reflection, throughout my childhood, over many years of research and while writing I was constantly bombarded by the categorisation of people in terms of race, colour, gender, culture, religion and so on. For me, these expressions were becoming almost meaningless in the sense that the person was, more or less, always subsumed, oppressed by group dynamics. Following my preoccupation which I had thus far applied in my writings, *Reimaging Britain* and *Arising From Bondage* (in the context of the Caribbean) deals with *difference* and *respect for difference* in relation to migration, settlement, home and belonging, freedom and human rights, thus shedding further light on the process and merits of these evolving ideas.

Now that *Arising From Bondage* was published in London and

New York, it also featured as New York University Press's 'Book of the Week.' This was a significant leap in terms of the book's reach. But, there was more to come: Given that it was a book about India and the Caribbean (a relatively new theme in international relations and studies) I learned more about the Caribbean publisher Lexicon's interest and their proposed Book Launch in Port of Spain. I was pleased because such coverage would assist in underlining the book's importance. Lexicon's planned Launch date was 25 May 2000; and once this was confirmed, on the 6 April, I wrote to its Chief Executive Officer Ken Jaikaransingh stating that I was 'relieved, delighted' that the books he'd been expecting had finally arrived. 'I am in full agreement with your proposed launch date of 25 May and will now make travel arrangements to be in Trinidad... Please keep me informed of progress in the coming weeks.'

While waiting for word from Lexicon, my thoughts were very much on the story of Rama. And so I wrote to various publishers hoping to interest them in publishing my first book length work of fiction, the novel *Rama's Voyage*.

By April 2000, it seemed I was riding the crest of a wave of popularity and was therefore not surprised to receive a letter from Laura Thomas of the 'Analysis and Research Team' of BBC News. She wrote: '*I hope you don't mind me contacting you out of the blue, I'm a researcher at BBC News and am currently working on a project which aims to increase the BBC's representation of Ethnic Groups on television and Radio. At present we feel in some cases Ethnic Minorities are only consulted on issues relating directly to their experience as a minority group living in Britain, such as police prejudice, discrimination and so on. We are keen to redress this balance and hope that the project will result in our having broadened our contacts to include a wide range of experts from minority communities who we consult on areas in which they specialise.*

I see from your entry in New Nation's Black Who's Who that you are a biographer, novelist and historian. Would you have any objection to being included on our database as a potential contact for cultural and arts related stories?...'

At that moment in time, given the accumulation of knowledge

over the years, I felt that Ms Thomas's description of my expertise merited agreement. But, the pressure of ongoing projects restrained me from pursuing the BBC's invitation. This was just as well for by early April, a three-way correspondence between myself, Michael Rolfe and Ken Jaikaransingh of Lexicon Books, concerning the Book Launch at the Trinidad Hilton ensued.

Why the involvement of Michael Rolfe? Because three years before, he was fully committed to filming me as I engaged with my two-day Whitbread Cardiff Lecture Itinerary and, it was now common knowledge that Mr Rolfe was working on *The Sand Road*, his Documentary film of my life. To advance this project, he now assured me that he would be *present* in Trinidad to film the Book Launch. A breakthrough! Such footage from Trinidad could only enrich the film, I thought. By 4 April, he wrote to me:

'*Yes the BAFTA Financing meeting was of enormous interest. And synchronicity was still…in the air that evening… There was a film preview taking place and who should walk out… - Saeed Jaffrey no less…I told Saeed (Jaffrey) that we had met… earlier and that things were progressing apace. A useful and positive evening all round.*

Graham was most impressed at meeting with you, I'm glad that it was mutual. Hope to hear from him, Diverse and… tomorrow… look forward to booking a flight as a result!

No problem making the alteration on the biography sentence. Consider it done…'

Meanwhile, in Trinidad, proceedings moved speedily and my expectations heightened. On 10 April 2000, Ken Jaikaransingh wrote saying he needed my arrival and departure dates urgently so that he could arrange the necessary Media Interviews.

'Could you also please advise whether that extended bio I requested,' he added, 'is en route to Ken (Professor Ken Ramchand)' He then outlined the following draft launch programme:

'*1. Welcome: 5 mins*
2. Ramchand on Ramdin: 10 mins
3. Brinsley Samaroo on 'Arising': 15 mins
4. Ramdin on whatever: 15 mins

5. *Vote of thanks: 5 mins*
6. *Cocktails*
   Any comments?
   Regards
   Ken.'

I replied immediately, positively and, to be sure, I sent a four-page 'bio' and an updated 'CV.'

My focus was now on travelling to Trinidad for what promised to be a Special Book Launch. As the date for this event drew closer, on 12 April 2000, I had news from Jane Stanton. She wrote:

'Dear Ron,
I am delighted to let you know that "The Unknown Soldiers,"… the regional documentary which explored the role of African, Indian and West Indian soldiers in the First and Second World Wars' has just won a National Award, receiving the Best Factual Television Programme from the Commission for Racial Equality – Race and Media Awards. Originally, "The Unknown Soldiers" was one of 50 entries and was shortlisted against two Channel 4 productions and one BBC production. Of course, the programme would not have been possible if it had not been for the kindness of everyone involved in the programme who assisted me with information and the wealth of their experience. So once again, Thank You.'

Ms Stanton's respect for my work as Historian and what talent I possessed was clear from the beginning of our association. Now, months after her film was shown, her honest letter roused a feeling of deep satisfaction within me. All the more so because *The Unknown Soldiers* had won that prestigious Award in the teeth of stiff opposition. Not a bad outcome, I thought, considering that it was the first time that a television Film Director had incorporated any footage of me in a finished film. Ms Stanton was not a 'political' type. She knew what she wanted; and having decided to include me as an important and integral part of her work, *The Unknown Soldiers* proved to be a winner! Ms Stanton reminded me of Ms V, one of the few managers in the British Library, who had treated me straightforwardly. In both cases, the result of working together was as it should be, excellent.

Knowing of Director Rolfe's intention of filming the Trinidad Hilton Book Launch, a few days later Ken Jaikaransingh wrote to him specifying that the date of the Launch of *Arising From Bondage* would be 25 May 2000. This email, copied to me, stated:

'*Dear Michael,*

Attached please find proposed publicity schedule and book launch budget for Arising from Bondage. The actual venue is to be confirmed pending estimates from the Hilton and the Normandie…

*We expect **a book as important as this** to be very well covered by the media. We are aiming at attracting as high profile as possible celebrities to the launch including all the "right" people.*

Please reply ASAP giving your thoughts, suggestions, etc.

Regards,

Ken Jaikaransingh

CEO.'

This communication was significant for it was only now that I had a flavouring of the thinking between Michael and Ken. This also confirmed my feeling that it was not going to be an ordinary Book Launch. The vibes were positive and my excitement grew when I received Ken's 'Publicity Proposal.' I was taken aback when I read the following itinerary which was just for the day of the Launch:

'Time	Venue/Agenda
6.00 am	Television: Live interview, TV6, 'The morning Edition'
9.00 am	Taped Interview, TTT/Information Channel, later Broadcast.
11.30 am	Press Conference, especially for print and other media
1.30pm	(At Lexicon Office)
1.30pm-5.00 pm	Free for Rest
5.30pm-7.30 pm	Book Launch (Vidalia Restaurant, or Savannah Terrace, Trinidad Hilton; Normandie Hotel.

Print Reviews: *Daily Express, Sunday Express, Trinidad Guardian, Sunday Guardian, TNT Mirror, T&T Review, BWIA Sunjet Magazine, Newsday, The Guardian.*

PR Profiles: PR for Launch All Radio.'

Impressive was the word that came to mind. But it was also a very demanding schedule and I wondered how many books (if any) in the history of Trinidad and Tobago had been so anticipated, publicised and planned for.

By now with the urgings of others and my interest enlivened, before flying to Trinidad, I wrote to the High Commissioner in London about the pending matter of being nominated for a British National Honour to which she replied: '*This is just to let you know that I have written to the Nominations Committee in support of the Nomination...*' Soon after, there was a change of High Commissioner and to this day, there the matter rested.

On the question of respect for one's work, I was commissioned by the Folio Society of England to write an Essay of approximately 4,000 words on 'Immigration Since the War' for *England 1945 to 2000*, the latest volume in the Folio History Series. The General Editor was the distinguished historian and Oxford University Professor, Felipe Fernandez-Armesto. As an historian, I was honoured to be among my peers as a Contributor to this prestigious history of England. With thoughts of having been an immigrant stranger on the shore and of Thomas Babington Macaulay's famous *History of England*, I began to write my Essay.

In the meantime, I had heard again from Mr Jaikaransingh of Lexicon Books. Plans were now more advanced. 'We are arranging television interviews for you,' he informed me, 'over the week you will be here.' To say the least, I was still stunned by how ambitious the jam-packed schedule was, just for the day of the Launch. So as time passed, there was much for me to do and think about. For one thing, before I flew to Trinidad, I realised that Michael Rolfe had yet to book his flight! I was very surprised, but he seemed unperturbed. He assured me of his presence in Trinidad and, of course, my hope was that we would travel together.

Time was now precious and with each passing day, I was expecting Mr Rolfe to inform me of the date and time of his flight. Perhaps, pressure of work was his problem, I thought. Nonetheless, I was anxious. But Mr Rolfe reassured me right up to the day before I had left London that he would be making the trip. Alas his assurances did not lessen my worry. At that point, my hope that he would be in Trinidad to film the Book Launch suddenly vanished. I must confess that his lie did jolt and side-track me for a while. But now there were urgent matters that I had to attend to.

The media were attuned to something big about to happen! Indeed I was getting ready to face the attention of television, radio and newspapers; and as my flight from London progressed southwards from cold to warmer weather, my thoughts were far from settled. I felt a chill run through me, as I prepared to deal with nothing less than a national Trinidad and Tobago Event without the additional filming of Michael Rolfe.

My comprehensive 'Media Schedule' was spread over consecutive days from 24-26 and 29 May, incorporating the TV6 Interview with Paolo Kernahan; the Trinidad and Tobago Television (TTT) Interview with Hansley Ajodha and the Information Television Channel Interview with the Reverend Cyril Paul, Moderator of the Inter-Faith Organisation in Trinidad and Tobago. There were also, of course, the radio Interviews, including Radio 104's Live phone-in and Radio 90.5; as well as print Interviews with *The Independent*, *The Express* and *TNT Mirror*.

Several days in advance of my visit, under the headline: 'RAMDIN RETURNS TO LAUNCH *BONDAGE*,' The *Trinidad Sunday Express* had stated:

'*... Ron Ramdin will return to Trinidad this coming week for the launch of his book Arising From Bondage. The book is a history of Indians in the Caribbean and is among the few works to address the topic taking into account the migrations of the indentureds to the French, English and Dutch Caribbean.*

The book, according to Lexicon, is a major contribution to the history of the Diaspora and will fill gaps that exist in the scholarship as it stands today…Ron Ramdin is a Trinidadian-born novelist and historian of note in the UK…'

On arrival at Piarco International airport, I was met by Chief Executive Officer of Lexicon Books, Ken Jaikaransingh, who was clearly delighted to be championing *Arising From Bondage.* A few yards away, my mother was waiting. (My father could not be there because of a recent hernia operation.)

This first meeting with Mr Jaikaransingh, was a pleasant one: 'It's good to meet you,' he said. 'I recognise you from your photograph.' Presumably he was referring to the photograph on the inside flap of the book jacket. With visible pleasure, Mr Jaikaransingh added: 'The President will be attending the Launch at the Hilton!' 'High profile' was an over-worked phrase, but in relation to this Book Launch, it seemed to be approaching its full attribution. Mr Jaikaransingh told me that the great and the good of Trinidad and Tobago would be present. Hearing this, I became even more positive about the Launch.

For one thing, the fact that President Robinson would be attending did not entirely surprise me. He had prior knowledge of my work, namely *The Making of the Black Working Class in Britain* and *Paul Robeson: The Man and His Mission,* books that were presented to him when we had first met in London some years before at the Lancaster House Luncheon in St. James's. His decision to be present at my Book Launch in Port of Spain was, I think, an acknowledgement of the quality of these books. Nonetheless, the forthcoming event at the Trinidad Hilton had the makings of a fairy-tale in the sense that to my knowledge, the Head of State attending a Book Launch especially in Trinidad, was unheard of!

Not only did Mr Jaikaransingh hand me the updated 'Media schedule' he also gave me a copy of the 'Invitation Card' at the back of which was the 'Official Launch Programme.' The attractively designed Card with *Arising From Bondage* printed in orange on a white background was another indication of the importance of the book and the occasion.

On the journey home from the airport, the glittering sun was setting. I could smell the air and was happy to gaze once more at the familiar countryside: at the flat fields of Caroni and south-central Trinidad. There were no more sugar cane fields, but evidence of the descendants of the indentured Indians who had come to labour on these fields, were everywhere. In spite of their long-standing presence, I felt that they were still largely unknown and therefore little understood. A few 'experts' had written on certain aspects of the Indians' presence and culture, hitherto for limited periods in specific territories such as Trinidad, Guyana, Jamaica, Surinam, Martinique, Guadeloupe and Grenada. But no one had attempted a book on the Indians in the Caribbean, as a whole. Moreover, a study of this diaspora necessarily meant filling a gap in Caribbean historiography. As we travelled further south, I thought about the major aspects of my book for use as possible sound-bites for my Media schedule. Earlier, I had made notes relating to the proposed 'Live' Interviews as follows:

' 1. Arising...fills a major gap in Caribbean historiography;

2.Arising...is the epic story of the extraordinary perseverance and courage of the Indo-Caribbean people since their arrival in British Guiana in May 1838 as cheap, disposable labour to replace the emancipated African slaves;

3. The Indo Caribbean people have contributed significantly in almost every sphere of Caribbean life in the former British, French, Dutch and Spanish colonial territories;

4. To date, Arising... is the most comprehensive study of the Indo-Caribbean peoples presence, dealing with their genesis and evolution: where they came from? How they got to the Caribbean? How they developed their communities and cultures and established their identities? It is a history which is synthesis as well as analysis, chronicle and text; a book which encompasses history, cultures and identities;

5. Arising...has the most comprehensive Bibliography to date. Both text and Bibliography will be essential for students of Imperial history, labour history, the history of the Indian diaspora and migration (complementing studies of Indian populations in other parts of the world) and, for those interested in the rich mosaic of cultures (and identities) in the Caribbean.

Taken together, Arising...fills a major gap in Caribbean historiography.'
I had also jotted down:

'Moreover, (1) between 1838 and 1917 more than a half a million Indians were transported to the Caribbean. (2) Today in the English-speaking Caribbean alone, there are one million people of Indian descent. They form the majority in Guyana and are close to becoming the majority in Trinidad. Arising From Bondage is about the Indo-Caribbean peoples history and culture and importantly how they developed their communities and established their identities.'

Dwelling on these jottings, I reminded myself that I would be in the hot seat, so to speak, and, of course, there should be no room for error. From the comments and information given to me by Lexicon Books personnel, most people in Trinidad and Tobago it seemed, would be listening and hopefully reading about the book. Bearing this in mind, I approached my presentation on the night of the Launch in the presence of the Head of State, as something of a national event.

Coming so soon after Emancipation of the African slaves, this first comprehensive story of the Indo-Caribbean people was, if anything, complex. And yes, it was a big story? Part of a continuum of 'New World' labour control and response. But in this country that had produced two of the Caribbean's greatest historians: C.L.R James and Dr Eric Williams, above all else, I reminded myself that my responsibility as Historian was also to present the story as simply and as clearly as possible. This was the acid test that awaited me in the hectic days of book promotion to come. For better or worse, the Trinidad and Tobago public would judge me on how I presented myself and the book. These were among my thoughts as the car stopped. Suddenly I was standing before the familiar wooden facade of the small house on the Sand Road. I was 'home.'

The next morning, I awoke at 3.30 a.m and sat on the bed in the back room; the new, much-needed extension of the house that I'd left in 1962. I reviewed my notes, shaved, showered, got dressed and waited to be taken to the Television Studios some thirty miles away in Port of Spain. I had set out early to be on time for my appearance on the 'Morning Edition' of TV6.

In the studio I was introduced to my Interviewer Paolo Kernahan
who said that as part of the 'Interview' there would be a national
Phone-In and that it was a Live show which would be 'On-Air'
for forty-five minutes. It was hot in the well-lit Studio. While
taking off my jacket, I observed that next to Mr Kernahan was a
copy of *Arising From Bondage* with several markers sticking out
from it. There was no doubt about the seriousness with which the
Interviewer was taking his job. He was, it seemed, as prepared as it
was possible to be. Mr Kernahan's reputation had forerun him; he
was well-known and respected. As it was, I met his interrogative
Interview-style with equanimity, though not lacking in enthusiasm
for my subject. I answered the questions as fully as I could; and
if there were loose ends, in so far as I could, I tried to tie them
up during the Live 'Phone-in.' Afterwards Mr Kernahan shook
my hand, a good sign, perhaps. Then I left the bright lights of
the studio. When I opened the 'Exit' door, the Receptionist with
telephone in hand, motioned to me. I moved closer.

'Dr Lloyd Best is on the telephone Dr Ramdin', she said. 'He
would like to speak with you.'

'Oh!' I said. 'Thank you.'

As I made my way to take the call, Chief Executive Jaikaransingh
was waiting in the foyer Lounge of TV6, where he had watched the
Interview on the big screen.

'Hello, Dr Best,' I said. We had not met or had spoken to
each other before but, of course, I knew well enough about Dr
Best's national status and reputation not only as a distinguished
Economist and Founder of the Tapia House Movement, but also
as a leading figure in Caribbean affairs.

'I watched your interview. You were excellent, Dr Ramdin,' he
said. 'When are you leaving?'

'In just over three weeks,' I said. 'I'd like to invite you for lunch
at my home before you leave Trinidad. My wife Suniti works for
TV6. Let me know when you can come. I would send a car for
you.'

'Thank you,' I said, 'I would be delighted to come.'

'Please take my telephone number,' he added. I did so and
promised to ring.

After putting down the telephone, I told Mr Jaikaransingh about

Dr Best's 'congratulations' and comments on my Interview and the Invitation to join him for Lunch at his home. The fact that Dr Best was clearly impressed was a positive *first reaction* to my Trinidad and Tobago TV grilling. A more distinguished and testing Caribbean viewer/commentator, I could not have hoped for.

Mr Jaikaransingh was also pleased with my performance, which added a certain lightness to our footsteps that morning as we walked across the way to the Hilton Hotel for breakfast. Thus the tone was set for what was to come.

Having seen the interview just minutes before, many people in the Hotel Lounge recognised me. One of them was a Mr Mahabir, who owned and was operating a new radio station. He hoped that I would, as historian and writer, be able to contribute to the programmes he was planning. I promised to keep in touch with him.

My next engagement was a Live Radio interview, after which I was presented with a green T shirt and mug. I returned south to my father's house where I spent the rest of the afternoon and evening.

The night was fairly restful before dawn broke on the day of the Book Launch. But this was not the only event scheduled for that day. I was up very early and was once more in my brother David's car, travelling back to Port of Spain to do another Live Interview: This time for Trinidad and Tobago Television (TTT). My Interviewer was Hansley Ajodha, Presenter of TTT's *Morning Show* which lasted forty-five minutes, including a fifteen minute Live Phone-In! Afterwards, I did a radio Interview. For both Interviews, I was accompanied by Mr Jaikaransingh. Publicity-wise we were up and running. Our next move was to travel eastwards to Lexicon's Bookstore and Head office on Boundary Road, San Juan, where I signed fifty copies of *Arising From Bondage,* one of which was for Prime Minister Basdeo Panday. While signing the books, a curious thing happened: A fair-skinned, white-haired Indian man in light-coloured shorts and sandals entered the Bookstore. For a while he scanned the book shelves not far from the table where I sat; then he disappeared. Suddenly he reappeared and stood before me.

'What do you know about Indians?' he asked. His combative attitude and hateful look, verging on scorn, made it easy for me to reply forthrightly: 'What do *you* know about Indians?' Without further ado, the man who was obviously not interested in books, never mind buying one, beat a hasty retreat from the premises. Was he one of the many local people who had seen my Interview on Television? I wondered.

Also present in the Lexicon office was *The Mirror* journalist Yvonne Teelucksingh with whom, as part of my Media Itinerary, I did an 'In-depth' Interview. The morning passed quickly and after midday, I travelled back south. I was determined to get about an hour's rest, before I showered and dressed. Soon I was making my way for the second time that day along the familiar highway to Port of Spain. This time it was for the Book Launch scheduled to begin at 5.30 p.m.

Thirty eight years before, virtually penniless, I had slipped away relatively quietly from the Sand Road and the village. Now I was on the threshold at the Trinidad Hilton, where I was met by Ken Jaikaransingh and members of his staff at Lexicon Books. Two lissom Indian girls, beautifully-dressed in colourful saris, came forward in the Reception area and greeted me. How truly wonderful to be so welcomed! Then, the 'official photographer' suggested that I pose with the girls: one on either side of me.

Just before 5.30 p.m. Mr Jaikaransingh and I made our way to the entrance of the Hilton Hotel for the arrival of His Excellency, the Head of State and President of Trinidad and Tobago, A.N.R Robinson. As we waited, I tried to steady myself: was this really happening to me? Then the Presidential Motorcade approached. It arrived promptly at 5.30 p.m.

When the President got out of his car, Mr Jaikaransingh duly made the formal Introduction. Almost immediately, President Robinson recalled our London meeting at Lancaster House. Together, Mr Jaikaransingh and I escorted the President to the entrance of the Savannah Gallery, where we stopped and stood at attention as the National Anthem was played. Tassa drumming followed as we approached our places in the front row of red velvet-covered, gold-painted high-backed chairs, fit for a Head of State and a celebrated author. After the President had taken his seat in the middle, my place was next to him.

Looking ahead, high above the Lectern on the raised podium was an extraordinary sight: A large banner spanned the stage. Emblazoned on it were the letters about a foot high: **RON RAMDIN**. This had a strange effect on me, especially because I was sitting next to the Head of State perhaps the most distinguished person in Trinidad and Tobago! Was this a homecoming? A celebration? A Book Launch? Or, all three combined! To my knowledge, no other Trinidad 'writer' has ever been thus publicised for a Launch. And once more, I asked myself: 'Is this a dream?' Certainly not! The time, the place could not be more real; and with the President beside me, I observed the elaborate decorations in the splendid Savannah Gallery: clusters of multi-coloured balloons were placed here and there; and just inside, near the entrance, there was an artistic display on a specially raised stand, as high as a school blackboard, with a large photograph of me surrounded by a few of my published books including, of course, *Arising From Bondage*. Overall, the Gallery and the entire scene was a sight to behold: the towering banner, the balloons, the President and Security officials, plus a glittering gathering of high-profile people. It all seemed to say: 'Welcome Home.' And how! It was extraordinary. Though I teetered on the edge, I did not allow myself to be overwhelmed.

Soon, Ken Jaikaransingh was at the microphone, his voice, clear, efficient, cutting through the air. On behalf of Lexicon Books, he extended warm words of 'Welcome' before leaving the stage. The next speaker was the well-known and highly-respected Professor Kenneth Ramchand. In 'Introducing Ron Ramdin,' he proceeded to speak on the theme: 'RON RAMDIN: ARISING FROM BONDAGE: *In 1996, the University of London conferred the degree of Doctor of Literature on Ron Ramdin,*' he began. '*This was not an honorary degree. It was earned by the candidate after a respectable academic institution had examined his published works in History, Race Relations, Industrial Relations and Labour History.*

It is incidentally, the kind of academic recognition that the University of the West Indies would honour itself by bestowing upon indefatigable researchers like...Ron Ramdin who have displayed a capacity to work independently, to maintain high standards without benefit of academic supervision, and to publish the results of his scholarship to a wider audience than the enclosed academic one.

Ramdin belongs to that increasingly necessary band of mental workers committed to the task of demystifying and democratising knowledge without encouraging disrespect for it.

A D.Lit Degree in London is a long way from the School Leaving Certificate which Ramdin collected after leaving Harmony Hall Canadian Mission School (1947 to 1955).'

Having absolutely no political ambitions, nonetheless, sitting next to President Robinson and various Government Ministers, I felt truly honoured as Professor Ramchand continued:

'When Ron boarded the P and O vessel S.S Canberra in 1962 he was not carrying a literary manuscript or a letter of admission to a University.

He had got into trouble with his father for tearing up in frustration the letters admitting him impossibly to Naparima College and Presentation College as a fee-paying student. He was an outstanding cricketer: as a fast bowler, he took five for five! But football was the sport that took a firm hold of him. You could say that for the next four years or so he was a handsome idler kicking ball at Union Park...

Later when the Trinidadianising Ron came to greater knowledge and understanding of his Indian heritage he would be able to celebrate his difference, accept it into himself and bring it to his fellow-Trinidadians as an enriching part of the identity of the Trinidad person.

But we are talking about the time of the "Busby Babes" and Ron's obsession with Manchester United may have been the only cultural impulse in a blind journey to the Mother Country...

Ron Ramdin's career is an impressive illustration at the individual level of a process which he describes in his latest book Arising From Bondage. This process can be captioned "the long march of people of Indian origin in Trinidad and Tobago and in other parts of the Caribbean including Guyana, Surinam, Grenada, Cuba, Martinique and Guadeloupe." It is a process beyond mere survival, and he seeks to document and construct it in two dimensions: as the social and material achievement of a people who came to the Caribbean as lowly indentured labourers; and as an inspiring moral epic...

As if to compensate for childhood deprivation, he has lived and worked books since that September of 1962. The Round Reading Room of the British Museum was a sacred place where men like Marx, Dickens, Wilde and Shaw had sat. Its high ceiling seemed to offer limitless prospects. From as early as 1969 he became associated with a corner seat M7 facing the... the sun's rays when they chose to shine. His first book was written at this seat, and he began Arising from Bondage right there.

I never appreciated till yesterday how deliberately and uncomplainingly, with what fanaticism, Ron applied himself to the task of rising out of privation and pressure.

In the Senate House library and in the British Museum he commenced his programme of self-education... At last he was qualified for entry as a full-time University student and he entered the London School of Economics where he obtained his BSc in Economics in 1982...

The titles of Ramdin's published books easily suggest the interests of a modern Caribbean person who has experienced the meeting of worlds! At the same time they tell the tale of his gradual discovery that all of we cannot be one if the one did not embrace and respect equally and take its changing shape from ALL ethnicities that meet in this place.

From Chattel Slave to Wage Earner picks up the story of African labour from emancipation, tracing from that time the history of the labour movement in Trinidad and Tobago. The book's heroes are Butler and Adrian Cola Rienzi and I read it now as a celebration of a threatened commodity, co-operation between persons of African and Indian origin.

The two major ethnic groups were united in popular opposition to colonial oppression in the late 19th century and in labour movements that struggled for our democracy in the 1930s and 1940s.

The book was coloured by the "Peace, Bread and Justice" March of 1975 which involved Weekes, Panday, Lennard and Jamadar; and in the INTRODUCTION James took the opportunity to criticise the politician Williams for being at the beginning of the dismantling of African-Indian unity...

Some time after the Graduate of the London School of Economics wrote The Making of the Black Working Class in Britain, a growing

*awareness of cultural and ethnic dimensions and of the specific
character of individual countries began to complicate the universalist
abstractions and the socio-economic approach that had allowed him
to include all non-whites in his understanding of "black." In his book
on Paul Robeson he noticed that Robeson would preach the oneness of
humankind and still affirmed all that he did was for the good of the
(African) race.*

*Significantly, the history of Britain that he published in 1999 under
the title Reimaging Britain: 500 Years of Black and Asian History
accepts the use of "black" to refer only to persons of African origin and
calls for a celebration of the creative potential of human difference and
the recognition of Britain as a country whose cultural diversity and
conflicting group interests need not lead it into ethnic wars against
itself!*

*Ramdin sees his latest book Arising From Bondage as a work making
the case that "Indo-Caribbean history and culture must be retrieved
from the margins and placed at the centre as an integral part of the
discourse on Caribbean historiography." He also makes the personal
confession that writing and researching it has been "a humbling and
deeply rewarding experience that has taken me back, as it were, to my
roots." '*

Professor Ramchand closed by saying:

*'I have tried to indicate that there is an enriching and intriguing
connection between Ron Ramdin's life and his writing.'*

When I had first started to write, I was aware of a void; the need
for knowledge and experience. Then as the 'university of hard
knocks' took its toll in the process of living, I gained in knowledge,
experience and observation and found my voice. Given that I had
something to say, Professor Ramchand's concluding words: 'there
is an enriching and intriguing connection' between my life and
writing, is valid for in essence, such a 'connection' I would argue, is
integral to *any* writer's work.

The Professor's 'Address' was followed by historian Dr Marianne
Ramesar, Research Fellow at the University of the West Indies. In
her appraisal of *Arising From Bondage*, she said:

'This (book) is a saga. A tale of sufferers and fellow sufferers; of

progress and setback. "Comprehensive" is the word which I would use to describe the text of this book. It covers most of the Caribbean territories to which the indentured immigrants migrated from India. Most of us writing on aspects of the history of Indians have limited ourselves to one or two territories - Trinidad or Guyana. Dr Ramdin, from his vantage point in the United Kingdom, deals with the fortunes of the Indians not only in the English-speaking Caribbean territories - British Guiana, Trinidad, Guyana and Grenada - but also the French Antilles, Martinique and Guadeloupe, and in the Dutch colony of Surinam.

The book covers a lengthy time period: from Emancipation to the era of present politics. The book is multidisciplinary. He works as a historian, a sociologist and a political scientist.

This is a general account; a factual account. Yet it is not impersonal. The voice of the author is heard throughout. We hear his concern for the people and his pride in their achievements. Ramdin exposes hardships of this period and the courage and resilience with which Indians faced these trials in a battle for survival, reminiscent of the ordeals of the African slaves. The author reminds us that many Indians still live in poverty. But Arising From Bondage celebrates the success of many others...

Arising From Bondage provides the knowledge and understanding which its author intends, not only of the Indo-Caribbeans, but of the "Caribbean people and their problems."

In the countries where Indians are in the majority, such as Trinidad and Guyana, he pleads for safe-guards for those who wish to retain much of their ancestral religion and culture. Likewise he defends those who prefer to participate in the local culture of their Caribbean communities.'

After these distinguished academics, it was the turn of a politician to speak. The person chosen to do so was Ralph Maraj, Minister of Foreign Affairs in the Government of Trinidad and Tobago. My memory of his speech was that he spoke so much about V.S. Naipaul (his hero) that at one point, I thought he came dangerously close to forgetting it was my book that was being launched! Nonetheless, this focus and over-emphasis on Naipaul's interpretation of Trinidad and its Indians (as if it was *the only view that mattered!*) was something that I would come to understand over the years as a cherished attitude on the part of many 'educated' Indo-Trinidadians of that generation. After Ralph Maraj's detour, it was my turn to speak.

Before an audience that was second to none, what I had to say was clearly spelt out and strongly presented.

'*Your Excellency, President Robinson, Minister of Foreign Affairs, Mrs Noor Hasanali (wife of the former President Hasanali), Distinguished Guests, Ladies and Gentlemen,*
For as long as I can remember, I have been bombarded from every conceivable angle by aspects of human difference. As a child, and years later as a young man, my lack of understanding was compounded by religious leaders and politicians, the one preaching about the "oneness of humankind" and the "brotherhood of man;" the other proclaiming from every platform: "All ah we is one!" In both cases the theme was unity. But therein lay, in my view, the core problem of human relations vis-a-vis human rights and freedom! The question of human difference has preoccupied me increasingly in recent years and, it seems appropriate on returning to my birthplace for this Launch that I should reflect upon the genesis and evolution of my book Arising From Bondage.
When he could no longer move about in his final bed-ridden state, I was told to shave him, which I did on several occasions. The hairs on his face and head were grey. He seemed to have always been grey. From the moment I first became aware of him to the day he died, he was always "old." But, of course, he was once a young man! In fact, it was in the full flower of youth that he was seduced by false promises of easy money on the Caribbean sugar plantations. The voyage from India was long and hazardous and when he arrived in Trinidad as an indentured immigrant it was with "little but hope to live on." He came here alone; a youth just nineteen years of age. He was my maternal grandfather.
As a child I was mesmerized by this man with the sad look, who stood out from the rest of those around him. No one made a fuss of him, though they may well have had his welfare at heart. Although he was a member of the household, he lived in a detached way; and because of overcrowding, it seemed his place was always under the small house on

wooden posts, where there was room enough for him to sleep.

After a lifetime of hard labour, I wondered whether spending his last days under the house had compounded the old man's loneliness. Certainly, the far away look in his eyes never left him!

Except for his daughter, there was little real meaningful contact made with him by other members of the family, essentially because he spoke no English. But, it should be said, he was the proud possessor of a Hindi-English Bible! No doubt he was grateful for the moments he spent with my mother with whom he spoke Hindi. She was his only child, born to a wife who had died soon after giving birth. He never remarried and for the rest of his life, it seemed, the longing, the loneliness and isolation, especially in his last years, did little to assuage the pain and loss.

When I became a teenager, things "Indian" were not hip. You had to be Westernised, creolized. You had to dress like a modern person and drink rum and coca cola. Hindi, Urdu and Indian music, though popular among older Indians was shunned by the wider society and younger Indians.

Though I could not then understand why, my grandfather remained a puzzle, an enigma whom local people made fun of when he wore his dhoti. As an impressionable boy with a "Trinidadian" outlook, I too, felt a little embarrassed because I did not understand the significance of my grandfather's pride whenever he wore his Indian clothes. I must add that he did not seem uncomfortable in shirt and trousers either.

Though he never spoke a word of English, I felt I knew him well enough. I was touched by his smile, his warmth and quiet dignity; and also by the tragic loneliness and longing I had come to know so well. But some 50 years of labour did not diminish his spirit. He never lost that strong sense of himself, a "sense" which I am convinced kept him alive! Was he pining for his Indian homeland? Or, had he settled for Trinidad as home?

Dignified and with an indomitable spirit, the old man dressed in his dhoti was among many enduring images that I harboured when I entered the ship that took me away from Trinidad to the heart of the Empire, where a decision taken in Parliament in the first half of the nineteenth century to transport Indians to the Caribbean, was succeeded more than 150 years later, by the decision to invite Caribbean *immigrants to work in Britain.*

So my grandfather's voyage and mine were connected. We were both uprooted, disconnected individuals. But he could not read and had few (if any) opportunities of doing so, while I, debarred of certain educational opportunities, was determined to develop my skills (whatever they were) and increase my knowledge. What was common to both of us, is that I was also nineteen years old when I left my homeland. We were both cut-off from our roots and had to cope with many years of adjustment. But there the similarity ends, for while his "journey" brought him to a life spent outdoors in all weathers tilling the land, mine, revolved indoors around books, art and literature. While he had little room for manoeuvre as bondsman and free labourer, I explored every available avenue and necessarily became increasingly engaged in the process of reinventing myself to survive in Britain.

Alienation generated profound questions, much thinking and a great deal of study. Scholarship led me to writing. Arising from my exile, many themes interested me: I tried to translate what I felt and experienced into literature. I was irresistibly drawn to research and to write books dealing with history, culture and identity. After six years of effort I was about to publish my first book which I showed to C.L.R James who wrote the "Introduction." In part, this is what he said in 1982 about Afro-and Indo-Trinidadians: "...there has been a division between (them) the blacks in advanced industry and the East Indians in the sugar plantation. They have made many attempts (to come to an understanding) but so far they have failed. Dr. Williams has written in public that one important thing he has done is to keep the Indian and African people apart...'

Since indentured Indians succeeded African slaves in the Caribbean, there has been tension between the two groups. James understood this and tried unsuccessfully to do something about bridging the gap politically. Both he and Dr Williams have written distinguished texts which provided Afro-Caribbean people with a vital and better understanding of their presence...

It has been 162 years since the Indians' arrival and settlement in the Caribbean. Until the early 1970s, apart from limited introductory background material, very little serious attention had been given to the evolution of East Indians in the Caribbean. Since then there has been a series of excellent theses, scholarly papers, monographs and articles, each emphasizing a specific aspect or aspects of the Indo-Caribbean experience. But their limitation has highlighted the importance of synthesis, analysis, chronicle as well as text.

By the mid-1980s, I had written extensively on colonial labour, British Industrial Relations, West Indian labour, on African-Americans like Paul Robeson and on Blacks and Asians in Britain; and having lived and worked in Britain since 1962, I became increasingly concerned with multi-culturalism.

In the years of my absence, Trinidad has remained an ever-present past: the economic struggle of my parents; the old man under the house rather than in it; his dhoti and the racial slurs (are all) dimensions of life that were precursors (albeit in different forms) of what I had come to know in Britain. Indians in Britain meant people from the Indian subcontinent and West Indians meant Afro-Caribbean people. Apart from Indo-West Indian Test Match cricketers, even today people like me in Britain are not regarded as West Indians or Caribbean people. So hidden has the Indo-Caribbean presence been that it prompts the question: how much do people in Britain (including Afro-Caribbean people!) know about them? The common assumption held by whites, Asians and Africans alike was (still is, to some extent) that Indo-Caribbean people are from India, Pakistan or Mauritius, assumptions that have been a continuing source of irritation, because many Indo-Caribbean people feel robbed of their identity.

Indo-Caribbean history and culture has tended to be subsumed in Caribbean and British discourse thus further obscuring their presence in the region. For many Indo-Caribbean people living in Britain, their sense of being overlooked, miscategorized and misunderstood was (and is) real enough.

Clearly this subsuming of Indo-Caribbean people and their history needed to be redressed. And over the years, I felt that the matter of identity needed serious attention, a major issue which raised more questions than it answered. Put simply, it was my story. This was the moment fifteen years ago when I decided to write Arising From Bondage: A History of the Indo-Caribbean People. My initial research quickly confirmed what I had suspected: that the Indo-Caribbean people's history was a "gap" in Caribbean historiography that needed to be filled. Ambitious though it was, I attempted to fill that gap. And what an incredible history of disappointments the process of research and writing this book proved to be! After many years of trying to "get it right"... an Indo-Caribbean publisher in London who, after the final proofs were corrected, refused to publish the book, for no good reason!

Then I showed the manuscript to Dr Lester Crook, managing Editor at I.B. Tauris, who said he had been "waiting for this book all his life!" So after fifteen years of stop-go, Arising From Bondage has finally seen the light of day; and so far the indications are good. Three weeks ago, New York University Press featured it on their world wide website as the "BOOK OF THE WEEK." It is significant that this comprehensive book provides Indo-Caribbean people with a text that should lead to a better understanding of their history, culture and identity.'

At this juncture, the voyages of my grandfather and myself, and migrations to and from the Caribbean, prompted my concluding remarks:

'At any given time (and this applies to each of us in this room) we are who we are and always will be. My grandfather, the India-born indentured labourer, understood this. Respect for each other can only be based upon this understanding. Over-emphasis on the group, on the society, tends to diminish the individual and should, because of its oppressiveness, be resisted. Understanding this has been at the core of my voyage of self-discovery.

In many ways what I had left in Trinidad is what I found in Britain; and thirty-eight years on I am still deeply concerned with ethnic groups and "race relations." Clearly the Caribbean is a multicultural region and in speaking about contemporary Caribbean cultural identity we must consider certain questions: Whose Caribbean? Whose culture? And whose identity? We should be concerned with the Caribbean as comprising complex societies in terms of age, gender, sex and family, ethnicity, language, youth, culture, class, politics and heritage; a diverse Caribbean with conflicting group interests. And not surprisingly, each of these groupings has its own interpretation of the Caribbean and none can claim to be solely representative because each is influenced by region, religion, education and profession. We should therefore speak in the plural, not of identity, but of identities. The Caribbean has been described as a unique field of good race relations and while there are areas where, from time and time, racism rears its ugly head, with the approach of Indian Arrival Day 2000, as we launch Arising From Bondage, we should not miss the opportunity at the millennium, not merely to acknowledge but also to celebrate the creative potential of human difference.'

Crucially, these final paragraphs (indeed the whole Address) were a refinement and application to the Caribbean context of the evolution of my ideas and philosophy in relation to the importance of difference and indeed 'respect for difference.'

After I'd spoken, Mr Jaikaransingh announced that I will present a copy of my book to President Robinson. As I did so, like a swarm, photographers and reporters crowded round to capture images for their newspapers and other publications. Then, Mr Jaikaransingh made another announcement: the presentation of my book to Ma. This poignant moment was also caught on camera. How extraordinary, I thought, for the irony was that Ma who could not read (but had taught me the ABC and how to hold a pencil to write) was here being presented with my book in the presence of the Head of State, the distinguished audience and in the full glare of the Media.

At the end of formal proceedings, Mr Jaikaransingh and I escorted President Robinson back to his car. When the motorcade had departed, I returned to the Savannah Gallery to face the photographers who needed more shots. After this 'Photo Call,' I was guided to a table where I signed books for the steadily lengthening queue that had formed. I was happy to inscribe every book and among those in the distinguished queue were Professor Bridget Brereton and Mrs Noor Hasanali. This sight would, I had hoped, make the Chief Executive of Lexicon Books and his staff proud of the Launch that they had so painstakingly and successfully organised. Also present, I'm delighted to say, was an old boyhood friend, the Reverend Cyril Paul, who expressed his pride in my achievement. The Reverend hovered around for a while and before he left, he said he was impressed by the way I'd conducted myself. I was not quite sure what he meant by this.

Later, I mingled with Guests among whom was someone I had hoped to meet: Isaiah Boodhoo, the artist. How fortuitous this meeting was. He looked frail, but I was glad to chat with him about his wonderful *Arrival* painting that was so apt for the book cover of *Arising From Bondage*. Towards the end of the evening, from the corner of my eye, I saw Pa who waved as he was leaving the Savannah Gallery.

When I returned home it was very late, but Pa was still up. He seemed relaxed as he smoked a cigarette. But I sensed he was in no mood to talk. Feeling strangely tired and happy with the day that I had had, as I untied my shoe laces no words about where we had been and what had happened in the Trinidad Hilton earlier that evening were uttered between Pa and I. 'Good night,' I said. 'I'll see you in the morning.'

In the back bedroom, I lay on the bed, but sleep did not come. Among my thoughts was the fact that given his hernia operation, because of my urgings I was glad that Pa had made the effort to be present at the Launch as did my brother David, his wife Kaye and my sister Annette and her husband Marlon. I vividly recalled leaving the Hilton (the 'Upside Down' Hotel, as it was referred to) and walking under a clear, moonlit sky, towards the car I had said to Annette: 'I have had some great moments speaking from platforms in many wonderful places in the world – I mean truly extraordinary experiences in my life, but what has happened here in Port of Spain is **very special**!' It was a memorable evening at the Hilton and overall the culmination of a very long, jam-packed day. For a while my thoughts wandered, before sleep overtook me.

The next day, I felt relaxed, but aware of more media commitments to come. Then accounts of the Book Launch appeared. The *Trinidad Guardian* published a photograph of me presenting my book to President Robinson under the heading: '**The Talk of Trinidad**' which referred to the 'Epic Launch.' The report stated: 'Historian Dr. Ron Ramdin retraces the path Indians have taken from the days of indentureship to where they are today in his latest book *Arising From Bondage* which was launched last Thursday at the Trinidad Hilton.' *The Express* newspaper also published a photograph: Their choice was of me presenting a copy of the book to Ma. These reports were followed by *The Sunday Guardian* which, in its cultural pages, published a photograph with the caption: 'RON

RAMDIN discusses his book *Arising From Bondage* with UWI's Deputy Principal and Professor of History, Bridget Brereton, at the Trinidad Hilton on Thursday. His book maps the history of East Indian indentureship.'

While the focus was very much on *Arising From Bondage*, something else appeared in the national press. On the eve of Indian Arrival Day, the Trinidad *Sunday Express* in its 'Reading and Writing' section carried the following article:

'THE OTHER MIDDLE PASSAGE. An Eye-witness Account of Indian Arrival:

Just in time for Indian Arrival Day, Hansib Publishing of London has published The Other Middle Passage by Trinidad-born writer and historian Ron Ramdin.

The book contains a facsimile reprint of the 1859 Journal of a Voyage with Coolie emigrants from Calcutta to Trinidad by captain and Mrs. Swinton of the ship Salsette.

During the early years of emigration to the Caribbean, voyages undertaken in relatively small ships were long and hazardous, especially in the 1850s, one of the most disastrous (decades) in terms of mortality. Ramdin's Introduction places the Journal of this 108 day voyage in its historical context...'

Still engaged with my Media Itinerary, the day after the 'Launch,' I was at Valpark Shopping Plaza off the Butler Highway where at 8.30 a. m I was interviewed on Radio 90.5; and after the weekend, first thing on Monday morning, I was interviewed on Television by the leading theologian Reverend Paul, who was Head of the Inter-Faith Religious Organisation. This Live 45-minute Interview which took me back in time to my roots, was conducted on the Information Channel.

In the wake of these major public broadcasts, on Tuesday 30 May 2000, the 155th Anniversary of Indian Arrival Day (now a Public holiday) was celebrated in Trinidad. For me, this was an intellectual milestone which coincided with the publication of *Arising From Bondage*. I drew satisfaction from the fact that though it was five years later than the 150th anniversary, better late than never. Like magic, for a while at least, all the disappointment that I'd previously felt lifted; and I was left with an unusually good feeling about the Launch and being in Trinidad.

On Indian Arrival Day in this millennium year, I went to Rio Claro to meet Bhagwatie Patteran who was said to be the last surviving Indian immigrant and perhaps the oldest person in Trinidad at the age of 106! When I met her, Bhagwatie's head was covered with a white orhni (a thin head cloth) rarely seen these days. As she spoke engagingly with me, I felt that I was in the presence of someone special as a unique Indo-Trinidadian story unfolded. I told her about my book on Indians in Trinidad and the Caribbean and to commemorate my meeting with her, I wrote down the following lines:

'Indians left footprints on the sands of time
Lives, of great men and women, all remind me,
We can make our lives
And departing leave behind us,
Footprints in the sands of time.'

Five days later, the *Trinidad Guardian* published a perceptive Book Review entitled: 'A Tale of Trial and Success' by Dr Diane Ramesar in which she concluded that the author is confident that Indians 'will continue to make valuable contributions to their Caribbean homelands.'

Following these hectic days of book promotion in Trinidad, I returned to London to some news that brought me great joy and satisfaction: In addition to *Arising From Bondage* being chosen as New York University Press's 'Book of the Week' I also learned that Curators in the British Library had selected and placed the book in the Open Access area for reference in the Oriental and India Office Collections Reading Room. So after all those trying years of its chequered history; of travel, work, worry and disappointment, eventually the book had emerged as a *winner!*

It was an amazing literary home-coming in that Trinidad and Tobago's most respected academics, politicians, journalists, media people, booksellers and book enthusiasts paid homage to *Arising From Bondage.* Of particular significance was recognition of the ideas of difference and *respect for difference* that I'd been exploring on my intellectual-literary odyssey. These 'ideas' were identified by Professor Ramchand in his perceptive remarks thus:

*'The titles of Ramdin's published books suggests the interests of a modern Caribbean person, who has experienced the meeting of worlds. At the same time they tell the tale of his **gradual discovery** that **all of we cannot be one, if the one did not embrace and respect equally and take its changing shape from all ethnicities that meet in this place.'***

Many years later, I was surprised to learn that soon after I'd mentioned the 'Indo-Caribbean publisher' in my 'Address' at the Book Launch, word had reached the unnamed London 'publisher' (who did not publish the book) about this reference. Who in the Hilton Hotel audience that evening could have relayed this information? I wondered. Whoever it was, as subsequent events have shown, the 'publisher' concerned received the news negatively; not as *the* truth, but as something of a slur (or attack) upon himself which was clearly not my intention.

The concentrated multi-level publicity, happening so quickly and on such a scale, was heady stuff. But I was ready to embrace it all. As promised, the car sent by Dr Lloyd Best duly arrived at the house on The Sand Road (now officially known as 43 Union Park Road) to pick me up so that I could keep my luncheon engagement.

Having seen photographs of Dr Best, on arrival at his residence, I saw the real person: a man of medium height, grey-haired and wearing a shirt-jack. In his office, he showed me issues of *The Trinidad and Tobago Review*. After riffling through them, he handed me the latest copy, plus a few back numbers before we left his office for lunch in the dining room of his house.

With no break in the conversation, we sat in the living room and continued to talk. I listened with great interest as the respected Economist and political commentator reminisced about his university days in England. I received a first-hand account of the formation, development and the ensuing struggles of Tapia House; an organisation which was not just symbolic. It was very much a physical and potent reality; an ongoing Movement.

When I said goodbye to Dr Best in his driveway, although it was our first meeting, given the remarkable ease with which we conversed on a range of matters over four hours, I felt as if I'd known him for years. As the car journeyed south, my thoughts played on what was a very pleasant interlude indeed: I reflected on the Economist's recognition of my intellectual worth having watched my television performance which, in turn, led to his Invitation, a most engaging conversation and overall generosity.

While writing these lines of my special Millennium sojourn to Trinidad, often I have had no choice but to resort to superlatives.

TWENTY-SEVEN

'KEYNOTE ADDRESS' INVITATION; FILMED AT THE BRITISH LIBRARY AND COMMENTARIES ON ARISING...

So far 2000 had been, to say the least, an eventful year. In the pleasant weather of early June, things looked bright. I received a letter from Iqbal Hussain, Ethnic Arts and Community Officer of the Education, Leisure and Libraries Department of Merton Council:

'I was pleased to discover your recent "Reimaging Britain: 500 Years of Black and Asian History," he wrote. *'As the son of migrant parents, born and brought up in this country and recently as a graduate in history what has excited me about your recent work is both your breadth of study and the quality of synthesis you have managed to achieve. In light of this, I would like to extend an Invitation on behalf of the London Borough of Merton for you to give a Keynote Address to launch our Black History Month on the evening of Friday 6 October 2000. I believe your contribution to the event would provide the Merton Community with an important historical overview. I hope your presentation could also assist in making the various parts of the community feel that they are part of Black History Month...'*

To this request, I responded positively; and reflected that for the 31 years, from 1982, *each year* I gave at least one public Talk or Lecture in Britain. In fact, since 'Black History Month' was instituted, I responded positively to invitations to participate, which meant travelling across the country.

After I'd written a 'Proposal' for a 90 minute Documentary entitled: 'Caribbean Mosaic: The Indo-Caribbean People' based on material from *Arising From Bondage* and the newly-published *The Other Middle Passage,* I contacted Mr Rolfe.

But still affected by the disappointment of his unexplained absence in Trinidad, I pressed on with characteristic optimism for given the success of *The Unknown Soldiers*, why shouldn't I be optimistic, I thought. Perhaps Mr Rolfe would, in good time, come to terms with his lack of transparency. Perhaps he would be encouraged and hopefully feel challenged by Jane Stanton's example in terms of her directorial recognition of me and my work. Indeed after *The Unknown Soldiers* had been screened nationally on ITV (and later on London Weekend Television) many of my British Library work colleagues, including the Director of the Department, thought it was a good programme and commenting on my performance, he said: 'You came across well!'

So fresh from my exhaustive Trinidad book promotions, British Library Oriental and India Office Collections Curator Hedley Sutton approached me. He said he had received a letter from 'Screenhouse,' the television company which was doing a *History Quest* programme for BBC 2. They hoped to begin filming in the OIOC Reading Room on the morning of Tuesday 27 June, arriving promptly at 7.45 a.m in order to start just before 8.00 a.m. According to Mr Sutton, the film's producer had spoken to Roy Greener of the British Library's Press Office who had informed Screenhouse that the British Library's Tony Farrington would not be available for filming on the 27th.

'We are trying to arrange for another Curator to be present,' Mr Greener wrote to Screenhouse. That Curator, it was agreed just the day before, would be Hedley Sutton; but after lunch that day, I found a note on my desk from him informing me that I was the person chosen to be interviewed early the next morning. 'Ron, All OK for tomorrow. They (Screenhouse) hope to start filming in the (OIOC) Reading Room at about 8.00 a.m. Roy Greener of the Press Office will also be in attendance. Thanks! Hedley.' What an extraordinary thing, I thought, that I should now be asked to appear On-Camera in the attractive, atmospheric OIOC Reading Room, when thirteen years before, another British Library Press Officer, Ian Haydon, had rejected any chance of me (an established and well-known author at the time) from being interviewed by Retake Films in the Round Reading Room.

So now with Mr Sutton's *fait accompli*, in spite of the very short notice, I agreed to do the television Interview. With impeccable timing, just as I was about to leave my desk later that day, Mr Sutton passed by to confirm that I would indeed be performing before Screenhouse's cameras in the Reading Room the next morning.

My job was to read passages from a selection of letters written by Indian soldiers during First World War. Written in difficult circumstances in the trenches, these were poignant letters of which my reading had to be nothing less than my best. In close attendance was Penny Brook, a Senior India Office Curator.

After this session, filming continued at other locations in the British Library building, namely (and this was a key aspect of the film) in the foyer at the front entrance when the Library opened its doors to the general public. For this important scene, my role was that of introducing a Reader to the British Library. I was directed to greet the 'Reader' in the Entrance Hall, then escort him up the marble steps and escalator to the first floor.

Before filming this sequence, the Director had instructed me to stand at a particular spot just inside the Hall, where I would meet and greet the 'Reader.' He then took a position high up on the Third floor balcony; and I waited for his call. When he shouted 'Action!' as I proceeded to greet the 'Reader,' one of the two women staff members at the Reception Desk broke the silence and my stride: 'Ron!' the voice reverberated in the Hall. I stopped in my tracks. 'Have you got permission to film here?' the person asked. For a moment, I knew not what to say or do. I moved closer to the women and looking up, I said 'Ask Roy Greener. There he is!' And if she didn't know who Roy was, I reminded her that he was the British Library's Press Officer. While I spoke, I struggled to contain my surprise and rising annoyance at the woman's outrageous assumption: Would I really bring in a large film crew to film me in this public space without the British Library's permission?

Following this rude interruption, Mr Greener and the film Director spoke to the woman and we resumed. Later that morning, from the seclusion of the Reading Room, the Screenhouse crew and I went out into the glare and open air of the Piazza, where I was filmed sitting at the base of the huge bronze statue of Sir Isaac

Newton as I read from two letters written by Indian soldiers in their trenches during the First World War. The film, I learned, related to a Memorial in Brighton to Indian soldiers who had lost their lives in service to the 'King Emperor' in the Great War. The Memorial was erected on the site of the funeral pyre of Hindus and Sikhs who had died in Brighton hospitals.

In all, the filming and my part in and around the brand new St. Pancras building, lasted an intense two hours, after which I was exhausted. Though I did not work officially as a designated Curator, hitherto my library experience and expertise was such that when the film was broadcast on BBC 2, my On-Screen appearances were credited as: '**Dr Ron Ramdin, Curator.**' This is, but one more instance (and significantly a public admission) of how over many years the British Library had used my knowledge positively and overall to good effect.

In the afterglow of that memorable morning's filming in of all places, the British Library, as I anticipated the BBC programme to be shown nationally, in Trinidad, the journalist Yvonne Teelucksingh's article appeared in the *Trinidad Mirror*. Under the headline: 'Author Tells of Bondage and Recounts a Grandfather's Crossing of the "Black Water," ' she was the first Indo-Trinidadian woman to Interview me, and I was interested to read what she had to say.

'*In his latest book, Arising From Bondage,*' she wrote, '*Dr Ron Ramdin avers that "Indo-Caribbean history and culture has tended to be subsumed in the Caribbean and British discourse, thus further obscuring their presence in the region."*

The Indo-Caribbean people's history was, therefore, "a gap in Caribbean historiography that needed to be filled " so the story of Indian peasants, uprooted and transported over the "black water" to neo-slavery with the accompanying "loss of religious and ethnic identity" might eventually be told...

As Ramdin states: "Put simply, it was my story." In his Preface, the author states that the main purpose of the book is to address certain imbalances in Caribbean historiography which have existed for years and, sad to say, continue to this day where those who feel that validation of their own identity dictates that they must negate that of others.

"For too long", he says, "the unrelenting struggle of the East Indians has been seen in certain circles, as a footnote to Caribbean studies, a view which it is hoped this ...book will help to correct." In other words, the history and presence of a people who make up a significant proportion of the Caribbean to the physical, economic and cultural structure of these islands cannot be challenged or gainsaid, has been largely and perhaps intentionally, ignored.

According to Ramdin: "If it is true that, until recently, Indians in the Caribbean have been ignored and, therefore, 'written out' of history, then it would be appropriate to assert that the time has come to write them in."

In an age when every Kirsten, Kwesi and Karamath seeks his root, this new book offers "opportunity for scholars from all over the world to direct their attention to neglected and emergent issues." In Trinidad and Tobago, Guyana and Suriname where the East Indian presence is most significant and where issues of culture and tribalism continue to foment racial discord, the relevance of such writing is the more valid.

Ramdin's own journey...across the Atlantic to the Mother Country bears striking similarity to his grandfather's crossing of the "Black Water."

It had taken the 19 year old lad four years to raise the 77 pounds sterling fare to England. There was the same hope of a better life.

The shock and feelings of betrayal which his grandfather, then also 19 must have felt on arrival at Nelson Island were similar to those of the young man when he arrived at Waterloo Station to face the "tragic loneliness and longing," another of Sam Selvon's band of "Lonely Londoners," "cut off from our roots" and having to cope with many years of adjustment. But there was one pronounced difference. Where his grandfather's "journey" had "brought him to a life spent outdoor in all weathers tilling the land, mine revolved indoors around books, art and literature."

While he had little room for manoeuvre as bondsman and free labourer: "I explored every available avenue and...became increasingly engaged in the process of reinventing myself to survive in Britain."

As Ramdin confesses:"My grandfather's voyage and mine were interconnected."

In London, Ramdin was "irresistibly drawn to research and to write books dealing with history, culture and identity. In 1996, the University of London conferred the degree of Doctor of Literature on Ron Ramdin, "a long way" according to Ken Ramchand "from the School Leaving Certificate which Ramdin collected after attending Harmony Hall CM School...

Ramdin's book proclaim "that all of us cannot be one if the one did not embrace and respect equally and take its changing shape from all the ethnicities that meet in this place."

Yet after some 38 years, he accepts that, like the Indo-Caribbean person after 158 years, his identity "is in danger of being negated"...

And yet there is not a trace of bitterness in the quiet well-modulated voice that reminds one of wonderfully aged vintage port.

Ramdin sees the same elements of racialism here in "God's country," albeit disguised as picong and an uneasy "tolerance." He identifies British racism as embracing in its tentacles not only White empathy toward Blacks but Black hatred of "other Blacks." He notes with a mixture of irony and amused tolerance that in the early days of Caribbean migration to Britain, Blacks from the various islands huddled together under an assumed solidarity of oneness, the "all ah we is one" mantra...

Arising From Bondage sets out to provide the Indo-Caribbean people with a text that would lead "to a better understanding of their history, culture and identity."

There is, however, a cautionary note. "At any given time," says Ramdin, "we are who we are and always will be; my grandfather, the India-born indentured labourer, understood this. Respect for each other can only be based upon this understanding. **Over emphasis on the group, on the society tends to diminish the individual and should, because of its oppressiveness, be resisted".**

The author challenges the sweeping Caribbean cultural identity where Carnival, Dub, steelpan, Soca and Calypso have been declared "we culture." He asks: "Whose Caribbean? Whose Culture? And whose identity?" He reminds us that we are "a diverse Caribbean with conflicting group interests with each of these groupings having its own interpretation of the Caribbean... Those who continue to preach tribalism and foment racism in this country where the two major *races continue to view each other with suspicion and contempt should recognise, as Ramdin and many others have, that "the Caribbean has...a unique field of good relations…" '*

This well thought through piece of local journalism, quoting liberally from my 'Address,' caught the essence of *Arising From Bondage* and, importantly, my intellectual-literary journey - a continuum of my grandfather's crossing of the *kala pani* (or Black Water) from India and I making a reverse crossing of the Atlantic Ocean to Britain. Perceptively, Ms Teelucksingh ended her article thus:

'And while there are "areas where, from time to time, racism rears its ugly head...we should not miss the opportunity at the millennium, not merely to acknowledge but to celebrate the creative potential of human difference." ' These were words that I had for years been continuously turning over in my mind; ideas that in one form or another I'd been consistently applying to my writings; and now its impact upon others was most gratifying. Imparting knowledge and generating debate were vitally important and Ms Teelucksingh's quotation above to end her piece, touched me.

Soon after reading what Ms Teelucksingh had written, my attention was drawn to another Indo-Trinidadian woman journalist, Indira Rampersad, who was more of a political commentator and as such she was a regular contributor to the *Trinidad Express*. On 11 June, 2000 she wrote about the Prime Minister in relation to my Book Launch pronouncements in an article titled: 'PANDAY - MARGINAL MAN':

' *"Trinidad and Tobago does not have an Indian Prime Minister...I am a Trinidadian born and bred and proud to be Trini" PM Basdeo Panday's volatile statement at the Divali Nagar site on Tuesday, May 30 (Indian Arrival Day) echoes Eric Williams' comment that there is "no Mother India, no Mother Africa, just Mother Trinidad."*
Panday's remark can be interpreted as politically correct electioneering, made in a bid to woo non-Indian votes for the next general elections. Or, it may be perceived as a highly irresponsible and inversely racist strategy of someone who has been progressively alienating Indians and

now wishes to identify with a faction where "Indianism" is subsumed by non-Indian elitist bourgeois values.

It can also be analysed as words of a confused leader who is still grappling with the phenomenon of multiculturalism in a complex society where he hopes to achieve national unity in diversity... There does exist some evidence of Panday's efforts to treat with multiculturalism, at least at the political level. Since 1995 he has been espousing the concept of "national unity" which has now extended to "the politics of inclusion" in his experimentation with a kind of multi-ethnic, multi-party Cabinet. He had recognised the challenge of governing a plural society, even as opposition leader in the 80s... it is in this phenomenon of multiculturalism that Panday's dilemma lies. As a political leader (of East Indian descent) of a plural society, he faces the enormous challenge of integration without assimilation, assertion without extremism...

Interestingly, the Indo-Caribbean presence seems to be unknown even to the Latin-Caribbean where knowledge is limited to that of the annihilated Amerindians and African slaves. There frequently arises an almost indignant need for the Indo-Caribbean individual to explain himself and his presence in the region. Indeed it is this very need which propelled Trinidad-born biographer, historian and novelist Ron Ramdin to write his most recent publication Arising From Bondage (San Juan, Lexicon Trinidad Ltd, 2000). During his book launch at the Hilton Trinidad on May 25 Ramdin elaborates: "... it has been 162 years since the Indians' arrival and settlement in the Caribbean. Until the early 1970s, apart from limited introductory background material, very little serious attention had been given to the evolution of East Indians in the Caribbean. Since then, there has been a series of excellent theses, scholarly papers, monographs and articles, each emphasizing a specific aspect or aspects of the Indo-Caribbean experience. But their limitation has highlighted the importance of synthesis as well as analysis, chronicle as well as text."

Through his personal experiences in Britain, Ramdin explains the consequences of this void in Caribbean historiography: "...Apart from Indo-West Indian Test Match cricketers, even today people like me are not regarded as West Indian or Caribbean people, but as Indians or Pakistanis." So hidden has the Indo-Caribbean presence been that it prompts the question: how much do people in Britain (including Afro-

Caribbean people) know about them? The common assumption held by whites, Asians and Africans alike was (still is) that Indo-Caribbean people are from India, Pakistan or Mauritius, assumptions that have been a continuing source of irritation, because many Indo-Caribbean people feel robbed of their identity."

Ramdin continues that "Indo-Caribbean history and culture has tended to be subsumed in Caribbean and British discourse thus further obscuring their presence in the region. For many Indo-Caribbean people living in Britain, their sense of being overlooked, miscategorized and misunderstood was (and is) real enough." '

Finally, Ms Rampersad recognised the main theme of my book: 'respect for difference,' as did Ms Teelucksingh, and concluded her piece thus:

'Panday's statement reflects the problems which emerges from the very definitions of multiculturalism. Ramdin recognises that "clearly the Caribbean is a multicultural region and in speaking about contemporary Caribbean cultural identity we must consider certain questions: Whose Caribbean? Whose culture? and Whose identity? We should be concerned with the Caribbean as comprising complex societies...; a diverse Caribbean with conflicting group interests... We should therefore speak in the plural, not of identity, but of identities." This,' Ms Rampersad concluded *'provokes the obvious question of whether Panday, once "Man in the Middle" has been replaced by the "Marginal Man" whose fundamental ethos is leap-frogged by the historical mainstream and subsumed by the West Indian milieu.'*

I found the above article most interesting, not least because, once more, my book's *essential message* had direct relevance not only to Trinidad and Tobago and the Caribbean, but also by extension to international politics. Thus the book was a valuable educational resource.

An additional expression of the value of *Arising From Bondage* came from Caribbean-born novelist Laxmi Persad who said she had used the book as research material for her fiction, the novel *For the Love of My Name.*

As if I'd not set myself enough challenges, ever-driven I felt the need to do more: in short, to extend my range. I began note-taking for synopses relating to two hugely ambitious historical works: namely, 'Parallel Narratives' and 'Empires.' Why? Because given the scope, depth and overlap of the serious reading that I'd done for *Reimaging Britain* and *Arising From Bondage*, I was able to identify certain 'gaps' and, excited by the prospects I proceeded to research and write two new book 'Proposals' and send them out to publishers. But writing such synopses were easier said than done. They proved to be time-consuming, challenging and demanding, thus confirming that a synoptic presentation presupposes great knowledge. There was, of course, always more to learn which I welcomed. So I pressed on because such historical works as I was about to propose were, in my view, necessary to understanding certain issues in the contemporary world. But being thus preoccupied, there were other matters to consider.

Among my daily post was a letter from Iqbal Hussain, Community Development Officer of the London Borough of Merton, with whom I had spoken earlier on the telephone. He wrote: '... *As we discussed, it would be good if you could address the Black History Month Launch event for between 20-30 minutes. If in your talk you could touch on the importance of History very much about more recent developments, as much as what has happened in the past, it would make an important point.*'

I wholeheartedly agreed with this approach. Mr Hussain went on to state:

'*The launch event will take place at Merton Civic Centre in the Council Chamber on 6th October 2000, starting at 6pm. The evening will open with a short introduction and then you will be invited to deliver the KEYNOTE ADDRESS... There will be a short cultural programme ... The audience would then be invited to view the Black History Month Exhibition, organised by a local study group, which I hope you will find of interest...*

The Event is the focal point of our activities for Black History Month in the London Borough of Merton and as such will receive considerable attention from local politicians, council officers and community groups. I know that your contribution to the event will be of interest to all concerned.'

I was, of course, interested to know as much as possible about what promised to be an important Event. Feeling honoured by this Merton Council's initiative and Invitation, I confirmed my participation, in part, because Merton was not a London Borough that I knew as well as others, but also because to a large extent, I felt that I would not be 'preaching' to the converted.

Meanwhile, having lived in the sprawling Metropolis for thirty-eight years, I was invited to do something quite different: I took the opportunity of seeing the capital through its nearest and most imposing landmark, the British Airways *London Eye*. From that iconic place in Westminster beside the River Thames, as my pod rose higher and higher, in every direction, the views of London were spectacular and wonderful. Such an overview of places afar and closer, was revealing. Nearby, there was Buckingham Palace; and overall the layout of the London streets, buildings and parks was breath-taking: the familiar looked so different, so magnificent, but my heightened views were ever changing as the wheel came full circle and I was grounded. Once more, while walking across Westminster Bridge, as it vibrated, I observed the choppy waters below; and with each step as though I was in danger of forgetting, I thought more and more of life's essence in relation to the great city's ever-evolving movement and change, from its early beginnings as *Londinium* to its present incarnation; the eternal city, symbolised by the turning wheel.

Since Anne McDermid's departure from Curtis Brown for her homeland Canada, I was effectively without a Literary Agent. Given my steady development as a writer, in the changing state of publishing, with a few projects in the pipeline, going forward I felt an Agent was needed. Having been in with Anne McDermid, now I approached Curtis Brown as an outsider. I wrote to Ms O: '*As I said during our telephone conversation yesterday, since my Agent at Curtis Brown Anne McDermid left, I had written several books including histories, a biography on Paul Robeson and I have just completed my first novel Rama's Voyage from which an excerpt* *was recently published in the prestigious...journal of international literature ... Wasafari.*

My reputation both in Britain and internationally... is now perhaps approaching its zenith following the recent publication of two pioneering and readable books Reimaging Britain and Arising from Bondage...Having just returned from my Caribbean Book Launch where, in media terms, I now have a high profile, I do hope you will be able to guide me to the right Agent who will not only help in the publication of my new novel and its film potential, but also to exploit fully the significant historical gaps which my books have filled. I hope you will agree with me that my books deserve national/international audiences and to reach them I need the most effective Agency.'

The cumulative effect of my visits to, and full media coverage in, Trinidad and the Caribbean had reminded audiences there of my growing body of work. Having received the congratulations of many people, on my return to England, one Trinidad citizen was so encouraged by my example that he put pen to paper:

'*Dr Ron Ramdin...*

Dear Sir,

I am an emerging Caribbean writer and I would like you to be my mentor.

I was born on the Corentyne Coast in Guyana. I got married in Trinidad fifteen years ago. Since I was a child, growing up with my mother's stories I promised her that I would one day record immortally the tribulations that she and her womenfolk survived. About a year ago this PROMISE started to haunt me. I finally had to write because I felt driven.

Since then I have come up with eleven books. I am working on my first novel. The tentative title is "TEARS: her destiny". It deals with the Indo Caribbean family between the periods of indentureship and independence.

I have seen "Arising" but cannot afford to purchase it. I looked at your interview on "T&T This Morning." If you can triumph after fifteen years, then so can I. I am looking for corporate sponsorship at present. I have a little (younger) brother who just finished his studies at Cambridge - MA in Finance on a World Bank Scholarship. He is on the Continent right now.

I have a BA in English from the University of London and I am proficient in four languages - one of which is Hindi. I teach in a secondary school.

I look forward very much to learning from you, but if you are too busy I understand perfectly. All the best in your future career and may God bless you always. Dios siempre esta contigo.

Yours respectfully,

E.R. Dewnarainsingh.'

To have so touched this Guyanese-born man, aroused in me a real sense of the value of my journey from Trinidad to Britain that was underscored every step of the way by the uncertainties of years of trying to educate myself as well as others. In retrospect, it shows how the desire and ambition that I had harboured and acted upon had, in turn, generated other dreams!

TOWARDS THE CHELTENHAM FESTIVAL OF LITERATURE

By now, my friendship with Sue Bradbury, Editor-in- Chief of the Folio Society was most cordial and had continued to develop since we met as fellow-Lecturers in Spain during the Murcia-sponsored 'Week of British Culture.'

After I'd been commissioned by the Folio Society to write the 'Post-War Immigration' Essay for *ENGLAND 1945-2000*, on 24 July 2000 Ms Bradbury contacted me to say *'The Essays and chapters are coming in thick and fast now, and I'm making a start on the editing. I'm assuming the end of August is still all right for you, but if there's any problem just let me know. I have promised to let Roy Jenkins (former British Home Secretary) have as complete a text as I can at the beginning of Sept. so he can write his Introduction.'*

One of my golden rules is: once commissioned, delivery must be on time; and so I kept a wary eye on the progress of my Essay. Being an historian, I regarded this opportunity as a bench-mark; as both prestigious and an economically good deal. While working on my Folio Society history contribution, I heard again from Iqbal Hussain of Merton Council:

'*Thank you for confirming that you will deliver the Keynote address for the Launch of our Black History Month celebrations. News of your participation in this important event has already generated considerable interest from both local Councillors, Senior officers and community groups. As **the focal event** for our celebrations, personal invites have been sent out to a large number of people. The event will also be well-publicised through a leaflet produced to promote the various activities. I have also had confirmation from a number of local artists, who will share songs and poems that celebrate the spirit of the occasion. All in all, it promises to be both a stimulating and important evening...The aim of the event is to benefit the community in Merton and to give them an opportunity to learn about and hopefully reflect on the issues raised.*'

He pointed out that normally the standard fee, with expenses, for Guest speakers to 'smaller Council events' was £75.00 - *almost as much* as I had to raise over four long Trinidad years of intermittent hard labour to pay for my passage to England! How ironic, I thought, even though the value of the pound sterling thirty-seven years ago was not the same as now Mr Hussain ended his letter saying that he hoped the fee offered, including expenses, would be agreeable.

Agreeable? Of course it was, especially because my earnings had not changed very much.

At least once, often twice each year, ever since I'd started work in England (the *raison d'etre* of my departure), I never deviated from the habit of sending money to Ma and Pa; and on each of my visits (on average once every five years or so prior to 2000) I took some additional money with me, just in case someone in the family was in dire need. As it was, my brother Jimmy's second daughter Nancy, a bright student, was offered the opportunity of taking the next step up in her education for which she needed financial help. I recalled only too well how poverty had denied me a 'College education' even when I *did pass* the Entrance tests! Fortunately, the payment of fees to attend College was a thing of the past. But on one occasion to ensure that Nancy would not be deprived, in so far as I could, I was glad to help. Just before she left to visit her mother in New York, on16 August 2000 she wrote:

'Dear Uncle Ron,

How are you? I hope you are fine. Well I am okay but I am afraid that I am NOT enjoying my vacation all that much. I am not allowed to go much places…PaPa… believes that I should spend my "last days" at home with him and MaMa…

Thank you very much for your letter and the Postal Orders, I really appreciate it. I received it since 9th August but it is only now I have got the time to write to you. I… assure you that I will listen to all your advice and I will spend the money wisely. Thank you once more and take care of yourself. I will be signing off now. God bless. Love, Nancy.'

I felt good reading Nancy's letter for having seen her as a child on my visits, now she was growing up into a fine, intelligent teenager. She needed and deserved all the support she could get. I had great hopes for her. Her father, of whom at one time I also had high hopes of a bright future, missed many opportunities. Knowing only too well where I'd come from, such 'home' matters in relation to Ma and Pa as Nancy had mentioned in her letter were familiar, but I tried not to dwell too long upon them.

Being self-motivated and disciplined, I kept a wary eye on my employment; and ever engaged with various books, now with more urgency, I spent a greater proportion of time on completing my novel *Rama's Voyage*. This meant some adjustment: a change in how I scheduled my days and weeks, alternating between writing fiction and non-fiction; a juxtaposition and an exercise that was a revelation, producing new meanings and therefore a better understanding of the processes of story-telling. In other words, I learned more about the difference between fact and fiction. Thus I embarked on a new phase of writing.

Overall, my disciplined work-rate continued; the way I lived was compulsive. Driven? Yes, but no less than before; and no one was forcing me in this (or any other) direction for my behaviour had its genesis a long time ago in the lack of opportunity in my youth, not only in employment, but also in education. This compulsion was indeed a hard-won 'way of life' that had brought me thus far;

and, given the respect shown by students, scholars and general readers both in Britain and abroad for my books, I was far from ready to give up. If anything, since those early days of writing short stories, now my energy and imagination had become more strongly engaged: I was increasingly preoccupied with fiction, as I shaped and reshaped *Rama's Voyage* using language experimentally, with more inventiveness, and through continued creativity I experienced a growing sense of buoyancy.

Since the impressive Launch of *The Making of the Black Working Class in Britain* in 1987 at the Trinidad and Tobago High Commission in London and the Commission's bestowal of the Scarlet Ibis Award upon me for my overall literary-educational-community contributions, I enjoyed an increasingly respectful and warm association with that diplomatic establishment in Belgravia. By now I had attended many high profile Soirees there; and had met a succession of High Commissioners who came, served their time in London and went. With the exception of Dr Eric Williams, I had met all the Trinidad and Tobago Prime Ministers and Presidents. Now news reached me from the incumbent Diplomat, the Honourable Ms Sheelagh de Osuna. In a letter dated 22 August 2000, she wrote:

'My Dear Ron,
I write to inform you that I shall be relinquishing my appointment as High Commissioner for Trinidad and Tobago in London at the end of this month.
I will be returning to Port of Spain to take up an appointment as Permanent Secretary, Ministry of Foreign Affairs. It is an appointment that I welcome.
I want to let you know how much I appreciate the relationship we have developed in these last years. Your support and advice have been invaluable. I do hope our paths will cross again, but in the meantime please accept my very best wishes for your personal well-being.
Yours Ever,
Sheelagh.'

I was very surprised that Sheelagh was leaving. Much too soon, I thought. Since I was introduced to her by Ulric Cross, my respect for her professionalism and warmth as a person remained strong. And given her appreciation of my overall contribution, especially as a writer, her letter confirmed my desire to press on.

Since my arrival in England an element of my personality that became more and more pronounced was an outgoing approach and an appreciation that in life there should be an element of fun. Free from the strictures of my life on the Sand Road, now in the maelstrom of London, more consciously (in so far as I could) I took every opportunity to express my need for more relaxation.

A few days after hearing from High Commissioner Shelagh de Osuna, I visited Woodbridge in Suffolk with my good friend Wendy. The weather was fine and having spent a wonderful weekend there on 4 September 2000, Wendy's mother June wrote:

'Dearest Ron,

Many, many thanks for your great kindness - not forgetting your excellent taste!

John and I "helped" each other with the lovely wine and the gorgeous Pannetonne ...

Thank you so very much...

With renewed thanks and our love.'

I was most appreciative of June and her husband John; and what a find Woodbridge was. Wearing my historian's hat, I was curious about this area. After reading a local inscription, I learned about a connection between Woodbridge and the Caribbean. It seemed that casks of rum had, at various times, been smuggled into England through Woodbridge.

The pace of life, the quiet streets, small shops and quaint houses in Woodbridge were very different from the noise and bustle of London. Soon after that weekend (during which we went to Aldebrugh and breathed the bracing air of the Suffolk coast) I returned to London refreshed. This served me well for in spite of Mr Rolfe not turning up for the Book Launch in Trinidad, my disappointment did not mark the end of our relationship. If anything, given the amount of filming we'd already done in Cardiff three years before, and elsewhere in London, my interest in our film projects seemed to have deepened.

Following the Summer Party at Saeed Jaffrey's house in Stratford-upon-Avon on 4 September, I wrote to Mr Rolfe: 'I tried (your latest email address) this morning, but my message was returned. (This had not happened before!) so I decided to write first to thank you for the invitation to Saeed's "Open House." It was good to meet and speak with this fine actor and man (and wife Jennifer) again in sparkling form…All in all, it was a very enjoyable afternoon and evening.'

During the Party (my second meeting with the great actor) as we sat under one of the marquees in his garden adjoining the River Avon, Saeed was in a lively mood and, at one point, he thought it a good idea to have one of his Guests take a photograph of us together. A few shots were, in fact, taken; and both Saeed and I were relaxed about this. But when, a few weeks later, I requested a copy of one of the photographs, nothing was forthcoming. This road-block, I surmised, was a clear indication that the celebrity brand had to be protected. I was, of course, respectful of this, but I hasten to add: it was clearly not a sycophantic desire on my part that had led either to the photographs being taken in the first place or to my request for a copy!

I was also delighted to meet Mr Rolfe's beautiful family.

On behalf of his own company Falcon Films Ltd, Mr Rolfe had, at last, sent me a formal document, a 'Terms of Agreement' to which I responded by saying that it *clearly embodies a great deal of deliberation on your part. As a legal document, it deserves the fullest consideration. It is therefore important that I seek as much advice as possible before I finally make a decision on the "Reluctant Voyagers" film project. Once that decision is reached, I shall, of course, let you know.'*

After seeing the document, I was much less optimistic about both *The Sand Road* and 'Reluctant Voyagers' film projects than I'd been before I went to Trinidad. But regardless of a sense of diminishing hope, I willed myself on: wait and see, was perhaps the best option.

Fortunately there was no chance of idleness for after being

deeply immersed in writing the best 'Essay' possible and eventually submitting it to the Folio Society, Sue Bradbury was again in touch. She suggested a few 'minor changes' and said that she and Professor Felipe Fernandez-Armesto, the Folio Society History Series General Editor, were agreed that 'everything you need to say is there...'

Meanwhile, there was increasing recognition of my books *Reimaging Britain* and *Arising From Bondage* at home and abroad. On 12 September, Marits Hashmikhan, a reader in the British Library Oriental and India Office Collections Reading Room, approached the Curator at the Enquiries Desk for assistance. He was from Surinam and was doing some work on the Indian diaspora. While conversing with the Curator, Mr Hasmikhan mentioned my name. When he was told that I was a member of staff in the British Library, Mr Hashmikhan said he would like to speak with me about *Arising From Bondage* which, as mentioned, was now officially a British Library Reference book in the Reading Room.

After meeting Mr Hashmikhan, I learned that he'd come to London via Amsterdam where, as an Indo-Surinamese Researcher, he was furthering his studies specifically on Indians in the Caribbean. We discussed various issues relating to my book, a copy of which he was keen to acquire. A couple of days later, he left a note for me. 'It is a very interesting book,' he wrote. 'Can we have a chat before I leave London?' I agreed to meet him again and when we did he said he would get his 'Institute' in Amsterdam to order *Arising From Bondage*. Pleased with meeting this student, the Surinam-Dutch connection augured well for the book, which I hoped would serve as a catalyst for other researchers.

AN ATTEMPT TO MAINSTREAM *REIMAGING BRITAIN*; THE FILM GAME AND TRIUMPH, AT LAST!

After the correspondence and telephone calls, at the beginning of October, at last, advance publicity about Merton's Black History Month arrived in the post. The enclosed Leaflet was titled: **'Cure the Fever: Launch Event. Featuring the distinguished Trinidad-born historian, Dr Ron Ramdin.'** Though not of the same pedigree or scale as the Whitbread Cardiff Lecture, I felt a great sense of expectation. In its own way, it had the makings of a very Special Event. Clearly, although other contributions were highlighted, the orientation of the 'Event' was largely to spotlight me as Historian. At the front of the leaflet, there was a photograph of me and an Invitation to the Public:

'Dear Friends,

I have great pleasure in inviting all of Merton's community to the Launch of Merton's Black History Month 2000. The event is the focal point of a varied programme of events which start in late September and run throughout October.

For this important occasion, I have invited Dr Ron Ramdin to help celebrate the contribution of the Ethnic Minority community in the UK. He is the author of several well known books, including Reimaging Britain:500 Years of Black and Asian history.'

My 'Keynote Address' was well-received by the packed audience in the Merton Council Chamber. It was followed by a short cultural programme featuring Afro-Asian artists who performed songs and poetry, celebrating the spirit of the occasion. This was followed by the official launch of a unique exhibition, a display of historical figures who were associated with the Borough: for example, Columbus Denniston ('Windrusher' 1948), Emperor Haile Selassie, Sophia Duleep Singh (Suffragette) and Couba Cornwallis (Healer of Lord Nelson). The exhibition was complemented by a display of "Positive Negatives," images recognising the valuable contribution made by Ethnic Minorities in Merton. Clearly the Council regarded this as an 'important occasion,' the start of a Week of Events that included a reading by the then relatively unknown author Zadie Smith, who was scheduled to appear later in the week's programme and read from her book *White Teeth*.

At the end of formal proceedings, I was introduced to dignitaries and officials of Merton Borough Council; and posed for photographs with the Mayor, who was unsparing in his dress, wearing the full regalia of his Office. Afterwards I was guided to a special display, mounted by *Books Etc* and did a Book Signing Session during which multiple copies of *Reimaging Britain* were sold. This was another indication of the book's growing popularity.

Making my way home on the train to North London, given the Merton Organisers' unsparing efforts, my hope was that after such an experimental night, they would indeed achieve a positive Launch response from the public. A week later, the Borough Council's Development Officer was in touch again. 'Thank you so much,' he wrote, 'for delivering your valuable Keynote Address. From all the feedback I have received, the Event was **a real success** and something that I hope we can repeat next year.' Thus, at what was an Inaugural Event, I was instrumental in spreading the word in yet another London Borough. Well done all!

After the spectacular millennium celebrations and now well into the New Year, looking back, I was confronted with a recurring, but sobering thought: although the cheque from Merton was very helpful and had made me more mindful of my economic circumstances, as always, the deeper satisfaction was getting the message of *Reimaging Britain* across to the widest British and international reading public. It was after all a book about Britain (and Britons) and the wider world from which historically we had all come! In fact at this time of racial strife which enshrouded the Merton Event like a dense fog, it seemed right that I should press on with the promotion and application of my *essential ideas* of difference and mutual respect, both in literature and as a public speaker.

At the time, the British media was full of reports of racial tension and violence. Over the years, I'd been speaking in the main to mixed (black and white) audiences, most of whom were from ethnic minority backgrounds. But now I felt the time had come to reach much further out into British society at large. If not now, when? Given my motto: Nothing should be taken for granted, I felt that British tabloid readers were a legitimate target. Having got through to Prince Charles, now I hoped to get information through to a wider audience. On 17 October 2000 I wrote to Piers Morgan, editor of *The Daily Mirror*.

'As an admirer of your sensitive coverage in The Mirror of the Stephen Lawrence case (which not only enlightened white people, but also informed and enriched the understanding of Black and Asian people)

I write to you, especially as we approach Armistice Day 2000 and in view of the National Debate generated by the publication last week of a Runnymede Trust Think Tank Report on the definition of the word "British" as it relates to Blacks and Asians in Britain...

Against this background, it is with much pleasure that I enclose a copy of my recently published book Reimaging Britain: 500 Years of Black and Asian History. It is the first history of Britain to take an inclusive approach which makes historical sense of the Black and Asian presence in Britain. This "landmark" book is not just another history book, but one that is underpinned by a philosophical point which is clearly (expressed) in the conclusion....

I respect the many calls on your time, yet I hope you will read parts of my book, especially the opening chapters, the sections on the First and Second World Wars and the final pages under the heading "Reimaging Britain: Literary and Artistic Identity."

I and many people with their ears close to the ground, whose views I respect...are at one in thinking that the book needs to reach a wider audience through serialisation in the national press. I hope you will agree and perhaps we could come to some arrangement whereby this could be done.

Thanks for your consideration and I look forward to hearing from you.'

A few days later, Mr Morgan replied. He thanked me for the book and said he would read it with 'great interest.' Having done my bit, now it was up to him; and in this he must be given the benefit of the doubt. But although I did not think that sending my book to historians and editors was an imposition, I began to get used to them going no further than thanking me and saying they would read the book. Educationally, unlike any other history, *Reimaging Britain* is a key text, but why would an editor who was so clear as to where he stood on the Stephen Lawrence case, *not* champion the book? I wondered. After all, I did not write it for financial gain.

In the afterglow of the Trinidad Hilton Launch and New York University Press's accolade of naming *Arising From Bondage* as their 'Book of the Week' I had entered a zone of possibilities, from where I continued to write to interested Producers as well as maintaining contact with those engaged in the art of film-making. In conversations with Mr Rolfe, I had heard about Ms Sarah Murch (a colleague of his) whom he said would be helpful to our film proposals. A person of this proven quality and high standing, I thought can only add to my experience, especially after working with film-makers Alan Benns, Eric Davidson and Jane Stanton. Thus far, given that only Benns and Stanton had completed films in which I had appeared, I wrote to Ms Murch on 19 October 2000:

'Dear Sarah,

I forgot to add in my email yesterday that last Friday at the invitation of Merton Borough Council, I gave the Keynote Address for Black History Month (and)…the filming I had done here at the British Library a few months ago (reading from letters written by Indian soldiers in the Great War) for the BBC Knowledge History Quest Series, will be screened on Monday 23 October…

I watched again last night Simon Schama's current BBC series A History of Britain (visually stunning and well-presented) and I am even more convinced now than when I enthusiastically put the idea to you of a five-part Television Series on the Black and Asian Presence in Britain based essentially on my recently published book Reimaging Britain: 500 Years of Black and Asian History.

Given my 35 years of dedicated research and writing in this field and the success of the above-mentioned book, among others, I am hoping that like Schama, I will write and present this long overdue Series, which will take a fresh look at Britain… a different angle from traditional "British" historians. My approach will be an integrative one, placing the History of Blacks and Asians in the context of the British Isles. Such a Series will clearly have a global audience, because no history of Britain can be of any value without the story of the Empire and Britain's post-Empire history which must be seen from that perspective. I see my involvement in the making of this Series as integrative, rather than consultative (i.e a mere fact-giver) and I hope you and I can together press this first project of its kind forward and towards its successful completion!

I do very much look forward to hearing from you.'

A day later, I emailed Mr Rolfe about the 'Terms of Agreement' which he had earlier sent to me for consideration:

'*...I too have been pushed for time of late! Anyway, I think enough time has elapsed during which I received a good deal of advice and have given much thought to both copies of Falcon Films "Agreement" to which I am afraid I cannot commit myself...*

In the past few weeks, I have reviewed the whole idea of this project and my paramount concern now is to get a film made about the Indo-Caribbean people, one which I will write and present. To this end, I hope we will continue to work together and, necessarily, with those key persons at the Television Channels, whose ultimate decision is crucial'.

Pressing my case for a television history was fortuitous; a form of communication and expression that propelled me. Indeed it was a sign of the times, a medium which added a keen edge to the various representations that I'd been making. Under the heading: 'Royal Jubilee puts Empire back on Map,' the *Sunday Times* had published an article which, in part, stated: '*Britain is to revisit its Colonial Past. Among measures being lined up to celebrate the Queen's Golden jubilee is one that will recall the nation's Imperial ambition and the building of the Commonwealth.*

Children are to be taught about the subject as part of a new course that will become part of the National Curriculum in 2002 the year that marks the 50th anniversary of the Queen's accession...

Tony Blair told Don McKinnon, the Secretary General of the Commonwealth that "Commonwealth Studies" is to become an important part of the new subject - education for citizenship - planned for all children aged 11-16....'

Having written for this age group in the Heinemann's Educational World series, namely the book: *The West Indies*, I read further:

'*Some teachers, unsure whether the conqueror represent imperial glory or colonial oppression, have shied away from the subject. But the proposed Course...will according to a briefing document at the Institute of Education, "explore in detail how the historical links between Great Britain and Africa and Asia and the Caribbean have influenced patterns of migration." One source said, "The Course will have to cover the origins of the Commonwealth and **that means examining the history of Britain's Empire."** '*

Indirectly, this piece was powerfully in favour of my proposed Television Series, I thought.

And so, with much hope, I waited to hear from film experts Michael and Sarah.

Other book ideas, arising from my research and writings, intruded. In the wake of the success of the *West Indies*, I suggested to my Editor at Heinemann's that I write another 'School text' titled: 'Britain's Imperial Past' for the same age group, 11-14 year olds.

After decades of painstaking research, with so much new knowledge at my fingertips, I was eager to have the opportunity for its dissemination. I needed the opportunity to present history through various stories of the past. Thus my willingness to explore all possibilities was undiminished; and I paused to reflect on this fact: that through reinventing myself, the years of gregariousness and engagement as a workers' leader and public speaker had dealt a mortal blow to any lingering vestige of shyness. Now increasingly I took time out from my regime of work, work, work to socialise; and over the years, I met many hundreds of people from all over the world and from different walks of life. Since my enrolment at the New Era Academy of Drama and Music my love of films and the theatre had continued to grow: I came to know a number of actors some of whom shared my passion for history and literature. Among them was the actress Judy Phillips, a woman blessed with talent and beauty. In her background, there was a Caribbean connection.

'*Dear Ron,*' she wrote, '*This is a very belated thank you for your book (Arising From Bondage). You know, it has only come home to me just now what miracles you work! Some people only write or only work, but somehow you manage to do both! And not just one book, but quite a few all contributing to our knowledge and understanding of the West Indies. What can I say? Genius (and good-looking too!!)...*'

Was Judy being over-generous? Deeply respectful of her intellect and professionalism, I didn't think so then and I don't think so now.

Soon after, I had met and spoken to Horace Ove, the Trinidad-born

Film Maker and photographer, who gave me a copy of 'The Stepping Stone:' a few pages about an 'historical review' of Trinidad, which I promised to read. Horace was reputedly the first black Film Maker in Britain to make a feature length film entitled *Pressure* which was well-received. (Lionel Nagakane, the black South African, had also laid claim to being the 'first'). On a few occasions, he and I discussed his photographic work and the possibility of working together. In spite of good intentions, the pressure of work on both of us prevented our collaboration on anything.

On the theme of film (now more wary of film-makers than I'd ever been) on 20 November 2000, between filming an episode of *Hollyoaks* Mr Rolfe emailed me:

'When I got home on Saturday it was after one of the toughest weeks filming I had had in a very long time...

So I was particularly relieved to get home. Even better, when I returned it was to find that you had sent me the message to which I am now replying. It's good to know that we are on course again and I do blame the pressures that we have both been under, especially me, for generating the wobbly ride we have had over the last few weeks...

I have responded to Sarah's (Murch) request to forward to her a title page for the proposal, she had retained a copy of everything but the title. However, I'm anxious to arrange a meeting between her, you and I to make certain that what she forwards to the BBC is exactly what we want her to forward...

I shall call her later today when I get to Liverpool... now that the main shoot is over I can speak to you on the phone again instead of having to email all the time - and we can take it from there...

It was great to see that email from you, it will be even better to sit with you and watch the first film rushes of our programme that we have persisted and won and that the completed programme is well on it's way to transmission. That won't be long now, I'm certain of that.

Speak soon, Regards, Mike'.

Mr Rolfe's friendly but business-like message left the door open for further co-operation, and it was in this mood of openness that Award-winning Film Director Jane Stanton's letter of 28 November 2000 reached me.

'*Dear Ron,*

*I thought I would write to let you know some more news about The Unknown Soldiers documentary. As you will remember in April of this year the programme won the Race In the Media Award for Best Factual Documentary; however, I am delighted to let you know that The Unknown Soldiers has just won a Royal Television Society Award!! I am also very happy to let you know that the programme will now be **transmitted across the country on ITV** on the night of 10th December at 11.50 pm. I do hope you will enjoy watching it again.*'

A second major award for *The Unknown Soldiers*. Incredible! A wonderful outcome to my much-delayed break-through. If Jane was 'very happy,' I was delighted by the timeliness of the National broadcast of what was now a *double* Award-winning documentary which I felt could give a fillip to my own proposals for television films.

'*In closing*', Jane added, '*I would once more like to take the opportunity to **thank you for all of your help and advice in the production of this documentary. I am grateful to have had your help, the privilege to explore this important part of history and to hopefully bring it to a wider audience for the recognition it deserves.***'

These sincere, heart-felt words of acknowledgement, about the *one* occasion when I was included in the final, fully-edited and transmitted television programme, brought into sharp focus all those discussions and performances when other film-makers had talked to me at length, but eventually chose to leave my contributions on the cutting room floor! Clearly, their agendas had nothing to do with professionalism, or perhaps with their own self-respect, for while fully exploiting my books and all that I'd said to them, they were determined not to credit my contributions!

If those who had deceived and disappointed me thought they'd side-lined me once and for all, the good news from Jane Stanton had generated positively good feelings for with my authoritative performance as historian in the forthcoming national broadcast of *The Unknown Soldiers*, I was now further emboldened to press ahead with my long-held ambition of translating the hidden aspect(s) of 'British' history and presenting it in the form of television films.

Thus as Educator (both as an On-Screen Historian and Script Consultant in relation to *The Unknown Soldiers*) I had broken new ground!

Following the Royal Television Society Award, on 4 December 2000, I thought it right and proper to write to Ms Stanton suggesting that '*like the excellent Simon Schama "History of Britain" series, I'd like to write and present a "HISTORY OF BLACK PEOPLE IN BRITAIN," a topic rich in visual images, which I have more or less already researched. Would the BBC be interested in doing such a timely television series to complement Schama's? I feel that for us the time is right!*'

Surely, I thought, following her stunning Directorial triumph Ms Stanton would give due consideration to my proposition.

THE FOLIO SOCIETY'S *HISTORY OF ENGLAND 1945-2000*

Meanwhile working closely with Sue Bradbury of the Folio Society, her colleague Neil Titman informed me: 'We are now making the final touches to copy before sending *ENGLAND 1945-2000* down to our production department for keying.' So, at last, the editorial work on my Essay was complete and ready for publication. At this juncture, it was perhaps appropriate that, as the only non-white author (in the multi-volume History of England Series), there were a few things which I felt needed to be said in my contribution to *England 1945-2000*. After seeing all the Essays, in his *Preface*, Professor Felipe Fernandez-Armesto wrote:

'*For the Folio History of England we have sought classic works by historians eminent in their day and influential since − books still worth reading for their status as literature or their contribution to historiography. Where no properly classic volume is available, recent works have been adopted − well-written, impactful at their first appearance and likely to endure. All the volumes are intended to represent important strands in the fabric of English history writing during the last hundred years. They have been chosen for their variety... They were written from a diversity of perspectives, with a diversity of methods, at widely separated moments from the first decades of the twentieth century to the last... The truth of English history if we could get at it −*

would consist of a totality of all possible perspectives: by shifting in and out of different viewpoints, the Folio history will therefore get closer to the truth than would a conventionally planned series unified by a very limited set of guidelines and shared assumptions...

The Series first appeared as the Folio Society celebrated its fiftieth year. As it draws to its close, England seems alive or alert with promise or foreboding. Reading about England's past is the best way of preparing for her future...'

The *Introduction* to this volume was written by Roy Jenkins, then Chancellor of the University of Oxford and former Chancellor of the Exchequer and Home Secretary in a Labour Government. He began by saying:

'Thirty years ago, Sir Keith Thomas, one of Oxford's most eminent historians wrote a famous book entitled Religion and the Decline of Magic. The period under review in these essays might appropriately be called Prosperity and the Decline of Belief. The belief which has declined however, is not so much religious faith (although that has diminished too) as faith in the destiny of the country...'

After a detailed historical analysis of the 'country' Lord Jenkins concluded:

'The essays which follow will help to show how the England which emerged from the Second World War got where it is today. I must confess to having very little idea what will be revealed by a similar volume another fifty years on.'

My Essay *The English Test: Immigration Since the War*, opened thus:

'Since Elizabeth 1 issued her proclamation of 1601 to deport "such... blackamoores which...are carried into this realm" because as she put it "there are already here too many considerynge how God hath blessed this land with great increase of people of our owne nation as anie countrie in the world," calls for a repatriation of "foreigners" from England have echoed down the centuries. But few could have imagined the changes that would succeed the traumas of the Second World War: namely that Shakespeare's "Sceptred Isle" which had for centuries so masterfully ruled the waves would through an influx of migrants be transformed

into a multinational state with a multiracial, multicultural society.

The insistent and unusual demands of wartime broke down barriers, but others were erected as large numbers of colonial people of various nationalities were uprooted from their homes, having accepted the challenge of serving King and country – a chastening and enlightening experience which led them to consider the prospect of employment in England.

West Indians, Africans, Indians and Pakistanis, the "colonial migrants," on the other hand, came to England in the post-war years at the invitation of the British government. Unlike the Poles and Italians (who, it should be said, did suffer some initial prejudice) the non-white migrants were overwhelmed by discrimination, and often deeply dispirited and disillusioned by the unpleasant experience of seeking employment and housing…

Post-War Black and Asian immigration remained a sensitive, volatile issue on the English political agenda, flashpoints being the Smethwick election in 1964, the Kenyan Asians Crisis in 1967 and passage of the Commonwealth Immigration Act in 1968 which represented (as one writer noted) a "major politicisation of racism in Britain and both parties had cooperated in its implementation." This was the period which also saw the rise to political prominence of Enoch Powell, spokesman against black and Asian immigration, whose inflammatory speeches loom large in English history…

Today, instead of embracing the enriching contribution of different religions, languages and cultures, many English people feel threatened believing mistakenly that a pristine Englishness is being corroded and will eventually be lost. They forget that an English racial and cultural mix has been evolving for centuries. Nevertheless, politicians, policy-makers and civil servants have, at various times, tended to demonise the "foreigner" for his difference. Not surprisingly, colour prejudice and racial discrimination have been highly contentious issues in English post-war history and, over the years, a number of measures have been taken to address them…

Queen Elizabeth II's England may need to change more than it has, but it has changed enough to recognise the merits of this challenge. Such writings as ("Listen Mr. Oxford Don") creations by people from the former British Empire are, in effect, redressing the balance by writing back in a new linguistic mixture, a vital and inescapable task at the heart of the post-colonial enterprise. (The actions that immigrants and their descendants) take proclaim that they too are integral to England's history by inscribing as a corrective to Western versions their own histories, participants in the act of social and cultural renewal.

So, in the wake of intra-British, European, African, Middle Eastern, New Commonwealth and Caribbean post-war immigration, the consequences have been enormous. And in speaking about contemporary English cultural identities, questions arise: Whose England? Whose culture? Whose identity?'

Thus, one more piece, incorporating the main ideas inherent in my writings, was concluded. My relief and sense of having done my best was palpable. And so in the wake of the multi-talented 'Bloomsbury Group,' as historian, (biographer, novelist and essayist) I followed Thomas Babington Macaulay. But interestingly (given his family's Colonial connections with the West Indies, Africa and India) ironically, I have come to write of an England which Macaulay could hardly have imagined.

LITERATURE:
RAMA'S VOYAGE AND IMPARTING BRITISH HISTORY

As the end of the first year of the millennium drew to a close, I used my Christmas holidays to review and complete the meticulous work of putting the final touches to my debut novel *Rama's Voyage*. The fictional journey to this point, has been a long and digressional one, but I was excited by its prospects as I began to consider publishers to whom the manuscript should be sent.

To begin with, the first recipient was Alison Samuel, an editor at the publishers Chatto and Windus. Why send it to her? Simply because she was recommended to me by a trusted colleague. She wrote that she was 'not quite convinced by the fictionalisation - in narrative story-telling and style' and added that she 'didn't feel that this was a novel which we could really effectively publish.' No ambivalence here: her message could not be clearer. After a few more rejections, I began to question Ms Samuel's dismissive words; two in particular which she used in her letter: 'effectively' and 'successfully.'

Given that book publishers are business companies, essentially commercial concerns, understandably maximising profits was uppermost in their minds when considering a manuscript for publication. With no further explanation, did these often used words 'successfully' and 'effectively' mean that only commercial viability was synonymous with the publication of a book? Given my far from straightforward experience with various publishers, this was a question that interested me very much. Such rejections as I'd received were tough, but fair enough, I thought. In other words, if the book (or manuscript) could not make money, there was no other criteria on which its publication could be 'effectively' judged. This, of course, raised another question: that of literary merit. Given that *only published* books (by recognised publishing companies) can be entered for Book Prizes, does it mean that if a manuscript could not be published 'successfully' or 'effectively' (for example, *make a profit*) it should be consigned to the slushpile as worthless?

If making money is the overriding criteria adhered to by publishers, then there must be thousands of manuscripts that will never become published books. Furthermore, the Man Booker and other prize-winners only get a look in because they would make money, rather than provide readers with well-written and moving stories. Surely, the essential qualities of a book's message, its contribution to the sum total of mankind's knowledge rather how much money it can make should be integral to the criteria of its *value* when it is being considered for publication.

Against the selective business-like reasoning, how many quality works of literature never see the light of day (and thus are not eligible for entry or selection for the Book Prizes!) one wonders; and we would never know! Should the 'value' of a book be so judged? Alas, the Agents and publishers work (and let's be real, they need money to survive) by the dictates of the 'market.' We should always bear in mind however that 'markets' are (like cultures) not God-given, but man-made! As an Economics graduate from the London School of Economics, I know this only too well. But as an author of several published books, I was also very familiar with the expression from agent and publishers: one can't afford to be 'hopelessly uncommercial.' And so with few exceptions in the last 20-30 years in Britain, far too many works of literature especially by Afro-Asian authors had been deemed "uncommercial" and therefore *unpublishable!* Sadly, this was (is) an ongoing story.

How diverse was published British literary output? Not very. But in spite of this hard fact and other goings on in the publishing industry, my pen was never still. Foolish you might think, but the approach to my literary output has been (and is) this: Now and in the future, what I write means far more than the price of its publication. But, as I continue to take great pride in writing, I do so with as much hope as ever of getting it printed and published.

Before the end of the first year of the Twenty-first century and thirteen years after publication of *The Making of the Black Working Class in Britain*, though still out-of-print, a friend and fellow-historian Dr John Gurney drew my attention to a recently published book by Professor Jonathan Schneer: *London 1900: The Imperial Metropolis*. The American scholar wrote:

'*The role of those who were descended from imperialised peoples but who lived in Britain has also exercised the minds of British historians. Ron Ramdin... among others have followed the example of previous historians who sought to rescue despised classes of earlier times from the enormous condescension of posterity, chronicling the lives and struggles of men and women previously unheralded.*'

Reading this, I was reminded of the words of another distinguished American, Professor Katznelson who, in his Book Review in *American Sociology* had written:

'*The title of the book (The Making of the Black Working Class in Britain) reveals the ambition of the author which is to do no less for the formation of Britain's Black working class than Edward Thompson accomplished in writing the history of The Making of the English Working Class...Ron Ramdin marries historical narrative, reportage, case histories, character cameos and vignettes to present the sweep of the story of the emergence of black consciousness and organisation from the outset of slavery (which placed some Blacks in British ports) to the present.*'

It was gratifying therefore to be reminded that my work recognised in American universities and colleges was helpful to Teachers like Professors Schneer and Katznelson among other Educators, authors and researchers. Thus the book's enduring value was confirmed through its national and international status.

With post-Millennium expectations still generally high, as the early weeks of the year passed, educationally, as news of the Award-winning success of *The Unknown Soldiers* was transmitted beyond Britain, for example, to the people of the Caribbean, an article to this effect appeared in the *Trinidad Express;* and through it more people were informed of my multifaceted work. In terms of filling gaps in British history, at the all-important Primary and Secondary School levels, I received the following letter dated 6 April from the Black British author Susan Okokon:

'I have just received confirmation from Hackney Education Authority with regard to the showing of your film and Lecture for 10 May 2001. The day is intended to begin at approx 11.00 a.m and I intend to forward a schedule based upon our discussions by phone earlier today, once I have conferred with Hackney. The Event will be taking place at Hackney Free School and will involve students from this school and History staff from two other schools.'

When my son was born, I was already doing the best I could as spokesman for British (both black and white) working men and women; and in the process, I'd learned a great deal about life on the ground. Slowly, but surely, having raised the bar, I'd become dedicated to education: to *lecturing* (in addition, of course, to writing) thus sharing my experience and disseminating knowledge to school children in Hackney, still one the poorest Boroughs in London. This shift from the workplace to schools, libraries, universities and through the media: radio and television to the wider public was significant; an extraordinary educational graduation.

Working class leaders with a tendency to be mired in Marxist Socialist ideology, rarely went to university or cared much about *writing* books. In fact many, in spite of their bullish rhetoric tended to defer to their university-educated 'betters'! As it was, many such 'colleagues' had been quite dismissive, even discouraging of my decision to move on in the direction of higher education: 'You are selling out!' they said. 'Far from it,' was my response then, as it is now.

And so on the morning of 10 May before a packed hall of eager faces at Hackney Free School (in the Borough where I had lived for thirteen years) young minds upon whom the future of the country depended, waited to hear what I had to say. The theme that I chose to speak on was 'The Unknown Soldiers and Our British History.' To begin with, I said:

*'British historians have tended to **separate** Britain from its Empire, as though the former was not dependent upon the latter for its "greatness." The important question that we should now ask is: How did the British people see their country? "Education, education, education!" we hear this repeated often enough by Labour politicians and their Conservative predecessors in Government. But in spite of such wake up calls, "Education, education, education" seems an irrelevance in terms of "British" history as it is taught in schools; and one wonders whether most (especially white) British historians have been asleep. Indeed, few of them have tried to truly "educate" the British people, to tell what has been done in their name, by relating to them the full, unbiased story of the British Empire. Or, at the very least (allow or offer) **another perspective**, an interpretation from someone with colonial experience.'*

The history lesson which I had decided on and I make no apology for elaborating it here, includes *'RACISM, EMPIRE AND LABOUR.'*

Aware of the diverse backgrounds of the young black and white Britons' before me, taking nothing for granted, I proceeded:

'No doubt there were (and still are) those who prided themselves on the fact that huge profits poured into Britain from the Empire, which helped Britain to become "Great" and which kept the British people fed, clothed and housed. But this, it must be pointed out, was a state of affairs that could not be maintained without British Imperial domination.

The "Imperial question" was therefore, as one British politician put it, a "bread and butter" question that could not be ignored for in essence, Imperialism means war which was the means that Britain used to overcome and subdue the indigenous peoples of the Empire…

When I ask the question: How long do you think Black African and Asian people have been in Britain? I get a variety of answers. Most white people think that Africans and Asians came to Britain in the 1950s, certainly after the "War." And when I ask "which War?" surprisingly few specify one or other of the two World Wars of the 20th century.

Anyway, the answer they usually give falls far short of the truth which is, that the Black Presence in Britain dates back to Roman times!

Asians have also had early contact with Britain, which goes back some 10,000 years, according to one source. Yet, in today's Britain, Black and Asian people are still regarded and branded as "alien," as strangers. Why is this so? In answering this (and related questions) an understanding of British history, importantly the history of the British Empire is, of course, fundamental…'

Pursuing this honest appraisal of the British School system, I went on to relate aspects of the 'Black' presence in Britain dating back 500 years before focusing on how the Empire evolved.

'We should also remember,' I continued, *'that the vast majority of the Empire's population were colonised, non-white people, the mainstay of an Empire that had to be kept under control. To ensure this, British rulers adopted a brand of racial superiority which was widely disseminated through literature (and, significantly through the British Education System), which inculcated in young minds the idea that Black and Asian peoples were innately inferior to the white people who ruled them. Armed with this myth, influential Britons, perpetuated the belief that Asians and Africans were incapable of governing themselves, essentially because they were like children!*

"Virtually every European concerned with Imperial theory and administration," as one writer put it, "believed that physical and racial appearance was an outward sign of inborn propensities, inclinations and abilities." So racial differences informed much of what passed for British colonial policy.

In India, British rulers expected and demanded obedience, loyalty and respect from their colonial subjects of whom they held a low opinion. Either as loveable pets or occasionally elevated to the status of school children, this Imperial perception of Indians justified the

Indians' exclusion and the paramountcy of white supremacy, which had a profound believer in Prime Minister Balfour, who led the British Government at the beginning of the 20th century.

So, the intertwined relationship between Britain and her colonial "possessions" bred inferior/superior perceptions and attitudes on the part of the British ruling elites, who were determined to penetrate every field of intellectual endeavour, starting with the very young in school, both at home in Britain and abroad. Teaching resources were vital. For example, in British schools, history books reflected the "British" version of Black and Asian people, who were portrayed as uncivilised. In India, Lord Macaulay, the historian and Diplomat had earlier issued his famous "Minute" on Indian Education, which set the standard for a generation of Indians who aspired to become "educated." However, amidst the heady cut and thrust of Empire-building, the effect of "Imperialist" ideas on children in Britain did not go unnoticed by all white people. More cool-headed observers felt the need to comment. J.A. Hobson, for example, the author of a famous book entitled "Imperialism" (1902) noted the "persistent attempt to seize" the British School system on behalf of imperialist designs, and warned, that by capturing the childhood of a country and poisoning its "early understanding of history by false ideals and pseudo-heroes, to feed the pride of Race, to fasten this base insularity of mind and morals upon the little children of a nation and to call it patriotism, is as foul an abuse of children as it was possible to conceive." If this was the problem in Britain, imagine how much more harmful this would have been for millions of children, the "victims of racism" who peopled the Empire. For the fortunate few among them, who received a British "colonial" education, school texts and history books in particular continued to propagate the essential idea that British guidance was imperative. In this literature, there was hardly a hint of recognition of the hard work, the talent, the creativity, the imagination of the Black and Asian people whom they governed so high-handedly. The oppression and violence (both physical and psychological) which underpinned the trade, commerce and profitability of the British Empire, were always targets of counter-aggression from the colonised peoples who had become caught-up in a long-standing and deeply involved relationship in which resistance and revolt were endemic.

Broadly speaking, it was against this British Imperial educational background that both the First and Second World Wars were fought. In these violent, global conflicts, millions of Black and Asian people showed their loyalty and respect for King and country by volunteering to fight for Britain. Poor, though they were, they risked everything. For those whose lives were spared on both occasions, the return to their colonial homelands brought bitter disappointment. As was the case before the two World Wars, there was no improvement in their economic and social circumstances afterwards. And so the disillusioned thousands who had served during the Wars returned to Britain to join those who had stayed on in the hope of finding gainful employment.

And when the struggle for colonial freedom was stepped-up in the post-war years, the British authorities chose to overlook the wartime contributions of their colonial soldiers and the poverty of colonial peoples generally by brutally putting down public protest marches and demonstrations and imprisoning the leaders, who were (more often than not) returned soldiers. In effect, the British were reluctant to recognise the full part played by millions of Indian, African and West Indian soldiers on the battlefields of Europe. But realising that they had been written out of British history, the "unknown soldiers," their descendants and other colonial migrants have been (and are) determined to set the record straight by writing about them in history books.'

Beyond the lonely, solitary act of writing books, the opportunity of speaking to pupils (many of whom were seen as 'problematic') was very special to me. What I'd said thus far was direct: indeed it was the essential message that I'd been delivering in various venues, in one form or another, for some thirty years; namely the adoption of a much-needed *inclusive* approach to history and culture and therefore to migrants and migration in Britain. I concluded by saying:

'And talking about history books let us dwell for a moment on what has happened in the British Education System some 50 years after the Second World War, when Black and Asian veteran soldiers and migrants generally are still being seen as "Spongers" and "foreigners." Why are they still being perceived in this way? you may well ask, after

all that these soldiers have contributed... The short answer must be sought yet again (as I mentioned earlier in relation to the pre-War literature), in **education,** in books, in what children are being taught in schools today.

How has generations of British people seen their Empire past? is a timely question.

"One of the preliminaries of the British vision of their past," as one white British writer argues "is that they learn about Britain and the British Empire from different groups of historians, often coming from different historical traditions...one group deals with the Metropolis, another with the wider world. As a result, the British are positively discouraged from seeing their homeland and their Empire as an indivisible whole." A long view certainly. But not, I would argue, as a monolithic "indivisible whole" for difference and respect for difference should/must be seen in the context of connectedness.

One of Britain's best known historians David Cannadine has recently sought to correct this by attempting "to put the history of Britain back into the history of Empire and the history of Empire back into the history of Britain"! Empire, he argues was "the vehicle for the extension of British social structures – to the ends of the world." The constructs which the British made in the Empire were primarily "the mirror images of the traditional individualistic, unequal society that existed in the metropolis." This reinforces the argument of the inequalities and impoverishment of colonial societies that had existed before and since the World Wars. But this, I must stress, is nothing new! As an historian, I have been writing about this in relation to race, colour and class and so on for many years. The award-winning "World At War" television series which is currently being repeated on BBC2, reveals the horrible atrocities committed by Hitler's Armed Forces. But let us not forget that the British Empire was also "essentially a Hitlerian project on a grand scale, involving military conquest and dictatorship, extermination and genocide, martial law and 'special courts,' slavery and forced labour, and, of course, concentration camps and the transoceanic migration of peoples."

If history and history books have much to answer for, the Post-War persistence of a few dedicated people (in getting stories that have been largely hidden across to a wider audience through the medium *of radio, film and television) should be applauded. And although, even today, there are passages in school textbooks about the massive war-time contribution of Indian, African and West Indian men and women, who fought and died for Britain, it is hoped that the screening of The Unknown Soldiers would indeed result in more pressure being brought to bear on the Education authorities to include this film (and accompanying literature) as integral reference material in the national school curriculum.*

*Coupled with this double award-winning film, books like my own Reimaging Britain, an integrative and **first inclusive history** of the 500 year presence of Black and Asian people in Britain, which places it in the context of the Scots, the Welsh, the Irish and the English. As such it breaks new ground and should be available in every school library. Thank You!*

10 May 2001.'

Heard perhaps for the very first time in Hackney Free School, the interest these words stirred among this young audience was encouraging. In turn, I expressed the hope of doing more 'Talks' of this kind because few 'History Lessons' could have been more timely and important for these eager young minds.

As I left the school and walked along Mare Street, I remembered when as a five-year old, my son was taken to school each morning by his mother; and once more this thought came to mind: soon after he'd started I had asked him what was the name of his school. 'Hackney Free "Parokium" School,' he had said. 'Parochial' was a big word, but he quickly mastered the correct pronunciation. In those early days, my hope for my son was that he would grow and learn to be as diligent a student as possible.

TWENTY-EIGHT

LITERARY EMINENCE ? THE CHELTENHAM FESTIVAL, WELLINGBOROUGH LIBRARY AND *WASAFARI*

As news of the newly-published *Reimaging Britain* by Pluto Press spread, towards mid-summer 2001, Neil Rowland, the Literary Development Officer of Northamptonshire County Council wrote ahead of time to 'formally invite' me to participate in the Council's celebration of 'Black History Month' in October at Wellingborough Public Library. *'We can offer a standard negotiable fee of £125 plus expenses... I look forward to reading your book "Reimaging Britain." Copies will be available for the evening for sale and signing.'*

With his letter, Mr Rowland enclosed Leaflets and Posters. This, he said, was appropriate promotion for a serious and valued writer. Northamptonshire, it seemed, was ready. I responded quickly, accepting the invitation because, I felt it was my *responsibility* to do so. And, as on previous occasions, while the 'fee' was most welcome, it was *the message* that mattered.

Soon after this communication, having travelled around the country giving 'Talks,' as an *Educator,* fast on the heels of the Northampton Invitation, I was called upon to undertake yet another speaking engagement. If hitherto the Whitbread Cardiff Lecture was my greatest literary moment, what was now being offered was of a different magnitude: very high profile indeed! Sarah Smyth, Festival Director of the Cheltenham Festival of Literature wrote to welcome me as a participant. She informed me that I was scheduled to speak on the 'First Day' of this great literary occasion, and would be sharing the Folio Society's platform with such intellectual giants as Professor Felipe Fernandez-Armesto, Richard Hoggart (legendary cultural guru and writer) and Peter Jay (former BBC broadcaster and British Ambassador to the United States of

America). The topic for us to debate was '20th Century Power.' As literary festivals go, those in the know regarded Cheltenham as the biggest and best.

My response to the invitation was immediate; and I received an equally prompt reply.

'*I am delighted that you are able to come and take part in the Festival this October,*' Ms Smyth wrote, '*and I am writing to confirm the details of your event (which has been) scheduled for the afternoon of 12 October and we have written the following copy for the brochure which goes to press on Monday 23rd July...*'

Reading these words I reflected on my gradual, but irrevocable rise to this literary position; and what a prospect it presented. From such a platform, I could speak about matters that hardly got an airing at such Festivals.

Over the years, I had always given due preparation before my public appearances and with the approach of the Festival, I felt as ready as I would ever be to engage in debate with my eminent fellow-Panellists who happened to be a few of the greatest minds of the day. And so my earlier and regular correspondence with Sue Bradbury of the Folio Society regarding publication of my Essay in the brand new beautifully produced book the Society's *England 1945-2000,* tied in nicely with the Festival's invitation. Naturally, my anticipation of the 'Debate' grew.

Later in the summer, on the afternoon of 11 September around 3.45 p.m as I was preparing to leave work at the British Library, my colleague in the office said there had been explosions, an attack on America. She was not sure, but thought that New York was the target. Normally, at 4.00 p.m, I would leave my office desk and head straight for Seat 60 in the Rare Books Reading Room in St. Pancras. On this occasion, as more people spoke about 'bombs,' I headed straight home. What I saw on the television screen had been seared in my memory ever since. Throughout the evening and night and the next day, all the talk in the media was about what had happened or was happening in America. Gradually, more hard facts emerged of what became known as '9/11.'

There were a number of co-ordinated attacks launched by the

Islamic terrorist group Al-Qaeda upon the United States: in New York City and the Washington D.C area. Four passenger airliners were hijacked by nineteen Al-Qaeda terrorists so that they could be flown directly into buildings in suicide attacks. Two of these planes, American Airlines Flight 11 and United Airlines Flight 175 were deliberately flown towards and crashed into the North and South Towers of the World Trade Centre complex in New York. Within two hours both towers had collapsed with debris and resulting fires causing damage to surrounding structures. A third plane, American Airlines Flight 77 crashed into the Pentagon (the headquarters of the United States Department of Defence) leading to a partial collapse of its western side. A fourth plane, United Airlines Flight 93 was targeted at the United States Capitol in Washington D.C., but crashed into a field near Shanksville, Pennysylvania, after passengers tried to overcome the hijackers. In total almost 3000 people had lost their lives, including 227 civilians and 19 hijackers aboard the four planes.

As an autumnal feel was ushered in and hours of daylight were reduced and while the days dwindled down, on 28 September 2001, Bridget Frost, Administrator of the Cheltenham Festival of Literature informed me of final details:

'I thought I should confirm arrangements for Friday 12 October. The Event will be held at the Everyman Theatre, Regents Street, at 4pm. The Festival organisers ask that participants arrive an hour and a half before the event for a Sound Test so please aim to be there by 2.30 p.m…below train times may be helpful. Paddington, Bristol Parkway, Cheltenham.'

Got it! The route ahead was clear.

Being born almost on the Union Park Race Course in Trinidad and, as a fan of horse-racing, over the years I'd heard about the Cheltenham Gold Cup and the 'Cheltenham Festival,' essentially about hurdling (jumping fences) rather than flat-racing which I was more used to. But having never been to Cheltenham, before boarding the train at Paddington Station on the morning of Friday 12 October, I was reminded of another literary journey that I'd made just four years before to Cardiff Central. Now as the train to Cheltenham moved slowly away, then gained speed, I glanced around in the carriage and just ahead were two people who looked familiar. Physically, they were remarkably alike. This was all the more interesting because I recognised one of them as Ian Baxter, a Curator and a distinguished expert on India Office Records, whose desk in the British Library was just two yards from mine. These men could be going anywhere, I thought, as the train travelled further into the countryside. But after it had left Bristol Parkway Station on its way to Cheltenham, I noticed that Ian and his companion were still in the carriage. Just before I got off, I spoke to him. 'We're on our way to the Cheltenham Festival of Literature,' Ian said. 'This is my brother.'

'I am also going to the Festival,' I said. 'I will be speaking *this* afternoon in the Everyman Theatre,' I said

'We'll be there!' Ian said. He'd obviously consulted his programme.

Outside Cheltenham Station, I made my way towards someone who was holding a placard with RON RAMDIN on it. As arrangements were being made to take me to the hotel, where I was booked to stay, a tall attractive woman approached. My first impression was that she seemed worried. A second look confirmed that something was wrong: Her face was flushed a reddish-pink. A taxi drew up; and as if cued by its arrival, the woman said: 'I have left my computer on the train!' An unfortunate thing to have happened and my immediate reaction was one of sympathy and empathy. There was little I could say other than 'I'm very sorry. Have you reported it at the station?' Too upset to speak, the woman moved away. As she headed back towards the station, I got into the taxi which took me to the Queen's Hotel on the Promenade.

I relaxed in my room for a while, then had a quick look at my 'Presentation' before walking over to the *Everyman Theatre*. In the Guests' lounge, I was greeted by Sue Bradbury, who introduced me to Felipe Fernandez-Armesto, Richard Hoggart and Peter Jay, my three co-Debaters, all of whom I had heard on radio and television and had read a great deal about. They'd been at the top of their professions for years and were eminently qualified to debate now.

After I had met them for the first time, as was customary, we were asked to go onstage for a sound check of the microphones, one placed before each chair. I was curious about the *Everyman Theatre* and having pre-checked its history, I learned that Richard Burton had appeared there in *Dark Summer*. He was followed a year later by Roger Moore in *Miss Mable*. Sitting on the chair designated for me, I surveyed the empty auditorium as Festival technicians and officials checked and re-checked the sound system. Twenty minutes later, the doors of the Theatre were opened to the public.

When we eventually took our seats on stage the Theatre was jam-packed. Professor Felipe Fernandez-Armesto chaired the *Debate on 20th Century Power* and after each speaker had given a Five-minute Presentation, he opened the Debate by putting the first question to me. I was somewhat taken by surprise, but responded positively. Richard Hoggart and Peter Jay great professionals that they were, predictably spoke with authority; and as the Debate progressed, guided by Chairman Professor Felipe Fernandez-Armesto, time and again, I referred to immigration and multiculturalism in post-war British society. The Debate was then open to the floor. Another surprise, was being asked the first question from the audience. This was followed by several others. During the exchanges, I remember making reference to difference and 'respect for difference' in relation to most of what I'd been arguing. In a sense, I felt confident enough to do so and importantly this was the first big public test (before a cross-section of British intellectuals and the public at large) of these ideas that I'd been exploring and applying to the realities of my life.

After our 'Debate' on this first day of the Festival, myself and the other three participants returned to the Reception area where there was a book display. We exchanged books. Richard Hoggart signed his book *First and Last Things*, while in his brilliant book *Civilizations* Felipe's inscription read:

'To Ron –
A civilizing influence, from a savage admirer –
Felipe Fernandez-Armesto,
Cheltenham,
12 October 2001.'

As we were leaving the *Everyman Theatre* through the Stage Door, the queue for the next event had snaked its way off the main road to the side entrance. The person following us onstage was V.S. Naipaul, who it was announced the previous day, had won the Nobel Prize for Literature. How strange, how extraordinary, I thought that two Trinidad-born writers who had followed very different paths would have appeared on the same stage within an hour of each other!

That night at the Town Hall celebrations for the 52nd Cheltenham Festival, I saw the woman who had forgotten her computer on the train. She looked very different: calm. Transformed. I learned that her name was Ruth Padel, the well-known poet. 'Hello!' I said. 'Did you get your computer back from the train?'

'Yes,' she said. 'Thank you!'

I was very pleased for her. As part of the evening's programme while she read one of her poems, I listened with great interest. Later, I learned about her family's lineage to Charles Darwin.

When I returned to work at the British Library on the Monday morning after the Cheltenham Festival, Ian Baxter congratulated me on my performance. Until he'd spoken, I was not sure if he and his brother were in the audience as he said they would be. The fact that he was present on the train and in the *Everyman Theatre* added to the specialness of the *Debate on Twentieth Century Power*, my part in it and the occasion, as a whole.

Without doubt, looking back, this was the grandest, the most prestigious Festival on the literary calendar in which I'd participated, pitting my knowledge and intellect with seasoned debaters; and doing so before a knowledgeable and opinionated audience was indeed an extraordinary experience and achievement. Three days later, on behalf of the Folio Society, Sue Bradbury, the guiding light, so to speak, of the handsomely produced book *England:1945-2000,* published to coincide with the Festival, wrote:

'Dear Ron,
Thank you so much for your sterling contribution to our discussion last Friday in Cheltenham. I felt privileged to have three luminous talents on the panel and of course supremely lucky to have Felipe as Chairman.
I hope you enjoyed the experience – it was wonderful for me having

you there – and I hope too that you had a good time for the rest of your stay. It's quite an eye-opener if you have never been before!'

She added that a case of wine would be sent to me and expressed the hope that we would meet soon. Eventually, a case of wine from the Merchants Berry & Rudd of St. James was delivered to my desk in the office at the British Library.

The Cheltenham experience was indeed in many ways an 'eye-opener' and I was delighted to read Ms Bradbury's personal and professional thoughts which were followed by Festival Director Sarah Smyth's letter:

'Dear Ron Ramdin.

I am writing to thank you very much indeed for coming to take part in the Cheltenham Festival of Literature this October.

I know that your event was greatly appreciated by our audience *and I hope you enjoyed it as much as we did! This year the Festival attracted an audience of more than 50,000 who came to over three hundred (300) events in total.*

Thank you again for coming to the Festival – it is very much appreciated – and I hope we might be able to welcome you to Cheltenham again in the future.'

Fifty thousand was quite a lot of people. In reply, I wrote that 'the entire experience of being in Cheltenham is one that I have enjoyed very much and will always remember.'

In the days that followed, being back in Bloomsbury where I had spent all my working life in England, I viewed the 'Village' as if I were a newcomer, but with the benefit of hindsight, I reflected on the literary pedigree of the famous Bloomsbury Group, the squares and leafy surroundings of the University of London. Taken together, my Cardiff and Cheltenham appearances and the Higher Doctorate, the D. Lit, were thus far, high-points of recognition in my literary career.

In the afterglow of these extraordinary successes, time passed quickly as I became busier. More travel, as expected, was in prospect. Before my Talk for 'Black History Month' in Wellingborough Library, Northamptonshire, Mr Rowland the Literary Development Officer ensured that sufficient publicity was being given. I never doubted this. Sponsored by Northampton Council and East Midlands Arts, the leaflets and posters entitled: 'WORD WORKS' carried the following message: 'Listen to Ron Ramdin the distinguished historian, biographer and novelist, who is based at the British Library. His new book is called *Reimaging Britain...*'

Tickets for this special Wellingborough event were reasonably priced at £4.00, and with concessions at £2.00, a good attendance was expected.

On the evening of my 'Talk,' I was met at Northampton Station by Mr Rowland who seemed pleased as he drove me to Wellingborough Library. Fresh from my Cheltenham appearance, I felt at ease; and as we entered the building there was a buzz of excitement arising from those who had gathered.

The evening's programme began with a stirring presentation of poetry by 'Sweet Sister Hood,' a colourfully dressed woman. After being introduced, I went to the rostrum and launched into my 'Overview' of the 'Black and Asian Presence in Britain' at the end of which Mr Rowland, as Chairman, invited questions.

A man at the back stood up and I anticipated the first question. I waited but he did not ask a question. Instead, he lectured me on the 'Nile Valley' and associated studies. He did this for several minutes during which I tried repeatedly to interpose, but he denied me the chance to speak. His harangue continued for some time before I was able to say: 'I am not qualified to answer questions on the Nile Valley, but if you have a question to ask about the Black and Asian presence in Britain, I would be happy to respond.' At this point, the man was eventually asked to leave the room and the Library premises. It was the first time in my thirty-two years of public appearances in Britain that such a disruption had taken place. I was nonetheless heartened by the man's stout defence of 'blackness' or, as he had put it, his 'Africanness;' a clear indication of growing pride and awareness of culture and identity in the black community.

Apart from this disruption, the rest of the evening's programme went ahead as planned. During the Book Signing session, like the Merton Council *Books Etc* experience, several copies of *Reimaging Britain* were bought. Overall, I had met and spoken to people from many different backgrounds; and on my way back from Northampton, I was satisfied with what turned out to be an eventful and exciting evening in Wellingborough Library. Time very well-spent, I thought. Why? Importantly, because it was another occasion when I was given the opportunity to listen, share experience and say something meaningful to a diverse group of people who were open (except for the heckler), ready and willing to learn about their place in contemporary and ever-changing British society which many people regarded as the 'Dis-United Kingdom' *educationally*.

The golden colours of the trees in autumn mirrored my feelings of the passing of time which transformed the environment. Given that landscape triggers feelings and memory, I reflected on my successful Merton Council, Cheltenham Festival and Wellingborough Library appearances. These high-points were followed by the Autumn Issue of *Wasafari*, the journal of international literature, which featured an Interview with novelist Bernadine Evaristo. The Interviewer was none other than the well-known and respected Dr Alistair Niven, an expert on African and Black British history and literature. Some years before, I had shared a Platform with Dr Niven at the Birmingham Arts Readers and Writers Festival at which we spoke about Black history. The need for education in this field was clear: For my part, in spite of over two decades of publishing books and delivering Conference papers, lectures, talks and giving radio and television interviews in Britain and abroad, incredibly a new generation and indeed most of the wider British public still hardly knew much about the long-standing Black and Asian presence in Britain. Against this background, Dr Niven's 'Interview' with Bernadine Evaristo was interesting. It opened as follows:

'AN: I was very struck by your final remark in The Emperor's Babe when you are giving some late acknowledgements you say that Peter Fryer's Staying Power was an influence over you and it was there that you really discovered that black people existed in Roman Britain. When did you read the book?

BE: I read it in the late 1980s. It was the first time I really realised

that there had been a black presence in Britain well before the 1940s...
It is important because it is an aspect of British history that hasn't
been fully recognised and that is still unacknowledged and that is still
invisible to most people.

AN: And do you think people like Peter Fryer and Ron Ramdin,
historians of the Black experience, are themselves unacknowledged and
should be better known?

BE: I think so, yes...'

Perhaps this was the correct thing to say. Knowing there were
gaps in the history of Britain, for those who cared to read it, I
felt my body of work should speak for itself. Celebrity authorship
was far from what my life-style had been as I continued to push
the boundaries, confronting the pressing political, economic and
social concerns of the day. By so doing, I revisited, reappraised
the issues of race, colour, class, gender, religion and so on as they
related to my unremitting engagement with cutting-edge debates
on historical and contemporary life. Significantly underscoring it
all, was my insistent engagement with exploring ideas and crossing
boundaries through different literary genres.

Surprisingly, in spite of my public appearances, before the end of
2001, the *only in-depth* Book Review of *Reimaging Britain* appeared
in the multicultural counselling Journal *RACE*. I was eager to read
it.

'*The title of this book*', reviewer Karen Bell wrote, '*was very*
intriguing. Before even reading the book, I started to think about what
the writer was trying to present. It highlights that black and Asian
people are very much part of British society (a positive part). Therefore
the title "Reimaging Britain" was very apt.

I found this book very informative and interesting to read. It enabled
me to gain further insight into the difficulties black and Asian people
experienced in this country and their own country of origin over a
500-year period.

It is not very often that you find a book that documents the
presence of black and Asian people in Britain before 1950. *More*
often than not the focus is on the period between the 1950s and 1960s.
This book does not negate the importance of this period, far from it! It

considers the historical importance of black and Asian people before, during and after this period.

As a black woman, reading this book enabled me to gain a greater awareness of the role black and Asian people played in the history of Britain and the former colonies, which I consider significant as to how Britain has developed to the present day. The author has also given some substance and value to the largely hidden histories of these immigrant communities, bringing their sufferings and achievements to the fore. **A lot of information about the black and Asian experiences is entwined with British history,** *which is encapsulated in this book.*

Ramdin's book is **a very uplifting read. It gave me a further sense of pride and belonging, with a most appropriate title which documents how Black and Asian people have been involved in Britain for centuries. Without writers such as Ramdin many people of African and Asian descent might not be totally aware of the length of time we have been involved in developing and re-imaging this country.**

This book demonstrates how we have become part of the fabric of British society. It recognises the changing face of Britain and how the Empire is no longer outside Britain but now within Britain.

Perhaps the time has come for this aspect of British history to be included in the National Curriculum to aid the developing mind of Britain's young people, giving them a true, overall reflection of British history.

For as Bob Marley said, "Half the story has never been told." Britain is a multicultural society with a diverse population of different peoples from around the world. Ramdin's book recognises this and demonstrates it well.' (Author's emphasis).

The positives identified by this experienced Counselling Professional was honest and refreshing. But how many who had read the book took what was said seriously, I wondered. Suffice it to say (and I remain hopeful) that the integrity of Reviewer Karen Bell's words would resonate in the minds of those who read *Reimaging Britain.*

Interestingly, unlike *The Times* Book Review of *The Making of the Black Working Class in Britain*, none of Britain's newspapers had reviewed *Reimaging Britain* which provoked the thought: How many people, including Book Reviewers, in London and in Britain's other towns and cities, can say that their own back-stories stretching over four generations (or less) does not have an immigrant ancestor! In fact, Britain is essentially a nation of immigrants, including those who, at various times, constituted 'The Establishment.' Scratch the surface of their past and much will be revealed. Personally, I love many things about Britain; indeed I have become rooted here and feel 'British.'

For me, identifying with Britain does not however preclude speaking out against social injustice, here or wherever I find it. This relates to a fundamental human tendency: the desire to be liked and, often appreciated. But too often this 'desire' tends to inhibit us from being more truthful about ourselves and others. This 'tendency' arises from something that I'd been trying to come to terms with over many years: namely, the 'fundamental dissonance of life' and certain essential ideas arising therefrom that I'd been exploring in *Reimaging Britain.*

Since I'd given the Cardiff Whitbread Lecture, socially I saw more of Professor Skilton, Andy McKillop (Director of Arrow Books) and Chris Hughes, the Whitbread Company Director. After we had met for dinner before Christmas 2000, the next day Andy wrote: 'Very good to see you last night and to catch up with your news... I've enclosed a copy of *The Healthy Flying* book I mentioned to you at dinner. It's the exercises section that will probably be most useful to you on your long flight in January to New Zealand for your son's wedding. How exciting! I hope it all goes well.'

The Lecture had brought us three together and now I saw Andy as a friend.

In the last days of the first year of the millennium, as if to test my resolve the bitterly cold temperatures of winter made me shiver, but I warmed to the thought that seventeen years on, **educationally**, *The Making of the Black Working Class in Britain* has continued to reach and teach people far and wide, one of whom was Professor

Jonathan Schneer while he was working on his book *London 1900*.

TO THE END OF THE EARTH

My grandchildren Georgia and Joshua were now six and four years old. My son Ronnie and his partner Melissa, were adjusting to a new life in New Zealand. The plan was that they would get married at a convenient time. Several months after they had left England, I received a Wedding Invitation from Melissa's father and mother, David and Moira Slater, to attend their daughter's marriage to my son. The Ceremony would be held 'at The Mudbrick Vineyard, Waiheke Island, just off Auckland on Thursday 10 January, 2002 at 11 a.m.' My one and only son was getting married at the southernmost end of the earth. Hard to believe, but true.

Just before the wedding, I flew from London via Los Angeles to Auckland. It was an extraordinary journey of twenty-five hours of flying! Hitherto unimaginable, the first part of the one-stop flight from London to Los Angeles lasted about twelve hours. During the stop-over of two hours, while passengers' baggage were checked, I was pulled over for questioning by officials because a shaving Wilkinson sword razor blade was detected in my briefcase. Once this was sorted, I rechecked-in my baggage and after another thirteen hours of flying, I landed early in the morning in Auckland, where I was met by my son who drove me to his house in Freeman's Bay.

Along the way, many colonial-style bungalows, painted cream or white and green, reminded me of those I had seen in my youth at the Pointe-a-Pierre Oil Refinery complex. Above all, it was a great joy to see my son again. He looked happy. Together again we could not be further away from Upper Street in London both in terms of mood and place: we were now at the furthest reaches of the planet near the vast forbidding ice-scape of the South Pole. Being there roused a joyous, warm feeling and from the moment of arrival and meeting the Slaters, I was made to feel most welcome and at home by my family to be.

The night of the next day was Ronnie's Stag Party before which a number of us (including the group of 17 people from London who had come to attend the wedding) visited the big Casino beneath the Tower in central Auckland. Afterwards, we stopped at a few pubs; and being in the company of Londoners made me feel less alien in the new environment. When the Stag Night crowd arrived back at Ronnie's Freemans Bay address, we all crammed into the fairly spacious house. At breakfast a few hours later, (as well as on the mornings that followed) on his Barbecue deck, Ronnie fried eggs and bacon. After the seemingly continuous celebrations, there were some hungry mouths to feed. Everyone seemed satisfied. Being in Auckland was the most unlikely thing; a great experience made all the more meaningful because it was for Ronnie's wedding.

The day before the wedding, Ronnie, Dean (Ronnie's Best Man and dearest friend from London) and I boarded a Ferry from Auckland Harbour which headed out to the island in the distance known as Waiheke, where we spent the night in a local hotel. The next morning we woke up early and was greeted by a perfectly clear, sunny day. After breakfast, we relaxed a while. Then Ronnie began to dress for his Big Day: First the shirt, trouser and cravat before donning his jacket. Fully attired, he looked very handsome and I felt a surge of pride. Soon, Ronnie, Dean and I made our way out and boarded a bus that took us to join Wedding Guests at the picturesque Mudbrick Vineyard.

On arrival we made our way across the lush grounds just outside the Restaurant and Wine cellars area. At intervals on the undulating green lawn there were large multi-coloured umbrellas under which were tables with glasses, jugs and bottles of drinks for the Guests, who had arrived on the Ferry from Auckland. Nearby, a String Quartet played as people milled about. It was a perfectly clear day. In the distance, I could see the blue Pacific and a number of islands. The edge of the lawn was bordered by the Vineyard, with its well-tended rows of vines that stretched up the gently sloping land. In all, the setting was beautiful, truly wonderful. The music floated on the steady breeze, as people chatted and sipped pimms and other drinks. Marvelling at the pleasant scene, I was overtaken by an encroaching reflective mood for here I was, a long, long way from London attending (apart from my own), the most important wedding. I remembered the *S.S. Canberra,* the Pacific and Orient Liner and the New Zealand teenagers aboard. How incredible that

I should be here now in the Pacific, I thought.

I looked on as my son talked to members of the Wedding party and Guests. Then my daughter-in-law to be Melissa and grandchildren Georgia and Josh arrived in a sleek American-style period limousine. Melissa looked stunning in her outfit and her children looked cute and beautifully dressed for the occasion. Altogether, Ronnie, Melissa and grandchildren Georgia and Josh were a handsome family. Then there were David and Moira Slater and their son Mark and daughter Kelly.

The marriage ceremony was held in the open air, and from where I stood the skyline of Auckland city was just visible beyond the officiating Pastor, a relatively young woman. As part of the 'Service,' I was called upon to say a few words. I was forewarned of this, and so before leaving London, I gave some thought to my contribution. This is what I said:

'*Charlotte played the piano extremely well. Eduard performed not quite so well on the flute; for, although he practiced diligently from time to time, he was by nature not patient or persevering enough to train such a talent successfully. Therefore, he played his part unevenly - some passages well but perhaps too quickly; in others he had to slow down because he was not familiar enough with the music; and it would have been difficult for anyone but Charlotte to go through an entire duet with him. But Charlotte timed how to cope with it; she slowed down and then allowed him to run away with her, fulfilling in this way the double duty of a good conductor and an intelligent housewife, both of whom always know how to preserve a general moderate measure, even if, single passages may not always be in the right tempo.*'

After the ceremony, the relaxed atmosphere enhanced the occasion. As we mingled, many 'Introductions' were made and I was very pleased to embrace my warm and welcoming New Zealand family and their friends.

Moving on to the Restaurant, we took our places for the Wedding Dinner: a delicious 'entrée,' main course, dessert, tea and coffee. The feast was followed by toasts and speeches, before music and dancing ensued. I much enjoyed my dance with Moira. Among the people I spoke with were Joan, Dorothy ('Dot') and John Murray, a friendly couple, who invited me to their home. Engaging and charming, they were also book-lovers!

As the dancing and talk continued, the merriment at Waiheke was gradually brought to an end when it was time for us all to make our way back to the quayside and board the Ferry back to Auckland. Ahead of us were the Bride and Groom in their special 'Wedding Launch' just for two, on which the New Zealand flag astern flapped briskly in the breeze. On arrival at Auckland Harbour, the newly-weds were greeted by officials at the Hilton Hotel, their honeymoon destination. The rest of us, family, friends and Guests made our way to a local venue where we danced until it was late. Finally, as that memorable day and night merged into the early hours of the next morning, on our way home, someone said he fancied a 'White Lady' and suggested that I have one.

'What is a 'White Lady?' I enquired as we walked towards an all-night Van-cum-food stall, which reminded me of a hot-dog seller. We were now in central Auckland and, arising from the oniony smell and comment, I realised that a 'White Lady' was a snack; a New Zealand Speciality. Judging from the person nearest to me in the queue who was holding one, it was the largest Burger I'd ever seen! Between the two halves of a bun were eggs, bacon, ham, sausage and cheese plus condiments. By the time, I was served I was hungry enough to tuck into the 'White Lady' with relish. It had been a very long day; and after the drinks we had consumed, a few of us were in need of some relief. But being in the city centre there was no available Public conveniences at our disposal. How very strange, I thought. Naturally one or two of the younger men sought dark, quiet places to relieve themselves. Interestingly, one of them was arrested by plainclothes policemen. This marked a surprising end to an unforgettable Wedding down-under in New Zealand. A few days later, referring to the 'pee' arrest, I dared to see the funny side of it and said to Mark and his father David: 'One day I would immortalise this incident in a short story titled: 'The Pee-nal Colony.'

In the days following the wedding, I made many enjoyable visits to the home of the Slater family, to beaches and other places of interest. And I had, of course, posed for photographs with family and friends, including one with a Special cloak, reputedly centuries-old and once worn by a Maori King!

In the days that followed, Ronnie and Melissa spared no effort in ensuring that all their guests from England were well looked after. Soon, one by one, or two by two (the couples) and individual guests left for the long haul back to 'Old Blighty.' As the last visitor to leave, I took the opportunity of visiting Melissa's relatives and friends and went to Sulphur Springs and the Slater's House on Bethells Beach where at night, I saw something wondrous - the night sky as never before, the starlit canopy of the 'Southern Cross' and other Constellations. On one occasion the Moon appeared larger and closer than I could ever have imagined it. Feeling the rising cool winds - the 'Southerlies,' I feared its potential power. Put simply, New Zealand was a beautiful and enriching country and strangely mesmerised, there was an indefinable something that I sensed which was also forbidding about the place.

A few weeks after the 25-hour return flight, I gradually adjusted to being in London again. It was Spring-time and I wallowed in pleasant memories of Ronnie, Melissa, my grandchildren and the extended New Zealand family. Being back, I was hopeful of news on a number of fronts, including two book proposals. Then in March 2002 I received a letter from Lester Crook on behalf of the Radcliffe Press, an associate of the publisher I.B. Tauris.

'*Thank you for your letter of 25 Feb. I too was glad to be able to speak with you the other day although I regret that our conversation was rather short. I shall look at the possibility of a paperback of Arising From Bondage. It should* **certainly go into paperback** *and this was* **always my intention**.' (Author's emphasis)

Having earlier sent the Proposal 'The Great Cause' to Dr Crook, more recently I followed this up with another book idea to which he responded:

'*Thank you for the outline of your proposed biography of William Wilberforce: A Life. I regret of course that we are not at the moment going ahead with "The Great Cause" but I understand the reasons...*

I agree that the approaching 200th anniversary of the abolition of the Slave Trade is a good one for a new biography of Wilberforce. But what would be the real attraction of the book? I think this must revolve around the way in which Wilberforce is portrayed. It must be above all an outstanding biography - the life of one of the most extraordinary figures in an age which produced a number of giants! How will Wilberforce spring into life and how Wilberforce would take the reader along and prove an irresistible attraction? What I am attempting to say is this: however well the scholarly and wide raging source material is used...and however outstanding the scholarship the book must make the man live and form a powerful and lasting impression on the reader. Perhaps Wilberforce might be regarded as being rooted in the mores of this period but I wonder whether he might not be regarded as being an important figure for any age.

I much look forward to discussing this proposal with you.'

These were valid points of which I took note for future reference.

TWENTY-NINE

'PATRIOTISM:THE LAST REFUGE'
ANOTHER GREAT BRITISH DEBATE

Another ongoing, significant literary matter was the submission of a draft of Chapter One of my novel *Rama's Voyage* to the *London Magazine* in the hope that they would publish an excerpt of it as a novel 'in progress.' Sebastian Barker, the *Magazine's* editor had cast his critical eyes over the 'draft' and made bold editorial marks on my typescript. As the son of the poet George Barker and a man of scrupulous literary and editorial judgement, I much anticipated his comments which eventually came. In red ink on the title page of the manuscript, he wrote: '*The novel (Rama's Voyage) is important because it has perfectly fictionalised the truth. Many novelists now writing are not capable of this. Instead, they fictionalize fiction. This is of course legitimate, but on a rung lower down the ladder of literature.*' How unlike the Chatto & Windus editor Ms Samuels's comments Mr Barker's were, I thought. Her outright rejection, indeed the dismissive statement that she was 'not quite convinced by the fictionalisation' ran counter to Mr Barker's view of what he had read as being '*perfectly fictionalised.*' To underline his opinion, lower down the page on which he had written, he commented further on the novel: '***Cool, sober, intelligent observation from a perfectly realized boy narrator. A true work of fiction trying to be born here.***'

Just over a fortnight later, I received another letter from Mr Barker. '*I am writing to you about "Rama's Voyage"… I like the story a lot. It will make an excellent piece for the Magazine…It is an honour to be associated with it…*

   If you wish to discuss these proposals, please write to me.'

The next day, I replied:

'*Dear Sebastian,*

Your letter just arrived and I hasten to respond. I am, in turn, honoured that you are interested in the story Rama's Voyage and I would, of course, be glad to discuss the "heavy editing." Please let me know when it will be convenient for us to meet.'

Mr Barker's glowing appreciation of what he'd read of *Rama's Voyage* was more than I'd expected and, of course, most encouraging. One of the publishers to whom I had sent the entire manuscript of *Rama's Voyage* was Peter Owen. On 14 May 2002, he responded:

'Thank you for sending me your MS. I have looked at it but not the whole book, and it certainly has quality.

Our current position is, the fiction market is so bad and there is a price restriction, so that we are not at this point buying any fiction. However, we are in negotiation with the Arts Council and it is just possible we may get some help there. If this is the case, then we would look at your book further and it might be possible to publish it...

Of course, if you wish to submit it elsewhere that of course, is fair enough as I cannot guarantee anything at this point.'

This lack of a 'guarantee' alerted me to the futility of taking the matter further with Peter Owen. But, I was determined to explore other options.

While considering the appropriate fiction publishers for *Rama's Voyage*, I turned my attention to a brand new and hugely significant proposition. As I'd always done, especially since I became a published author, while accumulating knowledge, my habit of giving of my time and expertise to researchers and students never waned. Thus as word spread, a few people like Ms C, a Senior Curator in the British Library, regarded me as a highly knowledgeable person who should be consulted. Among my contacts was a meeting with David Thomas, Head of E-Access at the National Archive (the Public Records Office) at Kew. At our first meeting, Mr Thomas and I discussed the ambitious 'Moving Here Project,' a PRO initiative, the aim of which was to provide a *pioneering website* for various groups of people from different parts of the world who had migrated over time to Britain. After further meetings, eventually I was selected to write the crucial Asian and Caribbean 'Briefs' that would form the basic structure: In other words, the documents that would start this core 'Project.' In the scheme of things, this was both an honour and a challenge. And so on 31 May 2002 I received the 'Moving Here Commissioning Letter' from the Public Records Office, the National Archive.

'I am writing to confirm the arrangements we have agreed concerning your contribution to the Moving Here website. By contribution we refer to the written material which you will provide and for which you own the copyright. It is understood that the development of the website and its content has been funded by a Grant from the New Opportunities Fund. It will cover information and stories about migration to England by people from the South Asian, the Caribbean, Irish and Central and Eastern European communities. In addition, for your information the contribution may also be used by the New Opportunities Fund (including to promote the site) and their licensees: The People's Network, the National Grid for Learning or other similar Public Sector sites. Your contribution will be written in accordance with the brief already agreed between us (a copy of which is attached to this letter. You will deliver your contribution in batches as outlined in the attached brief. These Batches will be delivered to us no later than the dates listed in the enclosed schedule, time being of the essence of the contract and in accordance with the following Terms & Conditions (12 listed)...

I would be grateful if you could sign both copies of this letter below as confirming acceptance of these Terms and Conditions and return one to me as soon as possible.

Signed Dr Ron Ramdin.........

Author/Writer (10 June 2002).'

After reading this letter, there was no doubt about the importance of my role in this new national-international enterprise.

Characteristically, I embraced my responsibilities fully: first I duly signed and returned the Commissioning letter; and on that same day 10 June 2002, I wrote to Sam Seager, Head of this National Archive's Moving Here Project: *'In accordance with our Agreement that I am "WRITER" of the "Caribbean Narrative" of the Moving Here project, I enclose a copy of the "Commissioning Letter" with my signature on it.*

I look forward to receiving a copy (of the "Agreement") with both signatures.'

And so I buckled down to work. To begin with, I composed my 'FRAMEWORK DOCUMENT: THE CARIBBEAN NARRATIVE.' Thereafter, from my 'Original Brief' of this aspect of the Moving Here Project, I incorporated many themes: Prologue; Origins; Journeys; Settling; Growing Up; Working Lives; Politics; Culture and Festivals and Establishing Identities. I also wrote a Time Line from 1840-2000.

Taken together, this 'Framework' formed the 'original' structure from which this aspect of the present 'Moving Here' website developed.

My signature on the 'Briefing Documents' and commitment to the rest of the 'Project' marked a major departure from all that I had done so far: for example, from being a pioneering historian and workers' leader concerned over many years with diversity and community issues, now appropriately, I was given the responsibility of 'authoring' the template of a seminal resource for twenty-first century Britain (and the world) through the new National Archives website.

Predictably, this work on Moving Here brought me in contact with key figures; indeed many leaders in their field, among whom was Alison Taylor, a regional expert on Caribbean migrants in Bedfordshire who had contacted me. In turn, I wrote:

'Thanks very much for getting in touch. Your contribution to the Moving Here Project is, of course, very important. I have just done a draft of "ORIGINS" and "JOURNEYS" and have started "SETTLING" and "GROWING UP" of Level 3 of the Caribbean Text. I found our "Content Meeting" very helpful as to who has got to do what and I recall the many examples of things you said you have at Luton. They would complement the text... It would therefore be most helpful (and timely!)

If you could, remind me of the specific images/items you have and, particularly those that are relevant to the above-mentioned sections of the Caribbean Narrative.

In anticipation of your response...'

Given that much time for the deadline of my submission of the 'Briefs' had already elapsed, four days later, Ms Alison replied:

'Many apologies for taking so long to get back to you...

I'm not sure how much of the info I previously supplied to others at Moving Here has made its way through to you, so perhaps it's best to start with basics. I think our main contribution will be oral testimony, some of it written and some in audio form. I have Tapes of 4 interviews which I did in connection with the Museum's "East-West, Home's Best" Exhibition some time ago. They will need quite a bit of editing before they can be added to the website, and therefore I do not think I can have them ready for the November Launch... In fact, we had originally said that Luton could make no contribution to MH until 2003 for this reason. Coming to the Content meetings and talking with the researchers/writers has made me realise that I need to provide some material in time for the Launch, but I must confess that it's proving a struggle.

However, the best info from the audio Tapes is already transcribed into written form as "Caribbean Reflections-Memories of Island Life." This was an information file produced in connection with the exhibition, and in addition to extracts from the 4 individual interviews it contains memories which were disentangled from a very confusing recording of a lively group meeting, which no longer exists in audio form. I attach the text of the file below - as you will see it concentrates on life in the Caribbean but also looks at moving to England, and issues of identity and reconnecting. Very much the structure of the MH site, in fact.

In connection with the same exhibition we borrowed and copied personal photographs from local people who helped us to mount the display. They have verbally agreed that most of them can be used for MH though I have yet to get written consent. I attach the images below...

There are also some more recent oral history interviews gathered primarily for our redisplay project which looks at life and work in Luton. They concentrate on the lives of a few African Caribbean individuals during their time in Luton and are not specifically concerned with their cultural background, though there are mentions of experiences of racism etc. We do not have complete transcripts but I attach summaries below to give you an idea of the content. If you want them… I could probably provide them in time for November.

I thought that some of the objects which we used in the East-West exhibition could be photographed for inclusion in the website. However, I think this will have to wait until next year.

This is more or less everything. I'm sorry this is such a long email and apologies for bombarding you with all this at once, but hopefully it gives you a clearer picture. Looking back at my original email when I asked you what your priorities were, it seems that I am now dictating them myself. I fear this may be unavoidable given my other heavy commitments at the moment, but hope the material I have suggested for November will be enough to meet your needs.'

All that Ms Taylor had mentioned was relevant, but more was needed. The emphasis was still on the Afro-Caribbean Experience; and of the many photo images and archival material that I'd been considering for incorporation was a War Office Document: WO 339/90293 concerning the demise of a then little known stalwart Black Briton of Afro-Caribbean English descent, a Black Briton of whom I had knowledge many years earlier. His name is Walter Daniel Tull who was 'killed in action' on 25 March 1918 in France. Tasked with integrating such material into the 'Moving Here' structure, just handling the Document, it must be said, had its own arresting power, which made me pause for reflection.

I had no illusions about the demands of authorship, both of writing and expanding this 'Brief'; and as it evolved, I was excited about bringing together the steadily accumulating mass of material as never before (archival and illustrative) and aligning the various themes into a coherent and clear perspective. So it was that I remained intensely focused, engaged with the main professionals, archivists and others, as the day for the Launch of the Moving Here Project at the Public Records Office, approached.

A GREAT BBC DEBATE

Never far from my thoughts was the need for money especially at Christmas time. Propelled by this 'need', on 6 November 2002, I wrote to Sam Seager (Head of the MH Project) about payment of an Invoice that I'd submitted some weeks earlier for work done. By my reckoning this sum would ease the financial pressure upon me until well into the new year. In addition to the payment of £500 for the Cheltenham Festival appearance, I was rather pleased to receive another offer that was less financial than it was prestigious and with the potential, as one publisher put it, of uprating my public profile and reputation without the razzmatazz. The 'offer' I refer to is an opportunity that had arisen after I'd appeared on the first day of the Cheltenham Festival of Literature.

Michael Blastland, a Producer at the BBC had invited me to participate in the highly-rated Radio Four Programme ANALYSIS which, at the time, was presented by Professor Felipe Fernandez-Armesto. On the day of this engagement, I was met by the Professor in the foyer of BBC's Broadcasting House in Langham Place. The theme of this Current Affairs programme was 'PATRIOTISM: THE LAST REFUGE.' This recorded programme was first broadcast on 7 November 2002.

The participants in the Debate were Oliver Letwin (Shadow Home Secretary in the Conservative Party); Professor Brendan O'Leary (Professor of Political Science and Director of the Solomon Ash Center at the University of Pennsylvania); Professor Lindsay Paterson (The Institute of Governance at Edinburgh University); George Schopflin (Jean Monet Professor of Politics at the School of Eastern & Slavonic Studies, University College, London); Marianne Talbot (Lecturer in Philosophy at the Department of Continuing Education, Oxford University) and myself, introduced as Dr Ron Ramdin the author of *Reimaging Britain.*

Patriotism is of course, an interesting, complex subject and the BBC as provider of the biggest platform of radio broadcasting in Britain (perhaps in the world) granted the distinguished speakers and I the opportunity of saying something meaningful to a national audience of millions of listeners, not only in the United Kingdom but around the world.

I first heard the full fascinating Debate over a car radio when it was broadcast on 7 November 2002 and I think it is worth quoting parts of it at length.

Opening the programme, Professor Fernandez-Armesto said:

'*Patriotism is a virtue. It is altruistic: it puts community - the patriot's state as nation - above self. It is generous: patriots make sacrifices for their country. Patriotism is progressive, because citizens who want to make their country the best strive to make it better.*

And yet, if you are patriotic, I think you shouldn't be. Not that patriotism is a bad thing: like maths and dancing, it fills one with wonder, because its hard for a half-Briton, half-Spaniard like me. But in the materialist, consumerist, individualist, atomised, kaleidoscopically mutable kind of society we inhabit, all patriotism seems surprising. Chauvinists and xenophobia give it a bad name. Abandoned traditions leave others little to be patriotic about. So how does a patriotism survive - how does it survive nowadays?

Oliver Letwin, the Shadow Home Secretary, is the son of Jewish immigrants from Germany. How does he define his patriotism?

LETWIN: '*I'm like my fellow citizens nurtured by Britain - the country that gave me freedom under the rule of law and a very good standard of living and protection from marauders - and so I have a duty as I see it to support this country against its enemies..*

FA: *So it's quid pro quo - its what the country done for you that makes you patriotic.*

LETWIN: *Yes, exactly.*'

In turn, Professor O'Leary said: '*Patriotism, I think, is associated with loyalty to a political community, a state in our contemporary language and there's a rationale behind that, namely that loyalty to the state should be based on some notion of rights and duties accompanying one another...Its not surprising that with the great role that contemporary states play in the organisation of contemporary lives that they should be the residual site of some degree of affection and a natural obligation. I think one can write and speak a history particularly of the working class which would say that its patriotic attachment to the state has grown in proportion to the welfare state and that its much more rational and rooted in its self-interest than it might have been in previous times.*

FA: *Brendan O'leary is Irish and therefore knows something about the struggle for Statehood. He says patriotism is traditional - a deal you make with the state. States buy patriotism from their subjects with services, protection, nurture...Britain may have jettisoned a lot of the traditional baggage of the patriotism of the past, but a regime of political rights and social welfare has created a new focus of allegiance. Oliver Letwin is susceptible to this idea even though he's from that conservative tradition which is suspicious of the state.*

LETWIN: *I have been happy enough to live under its laws and to benefit from it so it has a right to expect from me a return.*

FA: *And that would include things like the benefits of the Welfare State?*

LETWIN: *Yes. That is part of it...It's the whole structure of a liberal democracy.*

FA: *I found this a tempting but unconvincing explanation of patriotism;...I'm sceptical about the role of rights and welfare in generating patriotism because people sacrificed themselves for their country long before States began to take on those responsibilities. Patriotism isn't proportionate to the beneficence of the state. Professor Lindsay Paterson cites ...Central Europe.*

PATERSON: *People got a pretty raw deal out of the various states that were set up there and yet there's NO suggestion at all that they stopped being patriotic Poles or Bulgarians or Czechs or Slovaks or whatever. They retained their allegiance to their cultural groups sometimes in opposition to the State which was often seen as being an alien importation from the Soviet Union or from Russia. Roughly the same has been happening in Western Europe as well actually,...People have often seen politics as almost polluting the cultural essence of the nation.*

FA: *So "the cultural essence of the nation" attracts a kind of higher allegiance which makes patriotism impervious to political change. Could this be the last refuge for a would be patriot under any uncongenial regime? But cultural essence is rather an elusive concept: doesn't individual judgement vary, isn't what matters in culture infinitely redefinable by personal caprice? Part Hungarian, part Scot, George Schopflin is Jean Monet Professor of Politics at the School of Eastern European and Slavonic Studies, University College, London.*

SCHOPFLIN: *Every country has its sort of sacred shrines. I suppose the Tower, Westminister Abbey to the Cenotaph - whatever. These are very sacred British, probably English sites. If you come here as a tourist you will look at them as an outsider and you'll think, okay, well that's very interesting, that's HOW the English do it. If you go to Paris, self-evidently it's Eiffel Tower, its Arc de Triomphe; if you go to Rome its the Altare Della Patria and you can find equivalents of this practically and virtually quite alike in some way.*

FA: *Are you saying that these shrines are sacred for all the people who identify with these communities?*

SCHOPFLIN: *Cultural allegiances can survive political change because they're mythic: They can therefore withstand factual undermining. It is in the nature of myth to resist reality. This helps to explain patriotism's durability but not its credibility.*

FA: *...what about when the culture changes too? British reserve has been replaced by emotional self-indulgence. The stiff upper lip has turned wobbly. The food has gone foreign. Fair play and the cult of the underdog seem as old fashioned as warm beer and bowler hats. The Corinthian Spirit has vanished from Westminster as from Wembley. The class system has yielded to the Celeb system. The workshop of the world has been sold off, green and pleasant land has been drearily redeveloped... The Britain my father wrote about - is barely recognisable in Britain today. How can patriotism survive this national self-reinvention? Cool Britain is something you can only be lukewarm about? How much change can Oliver Letwin stand and still be patriotic?*

LETWIN: *...patriotism does depend to a degree on continuity. Its an allegiance to history and to everything that history has created to a culture, to the institutions that symbolise the history and the culture, to a language, a sense of humour, to a literary tradition, to the music and the poetry, to the place, to the look of it. The romantic side of patriotism is extraordinarily intangible...*

FA: *For some, welfare is the bottom line; for others its bread and butter. But material culture perishes! Even pudding goes stale. Symbols get discarded. Robespierre's France; Lenin's Russia, Mao's China all transformed their traditional identities with amazing speed and zeal; but patriotism survived...Surely there must be something deeper to sustain it, harder perhaps to trash than the matter and symbols of culture. Marianne Talbot thinks there is! She's a lecturer in Philosophy at the Department of Continuing Education, Oxford University and was on the Crick Committee which advised the government on citizenship.*

TALBOT: *Through a regime change...one can continue to remain loyal to what one believed are the core values of a nation, a country and believe...or at least hope that one day it will come back and thereby remain loyal to the idea of the country, even whilst not respecting the actuality of the country at the time. If for example, a government were to come into Britain which was like Hitler's Government and changed a lot of what was going on in Britain, I would continue to think that the true values of England were what I value and that the current government didn't represent them properly. I think what changes is the way in which we order our values. I mean, I think for example, the Victorians valued personal happiness just as we do, but they didn't put it as high as duty! Also, these values are not inconsistent with the values of other communities. I mean I don't suppose there's anything I've mentioned that wouldn't be valued by people in France, Germany even in many cases, Iraq.*

FA: *Talbot's answer to the problem of continuity is that the values which endure are universal. Clearly, however, you can't erect patriotism (which is directed towards a particular country) on the basis of universal values. Such values are more likely to make us espouse humanity indifferently and separate the professed patriotism from the supposed object of patriotism: the State. Paterson expects this to happen soon, if Britain goes to war against Iraq.'*

Listening to the Programme recently, I reflected on the pros and cons of the disputed Weapons of Mass Destruction (WMD) debate just before Britain went to war against Iraq. Professor Paterson said: '*I'm pretty sure that if the UK Government decides to join in the war against Iraq... there will be support for our troops out there facing danger. At the same time, however, I doubt if that will actually still debate here. So I think what we see there is a very deep attachment to the liberal freedoms that we were in fact supposed to be defending allowing people to continue to debate the validity of the war even while it's in progress.*

FA: *So is that a form of patriotism. I mean, are those liberal values precisely the culture to which people feel allegiance?*

PATERSON: *Yes. I think that's the key point here. We don't any longer if we ever had it, have a notion of our country, right or wrong.*

FA: *...whether you advocate values or Culture as the underlying generators of the continuity of patriotism, the problem is particularly acute in Britain today; not just because we're facing the prospect of a war which will galvanise some peoples patriotism and dissolve that of others. There are deeper, long term structural difficulties. We're living in a country of rapidly multiplying loyalties...*

O'LEARY: *The notion of a British Patriotism that there is a civic territorial identity which unites the Scots, Welsh and the English - that's begun to fragment and its quite clear that significant proportions of the Welsh and Scots populations either have vigorous dual identities and in some cases strongly nationalist identities they prefer to see the break up of Britain and it will be a major challenge for the power holders at Westminster to maintain the notion of a British patriotism in the circumstances of running a multinational state.*

PATERSON: *I think actually most people in Scotland find it perfectly possible to be both Scottish patriots and British patriots.*

FA: *So the Irishman O'Leary fears conflicting patriotisms may be uncontainable in a single state; the Scotsman Lindsay Paterson is confident that they can coexist...How elastic is this sort of patriotism, which can embrace difference and sanctions uneasily compatible allegiances?*

LETWIN: *There are both practical and spiritual losses from fissiparation within the UK. But I'm not a pessimist about this in the sense that I think that most people think themselves as both English and British or both Scottish and British or both Welsh and British. (Except for Northern Ireland) on the mainland I think there always has been and there remains bifocalism.*

FA: *And, of course, that bifocalism could become trifocalism, you could have European patriotism... Of course, its not just devolution and Europeanisation which are blurring loyalties. There's immigration too.*

O'LEARY: *The most difficult thing about contemporary times, I think, is that to a significant degree in a range of northern world democracies, immigrant populations now include people who have a high culture, who are fully literate, fully ...trained and educated in their cultures of origin. Because of modern mass communications they can preserve their original culture much more successfully than in the past. If you're a state which is taking significant populations of peasants in, they're quite happy to be socialised in return for citizenship. Its somewhat more problematic I think for current states either to homogenise or to integrate to their immigrant population.*

FA: *So if O'Leary is right how loyal can we expect our present and future immigrants (more carefully selected, more highly educated than ever) to be? Paterson points out that patriotism for the host country can be acquired in surprising ways.*

PATERSON: *Let's take, for example, the role of Islamic culture... in 50 or 100 years time, will we not in fact have a variety of Islams in Western Europe just as we have a variety of Christianities. I'm not just talking here about the distinction between Protestantism and Catholicism but actually the way in which the various Protestant churches and indeed, the various branches of the Catholic Church, have quite recognisably distinct national characteristics.*

FA: *The Britishness of British Islam then, will become a source of patriotic pride for British Muslims! For Paterson patriotism which seems so elusive and insubstantial can actually be stronger than culture, absorbing and redirecting culture of foreign origin. There doesn't seem to be any logic to this but historical precedent on Paterson's side...But what if he is wrong? Isn't it more likely that mixed cultures mean divided allegiances? Dr Ron Ramdin arrived 40 years ago from the Caribbean (Trinidad.) His book Reimaging Britain, is about British identity. Does he think the British today can sustain patriotism of the past?*

RAMDIN: *The truth is they can't sustain it because we are in a new British society, a new situation of multiculturalism in which there are many diverse groups. And one has to ask the question today, whose Britain, whose culture and whose identity we are talking about. So you cannot invoke that sort of patriotism anymore. In my view, patriotism now will have to be a sense of belonging that would help to make the affected excluded groups feel a sense of belonging with no one culture imposing its will upon the others. For example, if patriotism was problematic for the Scots, Welsh and the Irish during Empire days with being "British," it has become even more problematic in today's devolutionary pro-European Britain which is confronted with harnessing the creative potential of cultural difference to formulate a new political community. So everything is in a state of flux - nothing is static, its evolving and...*

FA: *How can you be patriotic about something which is always changing, which is always shifting, which is always in transition, which doesn't have any stable values?*

RAMDIN: *That's the reality today. Britain today is not what Britain was 50 years ago. It's this constant reconstituting of what the values were, are and will be. All my life I've looked for something that would give me a sense of security in which I believe in and what I came up with time and again...(in spite of disappointments) is to reassess, renegotiate and I feel quite secure in that now.*

FA: *Oh you feel secure in your state of flux?*

RAMDIN: *Yes - in **my** state of flux.*

FA: *Can the British lion become a chameleon? Ron Ramdin's starting point is unchallengeable: patriotism has to adapt to survive. His analysis recalls working class patriotism in the nineteenth century - which was also perhaps confidence in a process of regeneration towards an evolving, increasingly democratic image of Britishness. I can see that some people might like an environment of perpetual renegotiation: it may enhance their sense of freedom. They may want to fight to defend it. This sort of sentiment could, perhaps replace patriotism, but it can hardly become patriotism. On the contrary, renegotiation could adulterate loyalties or create new conflicting ones, as communities of different ethnic origins define themselves in relation to each other. This is suggested not only by apparently unbridgeable fissures which divide some ethnic groups, but also by psychological studies of the way patriotism happens.*

PATERSON: *The conventional wisdom would be that young people start off with very stereotypical views of others...Now the interesting thing is, in this recent research, is that actually adults operate with a lot of stereotypes as well...And the social psychologist seem to suggest that this holding of stereotypes is actually...*

FA: *So we're psychologically programmed to form allegiances which are based on stereotypes and directed against the different.*

SHOPFLIN: *Each cultural community has a particular way of putting its case. I think the technical terrain for this is a thought style. In the case of the Anglo-Saxons its emphasis on pragmatism, if you like empiricism, of dealing with a problem that's immediately in front of* us. And secondly, I think its very strong in this country, people say, only we are pragmatic, those continentals - they're ideological. I've heard this countless times. Now when, however, the French who likewise have certain forms of pragmatism do something like that, the English will say, that's opportunism, unprincipled.

FA: For George Shopflin, these are fictions - but they really shape the way people feel. Is this why so much of the residual patriotism which has survived change in Britain gets muddled and muddied with nationalism and xenophobia? Is it just an ugly mask behind which all the real features of patriotism have rotted away? There is something odd about British people who are willing to abandon or abolish their own traditional and historic peculiarities of culture, yet anxious to impose loyalty tests on immigrants. For British louts abroad, hatred of foreigners seems to be their last refuge, the closest they come to patriotism. Maybe in multicultural society and a multicivilisational north we would be better off without patriots.

TALBOT: I think that in a way, being patriotic is precisely self-differentiation, the same for feeling identity with your brownie pack...I mean I don't think there is anything particularly bad intrinsically about distinguishing oneself from others. It is one's attitudes to the others from whom one can draw an analogy here with the Bully in the playground who doesn't respect himself and so takes it out on others. He, because he has a lost sense of self-esteem, distinguishes himself of from others and needs to put others down in order to bring himself up. I think if you don't feel a sense of belonging in your own country, culture, you're likely to turn into a cultural bully.

FA: For Marianne Talbot, patriotism can give you confidence for coexistence - self-respect - which precedes respect for others. Plausible in theory. But has Ron Ramdin found that it works?

RAMDIN: In the way that patriotism has affected me at the time (of my migration and thereafter) negatively, terribly negatively, I felt no it can't be a good thing. But then, you know, there are positive things about belonging...For example, having been in Britain for many years I've had many opportunities to do things. I look at that as positive. Whether or not I'm a patriot is another thing, but I do feel BRITISH.

FA: Perhaps true patriotism survives if we don't think about it too much, for this is a field in which scrutiny leads to scepticism. Perhaps

there are abiding values concealed at present which may re-emerge,
as they did in Russia or France or China after the revolutions. Those
bifocal and trifocal allegiances of which we have heard are testing
many countries' patriotism today. In some, including Britain, it may
fragment into regional patriotism or dissolve amid renegotiation or
vanish into some future super-state. For as long as it lasts, it will surely
be abused. I suspect however that in Britain, at least, it will go on
surprising us by its durability as well as its mutability: because an
attachment which has so little for so long clearly has amazing powers
of adhesion.'

The high regard and importance of this topic on the ANALYSIS
Programme was reflected in widespread interest. When I requested
a copy of the Transcript, BBC Producer Mr Blastland informed me
that Professor Bernard Crick of the University of London was one
of the first to do so!

Looking back, it was a rare opportunity for me to have been
invited to engage in debate not only with Felipe Fernandez-
Armesto, Richard Hoggart and Peter Jay at the Cheltenham Festival
of Literature, but also to join a distinguished international Panel in
another great National Debate, this time far beyond the confines of
the *Everyman Theatre* and reaching out across the airwaves through
the BBC's flagship Radio Four. The ANALYSIS programme on
'PATRIOTISM' was broadcast twice in a week: on the 7th and
10th November 2002; a great Debate which I hoped had stirred
the thoughts of millions of people.

GOOD NEWS, BAD NEWS

Against the background of unprecedented national exposure, my
efforts to find a publisher for my novel *Rama's Voyage* never flagged.
Nothing, as I knew from experience, could be taken for granted.
Rather than concentrate on a few publishers, on the eve of a visit
to Trinidad, I extended my search. I wrote to Ken Jaikaransingh
of Lexicon Books in the Caribbean and informed him that '*The*
London Magazine will be publishing an estimated 6,000 words of my
novel Rama's Voyage. Given this seal of approval, I am now hoping
to place this (first work of fiction of its kind) in the hands of the right

publisher. In my opinion, a Caribbean publishing interest will be best for this book, which should reach the widest (local/international) audience. I will be visiting Trinidad in the next few weeks and would be glad to know if...Lexicon will be interested in publishing and promoting this novel as a publishing event. If you would like to see the whole text or sections of it in advance of my arrival, I shall be pleased to oblige.'

Mr Jaikaransingh replied:

'I would welcome the opportunity to talk to you about publishing your novel. Let's talk when you get to Trinidad.' I noted his lack of enthusiasm, his emphasis on 'talk,' but I reasoned that he could not, of course, say more until he'd had a chance to read the manuscript. Given his appreciation of *Arising From Bondage* (albeit non-fiction) which was a positive connection, I felt there was hope.

Meanwhile, with little time to spare, pressing on with the urgent work of the National Archives Moving Here Project I wrote again to Mr Seager thanking him for his much anticipated 'message' and enclosed my Invoice which I stressed was 'in line with your calculations...'

My return to Trinidad at this time was the first visit to coincide with the Festive Season since my departure as a teenager. I very much looked forward to the Christmas experience as a chance to rekindle childhood memories. As it was, I was able to relax, a marked change from my London life of intense work: of earning a living at the British Library, of writing to meet deadlines, of making public appearances, broadcasting and so on. Surrendering to the pleasure of the fine weather and meeting many warm, less guarded people, I recalled my first six Christmas Days in cold England, especially the first and coldest that I had spent, wrapped up and alone in bed. Such wintry thoughts heightened my awareness and appreciation of being on the sunny Sand Road for the celebrations.

Just two days before Christmas, as expectations rose and Yuletide sentiments were gladly expressed, myself and family received shocking, numbing news: my sister Lydia had died. She'd been suffering for some time from cancer. All Christmas plans in Trinidad were immediately shelved as myself, Ma and sister Annette made arrangements to travel to Canada. How sad, how awful these moments and days were. Eventually we arrived in Toronto and were met by my brother Joel and his wife Benigma with whom we stayed.

Before the funeral, I was asked to deliver the Eulogy. Even though this was expected of me, time was of the essence. As soon as I could, I removed myself from my distraught, mourning family and found a quiet place to write the important words that I would speak. Having never delivered a Eulogy, I approached it as best I could. Working in the basement of Joel's house, thoughts of my departed sister, whom alas I wished I'd known better, concentrated my mind. Composed of fact and certainly not fiction, such a piece of writing was, in many ways, a big test: I dredged my experience and memory. Lydia was just two years old when I had left Trinidad. On my visits over the years, it was wonderful to observe her as she grew up from girl-hood, ever taller and into woman-hood. Though we had spent far too little time together while she was alive, in death she commanded my fullest attention. Writing my last words about Lydia was surreal; I felt terribly alone in the basement. Once I'd completed the Eulogy, I rejoined the family.

The next day around mid-morning myself and the family arrived at the Chapel where Lydia's body lay in an open casket. Having not seen her for ten years, now she looked as if she was asleep; and strangely, very beautiful. I stood for a while gazing at her clear unblemished face in peaceful repose. Then I touched her hand and said 'Goodbye sister.' Moved by what I'd seen, I shuffled to a corner of the room where Maria, Lydia's daughter sat. How remarkably like each other they looked. The room was crowded, but amidst the quiet milling around, the sounds in the room were more respectful whispers than noise. Then a disturbing, guttural moan came from the opposite end of the room. It was like nothing I'd ever heard. I was forced to listen. It rose as if from a deep well or cavern and increased in volume. In spite of the trance-like state of mind that I'd been in, I realised the cry was coming from Ma. The seemingly undignified bawling that followed was almost inhuman. Having lost her two still-born babies Emma and Louisa, now Ma's first daughter to survive child-birth, her beloved Lydia, was no more. I was always there in the small wooden house when Ma had suffered the traumas of everyone one of her eight childbirths. Now all the pain of the previous losses were compounded at this moment of farewell; and, for a while, Ma's groans and bawling became a disturbingly soulful cry that I shall never forget.

Soon the casket was closed and we followed the white men dressed in black: the coffin-bearers as they entered the Chapel for the Funeral Service. After a few hymns, prayers and readings, as the order of Service stated, it was my turn. My walk to the pulpit was slow as I tried to steady myself. I faced a jam-packed Chapel audience. This is what I said:

'Just over two weeks ago, I had arrived in Trinidad to spend Christmas Day, not having done so for forty years. My mother had returned distraught after visiting her terminally-ill daughter Lydia in Toronto. With pride and deep sadness, she showed me a long-forgotten black and white photograph. In it were two children – Lydia, at the age of two, and her brother David, who was two years older. David was looking at Lydia with care and concern. But Lydia was not looking at him. Her gaze was fixed ahead, directly at the camera or whatever else that had caught her attention. It was at once, a look of curiosity and of being challenged by what was before her. There was much in her expression which defied explanation.

Lydia was born in a small, but "special" place in Trinidad. To be more precise, she came into the world at number 43 Union Park Road, Marabella. She was the sixth of the seven children of her parents Peter and Florence. The family was large and far from wealthy. But Peter and Florence were rich in certain values which they passed on to Lydia, values such as strong religious/spiritual beliefs and a sense of caring and commitment to family, friends and to people generally.

It is significant too, that although our parents were poor, even in the hardest times, they provided us with food. What is even more extraordinary is the fact that they did not just provide food for their children, but also for anyone else (regardless of numbers!) who happened to be present. How they managed to do this when I was a child (and continued to do so to this day) remains an economic mystery. What is extraordinary about this ongoing act of sharing is that it is not charity or a trade-off between giving and receiving. It was (and still is) an expression of my parents' innate generosity of spirit and their humaneness. This is indeed the mould from which Lydia sprang. She was kind, caring and sensitive; and her vitality, her zest for life, her determination and courage in adversity were core values that became the hallmark of her warm and engaging personality...

Over the years, I watched with brotherly pride as Lydia, the gawky, but attractive teenager became a beautiful young woman. The attention she received from admirers was legendary and, naturally, this worried her father. The warning he delivered to her could not be clearer: "Don't bring a baby to this house!"

Eventually, Lydia was married... She had two children – Maria and Mario. Later, married life in Trinidad gave way to a new life in Canada. This was not an easy transition, and the stresses and strains took its toll on the marriage...

Almost ten years ago, when illness invaded Lydia's body, I visited Toronto. A few weeks after I had returned to London, she wrote one of her rare letters to me to say that a "miracle" had occurred: she was cured. I was overjoyed! Then, about a month ago, I was told that Lydia was terminally ill. I had already booked my ticket and was anticipating a well-deserved Christmas break in Trinidad. I had not known that arrangements were made to take Lydia back to Trinidad where she would spend her last days. But this was not to be: Lydia broke her hip and had to remain in hospital. This double tragedy meant that her father had to make the trip to Canada to see his daughter because he was told she had only two months to live. My father had left for Toronto the day after I had arrived in Trinidad and, because of daily improvements in Lydia's condition, I decided to defer my trip to see her until early in the New Year.

Then, quite suddenly, Lydia passed away – peacefully, I was told, and surrounded by her father, Maria and Mario, my brothers Kenrick, Joel and his wife Benigma... among others. In these final moments of her life, like the photograph that my mother had shown me, from accounts I received from those present, I have another haunting, enduring image of Lydia and David. Her last request was to David: "Rub my back," she had said to him. And while David did so, as in the old photograph of them as children, now David was looking at her (attentive and with characteristic care and concern), but Lydia was not looking at him;

she was again looking at something that compelled her attention. This time, she summoned up all her strength. She craned her neck forward. She looked up, her eyes fixed upon something above! Soon after, she died. This final image of Lydia and David, prompts the question: did the deeply religious Lydia finally recognise what she may have been looking for?

In the last two weeks of her life, deliriously happy to see her father and David at her bedside, Lydia joked and laughed often in spite of her pain. On one occasion, she reminded her father of the time when he had warned her about bringing a baby in the house.

"I did not let you down," she was pleased to say to him.

She had also said: "One day I'll bring this family together!"...Before Lydia had died, it did not seem possible that I would see my brothers Kenrick and Joel this year, and certainly not before Christmas. So when I woke up in Toronto on Christmas morning, I could hear the echo of Lydia's words: "I will bring this family together!"

Instead of the Party that was planned for Lydia at the hospital on Christmas Day at which she had looked forward to wearing her green dress and red shoes, she did indeed bring the "family together," but it was no Christmas Party!

And so the life of Lydia which began 43 years ago at Number 43 Union Park Road, ended in Toronto. "Death is not extinguishing the light," Rabindranath Tagore wrote: "it is putting out the lamp because dawn has come."

As Lydia's eldest brother, who arrived too late to see her alive, I bid her farewell with the words of a poem: "I may keep memories of you, but not your essence, for that will pour forth tomorrow."

While in Toronto, I met members of my extended family following my brother Joel's marriage to Benigma, who was originally from Portugal. The visit of Ma and Pa to Toronto was their first: a double flying venture on an airplane, and a baptism of chilliness in frosty, winter-bound Canada. Amidst the Arctic cold January weather, Joel's wife and her large family were especially warm and supportive. They got on well with my parents; and when I returned to London, on 16 January 2003, I wrote to Benigma:

'Following the death of my sister Lydia on behalf of the Ramdin family I write to express our grateful thanks and deep appreciation for

the empathy and sympathy and for the generosity of your good self and your entire family including Franco Luiz, Joe Luiz, Franco Almeida, John Cout, Antonio Luiz, Juoa Couto, Isobel Bettencourt, Maria Candida, Maria Amelia, Merces, Maria, Jonas, Eugenia, Elma, Mary Rocha and Fernanda.

Our family will always remember the light that you all brought into our lives during those dark days with special fondness and with love.

God Bless You All.'

WORK CONTINUES ON A BIG NEW NOVEL; NEW BOOK PROPOSALS

The shock and realisation of my sister's death had a devastating effect on my parents, myself and the family. Predictably bereavement was a time of reflection. In the previous three years or so, I had become increasingly engaged with my very important second novel *The Confessions of the Reverend William Wragg.* I also began to think seriously about taking 'early retirement' from the British Library. Why? Because this book was of such value that it pushed me to seriously consider not staying on until the full retirement age of sixty five. Accordingly, I made a formal request to terminate my employment two years before. After this decision, I became deeply immersed in *The Confessions…*; a novel which I had first conceived some twenty years before. Now I was determined to complete the book *before* retirement from the British Library. Every hour outside office time, I worked intensely on the novel. I was far too busy to worry about the full implications of the fast-approaching date when I would be 'out of work' for the first time since my depressing 'Dole' experience, some forty-three years before.

After fulfilling my Contractual obligations for the Public Records Office's 'Moving Here Project,' namely writing the 'Briefs' and Caribbean 'Narrative' - my circle of professional contacts in Britain had widened. And given that *The Sand Road* film project had stalled, I began discussions with Tuareg Productions about a one-hour Documentary film titled 'Making A Difference.' The word 'difference' was significant in that it mirrored even more clearly now, my ideas and exploration of the social realities that I'd been writing about. Tuareg Productions stated:

'*This Documentary is about a very unusual life: the life of Ron Ramdin, an uplifting story of a teenage boy's courage and determination to gain experience and knowledge. Put simply, it is a story of self-discovery, dedication, compassion and hope.*

How does a relatively unschooled "country" boy… (who dreamed of an education he could not have on the island) engage in a multiplicity of areas of public life and living in Britain.

The almost miraculous thing about this story is that Ron has achieved all this on a shoe-string, in his "spare time" because he's had to remain in employment to "stay afloat". Thus far, his exemplary life has been a model for people from different walks of life, including students, many of whom are researching their PhDs. But Ron is no ivory tower academic; his story and this film will challenge the viewer and should not fail to encourage anyone (especially the young) who watches it…

Ron's life and work has made a difference to many, and certainly to Ron himself. He believes that respect for each other can be genuine only when, as he says in Reimaging Britain, we recognise and "celebrate the creative potential of human difference." '

For a while, I worked closely with Tuareg Productions, but as discussions proceeded up to the point when the focus shifted, I decided not to pursue the idea. Alternatively, I spoke with Film Director Paul Balmer; and after we'd collaborated on the key matter of production costs, as with Tuareg, our paths also diverged. And so, 'Making A Difference' (Tuareg's title of its film about me and my work) more or less, went the way of my earlier collaboration with Mr Rolfe on *The Sand Road*.

Set against this disappointment, the steady, but at times intermittent work on *Rama's Voyage* had finally been realised in the form of a completed manuscript. Considering the various demands on my time, creating *Rama's Voyage* was an achievement, a source of encouragement which, in turn, generated even greater interest in writing fiction.

In the early weeks of 2003, I received a telephone call from Makeda Coaston, the African-American activist whom I had met some years before. Following our long association on projects/

programmes relating to 'Black' history and culture in Britain she informed me that she was in the Culture Team at City Hall in London. With Ken Livingstone in post as London's first elected Mayor, she spoke about the Mayor's initiative – the setting up of a Mayor's Commission on African and Asian Heritage. In due course, Ms Coaston was pleased to inform me that the Mayor would like to appoint me as a Commissioner to serve on the pioneering Commission. This invitation was timely and therefore crucial. Why? Because in all the decades that I had been engaged in campaigns of one sort or another, I'd never heard of a bolder initiative from a top politician on such a matter. Later, when Ms Coaston and I met to discuss the appointment, she reiterated that my contribution would be valuable.

Meanwhile, there was still the manuscript of *Rama's Voyage* to be hawked around. There was also the very important work that I'd begun of researching and writing a biography of William Wilberforce; a familiar subject which preoccupied me to the extent that I shifted perspective: I felt a new approach to writing about him was needed and decided against a biography. After more reading and thought, I wrote and submitted a new Book Proposal titled: *'ABOLITONISTS: EQUIANO & WILBERFORCE: Parallel Lives,'* which included a Prologue, 26 Chapters and the following 'Synopsis':

'ABOLITIONISTS: EQUIANO AND WILBERFORCE
Parallel Narratives

'After many years of research on the FIRST full biography for twenty-seven years of William Wilberforce (the Abolitionist/Liberator who led the great campaign to free enslaved Africans in Britain's colonies), I recently attended an International Conference on Olaudah Equiano, and the more I read about Wilberforce, the more I thought about the less well-known contribution of other abolitionists who had played important roles in what Wilberforce described as the "Great Cause." One of these lesser known figures was Olaudah Equiano, the slave who bought his freedom and became the foremost black writer and leader of the eighteenth century Black community in Britain. In the

wave of abolitionist sentiment that swept through the country, this extraordinary man wrote his autobiography entitled The Interesting Life of Olaudah Equiano, or Gustavus Vasa, the African, Written by Himself, a bestseller which was accredited with nine editions within six years. After attending an Equiano Conference, I felt that my work on Wilberforce alone would be inadequate.

To juxtapose (compare and contrast) the life of the slave and Abolitionist Equiano (who aspired to, and almost became an "English Gentleman") with the life of Wilberforce the "English Gentleman" par excellence is, in my opinion, a much more exciting and enriching approach in telling the uplifting story of two epochal moments in human history - the abolition of the African Slave Trade and the eventual overthrow of the Atlantic Slave system. I therefore decided to write a double-biography namely: **ABOLITIONISTS: EQUIANO AND WILBERFORCE - Parallel Narratives.**

My aim is to write this book in an engaging and accessible style (without compromising its scholarship) for the widest audience. This work will necessarily draw upon a variety of sources including diaries, letters, parliamentary papers, contemporary biographical sketches, autobiographies, the most recent academic research papers and other (printed) source materials.

Given that I would like to complete this important book before the 200th Anniversary of the Abolition of the Slave Trade in March 2007, time is of the essence. This means submission of the final manuscript in 2005!
Copyright, 2003
Ron Ramdin.

After completing this 'Proposal' I felt unburdened, even uplifted, as if a path had been cleared that allowed me to see more of the road ahead. Contributing to this was, of course, the invaluable work that I'd already done on 'The Great Cause' and the biography on Wilberforce.

A few days after my first submission of 'ABOLITIONISTS' to Flamingo, an imprint of Harper Collins publishing, I received a non-committal reply, stating that while I'd raised 'some interesting themes and ideas,' they were unable to offer me a Commission at this time. They added: 'However, we would be more than happy to consider your completed manuscript and would welcome its submission when you have finished writing.'

Building the house without a mortgage was the expression which immediately came to mind. But while I was familiar with the overriding financial constraints of the publishing world, I did not allow Flamingo's response to dampen my enthusiasm. I duly approached other publishers.

At this time, I was also re-reading *Rama's Voyage,* a process which was quite revealing: I felt empowered; indeed much better placed to evaluate and appreciate the merits of fiction (the novel) and non-fiction.

Having not seen or heard from my friend the novelist and publisher Allen Synge for quite some time, in a letter dated 3 June 2003, he wrote thanking me for a copy of *Arising From Bondage* which I'd sent as a 40th birthday present for his son Daniel. Over many years in Bloomsbury, I had had the pleasure of Allen Synge's company: he was a raconteur with whom I'd shared the desire and ambition of writing and publishing more. His favourite saying was 'Attack! Attack! Attack!' Whenever we met socially on Thursdays or Fridays in Bedfordbury, Covent Garden, we did an unpopular thing: we 'talked shop' with great interest and mutual encouragement. Allen closed his letter saying that he looked forward to another meeting soon. Although he was of good pedigree (a relative, on his mother's side, was J.M. Synge, author of *Playboy of the Western World*) he was never boastful. As an author, he displayed an energy, seriousness and respect for writing which appealed to me. As far as friendships go (and I had precious few of them!) I always looked forward to seeing this person who, in essence, was an esteemed literary friend.

FIRST IMPRESSIONS OF SOHO;
APPOINTMENT AS COMMISSIONER BY MAYOR OF LONDON

In the continuing hot Summer days of 2003, to coincide with London's 'Soho Festival,' the Soho Society's journal *The Soho Clarion* published my commissioned article: *First Impressions of*

Soho. Previous 'First Impressions' were written by well-known writers and personalities. This was a wonderful opportunity, I thought. Why? Because apart from my books about the changing face of Britain, my article would be read by thousands of people from all walks of life, including tourists from all over the world who flocked to London each year, particularly to the West End and Soho, especially in the summer. As a writer and resident of long-standing, this reflective article brought me closer to this great city, to its central area known as 'Inner London,' and thus far, to reflect upon my life and autobiography.

I was but a youth, just past teenage-hood and within a few months of arriving in London, after receiving my second pay packet, I headed for the 'West End.' It was a Friday evening and while making my way through the jostling crowds, caught up in wall-to-wall people, I wandered off from Piccadilly Circus and up Shaftesbury Avenue before strolling along Soho's Greek, Frith and Old Compton Streets, then, for better or worse, I turned into Dean Street. Memories of this time were remarkably vivid and so I began to write my *Soho Clarion* piece:

'From the small horse-racing village of Union Park in Trinidad to my arrival in Central London is a long way and was a long time coming. It was a dream come true. On my first stroll around Piccadilly in the early Sixties, as night fell, I wandered off Shaftesbury Avenue into Greek Street. Someone whistled. I stopped and looked up. A beautiful young blonde woman was leaning out from a first floor window.

'Hello!' she said. Her voice and manner could not be more friendly and inviting. 'I'll be down in a minute,' she said. She seemed as good as her promise as she stood before me. Behind her, on either side of the front door, the flames of two torches flickered. This is no ordinary house, I thought. 'Please come in', the woman said. I followed, unable to restrain my youthful optimism. Just inside the dimly lit room, there were cubicles. She sat down in one and invited me to join her at a table. "If you give me two pounds," she said, "I will spend half an hour with you. A fiver for an hour." Money was my biggest problem, and suddenly, she no longer seemed attractive. "And, for a tenner," she continued, "I'll come home with you for the night!" My face reflected my lack of interest in her sales pitch. She did not hide her

disappointment, nor did she ignore my discomfort. "Okay, how much have you got?" Just then, I noted a large man standing with muscular arms folded at the front door. I reached for my wallet with a heavy sense that I would not be able to leave without incurring some expense. Some kind of payment seemed unavoidable. I had about £9 and did not offer to buy her a drink.

"Let me see how much you have," she said.

I held up my wallet before her. She counted the few notes. I did not have a "tenner."

"Would you like to spend an hour with me?" she asked. At that point, I removed the five pound note from my wallet and handed it to her. "You need this more than I do," I said, proud of my magnanimity, but with some mixed feelings, knowing that I would be left with just four pounds for the rest of the weekend and the following working week. As I began to make my move, she followed me past the unsmiling strong man at the door. Then walking away briskly towards the brighter neon-lit Old Compton Street, she shouted "You cretin! You cretin! Cretin! Cretin!" I did not know the meaning of the word. It might as well be Greek. Just the sound of her voice was enough for me.'

After this episode, some months later, I was back in Soho. This time, as mentioned earlier I was guided there by my two rich African-Indian friends who, having won a large sum of money on the horses, had invited me to join them for a drink in London's West End. Reflecting on my *First Impressions*, I continued:

'We strolled along Dean Street from the Oxford Street end, taking in the sights and sounds of this part of the city and I found myself in a small, unusually crowded bar. It was unlike any other public place. I recognised its uniquenesss immediately. "This is a wine and champagne bar" one of my rich friends said grandly, trying to impress me... There was hardly elbow room, but the buzz was exciting. And, as I confessed to my friend, I had never tasted champagne before. So both his big win (on the horses) and my introduction to this strange, fascinating place, were moments to savour. We stood at the West end of the bar, sipping and talking and after a while, with the champagne working its magic, I became more aware of the surroundings and of a well-dressed man with an unusual moustache who surveyed the scene from behind the counter. "That is Gaston Berlemont," my friend said. I considered

Gaston and his audience. This was theatre; and he was centre stage. There were two other men assisting him. There was also something (which I could not then identify) about the people...that gave the space its extraordinary ambience. What was this place? Who were these people? After the second glass of champagne, as my shyness gave way to emboldened observation, I noticed a woman wearing a hat. She was chatting gaily with a small, long haired man, at the opposite end of the bar. They were staring in our direction, perhaps because we were the only non-white people there at the time... Moments later, the... man appeared next to me. "Excuse me," he said, "the lady over there (he pointed at the woman with the hat) would like to buy you a drink. She would like to have a word."

My friends smiled and I followed the man to the other side. "I'm a freelance photographer for the Sunday Observer Magazine," he said. "This is Lady..." The Lady... offered me a drink and introduced me to several people – artists and writers... I took their particulars and promised to call.

By the time that I had left the French House, I was imbued with a heady mix of thoughts and ideas about Soho. My friend's success as a punter had led me to an establishment of quality; to people that left a first impression so indelible that (having just turned twenty and with my temperament and curiosity heightened by the boundless potential of my presence in London) I didn't have to be a gambling man to know that Soho would be an odds-on favourite with me in the years to come.'

The publication and distribution of this personal view of such a popular place in London was most gratifying. Put simply, being given the opportunity to write the article, reflected my standing in the community (encompassing Theatreland and the film world) to which more famous people came and went than anywhere else in Britain and perhaps the world.

Soho, as I came to know it socially, generated historical interest. It was an area where Huguenots (French migrants) had settled; and over the years, other newcomers, including Jews, Italians and Greeks had become part of a burgeoning community that welcomed other ethnic groups. My friend Wendy, who had commissioned the piece as Editor of *The Soho Clarion*, had also been a deeply committed administrator of *The Soho Society* for many years. Right at the heart of this 'Inner London' community was The French House.

With the passage of time, as I became more familiar with the area, the well-known journalist Sandy Fawkes had published her book: *The French House*. In it, Ms Fawkes cited herself and I as two of publisher Peter Owen's authors. 'Quality,' is how Peter had described two of my books; and it is that very word which I would use to describe his publishing house in its heyday.

The positive feedback from my *First Impressions...* was most welcome, but I did not allow myself to wallow unduly in the positive response of the Soho community. Alas, there was far too much that preoccupied me.

Towards the end of the summer after a further meeting with Ms Coaston, in her role as Senior Strategy Officer at London's City Hall, I received a letter which stated:

'*Dear Ron Ramdin,*

We are very pleased that you have agreed to serve as a Commissioner for the Mayor's Commission on African and Asian Heritage. With your expertise and experience, we believe you can make a significant contribution to the Commission, which should provide a platform to advance diversity in institutional practice and help to ensure that London more fully reflects its varied histories and heritage...'

This 'letter' from the Mayor's office came with an 'Outline' of what lay ahead in terms of my work as a Commissioner. Ten Commission Sessions were scheduled between August 2003 and March 2004. By any standards, this process would be a testing and intense exercise, but having sat on a few London and National Committees with an educational orientation (for example, the Inner London Education Authority of the 1970s and more recently on the Arts Council of England Cultural Committees) I looked forward to the challenges facing this Inaugural Commission.

Ken Livingstone, as the first elected Mayor of London had, in consultation with his key advisers, made the appointment which I duly accepted. How interesting, I thought, that my decision to continue to research and write; to provide a few books for schools and libraries (that would fill gaps in our knowledge of 'British' history and hopefully lead to a ***better understanding*** *and appreciation of each other*) should now lead to this top-level Appointment. At last, the messenger would be able to present the message in a major policy-making forum.

From the outset, I left my fellow-Commissioners in absolutely no doubt about my commitment. Although I was clear about my decision while at the LSE (and after) that I should not aspire to either become Prime Minister of Trinidad and Tobago or the first non-white Prime Minister of Britain, now twenty-one years on, in my capacities as historian, biographer and novelist, I realised that my choice was clearly the right one. Having been on the staff of three of the greatest libraries, the decades of employment, study and writing books had merged; and, in spite of the ups and downs, now those all-consuming aspects of life melded and felt like the perfect combination.

So I considered my 'Appointment' to the Mayor's Commission and how it would relate to the British Library which I hoped would, as the leading institution of its kind in the world, become a key player in the Museum, Libraries and Archives sector in London and nationally. Instead of the British Library authorities hearing of my 'Appointment' through the Mayor's Office or City Hall networks, I decided that as a Commissioner I should approach the British Library directly. To begin with, I thought it appropriate first to inform Graham Shaw, Director of my Department, the Oriental and India Office Collections (renamed 'APAC'). So on the morning of 19 August 2003, I emailed:

'*Dear Graham,*

Just to inform you that Mayor Ken Livingstone has appointed me to serve on the Mayor's Commission on African and Asian Heritage (MCAAH). It is, of course, a great honour to be a member of such a "pioneering project," a Heritage Strategic Initiative that will play a ground breaking role in establishing landmark partnerships and a programme for action that will address the deficit of effective representation, preservation and interpretation of African and Asian Heritage. The Report and Recommendations of this "High Profile" Commission will guide and hopefully in time change perception and attitudes toward heritage in London and in Britain as a whole.

Best Regards,

Ron.'

Later that day, Graham replied:

'Dear Ron,

Congratulations! I'll be very happy to discuss with you further about this once you get "up and running" - whether there are any initiatives into which the BL can (hopefully) be "worked" or ideas that we can put into the mix, etc.

*NB I would let Strategic Marketing and Communications know about this asap i.e that you have been appointed in your own right as a well-known writer on African and Asian heritage and the UK. Do you know anyone there? Heather Norman? Isabel Oswald? This is because they are negotiating closely with the London Development Agency over the Innovation Centre and will no doubt want to be informed of any contacts with Ken! (Mayor Ken Livingstone.) It would also make an excellent story for **Shelflife** (the in-house British Library magazine) but let Strategic Marketing and Communications know about it first.*

Regards,

Graham'

All things considered, sitting on the Commission was, it seemed, a logical placement for me. It was a major achievement as Mr Shaw had said 'in your own right' and, to some degree, an acknowledgement of my life's work thus far. Put simply, it was an opportunity to contribute at the highest level in relation to neglected areas that had been of pressing social and economic concern to me since my days as a Trade Union leader in the British Museum and the early years of the British Library. Given that in the late 1960s (and especially in the 1970s) racial discrimination at the workplace (as elsewhere) was rampant, the fact that as a 'man of colour,' so to speak, to have been at the forefront as a central figure in the delicate, but tough business of rank-and-file working class struggle', I was determined in my negotiations with management to engender trust that would make recruitment and staffing at the British Library more flexible. In other words, more *inclusive*.

Raising issues of race and immigration were unheard of in the British Museum when I was first elected as workers' leader and, significantly, the *vast majority* of those who had voted for me at each year's election were white. I was the long-serving face of Staff representation, not only in the British Museum, but also in the British Library. Embracing my responsibilities was therefore **challenging, pioneering work**! Slowly as the composition of the work-force changed with the recruitment of more people from different ethnic/racial backgrounds, I repeated my calls for an end to discrimination on the grounds of race, colour or gender and for the implementation of fairness: equal rights and equal opportunities. These day-to-day issues were, since my leadership role began in 1969, contentious. And so thirty-three years later on my journey from the grassroots to becoming an historian of an ever-changing Britain, I had kept a steady course while campaigning with others in the diverse Black and Asian communities against discrimination and importantly for a Race Relations Act. Getting something on the Statute book was for us crucial.

Against this background and, given my experience and historical understanding, each time I went to City Hall as a Mayor's Commissioner I never missed an opportunity of debating the challenging issues of social injustice. The hope was that such debates would point the way forward so that London would be seen as a *model* of *ethnic inclusiveness* by other cities in Britain and Europe.

At this juncture, being on the Commission marked a highpoint; and with the publication of *Reimaging Britain* and *Arising From Bondage,* complemented by radio, TV appearances and lectures at various London venues and across Britain, my fast-paced life became busier. Thus success exacted its price!

Our first MCAAH meeting in City Hall's splendid Debating Chamber was an unusual event: an assembly which included a Who's Who of 'experts.' On the face of it, everyone seemed comfortable with each other and this augured well for the future. For my part, regardless of what the other Commissioners thought, my attitude remained positive: It was in this frame of mind that I approached the meetings to come.

By contrast, in the British Library I was regarded with no more respect than any other employee on the Administrative Staff. Predictably the dominant voices were those of the Chief Executive,

Directors and managers. Within this structure, it was significant that there was now a 'Diversity Manager,' a woman of Indian descent. This appointment, unthinkable ten years before, was however not lost on me for having consistently campaigned for such a post, I drew enormous satisfaction from this shift in thinking; an appointment which justified in word and deed, my relentless 'one-man crusade' (as an American observer and London resident had described my continuing efforts) against discrimination and for inclusiveness.

Put in perspective, given some persons stubborn, negative attitude towards me, the placement of a Diversity Manager, a clear progression from the original EOO was, to say the least, a good start. This attitude to diversity was, I felt, an advantage which should be pressed forward from my new position on the Mayor's Commission. Why? Because recent results had been encouraging. In the British Museum, since my intense campaigning days there, after years of gestation, an African Gus Casely-Hayford had been recruited as a Curator; and more recently, a black woman, the American-born Bonnie Greer, had stormed that bastion of white male membership, by being appointed to serve on the Board of the British Museum. After serving for a few years as a Trustee, Ms Greer was promoted to become Deputy Chairman of the British Museum Board of Trustees. The appointments of Mr Casely-Hayford and Ms Greer at Senior levels (considering my pioneering, ten-year long efforts way back in the 1960s and 1970s at the British Museum against racial discrimination and sexism; indeed for greater *inclusiveness*) were very significant developments from which I derived great satisfaction. I was reminded of the fact that: *we stand on the shoulders of those who came before us!*

In the British Library, the men and women with a 'vision' for the future were concerned with the next steps that the organisation should take. After informing Mr Shaw about my position on the Mayor's Commission, I had made it clear to him that I was on the Commission as an historian and not as a representative of the British Library. Mr Shaw was happy that I was on the Commission and having said: 'The BL would like to buy into this. I will be glad to speak with you…and colleagues in the Strategy Team,' a few days later on 26 August 2003, Clive Field, Head of Special Collections in the British Library contacted me: *'As you can see'*, he wrote, *'Graham had relayed your news to me. This is indeed, a very great honour for you to have been invited to serve on the Commission. I offer my heartfelt congratulations to you and look forward to hearing how the Commission's work progresses. **I hope that there will be a good opportunity for the BL to engage with it.'** (Author's emphasis)

Early the next day, I responded:

'Thank you very much indeed for your email. While it is a great honour for me to serve on MCAAH, I do agree with Graham and yourself that a British Library engagement with this Commission (perhaps in the form of a Presentation) is an opportunity not to be missed. When I had raised this possibility with the Commission's Senior Strategy Officer towards the end of last week, her response was immediate and positive. Given that time is of the essence, please contact Ms Makeda Coaston…'

Soon after, Clive Field replied: 'I will ask Graham to make contact with her (Ms Coaston). If she comes in, I would be very pleased to meet her and the two of you'.

After discussions between Mr Graham Shaw and Mr Field, Ms Coaston was contacted, but I was not invited to the meeting. Nonetheless I spoke to Mr Shaw and urged him to attend the forthcoming 'Round Table Discussion' at City Hall.

Soon after, the Strategy Team had been in consultation with their 'Diversity Manager' as to the next steps for the British Library vis-a-vis the Mayor's Commission. This internal British Library link could only be helpful, I thought. And, as important, if not even more so, was the contact that had been made between the British Library's Strategy Team and the Commission. In relation to my position on MCAAH, I felt the presence of a Diversity Manager in the British Library, was timely.

On reflection, I considered the fact that since 1972 I'd been speaking in public; and with regularity from 1982, I'd been delivering either a 'Talk' or Lecture every year. Now on 28 August 2003, I was contacted by the Museum of London's 'Access and Learning' staff who were delighted that I 'will be providing the "Pan Africans in England - An Overview" ' Talk on Saturday 18 October 2003.

This was a well attended Event and the Museum of London's organisers were pleased with the outcome. Why? Largely because so much of African and Asian history was still not adequately researched and articulated in the context of Britain. As I'd been saying for many years, these were not simply minority 'ethnic' stories, but integral aspects of *British history.*

In relaxed and reflective mood, I thought of the evening when Sir Richard Attenborough had celebrated his 80th Birthday at the South Bank's Festival Hall. My friend Wendy had invited me to attend; and as we moved amidst the large gathering of the good and great, sipping drinks and munching canapés, I found myself standing next to Ben Kingsley, the actor who played the title role in Attenborough's film *Gandhi.* After I'd complimented Mr Kingsley on his powerfully nuanced performance, he leaned closer and whispered in my ear: 'You have a crumb on your lip.' These few well-timed words were spoken almost musically, a cadence reminiscent of Shakespearean delivery. I turned aside for a moment and somewhat shame-facedly while brushing my lips, I caught the stares of actors Richard E. Grant and a woman who looked like the actress Julia Sawalha. Resuming our talk Mr Kingsley enquired about my work as a writer and expressed an interest in a copy of *Reimaging Britain.* He gave me an address to which the book should be sent and we both moved on: Kingsley to where Richard Attenborough was standing; and I closer to Wendy.

My engagement with the Mayor's Commission confirmed my appreciation of the value of history and therefore my continuing ambition to fill gaps wherever I perceived them. After many months of research, I approached my publisher I. B. Tauris with the book proposal titled: *EMPIRES: A History from Ancient to Modern Times.* This theme reflected my ever-broadening interest and growing confidence in linking the particular with the general; not only in relation to my colonial upbringing within the British Empire, but in Empires from ancient to modern times. And, as I read a great deal more, I felt the *need* to use the knowledge gained to understand great civilizations of the past. Bearing in mind that it is *in the present* that we make sense of the past, my enthusiasm for the subject was seemingly boundless as I sent off the 'Synopsis' and 'List of Contents' to I. B. Tauris and waited with much hope. A reply from history Editor Dr Crook was not long in coming. He wrote:

> *'I included this book (Empires: A History from Ancient to Modern Times) on the Agenda of our last Editorial Meeting and argued that this was a bold and timely project with the emergence of a new global USA Empire. I think that the general reader as well as the student would be very interested in a book which will give a survey of imperialism. We would therefore like to take on the book and I will obtain the costings and go to financial profile and contract stage.'*

At this point, I paused and thought, how very encouraging to have had such a positive response. Then I read further:

> *'I envisage a book of 352 pages in hardback with a good dust jacket and illustrations and of course the price would be within the range of the general reader and student. I would like to discuss this in detail with you. I think that the ideas of imperialism in your outline should be simplified for general readers and I feel also that Hobson's definition is too vague and that his "Imperialism" represents a particular strand of historiography. I think that the study should be a survey of the developing idea of an empire but will be attractively written and evolve into an engaging history which brings together ALL the Empires from the dawn of "civilisation" through to the present...This could be a remarkable book...*
>
> *I look forward to your response.'*

I replied immediately to Dr Crook's letter and, once again, I waited.

In the following weeks, it was fortuitous that the "Round Table" discussion on 'Exploring the Heritage Landscape' marked the opening of proceedings of the Mayor's Commission and, as I had hoped, Graham Shaw, Director of the Oriental and India Office Collections was present. A few days later Mr Shaw reported to his colleagues, namely Jill Finney of the Strategy Team, Clive Field and British Library Chief Executive Lyn Brindley. Rating the importance of this email to me as "High," Mr Shaw, acknowledged the Commission's eight key areas of concern: Representation of Ethnic Minorities on Boards of Cultural Institutions; the 200th Anniversary of British Anti-Slavery legislation in 2007; Mainstreaming; Interpretation; Representations; Mapping of Collections; Ethnic Minority representation in the Staffing of Cultural institutions and Visitor Profiles.

Clearly, there was a great deal of work to get through and all Commissioners knew this only too well. There was never any doubt on my part that the work before us would be done; and importantly that the crucial 'Report and Recommendations' would be written and published. The real difficulty was the very tight schedule which was a pressing concern. Coincidentally, the time had come to celebrate the British Museum's 250th Anniversary 1753-2003; and as a Commissioner, I was invited to attend a lavish Reception Party which was held in what was now the spacious and breath-taking new British Museum Great Court designed by Norman Foster. Several weeks before the Court was formally opened to the public, I remembered the day only too well when, after wearing a hard hat and boots, George Reilly, one of the Engineer-Builders had guided me up the construction steps to the top of the forest of scaffolding as the impressive glass roof beneath which I now stood, was being put in place.

Amidst the lively commotion and chatter that filled the circular new space, much champagne was consumed and I met some of those who were, in the heritage, museums and galleries sector, regarded as the 'good and the great,' an expression which, as I now knew, was an ever-shifting social constituency. There were many distractions at this Reception, but as I stood here and there, I could not ignore the fact that the Great Court was flanked by two rooms: the Egyptian Gallery to the west and the former King's Library to the east; the latter's former collection of books were now housed in the great glass book-case at St. Pancras. And how could I not be aware of the former Round Reading Room at the centre of the Great Court? Alas, the Great Court was the main attraction and the Round Reading Room's devaluation from its glorious position as the world's greatest Reading Room to being an Exhibition space was now sadly complete. Though loss of the reading room was a matter of the greatest regret for me personally, as I moved around the Great Court, I remembered the rows of book-stacks that had once occupied it, including the old 'Iron Works' site that had for so long seemed like an immovable fixture at the south-eastern corner where one of the British Museum's Information Desks now stood.

The fizz of champagne seemed to enliven and deepen nostalgia; my sense of the place where so much of what I had yearned for over the years (primarily the desire to write and publish books) had happened; a location where a totally transforming phase of my life was lived! No one else among the hundreds of beautifully-dressed Guests shuffling around me either knew, or would ever know, what I knew and had experienced in that area before it became this splendid setting. I looked up and surveying the magnificent ceiling, having seen old prints of the original British Museum building that had housed Sir Hans Sloane's Collections, given my acute awareness of the passing of time, I felt enriched and strangely moved to be celebrating this great institution's Anniversary.

MARTIN LUTHER KING JR; THE 'COMMISSION' SITS; ORAL HISTORY; 'DOT' DIES

At this time, among my options was the possibility of writing a book on Mahatma Gandhi; a proposition which I'd put to Barbara Schwepke of Haus Publishing for whom Nigel Cawthorne had informed me he was commissioned to write a book. After corresponding with Ms Schwepke, I invited her to meet me at the British Library, where we discussed my 'Gandhi' book proposal, but eventually agreed that I should write a biography of Dr Martin Luther King Jr instead. This prompted a legitimate question: what was there to say about the life and times of the American Civil Rights Campaigner that had not already been said in the millions of words in print? To say that I was not under pressure to write a book that would not be prolix, but one of quality, would be an understatement. Undaunted and commissioned, with characteristic excitement, I was ready to meet the challenge.

As I had previously informed Clive Field, the British Library's engagement with the Mayor's Commission (perhaps in the form of hosting a Forum) 'is an opportunity not to be missed.' Brimming with optimism, I felt very hopeful of the Library's involvement in something that had long preoccupied me: meaningful diversity. In his report back to the British Library Mr Shaw concluded: '*There is the option of our making a formal submission or presentation to the Commission and clearly this is something we should discuss asap. On Monday I have invited Makeda Coaston, Senior Strategy Officer - Culture Strategy and MCAAH Programme and Project Manager to Lunch at 12 to try and find out more.*'

So far, I had encouraged the British Library to become more than just interested. But once the key Library players had become involved and more conversant with 'diversity' (an increasingly used word) they immediately distanced themselves from me and my Commissioner's role as they proceeded with their meetings directly with Commission administrators at City Hall. Furthermore, just over three weeks after the above email of 5 September was sent to Ms H, Mr Shaw had forwarded it to sixteen other members of staff in his directorate. The next day one of the sixteen contacted me: 'You don't seem to have been copied in to this...'

Soon after receiving this message, a 'Special Black History Month Launch' was planned at City Hall, during which a '**Public Debate**' was due to take place in the Grand Chamber. I was selected as one of the Speakers; and among the other Debaters were Professor Lola Young, Head of Culture (Greater London Authority); Lee Jasper (Policing Director) and Jeanette Arnold (London Assembly Member.) Attended by a packed audience, the evening's proceedings were opened with an Address by Mayor Livingstone, which had added significance because he was London's *first elected* Mayor. The sense of occasion was palpable. After speaking in the Debate that night, I left the Debating Chamber and City Hall and as I walked along the River Thames, I felt even more confident than hitherto about a positive outcome from our deliberations on the Commission.

Like a delayed reaction, a few days later, while steeped in work, on18 October 2003 an article appeared in *The Trinidad Express*: 'Trini Novelist to Serve on London Committee' which stated:

'At the Mayor's 2003 Black History Month Launch "Debate" (in

London's City Hall) Ron Ramdin did us proud with a distinguished presentation.' News travel fast, I thought, and this was all to the good.

By now, I had completed several drafts of *Rama's Voyage*; and with the *London Magazine's* forthcoming exposure, giving pride of place to an excerpt of the novel as the 'Lead Story' in the forthcoming October/November issue, my hopes of finding the appropriate publisher for the novel were raised.

Around this time, a past life became a matter of importance which needed to be recalled. Why? Because of an approach which came from Pavel Alam of the Workers' Educational Association, inviting me to contribute to the 'Black Trade Unionists Oral History Project' sponsored jointly by the WEA, London Metropolitan University and the Trades Union Congress. After further meetings, arrangements were made for me to do an In-Depth tape recorded biography of my life and work in the British Labour-Trade Union Movement. What a rare and historic opportunity this was? Given that the devoted manner in which I'd represented workers was an essential part of my British experience, although I'd left the 'Movement' twenty-four years before, now I was seen by a new generation as having an important, unique story to tell, one which, those who knew best, were ready to receive.

For this exciting 'Oral History Project,' I signed the '**Consent Form'** which, in part, stated: '...*I have been given information about the research project and the way in which my contribution will be used. All material will be preserved as a permanent public reference resource for use in research, publication, education, lectures and broadcasting.*

My contribution will be kept safely and securely with access only to those with permission from TUC Library collections at London Metropolitan University...

I give my permission for the interview, which I am about to give... for the above project to be used for research purposes only (including research publications and reports)...

*I hereby **assign the copyright** in my contribution to the TUC library, London Metropolitan University, London North Campus, the Learning Centre, 236-250 Holloway Road, London N7 6PP.*

Signed: Dr Ron Ramdin, 30 October 2003
    (Interviewee)
Signed: P. Alam (Researcher" 30 October 2003.'

Soon after consenting to the archival recording of this aspect of my story for the London Metropolitan University and the TUC, the idea suggested by Graham Shaw of doing a *Shelflife* article came to fruition when this fortnightly 'newsletter' for British Library staff published the following:

'HERITAGE Partnership: Ken Livingstone has appointed Dr Ron Ramdin of Asia, Pacific and Africa Collections to serve on the Mayor's Commission on African and Asian Heritage (MCAAH). This project, a Heritage Strategic Initiative will play a ground-breaking role in establishing partnerships and a programme for action that will address the dearth of effective representation in London.

Since Ron is serving on the Commission, as an individual, the Library was represented by Graham Shaw, Director of APAC, at an Open Session at City Hall. Among the issues raised were the need for community involvement in the Curatorial interpretation of objects and ethnic diversity in the staffing of institutions. 2007 is the anniversary of anti-slavery legislation in Britain and the Mayor's office hopes that institutions like the BL will curate activities connected with this anniversary. The Library is considering various activities at present, including an Exhibition.'

I felt great joy reading about an 'Exhibition' in relation to the Mayor's Commission and the British Library. Words, words, words! Countless words, mostly *written and spoken* by me, over many years, would hopefully soon be put *into practice*. At Last! I thought. I was now convinced of the British Library's commitment *to act* and thus truly reflect the modern community it served.

I could not help but reflect on those early years when I had spoken out on behalf of the poorly paid, when I was perceived and demonised as a 'Communist' and branded a 'black sheep,' not one of the British Museum-British Library fold. But, all along, I never deviated from my belief in genuine, meaningful social relations; indeed in the *practice* of, *respecting difference*. So with publication of the 'Heritage Partnership' piece, through continued input on the Mayor's Commission, my hope for *greater inclusiveness* in the British Library was higher than ever.

Eventually the WEA recording of my Trade Union experience took place over several hours at a studio in the Communications Workers' Union headquarters in London. As I spoke, I was surprised how deeply I felt about those heady, pioneering days of heightened tension and industrial strife in Britain, when almost everything that I did was a first; engagements that pushed boundaries. Little did I know that I was in deed *making* history! As part of the 'Oral History Project' my recording is now in the Trades Union Congress Library Collections at London Metropolitan University, where it can be accessed by researchers and interested members of the general public. And so my contribution to British working peoples' history was archived for posterity; and thus it became a research resource for generations to come.

After revisiting my leadership role in the turbulent 1970s, I looked back on my intellectual journey and realised how far I had travelled. This 'journey' was certainly not a straight line: it was, in essence, multi-stranded, multi-dimensional, often disorientating, but always forward-looking. For now, however, my pursuit of getting *Rama's Voyage* published remained intense: I continued to send copies of the Synopsis to editors and Agents and even wrote to Anne McDermid (my former Literary Agent) who was now back in Canada.

At this time of the Commission's deliberations, a crucial juncture was reached: after debating various issues, the time had come to appoint a 'Writer' from a list of five candidates, to write the Mayor's Commission Report. A panel of Commissioners appointed Richard Ings; and at once, given my historical understanding, the name reminded me of one of the accused in the 'Cato Street Conspiracy!'

Thereafter, Commissioners discussed the 'Workplan Milestones:' a schedule of meetings from 2003-2004. In this document, the projected date for the much-anticipated Launch of the Commission's

Report was set for March 2004. Before then, however, as all Commissioners were well aware, there was a great deal of work to get through. While some were excited and optimistic that a 'Report' would be written and submitted on time, others were less confident. For my part, as I'd been at the very beginning of 2003, now there was never any doubt. My optimism related not only to the Commission's findings, but also my wider work; my decades-old reading and research habits and activity: not only in relation to various London Archives, Museums and Galleries, but also more broadly on British history.

At one of our sittings, it was rumoured that a 'Chairman' was expected to be appointed to head the Commission. Was this necessary? Yes. The person appointed was Dame Jocelyn Barrow. And so twenty-one years after she had spoken as an 'Educationist' in praise of my first book *From Chattel Slave to Wage Earner* at its Launch in Knightsbridge, I was about to meet Ms Barrow on the core matter of our mutual interest: **Education** as it related to the history, culture and identities of Africans, West Indians and Asians in Britain.

Of the many wonderful people that I'd met on my trip of a lifetime to New Zealand, apart from the Slaters and Joan, were the Murrays, John and 'Dot.' This couple were not only pleasant people, they also cared passionately about music and literature. Indeed, Dorothy was the author of *Gently Down the Stream: A Social History of New Zealand and the Shoebridge Family* which was published in 1996. She kindly presented a copy to me and signed it: 'To Ron, On the occasion of your visit to New Zealand.' Below this inscription, were the printed words:

'Row row row your boat
Gently down the stream
Merrily merrily merrily merrily
Life is but a dream.'

Meeting Dot was certainly not a dream. A few months after I'd returned to England, I was deeply saddened to hear that she had died. From his Sealy Road home in Torbay, Auckland, on 19 December 2003, John took the time to write to me:

'*Dear Ron,*

Christmas is almost upon us and I am still sending off cards every day, still, it is good to keep in touch with friends and family.

It has been an unusual sort of year for me without Dot, but I am soldiering on because life must go on. I am selling our old Sealy Road home in February... Of course, the hard part will be sorting out and disposing of a lifetime of memories and treasures...

I am still in regular touch with Moira, Taffy and I saw Ron and Melissa and Georgia and Josh a couple of weeks ago. They are all happy and in good health and living busy lives, which is a good thing... If I am lucky enough I hope to catch-up with them all at Bethells Beach on Boxing Day.

Ron, congratulations on your novel and thank you for the Extract you sent. It has an intriguing beginning and it will be interesting to find out what happens to Rama and the little band of waifs he starts out with. I wish you every success and hope we can get some copies here in the antipodes, for I will surely buy one. Thank you also for your lovely card. Most of the cards we still send are winter scenes. I suppose in deference to our old British ancestors. Of course we will probably be roasting in the Xmas heat – out here... Last weekend, they had the Concert in the Park again. I didn't get once to town to see it, but watched it on television and thought of how the last one went as you were here with us too. Unfortunately like all good things it is about to change. Since you were here, they have constructed a massive new hospital on the old site, just up the hill and the concert is now considered too noisy for the hospital people and the crowds make traffic control in the city area too difficult. They will shift the event no doubt to some Stadium in the suburbs ad it will never be the same again, because for 50% of the old audience it will be too far to travel.

Well Ron, I hope you have a very successful 2004. We are often thinking of you, you will have to come back one year soon.

John -

P.S. The music and literature are definitely going with me, to the new house – a lot of the memorabilia too. Robin Dudding (of the New Zealand Literary Review) sends his kind regards and hopes you have a festive season. He still spends most of his days in the garden. He is compiling an anthology of New Zealand poetry next year.'

John's letter was heartfelt and re-reading it now evokes warm memories.

Two months into the new year, once more, travel overseas beckoned. Before setting out to visit my fast-ageing parents in Trinidad, I'd met a friend for a pre-travel drink in a pub in King's Cross. A football game was being shown on a large screen, and as the centre of interest, it was watched by high-spirited customers. From time to time, our conversation was interrupted by oohs! and aahs! and shouts of goal! At one point, I was standing next to an excited young Englishman. 'A good game,' I said, careful not to take sides. The youth gave a friendly nod and said: 'I'm a Manchester United man.' Mentioning this club, reminded me of my teenage obsession with English football and in particular, Manchester United which, as a player in Trinidad had added further encouragement for me to emigrate. Filled now with the spirit of the game, amidst the good-natured mood and camaraderie of the clientele, I ventured the following remark: 'I played first Class football when I was younger.' A quizzical look spread across the young man's face. 'How many drinks have you had?' he asked.

No more was said; and in the awkward silence that ensued, the young man moved to another corner of the pub. This was, however, not the end of the matter for me.

After that brief exchange, I thought of something that had concerned me ever since I came to England: This relates to a report that I'd read (but interestingly I could not now be sure that I had) either in the Trinidad *Evening News* or the *Texaco Sporting Star*. Did a report of my playing days *really exist*? Or was my imagination playing tricks with me? I wondered about these questions as the television football commentary overlaid the general buzz of lively customers. To exaggerate or lie about a boyhood experience (or some long past event) is what some older men got up to. But as an historian, I knew the importance of 'evidence.' Like the young man who questioned my claim, no one would ever believe me unless and until I was able to produce the evidence. So, on the eve of my departure from London, over four decades later, once and for all, I decided to investigate if there was, in fact, a surviving report or perhaps a photograph of me as a footballer in existence. From those moments that day, increasingly, finding this information took hold. To begin with, I was almost certain that Texaco Sports Club with its organisational and sporting prestige would have kept copies of its journal *The (Texaco) Sporting Star*. But that was very long ago, I reminded myself. Nonetheless, it would bring me pleasure to see and/or read something about those wonderful games in which I had played, the memory of which was still ever-green.

And so, soon after arriving in Trinidad, I said to Isaac, an employee of Texaco: there must be a library or similar repository in the Texaco Company where this journal could be found. Isaac suggested a few places, but he seemed unsure. As we explored, he took me deep into the inner preserves of the Texaco precinct to the only place where he thought surviving copies of the *The Sporting Star* may have been stored. The Librarian was positive: 'Yes we have copies of *The Sporting Star*.' Ah! I breathed a sigh of relief. I was ushered into a room and three large bound volumes containing copies for the years between 1958-1962 were placed on one of the desks. After I'd leafed through the first two volumes, my heart sank more than just a little, but with great hope I scanned the pages of the third volume. Past half-way, I was fast running out of pages. My disappointment grew as I slowly turned the remaining pages. Then I came to *The Sporting Star*, No. 46: Yes, there it was! The Match Report commentary that I'd seen so many years before. With great deliberation and excitement I refreshed my memory as I read:

'*The Texaco football eleven after suffering some early setbacks, has now settled down to the Don Revie "M" "W" plan, and it is apparent by their most recent performances that the Star boys intend to get even in a manner that will make coach McDonald Durity feel really proud of them...*

With Ramdin and the other players improving with each game, fans are in for some real top-grade soccer by this young and fast-moving Texaco Team.

Reason for their early failures was the inability of the wing-halves to adapt to the new plan which should be "M" in attack and "W" in defence. But Durity had faith in his conviction that the plan could not be expected to work smoothly all at once and so it was Shell's fate to receive the first blow. Texaco won 3-2…'

This was more than just confirmation of my sporting prowess of years past. To be picked out for special mention by the respected Sports Writer K.O. Williams was especially gratifying. Also on this page, was a precious find: A full report of all of Texaco's recent matches and for the record, a number of the best-known footballers of that generation were mentioned, including Edgar Vidale, Noel Daniel, Ken Merrick, Terry Lane, Pat Gomez and two former Inter-Col (Inter-College) players (who later became better known: Bobby Sookram and Henry Quanvie.

Reading these 'Round-Ups' was a vivid reminder of my youthful self. Then, as a withdrawn seventeen year old, I faced my biggest challenge: wearing the distinctive Texaco green shirt with the red star and running out on to the carpet-like turf of Guaracara Park to play my first game. Now, with the evidence before me, the memory was all the more vivid and reassuring.

As nostalgia gripped me, there was another surprise in store: when I turned the page I found further evidence to support the claim that I'd made in conversation with the young man in London. I was stunned to see photographs: one in particular, in which I appear on the Guaracara Park ground with Coach McDonald Durity and four other players: the Coach was conducting a Training session. I remember well the usual drill: heading, trapping, passing, dribbling and new skills. The photo's captions read: 'MC DONALD DURITY puts his players through their paces at Guaracara Park, Pointe-a-Pierre. Texaco plan to play the "M""W" Don Revie system…For them its football the Hungarian Way.' I made several copies of this 'evidence.'

Soon I was back in London and having seen myself as that teenager learning to play football the 'Hungarian Way,' the memories came flooding back: Football was then an obsession, but I also remembered those heady days and weeks as a time when 'going to England' was the dream, very much *the* goal! And given the ongoing heated Debates far away in the British Parliament, I was also aware that being an *immigrant* was a very contentious issue, as I tried desperately to raise the money and pay for my passage to 'Beat the Ban.' That was a very long time ago. Now, after seeing and reading the *Sporting Star's* report, I thought of the effect of large scale post-war immigration and the settlement of Commonwealth citizens. In particular, I considered the more recent debates in Britain on 'new immigrants' and certain themes: 'Common Values,' the 'Muslim Divide,' the 'Call to Race Relations' and 'Multiculturalism.'

Against this background and while the Mayor's Commission on African and Asian Heritage got on with its work, following the *Shelf Life* article on my appointment by Mayor Livingstone I was contacted by Andrew Simons, Curator of the British Library's 'Modern British Collections' who wrote:

'Dear Ron,

You're involved in the Mayor's Commission on African and Asian Heritage. With the recent success of the Reaching the Regions project, the Library is keen to form partnerships in, for now, the Northeast and the Southeast. Graham Shaw has been copied to me, wondering whether this Commission could involve the Library in the Cultural Strategy for London.

My Black & Asian Working Group would like to know of the progress of the Mayor's Commission so please keep us informed.

Also, are you on the Commission as the BL representative or as an independent historian?

We haven't really met yet, but I hope we can soon after the Easter holiday break. I came to the BL ten years ago as the now-redundant Jazz Curator and am currently a book curator in social history. Previously I was the Head Archivist at the American Research Centre in the States (http//www.armistadresearchcenter.org/) and so I have an interest in pursuing this.

Thanks.

Andy Simons

Modern British'.

Again that question: '…are you on the Commission as the BL representative or as an *independent historian*?' Clearly Mr Simons had not read the *Shelf Life* article.

What struck me about his message though was the thought that after 34 years of seeking workplace recognition for minority 'Ethnic' groups in the British Library (the treatment of all with fairness in promotion and other matters!) now, at last, there were others ready and willing to engage. This was heartening, very encouraging. But there was also something proprietorial about this message: '*My*' Black & Asian Working Group which was reminiscent of the leadership style of those British Library union representatives who had succeeded me as Secretary of the Whitley Council Staff Side and as CSU Branch 849 Secretary.

Overall, I appreciated Mr Simons's work and welcomed his move. The earlier groundwork that I'd initiated and pursued was proving to be a fertile field at an opportune and opportunistic time, upon which the 'Black and Asian Working Group' could maintain its existence and grow.

In a busy life, I tried to allow some time for socialising. One evening on my way to visit my good friend Wendy, I stopped at Vintage House on Old Compton Street and bought two bottles of Evian water. The next morning, Wendy was unusually upset. Why? She explained: when she had got up in the night to have a drink of water, she realised that one of the bottles contained 'white spirit!' instead of water. I was stunned. I duly wrote to Mr Mullins, the Vintage House manager, expressing my shock as well as to Brian C. Robins, Legal representative for Mr Mullins of Vintage House.

'*Dear Mr Brian C. Robins,*

Your letter has made the case for Mr Mullins very well. You have made much of "due diligence" and "reasonable steps," which although understandable does not compensate for Vintage House's incompetence at the point of sale, meaning the lack of diligence on the part of the staff who, I might add, was keenly observant about the payment I had made, but nowhere near as vigilant or observant of the contents of the item they had sold to me.

What is most disappointing is that you have not once alluded to the seriousness of selling white spirit in an Evian water bottle! This may well be a genuine mistake and I appreciate that Mr Mullins cannot be everywhere at once, but this was clearly negligence on the part of his staff in spite of what you say. They are culpable.

As a regular customer for as long as VH has been there, I shudder whenever I think of the seriousness of the matter. It was a miracle that neither myself nor Wendy had opened that bottle in the night and gulped downed white spirit. When Wendy rang me the next day to say that I had bought her white spirit, I was horrified. "Where did you get it?" she enquired. She was unusually upset.

May I remind you that it was Wendy's " due diligence" that saved us both from being unfortunate customers and Mr Mullins and his staff from deep trouble!'

Having come so dangerously close to disaster, to this day, I shudder at the thought. Always expect the unexpected was the lesson learned.

If immigration had been a perennial problem before and since my arrival in Britain, now it hit the headlines and remained in the news. On 1 May 2004, the *Daily Mail's* article: 'Next Stop Britain' stated:

'As the EU (European Union) celebrates expansion, 40 Poles from one small town head here to find a better future. JOBS WARNING: Romano Prodi (Italian Prime Minister) cast a shadow over the celebrations marking the EU expansion with a warning that cheap labour would undermine unskilled jobs in richer nations'.

Reporting on "Legal Bills" the newspaper reported:

' The cost to taxpayers of providing asylum seekers and immigrants with state-subsidised lawyers soared above £200 million last year, it was revealed yesterday...Today 10 more countries join the EU. It should be a cause for celebration - but the shambles of Britain's Immigration policy has tainted this historic moment.'

Enoch Powell and Powellism of the 1960s and 1970s had had its day, but few British newspapers were as touchy about immigration as the *Daily Mail* which dug up as much material as they could find; and, given their political orientation, the stories they ran were often sensational.

Propelled by the possibility of translating my literary work on film, on 26 May 2004 Paul Balmer, film-maker and Director of 'Music on Earth,' was interested in working with me on his 'Descendants Project' for which he was seeking funds. He had made a fine film about Tunde Jegede - the brilliant kora player-cum-all-round musician and composer. He was the person that I had turned to after I'd left Tuareg Productions. Keen to make a film about the Caribbean community, using my name as a 'Mayor's Commissioner,' Mr Balmer approached the Heritage Lottery Fund for financial backing. We were, of course, hopeful of a good outcome. Alas, this did not materialise. Thus Mr Balmer had joined the preceding two film-makers who, in their dealings with me, were also in search of money.

As a Public Holiday in Trinidad, Indian Arrival Day was also celebrated among Indo-Trinidadians and members of other groups in the wider West Indian communities in Britain. On 30 May 2004 under the sponsorship of the Trinidad and Tobago High Commission in London I gave the Indian Arrival Day 'Keynote Address' in the presence of the newly-installed High Commissioner, Glenda Morean-Phillips. This was a grand occasion held before a large audience at the historic Kingsley Hall, where Mahatma Gandhi had stayed during his visit to London.

Later, the *London Mission Newsletter* issued by the High Commission, reported: 'A large gathering of nationals attended the first Indian Arrival Day Celebration in London under the auspices of Her Excellency the HC Mrs Glenda Morean-Phillips... The celebration took place on Sunday May 30 and featured addresses by Dr. Ron Ramdin who spoke on the Indo-Caribbean experience...'

The report was accompanied by a photograph of me on stage giving the 'Address.'

This was a successful event and among the other speakers was Shirley Sookraj, one of the event's organisers. In the afterglow of the Celebrations, on receiving a copy of *Arising From Bondage: A History of East Indians in the Caribbean*, Ms Sookraj wrote:

'*...In many a sense, as we celebrate our fore-fathers arrival I feel so strongly that we, their children, have also arrived...but to speak of "arrival" and no more is in some ways to invite perception of* *stagnation...stagnation of our intellect and our achievements and our hopes for the future. So we must move forward not only to secure our inheritance from our forefathers, but for it also to become our legacy to our descendants. This is why receiving your book has brought so much joy to me today!! Our forefathers were not without knowledge or intelligence. They were simply a people without literacy. But they overcame even if the price they paid was (costly)... Hinduism and Islam... They learnt letters from a new language called English, letters which they were taught to select out of a choice of only 26, to make words...*

Books like yours! and the many authors whom I have no doubt your bibliography honours... have immortalised their history of our people, so that descendants like myself can erase their ignorance. To simply thank You is insufficient! To pray that God, or more accurately, my mother Saraswatee, the Saint of Intellectual Prosperity in Hinduism, will bless your intellect bountifully (even if you have no religion!) seems so much more appropriate to commend your generosity in giving me your book.'

Coming from someone so passionate about standing on the shoulders of our forebears, confirmed the importance that I'd attached from the outset to *Arising from Bondage* and, especially that fateful error and the sense of devastation that I felt on the morning after the book had been erased from my computer. Two days after receiving the above-mentioned letter, High Commissioner, Glenda Morean Phillips was also forthcoming with her thoughts. She wrote:

'I wish to thank you for your contribution to the celebration of Indian Arrival Day which took place on Sunday May 30 2004. It was a pleasure to observe the support given by nationals in putting together such a varied programme. The combination of speeches, literary contributions, music and Indian cuisine all contributed to making the day a memorable occasion.

I look forward to continued contacts with you.'

This official response from the new diplomat, augured well for good relations. In fact, she requested a copy of my 'Address'. But given my 'marginal' social position ever since I came to England in the hope of sustaining my multi-dimensional interests, I remained inventive and creative, continuously alert to what interested and moved me as a man and a writer.

THIRTY

GARY SOBERS, SIR GULAM NOON, ZOE WANAMAKER AND 'AMERICAN VISIONARIES'

My playing days in Trinidad, founded on the British cultural legacy of 'Hoofbeats and Footsteps': horse racing and football continued to interest me in England, but not to the same degree as before. Having had the honour of meeting the sporting legends 'Ram and Val' (Sonny Ramadhin and Alfred Valentine), early in June, to mark the 75th Anniversary of West Indian Cricket I received an Invitation from Clem Seecharan to attend 'An Evening with Sir Gary Sobers' at London Metropolitan University.

News of this event triggered thoughts of another great West Indian Cricket 'great': Viv Richards. From the Stands at the Queen's Park Oval in Port of Spain, having watched him bat, we had eventually met at a Reception in London. Now, in another London setting, I was in the audience awaiting the entrance of Sir Gary Sobers who was also 'great' and revered.

It was a delight to hear Sir Gary reminisce about the high points of his sporting career, including the extraordinary six sixes he'd hit in one over of six balls or deliveries! Afterwards, as I left the Lecture Hall and walked towards the University's Staff Café for the Reception, the possibility of writing a biography of Sir Gary crossed my mind. Why not? Through this literary genre, I thought, I could gain further insights into the man, rather than the myth or legend. I also thought it would be a good book.

After putting the matter to Sir Gary and discussing it for a while, he did not commit himself. Nonetheless I was glad to have spoken with this iconic sportsman whom many knowledgeable commentators regarded as the greatest West Indian cricket all-rounder of all time. As it was, I was quite content to continue researching my biography of C.L.R. James, author of the classic book on cricket, *Beyond a Boundary*.

On this matter of sporting legacies, with a sense of amazement, I looked back on having, within a relatively short space of time, met two Knights of West Indian Cricket. (I'd often wondered why no Indo-Caribbean cricketer had achieved this status). As a barefoot boy listening with wonder to the radio Test Match commentaries, the chance of person-to-person meetings with sportsmen of this stature was seemingly impossible. Truly extraordinary, I thought for in most people's experience such encounters were well beyond a boundary.

By now, I was in the thick of things as a Mayor's Commissioner and as the Commission continued to meet, accompanying our deliberations various documents were passed around and, time and again during debates, I was reminded of the grim realities, the ups and downs of Black and Asian migrants' lives. In discussions, Commissioners were unsparing: exploring every avenue, we aimed for all that was valuable; for uplifting stories.

Between the Commission's sessions, I attended other meetings and events which altogether formed a rich and varied tapestry of activities, social, cultural and economic, including one that was held in the British Library's Conference Centre where I heard Sir Gulam Noon, a hugely successful Indian businessman speak of his entrepreneurial rise and rise in Britain. That evening, during the Reception (held in the Library's Front Hall and Upper Ground Floor areas) I spoke to Sir Gulam. A few days later, I thought his life and work was worthy of a biography. He was an inspirational figure.

I contacted Sir Gulam. He responded by inviting me to meet him in his London office at St James's Gate. On arrival at this address, I was met by his Secretary, a professionally friendly, but business-like woman of a Caribbean background who ushered me in the Reception room. After a few minutes, she led me to Sir Gulam's inner sanctum. He was immaculately dressed and seated at his desk in an attractive, spacious office, studded museum-like with memorabilia. During a most encouraging meeting Sir Gulam presented me with a signed copy of one of his books; and in furtherance of my objective - a biography of him, he was most encouraging. He offered me his bio-data and a Compact Disc of his 'Guest' spot on the BBC's popular Desert Island Discs programme. Whilst we chatted, I glanced around: the office was very pleasant, almost a private haven. Among the framed photographs was one of Sir Gulam with Tony Blair and nearby, there were a couple of cricket bats and a few faded, used balls - souvenirs, personally signed. Having met Sir Gary Sobers, I mentioned the chat that I had had with the much-admired cricketer; and for a while, in manner and speech, I saw a less formal side of Sir Gulam. Overall, the meeting augured well for future collaboration and when I left the entrepreneur's office clutching the material he'd given to me, I was quietly encouraged by what was a positive Interview. Now, it was up to me to advance the biography idea a step further.

I wasted no time. Having listened to the CD and reading the relevant materials to hand, after much thought, I decided that the working title of Sir Gulam's biography should be: 'FOOTPRINTS: The Authorised Biography of Sir Gulam Noon.' Soon after, I wrote to him:

'I found our meeting most stimulating and have since done a List of Contents and two versions of the Synopsis of FOOTPRINTS...a first Draft of five pages and the enclosed shorter version, which is for presentation to HarperCollins. I hope both will be agreeable to you, as essentially working drafts.

While writing the SYSNOPSIS I realised that the 70th Anniversary of your birth is on 24 January 2006. It would be nice to complete the research and writing and have the book published by then, which means getting a publishing contract very soon. It would therefore be most helpful if you could pass on the enclosures to the Editor concerned at HarperCollins with your endorsement.

I look forward to hearing from you.

Yours sincerely,

Ron Ramdin.'

My 'List of Contents' for FOOTPRINTS contained fifteen Chapter headings plus a Bibliography and Index; evidence of a good deal of time and effort. My hope was that as an historian of the Black and Asian experience in Britain, I would present this book as one of the great migrant success stories of recent times. But without in any way demeaning its importance, apart from this project, other ongoing literary matters necessarily played on my mind.

By now, I'd completed a second and possibly the penultimate draft of my 'big' novel *The Confessions of the Reverend William Wragg*. It was a significant juncture for this book had been conceived some two decades before; and as my early retirement from the British Library loomed larger, I felt compelled to complete *The Confessions*...as soon as possible. Bearing in mind that I had never been out of work since I was first employed at the Senate House, I could not ignore the fact that my working career in the British Library had less than a year to run before I departed. My awareness of time which had so preoccupied me, now assumed an even greater preciousness.

For some years I'd been meaning to contact my previous employer, the University of London Library, about the transfer of my seven-year Pension contributions from them to the British Library Pension Scheme. Looking back, how incredible, I thought, that just weeks past my twentieth birthday, escorted by Mr Boxer, I was ushered into the University's Personnel Office to discuss my Pension! My Pensionable age was then an unimaginable distance away; an almost unthinkable thing. But time had slipped by, and now here I was staring at retirement. And so, thirty five years on, I wrote a second letter to the Personnel Officer at Senate House saying it would be very helpful if he could let me have all the relevant information regarding my '*rights/dues as it relates to the years of my payments into the University Pension Scheme.*
I do look forward to hearing from you.'

Appended to this letter was the copy of a letter from the Pay and Pension Section of the University of London, which informed me that according to their records, I had been paid-off and therefore had no claim! When was I paid off? I strongly disputed the University's spurious argument of payment to me; and for many days, this matter so played on my mind that I had no choice but to seek redress from the Ombudsman. Money, a constant preoccupation throughout my life, continued to worry me all the more now that my wage-earning days were numbered.

With just about a year to go before I left the British Library, some projects became more urgent than others: for example, I felt my Interview with Sam Wanamaker, recorded at Shakespeare's Globe Theatre in 1987, should be made available not only to the British public, but also to an interested international audience. To this end, I spoke to a few people in the theatre world, especially actors. Zoe Wanamaker, the well-known actress and daughter of Sam Wanamaker, had been informed of her father's Interview with me. Subsequently, while at work, I received a surprise telephone call from Zoe. She said she was interested in hearing my Interview which was done when the Globe Theatre was being built on Bankside, London. This rare recording on cassette tape was of 91 minutes duration. Thanks to the British Library, to whom I had donated a copy of the original recording, a two CD set of it was made for me.

Zoe had learned of the existence of this 'recording' through actor Nick Gecks and photographer Nobby Clark who knew her, it seemed. When we spoke on the telephone, she said she would like to visit me at the British Library. On the appointed day, I met her in the foyer and invited her for a cup of coffee in the Upper Ground Floor Café where we had a most enjoyable conversation which lasted over one and a half hours.

We spoke of many things, including her father, certain family matters and, of course, acting in relation to her roles past, and those which she had hoped would come. I presented her with a copy of the 2 CD set of Sam Wanamaker talking with me, not only about Paul Robeson, America, racism, fascism, acting and Shakespeare's *Othello*, but also about the 1959 Stratford-upon-Avon Production directed by Tony Richardson, which starred Paul Robeson as Othello and Sam Wanamaker as Iago. Zoe was very keen to listen to the Interview and I empathised with what was an understandable eagerness to know what exactly her father had said to me seventeen years before.

When the meeting with Zoe had ended, I walked back from the Café with her to the Reception area and said goodbye.

The next day, I was amused when a female member of staff stopped me to say: 'Guess who was in the Library yesterday?'

'Who?' I asked.

'Zoe Wanamaker!'

'So you didn't see *who* she was with?' To this question, there was no response. Was this woman's question meant to be playful?

After that encounter with the star of stage and screen, naturally, I was curious to know what Zoe's thoughts were about her father's views. I did not have to wait long. On 28 June 2004, she sent me a postcard. '*Dear Ron,*' she wrote, '*I am sorry not to have spoken with you since our nice cup of coffee.*' She added that while listening to CD 1 she found herself urging her father to 'answer the question. He repeats himself and rambles.' The second CD about the Sam Wanamaker-Paul Robeson connection, in particular, their acting relationship was much more to Zoe's liking. But responding to my expressed interest in writing a book about Sam, she wrote: 'I've met someone who is willing to do some research with a view to writing a bio of Dad and this recording is just fabulous for that.' Furthermore, she felt the recording was 'good enough for a radio programme on its own' and said she would approach Sue MacGregor (the former BBC Radio 4 'Today' Programme Presenter) 'to see what she thinks... Please Keep in Touch...I can't thank you enough!'

I was very pleased that Zoe liked the Interview, but although I was disappointed by her lack of interest in my biography idea, my intention to write about Sam Wanamaker and Paul Robeson was undiminished.

In fact, for sometime before, and especially since Zoe came to see me at the British Library, the impulse to write a double biography of Robeson and Wanamaker gained momentum and I proceeded to write a Synopsis titled: *AMERICAN VISIONARIES: Paul Robeson and Sam Wanamaker.* I prefaced this with these quotes from Sam Wanamaker and Paul Robeson. '*If the performance does not reflect social reality, it is not art,*' Wanamaker had said to me at Shakespeare's Globe Theatre. And many years earlier, Robeson had declared: '*The artist must take sides.*' After much thought and more research, I completed a List of Contents and the following Synopsis:

'*Hitherto 1987, I had come to know a great deal about Paul Robeson, but also about Sam Wanamaker, the visionary whose name will forever be associated with Shakespeare's Globe for had he gone back to America, the Theatre on Bankside, London, would not have been recreated and reopened in 1997. My interest in both men had started when I began researching and writing about Robeson in 1982. By then, Robeson had passed away, but I had met his son. Thirteen years later, not only did I meet Sam Wanamaker, I also met Zoe Wanamaker. The fact that I had met the offsprings of both men added a further dimension to my interest in this project.*

In spite of their physical differences, both Wanamaker and Robeson had much in common: both were born in America and both became actors. As men of their times, both found common cause with progressive movements at home and abroad. They were against racism, (segregation in American theatres) fascism and cared passionately about America, art, acting, the theatre and Shakespeare's work, especially Othello. While Robeson had played Othello three times, Wanamaker had graduated from being a fine actor and director to becoming the Founder of Shakespeare's Globe Theatre in London.

Robeson's first attempt at playing the title role in 1930 found him playing opposite Peggy Ashcroft as Desdemona. Thereafter, he played Othello in 1942-1943 in America and then for the last time in 1959 when he and Wanamaker came together on stage as actors in Shakespeare's birthplace Stratford-upon-Avon. In this celebrated production, under the direction of Tony Richardson, Wanamaker played Iago. It was an extraordinary and revealing experience. As a researcher, I felt sure that Wanamaker would have gained many insights into Robeson's ability as an actor which is why I had contacted him.

While there are many accounts of Robeson, to date, there is NO biography of Sam Wanamaker. Fortunately, my recorded Interview with Wanamaker is not only the FIRST tape recording ever made at the Globe, but also arising from it, is a remarkable unpublished Transcript of the full Interview, the closest thing to an autobiographical account of Wanamaker's life.

Significantly, underscoring both men's lives is the fact that because of their progressive, pro-Communist views, both were subpoenaed to appear before the House Un-American Activities Committee: one of them, Robeson, answered the call and his career was destroyed; the other, Wanamaker, who was in England at the time, chose to stay there. The rest, as they say, is history.

To date, there is no biography of Sam Wanamaker and given his key role in a relentless campaign to rebuild the Globe Theatre, I hope that publishing the intertwined stories of both men would shed light on a dark period in the history of America for they were men who lived in a black and white 'Cold War'-oriented world, far different from what exists today. The book I propose is timely for Sam Wanamaker and Paul Robeson were truly men of their times: visionaries.

__AMERICAN VISIONARIES__ will be written in an accessible style and I anticipate a global demand for it.

List of Contents:
Prologue
1. America (Pre-1929)
2. Finding Their Voices (1930-1940)
3. From Interpretative Artists to Political Artists (1940-1946)
4. From Great Americans to 'Un-Americans' (1946-1949)
5. Dilemma of the Political Artists (1949-1958)
6. Last Journeys (1949-1958)
7. Last Years (1959-1993)
Epilogue.'

After completing this proposal, I began the process of selecting the first publishers to whom it should be sent.

Meanwhile, like a voice growing ever louder, nagging me was the fact that in almost exactly a year's time, I would be ending my employment in the British Library after thirty-six years of service. If the University of London's Senate House Library was a Tower of books, the British Library, the greatest repository of its kind was a Temple of books in which the cathedral-like silence of the Round Reading Room had fertilised minds to produce great literary works. But while retirement was the goal for many people, the mere thought of it did not sit easily with me. It was just as well that I was busy.

Among my urgent concerns now as I waited to hear from Sir Gulam Noon was the hope that I would receive a positive reply to the Synopsis into which I'd put so much effort. I'd more or less thought the story through and was ready to get on with the biography. Twenty days after we'd met in his office, Sir Gulam wrote to me:

'Many thanks for your letter dated 10 June... I am flattered that you found my personal life as a subject worthy of a biography. Having considered it more seriously, at this moment in time I am not ready for it.'

At the age of seventy, he was 'not ready.' Fair enough, I thought. But 'being not ready for it' was not the reason his Secretary had given to me very soon after I'd received Sir Gulam's letter. Dutifully she telephoned me to say that cash was a problem. Indeed, the words 'strapped for cash' were used. Strange language, I thought; but stranger still in Sir Gulam's case. Though I was a relatively 'poor man,' to say on behalf of one of the richest men in Britain's immigrant community that he was 'strapped for cash' was rubbing salt into the wound, implying that I was in it 'for money!' This, I felt was an affront to my motivation which was to portray Sir Gulam Noon, an exemplar of enterprise and self-belief, as a role model for young people, not only in the Asian and Black communities, but also in Britain generally.

Nonetheless, spurred on by other inspiring figures of our time, the genre of biography held my attention and on my 'list' of notables at this time was Nelson Mandela. Having made a written request for an Interview, on 9 July 2004, John Samuel, Chief Executive of the *Nelson Mandela Foundation* wrote:

'We acknowledge with gratitude receipt of your letter dated 15 June 2004.

Mr Mandela will unfortunately not be in a position to grant you the Interview as requested due to time constraints. Mr Mandela is overwhelmed with requests from media representatives from across the world and we find it increasingly difficult to accommodate these requests...He is also currently working hard writing his book on his Presidential years and the time therefore available for other engagements is extremely limited...'

Considering this response, in the wake of Mandela's much publicised autobiography *Long Walk to Freedom* and the writing of his Presidential memoir, I felt my biographical interest in the South African Freedom fighter was best left alone.

'WHO DO WE THINK WE ARE?'; ADDRESSING THE LONDON MELA; 'EXHIBITING DIVERSITY'

Talking about autobiography and biography, I was invited by the Heritage Lottery Fund to attend a Special Conference on 'Who Do We Think We Are?' to be held in the BP Lecture Theatre at the British Museum.

Chaired by Melvin Bragg, the terms of reference were: 'to take forward an important discussion about individual and shared national heritage and identity in wider society. What are the links between heritage, identity, social cohesion, pride and citizenship. Can understanding the past help us by bringing communities together for the future or does the past divide us? What do our views of our heritage (shared and diverse) tell us about ourselves as a nation?'

There was much to discuss; and after listening to various speakers on the panel, I asked a couple of questions in relation to education through the medium of a television series on Black and Asian history in Britain. On this matter, instead of giving an answer, Liz Forgan, Chair of the HLF and one of the Panellists, suggested that I should speak with her after the Event.

On 14 July I wrote to her:

'Dear Liz Forgan,

It was good to meet you again at the Conference which you and the HLF hosted at the British Museum.

In the debate on "The View From the Media" and throughout the day's proceedings it was abundantly clear that in terms of educating the British public, after Melvin Bragg's Series on the **History of the English Language**, Niall Ferguson's **History of the British Empire** and Simon Schama's **History of Britain**, there is still no History of the Black and Asian Presence in Britain. As I said during the discussion, I have been knocking on the door of media producers to write and present a long history of this 'Presence' for many years. Why not Ron Ramdin's 'History of the Black and Asian Experience in Britain' on Video/DVD for schools and communities across Britain?

After Tuesday's "Who Do We Think We Are?" Conference (and with the approach of the 200th Anniversary of the Abolition of the Slave Trade) I am even more convinced and determined to write and present such an educational video/DVD of the hidden histories of Blacks and Asians that are so integral to British history. Your comments, and those of others, on heritage, identity and inclusiveness, on roots and routes, have been the focus of my writings, lectures and talks for the past 25 years on television, radio and at universities and schools. I hope, with your help, my Four Part proposal (please see enclosures) to make an educational video for schools and communities will be realised sooner, rather than later.

I do look forward to hearing from you...'

Since my earlier proposal in collaboration with Eric Davidson for a 13 Part Television Documentary about the Black Presence in Britain had foundered and lapsed, I was again 'knocking on the door' to present a Television Series. I was doing so at a time when many people had seen a repeat national showing of the award winning *The Unknown Soldiers,* as well as my more recent appearance on BBC Two's History Quest programme *Chattri* of which my part was filmed in and around the British Library building in St Pancras. If I wasn't ready now to write and present such a television Series, I never will, I thought. I was also keenly aware of the passage of time which, in turn, alerted me to other areas of life that were of social concern. My membership and role as a Mayor's Commissioner was seen as advantageous to others who requested my assistance in seeking funds. So once more on 20 July 2004, I approached the HLF. On this occasion, the theme was 'Trade Union Archiving' and I wrote in support of the application for funding from London Metropolitan University, the Trades Union Congress and the Workers Education Association:

'*To Whom It May Concern,*

Several months ago I was approached by Pav Alam of the Black Trade Unionists' Oral History Project to record my many years of experience at various levels of the British Trade Union Movement... Since then, and after graduating from the London School of Economics, I have written a few pioneering books and lectured internationally. Each year, including Black History Month, for over 25 years, I have been a speaker on black and Asian history and culture in Britain in universities, schools, Town Halls and public libraries across the country. I was recently appointed by the Mayor of London, Ken Livingstone, to serve on the first Mayor's Commission on African and Asian Heritage (MCAAH). The Commission's pioneering Report will be launched in November 2004 and arising from our Recommendations, it is hoped a model will emerge that will be implemented by policy-makers in the Heritage sector.

Having spent many years of my working life as a Trade Unionist, it is with a deep sense of appreciation and understanding of grassroots communities' work experience at both local and national levels that I fully support the BTUOHP's bid for a much-needed Heritage Lottery Fund Grant.

Yours sincerely,

Dr Ron Ramdin.'

Three days after the above letter was written, Ms Forgan replied to my initial letter:

'*Dear Dr Ramdin,*

Thank you for your letter of 14 July 2004. It was good to meet you at our "Who Do We Think We Are?" Conference and I do hope you enjoyed it.

*A history of Black and Asian experience in Britain **certainly needs to be made** and I understand that you have been in discussion with colleagues here in our London Team. I should **warn you** though that a DVD educational video by itself **is unlikely to meet our policy and priorities** which are focussed on the active involvement and*

engagement of people exploring and identifying their heritage, nor would we be able to fund you to write the history. However, if there is scope to explore, in partnership with others, a wider education and learning programme with learning-based heritage activities around the history of Black and Asian presence, the London Team would be delighted to continue to have talks with you. Please do get in touch with them.
Yours sincerely,
Liz Forgan.' (Author's Emphasis)

To this insistence on denying the funding of a television history of Blacks and Asians in Britain (along the **inclusive** lines of *Reimaging Britain* and the popular BBC programme *Who Do You Think You Are?*) I replied to Ms Forgan on 4 August 2004:

'Thank you so much for your letter dated 23 July.
I enjoyed the conference enormously. It was unusually stimulating and I left with many ideas, one of which was reinforced by your strong support for a history of the Black and Asian Presence in Britain. Given the constraints of your criteria, I do appreciate the difficulties that an educational Video "by itself" would meet, but surely we both can't be wrong about the need for a LONG view of this integral but neglected strand of British history.
I am very encouraged by your letter and will be getting in touch with the London Team to advance my Proposal for a Heritage-oriented history.
With All Good Wishes.'

Unlike Simon Schama and Niall Ferguson, I was willing to see how best these strands of British history could be made, aired and, in practice, taught. All these road-blocks (warnings) when it came to the national purse and funding a television history of the kind that I proposed was proving to be a distraction. If I could not get funding from the HLF to do it as an *integral part* of the history of Britain, I would have to look elsewhere.

Amidst all that was going on, there was a growing demand for me as a speaker. On Sunday 15 August 2004, for example, I was invited to speak at a new event billed as the 'LONDON MELA.' This turned out to be a huge Cultural Festival which was held in Gunnersbury Park, London from 12.00 pm-8.45 p.m. During my particular slot between 15.35 p. m - 16.50 p.m, a film was shown after which I gave my Talk on celebrating the very rare and much-neglected subject of 'The Indian Influence on Trinidad Carnival.'

In essence, my presentation, based on research that included the most recent articles and literature, was as follows:

'Much has been said and written about the Trinidad Carnival and the steelband or pan. But a little known aspect of the story is the Indo-Trinidadians' cultural contribution to the development of the steelband and Carnival in Trinidad, namely, their Tassa drums and the Hosay or Muharram Procession.

Since 1845, the Indians' repertoire of songs and music which they had brought with them from India, gradually impacted on the development of a Creole culture in general and, on Carnival in particular. The Hosay or Muharram procession in St James in the later 1840s was a cultural reservoir for the convergence of peoples and cultures. Creativity and craftsmanship were expressed in the construction of floats and effigies and in parades, songs, dances, tassa drumming and stick-playing. The musical instrument which linked all these was the Tassa. The Tassa drums are basically used in Indian culture as a means of communication to, and in the praise of, God. The drums are semi-oval in shape, consisting of a metal or plastic cylinder with a goat's skin stretched tightly over one end. The early (oral) history of Indian musical instruments in Trinidad reveals that a type of Tassa known as the Tayreen, was much in use and increasingly attracted members of the African community in Port of Spain. These drums were prominent during the Hosay celebration in St James.

Given that the Tassa has not been fully explored as a percussion instrument and although a variety of melodies cannot be played on it, one is amazed that such a range of tonal shades and nuances could come from so flat a surface. The Kalinda is the simplest rhythm pattern, which Indians believed was brought to Trinidad by their forefathers from India. There is documented record however, to the contrary, that

Kalinda rhythms were played by Africans during West Indian slavery. This adoption of African rhythms to an Indian drum, speaks of an early social and cultural contact and exchange. In Trinidad, communal Indian-African separatism began to disappear. Music had a unifying effect and the commingling of Africans and Indians grew over time. Africans' consistent contact with Indian culture dating as far back as the 1850s, is reason to believe that Carnival in general and pan in particular drew some of its features from Hosay as more and more Africans participated in Hosay and Tassa drumming. One consequence of this, was the coming closer of the Tassa with the Steelband.

When Carnival came to St James, Indian Tassa drummers saw an opportunity of extending their music-making into a secular affair for the first time. This practice has still been retained in St James and some parts of South and Central Trinidad...St James is especially interesting for it is considered the home of the annual Port of Spain Hosay and had close relations with the steelband movements. The possibility existed that some features of the Hosay would "rub-off" on the Carnival celebrations especially when the participants and venues were more or less the same!

The Belmont area which had a substantial number of Indians to accommodate a Hindi class in the late 1930s was also a nucleus for the meeting of Indian and African cultures. But how much of an influence was the Tassa? According to Errol Hill, the drum was as prominent in Indian music as in African, and the arrival of the Indians helped to reinforce and enrich the already strong rhythmic foundation of native music.

During the annual Hosay parade, Africans not only observed, but also participated in playing the Tassa. And, it has been argued, the seed of the steelband then, was nurtured by the search for a new cultural form related to, but not the same as, the Tassa! Significantly, the Tassa was played with two sticks and hung from a strap around the neck for convenience, and the technique of tuning a Pan with the application of heat had its origin with the Tassa and did not come about by "accident" as some historians try to explain.

Anthropologist Dr J.D. Elder concurs with another writer Mr. Simmonds on the point that pan, like Carnival and calypso "is a result of cultural mixture of European, Asiatic and African strains"...

The burning of sugar canes before reaping was celebrated during slavery by the beating of drums during the Cannes Brulee or Canboulay procession. Thereafter, with Emancipation of the slaves in 1838, the banning of African drums was rigidly enforced; and after the introduction of Tassa bands by Indian labourers in 1845, the common meeting ground for the two cultures was Hosay and Carnival where Kalinda "hand" of the Tassa as well as the Tassa and, Tamboo-Bamboo orchestras provided music for the gatka and Creole stick-fighting.

The Tassa, secured by a chord around the neck made of metal cylinder and played with two sticks, was structurally closer to the pan. This manner of playing reflected the tempo of the times which demanded that melody be played on a durable and mobile instrument.

Great controversy rages on the origins of the steelband. And to attribute the beginning of the steelband movement to a single individual or band or place would obscure its true significance. It was a National community effort which bore fruit after years of evolution. No amount of collection and collation of documented and oral information could give an accurate account of the history of Pan until researchers pay cognizance to the Tassa-Drumming which was played annually during Carnival and Hosay to the delight of Afro-Trinidadians since the 1850s.'

I concluded:

'In considering the Trinidad Carnival and Steelband music, we should remember that Indian culture in Trinidad had never been seriously considered outside its own sphere of involvement.

Despite the attempts of some purists "to dismiss the fact that Tassa was influential in the making of the Pan, the artefactual elements of the Tassa, it was argued, is still visible in the steelband's two sticks; metal cylinder, heat to provide tonal quality; posture of the musicians; and of late, the thong around the neck. The steelband is related but does not belong to the family of African or Indian drums." It is, a product of Trinidad of which both Afro-and Indo-Trinidadians should be proud.

The connection of the Trinidad Carnival and steelband music with India is therefore clear and, it is in this context that we should view Ms. Ali Pretty's timely and beautifully made film Din Shuru. Importantly we should bear in mind that it was the mutual influences of Africans and Indians and their descendants who were instrumental in creating the steelband and Carnival in Trinidad.'

Predictably, a lively discussion followed my Talk. As I left the scene, I was glad to have contributed to this huge, unprecedented London gathering, especially pleased to put forward the little known but vitally important connection between the Indian influence on Pan music and Carnival in Trinidad.

On 17 August, a fortnight after the 'Mela' (attended by the Director of the British Library's Asia, Pacific and Africa Collections - formerly OIOC), I was contacted by a Senior Manager, Ms H who, knowing well of my "position" on the Mayor's Commission informed me that the Library was planning to hold an 'Event.' She suggested that we meet; and during the brain-picking exercise that ensued, to the various questions put to me, I responded positively. For one thing, it felt like music to my ears to hear that 'The BL is considering holding a Conference...' I exulted. Why? Because after two decades of working, in a variety of ways, towards greater INCLUSIVENESS in various institutions particularly in the libraries, museums and galleries sector, the fact that the British Library was considering holding a one-day Conference on Minorities was not just a glimmer of hope: in fact, it had reached the stage of becoming a concrete Plan! Furthermore, as I soon learned, the theme of the 'Conference' was: 'Exhibiting Diversity.'

Difference, diversity and *inclusiveness* were words that I'd long held dear; indeed I'd tried consistently to effect change so that such words would become meaningful not merely as a policy, but as practice in the workplace. Now when Ms H said 'We are looking for a "high profile" person from the black community to oversee the Conference,' I put forward the name of Mike Phillips, the Caribbean (Guyana-born) journalist and writer. In the conversation that followed, either knowing (or not knowing) that I'd been living, working and writing about 'diversity' in Britain for 42 years, Ms H (as a Library 'Consultant') not merely inferred, but made it quite clear that I was a relatively new immigrant whose presence in Britain was *preceded* by other groups. It seemed that in her view, immigrants from East Europe or the former Soviet Union and Afro-Caribbeans were much longer settled here and therefore more integral to Britain (more British) than an 'Indian'-looking person like me from Trinidad. This was the first time that I'd experienced the undisguised privileging of one minority over another in a major British institution. In terms of 'race' and racial superiority, this prioritising and privileging of one group over another is indeed what was used to initiate, consolidate and perpetuate the all too familiar horrors of slavery. And so, after my suggestion of the 'high profile' black candidate that Ms H sought was passed on to the British Library Strategy Team, I received the following letter from Jill Finney, Director of Strategic Marketing and Communications:

'Dear Mr Ramdin,

EXHIBITING DIVERSITY

Exhibiting Diversity was instigated by a meeting I attended with colleagues in the media and cultural sectors who share concerns that we are not attracting wide ranging audiences for, in particular, major exhibitions. I offered the facilities of the British Library for an event to address these issues.

It is clear that both goodwill and good intentions are now widespread within the museum, library and archive sector. What remains to be established, however, is a consensus within our national institutions about the mechanisms and structures which can deliver imaginative and credible exhibits for the foreseeable future.

It is with great pleasure that I am inviting you to join me at a day workshop, as a Guest of the British Library, on Monday 27th September 2004. The purpose of the workshop is to kickstart a campaign of debate and action aimed at encouraging new thinking and new models, reflecting not only the diversity of our audiences, but also the diversity of their thoughts and aspirations.

I am delighted that Mike Phillips HLF trustee, academic, writer and broadcaster - co-author of Windrush - has agreed to facilitate the day. Dr Alistair Niven, Principal of Cumberland Lodge has accepted the Chair for the day. Exhibiting models of good practice will be presented as will topics against which to test them. By the end of the day we hope to see some routes forward to embedding within our exhibits the interests of the full spectrum of our ethnically diverse potential audiences.

The places are limited and so I would appreciate your response by 3rd September. I am asking you to commit your time for the day (9.45am-5.15pm) and to take part later in the follow-up which will be outlined during the day. I look forward to meeting you on 27th September at the Institute of Physics in Portland Place, London W1B 1NT.

Yours sincerely...'

This positive outcome (and the fact that she had accepted my recommendation of Mike Phillips) was directly due to a chain of events which started with and had gained momentum after I'd informed Graham Shaw and the Strategy Team of my appointment to the Mayor's Commission. Of this, I was truly proud! And so, I replied to the Invitation letter from Ms Finney: *'It is with great pleasure that I accept your Invitation to attend the "EXHIBITING DIVERSITY" workshop as a Guest of the British Library on Monday 27th September 2004. I do look forward to meeting you!'*

ENCOUNTERS: SPEAKING AT THE
VICTORIA AND ALBERT MUSEUM

Having submitted the finished manuscript of my new book: *Martin Luther King Jr: Life and Times* to Haus Publishing, the first response and reports from publisher Barbara Schwepke and her editor Robert Pritchard were warmly appreciative. So much so, that as the book's proof copy was being prepared, I was emboldened to suggest a Book Launch at the British Library. This was a speculative suggestion, but as the publication date approached, I hoped for the best.

Soon after receiving the 'Exhibiting Diversity' letter, Irna Quereshi of the Victoria and Albert Museum, invited me to give a 'Talk' as part of the much-anticipated 'ENCOUNTERS Exhibition' at the Museum. I agreed and soon after, Ms Qureshi enclosed a handful of leaflets and a poster advertising the 'education' programme. From the advance publicity, the importance of the event was clear; and to promote and complement the Exhibition, an exciting line-up of Events was scheduled, including my presentation on the 'History of Asians in Britain' on Sunday 24 October 2004 in Seminar Room

3 from 12.00 – 12.45 p.m. This was another opportunity for me to provide the context to the presence of Asians in Britain, which I gladly did.

I opened by saying:

'In 1498 the Portuguese explorer Vasco Da Gama had landed in India. Why did he go to Asia? Because there was a demand in Europe for spices and luxury products. In time, this encounter would lead to burgeoning trade between Europe and Asia. The relationship between India and Britain was especially dynamic. By 1600, with the establishment of the East India Company, trading began to have an impact on social relations between Indians and Europeans...'

My closing words were:

'If diversity and divergence between the various ethnic minority groups have become clearer in the 1990s, there is no doubt that today, Asians in Britain are responding to the challenges facing them, with creativity and imagination, as their forebears had done, ever since the 15th century encounter.'

Speaking for the first time at the Victoria and Albert Museum was indeed a pleasure and an honour. My 'Talk,' according to the Organiser, was a success which made the occasion and, of course, my subsequent tour through the impressive ENCOUNTERS Exhibition all the more memorable.

Against this background, I received the page-proofs of my biography *Martin Luther King Jr.* and wasted no time making final corrections before returning to the publisher what for me became a precious manuscript. Before the book was published, I also wrote to Haus requesting their support for a Book Launch in Trinidad, where the American Civil Rights leader, Preacher and activist was no less a hero than he was in other parts of the world. Given that my book on Paul Robeson had been well received in Trinidad, generally the prospects for the King book looked promising. So impressed was Haus Publishing by my King biography that they offered me another Contract to write *Mary Seacole: Life and Times.*

Thus the systematic alternation between the day-job and writing, now finely-tuned, persisted, but I was never too busy to be of help to others.

When Dr N. Kumar Mahabir, a Trinidadian academic, contacted me to request a Review Blurb for the 'Dictionary' he was about to publish, I obliged. '*The languages which Indians brought to Trinidad,*' I wrote, '*were vital links that strengthened their sense of camaraderie, continuity and identity as the experience of indentureship devalued and threatened their survival. Their history and culture affirms this. The appearance now (2004) of this first lexicography is, at once, an historical and contemporary reference, an invaluable dictionary which informs a new generation of Indo-Trinidadians (and Trinidadians generally) of their essential linguistic heritage.*'

After this 'good turn' given my rapidly diminishing time as an employee, looking back I felt there was little more that I could have done to effect change in the British Library. Now, as a Mayor's Commissioner (and having sat on a number of 'high powered' Committees at local, regional and national levels over the years), given the paucity of non-white faces, I felt the time was right for those in our communities with the requisite experience and knowledge to be recognised. Indeed, I felt it would be appropriate for the British Library to appoint a non-white Board member. The person I had in mind was Professor Stuart Hall. On 22 September 2004, I wrote to him:

'*Dear Professor Hall,*

I am an historian, biographer and novelist and a member of the recently constituted Mayor's Commission on African and Asian Heritage (MCAAH). The objective is to mainstream diversity, to ensure that museums, archives and libraries reflect the diverse communities they serve. At the moment, we, the Commissioners are fine-tuning MCAAH's Report and Recommendations which is expected to be launched in the New Year.

As one of the longest-serving members of staff, for some time now, I had been thinking of you as a possible Member of the British Library Board. I think your presence here will make a difference. I have spoken to a few key individuals, but would now like to know if joining

the British Library Board is an appointment that would interest you'.
I do look forward to hearing from you.'

Eight days later, Professor Hall replied:

*'My apologies for not replying to your letter but it has taken some time
to reach me from the Open University from which I retired some time
ago. I'm delighted to hear of the initiative launched by MCAAH and
look forward to seeing a copy of your final report. This is, as you know,
a subject close to my own heart. It is kind of you to think of proposing
me as a member of the British Library Board but I'm afraid it is not
possible for me to take on new commitments of this kind.'*

That he was unwell and unavailable was unfortunate. Nonetheless
I took the opportunity of congratulating and thanking Professor
Hall for his academic-intellectual contributions over the years.

By now, an important day in my long relationship with the
British Library had dawned: It was the morning of Monday
27th September 2004 and I travelled by tube to attend the
EXHIBITING DIVERSITY CONFERENCE at the Institute of
Physics at 76 Portland Place, London. On my way there, I recalled
another national institution – the BBC that had also recognised
diversity and held a One-Day Conference for which they had
chosen me to deliver the Opening Address. The difference now
was two-fold: I was not the person opening the British Library's
Conference and there was no chauffeur-driven car to bring me
to this Event. The irony was that after all the decades that I'd
spent studying, researching, writing, lecturing and broadcasting,
in short championing the cause and hoping for the recognition of
diversity, now that the British Library had organised a 'Diversity
Conference,' alas, I was but a minor player!

Nonetheless, that morning of the Conference, on arrival, I was
greeted in the foyer of the Institute by Dr Alistair Niven, with whom
seventeen years before I'd shared the *Roots in Britain* platform at
the Birmingham Festival of Readers and Writers. At that time,
the theme and our presentations were relatively new, pioneering.
Now on being reacquainted with Dr Niven (and, given that I'd
been writing 'Black history' many years before Peter Fryer) I was
reminded of his Interview with novelist Bernadine Evaristo, during

which he had pointedly asked: *'And do you think people like Peter Fryer and Ron Ramdin, historians of the black experience in Britain, are themselves unacknowledged and should be better known?'*

Ms Evaristo's reply was equally forthright: *'I think so, yes... I think that it is important that these books (Staying Power and The Making of the Black working Class in Britain) are brought to light and that we re-examine British history from this perspective.'*

Bearing Ms Evaristo's words in mind, I was also reminded of an interesting conversation that I'd overheard on a bus one day: A reader of popular books as advertised in the print and image-saturated media when asked about the writings of the celebrated writer Samuel Coleridge unashamedly admitted to knowing nothing about him, but was quick to add: 'If he was any good, I would have heard of him!'

Interestingly, the Exhibiting Diversity 'Handout' proclaimed: *'Cultural Diversity has become one of the current buzz-words in the Museum and Archive sector. On the other hand, although almost everyone would subscribe to the concept, everyone is also likely to have a different view about what it is and its place in their everyday practice. In principle, this could allow everyone ownership of the label which might be a fairly healthy situation. In practice, the sector's view of cultural diversity continues to be deeply influenced by the legacy of our imperial past. Historically, our national institutions were showcases at the hub of the Empire, illustrating the variety and diversity of its populations and at the same time demonstrating the implicit power and control of British administration.'*

In effect, this was saying nothing more than I'd been writing and speaking about for almost two decades. But what followed in the 'Handout' was relatively new:

'In recent years, however, the role of the (diversity) sector and the needs of its audiences have undergone fundamental changes. Over the last 50 years in Britain there has been a step change in the legal and constitutional status of British citizenship and British audiences are no longer the product of an established consensus about their heritage and identity...

While cultural Diversity may well be part of some institutions' self-

image as sites of international excellence, their routine processes do not offer many challenges to traditional views of national collections, or create an incentive to embrace inclusive practice.

Some of what we need to do in creating new models therefore is to encourage institutions to consider with fresh eyes the opportunities and the obstacles which are already implicit in holdings and acquisitions instead of simply seeing diversity as a programme of importing prefabricated "ethnic" models. Exhibiting Diversity is an opportunity to pursue a new approach, joining a campaign of debate and action aimed at encouraging new thinking about how to reflect not only on diversity of our audiences, but also the diversity of their thoughts and aspirations...'

Put simply, at the outset, the Conference's message was 'how to construct ways of meeting the challenge of cultural diversity.'

That word 'Diversity' was clearly a step in the right direction. A Challenge? Yes, an enormous, but necessary challenge as it had long been. But after 35 years of championing *'Diversity'* (representations that had subjected me to so much scrutiny and negative perceptions from management) thankfully it was no longer a word whispered to me confidentially either by a Director or manager in an office or corridor in the British Library, but now openly proclaimed at a Conference of professionals.

In his opening remarks, Convenor Mike Phillips said that he and I 'go back a long way!' True. (Indeed some years before at a literary party, he admitted to me that he'd 'cannibalised' my book *The Making of the Black Working Class in Britain*), an interesting compliment, I thought. And, on the theme, "Hidden Histories," various 'Presenters' spoke about colonialism and slavery, but there was no reference to India in relation to 'Black' (meaning non-white) migration and Settlement in Britain in spite of a voluminous body of literature on these topics; nor was there any mention of educational resources like the rare and comprehensive texts: *The Making of the Black Working Class in Britain* and *Reimaging Britain* in which, like never before, such themes were extensively explored. Neither book was mentioned in the Conference's literature, as if such texts were entirely irrelevant to today's challenges. But worse still, was the fact that the Conference's Presenters were, it seemed, largely unaware of the existence of these books which revealed a great deal more about Britain's 'hidden' histories than other texts.

Furthermore the 'Handout' informed Conference delegates that the *Moving Here* - PRO/National Archive Project (for which I'd written the original Caribbean-Asian 'Briefs' and of which, it seemed, the British Library Conference Organisers had no knowledge!) was now proclaimed as the biggest *'data base of the digitised photographs, maps, objects, documents and audio items from 30 local and national archives, museums and libraries which record migration experiences of the last 200 years.'*

In essence, the *Moving Here* catalogue items were used to explain the migration experience of the Caribbean, Irish, Jewish and South Asian communities. Ironically, my writing the 'Briefs' was only possible after decades of research covering a long period of British-Colonial history, migration, settlement and culture in Britain, as contained in *The Making of the Black Working Class in Britain* and *Reimaging Britain.*

So, the 'hidden histories' that had preoccupied me for so long (when few of us cared much about its research, never mind writing books aimed at raising awareness!) was now presented to the British Library Conference as new material, new discoveries! In reality, prior to this Conference (well before 'Black History Month' became a regular feature in Britain and every year since 1972) as mentioned I'd been travelling across the country giving Talks, Lectures, radio Interviews and discussing issues of race, immigration and settlement, as gradually the expressions 'diversity and inclusiveness' became increasingly more familiar.

Now on this day of 'Exhibiting Diversity,' having listened to various speakers (the 'professionals') I seriously wondered how many of them knew or really cared enough about the histories that were 'hidden' and therefore no longer taught to children.

By the end of that 'Exhibiting Diversity' day, I had no doubt that what had transpired was, to some extent, an exhibition of ignorance of 'British history' frequently alluded to, but little understood. Nonetheless, that day was, given my three and a half decades of harbouring hope, an admirable, timely and positive move by the British Library. Encouraged, I took every opportunity to add new insights to some of the things that had been discussed and by so doing I continued to contribute as fully as possible as a

Commissioner on the Mayor's Heritage Commission.

EDUCATION: THE 'COMMISSION'S FINDINGS; *RAMA'S VOYAGE* AND *MARTIN LUTHER KING JR*

So far during our sittings, one thing had become quite clear to me: never take anything on the Mayor's Commission for granted. Thus I debated and sought clarification on various aspects of every issue. My keen sense of history was especially important; and all the more so because the key objective of the Commission was to publish its findings on Museums, Archive and Libraries in a Report. From its earliest days, I must say, there were a few people who did not think such a 'Report' would, given the time limit, be completed.

But as time passed, we persevered with MCAAH's work. And in spite of the daunting task of fifteen individuals often necessarily disagreeing while debating and discussing a range of issues with the goal of producing a Report and Recommendations, I sensed an air of excitement among most Commissioners. Knowing well the Commission's historical significance, my innate high level of enthusiasm found expression in both verbal and written contributions. As we progressed towards the Final Draft of the Report, Ms Coaston, as Senior Strategy Officer on the Commission requested that I write the Report's 'Historical Section.' I responded positively for once more, I was called upon to write a major document. In effect, Ms Coaston's request was that I should provide a crucial first draft manuscript that would underpin the Report.

To circulating drafts of other sections of the Report, I duly commented: On 'EDUCATION FOR LIFE,' for example, I responded: It 'is well written, a clear exposition, which raises all the key issues and makes excellent use of the 'evidence.'

I also felt bound to offer two small additions:

'The first is the inclusion of "indentureship" after "slavery" in Section 7 on page 14.

The same word again should follow "slavery" in Section 5 on page 16.

The second addition refers also to page 16. My understanding is that the children were placed in ESN Schools, ESN referring to Educationally Subnormal.'

I commented further:

'Given that this crucial chapter exposes the paucity of historical resources - what is missing and what are needed as correctives, what comes through powerfully is the urgent need for, as the Chapter states, a "holistic," "integrative", non-Eurocentric' text and context, a history that is inclusive; a history about roots and routes that provides not only a general framework, but also illustrative detail; that takes a long view; that is an alternative...to traditional "British" histories. In other words, a history that covers a 500 year period and necessarily encompasses colonisation, slavery, indentureship and migrations (from the Empire and the "Empire Within"), difference, identities and cultures.

Certainly as a starting point, most, if not all of the main concerns, the perceived gaps in the History/Education Chapter are contained in an INCLUSIVE history of Britain entitled **Reimaging Britain: 500 Years of Black and Asian History**.'

I also wrote to the particular Commissioner charged with writing the 'Education' Section. Why? Because to my great surprise (yet another example of those 'professionals' who write and determine educational policy) she knew nothing about the above-named and well-known book. I stated:

' This is the only history book of its kind! I have seen no reference to this text (though websites and the Runnymede Trust Guide are mentioned) which may well be an understandable oversight: nonetheless, it raises the question: has this book (with its wealth of reference material and comprehensive Bibliography) been read by Commissioners?

Having thought a great deal about this over the weekend, I feel bound to raise the matter because WE, on the Commission, should guard against the charge we make of "deracination" and the fact that British publishers are not publishing our "hidden" histories, when we ourselves may omit fundamental resources that **do** *exist.*

Yours, Ron.'

In spite of so much talk about Empire, history and diversity, I still had to argue vociferously for consideration and inclusion of the books that I deemed to be key and timely educational texts; vital resources for British schools and universities.

It was the end of September and by my reckoning, as a member of British Library staff, there were approximately five and a half months left before my early retirement was due. The thought of this, at times, made me apprehensive for once more I would be placed in a situation of being unemployed which I did not have to deal with for thirty- three years. For now, thankfully, my relentless work-writing schedule had kept any insecure feelings of unemployment at bay.

On 1 October when the distinguished photographer Stefan Cagnoni arrived in the British Library's Front Hall at St. Pancras, his assignment was to do a 'Photo Shoot.' His subject was me; and I smiled at the thought of the Harry Diamond Shoot in Bloomsbury some thirty years before. Mr Cagnoni's Shoot was at the request of the Public and Commercial Services Union that had merged with the CSU to form the largest Civil Service Union in Britain, of which I was still a member. Why was Mr Cagnoni directed to find me? Because I was the author of the recently published biography *Martin Luther King Jr.* It was primarily this new book, and not just the fact that I was preparing to leave the beloved British Library after a long library-orientated career which included the University of London's Senate House Library and the British Museum Library.

Lying on the tiled floor, Cagnoni took several shots of me sitting on the bronze Open Book sculpture (an iconic fixture) in the British Library's Front Hall, holding a copy of my book: *Martin Luther King Jr.* He then suggested that we proceed to other parts of the building where he photographed me facing this way, then that, until two rolls of film were used. One or more of these photographs, I was told, would accompany a 'PROFILE' of me to be published by the national *PCS Magazine*.

Soon after the 'Shoot,' the Editor of the Magazine rang me to ascertain details about the 'piece' she was writing. So until the *Magazine* was published, my expectation of seeing it and Mr Cagnoni's selected photograph, was put on hold. After being the subject of this big Shoot in the new British Library building, apart from Harry Diamond's work, I also recalled Zac Macaulay's Special Shoot of me at the British Museum.

Between my histories and biographies, my interest in writing fiction (my first love) had intensified and I was very pleased to have completed *Rama's Voyage*. I had yet to interest a publisher, but I was hopeful and reasonably pleased when I'd submitted the first two chapters of the manuscript to the *London Magazine*.

After our initial contact and, as cited above, a regular flow of correspondence with editor Sebastian Barker, an excerpt of *Rama's Voyage* eventually appeared, significantly as the 'Lead Story' in the October/November issue of the *London Magazine*. In terms of my debut novel, such a 'lead' publication was a huge vote of confidence, as was the excerpt published in *Wasafiri*. After its long gestation, maybe now, a reputable publisher would see the merits of this little known, but powerful story, I thought. Having set the novel in British India, taking a synoptic view, I noted: 'Alone in the great city, Rama is befriended by two street-children and he joins their group. He learns hard lessons and in desperation embarks on a "Coolie ship" bound for the sugar plantations of the Caribbean.'

After the book's 'DEDICATION: To the homeless children of Calcutta and the world who seek and hope for a better life,' the opening paragraph reads:

'*While many people consciously seek the truth, there are those to whom it is, in an extraordinary way, revealed. When Rama arrived at Mukherjee's bazaar, the still Calcutta morning air and stifling heat added not only to his physical discomfort, but also to the general uneasiness he felt about his life. But necessity being the mother of invention, he understood well why his immediate thoughts were, for the most part, on the job. He was not a ditherer. So, his feelings about himself and what he had been doing merely to survive were no different that morning than any other. And judging from its unpromising beginnings, he took for granted that it would be another frustrating and, for sure, exhausting day; nothing more, nothing less. He was wrong.*'

After the unrelenting horrors of almost three months at sea, spending his first night on land in the barrack room, the novel ends thus:

'*All is still. And the deepening silence, greater than he had ever experienced, amplified his heartbeat. Images of India danced across his vision at random like the mosquitoes that were now zeroing about his head. He thought of some of the extraordinary events that had overtaken him; of the day when he had left the orphanage and boarded the train for Calcutta and that fateful morning at Mukherjee's Bazaar when the sweet-talking recruiter excited his boyhood imagination with rosy pictures of greener pastures. And then his thoughts shifted to that moment of arrival after he had left the ship and was grounded again, when he saw the rainbow, but had little time to fully consider it. But soon after, as he now recalled, he pondered the rainbow's promise.*

Kapoor's snore was audible again; a gentle laboured sound. Then, once more, there was utter silence. In the unnerving, quiet moments that followed, as if he was still on the ship, Rama could feel the rocking sensation of being carried forward, even though he was lying motionless on the unyielding wooden planks of the slave barrack-room floor, enfolded in darkness but thinking of the Trinidad dawn.'

In this first imaginative epic of its kind, the narrative navigates the choppy, treacherous waters of British-Indian relations endemic in Rama's extraordinary journey, during which he meets a host of characters, significantly the English woman Caitlin Fairweather.

Rama's Voyage deals with themes rarely explored in fiction. It is a story assailed by tragedy, by man's inhumanity to man, but it is also evocative of incredible courage and endurance, love and romance, revelation and self-discovery.

Pondering these words, I was imbued with renewed hopes that others would soon be able to read the novel in book-form.

A short while later, Cagnoni's photograph of me sitting on the British Library's bronze book sculpture in the entrance hall appeared in the *PCS Magazine*. Under the heading 'ACCLAIMED AUTHOR SHOWS OFF LATEST BESTSELLER' the article was an eye-opener for many members of staff in the British Library who thought they 'knew' me. It stated:

'*Renowned historian and PCS member Ron Ramdin celebrated the 75th anniversary of the birth of Martin Luther King, Jnr in October with the publication of a new biography of the American black rights campaigner.*

With a long-term interest in black and Asian history and eleven books under his belt, Ron is no stranger to seeing his work on bookshop shelves. Nevertheless, "it is still an exciting feeling to know that people are reading the words I have worked so hard on. Everyone is interested in King," explains Ron, "so this book was a huge challenge."

Born in Trinidad, Ron has worked for the British Library for over 30 years. As well as a demanding day job overseeing the microfilming of the India Office Records and Archive, Ron is keen to maintain his long-term interest in unions – "I was the first elected Secretary of the Whitley Council when the British Library was formed " – as well as in African and Asian culture (as a recent appointee to London Mayor Ken Livingstone's pioneering Commission on African and Asian Heritage) and, of course, writing.

Over the years Ron has received recognition for his work from both fellow historians and writers in his country of origin and in Britain. And in 1997, he received the Doctor of Literature (D. Lit) from the University of London. So what would Ron's message be to other aspiring writers? "If I can do it so can you," he says simply.'

The article concluded:

'Two lucky members could win a signed copy of "Martin Luther King Jnr" by Ron Ramdin. To be in with a chance please send a postcard marked "Martin Luther King" to PCS, Campaigns and Communications Department, 160 Falcon Road, London SW11 2LN.'

While reading this piece, I was struck by it as the stuff of dreams! In fact, when I was engaged in the thick of things as Organiser and staff leader in of all places the British Museum, I was not sure how long I would last in such an overwhelming and demanding role. Perhaps a year, at most. But, for better or worse, having *voluntarily embraced* the challenge of my manifold and onerous tasks in relation to aspects of the social, industrial and cultural life of the 1970s, I learned about 'Man-management' and more broadly and deeply about human nature: Tell a man or woman that he or she is about to lose their job and, in my experience, the reaction was always interesting, to say the least.

Regardless of the negativity of a few managers and the pressure of life and living generally, I maintained my passion for books, and an abiding interest in the art of literature, conscious of genres and styles. I wrote countless letters, notes, official minutes and reports, which not only served their purpose, but were also an apprenticeship of sorts that taught me a good deal about writing. Unlike my first attempts at fiction, learning to write clearly and thus effectively was at the heart of my success as a communicator and Organiser. As time passed, this disciplined approach was intertwined with my authorship of books which, at this juncture, encompassed four genres: history, biography, short stories and novels.

So now with publication of the *PCS Magazine's* headline 'Acclaimed Author Shows Off Latest Bestseller,' I was unreservedly, proudly presented to the Union's huge national readership of hundreds of thousands, not just as one of its members, but as something of a role-model for other working men and women. The PCS's pride in promoting my work as a *writer* who should be read was indeed recompense for an attitude that I'd adopted and applied, especially since I'd started work in Britain at the *very bottom* of the employment hierarchy: *What you put in, is what you get out*!

On 5 October 2004, I was reminded of my job's wider interest (indeed my overall range of activity) when I received a letter from Ramona Mitrica, Director of the Romanian Cultural Centre in London. Knowing of my involvement in the British Library, her letter to me was most gratifying.

'*Dear Ron Ramdin,*
It was a truly interesting experience to take part in a programme such as "Exhibiting Diversity" organised by the BL and to meet so many exciting people. The matters presented are of real importance for today's Britain and, as Director of the Romanian Cultural Centre in London, I can only hope that in the not so distant future we will be able to talk about the Romanian contribution to cultural diversity in Britain and, of course, in Europe.'

The ripple effect of the pebble that I'd thrown into the pond of national-international diversity was spreading. This Romanian Cultural connection coming so soon after the British Library's Conference was a significant reference point in relation to diversity in Britain and Europe. At once, though thirteen years on, I was reminded of having **introduced** students at the University of Seville to such 'diversity' during the lecture that I'd given in Seville on Ethnic Minorities in Britain and Europe. In fact, thus far, I had spoken and written repeatedly, year on year, about culture and difference in Britain and Europe and hoped to do so again elsewhere in Spain. Ms Mitrica's letter continued:

'I would like to know more about your programmes and projects, so please include me in your emailing/mailing data base. I am sending you some information about one of our major events starting this Friday: The Romanian Film Festival...The Romanian Cultural Centre and the volunteers connected with us invite you to come and share Lucian Pintile's vision. It may be your first opportunity to see in cinematic form, expressions of European culture from which other well-known artists like our great sculptor Brancusi have emerged.

The RCC has been the focus of the organisation of this event with the collaboration of the National Centre of Cinematography in Bucharest,... We would be very happy to have you join us at any or all of the film presentations. I look forward to hearing from you.
Ramona Mitrica.'

Ms Mitrica's interest and kind invitation added to the enriching mix of cultural diversity in Britain. I appreciated her work, in particular, her attitude of reaching out; a good example of my crystallizing core idea of 'respect for difference' and its inclusion and relevance to an expanding vision that is evident in my literary works.

The Autumn of 2004 was a time of feverish and quite extraordinary activity for me. The fruits of my labours were visible in the form of my latest publication; a book which caught the attention of the British Library's Events selectors. When their *WHAT'S ON, WHAT'S WHERE* booklet, a programme of Events for October/December 2004 was published, multiple copies were displayed in the Front Hall. Inside this Guide were forthcoming 'Literary' Events to which the public was invited to meet the selected authors. On 26 October I was scheduled to appear as part of 'Meet the Author' series in the British Library's Bookshop where I was expected to give a Talk about my new book: *Martin Luther King Jr - A Life*. For this occasion, at the entrance to the Bookshop, were two large Poster versions of the impressive front cover of the book jacket: a striking profile image of Dr King.

Barbara Schwepke, my publisher at Haus introduced me to the packed Bookshop audience. This was an exciting, but also a strange time: for here I was presented as a distinguished author at a major British Library event, yet six years before, I was banned from entering the Reading Room as a Reader! But conscious of this Book Launch in the British Library, as I'd been with all my public appearances, I was careful that my 'Talk' should be as good as I could make it. To reiterate my earlier concern when I'd begun to write the book, what more could I say about Martin Luther King Jr that would hold the already well-informed audience's attention? All things considered (including my hope, as well as the publisher's that copies of the book would be bought) I began my presentation 'King, The Talk' with the following excerpt from my book:

' *"We are here this evening for serious business. We are here, in a general sense because first and foremost we are American citizens and we are determined to apply our citizenship to the fullness of its meaning."*

These were the words of the 26 year old Martin Luther King Jr on the night of 5 December 1955 as he addressed a mass audience in his church. This speech marked the beginning of King's public campaign for Civil Rights in America.

With no leadership experience to speak of the young Preacher talked about his people's disinheritance and their tiredness of having endured the "long night of captivity." Now their quest was for freedom, justice and equality. This was Montgomery's "Moment of truth" and King had become the Leader of the protest Movement that would eventually elevate him to the pre-eminent position of becoming one of the "makers of the 20th century."

Eight years later, in a speech before an even bigger audience, he spoke about his American Dream that had arisen from the grim reality of a deeply divided country. He was confronting an "aggressive system." '

After reviewing his early life through his Theological Studies, various campaigns and so on, I ended as follows:

'He was a complex man in whom the elements were mixed. By the time he had reached Memphis on 3 April 1968, he seemed to have come to terms with himself. Having lived with the spectre of death each day for so long, he was filled with a strong sense of his mortality and had no qualms about going public with his feelings. "Every now and then," he said in one of his last sermons, he thought about what he would like someone to say at his funeral: that he had "tried to give his life serving others;" that he believed in love, justice, peace and yes that he was also against war and violence. By helping others, he hoped his "living would not be in vain."

So, after years of foreboding, at times, of desperate personal anguish, he was now foretelling his death. Much as he would have liked to live a long life "it really doesn't matter now" he said, "because I've been to the mountaintop." It was a privilege to have seen the promised land but, he warned, "I may not get there with you." After preaching these prophetic words to a large gathering of the faithful on the night of 3 April 1968, he retired to his Motel room exhausted.

The next day, he seemed more at ease, but it was not one of his bright days. On his journey thus far, he had met the movers and shakers of his time but, few, if any, had truly impressed him. He was just 39 years old, but looked older. Now, as evening approached, he was dressed and ready to leave the Motel for dinner…He was anticipating the "Soul food." Those who were with him on the balcony left his side and for a brief moment he was alone. Then a loud sound was heard and moments later he lay mortally wounded by an assassin's bullet. Ralph Abernathy was first at the scene and called out to his friend: "Martin, can you hear me?" There was no reply from King.

In death, King was released from the redemptive suffering endemic in the non-violent pursuit of his "Dream." But although the bombs continued to rain down on Vietnam, he could hardly have imagined that his "living had not been in vain." For as he had said of Mahatma Gandhi, now he too belonged to the Ages. He was not a Saint, but *a man. His genius, in part, lay in his ability to translate complex arguments of his time into simple language: "Make it plain son, make it plain," his proud father urged him on early in his pastoral career. He honoured this dictum and, as the maturing Preacher King became the King of Preachers, less concerned with the hereafter than he was with life on earth, he created his own rich mosaic of expressions that were (and are) eminently quotable. "We must accept finite disappointment" he said, "but we must never lose infinite hope." It is this abiding belief in the transforming power of his vision that moved King to speak on ethical and moral issues in a voice that at once touched the hearts and minds of people everywhere. Then, as now, the resonance inspires other dreams.'*

After taking a few questions, I was guided to a table on which was a pile of books, hopefully to be bought and signed. In the extended queue that had quickly built up was David Blake, a Senior member of staff in the India Office Manuscripts and Records Department. Interestingly, with the exception of Mr Blake, no other British Library Curator attended. I'd heard about 'Gradism' in this institution, but how much of this attitude could be attributed to the 'Gradism' of certain Curators and hence their absence from the Launch that evening I could not ascertain. What was clear, however, was the fact that this Event had placed me as an 'internationally recognised author' by British Library Bookshop selectors. This realisation reminded me of something that I'd said some thirty four years before when I'd first started work as a Library Assistant in the British Museum's Round Reading Room: 'One's intellect and innate ability should not be judged by the job he or she happens to be doing, **at any given time**.' Thus, the absence of those Curators whom I had invited to the Book Launch was, in large part, attributable to this Gradist sense of an uncrossable line defined by the status quo.

In every other way, for myself, my publisher and the Bookshop, this *Meet the Author* Event was a success! I am pleased to say that many people outside the curatorial grades on the British Library Staff did attend as well as a cross-section of members of the wider reading-literary community. On the whole *Martin Luther King*

Jr: Life and Times was creditable: many copies were bought and Barbara Schwepke, director, publisher and connoisseur of books, described the biography as 'wonderful.'

In the queue awaiting my signature on his copy of the King book was a Caribbean-born young man, of African/Indian descent. He was also clutching one of my other books *Arising From Bondage: A History of the Indo-Caribbean People* which he asked me to sign. As I did so, he declared: 'it is a masterpiece.' Such heady praise for a book published four years before to a large extent, underlined my authorial power and the significance of that evening.

Overall, in terms of attendance and sales satisfaction, that 'Meet the Author' evening in the British Library Bookshop was a personal triumph, which I took in my stride; and as usual the next morning, I showed up in the office for work as if nothing very special had happened.

Within days of this Library Book Launch, I'd reached another literary milestone: the long awaited publication of my first novel *Rama's Voyage*. Academic and author, Noor Kumar Mahabir of Chakra Publishing in Trinidad described *Rama's Voyage* as a 'lotus flower of a book,' a novel which he confirmed had never been attempted before. Clearly the next step was not if, but when I would be able to visit Trinidad to promote the novel.

For now, I considered the consequence of work that I had previously done and what developments had taken place since. At last, the first publicity Brochure for the PRO's project MOVING HERE: 200 YEARS OF MIGRATION TO ENGLAND appeared. Attractively produced, it contained photographs, the *Moving Here* logo and website address. 'Moving Here,' the Brochure stated, '*provides free online access to original items from 30 museums, archives and libraries. All records on Moving Here illustrate and record the migration of Jewish, South Asian, Irish and Caribbean communities to England over the past 200 years.*'

So the original 'Project' had extended widely and, as a record of waves of migration it had set the tone as a template for the continuing influx of people to Britain. As an immigrant, the fact that I was recruited by the *Moving Here Project* at its inception, engendered a special and deeply satisfying feeling of the value and importance of this work which, in various ways reflected essential multifaceted aspects of the centuries old migratory inflow to the British Isles.

MEETING V.S. NAIPAUL; *RAMA'S VOYAGE*

Although preoccupied with matters literary, given that it was four years since he had followed my appearance on stage at the *Everyman Theatre* in Cheltenham, quite by chance, I met V.S. Naipaul. The occasion was a Diplomatic Reception held at the Trinidad and Tobago High Commission to mark the visit of the President of Trinidad and Tobago to London. On arrival, at the entrance to the Reception Hall, Deputy High Commissioner Sandra McIntyre-Trotman said to me: 'Vidia is here!'

'Is he?' I responded.

'May I introduce you to him?' she asked.

'You may,' I answered.

I followed Ms McIntyre-Trotman into the Hall. Naipaul and his wife were standing near the southernmost window facing Belgrave Square. Obliquely opposite, at the other end of the Hall, a lively sound came from a group of guests who chatted over drinks. Naipaul was holding a glass in one hand, and a canapé in the other.

'Sir Vidia,' Ms Trotman said, 'may I introduce you to another of our distinguished writers?'

The Nobel Laureate observed me closely.

'Hello!' I said with characteristic lightness. 'Good to meet you. My name is Ron Ramdin.'

After I'd spoken some more, at one point, he looked beyond my left shoulder and glanced at the walls of the spacious room. 'I've never been here before,' he said.

I did not expect to hear this. Why? Because Naipaul had lived and worked in England for most of his life.

'You surprise me,' I said.

Then the writer, famous for his forthright and sharp comments asked: 'What did you say your name is?'

'Ron Ramdin,' I said.'

Without hesitation, he said: 'I have one of your books on my shelf.'

'Which one?' was my immediate response, not intending to be either condescending or too questioning.

I told him about my Whitbread Lecture *Homelessness and the Novel* and my book *Arising From Bondage: A History of the Indo-Caribbean People*. He expressed an interest in seeing both and I promised to send him copies. 'Send them to my Agent,' he added.

'Who is?' I asked.

'Gillon Aitken,' he said.

'I will.'

'Who is your publisher?' he enquired.

'I've had several publishers,' I said. 'You see, I have written not only histories and biographies, but also a novel *Rama's Voyage* which is my latest book.' After saying this, I realised how versatile I'd become as an author and hoped that I did not come across as boastful. I felt remarkably at ease in Mr Naipaul's company.

As we spoke, more people arrived; and for a while, Naipaul's wife who had been standing nearby, almost circling us, swooped. Soon they were gone.

When I had joined the lively gathering at the far end of the crowded room, I overheard someone say: 'Vidia is here!'

'He *was* here,' I said. 'He left just a while ago.'

Strange, I thought, that he did not stay to meet and mingle among his compatriots for there were many who, though finding some of his views disagreeable, had hoped to meet him. Because I had more respect than reverence (as many do) for V.S. Naipaul, on reflection, I remember that unexpected meeting with him as a pleasant interlude; a chat that had uninterruptedly lasted a good fifteen minutes. (A few years earlier, in that very room I had also met and talked with Derek Walcott, another Caribbean-born Nobel Laureate).

Following publication of the excerpt from chapter one of *Rama's Voyage* in the November 2004 issue of *The London Magazine*, although there was a great deal going on in the days that followed, I gave precedence to the promotion of the novel in Trinidad. Before leaving London, on 23 November, *Newsday*, the Trinidad newspaper, headlined: 'Ron Ramdin to Promote Rama's Voyage. Acclaimed Trinidad-born writer Ron Ramdin arrives in Trinidad on December 8 to promote his epic book Rama's Voyage...' This was followed by a major Book Review on 5 December in the Trinidad *Sunday Guardian* by Hafiza Seesahai. Under the heading: 'RAMA'S VOYAGE, VIVIDLY WELL ORCHESTRATED' she wrote:

'The title of this book Rama's Voyage was somewhat misleading. I was expecting Rama's Voyage to start in Ayodhya and progress through all his adventures ending in the final and famous battle at Lanka. It soon became evident that this was not mythology but realism.

Rama reminds me of Voltaire's Candide through whom we experience the suffering of the underdog and the underclass. Through him we see man's inhumanity. We see the inverse when many can rise up and help each other in spite of their helplessness. Through him we see all the hope and the ambition of our forefathers in spite of their suffering. For like the sysyphus ordeal with the rock, he never gave up.

*Here is a child who has lost his parents, his past, his country and must make a future with nothing but hope, tenacity and ambition. The novel opens up like a painting where each character reveals a story in its own right yet each is used to cement a powerful story. It is like a tapestry where all the threads are woven only to finally form the finished product. For example, in the beginning, through Rama we see the man with the "box" and to the very end the same man plays the harmonium to celebrate their arrival. **The characters are so well co-ordinated that it is like an orchestra using all its players to perform a piece of great music.** We have the opposites of characters - the Captain and Caitlin – one rough and ambitious whose only interest is to keep the "Coolies" alive for pecuniary gains; a nuisance but necessary. On the other hand, there is Caitlin, a compassionate English rose, soft,understanding and sympathetic.*

Then the crew in their boredom and sexual starvation transform into sadistic thugs, who use their power over the helpless "Coolies." They dehumanise them, then had their way with them...

This book is evocative, vivid and direct. The author plays with words. We travel with him, feeling the seasickness, the high winds and waves, the hunger and thirst. We feel the beatings of the crew on the weakened

"Coolies." We sympathise with the victims of rape. We follow the author on Rama's journey and experience how the master exploited and brutalised his slaves. We pity Caitlin who is trying to give some meaning to her sad, unfulfilled life.

The author has a deep understanding of human emotions and human nature, noting every detail and conjuring up the behaviour of all his characters, bringing "life" to the scene. We see the consequential effect of one behaviour to the other. This understanding of human emotions as well as the powerful imagery, gives depth to the plot and allows for interpretation on different levels...

The novel is dotted with powerful imageries and descriptions all of which evoke memories of different kinds... We see the author's fondness of allegories – the work is filled with a bitter-sweetness and melancholy, and yet so realistic. The visions are those of a dreamer, the compositions are neither unified nor centrally focused.

CHAINS OF CASTE

In order to read Rama's thoughts, the reader must shift from his own to follow the movement of the undulating ship and the tones and rhythms of the drums as these get louder and louder and then fade out. When the Guru dies we see the end of a past and the marriage to Indeeya marks the beginning of a new life in a new world where one must move on and unburden the chains of caste.

The novel is extraordinarily powerful as it traces from beginning to end, the plight of the indentured labourers. The author has poignantly expressed his own wish to pass on the truths of yesteryear when he tells us of the Captain's speech about the deaths of the immigrants. "Their deaths... were simply and clearly caused by carelessness, disease and very bad weather, three factors which will be remembered by historians and chroniclers in years to come. Nothing else can and should account for this high rate of mortality."

However, the author has conveyed to us that part of the chronicles that is not told to the masses.'

So in the wake of Rama's journey, as recounted above, I arrived in Trinidad. The novel's wide distribution by 'Periodicals' Distributors Limited, was accompanied by Media coverage in the form of two live Television Interviews: The first on Trinidad and Tobago Television's 'Morning Programme,' the other, on Gayelle Television.

The Interviewers were young women: one Indo-Trinidadian, the other Afro-Trinidadian. To begin with, both asked more or less the same question: 'Is this an historical novel?' Not anticipating such a question and given that it was six o'clock in the morning, to the first of my questioners at TTT, I replied: 'I'm glad you asked that question,' and within the brief space of time that it took to speak those six words, I quickly collected my thoughts and answered: 'History is based on evidence, and there are gaps in the evidence. Where history ends, story begins. All that you've read (or will read) in *Rama's Voyage* **did not happen**. It is a story; and the characters are fictitious.'

The rest of this Interview went well, as was my Interview on Gayelle Television. Amidst the warm weather in Trinidad, I thought about the cold London days when I was writing and finishing the book; and on the positive responses from my friends Wendy Greenbury, Leena Mitford, Jackie Ali, John Saliba, Paula Lewis, Annette Bush, Ann Marie Cheddi and Hafiza Seesahai. For them, and many others who had read and liked the book, the feeling and expectation was the same: 'I cannot wait for the sequel.'

THIRTY-ONE

AN ARCHIVE DESTROYED IN THE BRITISH LIBRARY

Time passed quickly. With only a few months of employment left in the British Library, a matter that had been at the back of my mind now came powerfully to the fore and I reasoned: better to do some things while in employment than afterwards. But time certainly was not on my side. The most urgent thing that concerned me was a matter that I'd postponed for many years. It related to accessing a copy (or copies) of a foundational document for research purposes such as the Minutes of the *first* British Library Whitley Council Meeting and copies of some other important papers and correspondence relating to the heady first two years of the British Library's existence, when I had presided as the *first* elected Staff Side Secretary. With hindsight, the accumulation of 'firsts' gave additional significance and thus value to the documents that I sought.

After enquiries, I was able to meet the incumbent Staff Side Secretary, Ms N. During a brief conversation, I asked about the relevant papers and Ms N said she would look into the matter. Just before the end of 2004, apart from the material requested, I also felt the need to see some of the 40 or more files that I'd carefully filed and left in the Staff Side Office. As more time elapsed, I again approached Ms N who told me that the Files were certainly not in London; they were more than likely to be in Boston Spa. Later, when I pressed her for a definitive answer about accessing these papers, she said the files were *not* kept.

'Destroyed?' I dared to ask.

'Yes,' she said.

And when I queried 'Why?' the simple, nonchalant answer given was: a 'lack of storage space.' My heart raced. I was deeply shocked to hear this. Then Ms N surprised me again: 'And anyway the "Agreements" in those files are now out-of-date.' Absolutely incredible! I was devastated, numbed. I could hardly speak. Thus an accumulation of hundreds, more accurately, thousands of British Library documents were deliberately destroyed by members of staff in the British Library. Who was the person (or persons) who did this? Who were they? Surely the twelve Staff Side representatives on the Whitley Council did not *all agree to destroy* their own collective British Library records? I questioned. Then I asked myself: are the current staff representatives in 2004 aware that such a collection of documents were no longer in existence? And anyway, these papers-correspondence were integral to any credible understanding of the history of the British Library and thus of Staff-management agreements, procedures and practices that governed the wider Collections. This archival vandalism committed within the National Library by a member (or members) of staff, nagged me for days and months. Even now, it touches a raw nerve.

Professionally, wearing my historian's hat, I was at a loss to understand this wilful, wanton destruction of invaluable papers, now lost forever and thus denying future historians and generations of interested researchers access to these seminal records! This unilateral destruction echoed and compounded similar sabotage committed earlier by a member (or members) of staff – twenty-two years before when a Mr Wagu became my successor as CSU Secretary in whose keeping I had left thirty-four Manila folders; a precious ten-year accumulation charting the emergence and development of Branch 849 in the British Library.

So it was that after the crucial years of teething problems, Industrial Relations practice reflecting vital and steadily improving staff-management relations (in effect necessary changes in working practices which saw the transition from British Museum Library to British Library) contained in the destroyed records was unquestionably a great loss. (This 'loss' was recently confirmed by Lyn Young, the British Library's Archivist). After Ms N had delivered the shockingly sad news, I found among my personal papers at home a folder containing a copy of the sought after first British Library Whitley Council Minutes, as well as some letters, including a few that I'd written to the British Library's first Chief

Executive and Deputy Chairman of the British Board, Dr Harry Hookway.

If the serving Staff Side representatives were blissfully unaware (as were Mr Wagu's Branch members) the irony consequent on the destroyed archive is that a hard-won 'Agreement' which I'd successfully negotiated with John Sheldon at the Civil Service Department in The Mall during the early 1970s (which ended the unpopular Weekly Day Off- WDO-system) was, some 30 years later *re-introduced* in the new British Library building at St. Pancras! This happened because the Union representatives and Staff knew nothing of the 'Agreement.' How could they? when this and many other 'Agreements' were destroyed by members of staff who were *in charge* of the Staff Side Archives. If knowledge is power, the staff and their representatives' unawareness of the 'Agreement' that was reneged on, and *reintroduced* as a new WDO System were, to put it mildly, cheated; a very sad and awful thing!

As time passed and I prepared to come to terms with ending my working life in the British Library, I made this observation: to a large extent the new 'Staff representatives' attitude was at best lacking in spirit or interest in what they were doing; and those they represented seemed to have succumbed to a sense that their roles were not valued. Indeed many of the new generation ('Thatcher's children') had no idea what trade unions were. Some were downright hostile to staff representations which they regarded as irrelevant. And whenever any form of Industrial Action was taken, more often than not, the question was asked: why should they (rogue strikers who needed just a few pennies more!) be allowed to hold the country to ransom? At this interesting time of my life, I vividly recalled reading about Mr Moneybags' who in Karl Marx's book *Capital* (or *Das Kapital*) was primarily concerned with the exploitation of workers. Such unbending employer attitudes towards some of the poorest of the lower-paid working people, I've found great difficulty in understanding. But life being far from straightforward I was also reminded of the French writer Michel Montaigne's remark about oppressed slaves who, for the most part, tended not to rise up *en masse* against their Masters.

Having been a central player at an important time when new

national institutions were being incorporated within the British Library, the archival vandalism that occurred in the British Library will always be *deeply disturbing to me*. Unlike the perceived 'rogue strikers,' the real violence and the act of destruction, came from those with authority either to preserve or destroy. Over the years, I'd worried and kept this matter largely to myself, hoping against hope, that the files were indeed in Boston Spa or safely stored away. Now that I knew what had actually happened to the documents, for the first time, I am setting the record straight. But nothing could ever compensate for the loss of the voluminous archive. Surely the destruction of both Branch 849 and Whitley Council Staff Side records (altogether at least 78 files) in, of all places, the National library, were illegal acts. Shouldn't those responsible be brought to book?

The continuous inflow, the toing and froing of crowds into and within the vast London sprawl excited and generated an increasing gregariousness which, over the years, bought me in contact with many people. The accumulation of experience had engendered in me a remarkable capacity for getting on with others. I learned a great deal about being sociable and socializing. And where better than the 'London scene' to have been so apprenticed!

Having lived in several boroughs, the core attraction was Central London, particularly Bloomsbury, Covent Garden, the South Bank, Fitzrovia, Soho and the West End. Many writers, actors and artists, who were counted among the 'good and the great' were to be seen in these areas. Though far from being like Bloomsbury and the 'Bloomsbury Group,' Soho also boasted its attractiveness to a number of luminaries, including Dylan Thomas, George Barker, Francis Bacon, Lucien Freud, Michael Foot, Muriel Belcher, Brendan Behan, Gaston Berlemont, Colin MacInnes, Ronnie Scott, the *Private Eye* people, great actors and playwrights, Peter O'Toole, George Melly and Keith Waterhouse, among many others.

Very gradually, as and when I visited the West End, Soho in particular, my historical sense and innate inquisitiveness helped me to understand more and more of its multifaceted character. I was fascinated to learn that William Blake had lived on Broadwick

Street, just off Berwick Street and its famous Market, which I'd frequented when I knew Wendy who had lived at Number sixty-nine Berwick Street. These were wonderful years; a time when Wendy played a central role in the Soho Society, organising and participating in the Community's well-known activities. St. Anne's Church was a hub; and cultural events such as the Soho Pantomime and the Soho Fair and Festival were annual highlights. At the time, I'd come across two songs about Soho Village: 'Berwick Market' and 'The Bells of Soho' which I think captured the essence of the place.

'BERWICK MARKET

The shadows are falling, the long day goes by,
The lights of the market sail up to the sky;
The organ is braying and playing a song,
And hundreds are hustling and bustling along.

There's plenty to buy if the money you've got,
And plenty to long for and save for if not!
And everyone's happy and everyone's bright
At old Berwick market on Saturday night…

Come sweet London lassie and don't be shy,
There's sure to be something that pleases your eye!
A dear little hat that's just made for your crown,
A pair of white shoes or a beautiful gown!
And you London lad, there is something for you,
A ring for your sweetheart, a trinket or two,
Or something in music, or something in fruit,
And if you're a dandy, a scarf or a suit.'

And

'THE BELLS OF SOHO
Waken, awaken! The red dawn is shining,
Fresh from the country the glad breezes blow;

Forth to your work though the sunlight be passing,
"Wake to the dawn!" ring the bells of Soho!...

Hark then, good people! As days go a-flying,
Hark to that message, "Leave sorrow and woe!
Lift up your hearts ev'ry wonderful morrow!"
Hark, one and all, to the bells of Soho!'

In my experience, more people in the arts were to be found in and around Soho than anywhere else in London and perhapsthe rest of the country. As we've seen, the celebrated artist Francis Bacon was a regular in the French House. Often wearing a black polo neck jersey, he was rarely alone; and his conversations always struck me as being involved and intense; private matters conducted in a public space. I'd observed this many times. If the round shape of his face was striking, his piercing look, drew you in. He spoke softly, and though friendly, he was not always approachable. It was not the done thing to point out who was who (either in the 'French' or the Colony Room Club) but very gradually through the nods, the 'Hellos' and 'How are Yous,' Francis Bacon's presence as the artist of the *Tryptich* and other works, could not be ignored. An abiding memory was seeing Bacon and Freud in the jam-packed French House where together, they seemed isolated in a private conversational huddle. Lucien Freud, a man of slight build and sharp features was the possessor of no less a severe gaze and intensity than that of Francis Bacon. And as if to confirm what I'd first thought, there was something mysterious and very special about their eyes!

The link between myself and these two great modern artists was the enigmatic, highly regarded photographer Harry Diamond with whom I conversed more often than not. Memorably having used more than one roll of film on me as the subject of his 'Shoot' in the courtyard of the British Museum and the environs of Bloomsbury, over the years, as I wrote and published more books, I got to know Harry (if that was possible!) a little better; and to our credit we never ignored each other. The trio: Harry, Francis Bacon and Lucien Freud were not mere acquaintances; they knew each other very well and, of course, Lucien Freud did a large portrait of Harry which was recently exhibited at the National Portrait Gallery. With the passage of time and a growing reputation, Harry became a highly collectable London photographer. Among his works were those of the great musicians who had appeared at the famous Ronnie Scott's Jazz Club in Soho.

Outside the world of professional art critics, as a mark of Francis Bacon's greatness in the exclusive preserve of the more or less exclusive Soho 'in-places,' the proprietor of the French House had placed a framed black and white photograph of Bacon on the south wall: it was one of the few images of a living painter to have been on *continuous display* in this West End establishment.

Given that each of the walls, especially those facing east, west and north were adorned with pictures (it was becoming more and more of an Art Gallery) one day in November 2004 when I visited, Lesley Botham, the French's new proprietor/manager drew my attention to a recently placed photograph: a black and white image. This photograph of myself was taken by John Claridge earlier in the summer. It was quite a large photograph set in a wooden frame, and given the special honour of being hung on the East wall, next to five or six prominent personalities in the world of the arts and literature. I was in the famous West End and I could hardly believe what I was seeing! On each of the other walls there were historical and contemporary photographs of the good and great from the world of the stage and screen: I clearly remember seeing some years before a number of pictures and was particularly struck by one of Rex Harrison when he appeared as Professor Higgins in the London stage production of *My Fair Lady*.

Historically, of course, the French House was connected with the French Resistance during the Second World War. Here, it was said, Charles de Gaulle master-minded the crucial 'Resistance' strategy. The French House's façade of being a social meeting place served as an effective disguise for General De Gaulle's behind-the-scenes machinations. Having my photograph on public display here in London's West End was, for me, a mark of real distinction.

As Christmas 2004 approached, the photograph reminded me of my first visit to Piccadilly Circus and to that unusual, crowded social space when, as a youngster, I hardly knew anyone. I was adrift in the maelstrom of the greatest of world cities. Now, during the Festive Season, at the bottom right hand corner of my photograph's frame someone had adorned it with a sprig of mistletoe. Merry Christmas indeed. What a contrast, I thought, to those first six Christmas Days that I'd spent alone in a cold bedsit. The 'Claridge photograph,' as I called it, remained on show for many months in that West End Establishment which had the reputation of being visited by, and had close association with many exceptional people, including writers and, of course, actors such as Paul Robeson, Rex Harrison, Richard Burton, Peter O'Toole, Paul Newman, Tom Baker, Struan Rodger, Nick Gecks and others too numerous to mention here. From the Sand Road to Bloomsbury and London's West End, my feelings about this incredible journey as I stared at the large photograph of myself displayed alongside iconic images was odd, but strangely exciting too.

Early in 2005, while standing in the morning coffee queue in the British Library's Café on the Upper Ground Floor, I saw Kerry Hooper, a former work colleague and manager on the Book Moves Team. For a long moment, she stared directly at me, a curious look, I thought, as if she did not know me. Eventually she spoke: 'I was in the West End over Christmas with my partner,' she said, 'and we went into the French House where I saw a framed photograph of you on the wall: I know that man, I said to my partner. It is Ron Ramdin. He works with me!' '

The distance between what she *knew* of me and what she'd seen on her night out, was, it seemed, at odds and quite puzzling. The fact that we were no longer working in the same department gave added significance to my photograph being 'On Show' in the West End. Like so many people that I knew in the British Library, who had either heard that I was a writer, or may have thought that I was a dabbler, a 'walter-mitty' poser, the public display of my photograph in the French House may have changed Ms Hooper's perception of me even though she knew little or nothing about the truth of my life and work as campaigner, educationist, lecturer and writer! In the court of public opinion, this public showing was perhaps one of the tests of having 'made it!' Naturally, such recognition reminded me of those earlier years when there were markedly fewer non-white people in Britain than there are today and my very first visit to Gaston Berlemont's Establishment, where I was perceived as a strange-looking black youth amidst a sea of curious (even intimidating) white faces; a time when, as one writer later put it, I was a 'green-horn' and clearly overwhelmed by the unfathomable Metropolis that was London.

A POEM REDISCOVERED

Early in the New Year, Phil Salman, a former American University lecturer and regular reader in the British Museum Round Reading Room had handed me an envelope. In it, there was a note attached to a poem entitled: *The British Library* which he'd written twenty-five years before in November 1980. A quarter of a century later, we were still Readers, but no longer in the British Museum. Now sitting at Seat 60 in the Rare Books Reading Room at St Pancras, I re-read the contents of Phil's envelope. 'For your recreation,' the note stated. 'Any criticisms welcome...Phil.'

I had no criticisms and because it was one Reader's thoughts of the former iconic 'Room' written at a time when I had worked there both as a member of staff and reader, I have decided to include it here.

'THE BRITISH LIBRARY
...Panizzi's design runs long desks out
under the dome. They parallel
high mullioned windows, but do not
curve. The curve of the dome, at night,
above the lights, gives back the crystalline sphere,
the bowl of the heavens where the zodiac
might curve in the south or Orion and the Bears
might rotate and curve
But there are no stars, not even
painted ones. Blue, yes. But no planetarium
or no cherubs around aresident
allegory, Library Rising to Heaven Conformed

to the Father. That was left to the readers
down among the lights, seated along
the spokes, mostly silent, but coughing,
laughing occasionally, whispering among
the snap of catalogue books, blue
beavers' tails, into their shelves,
Their minds move on silence.
They read by their lights
and must produce light as mirrors
of what they read. I am pleased
as the Library darkens, the lights
come on, and the readers, making
categories, confound categories.
London, November 1980.'

These lines reminded me of a piece of paper that I'd seen within weeks of starting my employment at the British Museum Library. It was sticking out from one of the many books on a barrow while I was engaged in that morning's book replacements. I had unfolded the paper and looked briefly, casually at the type-written words by Louis MacNeice, whom I had then not heard of! Some years later, I came to know of MacNeice's work and tried very hard to remember the book and find that original 'piece of paper' containing his poem about the 'Reading Room.' To this day, I think of it as the one that got away.

From poetry, I was confronted with familiar prose. After many day-long sessions and in-depth discussions, as the Mayor's Commission Report began to take its final shape, Commissioners were circulated with drafts of the 'Chains Preface' and the 'Executive Summary.'

These written sections pleased me greatly as I pressed on with my own first Draft of the 'Historical Section' which included biographies of Blacks and Asians. As the Commissioner charged with completing this work on schedule (after the exercise of writing the 'Briefs' for the PRO's *Moving Here*) I felt compelled to appreciate that having served a very long apprenticeship, I was now the right man, in the right place, at the right time. But, I also realised that such a feeling did not come about by chance. Significantly, having had no benefactor at any stage in my life, I was powerfully reminded of a hard fact about myself: I had indeed 'made my own luck.'

On my return to London from Trinidad, I received a letter of acknowledgement after a visit to the Holy Faith Convent School on Clark Road, Penal, where my sister Annette was employed as a Teacher. Ms Valerie Bethel, the Principal, on behalf of the Teaching Staff and students of the Convent, wrote of her *'wish to extend sincerest congratulations'* to me on the publication of *'yet another masterpiece. We wish you God's blessings as you continue to produce work of a high standard and of international appeal.*

Thank you for the copy of Rama's Voyage which you have so generously donated to our Library.

Yours respectfully.'

This letter had a strong resonance for it reminded me, lest I forget, that my books, both non-fiction and fiction, were being received as rare and *'important'* (Sam Selvon's description of my first book!) **educational resources** germane to many levels of education, not only primary, but also Secondary and for general readers.

Apart from literature, with the increasing influence and value of images on the silver Screen between 23-24 February and 24 March 2005 I wrote to a number of people including Sir Richard Attenborough, Steven Spielberg and Sir Gulam Noon about the film potential of the novel *Rama's Voyage*. I also had a meeting with a Literary and Film Agent at David Higham Associates. In a word, my hopes for the little known story that was *Rama's Voyage* were ambitious.

Living in my head, so to speak, after years of relentless effort, I could not ignore the wear and tear on my body. For several weeks, I had been dogged by intermittent pain in my groin area. As the pains became more regular, I went to see my doctor who referred me to St Mary's Hospital in Paddington, where I began a series of checks in relation to my prostate.

Meanwhile, I received the following from a Writers' Directory of international repute:

'It gives me great pleasure to enclose a typescript of your entry as it will appear in the Thirty Second Edition of this prestigious title which is due for publication in mid-2005: *Dictionary of International Biography.*' As requested by the editor, I duly updated my biographical details and submitted an updated list of publications. Being part of the community of writers, I saw the DIB entry as further recognition of my writings. Already, I'd been listed in other author's directories including *International Whos's Who* and *Contemporary Authors.* To be included among my peers in these internationally recognised Dictionaries was surely a mark of authorial excellence.

Alternating between projects (which I'd been doing for over two decades) as if they were energy-giving sources, I not only maintained, but also increased my writing work-rate; and coincident with completion of my biography of Mary Seacole, it was fortuitous that she was making the news headlines. Why? Largely because a long lost portrait of the 'Crimean heroine' by Charles Challen, was found. This, the experts argued, was the only known oil painting of Mary Seacole; and in March 2005 it went on display in the National Portrait Gallery. For this 'Nurse' of the Crimea, a feverish interest in her life and work began to spread. Apart from books like mine, her life and times were explored by other media.

Paul Kerr of October Films contacted me about a Television Documentary Film he was making on Mary Seacole. My authorship of this outstanding Jamaican, prompted an invitation from Mr Kerr to do an 'On Camera' Interview for his 'Film.' A special set was prepared at a location in London and after my Interview, I was duly paid. Several weeks later, on 9 March 2005, Mr Kerr emailed me:

'*The documentary is nearing completion (just the music and sound effects to be added now) and is likely to be screened on C4 in late Spring or early this summer.*' Then he added: '*I'm afraid, however, that we have ended up not using your Interview as we also did some late additional interviews in Jamaica and London and had to make some* hard choices about which ones to use. A Channel Four hour is only 49 minutes of screen-time and simply can't accommodate everything we hoped to include. I hope you aren't too disappointed.'

These words echoed the past: the same old story, I thought. My face didn't fit, though what I'd said during my Interview was a different matter. So yet again, I experienced what was another 'Paul Robeson moment' for much of what I'd contributed was incorporated in the 'voice-over' narrative for which the Mary Seacole film-makers could justifiably have argued they had already paid and thanked me! But, as with books, talks and lectures, of course, these paltry fees were never the motivation for my acceptance of such invitations. Thus the story of my **one-man Crusade** in the face of Film directors and producers, continued.

That very day I responded to Paul Kerr's message:

'I'm sorry you will not be using my contribution, all the more because I have just submitted an original article to The Times and The Observer entitled: "PARTNERS AND LOVERS." In this piece I argue (using the evidence from Mary Seacole's autobiography) that the 20 year relationship with the Englishman Thomas Day was much closer than we think. Indeed, it was crucial to the setting up of the all-important British Hotel in the Crimea which resulted in Mary becoming the Crimean heroine… the argument I raise would, I think, be an exciting one for future research.'

Within hours, Paul Kerr replied:

'On second thoughts you must have discovered something very new about Thomas Day beyond which Mary herself tells us, because if memory serves, she only admits to meeting him in 1853/4 in Escribanos and she obviously can't tell us about anything after 1857. So where did you discover their 20 year relationship?
Yours fascinated,
Paul.'

I would not have written the 'Article' mentioned above if what Paul Kerr believed was not in question. I did not, however, feel it would, at this stage, do either of us any good vis-à-vis the Seacole 'Documentary' film and so I did not answer his query.

After this unsatisfactory outcome, with time hurtling on, other things jostled for attention: for example, my growing awareness that decades of continuous employment, now reduced to a few months, was coming to an end. Awareness of this impacted with a force that surprised me, particularly when I received and read a letter from Dr Clive Field, Director of Scholarship & Collections.

'Dear Ron,

As you near your retirement from the Library, I write to thank you for your contribution over the past 35 years, most recently on the preparation of India Office Records volumes for preservation microfilming.

However, on a personal level, you have also undertaken significant academic research for your publications on the history of the Caribbean and of Afro-Caribbeans in the UK and, as a result, have been invited by Ken Livingstone to be a member of the Mayor's Commission on Africa and African Heritage. I hope that your retirement enables you to devote more time to these successful academic pursuits.

On behalf of all your colleagues in the Library may I wish you a long and happy retirement...'

My 'Afro-Caribbeans' work was but part of my contribution. Nothing was said about my Secretaryship of my decade-long engagement with vital Staff and Management issues as we worked through knotty problems towards the viable functioning of the British Library. Either Mr Field knew about my past British Library Whitley Council contribution and decided to omit it from his letter or, as I thought most likely, he knew absolutely nothing about it! And why didn't he know? Because there had been a significant change in policy-orientation and perspective: from being collaborative to a culture that led to such matters as good management-staff relations being relegated to low-priority and thus to the destruction of the records that did not, in retrospect, fit the 'perception'! The pertinent question to ask is this: did Mr Field or anyone of his authority know of this destruction? As Director of Scholarship and Collections and Keeper of the national collections what would he have said about any form of Archival destruction in the British Library?

Receipt of my Official 'Retirement letter' led to a frantic rush to sort matters out at work: for one thing, my desk needed to be cleared before my separation from the Library. Time passed remarkably quickly. As the months were now reduced to weeks, more than ever, I considered my life and work: what did it really represent? In terms of experience, one thing was abundantly clear, the thirty six years that had passed in the British Library was far from being dull. Indeed, it had been unceasingly eventful, if not always happy.

Unlike my fellow employees at the Senate House Library, a habit that I'd developed at the outset of my working life in Britain: coming in very early and leaving late (which I continued to practice over three and a half decades) helped me to use *time* well and thus I gained knowledge not only about the British Library, but also about the world and life generally. It would, of course, take much more time to expand on what I knew. Nonetheless, in terms of autobiography, the die was already cast in the form of my *Carnival in Trinidad* extended Essay. Even then, I'd already decided that my story (both of life in Trinidad and Britain) should be a continuous narrative contained in one book.

Although I'd begun to write sketches of my back-story, as early as the late 1960s, after years of suggestions from various people, especially after I had given the Whitbread Cardiff Lecture and at the urgings of Film Director Mr Rolfe (with whom I was working on *The Sand Road*) writing my autobiography had gained momentum. By then, I was well on the way to completing a draft with the new working title: 'Making a Difference.' So as my British Library career was nearing its end, on the theme of 'legacy,' as I saw it, on 15 April 2005 I wrote to Sandy Nairne, Director of the National Portrait Gallery, whom I'd met on a few occasions in my capacity as a Mayor of London Commissioner:

'Dear Sandy,
After 44 years of work in three of the greatest libraries in the world (the University of London, Senate House Library: the British Museum Library and the British Library) and a varied career as Historian, biographer, novelist, broadcaster, international Lecturer and trade

unionist, I will be leaving the British Library this year. As I am about to do so, yesterday, I was informed of my inclusion in the Cambridge Dictionary of International Biography. A nice rounding off, you might say...

With my book Mary Seacole due out... I look forward to the wonderful prospect of writing full time and, importantly, to completing my autobiography entitled "Making a Difference: From Trinidad Village to the British Museum and British Library."

Given my long, multifaceted career/contribution to community work and to British society generally, I decided to write to you to offer to the National Portrait Gallery, two items on permanent loan: an impressionist painting of myself by Dalia Daza (an artist whose work, especially her Exhibitions of Flamenco Artists are well-known in Spain) and a bronze bust of myself. I also have four rare photographs taken in Bloomsbury (London) 33 years ago by the celebrated (collectable) photographer Harry Diamond.

Please let me know if you would like to see copies (photographs) of these images.

I do look forward to hearing from you.'

After contacting Sandy Nairne in April 2005, I had received a letter from Ruth Kenny, Assistant Curator, at the National Portrait Gallery. Now she wrote to me again:

'Dear Mr. Ramdin,
Further to our correspondence, we have had the opportunity to discuss the Harry Diamond photographs you kindly brought in with our twentieth century Curator.
We would be pleased to acquire one of them for the National Portrait Gallery Collection, but before we proceed any further would like to confirm the terms of your offer. Were the photographs intended for purchase or as a gift to the Gallery? I hope you will understand that due to our extremely limited annual budget, we would only be in a position to accept the photograph if it were the latter. I would be most grateful if you could let me know at your earliest convenience.
Yours sincerely...'

My decision in relation to the photograph of myself was to donate it.

Six days after her first letter, I heard again from Ms Kenny: '*Thank you… for so generously agreeing to offer one of your Harry Diamond photographs as a gift to the Gallery. I have asked our Collections Manager, Dr. Tim Moreton, to contact you in order to make the necessary arrangements.*'

For years since the British Library was formed, I'd listened to, and participated in, countless meetings and debates; and thus far among the most vigilant monitors of British Library developments was the Regular Readers Group (RRG). Now, seventeen years after the new library building had opened its doors to an interested and, at times, sceptical British public, in addition to the 'Group,' there were other interested parties, other voices: in fact, a growing, even shrill chorus. In April 2005, a thought-provoking article appeared in *The Guardian* under the title: 'Fancy Sitting down with a good book? You'll be lucky.' The writer, John Sutherland wrote:

'Finding room to read at the British Library is no mean feat for established users, as seats are increasingly filled by twittering students fiddling with their phones. Ask most academics what single building represents the brain of Britain and they'll reply "The British Library."

But the Brain is bursting. And the current problems at the British Library site at St Pancras are a grim portent of what lies ahead for the country's industrial-intellectual infrastructure: its universities.

For a century and a half, the BL has been one of the nation's glories. Writing about Panizzi's British Museum Reading Room, shortly after it opened in 1857, the novelist Thackeray wrote:

"I have seen all sorts of domes of Peters and Pauls, Sophia, Pantheon - what not? - and have been struck by none of them so much as by that Catholic dome in Bloomsbury, under which our million volumes are housed. What peace, what love, what truth, what beauty, what happiness for all, what generous kindness for you and me, are here spread out! It seems to me one cannot sit down in that place without a heart of grateful reverence."

Indeed, the Dome in Bloomsbury suckled the nation's intellect. Philosophers, revolutionaries, poets and scholars drew sustenance from the ever accreting store of books. Whatever you sought was delivered to your desk in hours. *The BL was the perfect research machine. But even the grandeur of Panizzi's structure was inadequate to house the exponential increase of reading matter after the second world war - now 20 times greater than the million volumes that caused Thackeray to wonder...*

Over the years, the new BL project swelled to become, one was told, the most expensive public building undertaking in the UK. It was cursed by interminable delays, grotesque cost overuns and gremlins...

At long last, the new building opened in 1997. And, surprise surprise, everything worked reasonably well. After a while, one got used to it and even fond of the new BL. Until, that is, a month or so ago. It has always been the case that the BL kept users down to manageable levels through a series of polite, but formidable barriers. You were interviewed, and had to demonstrate a need to use the library. A reader's ticket was, one understood, a scholar's privilege, not a citizen's right. Above all, the BL was at pains to keep at bay London University's 100,000 students. But, in the last few months, undergraduates have suddenly been made very welcome. Word of mouth means more are streaming in every day. Even as one member of staff complained to me, sixth formers can now get a reader's ticket. Why is the BL now Liberty Hall? One assumes that new "targets" have been issued. More users means more clout, and more funds. Lift the portcullis: let in the students. And, if that doesn't work, let in the winos and the street people. Bums on seats is MISSION STATEMENT 2005. And, if there are more bums than seats, its hard luck for the seat-less. There have been furious complaints from the "real" BL users (as they see themselves). Unless you get in at the crack of dawn, you won't find a desk. Karl Marx would have to go to King's Cross station to write Das Kapital. Virginia Woolf would have to go home to the room of her own. No entry today, Mr Thackeray. If you want to sit down with a heart full of grateful reverence, come tomorrow - very early.

These hordes of new young users, their elders lament, have no sense of library etiquette. They use their mobile phones. They rather text than read! They chatter like parakeets in an aviary. Above all, they are not serious. They are in the BL because its warm, handsomely appointed, has free input for laptops and an ace cafe attached. It's a good place to hang out.

There's a moral here, if the DfES cared to look. It's not just libraries that are easily swamped. Target-driven planning (50 per cent of school-leavers in university, 100 per cent occupancy of the BL) doesn't work. You don't believe me? Go to St Pancras. You won't have any trouble getting a reader's ticket. But you will have trouble getting a seat.'

This was a new argument, a real problem which the administration of the new British Library building would have to deal with. Among the complainants of this seating issue at the British Library was none other than my fellow-User Lady Antonia Fraser, whom I'd known when she sat next to me for several months in the M Row of seats (M6) in the former British Museum Round Reading Room. Recently when Ms Fraser visited St. Pancras eager to use the British Library, she could not find a seat. Unlike the Museum's Reading Room, the British Library was now an over-subscribed public library which, in effect, meant those who came in early got a seat. Those who didn't, were shut out! Indeed such was Ms Fraser's experience that she complained. On another occasion when she arrived at the Library hoping for some improvement, she found that things had not changed. Tough! Then it occurred to me that soon I would be like Ms Fraser (or any other reader) an *outsider*, for my time as a Staff **insider** at the British Library was getting shorter.

Then, as if it was meant to lift my spirits from being submerged by encroaching worry, I received a Book Review of *Rama's Voyage* from Jawaharlal Nehru University in India. The Reviewer, Dr Priti Singh of the University's School of International Studies wrote:

'Rama's Voyage is more than a voyage. It is a quest for indentity and self-definition, a search for individuality denied to the peoples around whom the story is woven — the indentured labourers from India on their way to Chinidad as they knew it. While there are many others on the voyage who stand out, the journey is centred around Rama, a simple yet powerful name in Indian mythology. It is this simplicity and strength of character that is brought out in the portrait of Rama.

Rama, an orphaned child, personifies many traits — courage, valour, humanity, love, forgiveness, but also personalized by a lack of identity. He has no surname and no home. He is a child yet to discover himself; a wanderer lured by a "silver tongue" (recruiter) onto the ship, because like most of the others on the voyage he wants to move forward to a better future. He feels a "general uneasiness" about his life and is one of those who are "in the middle of nowhere but going somewhere" in search of truth and a sense of belonging. Unlike others who consciously seek truth, to Rama the truth is, "in an extraordinary way, revealed."

Was India not home for the indentured labourers? Yes, it was but they carried a part of India with them wherever they were, even in the middle of nowhere on the ship. Eventually, the voyage brought the Indians closer together because it was together that they could help each other to survive. "Mother India" was for them "so far away, and yet so near."

Interestingly, it was in the final lap of the voyage, Rama discovers his true identity. Not only is his past and parentage unfolded to him, he is also assured a part of his future. About his past, he discovers that he is the son of a king and one of his mistresses — both of noble birth and an untouchable. At the same time, he is betrothed to Indeeya so that they can start their new life together in Chinidad. Just as he is reaching Chinidad he is no longer alone. All his life, whomever Rama forms an attachment with he loses. Yet, he survives. He discovers himself. And that is what the voyage is all about - discovering one's strength in the struggle for survival in spite of being "captives cocooned in the bowels of the Trinity Hills, a capsule of sea-sickness, melancholia, disease and death." The adverse circumstances eventually drew the Indians together like "moths to the flame of their common humanity," irrespective of their class and caste. Survival, not social rank or caste, was of vital importance on the voyage. While some of the higher caste still looked down upon the lower castes, to Rama it made no difference. "This was a matter which he little understood...It did not bother him. For him there was no going back. It was as simple as that." The experience of the Indians brought them together creating a "Jahaji Bhai" spirit, the brotherhood and sisterhood of the ship." It was a new beginning. A new life in a new country that would demand great love and courage.

The message is clear: "Truth is one, the sages call it by different names." Therefore wherever you go, it is ultimately the "self" that matters and one's ability to rise above the self. To meet the challenges, life brings one's own way and to find the "truth." It is a voyage unto oneself to discover the truth and to cross the dark waters (kala pani) of the once-

in-lifetime voyage and to make a future out of it. To meet one's destiny and to end one's homelessness, the sense of "un"belonging or lack of identity in the "new land of the virgin West." This is the "other place" where "homelessness would end." Rama is greeted in this new land by majestic mountains which remind him of the Himalayas and high above the mountains a brilliant rainbow appears. Rama then feels that "there was something extraordinary about him being there." For the orphaned Rama the voyage had been an odyssey towards hope, in search of the truth and a home. This then was home.'

The understanding that Dr Singh had brought to bear in this deeply perceptive Book Review was commendable: it was reason enough to feel encouraged. Both the *Trinidad Guardian's* in-depth Review and Dr Singh's perspective from India in the fictional work *Rama's Voyage* pleased me for they not only marked a significant milestone in my literary career, but also encompassed an ever-hopeful quest from the ancestral East to the West for home and belonging.

THE SAM WANAMAKER SHAKESPEARE'S GLOBE THEATRE INTERVIEW

During the gorgeously bright Summer days of 2005, I felt anything but in holiday mood. Each morning as I walked across the Piazza, through the front doors then up the marble steps to my office on the third floor of the British Library, I tried to dispel from my mind the stark fact of early retirement.

As it was, I had little time to reflect upon, or to concern myself unduly with, leaving. My nagging worry was the recurrent pain near my groin and lower abdomen! But even this could not deflect my attention from even more urgent matters.

With less than a month before my departure as I began clearing my desk which was piled with papers: correspondence, manuscripts and books, I realised that much of the material that I'd accumulated over the years, plus what I had at home, was of value: a rare archive, and I wondered how much of it was worthy of becoming part of the British Library Collections. This accumulation surprised me for as the years passed and dog-eared manuscripts became published books, I kept the originals; as well as BBC and other British and

Caribbean radio and television recordings: cassette tapes and audio-visual DVDs. In terms of manuscripts and Posters relating to public appearances, my 'Collection' was now significant: a unique 50 year record of British literary and social history and, as such, I felt it merited inclusion in the national Library. So while composing this autobiography, I discussed archival matters with a former Senior British Library Curator who recognised its scope and depth; and thus the uniqueness and value of my 'papers' and recordings.

Taken together, my 'Collection' was, I felt, significant. And so with just days left before I was due to leave the British library, on 21 May I contacted Stephen Cleary, Curator of the National Sound Archive:

'*Some time ago, I'd written to you about an ORIGINAL 90 minute audio tape of an Interview with American Actor-Director SAM WANAMAKER talking to me about PAUL ROBESON: How they met in America, their acting careers and collaborative efforts in bringing about what is regarded by many as one of the greatest productions of Shakespeare's Othello at Stratford-upon-Avon in 1959. I would like to donate a copy of this rare recording to the British Library's National Sound Archive Collection. Please let me know how I should go about this.*

I would also welcome your guidance in the matter of transferring the music (4 songs) from a master tape to a CD. I also have a Vinyl recording (a 45 rpm) which I would like to donate ...'

Later, I wrote:

'*...Since our meeting, I have been reviewing the other precious items in my collection, which I would also like to submit to the British Library/NSA in the near future. Please let me know when you will be free to meet.*'

Eventually Stephen Cleary replied:

'*Thanks Ron. I have passed the three items you kindly donated to the Sound Archive to our studio engineer..., who has scheduled them for dubbing. I will let you know when the job is finished... Best, Steve.*'

Soon after this correspondence, I met Nick Gecks, the actor and writer, with whom I had discussed the possibility of a BBC radio broadcast of my Interview with Sam Wanamaker, especially as the Tenth Anniversary of the opening of Shakespeare's Globe Theatre approached. Nick suggested that I get in touch with Hannah Sim, a radio, broadcaster/producer. Time was of the essence; and without further ado, I wrote to Ms Sim,

'On this Tenth anniversary of the opening of the Globe Theatre, after a meeting with Nick Gecks yesterday, he suggested that I contact you about an ORIGINAL 90 minute Tape Recording in which SAM WANAMAKER talks to me about Paul Robeson... and Shakespeare's Othello with special reference to the acclaimed 1959 Stratford-upon-Avon Production of Othello. This is a first, engaging, revealing and as Nick said "volcanic"... evocation of the innermost thoughts and feelings of one of the Twentieth Century's greatest men of the theatre. On this important Anniversary of Shakespeare's Globe Theatre, the realisation of Sam Wanamaker's cherished dream, it is therefore timely and fitting that this rare, historic recording "SAM WANAMAKER Talks to RON RAMDIN" should have its inaugural airing on the BBC's Radio Four.

I do hope you will be interested in producing such a programme or programmes.

*I am an historian, biographer and novelist and my work is known both nationally and internationally. I am presently serving on the Mayor of London's pioneering Commission on African and Asian Heritage. (Further details can be found on my website: **ronramdin.com**)*

Given that time is of the essence, I look forward to hearing from you...'

After our correspondence, I went to see Stephen Cleary. He was most helpful in monitoring progress of the Library's copying of my original Cassette to CD. This acceptance of my work was crucial. I was encouraged and considered the prospect of the British Library as the repository of the rest of my 'Collection' or archive, and all the more so, because I had already embarked on the increasingly serious matter of writing this autobiography, the pages of which contain numerous references to that archive.

The continuous alternating between projects moved apace. By now, all of the Heritage Commission's scheduled and emergency meetings, as well as the writing of the Report, were completed. My 'Historical Section' Draft had run into several pages; and after circulating it, the feedback from fellow-Commissioners was positive. But, as with all such collaborations, there were final checks to be made. Just before the Report went to press on 6 June 2005, in response to a query from Commissioner Melissa Di Mello, to allay any doubt I emailed: 'I was not here yesterday and hasten to send this on. Having double-checked, I informed Makeda (Coaston) on Monday that the 10,000 year Asian presence in the first line of my piece relates to Europe (not specifically to Britain) and therefore after "The Asian presence" in the first sentence, the words "in Europe" should be inserted.'

My quick response to the query was entirely dependent upon my store of knowledge. This, and similar responses to various queries, further justified inclusion of my history: *Reimaging Britain: 500 Years of Blacks and Asians* in the final draft of the Report's educational resources recommendation.

Having had the pleasure of a surprise telephone call and a meeting with Zoe Wanamaker (whose national popularity on television was increasing, while also carving out a distinguished career in the theatre) I queried my rights of ownership of the Sam Wanamaker recorded Interview with the British Library experts. On 8 June 2005, I got in touch with Mr Cleary informing him that 'I am very concerned about securing my copyright of this recording. Can you offer any advice as to how I should proceed towards protecting my Copyright?'

Now that I'd given Ms Wanamaker a copy of the recording, I felt copyrighting it was vital. To my query, Mr Cleary responded:

'I have spoken to Richard Fairman, who is our "authority" on copyright. His advice is given below. I think this answers your question.

We can supply Zoe Wanamaker with a CD copy if you like, but I must stress we would not do this without your written permission.'

That very day, through Mr Cleary, Richard Fairman gave his much-valued opinion:

'*If Ron Ramdin made the recording, the copyright in the recording is his. If he speaks on the recording as Interviewer he also has rights in his part of the content. It would help if he had some written agreement in the past with Sam Wanamaker to have the interview recorded and the terms of use, though I guess that he doesn't. If Ron is concerned there could be a dispute on the issue of ownership of rights, I suggest he supplies Zoe Wanamaker with a copy of the recording marking the cassette or CD with a title such as "Ron Ramdin Interviews Sam Wanamaker" his words "Recording made by Ron Ramdin" and (if he thinks it necessary) copyright Ron Ramdin.'*

You can't get fairer than that, I thought; and Mr Fairman's advice was fully taken. Then on 9 June, I had the added benefit of Rob Perks (Curator Oral History and Director of National Life Story Collection in the National Sound Archive) clarifying copyright in relation to my recording.

Knowing that the Tenth Anniversary of the opening of Shakespeare's Globe Theatre to the public was pending, I searched among my papers and found the fifteen pages that I had painstakingly transcribed from the original cassette tape recording. This Transcript which I titled: '*Sam Wanamaker Talks to Ron Ramdin about Paul Robeson, Acting, America and Othello with special reference to the acclaimed 1959 Stratford upon Avon Production of Othello,*' was a ready textual reference and it was with some confidence that I awaited a reply from Hannah Sim.

Towards mid-summer, I was unusually aware of how surreal I was feeling as my final days on the staff of the British Library drew nearer. In my end is my beginning, and more than once, I thought about that first day of my first job in England at the Senate House Library when the Foreman Mr Boxer had said: 'After your tea-break, I must take you to Personnel to see about your Pension.'

'Pension?' I asked.

'Yes, your pensionable contributions!' Mr Boxer had said impatiently, as if I should know. Only a few weeks past my teens, thoughts of a Pension was the furthest thing from my mind! Now, with just ten days to go before my forty-three years of working life in England (thirty-six of which were spent in the British Library) would come to an end, I made it clear to Ms P who was overall in charge of my Section that I did not want a "Leaving Card"; a request which she respected. Then, in the final hours of my last day, Margaret, a relatively new and 'Temporary' member of staff, approached my desk with a large thing wrapped in brown paper.

'Here you are Ron!' she said unceremoniously, as she placed the object between us. I stood up and instinctively knew that the wrapper contained something to do with my leaving. 'It is from your colleagues in the office!' Margaret obviously did not know of my previous request to Ms P. I had no choice but to unwrap the object. What a great surprise! It was the largest 'Leaving Card' that I'd ever seen: its dimensions, I was told, were twenty two inches long and eighteen inches wide. It was a hand-made work of art; beautifully designed: two-thirds of the lower part was an historical map of the world in colour, showing the pink areas that formed the British Empire. At the top of the map there were three cherubic figures holding banners with the words: 'Freedom,' 'Fraternity' and 'Federation.' Just above, was a gap which marked the boundary of an insert with the following words in larger than usual print:

'*Ron's Voyage*

Mr. Ramdin's work represents a remarkable scholarly odyssey...Far from cutting corners he has been truly adventurous and ingenious in discovering new sources and adding new dimensions to his chosen subject.'

This quotation was an excerpt from the citation of my Higher Doctorate, the degree of Doctor of Literature from the University of London. These two parts of the Card were bordered on all sides by spaces of between two to four inches on which the scribblings and signatures of sixty-five people (only those employed within the OIOC Department of the British Library) were inscribed. How many more signatures could there have been, if leaving messages were solicited Library-wide? I wondered. One of the Card's messages was from Kwame, my Nigerian friend of many years:

'*Dear Brother, Comrade and friend,*

I hope your leaving here won't be the end of our great Friendship and political discourse. Please don't rest on your laurels and do continue to advance knowledge through your great works.

Good Luck and Best Wishes.'

Another was from Curator Hedley Sutton:
'*There was a young fellow called Ron,*
A writer and scholar bar none,
He's accomplished his goal,
With his book on Seacole,
And we're sad he'll shortly be gone.'

It was a big surprise that the organiser (or organisers) of the Card were able to get all sixty-five people, a cross-section of the Department's ranks, including Director Graham Shaw and a few scholars of world renown. One such scholar was Dr Frances Wood, whose father Lawrence Wood (a former Keeper) had sat on the newly-formed Whitley Council during my watch as Staff Side Secretary in the British Library. Was this Special Card solely Margaret's idea? I think it was; and, of course, I appreciated the thought, patience and artistry that had gone into making such an ambitious and beautiful leaving present. In particular, I marvelled: how did Margaret, within just a few months of knowing me, achieve this? Deeply touched by this magnanimous gesture, I arrived home from work that evening for the last time as an employee of the British Library and realised that the regular wage-earning phase of my life had ended.

Re-reading the short messages on the Card, I was overwhelmed by the thoughtfulness and respect that so many of the OIOC staff had shown. To this day, I have maintained good relations with many who still work there, including David Blake and Leena Mitford. Being the last of the many areas in the British Library where I'd worked and, having been the recipient of this unusual Leaving Card, on reflection, I wondered if such a thing could have happened in any of the other departments where I'd worked. The ethos of respect for scholarship and hard work among many in the OIOC during my last eight years in the British Library had engendered good feelings, a strong self-awareness and a sense that the decades of habitual reading, writing, publishing, travel, lecturing and broadcasting were, to some extent, recognised. And so after countless twists and dramatic turns from the ridiculous to the hilarious, the curtain came down on a deeply-committed, varied and honourable career; the culmination of a work-writing life spent in three truly wonderful, precious libraries – The University of London, the British Museum and the British Library - all in Bloomsbury, the heart of London which was, for me, ever since I had arrived, the centre of the world.

With no need to go to the office anymore, now mentally and physically I had to get used to treading a very different path: I had to adapt to a new set of circumstances. No longer would I be seeing the same people with regularity each morning and during the day; and worryingly, I had to cope with *less money*. On the other hand, the compensatory fact was that I would have *more time* at my disposal. In effect, the long-held dream that I had since the Sixties of becoming a *full-time* writer, had become reality. I could hardly believe it!

In the last days of June 2005, a strange period of transition, there were many things on my mind. Most prominent was finishing the final chapter of the third draft of my novel *The Confessions of the Reverend William Wragg*. This second work of fiction had been gestating for some seventeen years - since the summer of 1988! While writing, it proved to be a challenging and deeply satisfying experience. But now that the book was almost finished, I was not sure how my severely reduced income would work out in terms of paying the rent, as well as keeping body and soul together.

Money, so long a preoccupation, remained a major concern. For one thing, my British Library Pension was far short (*half* of my former income) of what I needed to live on; and depressingly, it would be as long as two years before I qualified for the all-important Government Pension. Until then, to meet the shortfall, I had no choice but to seek employment through Job Centre Plus.

And so forty three years after I'd first visited the 'Unemployment Exchange' on Medina Road, Finsbury Park, now I was back in an Unemployment office filling-in Forms: this time, not just a single sheet of paper but a thick booklet of questions to answer, which included several boxes to tick. After I'd completed the task of entering the details, I realised that because my severance pay after leaving the Library was marginally just above a certain amount, I did not qualify for 'Benefits' beyond the paltry sum of £40.00 a week. To qualify for this weekly sum, I would have to register each week in person at Job Centre Plus and be ready for work as and when a vacancy arose.

Meanwhile, the still unfinished novel *The Confessions of the Reverend William Wragg* was very much on my mind. In these demanding stages before completion, I needed to work systematically each day on it; and the prospect of doing another Full time job posed a problem. Economically, I was between a rock and a difficult place, so to speak. The dilemma was real, the acid test being: how important writing really was to me! Eventually, I made the hard decision of foregoing the Job Centre Plus option which meant supplementing my inadequate Pension by dipping into my small precious savings each week.

As time passed, the worry did not lessen; I felt hard-pressed, very insecure. Cast adrift! was not putting too fine a point on it for, once again, I could not push aside my experience of that unforgettable first summer of unemployment in 1962, when I'd lived on £1 a week. Now such thoughts were never far away, as I reasoned perhaps irrationally, that supplementing my small pension was less important than the urgent need to finish my novel. Why? Because since I had started it, I'd been hoping to get the book published early in 2007 on time for the 200th anniversary of the abolition of the African Slave Trade. Meeting this deadline was my main objective.

To add to my anxiety, the acute pain near my groin that had begun a few months before leaving the British Library, increased and I was forced to seek medical advice.

About this time, after he'd approached me to write about him, I had my first formal meeting with Sonny Blacks who had distinguished himself as an Entertainment Impresario both in Trinidad and in England. Over the years, we had met often at the Trinidad and Tobago London High Commission receptions and during snatches of conversations we discussed the idea and possibility of my authorship of his biography. I'd heard about him when I was a youth in Trinidad in relation to the arts and culture (particularly

Calypso and Carnival), but I confess that my knowledge of Sonny Blacks remained vague until we had met and began to talk about his life and times.

Sonny came prepared with a number of documents and newspaper cuttings. I was fascinated by what I had read and concluded that I would be glad to collaborate with him. In fact, I agreed to be his biographer providing we could get some funding to enable me to do the necessary work. On this understanding, before we parted company, he handed me a copy of his impressive *Curriculum Vitae* which, in part, stated that Sonny Blacks, the Trinidad-born Promoter 'came to the UK in 1961 together with the Dixieland Steel Orchestra, winners of the Islandwide Steelband Festival. Prior to this, he was the first to promote a young calypsonian named Francisco Slinger (the famous Mighty Sparrow) in Port of Spain and a series of successful concerts in Trinidad and the Caribbean islands, concentrating his efforts on the development and showcasing of calypso and steelband music. He was also the **first** person to promote steelband concerts and calypso shows at the Queens Hall in Port of Spain, Trinidad, which featured amongst others: The Trinidad All Stars, Invaders, Dixieland, Ebonites and Starland Steel Orchestras.

After a brief period in London, he travelled extensively throughout Europe, gaining first-hand experiences in concert promotion and management, working with many new artistes such as Jackie Edwards, Jimmy Cliff and Boney M.'

Reading the fascinating material on Mr Blacks, I was reminded of another Trinidadian: the talented steelband musician/composer Bobby Mohammed, who had also asked me to write his biography. I had considered writing about Bobby, but again funding was not forthcoming. Time was money. In relation to the Sonny Blacks' biography, I had had no more discussions and, unfortunately, the project went no further. Nonetheless I very much look forward to reading about Mr Blacks's life and times when the appropriate biographer has done his or her work and the book is published.

Still on the theme of Show Business, Pearl Connor, Theatrical Agent, and former wife of the Trinidadian actor Edric Connor, had insisted that I have a look at her Archive on Black artists in the theatre and television in Britain. Pearl and I were among the first Awardees of the Scarlet Ibis Award from the Trinidad and Tobago High Commission in London. Whenever we met, we spoke about the possibility of a book on her life and work. Sadly, this project came to nothing. But in addition to Pearl's efforts, my writings on Blacks and Asians were never narrow or confined. Necessarily, they were in principle, inclusive of intertwined histories, cultures and identities. As one who had consistently championed various causes over the years, now I felt no less involved than I'd previously been. In fact, July 2005, marked an historic moment: at last, the Mayor's Commission on African and Asian Heritage's Report *Delivering A Shared Heritage* was published, thus proving the doubters wrong.

The grand Launch was scheduled to take place at the Victoria and Albert Museum in Kensington, London. On that day, just a few hours before the Ceremony, Makeda Coaston, Strategy Officer at City Hall, telephoned me at home requesting that I arrive at the Museum around 2.30 p.m. A call from her now? Why? I wondered. But such thoughts didn't matter because I was already getting dressed to attend the event anyway.

When I got to the Museum Makeda said that she would like me to contribute to the Launch Programme. In what way? She explained that I would speak a few words, not once, but four times during the Launch. As a Commissioner, I accepted this responsibility. By now there was an impressive gathering of hundreds of Guests. Once more, I was among people regarded as the 'great and the good,' this time under the Museum's chandeliers as the champagne Reception got under way. As 'Big Nights' go, for a number of reasons, the Launch of MCAAH's Report held great promise. Everyone who was anyone in the Education-Heritage Sector, it seemed, was there.

After Mark Jones, Director of the Victoria and Albert Museum had spoken words of welcome and made his Opening remarks, a stirring African drum roll sounded to signal my appearance on the podium. I stepped up to the microphone and said: '*We stand on the shoulders of those who came before us. Let us celebrate* Olaudah Equiano.' I was followed by an actor dressed-up to look like Equiano. He recited passages written by the former slave and anti-slavery campaigner.

Then Mayor Ken Livingstone, who had appointed the Commission, was next to speak. He told the audience (among whom were key Government administrators, including a Government Minister, policy-makers and others connected with Archives, Libraries, Museums and Galleries Sector) about the Commission's importance and purpose. As Mayor Livingstone spoke, I remember sitting beside him just before the Launch proceedings began. In those moments, he seemed to be within himself, composed; and I was too preoccupied with my own thoughts to say anything to him. After the Mayor's speech, another drum-roll sounded. This time, the drum-beat came from an Indian Tabla, my cue to return to the podium. Once more, I said the words adding a new name : '*We stand on the shoulders of those who came before us. Let us celebrate* Dadabhai Naoroji.' An Indian actor followed me to enact an excerpt from Naoroji's life.' Afterwards, the Minister of Culture, David Lammy spoke about the Commission's work in relation to larger national goals. Another overture, played on a Chinese stringed instrument, preceded my third appearance to say the words that I'd spoken earlier, at the end of which, I added the name of Lao Tse, the Chinese writer. Then, for the final time, another drum-roll recalled me to the microphone to repeat the introductory words before identifying Olive Morris, the Jamaican-born activist and trade unionist. In turn, a woman stepped forward to speak about Ms Morris's life and work.

My four appearances were significant in that it connected the major speeches and dramatic performances of the entire Launch Programme. By the end of that long evening, I was both exhausted and excited, but thoroughly satisfied that having sat from 2003 through to 2005, the Commission had finally delivered. Of this achievement, from the outset, I had no doubt. Whatever happens in the future, I thought, the Report and Recommendations would stand as a record of our combined efforts and that evening in Kensington's Victoria and Albert Museum, was a celebration of the realisation of *Delivering a Shared Heritage*. Indeed it was gratifying to see in Chapter 5: 'Fostering Inclusive Education' the following statement: '*Peter Fryer's Staying Power, Rozina Visram's*

Asians in Britain and Ron Ramdin's Reimaging Britain, for instance, are a few overlooked volumes that detail an inclusive history of Britain and should be compulsory reading for all Teacher Training Agency (TTA) Staff and those in teacher training Institutions, the Department of Education and Skills (DfES) QCA and Ofsted.' Coupled with the PRO's *Moving Here* 'Briefs,' I felt that my life dedicated to such integrative work (and myriad other engagements) was fully justified; and, that now I had to move on and proceed with the job in hand. But it was so significant and exhilarating a night that I felt the need to pause a while for reflection.

Having been an 'early riser' since I came to England (especially from my first day of gainful employment) what was then unimaginable had become real: now retired, rising at the 'crack of dawn' was no longer compulsory. But I was faced with the question: how would I be affected by never again following the beaten paths along which I encountered many people on a day-to-day basis on the streets, on buses, tube trains and, more familiarly, in the workplace? Such thoughts were thankfully, only temporary; and in perspective the least of my worries for having long desired to write full-time, now I had the opportunity to do so. But pursuing this new way, clearly I would have to live on half-pay for the next two years before the Government Pension was granted. Until these tough months had passed, my problem would be: how to live on £100 per week? A grim, challenging prospect, to say the least.

Although money could not, certainly at this stage of my life, buy time, the trade-off of being able to write full-time had to be weighed against my economic dilemma. Pragmatism kicked in: Yes, I needed money and there was no alternative but to seek it. So once again, I visited Job Centre Plus and filled-in Questionnaires. But after doing so, I realised there were insurmountable difficulties facing me in the job-seeking process. Then one thing became abundantly clear: in order to complete my novel, there was no alternative but to forego the 'Job seekers allowance' and live *within my means.* This was the nettle that I had to grasp; and I did. The literary effort of finishing the novel *The Confessions of the Reverend William Wragg* was of the greatest urgency and importance. Why?

Because I had high hopes of it being a good, meaningful book; and therefore well worth the sacrifice. But there was also another important matter: *I had yet to find a publishe*r which, as I knew only too well, was crucial in achieving my goal of publication **before** March 2007! Why the deadline? Because this date would mark the historical milestone that was the 200th anniversary of the abolition of the African Slave Trade. As it was, the campaign for this 'abolition' formed the backdrop against which *The Confessions of the Reverend William Wragg* was set.

THE SEVENTH OF JULY BOMBINGS; HISTORY-EDUCATION; *MARY SEACOLE:LIFE AND TIMES*

My new life of being a non-British Library employee dramatized the passage of time and how best to manage it. Being older had not diminished, but heightened my concern with *time*. Indeed eighteen days after I'd left the British Library, as part of my 'working day,' I was determined to get into the Readers' queue at a reasonable time before the Reading Rooms in St. Pancras opened at 9.30 a.m. It was the morning of Thursday 7 July, 2005, and there was a tube delay on the Jubilee Line. Alternatively (and unusually) I boarded a bus on Kilburn High Road for Oxford Circus from where I took another bus to the British Library. It was around 9.00 a.m and travelling north along Tottenham Court Road towards Euston someone in the bus said a bomb had exploded in London.

At the next stop, a person who had got on the bus said that there was more than one bomb explosion. Where had these explosions taken place? There was confusion. No one could say. But soon the bus stopped before reaching Euston Road and passengers were told to get off. Of course, I wasted no time and headed directly towards the British Library. My haste was checked well before reaching the Fire Station on Euston Road, where a cordon and policemen barred the way of anyone travelling East: 'Stand back! No one is allowed past this point. Stand back!' one policeman barked at the ever increasing, curious crowd.

The cordon was about 200 yards west of Southampton Row, but there was a clear path southwards which I took still hoping to under siege.

Until recent years, mainstream British historians have been notoriously disinterested in the Black and Asian presence in Britain. When they did show interest, they betrayed a lack of awareness and respect for the works of certain authors. Worse still was the fact that being 'professionals,' a few historians with reputations, usually Heads of Departments, were not always the best persons to promote the broader view of history and culture. In 2004, according to the Director of the Runnymede Trust, as stated in *Delivering A Shared Heritage*: '*What I would like to see in two years' time is to walk into a room full of 200-300 teachers and not have a single one of them tell me that they can't find resources on Black British history.*' That very year, the Black and Asian Studies Association complained: 'We have learned from colleagues around the country that teachers find it very difficult to include the history of black people in their teaching. This is hardly surprising as generally they are themselves ignorant of it.'

In his earlier study: *How the West Indian Child is Made Educationally Sub-normal in the British School System* Bernard Coard had concluded:

'*The Black child acquires two fundamental attitudes or beliefs as a result of his experiencing the British School system: a low self-image and consequently low self-expectations in life. These are obtained through streaming, banding, bussing, ESN Schools, racist news media and a white middle class curriculum; by totally ignoring the Black child's language, history, culture, identity. Through the choice of teaching materials, the society emphasizes who and what it thinks is important – and by implication, by omission, who and what it thinks is unimportant, infinitesimal, irrelevant. Through the belittling, ignoring or denial of a person's identity, one can destroy perhaps the most important aspect of a person's personality; his sense of identity, of who he is. Without this, he will get nowhere.*'

Since this statement was made in 1971, in a multiplicity of ways, I have been addressing the issue, importantly through my books and lectures. Yet, the 'educated' among us, whom we take for granted and who should know better, persist in ignoring what was glaringly obvious.

When the erudite and popular historian Simon Schama published an article in *The Guardian* on 31 August 2005, my publisher did not let it pass without comment. Helen Griffiths of Pluto Press in her letter to *The Guardian* wrote: 'Simon Schama ("Death on the Grain Coast")...writes about the "forgotten tragedy" of Granville Town. Not by all. *Staying Power: The History of Black People in Britain* by Peter Fryer deals extensively with this subject. As does Ron Ramdin's *Reimaging Britain: 500 Years of Black and Asian History*, another stalwart...'

What makes this letter in *The Guardian* especially relevant is the fact that after the 'Voice of the Century' Lecture given my Mr Schama at the Queen Elizabeth Hall, South Bank, I had personally handed to him a copy of my book *Reimaging Britain: 500 Years of Black and Asian History* which Ms Griffiths had cited. Mr Schama had said he was flying back to the United States soon and asked if I'd 'left a note in the book.'

'Yes,' I said.

At this time, there were a few more episodes of Mr Schama's popular *History of Britain* to be screened. With my book safely in his hands, having been gifted the great opportunity of presenting his television history, I was interested to see if Mr Schama would, at least, acknowledge the centuries-old Black and Asian presence in Britain. To this day, I have not received an acknowledgement from Mr Schama about *Reimaging Britain*; and when the final episode of his *History of Britain* series was broadcast, there was no mention of any aspect of the *long history* of the Black and Asian presence. If Mr Schama had bothered to open *Reimaging Britain*, he could not have failed to see the connection between the 'Sierra Leone Experiment' and the 'Grain Coast.' To be fair, I can only surmise that he was either too busy or not interested in reading the book. More seriously, I wondered: was this another example of a more general, dismissive attitude and attempt to consign *Reimaging Britain* to being a 'rant'?

All things considered, the letter to the *Guardian* from Pluto Press did not surprise me. Essentially because, as I'd been arguing thus far, most of the 'highly-respected' British historians still did not see find my way to the British Library, which was tantalisingly close. Gradually, as I moved further south, I could see the remains of a red double-decker bus, its top sheared-off and jagged bits stuck out. 'That is the bus which was bombed,' a man near me said. The wreckage was very near the British Medical Association building on Southampton Row; and no one around me knew very much about what had really happened.

By now, as time ticked away, anticipation of that day's work on the final draft of *The Confessions of the Reverend William Wragg*, was so disrupted that I felt out of sorts. Uncharacteristically, for a long while, I stood around that morning seemingly purposeless; my thoughts suspended by the audacious atrocity of a bomb on a London bus. I had made thousands of journeys on these iconic red London buses and considering that I could have been on that bombed one, my need for more news about what was going on, grew. Now instead of being a frustrating day in terms of work on my book, like millions of Londoners, I was caught up in a mood of curiosity and disbelief, compounded by the fact that the horrible thing had happened at a time when I was just coming to terms with the shock of being unemployed! Although it was a bright summer's morning, shades of uncertainty were ever-present and threatening to unnerve me. That day, in many ways, I found myself in unfamiliar territory; and after standing idly by for more than an hour, I walked away from the scene of the atrocity.

Throughout the afternoon news filtered through; and by the evening, the television coverage provided a fuller picture of the horrors of the bombings. Reporters told of a 'series' of co-ordinated suicide attacks in London which targeted civilians using the public transport system during the morning rush hour. Four young British-born Islamic terrorists had detonated four bombs, three in quick succession aboard London underground trains at various locations across the city and later, a fourth on the double-decker bus that I had seen in Tavistock Square. Fifty-two civilians had lost their lives, four bombers were killed in the attacks and over 700 people were injured. The explosions, it was reported, were caused by home-made devices packed into ruck-sacks. Two weeks later, there were more attempted attacks. London, it seemed, was the Black and Asian experience, spanning 500 years as germane to many aspects of British life and therefore integral to *British* history. This lack of awareness or interest are among the things that I had been continuously trying to counteract; and sadly, to a large extent, it may help to explain why my repeated attempts to write and present such 'hidden' histories for the general public on British television screens never came to fruition.

Meanwhile, living with intermittent, at times, excruciating pain, I continued with my Tests at St Mary's Hospital. This ailment hastened work on the final Draft of *The Confessions of the Reverend William Wragg* and one fact that can be expressed in four words, loomed larger than ever: *money can't buy time*! This realisation put the value of the novel in perspective, in particular, my goal of completing the novel to meet the forthcoming Anniversary deadline. Thus 2005 was a watershed in my life; a year which saw the culmination of many things. Indeed it was a year that spanned 35 years of making various representations, including contributions in the Museums, Archives and Libraries sector in Britain. In essence, this reflected an extraordinary way of life underscored by a passion and determination to do a number of things that, in my view, had been in need of attention.

Just past midway in December, 2005, I had completed my first six months without employment; and during the Christmas break, I was plunged into depths of the unknown, anticipating the future, but also looking back. Miraculously, I had survived, I thought. Then I became more reflective; a mood that in the hectic years of my working life, I'd been too busy to engage with. And so things that I'd regarded as 'less urgent,' like the reading of certain articles and books, lapsed. For example, among my papers was an essay entitled 'The Role of the Individual in Society' which I promised myself I would read one day when I had more time: that time had come!

As I read, I thought of the Marxists and Socialists that I'd known who hated the idea of the 'individual.' They thought that one was a greater person for surrendering to the totalising effect of the social whole. 'A great man is great not because his personal qualities give individual features to great historical events, but because he possesses qualities which made him most capable of serving the great social needs of his time, needs which arose as a result of general and particular causes.' But Carlyle in his well-known book on heroes and hero-worship, 'calls great men beginners. This is a very apt description. A great man is precisely a Beginner because he sees further than others and desires things more strongly than others.'

I pondered these words in my quiet moments, of which there were now many. My readings took a more deliberate, emphatic turn towards matters beyond cause and effect to include philosophy: Greek-Roman, Indian, French and German. And in relation to the individual and society, the general and the particular concerned me much as ever. But my writings thus far regarding the Black and Asian presence in Britain in relation to Empire, labour, migration, settlement, race, class, colour and gender highlighted *groupings*, categories that led me irrevocably in a certain direction: not simply to recognise race and racism or sex and sexism and so on, but to something deeper, more elemental and fundamental to human social formations and life. This was revealing itself more clearly to me as a writer seriously and increasingly concerned with DIFFERENCE, with connectedness and belonging; with human rights and freedom. And soon, I began to see difference as *central* to life: to nature, evolution, civilization, to communities, to society and philosophically to the journey of homecoming. In fact, I now saw difference as the DNA of social relations and had thus coined the phrase: *What is common to us is our difference.* But was *difference* (and more fundamentally **respect for difference**) the key to so much as I'd been claiming for it? I wondered. The application of this idea and philosophy, arising from experience, study and observation to my writings thus far would, I hoped, continue to evolve and become clearer.

MARY SEACOLE: LIFE & TIMES

Soon after I had submitted the final manuscript of my book *Martin Luther King Jr*, Haus Publishing commissioned me to write *Mary Seacole: Life and Times*. And so, well in advance of the publication of King's biography, I began work on Mary Seacole. Adhering to a strict schedule of writing, I submitted the final manuscript on time and soon the attractively-produced Seacole book was before the reading public.

Just prior to its publication, in Britain the rising feverish interest in the 'Yellow Doctress' was fortuitous. The book opens as follows:

'Mary Seacole was born in Kingston, capital of the British island of Jamaica in 1805. She did not give us this year herself nor the precise day or month of her birth. She was shy of divulging such details and, in response to the question in later life, she wrote that "as a female and a widow, I may be well excused giving the precise date of this important event. But I do not mind confessing that the century and myself were both young together and... we have grown side by side into age and consequence."

In the early 19th century, the question of colour was a major issue in Jamaica...researchers have commented that in order to fully understand Mary Seacole's achievements, her work must be measured against the time in which she lived and the restrictions under which she had to operate. In 1807, two years after her birth, Britain had abolished the Slave Trade, but the institution of slavery persisted. In order to enjoy civil rights in Jamaican society at this time, colour was all-important and throughout her childhood and for the rest of her life, Mary would have been aware of its relevance...'

After traversing her life's journey in nine chapters: 'Early Life; Travels; Business and Nursing; Determined to Serve; Onward, At Last; Prelude to War; The British Hotel; Amidst the Carnage; Aftermath; and Last Years: Crimean Heroine,' I arrived at her life's end and concluded:

'Mary was buried in St. Mary's Roman Catholic Cemetery in Kensal Green and was quickly forgotten. Then, 67 years after her death, a shipload of Jamaicans arrived aboard the appropriately named SS Empire Windrush, heralding an influx of Commonwealth migrants including a number of qualified and trainee nurses. Although Mary Seacole was the 19th century precursor of these 20th century Caribbean nurses, few if any of them knew who she was. With continued migration and settlement the children of Empire and their descendants in the post-war 1950 era engaged in struggles of race, class and colour in Britain

and began to assert their identities and claim their heritage. There was a search for knowledge and researchers abounded. Thus history and culture came into play and answers to the migrants' questions revealed the hidden histories of heroic figures including Mary Seacole. In 1973 her memory was restored with a ceremony at her graveside; and in 2004, she was voted the "Greatest Black Briton." So, 148 years later, in post-colonial Britain, Mary's reputation is greater than it was in 1956. Tirelessly remedying ills on three continents, she was truly international, a one-off ahead of her time. In recognition of her heroic struggles, the Jamaican government had in 1996 awarded their Order of Merit to her. And as if in recognition of these developments, the long lost portrait of her, an oil painting by Charles Challen was recently found.

Whether or not she was the greatest Black Briton few could doubt the happiness and pride with which she demonstrated her Britishness. But while the particularity of her "blackness" is important, it was her enduring goodness of heart that is the hallmark of her greatness. As an individual, she fought prejudice (some argue she could have done more) and treated it with the contempt it deserved. It was her way of confronting racism, of trying to humanize negative "Britishness" which to a degree she had achieved when she won hearts and minds and became "Mother of the British Army."

Today the "lost" painting of Mary Seacole in profile is proudly displayed at the National Portrait Gallery which ironically was the former site of the barracks from which troops bound for the Crimea had left in 1854. This image captures the enigma that is Mary Seacole, a powerful evocation of the care-worn, but determined face of a matronly, self-possessed humanitarian.'

Ever since I had Interviewed Trevor McDonald in 1982 in my capacity as a BBC Journalist and having enjoyed his company on that occasion, as a fellow-Trinidadian, I had kept in touch with him through my writings. That 'Interview' was a marker; a time when I'd decided to continue as a writer instead of becoming a broadcaster. Having sent him copies of my latest books, including my biography of *Martin Luther King Jr*, from his ITN office in Gray's Inn Road, he wrote:

'Dear Dr Ramdin,

Thank you so much for sending me your latest books. And thanks for remembering our lunch in Richmond. I am so pleased you ignored my advice and stuck to writing.

I look forward very much to reading the books and I hope your career as a writer goes from strength to strength.

Sincerely,

Trevor.'

THIRTY-TWO

METAMORPHOSIS: FROM THE CONFESSIONS... TO THE GRIOT'S TALE

Six months into 2006, I increased my efforts to find a publisher for *The Confessions of the Reverend William Wragg*. Time remained of crucial importance and not surprisingly I'd become more anxious about the novel's publication to coincide with the 'Anniversary deadline' which was just two years hence. Then something quite unexpected happened. While re-reading the third and final draft of this second novel, I was faced with a major decision: either to leave the work as it was, or make a fundamental change. I opted for the latter and thus *The Confessions of the Reverend William Wragg* was transformed into *The Griot's Tale*. This was not an easy decision or transition for as a consequence, I had to do much rethinking; and to effect its reorientation, I rewrote the text. For one thing, instead of a third-person narrative, the story was now told in the first person. This was a major change which dramatized the novel's gravitas and timeliness; and after close readings, the final text of *The Griot's Tale* was ready for publication not just for British readers but for a world audience.

As it was, an Asian publisher, Pied Piper Books, expressed an interest, not only in publishing *The Griot's Tale*, but also a British edition of my first novel *Rama's Voyage*. It was the perfect arrangement; and I couldn't be more thrilled about getting both novels in the hands of the readers. The prospect was very exciting. Thereafter, the publisher and I agreed to meet and finalise plans for publication.

Having written to Zoe Wanamaker about my intention of writing a biography of Sam Wanamaker, her reply that 'there are two other people in the frame for writing Sam's biography' surprised me.

To be fair, Zoe had made no promises to me; and although I had thought it was wise to bide my time, her clear statement prompted a more determined interest and pursuit of my larger project 'American Visionaries: Paul Robeson and Sam Wanamaker.'

Since I first began writing Short Stories, I had had to learn fast; and now from the experience gained, the continuous day-to-day process of writing underlines the indivisibility of art, literature and life. Further thought on this matter, especially in relation to my proposed book: '*American Visionaries: Paul Robeson and Sam Wanamaker*,' left me in no doubt that fundamentally **art is a symbolisation of the experience of Being.**

THE GRIOT'S TALE: A FIRST 'BOOK REVIEW'

A few weeks after finishing *The Griot's Tale*, Dr Ariella Atzmon to whom I had passed a copy, had completed her pre-publication Review. She was the first person to see and read the book in its entirety. I had first met her at the time of her visit to the British Museum's Round Reading Room when she was researching and writing her PhD thesis. Soon after, she had read my books *The Making of the Black Working Class in Britain* and *Paul Robeson,* as well as some of my other published works. Now, many years later, I felt she was well-qualified to undertake the task of reviewing this second novel; and so with due respect and anticipation, I read Dr Atzmon's Book Review. Significantly, it was not a one-page summary, but an in-depth examination spread over three pages.

Overall, it was an unusually perceptive and well written appraisal of the novel. Among other things, Dr Atzmon's Review caught, in large part, what my intentions were in telling the story. She wrote:

'*The more ideas that can be drawn from a book the greater is the value of the book.*
Besides the pleasure I gained from reading The Griot's Tale, this new novel by Ron Ramdin, enriched me with many insightful thoughts about the written and the spoken word, the acquisition of language, the sense of belonging and heritage.
As a philosopher being absorbed for many years in the theme of language

and its vicissitudes, I was amazed by the way in which the intricacies of the subject were so poetically dealt. The Griot's Tale proves how sensitive writing thinks, respond and recalls poetically and has the power to replace abstract philosophizing about the human condition, knowledge and reality. The Griot's captivating tale starts in the distant past in Africa. In a saga style, this is woven from childhood, adolescence and maturity and goes through a long pensive duration of the protagonist being behind bars. It is a story told in a non-chronological order as a puzzle of weaved episodes written and recorded, told and retold as the life and times of the main figures are expressed in notes, letters and confessions.

The main theme of the book is the passion of writing. As the Griot says: "Perhaps the true value of my 'Tale' is that it should stand as a faithful record of the truth of my life and times, which I hope and pray I shall live to complete. Indeed I'd like the story to be passed on not only to those who live now, but also to those yet unborn." It is the protagonist's deliberate choice to shift his ancestors' oral tradition into writing. I would say that this choice marks the embodiment of an ethical act. By being engaged in expressing his most genuine reflective impressions through the written word and simultaneously the intensive attempt to get a hold on the language, the Griot encounters the sublime.

In and between the boundaries of the words freedom, liberty, independence and emancipation as contrasted with slavery, captivity and imprisonment, the novel weaves a plot that ignites thoughts about human chains, about diverse versions of confinement, and the many notions of being enslaved.

Despite the way the protagonist is treated, and the many wrongs done, we do not grasp any sense of bitterness or rage. The Griot is motivated by an audacious need to understand and interpret. The word interpretation emerges again and again as he craves to explore, to see **beyond** the words, to unveil intentions disguised by flattering words. The notion of interpretation is also associated with the way the Griot interprets the pursuit of preaching. **"It is not simply a new interpree-tay-shun, it is also taking a different position...where the Old Testament can be read and interpreted in different ways."**

With tenderness and compassion, the act of interpretation is carried out by the creativity of reflection. There is no binary, no absolute good and no complete evil; there are many positions and subtleties which one should reflect upon with empathy and good will. And thus Ron Ramdin presents us with the Griot as The Man that strives to be an ethical being.

The protagonist's life is enfolded as a story within a story in a non-linear style where unpredictability prevails. Through the plot we encounter the inexorable dictate of arbitrariness that authorizes all human lives. We learn that human existence is not an organized construction, where events are arranged by rational causality subsequent to the imperative of punishment and reward. There is no way out. As human beings we all are destined to submit to the rule of unpredictability. Therefore, the reader will not find fury or anger in this novel, but rather meditative thoughts, reflection and compassion.

This theme of the erratic nature of the human condition should provoke some thoughts regarding the arbitrariness of the legal system as opposed to morality and ethics. The Griot's Tale is the story of a case where the law is blind to justice.

The Griot's Tale is absorbing from beginning to end. The tension grows and the reading gets more adventurous from one episode to the other. In wonderful, fluent writing Ron Ramdin transmits the breath of those minutes in time, the odours, particular intonations of speech, where the reader can listen to the sounds coming from the crowded, lively spaces around. It is as if one has been taken for a walk from "Clock Face Circus" along Sugar Loaf Lane and up to the St. Hilda's Rookery area.

We may say that every novel is weaved around a specific theme or kind of plot written in a unique style, but it is rare to meet with a literary work where the plot and the style are a message in themselves. The Griot's Tale is a novel about writing a tale which is dedicated to the pursuit of writing. The Griot's writing is the courageous decision to replace the oral by the written word, where words say more than it speaks and means more than it utters. It is a quest for words where the search creates a melody that is read poetically between and beyond the words. There is something immortal in the Griot which is enduring. The sparks of the Griot's inspiration will keep coming together eternally revived as a new flame. The revelation of The Griot's Tale is that those *who can genuinely encounter with the sublime, do not die but are touched by that which is within us as mythical immortals.'*

With due consideration to the structure, style and characterisation, coming from Dr Atzmon who was based at the Hebrew University of Jerusalem, such a positive response would, I thought, after its decades of gestation, nudge the manuscript of *The Griot's Tale* closer to becoming a published novel.

Following medical Tests at St Mary's Hospital, Paddington, and the relief of knowing that my ailment was not cancer of the prostate, but a hernia, nonetheless the Surgeon informed me that I would have to undergo an operation. Subsequently, I learned that this could not be done as soon as I'd hoped. National Health Service queues for certain operations were, it seemed, not getting shorter; if anything, the chorus of complaints was growing louder as waiting times increased. Eventually, a date for my operation was given; and when it was done, I was mightily relieved!

Now, after the months of worry, I felt freer to refocus on the pressing matter of securing a publishing 'Contract' for *The Griot's Tale* which I eventually received from Pied Piper Books. This was the culmination of many weeks of phone calls and emails between the publisher and myself. Importantly, the Contract incorporated the publication of both *Rama's Voyage* (a British edition) and *The Griot's Tale*. The 'Agreement' was duly signed and I reflected on a publishing arrangement which was much better than I could have hoped for. All the more so, because the publishing Director assured me that in view of the impending 200th anniversary in March 2007, *The Griot's Tale* will be published **on time** to coincide with the commemoration. Furthermore, soon after we had signed the Contract on 3 July 2006, once again, the Director expressed his unreserved enjoyment of reading *The Griot's Tale*.

Given this positive response, I sent him a copy of the pre-publication Book Review by Dr Atzmon. He was impressed enough to say 'we could use it at the back of the book.' I agreed. A while later, he also said he had *three* African artists working on the Book Jacket. Again I fully supported his positive approach. 'We must get it right!' he said. Quite! So with utter confidence in the publisher's attitude towards the novel, I concurred with his plans. Bearing in mind the fast-approaching Abolition Anniversary deadline, we also spoke about a reasonably-priced paperback edition of *The Griot's Tale* to reach the widest readership.

In the meantime, at a function held in the Trinidad and Tobago High Commission in London, quite unexpectedly a Special honour was bestowed upon me. In my absence, on my behalf, Jim Mungal, a fellow-Trinidadian, collected the *Award for Outstanding Achievement*. Like the *Scarlet Ibis Award*, this was also an historic occasion in that I was among the first recipients of this Award which was bestowed upon only three recipients: the other two were Baroness Floella Benjamin and Rudolph Walker, the distinguished actor. Later, an article appeared in 'The London Mission' Bulletin under the heading: 'Trini…A Synonym for Excellence.' In commemorating our 44th Year of Independence, it stated, 'we highlight the past and present accomplishments of two high-achievers from Trinidad and Tobago: Ron Ramdin and Joffre HQ Chambers…' To be so appreciated, pleased me greatly.

Before the end of 2006, a wonderful moment came when Pied Piper Books presented me with the page-proofs of both *The Griot's Tale* and *Rama's Voyage*. In order to prevent any further delay, I worked intensely and, in great haste, to correct and return the manuscripts before I left London to spend a long-deferred Christmas with my parents in Trinidad. Ensuring that the proof corrections were done on time was especially important because *The Griot's Tale's* **publication deadline,** the Anniversary date was fast approaching; in fact it was just months away. Having corrected both sets of proofs, I posted them with due haste to the publisher. So, on leaving London, I was not only relieved, but also happy and hopeful.

While in Trinidad, over the Christmas holiday and early in the New Year 2007, I spoke with confidence to interested parties about *The Griot's Tale* and often the question put to me: when will the book be published? My answer was positive: 'Next year.'

But occasionally, as time passed, I began to have slight doubts; reservations about the publishing deadline. Why? Because even though there was no reason to doubt the word of the Director of Pied Piper Books, I had yet to see evidence of a draft of the much talked-about book jacket.

On my return to London in January 2007 after the *Trinidad Express* had published an article about the impending publication of *The Griot's Tale* (a copy of which I had, with due urgency, sent to the publishing Director) I was keen to express what had now become obvious: my growing concern, verging on worry, that **time** was of the essence. It was clear to me, and hopefully for the Director, that he needed to act quickly.

Hitherto, I'd done all that I could to impress upon him the importance of publication for the 'Abolition' Anniversary, now only a few weeks away. All the while, there was an air of expectancy about the 200th Anniversary. The media was awash with forthcoming celebrations and new publications of various kinds on African slavery. But now, instead of coming forward, for the first time, the publisher was reticent. Having been told that three African artists would be designing the book jacket, there was still no evidence of this. Nor did I hear any more about the corrected 'proofs,' in particular, *The Griot's Tale*. Sadly, my worst fears were realised. The Anniversary came and went; and as weeks and months passed, by the end of 2007 the book was still not published. Once more, I was let down by an 'Indian' publisher, this time, not in relation to history, but two impressively-Reviewed, significant novels: one of which had a twenty-year gestation and set in London, the other, uniquely about Indians and India! Regardless of such thoughts, I waited, hoping that something would be done, even at this late stage.

THE SHAKESPEARE'S GLOBE THEATRE CD

But having hoped against hope, eventually I confronted the stark fact that I was living through an unsettled an unsettling time of life. Then an idea came to mind: given the forthcoming Tenth Anniversary of the Opening of Shakespeare's Globe Theatre on Bankside in Southwark, after approaching the Administrator, I entered negotiations with Mr A and Producer Mr G, key figures at the Theatre, to do a version of the 1987 cassette recording of my Interview with Sam Wanamaker as a Compact Disc. This initiative, was a major moment for all concerned with such an historic project. 'Historic' because it was not only the first recording ever made on the Globe Theatre site, it was also to be the *first CD* production by Globe Editions, sponsored by Shakespeare's Globe Theatre!

To begin with, it was agreed at least verbally, to proceed with the CD Project on the understanding that a Contractual document was being drawn up by the men concerned in whom I had the fullest confidence. So while awaiting a written 'Contract,' I went along not only with the writing of 'Links,' but also travelling to the Pinner Studios in Middlesex to record the Globe CD version of my original cassette recording. For this purpose, at my urgings and with the firm guarantee of the Producer, I began and completed writing the 'Liner Notes' for the CD at the end of which was a Biosketch of myself in which I stated that *The Griot's Tale* was my forthcoming book. Mentioning the book here, I thought, was significant because at the time of writing, by going public in this way, I'd hoped it would have the effect of convincing the Director of Pied Piper Books that a quick decision was necessary. But before these words on the 'Liner Notes' went to press, once again, I was confronted with the nagging worry of having missed the Anniversary publication date of the novel. If not for the Anniversary, when was the novel likely to be published?

To be sure, for the umpteenth time, not only did I ring but also wrote to the publisher requesting that he finally commit himself to an *actual date of publication*. Meanwhile, I reflected on how quickly things had changed: Incredibly, just a few months before, at a function in the House of Commons to which I'd invited the publisher, we had both handed out flyers proclaiming the publication of both *The Griot's Tale* and *Rama's Voyage*.

Finally, when I did speak to the Director, I told him about the Shakespeare's Globe Theatre CD production and although much overdue, I took the opportunity of once more requesting a publishing date for *The Griot's Tale*. He assured me that 12 October, 2007 was his deadline. I trusted him enough because this date was, I reasoned, still well *within* the Anniversary year! Was I catching at straws? Yes. Soon I realised that I'd been deliberately and comprehensively misled. Although I had tried my best to speed things up, the matter unravelled very slowly, dragging on until finally after advice from The Society of Authors, I annulled the Contract.

Several months later, in 2008, by chance, I bumped into the 'publisher' at a special Black History Month Event at City Hall in London. I greeted him cordially and, at the end of that evening, as we were about to part company at the Tube station, he referred to the fiasco of his failure to publish either *The Griot's Tale* or the British edition of *Rama's Voyage*. As my train arrived at the platform and the doors opened, he said: 'I've been naughty.' These words were entirely irrelevant. Stepping inside the train, the doors closed behind me. It was the last time that I saw the publisher; a meeting which effectively ended my association with him. The question for now was: what would I do next with my two novels?

Starting from scratch, I began the search for a new publisher. Third World and British Publishing was described as specialists, if not the best publishers of certain kinds of books. Sounds perfect for my novels; and after much thought and some optimism, it was to this Publishing Company that I sent the manuscript of *The Griot's Tale*. Though it was early days, once more, I found myself waiting to hear from a publisher. How long was 'long enough' I wondered because several weeks on I was still waiting for an acknowledgement of receipt of the manuscript. Instead of being hasty, I allowed more time to elapse. Three months after submission, I enquired first to see if the Publishing Company had received the manuscript and was relieved to learn that they had. But of course, I was especially interested to know what they thought of the Synopsis and what parts of the book they may have so far read. Several weeks later, the publisher contacted me to say they had not had a chance to look at my manuscript; and anyway according to their publishing schedule, they were booked up until 2010, three years hence! Having already waited patiently and been strung along for two years by the previous publisher, in the absence of a commitment to publish, 2010 was much too far a projection into the future, I thought. More worryingly, if after four months, the publisher could just about acknowledge receipt of the manuscript, never mind being able to express an opinion on the synopsis of the novel, it was abundantly clear what my next move should be.

SPEAKING AT KING'S COLLEGE, LONDON

In October 2007 I received a letter from Professor Max Saunders, Director of the Centre for Life Writing Research at King's College, University of London. He invited me to speak at King's. '*For this 'Talk'* he wrote: '*I'm planning for 2007-08 with my colleagues... The general title is "Life-Writing at King's" but this year's focus is on 'Medical Lives.' The aim is to invite prominent autobiographers, biographers or writers about these forms, to lecture on any aspect of life-writing. We'd be extremely glad if you were interested in offering a lecture in the Series. As King's has a large Nursing Studies Department your biography of Mary Seacole of course made us think of you.*

The dates haven't yet been fixed, but the frame is mid-October 07 to June 08. We could offer you a fee... plus a reception and dinner afterwards...The Series is funded by the Alumni, and the aim is that the Talks should be accessible to the wider College community; though we anticipate the audience will consist mostly of people working in Medicine or the Humanities.

I very much hope you'll consider it. We had some tremendous talks last year, including ones by Andrew Motion, Ed White, Hermione Lee and Kathryn Hughes. It'd be a great thing for the College if we could tempt you to come this year.'

I accepted the invitation and the date agreed for my presentation was 26 March 2008 at 6.00 p.m. Having decided that the working title of my 'Talk' would be 'Mary Seacole: From Margin to the Centre,' just before Christmas 2007, I travelled to see my ailing parents in Trinidad. As I re-read parts of my Mary Seacole biography, I decided to change the title of my Talk to 'From Margin to Centre: The Mary Seacole Story.' This evolved in the early weeks and months of 2008 into a final draft which I retitled 'Mary Seacole: Medical Artist.'

As it turned out, on the evening of 26 March 2008, I spoke to a full King's College auditorium, an audience which included a fellow-Reader at the British Library, Ken Nightingale, who had expressed an interest in attending. (The name 'Nightingale' I thought was timely and interesting, because Mary Seacole and Florence Nightingale did meet in the Crimea!)

Once more, as I'd done in the case of Paul Robeson and Martin Luther King Jr, I took the opportunity of placing these personal stories in the wider context of Empire. With my understanding of British and colonial history, I reconsidered how a jaundiced view of multiculturalism had been preserved and perpetuated, as I had shown in my earlier Talk to the pupils at Hackney Free Parochial School. I knew only too well how many teachers and professionals in the British Education system were even now, lacking in knowledge of the dynamics of post-Empire British history of which multiculturalism was (and is) an integral, inescapable and therefore necessary part. And so, combining the particular with the general, I revealed to my King's College audience, hidden aspects of the fascinating life of Ms Seacole. In essence, this is what I said:

'In the process of reclaiming Mary Seacole's place in history, especially since the 1970s, many details of her life have become known and we have a fuller, more defined portrait of her. In this Talk, while I consider a few of the more familiar "details," I will also look at an aspect of her story that is either often overlooked or taken for granted in Mary Seacole's journey from Jamaican herbalist and doctress to heroic Nurse in the Crimea.

I first wrote about Mary Seacole 28 years ago and each time I re-read her autobiography and reconsider her life and times, I gain new insights. She is fascinating: frank, forthright in her expressions, bold in action, yet elusive. Yes, elusive! In spite of her fame, she was no social or political organiser. She had started NO mass movement. If anything, she looms large first and foremost as an individual, as someone who went about her way with a single-mindedness that leaves one breathless and full of admiration. Given the restrictive colonial society in which she was born and brought up, her keen eye never missed an opportunity and, in this sense, she could be said to be an opportunist. This, I think, is most important for in spite of the great odds against her, she triumphed and in so doing she has become an inspirational historical figure. Many superlatives have been used to describe her but who was this woman who nursed the sick regardless of background in many lands? And why and how did she make her incredible journey from the colonial margin of the British Empire to its Centre?

Researchers have commented that in order to fully understand Mary Seacole's achievements, her LIFE and WORK must be considered in the context of the time in which she lived. She was born in Kingston... (two years after her birth, the institution of slavery still persisted) and given that freedom was restricted to a small privileged elite in Jamaican society, in spite of her being in a relatively better placed position as a mulatto, throughout her childhood and for the rest of her life, Mary Seacole would, time and again, be reminded of the relevance of colour...'

At this juncture, and, for the first time since I'd been writing about Ms Seacole, I felt confident in putting forward the idea of a relationship between herself and 'Mr Day' (an Englishman) which I felt was perhaps closer than anyone had hitherto considered. And so I continued:

'On her return to England, Mary and her Crimean partner, the Englishman, Mr Day, with whom she stayed in Aldershot, were declared bankrupts. Thereafter, following publication of her autobiography, Mary Seacole enjoyed much deserved praise, publicity and celebrity. But, what can we say about Mr Day who, it seemed was so present, so central and instrumental at a crucial time in Mary's life? She mentions him some 15 times in her autobiography, yet he remains marginal, a shadowy figure. How important or inconsequential was he? Their "relationship" which lasted for many years, generated a closeness and confidence which, on Mr Day's part I think, bred an understanding and appreciation of Mary's uniqueness as a "Nurse." Perhaps, this is why Mr Day was drawn to her from the moment they had met in Jamaica, then in Central America, and crucially in London before they proceeded separately to the Crimea, where Mary would fulfil her destiny...

In this process of reclamation all aspects of the compelling Mary

Seacole Story demands our attention if we are to get closer to a fuller, more complete picture. To this end, the recent resurfacing of Charles Challen's long lost oil painting adds to and deepens our understanding and appreciation.

Another example of aiding our understanding, in my opinion, is Mr Day and Mary's friendship, partnership and/or close relationship, call it what you will, which raises interesting questions about Mary Seacole's journey from margin to centre. Long before War Correspondent William Russell and Punch Magazine had drawn the British public's attention to the extraordinary work of Mary Seacole, for better or worse, Mr Day had already sensed her unique qualities and potential greatness. Her performance on and off the battlefield confirmed this sense. Didn't Mr Day and Mary Seacole like and trust each other enough to commit themselves, through thick and thin, as partners in that risky Crimean venture?

I hope these considerations will not only shed some light on the shadowy Mr Day, but would also refocus attention on the perceived portraiture of Mary Seacole. Her legacy is too important to do otherwise.'

At this juncture, I quoted from my book Mary Seacole:

'...whether or not she is the "greatest Black Briton" few could doubt the happiness and pride with which she demonstrated her Britishness. But while the particularity of her "Blackness" is important, it was her enduring goodness of heart that is the hallmark of her greatness. As an individual, she fought prejudice (some argue she could have done more) and treated it with the contempt it deserved. It was her way of confronting racism, of trying to humanise negative "Britishness" which, to a degree she had achieved, when she won hearts and minds and became "Mother of the British Army." Today, as we look at Challen's painting, proudly displayed at the National Portrait Gallery, with the benefit of new knowledge, new insights and new interpretations, we invest the image with greater meaning! This is the inevitable consequence of engagement from generation to generation, in the ongoing process of reclaiming the inspirational enigma that is the Medical artist, Mary Seacole.'

The Talk was followed by a Wine Reception at King's College after which I was 'Guest of Honour' at a Dinner in a posh South Bank

Restaurant. A few hours later, approaching midnight, in drizzling rain Professor Max Saunders and I made our way to the tube station. On the way home I drew satifaction from my overall performance and the audience's warm reception of my knowledge and interpretation of Mary Seacole that were hard-won over many years.

THE *RAMAYANA* AT THE BRITISH LIBRARY

Between 16 May and 14 September 2008, an Exhibition of the *Ramayana*, India's great epic of love and valour, was held at the British Library. This was a very Special Event. As the 'Exhibition Guide' put it: '*For the first time, over 120 paintings from the British Library's lavishly illustrated 17th century manuscripts of the story are on display. The vivid, brightly-coloured scenes are packed with narrative detail and dramatic imagery: battle scenes with Ravanna, the ten-headed King, the monkey kingdom of Kishkindha, white elephants and exotic flora, and finally the moment when Rama and Sita are reunited.*

The Exhibition explores the story of the Ramayana and how it has been represented and retold over the centuries and in different countries and cultures, up to and including the present day. It is still regularly performed in dance, drama and shadow-puppet theatre around the world. The Ramayana manuscripts are brought vividly to life...'

As part of the Exhibition, on display in the British Library's Front Hall, were a number of books relating to the *Ramayana*. Among them was *Rama's Voyage*, the ***only novel*** on this theme; and as such, for ten weeks, my book held a privileged place in connection with this much-praised Exhibition.

Just over two months later, on the advice of an actor and screenplay writer who held *Rama's Voyage* in high regard, I wrote the following Screen 'Proposal:'

'*The Screenplay for a full-length movie entitled: Rama's Voyage will be of 120 minutes duration. It will be based on my novel Rama's Voyage and will follow the Indian boy Rama who makes a tortuous journey before he eventually enters the "coolie" ship The Trinity Hills at Calcutta from where he embarks on his incredible voyage overseas to Port of Spain, Trinidad.*

In this epic film, Rama will meet a host of characters (Indians, Europeans and an American doctor) including the English woman

Caitlin Fairweather, wife of the ship's Captain Timothy Fairweather.
Frame by frame, the film will evolve not only as an adventure story,
but will also deal with love and romance, displacement and belonging
(a key theme in today's global village) revelation and self-discovery as
the seemingly doomed ship and Rama moves closer to his New World
destination.'

Ma had been unwell for a while. Some months earlier, she had
suffered a stroke that left her partially paralyzed. After a period
of immobility, with the aid of a stick, she was able to walk a few
paces; and, as time passed, gradually she moved about with more
assuredness.

Through my regular phone-calls to Pa, I was kept informed of
Ma's condition and progress. I could not help remembering that
for nearly eighty years she had been waking up at the crack of dawn
to begin and complete all the chores she was expected to perform.
Now, though checked by her disability, the habit of a lifetime
persisted: she bravely showed her willingness and indeed attempted
to perform some aspects of her previous housework. I was amazed,
though not surprised, by her courage, but saddened that the stick
she carried had become so necessary.

Although the fee for my King's College 'Talk' had the temporary
effect of softening the hard economic edges of retirement, the
reality was that having foregone the Job Centre Plus option of
finding a job, I was forced to supplement my small pension with
intermittent earnings (as and when that was possible) until I was
qualified to receive the State Pension. Linked to my earlier decision
not to seek another job was, as mentioned, my determination to
finish *The Griot's Tale.* Having missed the Abolition Anniversary,
nonetheless I continued to press on with my efforts to get the novel
published. Eventually, the long gestation ended with its publication
as a Trafford imprint in April 2009. At last, I held the published
book before me with a sense of wonder, and naturally I recalled its
long gestation and all that had gone into its making. Opening the
book, I turned the first leaf and read the 'Dedication' to my son
Ronnie; and on the following page the epigraph: *'No future without*

remembrance.' Then the novel opens:

' *"Once upon a time…" The words reached me as a motherly whisper. They were inviting and enchanting. Magical words that foretold all manner of stories and I remember them now as among the first that I'd heard Ma say. But one day these four words were followed by another four: "there was a Trial" and the rest of a story which was the last that Ma had told me. In these years of story-telling, I remember her speaking other memorable words:*
"Look! Look!" she said, "Over there!"
"Where?"
"Look!…There!" her voice raised triumphant as she touched my shoulder and pointed in the direction of a blackbird, the sight of which I just caught as it took off from a branch of the majestic immortelle tree in blossom. The fragrance of this reddish-pink splash of colour perfumed the air and enhanced the daylight, a wonderful flowering that never failed to uplift me.
Ma breathed deeply, a sigh of regret. "It fly away," said she and was silent for a while. Moments later, she was more hopeful. "It will come back, son." For some reason I did not tell her that I did see the bird in flight that first day…'

The story is told from Books 'One' through to Book 'Seven' and ends with an 'Epilogue'.

In the final chapter of the novel, the Griot ends his Tale:

'*Tomorrow, the Prison Warder will come one last time. Tomorrow, the Prison Chaplain will also come to take me away. He will speak comforting words and will lead me to the scaffold.*
Tomorrow I will meet my Maker.
Now as I write, I remember proclaiming the Psalmist's words from the pulpit:
Blessed are the meek for they shall inherit the earth.
Then:
False witnesses did rise up: they laid to my charge things that I knew not. They rewarded me evil for good for the spoiling of my

soul.

*But now, with respek to the Psalmist, I Adamah, the Griot-Priest say for the last time that all of Ma's stories and experience has taught me the hardest of lessons: "Blessed are those who are **not** so meek as to think that they will inherit the earth without great struggle, for they too, are the children of God'.*

Is this hard-won inter-pree-tay-shun Blas-fee-mee? Or liberation? After all is said and done a man who feels free in himself, should express himself freely for a free man should not talk like a slave. And rather than wait for a dis-pen-say-shun from above, it is, I believe, the God-given right of those in bondage to free themselves.

I moved my legs and the rattle of the chains reminded me how leaden they feel; how deformed they've become since the injury I'd received in the "Great Sea Battle." I feel so weary now. My head feels sore, as if battered. Thank God the questioning is over. How tired I feel. Drowsy and drowsier, I sink lower and lower. Ah, the immortelle tree in blossom! A glorious, but fleeting thought. Then, shrill sounds stir me:

"Tweet! Tweet!" Am I losing my mind altogether? No. Is it therefore what I think? Yes. "Tweet! Tweet!" It is birdsong. How strange. I turned to see a bird perched on the ledge of the small window. Was it a mocking bird? Was it a jailbird? No. It was a blackbird! An exact copy of the one I'd seen so long ago on the island. My heart leapt! The blackbird cocked its head and took a long look at me. Then it was gone. In its wake, like a shadow filling up the cell, a dark depression overtook me and at this moment of my gravest crisis, Ma's familiar whispered voice consoled me:

"De bird Free! Free! Free!" said she, "not like we, lock up inside de Big House."

Then, as if it came from afar, I heard a humming sound and I remembered Ma singing "The Songbird":

"Red and yellow, blue and green,
Where oh where have you been
Oh my troubles,
Oh my woes,
Humming and singing as I go,

Sometimes high, sometimes low,
Bye bye blackbird."
I remind myself that for her the Blackbird was the spirit-bird, a "good
spirit," said she, "the carrier of messages to and from our ancestors."
Could the bird have been Ma's spirit come to say farewell? I comforted
myself with the thought.
Bye Bye, Blackbird. Goodbye Ma.

'Once upon a time…'

Very wearily now, I write these last words:
"Dearest Rachele,
Since my imprisonment, I've spoken little, but written much.
Alas, the time has come to say goodbye. You had warned me
often enough about my 'brothers' and now I'm reminded of my
favourite Tavern song about coming into the world crying and
leaving it laughing. I will always remember you fondly for your
courage, your jokes, your laughter, your friendship! Your LOVE.
God Bless the child. A little girl! And Thank God Almighty,
she's alive! God bless you. Be strong and of good faith.
Farewell my dear devoted friend and lover.
Eternally Yours,
The Griot."

It was late in the day and the cell was dark. I stood before the window
to face the dying evening light.

Weeping may endure for a night,
But joy cometh in the morning.
'Once upon a time…
This is a Tale to be retold.

The Griot's Tale.'

The novel's *Epilogue* begins:

'I, Elizabeth, daughter of Rachele has worked and lived for nineteen

years at the Manse of the Church of Our Saviour, residence of the highly esteemed Pastor…the Reverend William Wragg who passed away two years ago. My mother told me that I came here soon after my natural father had died…'

After Rachele had died, Elizabeth married Alfred, an African-American organist with whom she had a son, Adam. After perusing the Reverend Wragg's books and papers, Elizabeth concludes:

'On the front page of the first bundle of manuscripts the word "Confessions" was written in the Reverend's unmistakeable left-handed scrawl. Next to this bundle, there were six black-covered note-books tied together by a piece of white string. The first carried the title: THE GRIOT'S TALE.

I have just finished reading these notebooks and I am speechless. I am numbed by what is revealed. How wishful I am now. I wish my grandfather the Reverend Wragg was alive so that I could publicly acknowledge and thank him. But I ask myself: why did he not admit that I was his grand-daughter? Then, as I wallowed in my wishful thinking, I heard the church bells peel. They were ringing to announce that "Full emancipation" had, at last, come to the Griot's "sable brethren" on the island. I rejoice in the knowledge we now have for today we, their descendants, can celebrate. The sound of the bells was loud and clear as Alfred walked into the library beaming.

"I am overjoyed," said he.

"So am I," said I. "Thank god for this day!"

"A blessed day!" he rejoined.

As we embraced, Alfred whispered: "I hear the first "Coolie" ship from India has arrived with field-hands for the plantations. They are to replace the slaves."

I knew little or nothing about "Coolies" but I immediately realised the implications: "That's a great pity," said I, "but for now, it should not stop us from celebrating THIS DAY that had been so long in coming."

We sat down and remained for a while in prayerful meditation.

"Ma! Ma!" Adam called. "Look at me! Look! Look at me!"

I hurried to the verandah. Adam was running around in the yard below as the celebratory bells brought forth remembrance: I tried to imagine grand-mother Mina, my father Adamah, the Griot, and my newly revealed grand-father, the venerated Reverend Wragg. Then, as I reflect upon The Griot's Tale – I think of love and loss. I think of freedom and the meaning of bondage, for as the Griot said, "Slavery is also a state of mind." And that applies to both Master and slave. I think of life and living now and in the future.

"Ma! Ma!" Adam called out again before he sat on his favourite plaything: the wooden seat attached to a thick rope hanging from a branch of the old oak tree.

Moving slowly at first, he picked up speed. Then, as the tolling bells mingled with his carefree laughter, he moved faster, higher and higher; forwards then backwards. I watched, I must confess, anxiously at times, but with pride and full of hope, as the boy with blue eyes and black skin played on the swing.

"Once upon a time..."

This is a Tale to be retold.

The Griot's Tale.'

THE GRIOT'S TALE: BOOK LAUNCH IN LONDON

After the disappointingly anxious wait for its publication, the book was finally launched in London at the Trinidad and Tobago High Commission in Belgrave Square. Clearly to myself and those who had read it, *The Griot's Tale* was a long overdue work of fiction. It was therefore with a mixture of relief and pleasure that I emphasized its importance by saying:

'For three and a half centuries prior to the 1950s (perhaps with the exception of Shakespeare's Othello) there had been few works of non-white fiction and a notable absence of black heroes in British literature. In response to the view "that black people began coming to Britain in the 1950s and, as a consequence of this influx, a multicultural Britain had emerged," I questioned: Is this statement really true? What about the pre-1950 period?...It became clear this was an area of darkness that needed to be illuminated. Further reading confirmed that long

before 1950, there were few, if any, non-white characters in British fiction. Why not? I asked myself and felt perfectly justified in so doing when I learned that there was an estimated 10,000 black people living in London between the late 18th and early 19th centuries. More importantly, no novelist had bothered to write a serious work of fiction about that multicultural London when Britain ruled the waves and increasingly most of the world.

Given our Caribbean/British literary heritage, why this gap? I pose the question because this was a most interesting period: the time of Jane Austen, when there was much campaigning and comment on the great social and political issues of the day by popular writers and artists. National and local debates were polarised and apart from English liberals, there were few literate Africans who made their voices heard. But still there was no work of fiction about **multicultural** London of that time. Could it be that the novelists of the day felt that their creative work would have been seen as propaganda rather than art? This may well have been true but even so, it does not fully explain why 200 years on, such work was not produced. I was astonished by this fact and instead of perpetuating the erroneous view that "black and Asian people began arriving in Britain in the 1950s" I felt powerfully drawn to this early presence of people from different backgrounds who constituted the melting-pot that was London. Who were they? Why were they here? What were their fears, their hopes, their dreams? And how different were the answers to these questions in relation to multiculturalism in our time? The prospect was boundless. My heart raced! My imagination soared and my creativity was engaged.

So just over twenty years ago, I conceived the idea of writing a novel set in pre-Dickensian London, a story that would deal with some of the great themes of life and literature that have exercised the minds of humankind, themes that include love and loss, (lack of respect for) difference, betrayal and who is in bondage and who is free?

For over twelve of the twenty years since conception, the idea of composing and writing my novel glowed brightly, then for a few years it receded before the fire of creation was rekindled and burned so brightly for the last seven years that, in spite of a series of setbacks and a change of title, I completed writing the epic which is published as The Griot's Tale. This long gestation, I am glad to say, has justified the old saying:

"nothing ventured, nothing gained." And so, a gap in our Caribbean-British literary heritage was filled!...

Without giving too much away, I can tell you that the novel's main character is Adamah, the Griot (or African story-teller) who as a child is filled with wonder and curiosity by his mother's magical stories. As his life evolves and he is confronted with hard choices, the truth of his mother's stories are revealed.....'

Given that all stories are driven by time and in this sense they are historical, I continued:

'The Griot's Tale is, first and foremost, a work of art, a literary composition through which the Griot emerges as an exceptional figure, perhaps the most powerfully drawn black character in British literature, a man who is motivated by a deep need to understand and interpret his experience...'

After all is said and done, the book must, of course, SPEAK for itself. Ladies and Gentlemen, I now invite you to READ The Griot's Tale. Thank You Very Much!'

The book sold well for several weeks in the British Library Bookshop; and to my surprise, I was honoured when during Black History Month, the British Library invited me to give a 'Talk' to *members of staff* and sign copies. Prior to this extraordinary Invitation, all members of staff were informed through the British Library *Intranet* (the Library's email system) about the special Event entitled 'The Inspiration Behind *The Griot's Tale.'* Interestingly, before I had uttered a word of my 'Talk' 20 copies of the novel were bought and signed, something I usually do at the end of my Talks. A wonderful prelude! I recalled my Martin Luther King Book Launch and thought: how ironic that at one time, not so long ago, certain line managers (long departed) were against me using the Library's Reading Rooms and writing books. Through sheer self-belief and imagination, the transformative power of the art of literature had worked its magic. As these pages show, this latest 'Literary Event' in relation to me was but one more example of how I'd been instrumental over the years in initiating and helping to bring a change in perception among administrators and colleagues both in the British Museum, the British Library and elsewhere.

My next book promotion engagement for *The Griot's Tale* was in Trinidad. Before leaving London, I had sent a copy to novelist Earl Lovelace and, of course, Book Review copies to the main newspapers, including the *Trinidad Guardian* and the *Trinidad Express*. The two people who helped to promote the book were Ariti Jankie and Zorina Shah.

Returning to launch this second novel was an interesting experience. The event was held at the prestigious Trinidad and Tobago National Library and Information Services (NALIS) in Port of Spain which was, I think, the best venue. On arrival at the entrance, I was glad to see my friends Mulchan and Rebecca with whom I spoke for a short while.

Opening Launch proceedings, the Reverend Cyril Paul spoke about my rise from poverty to prominence and return to Trinidad with another outstanding book. The respected Reverend, Head of the Inter-Faith Religious Organisation (IRO) in Trinidad and Tobago, concluded his remarks with a prayer.

He was followed by Attila Springer, the popular young writer, who spoke appreciatively about *The Griot's Tale*. As the Launch programme stated, from a 'West Indian Setting' I read an excerpt from the novel. The next speaker was Khafra Kambon, the well-known historian, political activist and commentator. In his presentation, among other things, he pointed out that one of the strengths of the novel, so far (he had not completed reading it because of short notice) is the fact that the author had taken the reader back to a time in pre-colonized West Africa when the civilisation of the Griots had flourished.

Following Mr Kambon's address, I returned to the podium to read a much longer passage of the novel from an 'English Setting.' Afterwards, I presented Mr Kambon with a signed copy of *The Griot's Tale*. But this was not the end of the programme. I was pleasantly surprised and deeply honoured when the much-praised and respected Calypsonian known as 'Composer' took the stage and sang one of his fine compositions: 'True or Lie' in which he referred to 'Ramdin' and himself! As a youth, I had loved the lyrics and catchy rhythms of calypsoes and admired the style of calypsonians. Now, to have had one of the leading exponents (a Calypso-Griot!) sing for me and the distinguished audience, was beyond my wildest dreams. This may have been the first time that a Calypso was so performed by a performer of this stature at a NALIS Book Launch, especially for an Indo-Trinidadian writer! And so, by a twist of fate, my literary imagination which led to the creation of *The Griot's Tale* had, in turn, the power to move others.

After the formalities of the launch which was filmed, I was guided to a table just outside the Audio Visual Room where multiple copies of *The Griot's Tale* were attractively displayed. I was delighted to meet people wearing the bright colours of African National dress; and to see Ma, visibly much older, frail and carrying her walking stick, but remarkably happy and proud. She was very much in her element I'd say, as she talked easily with various people that she'd met for the first time.

Among the distinguished Guests were Winston Dookheran (Political Leader of the Congress of the People Party), Professor Ken Ramchand, Brinsley Samaroo, Willi Chen, an American Professor and Chris Laird. Many copies of the book were sold and among those in the Book signing queue were Winston Dookheran and the Reverend Cyril Paul. In close attendance were my sister Annette, Marlon and Mr Quan Kep who were most helpful before, during and after the Reception.

Before I left Trinidad, Reverend Paul had invited me to join himself, Alan McKenzie (former Principal of Naparima College) and Reverend Elvis Ilahie for dinner at a San Fernando restaurant. I have always enjoyed Reverend Paul's company and while discussing my novel, he commented on my 'trade union' work in England and the Griot's involvement in labour struggles. 'Isn't *The Griot's Tale* meant to be fiction?' he asked. I smiled and said: 'It certainly *is* fiction. Many black men were at the forefront of working-class agitation in late eighteenth and early nineteenth century England and Scotland,' I responded. But having said this, I thought it best to stop short of explaining the fictive process to the Reverend.

A few days later, another Book Launch took place in south

Trinidad; at the Carnegie Library (NALIS) in San Fernando. This Colonial building at the corners of High Street, Mucurapo Street and Harris Promenade was the southern Branch of NALIS. As a boy on my first visit to San Fernando, I clearly remember this red brick structure and was impressed by its solid, colonial-style façade. Interestingly, in all of the years spent in Trinidad, I'd never been *inside* the building. The plain truth is that before leaving Trinidad, I had no idea what that, or any library looked like. I never dreamed that one day I would be the Guest of Honour as the author of a major novel, there!

Ms Jennie Allen, the Librarian had distributed, in advance, several copies of *The Griot's Tale* to members of the 'Carnegie Library Book Club' so that when I arrived, the readers would be fully prepared to ask questions. Also present were the Trinidad Press personnel: journalists and photographers. Just before the Launch, I'd spoken to Ms Allen who said she enjoyed reading the book. Another person in the audience, an Indian doctor, perplexed about my choice of the main character in the novel, asked: 'Why did you choose to write about an African?' I answered: 'The novel is not about the Griot's *"race."* It is about his *humanity!*' At this juncture, given that the story was, in part, about multiracial unions and culture, a young woman, a Film-maker of mixed Indian and African parents said: 'Ron Ramdin should be congratulated for his courage in writing this book about the Griot, the African hero.' This vibrant woman had touched on the very essence of my book which was about identity, crossing boundaries and especially **respect for difference** with which I'd long been concerned and for which I have argued in my writings. It was this absence of 'respect for difference' that had indeed led to racial oppression and slavery.

Overall, the book was well received by Carnegie Library Book Club Members. But just before the end of the Launch, a man said: 'I do not want to spoil the evening.' What was he about to say, I wondered. The man continued: 'But it should be said that there is a group of people in Trinidad who do not like Indians writing about Africans.'

'Well,' I responded readily, 'such people should be reminded that Trinidad has long been a multicultural country and certain basic freedoms and human rights, hard-won by the people of all backgrounds, should be observed. The idea, arising from 'race' and racism, that only Africans should write about Africans is a notion that must be swept aside in today's diverse communities. This quest for *racial purity* here (and indeed anywhere else in the world) is therefore not only a sad commentary on multicultural Trinidad, it is also a redundant one.' Such an alarming attitude among many Afro-and Indo-Trinidadians towards each other may have inhibited greater success of *The Griot's Tale* in Trinidad. Throughout my childhood and since I had first left the island, I reflected: many things had changed, but some had not. Respect for difference remained the seemingly distant goal, but as ever, I hoped that attitudes would indeed change for the better, sooner, rather than later.

The next day I did two local Radio Interviews: one with 'Heritage' the other with 'WAQ' Radio; then a Television interview with Andy Johnson, a Top Presenter on TV6. By now, I had done many television interviews in Trinidad, but I always approached them with utter seriousness. Two years earlier, I'd been interviewed by Mr Johnson and local celebrity Morgan Job on a TV 6 Live 'Show' during which we discussed the Globe Theatre CD Version of my cassette recording featuring Sam Wanamaker and Paul Robeson. That Interview I thought went very well; but now Mr Johnson was my only interrogator. He was interested to know how and why I, an 'Indian,' had come to write about an African. Taken aback, nonetheless, I responded forthrightly as to what qualified me to write about the Griot, an African. Put simply, I said: I was born in Marabella and grew up amidst West African, Hindu, Muslim and Christian cultures, each influencing the other. At the age of nineteen I emigrated to England and had lived in London among Africans from various parts of Africa; and to date I have written several books on the African and Asian experience in Britain. This grounding, I told Mr Johnson, afforded me an understanding of what I was writing about. But apart from all this, *The Griot's Tale* is a story that I have created; a work of the imagination, and thus an expression of literary art.

'Did you have to take risks?' he asked.

Of course, there were 'risks' I said, because fiction, unlike non-fiction, is not a genre that deals with the certainty of alleged incontrovertible facts, but with the writer's creative vision. The story as a whole has to be *imagined*. When this recorded Interview was screened nationally a few days later, judging from comments made by many people especially Afro-Trinidadians whom I had met in Marabella, it was abundantly clear that what I'd said was well-received.

A few weeks earlier, Professor Chris Mullard had written to me:
'Dear Ron,
To celebrate Dame Jocelyn Barrow's 80th Birthday we would like to request your company at a formal Dinner at the Reform Club (104-105 Pall Mall) on Wednesday 22nd April 2009...We are writing today so that you can note this date in your diary and also make two requests. Firstly, we would very much like you to become a Founding Donor to the Dame Jocelyn Barrow (DJB) Trust which we propose to Launch at the Reform Club...Secondly, we are planning to present DJB with a Liner Americoron at the dinner on 22 April. This Book of Friendship will contain written contributions from relatives, friends... as well as a few statements that relate to DJB's public achievements...
We very much hope you can reply in the affirmative to our request, as we know you hold Dame Jocelyn in great esteem and appreciate as much as us her steadfast commitment to and work in the creating of a just and multicultural democratic Britain.'
Such a 'Dinner' would indeed be a fitting Tribute for Dame Barrow. How interesting I thought recalling the fact that twenty-seven years had passed since my first meeting with Jocelyn Barrow: the occasion being the launch of my first book *From Chattel Slave to Wage Earner*, the educational value of which, she had fully recognised. Since then, as passionate educationists, in our different ways, we have remained committed, and I felt it would be good to see Ms Barrow and to be in the famous Reform Club once again (the social meeting place of Britain's great men of power and genius), where ironically, one 'Colonial' would be celebrating another! Against this background, I responded positively to Professor Mullard's letter.

THIRTY-THREE

'LONDON: HOME AND BELONGING'

'*So this is London!*' I had said on emerging from the Underground train at the Archway Station. These were my first words when I saw the city streets on that June day of my arrival. What surrounded me then, was no longer a dream or expectation. I was in London and could hardly believe it. My heart-beat raced. And like a clock reset, from those moments, imperceptibly, I had begun to respond to a new rhythm generated by the energy and bustle of life and living amidst the overwhelming sprawl and complexity of the Metropolis of which the poet William Wordsworth in *The Prelude* had written:

'*How often in the overflowing streets,*
Have I gone forward with the crowd and said
Unto myself, the face of everyone
That passes by me is a mystery…
Amid the moving pageant, 'twas my chance
Abruptly to be smitten with the view
Of a blind beggar, who with upright face,
Stood propp'd against a wall, upon his chest
Wearing a written paper to explain
The story of the man, and who he was,
My mind did at this spectacle turn around,
As with the might of waters, and it seem'd
That in this label was a type
Or the emblem of the utmost that we know,
Both of ourselves and the Universe;
And, on the shape of the unmoving man,
His fix'd face and sightless eyes, I look'd
As if admonish'd from another world.'

The inner light that had guided my days in all weathers, in dense traffic and the ever-moving crowds for decades in the labyrinth of London (and wherever I had travelled to in the world) had brought me safely through to just past Spring in 2009.   In June, after publication of *The Griot's Tale*, I was invited to give the 'Heritage and Legacy' Lecture at the Museum of London in Docklands.   I accepted the invitation and began to compose my theme: *Home and Belonging in London*.   In essence, it seemed, my life and migrant's experience had been underscored by 'Home' and 'Belonging.'   In one form or another, these were persistent, enduring themes.   Twelve years before, when I gave the Whitbread Lecture *Homelessness and the Novel* in the Welsh multicultural city of Cardiff, I had said then: 'If expatriate novelists feel compelled to write self-consciously, it should not surprise us if the need to transform reality into a corrective art-form becomes less urgent.' For me, art is a symbolization of the experience of being and having not lived in the period in which the novel that I'm currently working on *Fields of Lilac* is set, through the imagination, the genesis and evolution of the story will necessarily come into being as a work of invention and inventiveness. It should come as no surprise therefore that this third novel is connected with migration and something that I had said towards the end of the Lecture: 'It is now thirty five years since I stood looking out at the shimmering bay for the last time as I waited to depart. Since then…I have been engaged in the fictive process, most recently in **creating** *Rama's Voyage* (the story of a homeless waif from the streets of Calcutta in search of a home oceans away in the new and hostile world of the Caribbean plantations) an historical, inextricable dimension of my own **imaginary homeland**.'

So given that difference is, as mentioned earlier, the 'DNA of social relations,' at this point in time in an increasingly more complex multicultural Britain, my focus on *Home and Belonging* for the 'Heritage and Legacy Lecture' was apt. By now, I had lived and worked in London for decades; and like the city itself, I'd been constantly on the move. Since my arrival, the hint of mist or haze that I'd first seen at the Southampton shoreline and more densely at the Archway Station, as well as the fogginess of the days that followed, added a touch of mystery to incomprehensible London: its huge structures: houses, public buildings, as well as its maze-like streets, parks and gardens. Everywhere I went, there were more or less wall-to-wall people; and with each day, I gained an added sense of the enormity of the place. Although I had had the privilege of views from above: first from the Tower of Senate House, then years later from a pod of the *London Eye*, the whole city was still impossible to fully comprehend. Nonetheless, seeing the streets at six o'clock every morning, at least six days almost every week for forty-eight years and, getting home late, I became more familiar with more places which justified my feeling that London was *home*, in spite of my complex relationship with it. Time and space; space and time. After living on the hoof, so to speak, and for so long, my attention was now fixed on writing something meaningful about 'Home and Belonging.' Given that London is a huge subject, where do I begin? I began with what knowledge I had accumulated and questioned myself repeatedly: what did I really know about this greatest of cities? This gigantic amalgamation of villages, neighbourhoods, districts and boroughs, criss-crossed by rivers, canals, bridges and viaducts, railway tracks (underground and overground) streets and roads.

As in so many other things in life, through hard experience, I learned that London meant different things to different people. For me, having been ensconced in libraries and innately curious, it was essentially a place of relentless learning; of continuous study. Put simply, living and working among books and having read widely, I had accumulated a great deal of knowledge about London which, according to some observers, had moved its inhabitants to produce the best that had ever been thought and written.

Peter Ackroyd, whom I knew for many years when he was a regular reader and fellow-author in the Round Reading Room had kindly signed a copy of his magisterial new book *London: The Biography* for me. In the 'City as Body,' he wrote:

'Some will object that such a biography can form no part of a true history. I admit the fault and plead in my defence that I have subdued the style of my enquiry to the nature of the subject. London is... half of stone and half of flesh,' which he adds is *'in a continual state of*

change and expansion...'

Given this continuity, the idea and experience of being at 'Home' in London had, over time, assumed different meanings.

Geographically, London is ever-expanding from 'Inner London' to the Greater Metropolitan areas. And while all who live within its borders are 'Londoners,' could London be said to be a 'state of mind?' If London defies easy classification, it would, however, be correct to describe it as a 'global city.'

But who is a Londoner? Many millions of people regard themselves as "Londoners," even if they live many miles from the inner city. They feel *a sense of belonging* to the city that had been a place of continuous habitation over some two thousand years. And in spite of its solidity, it can rightly be called a 'visionary city.' Among others, it has been home to William Blake; and if the whole world of nations and races could be found there, it had been (and is) fundamentally a city of 'misery and suffering,' so much so that 'The bowels of God had opened and rained down shit upon London.' Indeed it is a city of contrasts, where poverty and wealth co-exist; and where, as Blake put it, 'Without Contraries' there 'is no progression.'

Within this diverse whole, it is the atomic spring and inventiveness of *difference* that has generated and generates, the ferment of endless creativity. For the millions of people who inhabit the city, there may be, as one writer has argued, as many different cities. In fact, it is well-known that Londoners born and bred, who visit other parts of the city, experience 'fear and alarm.' Why? In part, because they fear difference. It is nonetheless, this totality and variety of life in London that matters. As James Boswell had written: 'When a person is tired of London, he is tired of life...' So London as the city of possibilities and vision is a reflection of the inter-connected world. Here, a multiplicity of human thought had been expressed in literature: poetry, drama and the novel, through the works of Chaucer, Fielding, Blake, Jonson, Smollett and Dickens among others.

London artists, as well as others engaged with innovation and change, have expressed their vision too. Ackroyd captures this relentless flow well: 'Some of the great stories of London concern

1334 · TURNING PAGES · RON RAMDIN · VOLUME TWO

those who have taken on new identities and new personalities; to begin again, to renew oneself is one of the great advantages of the city. It is part of the endlessly dramatic life.'

Another account, *A People's History of London*, laments the 'forgotten history' of the city as the '*world capital of revolution. In the eyes of Britain's heritage industry, London is the traditional home of the Empire, Monarchy and power, an urban wonderland for the privileged where the vast majority of Londoners feature only to applaud in the background.*

*Yet, for nearly 2000 years, the city has been a breeding ground for **radical ideas**, **home** to thinkers, heretics and rebels from John Wycliffe to Karl Marx. It has been the site of sometimes violent clashes that changed the course of history: the Levellers doomed struggle for liberty in the aftermath of the Civil War, the Silk Weavers, Match Girls and Dockers who crusaded for Workers Rights; and the Battle of Cable Street, where East Enders took on Oswald Moseley's Black shirts... a city of pamphleteers, agitators, exiles and revolutionaries, where millions of people have struggled in obscurity to secure a better future.'*

I too, in my half a century of activities, including my long-standing role as a working class leader and thereafter, have continuously struggled to make a *Home* here and secure a better life.

As a 'sacred city,' we should also be mindful of London's stark contradictions and continuity:

'*If London were a living thing, we could say that all of its optimism and confidence have returned,*'Ackroyd argued. '*It has again become the "Capital of capitals" in every cultural and social sense....*

The levels of the centuries are all compact revealing the historical density of London. Yet the ancient city and the modern city literally lie beside each other; one cannot be imagined without the other. That is one of the secrets of the city's power.

*These relics of the past now exist as part of the present. It is in the nature of the city to encompass everything. So when it is asked how London can be a triumphant city, when it has so many poor, and, so many **homeless**, it can only be suggested that they too have always* *been part of its history. Perhaps they are a part of its triumph. If this is a hard saying, then it is only as hard as London itself. London goes beyond any boundary or convention. It contains every wish or word ever spoken, every action or gesture ever made, every harsh or noble statement ever expressed. It is illimitable. It is infinite London.'* These are grand claims, but they may well contain some truth.

Hitherto, I'd read a great deal about London's social history, but against this background, I had to formulate my own interpretation of 'Home and Belonging' as an inhabitant of the great city. I did so by looking at that all too often neglected dimension - the Black and Asian immigrant experience (after all, if there were no continuous influx of migrants, there would be no London!) essentially from an historical/literary perspective. On completion, what follows is what I had said during my Museum of London Lecture:

'Some of the greatest works in English literature have been imagined and written in London. From as early as the 18th century, men and women from Africa, Asia and the Caribbean had walked the streets of the city and some were moved to put pen to paper. For them and those who followed, the idea of "home and belonging" in London had been a major concern...

Because London has been (and is) "the world in a city," exiles from Third World countries have displayed the compulsions of history-as nightmare most ambiguously. Such writers are among the literary sojourners in the countries of the mind....and the more prolonged the absence from his homeland, the more idealised and like paradise it seems...the expatriates desire is of course, rarely fulfilled. He rationalizes his continued stay in London and faces rejections with some resolution and with hope that success will come one day.

*Nostalgia is central to the Black and Asian writers need to invoke ethnic origins, to become rooted somewhere. But their eventual return to their Motherland, years later, exacerbates the feeling of rootlessness after realising how distant they have become from the local peoples' culture. Such a person therefore feel marginalized, **homeless** in both cultures...*

Some writers could not avoid the ever-present and encroaching power of their past, and other displacement. Not surprisingly, houses and hotels figure prominently in their work...

Generally in Third World expatriate fiction, the effect of exile on characterisation is to create characters as symbols, men as ideals, concepts rather than particularised characters....

*Though writers through the ages have used allegories, expatriate novelists have created them more often than not. There is even an inclination, arousing them to lead the reader away from the experience to an **inner**, less accessible world. On the other hand, there is the vibrant, creative language of decolonisation, of subversion. Expatriate novelists experimented with language, drawing upon the whole spectrum of English language from "Standard" English to patois/West Indian English and a mixture of both.*

*If allegorical, abstract, self-conscious writing and the language of the rootless and isolated were salient features of expatriation and **unbelonging** by the 1970s Grace Nicholls declared: "Anywhere I hang my knickers is home": And, of James Berry, it could be said that his work reflected both where he had come from and the sense of life and being in the adopted city. Coincident with such responses to London was the effect of economic change on the immigrant communities. Between 1971 and 1976, unemployment in London rose with the loss of some 300,000 manufacturing jobs. Inner city areas, such as Lambeth bore the brunt of high unemployment, "estates" that were **"home"** for thousands of young Black and Asian people. But if the migrants' past was a hint of their children's future, soon enough, first and second generation Blacks and Asians (hardened and scarred by the school experience) entered the world of work and unlike their parents, they very quickly rejected "slave labour" and "shit work"...In "Yout Rebels" Linton Johnson encapsulates this new attitude:*

"Rough scene,
Braking away,
Takin the day
Sayin to the Capital neva
Movin forward hevva."

Increasingly in the Seventies, the relationship between black youths and the police went from bad to worse: "Sus" laws were introduced and enacted with alarming frequency. Race Relations deteriorated and then came the "Riots." Through the Eighties and Nineties in London, among the most outspoken were Johnson and Benjamin Zephaniah. With his ear close to the ground, Johnson evoked the rumblings, as police, at times with brutal force, broke up social gatherings:

"When nite come
Police run dem dung,
Beat dem dung a grung
Kick dem ass."

Some commentators regarded these words unfavourably. But with the death of Stephen Lawrence and the worsening of inner city Race Relations in the years that followed, there was among a new generation pent up anger. In the poem "Down De Road" the internalised violence of black youth was expressed thus:

"In the heat
Of the anguish
You just turn:
Turn on your brother
An you lick him
An you lash him
An you kill him."

Disturbing language indeed!

So from the "rootlessness" and "symbolism" of the characters presented by Black and Asian writers there had been a change in perspective as increasingly they turned to realism: their characters evoking rebellion and remonstrance.

With all that was happening in their home-grounds, literally on their doorstep (unlike their parents with no homeland overseas to escape to) these youths had no choice but to stand their ground and with time, their resistance, stiffened. In other words, they were adding to their vocabulary: They were saying **no** to "Slave labour," **no** to "shit jobs"! And no more intimidating harrassments. We **belong** here! **This is our home!** A reflection of this heightened awareness of oppression was the timeliness of a number of poems…In the early Nineties, there were also the "Yardie Trilogy" by Victor Headley, novels' portraying a world of the poor having poor education, poor social prospects and drug dealing. A bleak vision? Yes. But, we should also remember those voices of hope, *including that of the popular Malori Blackman.*

Taken together, the words of the above-named writers express "home and belonging" from different perspectives and at different times. For myself as a writer, my understanding of "home and belonging" is that to belong is to feel an integral part of, or, at least to be engaged to some meaningful degree with the community. To participate is to feel represented.

For those who practice the art of writing, why is so much black and Asian writing side-lined by the Publishing industry? For instance, not taken on and promoted by Literary Agents and mainstream publishers? In other words, why are these writers not better represented in British publishing? Is it really true that the Gate-keepers in the publishing industry believe that Black and Asian writing is largely a predictable rant and therefore not publishable? It comes as no surprise that one of Zephaniah's poems is entitled: "Political Poetry." Such a description of literature reminds me of Toni Morrison's clarity of expression in **Playing in the Dark**: *"Excising the political from the life of the mind is a sacrifice that has proven costly…a criticism that needs to insist that literature is not only "universal" but also "race free," risks lobotomising that literature and diminishes both the art and the artist." Thus literature in relation to British publishing, like African and Asian Heritage in London, is still placed in an exclusive rather than an* **inclusive** *relationship. The problem with Black and Asian Literature as with African and Asian Heritage in London had been (and is): How to mainstream it?*

Far from "Colonizin Englan in Reverse" as Louise Bennett, the Jamaican poet had memorably written, here in London, especially among black youths, the growing, deepening sense of UN-BELONGING is starkly reflected in acts of seemingly mindless violence.

Since Olaudah Equiano, Robert Wedderburn and Ram Mohun Roy had penned their words, in its making and re-making, London has been "HOME" for generations of black and Asian people.

The eighteenth century scribes and Mary Seacole were the precursors of those novelists, poets and writers, who followed. Historically, their voices have reflected the concerns of their times and this, it seems, is echoed today as many Londoners' struggle for integration, not assimilation,

Thus the quest for home and belonging in London is ongoing. And given the excitements and hope it inspires, this great eternal city will no doubt continue to inhabit the minds of writers in their feverish pursuit of both real and imaginary homelands.'

My presentation at the Docklands Museum in Canary Warf was so well received that afterwards a queue had formed and *all* the available copies of my novel *The Griot's Tale* were sold! This success led to the Museum's Bookshop manager ordering several copies. On my way home, walking through and past the splendid shops and sky-scraper setting of Canary Wharf (an impressive display of riches), I was sharply reminded of the ever-changing nature of London. Ironically, this was where West Indian sugar, molasses and rum (produced by African slaves and their descendants and indentured Indians and their descendants) flowed in and was stock-piled in warehouses over centuries. Thus *The Griot's Tale*, the theme of my Lecture *Home and Belonging in London* and the venue of its delivery, could not be more fitting.

'PLEASE SIGN MY BOOK-PLATE;' THE PHILADELPHIA FILM FESTIVAL

Soon after the Museum of London Lecture, out of the blue, from the Cotswold in Gloucestershire, Graham Young, a reader of my Mary Seacole biography was sufficiently moved to put pen to paper. On 16th June 2009, he kindly wrote to me:

'Dear Mr. Ramdin,

I very much enjoyed your book "Mary Seacole." I was born in Jamaica at Half Way Tree in 1935 of a Scottish father and English mother and came to UK when I was 6 weeks old and finally when I was 18 months. Even so I have a great interest in the country and in nursing – I married a Nursing Sister in 1962.

I found the book very interesting, if at times depressing. At p.1 "It took 3 generations to become a Jamaican white by law." I'm ashamed to say that both my parents were prejudiced until they died which I found very sad.

Mary Seacole was a quite remarkable woman and your story was a wonderful account. Well done: I'm sure it will do well – it certainly deserves to.

Would you please sign my book-plate.
Kind regards,
Yours sincerely
Signed
G.C.M Young.'

So meticulous a reader was Mr Young that he added: 'p.s. I spotted a typo at p. 20 first line "unplanned" has only one "n." To have survived the scrutiny of Mr Young with just this error was an achievement. It is easy to overlook such things; and to this discerning reader I was grateful.

As if I were riding the crest of a wave, on 28 August 2009 a 'Profile' of me entitled: ***Black Champion Who is Little Known Outside the World of Books*** was published on the Internet site, the *Latest. Com*. It was written by Clara Arokiasamy, formerly of the Heritage Lottery Fund. In part it read:

'Today is Trinidad and Tobago Emancipation Day. How fitting then that I should tell you about a man who has championed the contribution made to Britain by African and Asian Caribbean people yet it is little known outside literary and black political circles.

The publication of Ron Ramdin's new book The Griot's Tale coincides with Emancipation Day which commemorates the freeing of slaves of African origin. It is the latest novel from the British historian, biographer and novelist of Indo-Caribbean origin and provides a timely opportunity to draw attention to his works...

As I parted company with Ramdin at central London's Malabar Junction Restaurant close to the British Museum, I could not help wondering why, despite his achievements, this tall charismatic Indo-Trinidadian London resident remains a relatively unknown figure to the capital and the UK. Why are his books not used more widely in schools and museums and read by more adults, many of whom, still seem to believe that African and Asian people first came to the UK in the 1950s.'

Why, indeed are my books not more widely used in schools and museums?

For seventeen years I had been a resident in Northwest London and the *Brent Magazine*, a free publication 'for people who live and work' in the Borough of Brent, was supportive of my novel *The Griot's Tale*. With the front cover image of the Griot's mask spread over nearly half of its 'Competitions' page, the *Magazine's* editor informed readers of the story of *The Griot's Tale*. In relation to the Competition, the editor wrote: *'Author Ron Ramdin has intertwined Regency London with the Caribbean in his magical new novel.* **The Griot's Tale** *is a novel about* **multicultural London***. It tells the story of Adamah who is a Griot – a traditional story teller in African societies. With his Master, he makes the journey from the slave plantations of the Caribbean to England where he gains his freedom. The novel explores the Griot's life in Regency England as it twists and turns and he begins to reveal his special tale.*

Ron Ramdin who was born in Trinidad and now lives in Brent is the internationally known Author of other books, non-fiction and fiction, visit www.ronramdin.com

We have five copies of The Griot's Tale to give away. To win a copy of the book please answer this question. What is a Griot?'

In this November issue of the *Brent Magazine,* the Competition deadline was Friday 13 November. That would be a lucky Friday, I thought, for five people who, after reading the novel would hopefully pass it on to readers who were not so lucky. To add to the book's circulation and thus dissemination of the ideas it contained, the local bookseller Kilburn Books, in both its Kilburn High Road and Willesden shops, stocked *The Griot's Tale*; and the Librarian at Willesden Public Library had written to say the novel was now in their Collections. I drew the greatest satisfaction from knowing that the book was being *read,* rather than anxiously waiting and hoping that it would become a money-spinner.

As I had done the year before, over the Christmas holidays, I continued to work on a draft of my autobiography. The working title was: 'Making a Difference' though at this time, I was still veering strongly towards changing it either to 'The Stuff of Dreams' or 'Stuff of Dreams.' For several weeks into the new year, with renewed efforts, I worked without interruption on the autobiography, knowing well how quickly my writing priorities tended to change. At this time, I alternated between two half-finished projects, hoping to complete them before giving my full attention to this autobiography.

A PLAY: *PLAYING THEIR PARTS*:
SAM WNAMAKER REMEMBERS PAUL ROBESON

In March 2010, I contacted American-based film-maker, Cathy Sita Ram, whom I'd met at my Carnegie Library Book launch in San Fernando, Trinidad. I had sent her a copy of my newly-written play *Playing Their Parts: Sam Wanamaker Remembers Paul Robeson*, hoping that we could perhaps get it to a Producer who would not only consider its merits as a theatre production, but also as a film.

The play, constructed along the lines of an 'Interview Format,' relate to my meeting with Sam Wanamaker and the dialogue that followed including his thoughts and memories of Paul Robeson. My Synopsis of this Two-Man play in Three Acts is as follows:

'PLAYING THEIR PARTS

"*The artist must take sides*".
   Paul Robeson 1938.

"*I think everything we do has to have some relationship to society*".
   Sam Wanamaker Talks to Ron Ramdin at Shakespeare's Globe Theatre 1987.

RON RAMDIN, the historian, biographer and novelist, was in the final stages of researching his book on Paul Robeson and, after many attempts, at last one Saturday in the Spring of 1987, he made his way to meet Sam Wanamaker, the Founder of Shakespeare's Globe Theatre in London...For Ramdin, this was to be the last of a series of high profile interviews, including his meeting with Dame Peggy Ashcroft who was cast as Desdemona opposite Robeson, the first time he had played Othello in 1930.

At the time, the only knowledge that Ramdin had of Wanamaker in relation to Robeson were bald references to them as leading actors in Othello. Nonetheless for Ramdin there was something tantalising about being granted the opportunity of speaking with Wanamaker about Robeson. Why? Ramdin could only say it was a gut feeling that propelled him towards the Globe Theatre that morning 23 years ago. Since then, he has often reflected not only on what was revealed, but also the forthright and refreshing manner in which Wanamaker had spoken. Eventually Ramdin decided that the time had come to write **Playing Their Parts: Sam Wanamaker Remembers Paul Robeson**, a... play exploring the themes of art, acting and Shakespeare's Othello, with Special reference to the 1959 Stratford-upon-Avon production in which Robeson and Wanamaker starred.

Wanamaker was "thrilled" by the prospect of playing opposite his illustrious countryman. By this time, Robeson was in his Sixties and had been unwell for some time. But in spite of the emotionally fragile state he was in and the physical demands of Shakespeare's play, he prepared to face his most testing theatrical challenge.

Playing Their Parts reveals how the two Americans came together; and Wanamaker tells in fascinating detail, the story of the pre-production session he had had with Robeson as they talked about "emotional things" relating to their parts, the various scenes, improvisation and their characters. There were "problems" and Wanamaker spoke his mind about Robeson's approach and his understanding and delivery of Shakespeare's lines. Overall their rehearsals was an intense collaborative effort. Then, as now, the question was: what would be the outcome? From his professional vantage point, what was Sam Wanamaker's verdict on Robeson's final performance as Othello? Sam's answer was characteristically frank.

Set in the decades of the Forties and Fifties of the last century, **Playing their Parts**, evokes powerfully the connection between life and art which resonates powerfully today. It is at once historical and contemporary, instructive in many ways for a younger generation who seek answers to questions about themselves and the world they have inherited.

Paul Robeson died in 1978. Sam Wanamaker died in 1993. Both great Americans had lived through wars and struggled against segregation, racism, fascism and through the chilly years of the Cold

War. The bleak black and white world of their times, is a far cry from our multicoloured world, particularly the America of today, which has seen the recent Presidency of Barack Obama. In their lives Wanamaker and Robeson had played many parts and, as artists, they took sides. As Sam said to me: "If the performance does not reflect social reality, it is not art."

Playing Their Parts *is a powerful evocation of their legacy...'*

After receiving and reading my play, Film-maker Ms Sita Ram responded by saying that 'the universe has opened for you.' By this, she meant that the Philadelphia Film Festival Organisers were interested in presenting a One-Hour 'Staged Reading' of *Playing Their Parts* in the Ball Room of the Philadelphia Hilton Hotel during the 'Festival' in June. Obviously they liked the play. '*The universe has opened for you!*' The words evoking possibilities had a marvellous resonance. It was the opportunity of a lifetime; and I agreed with what was next proposed: 'Should we go ahead with casting?' Ms Sita Ram asked. She meant placing an advertisement in the 'trade paper' for actors in America who would read the parts of the principals in the play - Sam Wanamaker and myself.

'Yes,' I replied. Ms Sita Ram then asked me to provide a physical description of myself, so that she could place both advertisements in the paper in the hope of recruiting the appropriate actors. What exciting prospects could this important step bring?

Having set this process in motion for the forthcoming Philadelphia Film Festival, more immediately, my attention was turned to an important public event in London.

AN 'INDIAN ARRIVAL DAY' LIKE NO OTHER

Indian Arrival Day (a Public holiday in Trinidad) was about to be celebrated among Trinidadians in London. As I'd done at Kingsley Hall, East London in 2004, now I was honoured once more by the High Commission of Trinidad and Tobago which requested that I give the 'Keynote Address.' While composing this 'Address,' the General Elections results were announced in Trinidad. Unlike previous Elections, since the country had gained Independence in 1962, this year 2010 was different: there was a general feeling that the political mood in the country had shifted; and the results proved it. For the first time, Trinidad and Tobago's Prime Minister was a woman: her name, Ms Kamla Bissessar-Persad. Politically, this change was seismic and timely. The juxtaposition of an *Indian* woman Prime Minister on the eve of Indian Arrival Day was extraordinary. It was in these circumstances that I found myself sitting in one of the front row seats in The Tabernacle, West London, awaiting the start of the 'Arrival Day' event.

Before delivering the 'Address,' I was introduced to the new (Acting) High Commissioner Ms Serena Joseph-Harris. While talking with her she commented on my largely unaffected accent. Whatever that meant, her adopted American accent was pronounced and, of course, my hope was that the 'Address' I was about to deliver would indeed be enunciated clearly enough to be understood.

Given the confluence of factors attending this Indian Arrival Day Celebrations, after mounting the stage, I began:

*'Good Afternoon. Your Excellency Ms Serena Harris, Distinguished Guests, Ladies and Gentlemen. In 1838 when African slaves in the Caribbean plantations were Emancipated, Planters faced a major problem: **how to produce sugar without slaves**. The solution, as they saw it, was the introduction of Indian indentured workers which led to the institution of a new system of slavery. The theme of my Lecture this evening is: "**Homelessness, Arrival and Belonging**."*

India is a long way from the Caribbean and in spite of the Indians' long-standing presence in the region, by the late 1970s, the history of Indians in Trinidad was still relatively unknown... Today, Indo-Caribbean history is better known. Nonetheless the growing number of factual accounts, valuable as they are, present only a part of the story. Why? Because history is essentially based on evidence; and there are gaps in the evidence. Where history ends, story begins! Historians tell us what happened. The novelist tells us how the characters feel: how they think and act. It is this dimension (especially in relation to the Indians' motivation to migrate and their experience of the journey from India to Trinidad) that had been missing. One hundred and fifty nine years later, this pre-Arrival story, portrayed in a work of fiction was, at last written and published in 2004 as Rama's Voyage... Because the novel is essentially the story of a boy's homelessness, his feelings of unbelonging is the push factor in his decision to leave India. The boy's name is Rama and the novel opens with these words: "While many people consciously seek the truth, there are those to whom it is, in an extraordinary way, revealed." At every step of the way in his extraordinary journey through life, Rama is enlightened by revelation. For me, writing such a story posed many interesting questions: What was Rama's life like before he reached Calcutta? What was he doing in Calcutta? And why did he decide to get on a "Coolie ship" bound for Trinidad?

I will read from... sections of the novel. In the first extract, Rama is at the Immigration Compound awaiting departure... Rama boards the ship which left the port of Calcutta (the beginning of) his long voyage. "By any standard, this was a stern test of courage and after more than three months at sea, at last, land was sighted... When Rama's feet touched the land, he felt again a certain strangeness mingled with the familiarity of being on solid ground. But this earth was different! This was Trinidad and contact with it aroused feelings of gain and loss. Rama allowed himself one more glance at the ship. With relief and a rising sense of expectation, he strode towards one of the waiting bullock-carts, which stood against the backdrop of mountains. The prominence of this feature of the landscape surprised him, all the more, because he was, until now, paying closer attention to those immediately around him. The sun's rays were now behind him and facing north, he felt compelled to look up at the great height of greenness rising before him. He saw what the old man and the Guru had said he would one day see. And there it was! Like the Himalayas, he was overwhelmed by the sight of majestic mountains, the island's Northern Range, its highest reaches disappearing amidst a confusion of swirling, smoky mist and fast moving clouds. And like the Himalayas, here too, metaphorically, as the old man had put it, the earth met the sky. Rama was powerfully reminded and felt compelled now to think again about the mighty and mysterious Himalayas of India and the Guru's message:

"Mountains, swirling mist, cloud and sky portend,
That other place where homelessness would end."

He was lost for words. And to his amazement, above the mountains, as if girding it, a brilliant rainbow appeared... Whatever promise this held, he felt there was something extraordinary about him being there.

And from that moment, his interest in, and fascination for this land, was enlivened. That evening on entering the barrack room, Rama felt as if he was back in the belly of the ship. But now grounded, he remembered the Guru's words: "That other place where homelessness would end." Was this home? he questioned. Later, when the barrack-dwellers had fallen asleep, Rama lay wide awake listening to his shipmate's snores and sounds of frogs, crickets and owls; sounds now near, then deceptively far away. But above it all, he heard again Rajkumari's gentle, soothing voiced singing a familiar song of his childhood, no longer as a lullaby, but as she sang it more and more as he grew older, repeating the last two lines:
**"In search of the truth he will roam,
Until one day, he will find the Truth and a Home"** ...

How strange and confusing it must have seemed for this young immigrant. How unreal must it have been to be off the ever-tilting ship. Clearly, he did not consciously seek the "Truth" which was in an extraordinary way revealed…What follows, is the…final reading from the novel; the last paragraph.'

After this reading, I continued:

*'…While many Indian immigrants who came to Trinidad in the period 1845-1917 returned to India, the vast majority decided to stay. Removed from their Indian homeland, in Trinidad, the migrants were generally confronted with a double foreignness: a foreignness of place and language. Their isolation on the estates and their sense of separation had ensnared them in a "linguistic cocoon." Thus their distance from the wider society was bound to promote ethnic identity. Not surprisingly, like Afro-Trinidadians (who had invented their own Creole language) the Indians of necessity had to **create** new linguistic forms to give expression to aspects of their lives; and so through their languages they began to signify the manner in which they encountered and transformed their social reality. In turn, the way in which they articulated that reality, determined the manner in which they arrived at their sense of their people-hood and consciousness.*

Thus they developed a shared language known as "plantation

Hindustani" which facilitated communication irrespective of regional or caste origins. And so the Hindi dialect of Eastern Bihar, known as Bhojpuri became the Indian lingua franca in Trinidad. But with the spread of education and the changing perceptions of new generations, English has continued to be integrated and absorbed into what can be termed the Indo-Creole language which today is spoken by everyone in the various communities.

But if separation, arising from the economic demands of the sugar plantations had led to the Indians' estrangement from the wider society, there was always the possibility of closer alliances between Afro-and Indo-Trinidadians. Before and since the early 1980's, attempts at coming together have, of course, continued for difference and diversity so characteristic of Trinidad and Tobago must be cherished.

Having given this account, I concede that different writers will interpret the Indians' arrival, presence and contribution in Trinidad and Tobago differently. Rama's Voyage is uniquely my pre-Arrival novelistic presentation which goes beyond an historical understanding. It gets to a deeper truth, the truth of the heart. So now as I engage with writing my new novel "Fields of Lilac" (the sequel to Rama's Voyage) I am reminded of the following quote about the importance of the novel: "A novel is an exceedingly ordinary thing: it wades through lived experience," wrote Peter Nadas. Many agree that the novel certainly does wade through "lived experience." But is the novel an "exceedingly ordinary thing? Ordinary only if we mean that it arises from an individual's experience and speaks to everyone's need to understand why we must die, while yet we want to live." In his essay "Humane Literacy," George Steiner writes "All great writing springs from the harsh contrivance of spirit against death, the hope to over-reach time by force of creation." All great reading also "springs from that same source and in a great novel we readers participate with the writer in the "harsh contrivance of spirit against death." Art does no save us, but in our time art preserves for us a space in which we can be reminded of the story that is told by human beings in search of their humanity and the truth of their existence. It reminds us that the search is crucial to the love of life and that love of life is crucial to our search for the truth of our existence."

Through my Grandfather - the indentured labourer, his compatriots *and their descendants, I have learned a great deal about their quest for betterment. However, I also learned that their arrival was just the beginning of other journeys: for example, from being bonded labourers to becoming free men, women and children; from being perceived by the colonial authorities as "alien" immigrants to being accepted as Trinidadians, as citizens; from being marginal agricultural workers to becoming full contributors in almost every aspect of economic life; from being social outcasts, heathens who practised idolatrous religious rites within the confines of their villages to receiving national recognition. On this theme of **journeys**, I return to Rama's Voyage and the boy's predicament of homelessness. To the question: Where is home? some experts direct our attention to a place in the past full of childhood memories, while others regard home as being "neither here nor there." For Rama, there was no doubt: He knew very well, there was no ship waiting to take him back from whence he came, for all journeys are final. With this sobering reminder, today, 165 years on, we join the people of Trinidad and Tobago in celebrating the historic election of the first woman Prime Minister, an exemplar of that sense of belonging of which I speak and thus, another milestone in Indo-Trinidadians' odyssey towards new horizons.'*

On this Indian Arrival Day celebration in 2010, I had invited Film maker Tali Atzmon (wife of the highly praised Jazz Musician Gilad Atzmon) who had already set up her cameras and equipment in the auditorium of The Tabernacle when I arrived. The idea (in the absence of a Contractual Agreement) was to film me at the event, the footage to be used for a possible documentary film about my life and work. Overall, this was a prolonged session of filming and I was very impressed by Ms Atzmon's professionalism; her attention to detail. My 'Address' was well received and, of course, I had looked forward to seeing a copy of the film in due course.

MA'S FALL, DEATH AND MY EULOGY

After the Arrival Day 'Address' Official photographs were taken of myself with the High Commissioner, the newly crowned Miss Trinidad and Tobago and the colourfully- dressed Indian Classical Dancer, who had featured in the event. After saying goodbye to

Tali, I met Jacqui Chan, the Trinidad-born actress whom I had not seen for many years. She was with her sister; and while making our way from The Tabernacle to the Underground Station, Jacqui told me of her mother's passing. Given that Ma had been undergoing treatment for cancer, I expressed my condolences to Jacqui before we parted company.

It had been a long and tiring day and, on reaching home, I washed and went to bed. Sleep came quickly. Later as if it had been a faint sound from somewhere in the distance, gradually the unmistakeable tones of the telephone became louder and clearer. I got up immediately and answered. The caller was my sister Annette. Her soft-spoken voice, delivered harsh news: she said Ma had died. I needed more information. We spoke for a while with a surprising calmness perhaps because I'd thought of this dreaded moment many times.

Annette explained that Ma had fallen and hit her head. She had been in a coma ever since the fall. She never regained consciousness. Hearing my sister speak, suddenly my tiredness left me. It was now 2.00 a.m and I began to think about booking a flight within the next day or two, no later. After the telephone call, I could not sleep. I thought of composing a few words to say at Ma's funeral. Then I became more aware of what had happened. Oh my God! I could have shouted. Instead, I was quiet; still remarkably calm. But for the rest of those eerie early hours before dawn, I was in a very peculiar state of mind. Later, I realised that while I was giving the 'Keynote Address' in the Tabernacle, while praising one highly-educated Indo-Trinidadian woman Ms. Kamla Bissessar-Persad on the brink of playing her role on the national/international political stage, the life of another giant of Indo-Trinidadian womanhood, my mother was slipping away. I reflected upon the fact that unlike the new woman Prime Minister, Ma was unlettered. Nonetheless, Ma's interest in politics had grown progressively as she grew older. She had become very interested, a keen listener of radio and television news and debates; and I'd often wondered what she might have become had she been educated!

Once my flight was booked, things happened quickly. On arrival in Trinidad, the front yard of the house was obscured by a large tent under which a few hundred people had assembled. Such prayerful gatherings had been taking place every evening, I was told, since Ma had died; and was set to continue until the day of the funeral. The sense of grief was palpable; everything in and around the house was a reminder of the family's great loss. Within hours of being there, I began writing notes for Ma's Eulogy.

Although I'd spoken on big occasions all over the world, how well would I perform at Ma's funeral was anybody's guess. But this was not about performance, I thought; and soon enough I was sitting on the bed in the back-room with pen poised. What could I say? What should I say? These were strangely trying moments. Then I began composing Ma's Eulogy. Time was against me, but it was done; and on the day of the funeral I delivered it. After considering certain aspects of Ma's early life, I referred to her marriage: '*a union that had lasted some 70 years which I would describe as "**The Matchless Story.**" Matchless because for as long as I could remember my father was a heavy smoker; and as his cigarette-buyer, I knew the importance of matches to smoking cigarettes. Over the entire span of 70 years whenever I was in the house, Pa was always at a loss when he could not find his box of matches on the ledge near his favourite chair. "Who take away my matches!" he would bark. For a while, Ma would be silent until, the comments and accusations were repeated citing her as the culprit. This would break out into a row. For a long while, Ma would be silent again. Then she would go to him with a box of matches in hand and say very softly: "Where did you put your matches? It is mine that you always take!" At that moment, she would hand over the matchbox. At least once a week this used to happen; and I can tell you, the intensity of the rows and quarrels were at times, fierce: accusations and counter-accusations, resulting in raised voices and a parting of company followed sometime later by a truce; a cup of tea and peaceful talk.*

*After 69 years of being together, I had stayed with them last October for a month and sure enough, as if they could not help themselves, they argued as fiercely as before about the missing matches. I watched in amazement as I listened to them playing a scene, as if it was the first row they had ever had. In effect, this **Matchless Story** was like a device which they used to keep their marriage on edge and thus alive* *and ongoing!...'*

I talked about Ma's fair-mindedness and generosity and the fact that she disliked injustice, citing her concern about my dark skin as opposed to my brothers' fairness. She had done whatever she could, to minimize the devaluation of my complexion in colour-conscious Trinidad. I continued:

'*...no wonder that I wrote* **Reimaging Britain: 500 Years of Black and Asian History**; *the first history of multicultural Britain which identifies and proclaim the importance of* **difference** *in human affairs...So Ma in trying to equalize colour difference alerted me to something else... what she was attempting to do was the genesis of my new way of looking at the history of Britain, the Caribbean and all nations that reside on the earth. For as I argue, genuine mutual respect can come only through the acceptance of our difference, be it race, class, colour or gender...We cannot get away from our past, for it is that which makes us who we are...*

It was Ma who thought me to read the ABC...she was fond of picture books, especially those with brilliant colour photographs. Many years later, after I'd published several books, she said: "You should write a book with pictures." And so I did **World in View – The West Indies,** *which was distributed to schools worldwide. Those moments with Ma, marked the beginning of my odyssey as a writer. Then in 2000, when* **Arising From Bondage: A History of the Indo-Caribbean People** *was launched in the presence of the President of Trinidad and Tobago, ANR Robinson, an announcement was made that I will present a copy of my book to Ma. No sooner had her name been announced, Ma was already halfway down the Savannah Terrace of the Hilton Hotel. I duly presented the book which she held close to her as if it was the most precious of objects, even though she could not read it! The next day, The Guardian's "Talk of Trinidad" story, published a photograph of me presenting a copy of the book to President Robinson, while The Express newspaper carried a photograph of me presenting a copy to Ma!*

Those two photographs spoke volumes: the mother who could not read, was now, in the presence of VIPs (the great and the good) in Trinidad and being honoured in tandem with the Head of State! Reflecting on that poignant moment, I remembered something that my father had told me: "Your mother not backward, boy," he said. "She so smart, she does help me to fool her!" Now removed from us, thoughts come flooding back: enduring memories of a deceptively simple, but wise and saintly figure, who lived a life devoted to caring for others. She was my first teacher, the light that had guided me since she brought me into the world. Now is not the time for false modesty. All things considered, clearly, her greatness cannot be measured by ordinary standards. As we mourn her passing, we should also be mindful of celebrating the rare and wonderful human being that was FLORENCE RAJMA RAMDIN.'

At the front of the printed funeral programme, there was a quote from Pa: 'I thank you for being my companion through all the years. I'll never forget you till the end of my days, for there is **no future without remembrance**.' The last four words were particularly interesting. Not only was Pa quoting the epigraph of my novel *The Griot's Tale*, he was also expressing heart-felt feelings as the Griot had done in his last letter to his wife Rachele. So, in spite of Pa's often used phrase which I disliked: 'common sense before book,' intended to subvert my passion for writing, it would seem that in truth he had a secret and genuine respect for the printed word.

The Marabella Presbyterian Church was jam-packed. 'Your mother had a good turn out,' one respected Church-goer said to me. Many members of the Ramai family had attended and joined the Ramdin family in mourning. I was pleased to see them all.

Outside the Church, there were many people whom I'd not seen since I was a teenager; some were old, frail and almost unrecognisable. Over the years of my comings and goings, Ma had become increasingly matriarchal, surrounded by an increasing number of respectful grandchildren. And as if reflecting this, given that she was a long standing church-goer, the Pastor and Elders recognised Ma's dedicated support of the Church by presenting her with a plaque. In the evening of their lives, Ma and Pa had spoken openly about the end of life. On my visit before Ma had died, they talked casually about who would 'go first.' Pa said he did not want Ma to die and leave him. Privately, I felt, should this happen, it would perhaps be the right call. And so it happened.

Since my arrival for the funeral, I was more observant of Pa than usual. After the Funeral Service, held on Saturday 5th June, Ma's body was cremated at Belgrove's Crematorium in San Fernando. Pa did not attend; and remarkably, though unusually quiet, he showed no obvious signs of sorrow. Perhaps, I reasoned, because he was surrounded by family and friends. But what he may have felt privately when alone at night was, of course, another matter.

For many days, I had thought of Pa's use of my epigraph in *The Griot's Tale* 'no future without remembrance' and wondered: was this his way, not only of recognising Ma's hand in setting me on the then quite fantastic journey of becoming a writer, but also an indication perhaps of his 'forgiveness' for my sound and beneficial decision to leave 'home'? The latter was a good question, the answer to which I was unsure of. But to be clear, none of this mattered much now.

By this time, I'd reached an interesting phase of my work on the autobiography. Having considered various titles, at last, I found the appropriate one: *TURNING PAGES!* Patience was rewarded.

And now, the date that had been set for the scheduled 'staged Reading' of *Playing Their Parts* in Philadelphia during the Film Festival was 19 June. My attendance was, of course, cancelled because I had to be in Trinidad for Ma's funeral.

On my return to London, I resumed work not only on the early stages of my new novel *Fields of Lilac* (formerly titled 'Homeland') but also on the unfinished book *Isabella's Legacy: My Discovery of Spain*. My plan was to alternate between these works each week. But looming over them was the giant shadow of the continuous information-gathering and note-taking for my autobiography. Much as I'd wanted to devote more time to this, I had to wait. Priority was given to the long gestating book on Spain. With due diligence, after several months, I was able to complete *Isabella's Legacy: My Discovery of Spain*.

MA'S MEMORIAL AND A SPECIAL SCHOOL APPEARANCE

In January 2011, I had to forego another invitation from the Philadelphia Film Festival because of a Special Memorial Service for Ma in Trinidad. For this occasion, Marlon, Annette's husband and their children Brandon and Kimberley played the steelpan beautifully; and Khadine, my brother David's last daughter, sang. A year after Ma's death, my presence once more in the Church brought a flood of memories; poignant moments, hard to describe. Time had not brought healing enough as was evident on the faces of the bereaved. Regrouping with family and friends was nonetheless a welcome interlude. (By now, David's eldest daughter Candice had qualified as a Doctor, an achievement of which Ma was very proud).

While on this visit to Trinidad, through my sister, I was invited to visit the Holy Faith Convent School in Penal to give a 'Talk;' something 'inspirational' for the students of her class. No specific date was set and I had no idea what to expect. After dinner one evening, when Annette had casually asked if I would be ready to speak to the students *in the morning*, I was very surprised. Why? Because no date and time was fixed.

'Yes', I said. 'What time?'

'At 8.30 a.m.'

I had no idea of the number of students in her class, which I felt would give me a sense of the occasion. So I asked: 'And how many pupils would I be talking to in the morning?'

'About three to four hundred,' Annette said matter-of-factly.

This was, of course, far more than I'd thought. For one thing, clearly I would not be speaking to a 'class.' Being aware of the gravity of what was expected of me, I left the sitting room and went to the back-room, where I immediately got down to work on the 'Talk.'

Early the next morning, Annette drove me to the Convent School, where I met and was warmly greeted by the Principal Ms Bethell. This was our second meeting; the first was at Ma's funeral. Annette had told me what an understanding woman Ms Bethell had been during Ma's illness and I felt good about being invited to the School. The Principal offered me breakfast and after a cup of coffee, we proceeded to the large auditorium that was the Convent's Chapel-cum-Assembly Hall where I would meet the expected 300 students. Annette had under-estimated the gathering by a huge margin. Before me, there were an estimated 600 uniformed teenage girls; a more impressive sight I had not previously seen in a school in Trinidad.

After morning prayer, Ms Bethell addressed the Assembly on the theme: Inspiration. Introducing me as an 'Inspirational Speaker' she said: 'The epitome of an inspirational person is Dr Ron Ramdin.'

I had brought copies of my first and second novels *Rama's Voyage* and *The Griot's Tale* and after Ms Bethell's Introduction, I went on stage (this was no 'classroom') and talked about the books and what had inspired them. As I spoke, glancing to my right, then left, ahead and just before me, I was acutely aware of the attentive, eager faces of the girls: students, among whom were many who had earned high marks and excellent academic ranking in the Trinidad and Tobago school system.

Afterwards, I signed both books and formally donated them to the Convent School. In turn, the Principal presented me with a colourful and artistically-wrapped gift: it was an exquisitely cut drinking glass and a card. Although attending such a high-class institution was unrealisable when I was a boy, I was appreciative of the Principal's Introduction and the welcome of staff and students' in having me there. In fact, as I left the School, I was deeply reflective: moved by the generous reception. Why? Because I had come 'home' with two more rare literary works. And importantly, I took great satisfaction knowing that the novels were now in the Library Collections of this premier School where they could be read and studied by all who wished to do so.

ISABELLA'S LEGACY: MY DISCOVERY OF SPAIN

When I returned to London, I was not idle. Having completed *Isabella's Legacy*, I paused for thought. Like so many things in life, in spite of my sense of urgency, not only did it take longer to write than I'd expected, it also changed shape: it was now much larger. In this book of encounters, I began:

' *"Buenos dias senoras y senores," sounds that were to me clearly of a foreign tongue, words first heard in Hollywood films which I had seen as a boy in Trinidad, but never had I attempted to speak them myself until now. Slowly, clumsily I began to give voice, inflection and*

*intonation to each word. Practice rewarded me with familiarity if
not perfection as I repeated the words with growing confidence while
preparing to make the journey from London to Spain for the first time.
How ironic, I thought that Spanish should be a foreign language to me,
all the more because I was born and bred in Marabella just two miles
from San Fernando, the second largest town in Trinidad, the capital of
which is Port of Spain. These place names had been taken for granted,
but now on the eve of my visit to Spain, I questioned their origin. Thus,
contemporary thoughts demanded historical explanation.*

*Christopher Columbus, I learned in school, had travelled Westwards
in the hope of reaching India. But it was many years later that I
discovered a precious document. In a letter to King Ferdinand and
Queen Isabella, he began the Diary of his first voyage thus: "Your
highnesses commanded me that with sufficient fleet I should go to the
said parts of India; and for that purpose granted me great honours and
ennobled me…" Alas, his quest of reaching India was never realised.
But as a direct consequence of his voyages of exploration, here I was in
London (a descendant of Indians from India, born in Trinidad)…
preparing to visit Spain. Columbus…had introduced the sugar cane
plant to the West Indies on his second voyage, an act that would impact
upon me personally.'*

The manuscript recounts many episodes of my visits to Spain
prior to 1992 and when I had returned to Seville for the 500th
anniversary of the arrival of Columbus in the New World. One
of the highlights then was getting inside a replica of Columbus's
flagship the *Santa Maria* which was moored on the Guadalquivir
River.

Since then, I had not been back to Spain until 1999 when, at
the invitation of Dr David Walton of the University of Murcia,
I returned to give a Public Lecture in Murcia's Town Hall. Nine
years later, for the first time, I visited northern Spain for a weekend
break. In the book's *Postscript* I wrote:

*'For decades Barcelona has been a favourite destination for hundreds
of thousands of British people. Indeed, it is home for many of them.
That long weekend afforded me the great pleasure of walking many
miles in fine weather with teeming crowds, mostly tourists sightseeing.*

The most welcome stops for coffee and food in cafes and restaurants abuzz with chatter and enjoying the camaraderie of friends, were a delight but short-lived because there were many things to see, including fashionable shops, the squares and gardens, the Cathedral and, of course, Gaudi's architecture. Unfortunately I was unable to visit the Cathedral Familias, but was continuously, pleasantly surprised as I shuffled happily along the Ramblas with its beautiful market just off to the right, its art displays and artists; a long avenue that led to the broad expanse of an impressive waterfront.

Just before this, upon a tall column stood a magnificent statue of Christopher Columbus looking out at the sea. Almost at once, I was reminded of origins and my journey from West to East, from Trinidad to Spain. But this was not Andalusia. I was now some distance away in the northern province of Cataluyna; and how fitting, I thought, still gazing at the statue that I should end my tour of the wonderfully vibrant, artistic, modern city that is Barcelona, dominated by this towering iconic image evocative of travel and exploration. Alas, the "long" weekend proved to be far too short. With so much more for me to explore, Spain remains a place of complexity, fascination and ongoing discovery.'

And so, on its publication in 2011, the blurb of *Isabella's Legacy* proclaimed it as 'a unique book, a rare interweaving of travel, memoir, history, cultures and identities; a journey of surprises – stunning impressions, a meditation on world history and significantly on contemporary Europe. Above all, it is a narrative of my discovery of Spain which, in turn, has led not only to self-discovery, but also to a book which will hopefully enlighten and enchant the reader.'

Dr David Walton, who had taught for many years at the University of Murcia had read the manuscript and his appraisal of the book appeared on the book jacket. He wrote:

'Ron Ramdin, historian, biographer and novelist, and now travel writer, offers this candid, intimate and honest portrait of his travels in Spain. Following in the wake of Christopher Columbus, it is a voyage of discovery, a painstaking and insightful search for cultural roots that raises questions about cultural belonging and the effects of colonisation.

LONDON: HOME AND BELONGING' · 1359

It is also a tale of how personal friendships, chance meetings and casual acquaintances help the writer to explore and appreciate the land he so desired to know. Although the direct object of Ramdin's musings is modern Spain (mainly Andalusia), his Trinidadian origins provide the anchor point and the historical pointers that help him to navigate large geographical expanses and over five hundred years of history. If Columbus failed to discover India, Isabella's Legacy shows how a Caribbean West Indian was able to make his travels to Spain into a personal adventure that would help to shed light on the Columbus adventure.'

One of my greatest joys on finishing and publishing the book was the response of those who had been helpful. My *Dedication* reads: 'With deep affection and gratitude first to Marisa; Margarita, Nacho and family. And to the many people whom I had met on my Spanish journey. To them all, and to the beautiful cities of Seville, Granada and Barcelona, I humbly dedicate this book.'

A few weeks later in November, the book was launched in London at the Trinidad and Tobago High Commission. Speaking on behalf of the book, was Professor Clem Seecharan of London Metropolitan University. He gave a stirring presentation of the book and commented on my *place* among writers in Britain. After his speech, High Commission administrator Beverley Awonaya said to gathering and to Clem Seecharan: 'Professor, you read from Mr Ramdin's book as if it was from Shakespeare.' This perceptive comment and the Professor's praise were well-received by the knowledgeable and distinguished audience which included actor Rudolph Walker, former publisher Margaret Busby and friends Rey Bowen, Nigel Cawthorne, Paul Rowe, Roger Evans, Clara Arokiasamy, Ron and Silva Billings, among others.

Importantly, given its connectedness with Trinidad, I felt *Isabella's Legacy* should also be launched in Seville. To this end, I made enquiries and eventually contacted the relevant person at the University of Seville. Alas, he failed to engage further and what had seemed a promising proposal came to nothing. Nonetheless I had hoped to revisit Seville to promote the book at a later date. I also felt the need to take the book to Trinidad (and elsewhere in the

'New World') where there was very little being taught in schools about this earlier Spanish connection.

MY IMAGES IN COLLECTION AT THE NATIONAL PORTRAIT GALLERY

Before the end of November, I received an email from Inga Fraser of the National Portrait Gallery in London.

'Dear Ron,
I am currently indexing a number of prints, contacts and negatives by the late Harry Diamond. I came across this contact (attached) which we identified as yourself, and I wondered if you had any details to add about this shoot or Harry Diamond himself that you might like to share with us?
Best Wishes, Inga.'

Given that the 'Contact sheet' showed 23 images of me, including the one (a copy) which the National Portrait Gallery had earlier decided to add to their collection, I responded with the following contextual piece:

'HARRY DIAMOND AND THE SHOOT
In the early 1970s as a budding writer and member of staff in the British Museum, I became the first Black leader of the largest Civil Service Union in the British Museum and with the inauguration of the British Library was elected the first Secretary of the Whitley Council Staff Side when this new national institution was formed. Thereafter, at this heady time of industrial strife and strikes, I became well-known in London and nationally for my role as an Organiser. I had not only Produced and Directed the first (and only) Charity Concert in the British Museum for The Save the Children Fund, but was also instrumental in organising the closure of the British Museum by Industrial Action for the first time in British Museum history. "HISTORIC DAY AT THE BRITISH MUSEUM" was the big news headline in The Evening News. At this time, Bloomsbury was awash with intellectuals, radical socialists, writers and artists and one of its most distinguished and respected publishers, Tim O'Keeffe had

dubbed me: *"The Lenin of Museum Street."* It was **at this time** that HARRY DIAMOND approached me: *'I would like to do a shoot of you,'* he said. And so an arrangement was made for us to meet on location in Bloomsbury. The first shots were taken in the forecourt of the British Museum, then on Great Russell Street, in Gilbert Place (just off Museum Street) and in the then popular literary meeting place, The Plough on Museum Street.

After the shoot, I got to know HARRY DIAMOND better and was at times in his company in the French House and the Colony Room Club to which I was admitted as a member by owner and host Muriel Belcher. I was introduced to many of Harry's associates including Jeffrey Bernard and his brother Bruce, Francis Bacon, Lucien Freud, Tom Baker, Maurice Agis, Peter Owen, Sandy Fawkes and other well-known actors, writers and artists, too numerous to mention here.

HARRY DIAMOND, as I knew him, was a confident but seemingly 'shy' man. He always had a faraway preoccupied look; perhaps he was thinking of composition for he seemed to know the shot he wanted to take well before he snapped. I must say I enjoyed his company enormously and, in spite of his growing celebrity over the years, his attitude towards me was always warm and friendly. This quality, for a man of his standing (and given that he did not suffer fools gladly) I must say, was rare.

Of course, since the shoot, my reputation as historian, biographer, novelist and travel writer has been enhanced. Indeed in 2004, I was again fortunate when the much-in-demand photographer-film-maker HORACE OVE honoured me with a shoot (using two rolls of film) at various locations: On the steps of the British Museum, in its Great Court and in both the Egyptian and Greek Galleries.

Looking back, I am very pleased and honoured that I was one of HARRY DIAMOND'S subjects for he caught the mood and style of those extraordinary times of the early 1970s London and, especially during that period of the 'radicalisation' of Bloomsbury.'

After submitting this piece, Helen Trompleter, Assistant Curator of Photographs, at the National Portrait Gallery wrote:

'Dear Ron,

Following on from my colleague Inga's email I just wanted to thank you very much for the information you kindly provided on the photographs, and for sharing your memories of Harry with us. We will be continuing to catalogue and research the archive over the coming months and your help is greatly appreciated.'

Inga and Helen had both confirmed the safe keeping of Harry Diamond's work where it was destined to be. And so in death, Harry Diamond's work has re-emerged to form part of the national memory at the National Portrait Gallery; a collectable and iconic photographer whose lens had recorded images of me for posterity.

It was Christmas and without Ma, after their long marriage, Pa was a lonely figure. How tough it must be for him? Also in my thoughts was the fact that, on my regular visits, although Pa and I got on well there was a distinct cantankerousness, a tetchiness on his part, which spoiled our conversations; a tendency which almost always led to his raised voice and the end of our chats. So his behaviour had, at times, become erratic and there was no telling what would follow. When I went to Trinidad with my novel *The Griot's Tale,* it not only led Pa to seriously rethink the course of my literary journey, but also to reappraise me generally. One day he stared long and hard at me, then asked: 'Do you know who you are?' The question surprised me, but I smiled and said jokingly: 'You know, sometimes, I don't know.' What was he getting at? He was clearly puzzled about me: for in spite of his advice that I should go easy, take a break from the writing, 'retire,' as he put it, I continued to write books; and increasingly *in new genres.* He knew that the genesis of the long difficult journey that I'd undertaken in literature had nothing to do with his nurturing or practical help. I did it all on my own regardless of what he thought of me, and without malice. Being older, though he was proud of my achievements, each new book, it seemed, generated a certain ambivalence. When he had lost his temper on my last visit, it was already several months since Ma's passing and I put it down largely to him being alone. As he'd said to Ma in my presence, he would like 'to go first. I don't want you to die and leave me!' How strange, I reflected that this should come to pass; and now, especially at

Christmas, he must be feeling the full impact of the loss of his wife and companion.

These were my foremost thoughts when just a few weeks into 2012, I booked my ticket and within hours of doing so, I rang Pa to say that I would be coming to see him on 11 April. His phenomenal memory served him well; and later, when we spoke he reminded me that I had not rung him for more than two weeks, which was true. Then, at one point in the conversation he said: 'Now, what is it about the 11th of April…' His voice trailed off. Was there something else that I'd mentioned about my pending visit? I wondered. I had no idea what he was referring to. The important thing was that he'd got the message that soon we would be meeting! I felt good about this because his frailness when I last saw him made this journey all the more important.

PROFESSOR BRERETON'S BOOK REVIEW

Anticipating the visit, I worked harder on my autobiography. Then on 1 March the *Trinidad Express* published a Book Review of *Isabella's Legacy: My Discovery of Spain*. The Reviewer was the distinguished English-born Emeritus Professor Bridget Brereton of the University of the West Indies. Under the heading: '***Indies, Indians, Trinidad, Spain***', she wrote:

'Ron Ramdin is a Trinidad-born writer…who has published a remarkable range of books: biographies of Paul Robeson and Mary Seacole; historical studies of labour in Trinidad and Tobago, the black British working class and the Indo-Caribbean people (among other topics); and two novels…Rama's Voyage and The Griot's Tale.

His latest book, Isabella's Legacy: My Discovery of Spain (2011), tells the story of his visit to Spain in 1989, 1991 and 1992. It's part travel book, part a highly personal memoir, and part a meditation on what the idea of Spain meant to him when he was growing up in southern Trinidad in the 1940s and 1950s. And it is this last dimension that I found especially interesting…

Ramdin turned his visits to Spain, undertaken partly to give lectures and partly as holidays, into a personal "discovery" of the country whose history was so closely linked to that of his native island. He was a "Black British" person, a Trinidadian, a West Indian–and it was thanks to Columbus that he could claim that last identity. *As everyone knows, Columbus believed that he'd found the "Indies" - the East - when he stumbled on the islands of the Caribbean, and the term "West Indies" was coined as a result.*

Yet there was a further layer of irony: Ramdin was a Trinidad "East Indian." His grandfather Abraham Rattan, had been born in Madras and had come to Trinidad as an indentured labourer sometime in the 1890s or early 1900s. In Trinidad, he (and Ramdin) "had been known officially as an "Indian" or "East Indian" and, at times, less respectfully as a "coolie!"... As Ramdin puts it: "Ironically, 346 years since his (Columbus's) first landfall, those Indians from India that he had been expecting to meet were recruited by one of Spain's competing European neighbours, Britain, to labour in her colonial "possessions" in the former slave plantations, especially in the West Indies...So here I was in Spain, a direct descendant of those Indians, who had over the years imbibed the history and culture of the West Indies"...

"The Spanish legacy had been deeply etched in my mind," Ramdin writes, "but the connection with Spain remained submerged, the accumulation of layers of impositions by another imperialist power"...

He saw his presence in Spain as "a commingling of the histories I'd read and all that was before me, which altogether provided the context for this visit." These "meditations" on history and identity shaped the three visits to Spain, but especially the one in 1991. An obsession with Columbus and the "Discovery" led him to explore the places, buildings and museums linked to him and his men...He also visited while in Seville the famous Archivo de las Indias, the archive where the records of the Spanish American Empire (including those of Trinidad between 1498 and 1797) are stored. The great Andalusian city of Seville especially fascinated him, because it was the administrative and commercial heart of that empire. Ironically, Ramdin's "exotic" appearance - a dark skin, "Indian" features and long black hair-led to him often being mistaken for a Gypsy or Roma ("Gitano" in Spanish) in southern Spain - a further irony, of course, since the Roma descend from people who left India hundreds of years ago and their language is derived from Hindi. He became very interested in Roma culture in Spain, especially flamenco, the famous dance and music which may be partly of Roma origin.

*Ramdin's… meditations about Trinidadian, Indian, Spanish history
and identity make it an interesting read.'*

THE URGE TO SEE PA:
HIS SUDDEN DEATH AND MY EULOGY

Reading Professor Brereton's Book Review raised my expectations
about going to Trinidad which was now just weeks away. A few
days later, on Saturday 3 March, I woke up in London before 5.30
a.m and resumed the slow, relentless process of editing a printed
version of my autobiography *Turning Pages*. I had reached the
point in 2002 when I'd delivered the Eulogy at my sister's funeral
in Toronto. While reading from the manuscript what I had said
then about Lydia, melancholy feelings encroached, then overtook
me and lingered for a while. It had roused a mood which led me
to abandon my work on the manuscript. This had never happened
before. Going with the flow, I lay on my bed and perused a book
that I had never previously read: *The Spirit of Man: An Anthology of
Verses* in English and French by philosophers and poets. This was
one of Pa's books that I had some years before borrowed, but never
consulted. As I read the verses on various themes relating to life,
death, bereavement and after, I felt strangely lacking in energy and
a sense of disorientation threatened to engulf me. After pondering
certain poetic lines of lyrical beauty, still as if in a melancholy
trance, I got up and checked my emails. Two were from Trinidad,
both delivering the same message: Pa had died. I immediately rang
my sister.

Like Ma, Pa was now no more. He was just weeks short of his
90th birthday. Although I'd already booked my Ticket to go and
see Pa on 11 April, now I had to cancel it. I had to think and move
fast so that I would get to Trinidad on time for Pa's funeral. For the
rest of that Saturday afternoon, time moved depressingly slow; and
I had no desire to continue with my work on the manuscript. The
insistent momentum was now lost; and once again, the finality of
death had focused my mind on *time*, my own mortality and, more
interestingly now, the real importance of my autobiography.

A couple of hours later, news of Pa's death was overlaid by telephone
calls and more email messages. And once more my thoughts were

on writing a Eulogy. What *should* I say about Pa? I made notes and wrote a rough draft.

Then I arrived in Trinidad. As in Ma's case, there were many people assembled under a tent; and after meeting family and friends, I retired. The next morning I was up early. I did my best to refine and write the finished version of the Eulogy. When I'd done this, I was told there would be two other Eulogists: Annette and my youngest brother David. That was as it should be, I thought; and so with the passing of Pa, I found myself in a familiar place: the pulpit in Marabella Presbyterian Church.

'PETER HARDEO RAMDIN was the head of a family that was large and far from wealthy, but...he was rich in other ways,' were my first words. *'Always well-dressed, he carried himself with a certain dignity and, as everyone knows, he was one of the most sociable men of his time and place. He was a Talker, possessor of a strong voice and magnetic personality. He was in his element when he socialized and was known to have a drink or two. People liked his company. In fact, in a long life, he had made countless friends (young and old) in whose company he revelled, telling jokes (never vulgarly) that, more often than not, carried profound messages. I remember him telling me about a young man who, preparing for his Wedding Day could not decide on one last item that he would wear for the occasion: should it be a pair of white, brown or black shoes? As the Wedding day got closer and closer, he still could not make up his mind about the colour of the shoes, until he saw a man with one foot!*

An aspect of my father and his friends' behaviour when socializing was their tendency to make music. Singing in particular. In this respect... his rendition of songs earned him the nickname "Bing," after Bing Crosby, the American singer. But it was not a Crosby song that had in my estimation made his crooning outstanding. It was a melody made famous by Nat King Cole: "A Blossom Fell" which he sang often but never did I hear him perform the song badly. He gave real meaning to it. I will go so far as to say that while Nat sang it beautifully, my father interpreted it beautifully. And when his mother died in her sleep after a blazing quarrel with him, whenever my father heard another Nat King Cole song "Looking Back" he wished he had had the chance to speak a few final words to her. Sadly, "Looking Back" (the song) evoked a haunting regret.

My father was also interested in books; but he was no bookworm. He had a phenomenal memory. And often I'd been astonished when partaking of alcohol, unlike most of those around him, he would often quote verbatim wonderfully poetic words from Shakespeare, Wordsworth, Shelley, Keats, Omar Khyam and, of course, the Holy Bible. He was a free spirit who lived life to the full; and given his strong personality, he was a formidable opponent. Nonetheless, at the age of 15 in the face of high unemployment and a bleak future, I told him I was going to England in search of work. The consequences of my decision was terrible. Over a period of 4 years, he did his best to discourage me. And before I left, at least twice, he said with the greatest emphasis: "England is a pleasant place for them that's rich and high, but England is a cruel place for such poor folk as I!" In this, he was right, I could not have imagined how difficult things could be there! Indeed, over the years, it's been a life of austerity, enriched by extraordinary ambition!

Growing up I saw my father struggle in a Trinidad that has long since vanished. But he took things in his stride. He was young and belonged to Merry Boys Cricket Club. His friends were good, decent men. When they lost a match, they would take a drink. When they won, well, that was something else again. At Christmas, my father's friends would come to the house on the Sand Road; and at Easter time, they would go to the Union Park Races. As a boy, I observed my father closely; I and my brothers feared him; and with good reason. In later life, I came to appreciate how very lucky he was to have had a devoted wife…

What is …extraordinary is the fact that he and Ma did not just provide us with food, but also anyone else who happened to be visiting…

In later years, I reflected on other aspects of my father's life: on his formal education which did not extend beyond elementary school. Though self-taught, he was a formidable debater whose opponents, especially on the subject of religion, got short shrift. Many were the times when Reverend Ramjit, a former Pastor of this Church, would stop by on his bicycle for a chat. But within minutes, I would hear raised voices, and soon, much too soon, the Reverend was off on his bike. My father's so-called vices of smoking and drinking, were not the issues they quarrelled about. Their point of contention was Scripture, on which they were clearly at odds with each other; their different *views, a matter of belief.*

Nonetheless, ever since I could remember, hanging above my father's chair in the Gallery were two framed pictures: To his right, was the Sacred Heart of Jesus and behind him, the Rock of Ages. It was in this small Gallery, a warm and welcoming space, where I heard the most weird and wonderful things about spirits, phantoms, about voices in the night, Soucouyant, La Diablesse and Lagahou; about comic and tragic stories, the very stuff of life. It was there that my father entertained his friends. Among them was Gabriel, who played the most beautiful Harmonica music I've ever heard. Looking at me, Gabriel said: "Bing, this boy look just like you.' My father smiled and said: "Gabriel, apple can't grow cherry you know.' On another occasion, when I had returned to Trinidad to promote my first book... my father said to me: "From a bramble, a rose!" Such generosity of spirit, though very rare, was often insightful, remarkably wise and integral to his character. He was born at 43 Union Park Road where he lived all his life. Unlike me, he was not a wanderer.

In a long career, he had painted and decorated more houses (often as a favour!) than any man I know. His name was legendary in Union, Marabella and beyond. As a paint-mixer, he was second to none! I shall always remember him, left-handed and with elegant movements, applying paint to the wood-work; varnishing and polishing the furniture and floor, work which he did with joy and pride.

Over the years, since his retirement, I had visited him regularly and whenever I enquired about old Mr and Mrs so and so, he would jokingly say: "Those who are not dead, are badly wounded!" But when I last called him, he did not tell me that Mano, one of his closest friends and the last surviving member of Merry Boys Cricket Club had died. My father, even in advanced old age, exuded an air of well-being, so much so that it was easy, at least momentarily, to lapse into wishful thinking and overlook his mortality. "Death is not extinguishing the light," wrote Rabindranath Tagore. "It is putting out the lamp because dawn has come." As it was, my father died soon after dawn on the morning of Saturday 3 March.

Having spent many years among books and in the world of learning, I had discussed many matters with my father. We had many meaningful, enjoyable conversations; but in spite of my best attempts, especially in recent years, our difference of opinion tended to peter out badly. On one occasion, he veered off saying: "And when I die, tell them the truth. And," he added: Keep it short and sweet!" I respectfully bow to these requests.

Now beloved father as I say goodbye to you, I close with the words of a poem: "I may keep memories of you, but not your essence, for that will pour forth tomorrow.'

The loss of Ma and Pa, two towering figures who even though I'd lived away from them for fifty years, had continued to affect my idea of 'home.' After the funeral, all those who had come from all parts of the world to the Church Service, quickly returned from whence they came and I was left alone in the house. For two weeks, I sat in the gallery in my usual chair opposite Pa's having my morning cup of tea. These mornings were especially strange: an eerie, unnerving silence enshrouded the house. In the evenings when the few visitors had gone, I either watched TV or listened to Pop Music Hits of the Sixties. At one point, when *The Green Green Grass of Home* was played, I recalled the countless times in cold London when I'd heard the song and anticipated seeing Ma and Pa and this small, but warm home. Hearing the song for the first time here, I looked up at Ma and Pa's pictures on the wall, now garlanded with wreaths of artificial flowers and leaves. Though I'm used to my own company, I felt utterly alone and for the first time since I'd arrived for Pa's funeral, having kept cool and tearless, suddenly all the years of pent-up emotion came to a head.

A SPANISH TRANSLATION?
FAREWELL AGAIN TO THE SAND ROAD 'HOME'

In the last few days of my Trinidad visit, I had a call from Dr Mahabir of the University of Trinidad and Tobago who said he'd like us to meet. I agreed and a date and time were arranged. The person who kindly gave me a 'lift' in his car to attend this meeting was David Moulah Baksh, a teacher who spoke to me about a possible meeting with Norman Girvan, a Professor at the University of the West Indies. Later, David gave me the Professor's telephone number. When I eventually spoke with Norman Girvan, he said he'd read Professor Brereton's Book Review of *Isabella's Legacy*. In this connection, I asked Professor Girvan if he knew of a Spanish translator in the Caribbean or Latin America who may be interested in doing a Spanish translation of *Isabella's Legacy*. 'Yes,' he said. 'I know of one who is on a visit to Trinidad. She is from the University of Havana and will be going back soon.'

'Is it possible for us to meet before she does?' I asked.

'Yes', the Professor replied. 'How about lunch tomorrow?'

'I have a meeting tomorrow. Could we make it the following day?' I asked.

'I will call you back,' he said.

Eventually, a Lunch meeting was arranged for which I travelled from San Fernando to Port of Spain. Having heard so much about the Professor for so long, when we met I was pleased to see him clutching a copy of my book *Arising from Bondage: A History of the Indo-Caribbean People*. With him was Graciela Chaillou. Over lunch I learned that the Cuban historian and translator had been involved with the translation of many Caribbean classics into Spanish: *Black Jacobins* and *The Negro in the Caribbean*, among others. I had carried copies of both *Isabella's Legacy* and *The Griot's Tale* and at the end of the meal, I presented the books to Norman and Graciela. Norman requested that I sign these books plus, of course, his copy of *Arising From Bondage*. He said, he was impressed by the scope and depth of the work. When I opened the book to sign it, Graciela interposed saying that her name should be inscribed on *Arising From Bondage* instead of Norman's. At this juncture, I looked up at Norman and said that I could send him a replacement copy, if that was acceptable. Norman agreed to let Graciela have her name on the book.

After explaining the Spanish Translation process of English books at the University of Havana, Graciela said she would write to me. We exchanged email addresses.

Having been just names to each other for many years, the meeting between Professor Girvan and myself was timely and very interesting. In the taxi on my way home, I was hopeful that something would indeed come of this important and thoroughly enjoyable Luncheon meeting.

Following Pa's burial, on 3 April 2012 I went to Roodal Cemetery with Annette. We placed a wooden cross (Marlon's handiwork) on Pa's grave. Revisiting the site filled me with a renewed sense of loss; the inevitability of death, but also a heightened awareness of being alive. Standing there, I remembered the sticky mud around the graveside before interment of Pa's remains as well as Ma's ashes. Then, like an echo borne on the wind, their voices about who would 'go first' came to mind: Pa protesting that he did not want Ma to die and leave him. But the hand of fate had made it so; and now they were no more. Standing amidst the slanted weather-beaten gravestones, as the wind rose and fell, I stared at the wooden cross, then looking skywards, I thought: at last, they are now finally at rest; buried together here in the earth, not far away from another cemetery named 'Paradise.'

When Annette and I reached home, I was painfully conscious of Ma and Pa's absence. The delayed full impact of their deaths came forcefully at me in the form of occasional feelings of desolation that breached valiant attempts at controlling my emotion.

The morning of the next day 4 April, while sitting in the seat opposite Pa's 'Chairman's Chair,' remembrance of his voice and things he'd said were all-encompassing. In the last years, he had often said: '*Commonsense before book*!' Knowing of my many disadvantages while growing up in Trinidad, but blissfully unaware of my long, great struggle in England to become a writer, I thought his comment was insensitive, if not silly and out of order. In the aftermath of his passing, younger people were using the expression: 'Commonsense before book.' But instead of railing against those who were mimicking Pa's words, I held my fire. Why? Because this level of thinking, most surprisingly, was to be found among many in the wider community who regarded themselves as 'educated' and 'literate.' In fact, a few people unashamedly and with no sense of even mild concern had said to me when I visited Trinidad to launch *The Griot's Tale*: 'This is not a reading Society.' My forthright answer was: 'If it isn't, **now** is the time to begin to **make it a Reading Society**!'

On the day of my departure for London, while locking the front door of the house, I was conscious of the fact that it was something which I'd never done *before* Pa's death. Now, I was doing so for the last time before joining my brother David and cousin Michael who had taken my suitcase to the car. Holding the key, I slowly descended the steps and stood a while in the yard where once the cassarina tree grew green and tall. Compared with what it was a few years before, I also realised how bare most of the ground was. The mango tree was no longer there, nor was there the profusion of plants and flowers: bougainvillea, roses, hibiscus and morning glory, among others. And, as I'd done just a few months before when Pa had waved goodbye to me, now from the yard I looked in the direction of the 'Chairman's Chair.' As if he was still sitting there, like an unstoppable force from the deep recesses of my mind, long forgotten memories of my childhood and youth surfaced: I recalled the rain pellets on my bare back during heavy showers, the morning dew-drops on the leaves and flowers of the bushy garden, how Pa's love of his 'garden' had prompted compliments from neighbours and passersby; and now more philosophically, how at times, his gravelly voice articulated with great feeling lines from the poet Thomas Gray:

'*Full many a gem of purest ray serene.*
The dark unfathom'd cares of ocean bear:
Full many a flower is born to blush unseen,
And waste its sweetness in the desert air.'

Was this, I thought, a coded reference to a loneliness within himself?

Though its façade was unchanged, being larger, the house was now utterly empty; most definitely, it had changed forever. It was no longer '*home.*' I walked away from the yard and stood on the Sand Road from where I tried desperately to take a positive view of the absence of Ma and Pa.

IRMA DIES

Less than a week after arriving back in London, I was gripped by another wave of sadness. My son Ronnie emailed to say his mother Irma (who had emigrated from St. Vincent to New Zealand) was in a bad way; her former illness of a few years before had come back in an aggressive form. As the hours and days passed, it was clear Irma was gravely ill. Memories of her grew stronger with each passing day. She did not last long. When she died on 9 May Ronnie was utterly devastated and having spent many happy years together, I was overwhelmed by a renewed sense of sadness. My greatest regret was that I could neither speak with her, nor could I be with my son at this distressing time. What could be done from long distance, I did. I was very sorry and wrote 'PERSONAL THOUGHTS ON THE IRREPLACEABLE IRMA' which I asked Ronnie to read at the funeral service.

MY MEETING IN THE HOUSE OF LORDS

A few weeks later, on Wednesday 20 June 2012, I was in the House of Lords. My presence in Committee Room 3 was as a Member of the All Party Parliamentary Group for Trinidad & Tobago. The Theme of this Annual General Meeting was: 'Trinidad and Tobago – Celebrating 50 years of Independence…What's next for the future of the nation?' Among other matters being discussed were developments in the 'Energy Sector;' and on social policy, I raised the question of tackling the problem of Youth Unemployment and the importance of Job Training programmes.

On this occasion, aware of protocol, I arrived at the Houses of Parliament early and, with a few minutes to spare, I took a quick look around Westminster Hall. This is the oldest part of the larger building known as the Palace of Westminster which contained both Houses of Parliament: the House of Commons and the House of Lords. Westminster Hall is an awesome space, I noted. Apart from being used for the 'lying in state' of Monarchs and Prime Ministers, Oliver Cromwell's head was impaled there; and having seen the film *A Man for All Seasons*, I recalled that it was in this Hall that the Trials of Sir Thomas More (Adviser to King Henry VIII), Guy Fawkes and King Charles 1 were held. All of these men were sentenced to death. Until 1882, a brochure informed me, the Hall had served as the Royal Courts of Justice before its present location in The Strand.

After mounting the steps at the west end of the 'Hall,' turning left, along the way towards Committee Room 3, I passed busts and statues of politicians at which I glanced, but did not stop to look. From my decades-long research and writings, I knew well how fitting it was that those who held power should deem this as a place fit for British heroes; for men who held sway over momentous decisions of conquest, war and peace. To say the least, this visit to the House of Lords was an eye-opener.

In 2013 I received 'Congratulations' from Graciela Chailloux, Translator of the University of Havana and the prestigious publisher Casas de Las Americas with an accompanying letter from Senor Malagon, the Director of Arte y Literatura. The Director informed me that it was an honour for Arte y Literatura to publish a Spanish Translation of my second novel *The Griot's Tale*. He pointed out the prestige attached to my novel being included in the publishing house's Catalogue of Universal Art and Literature.

(Ms Chailloux also referred to her Spanish Translation of my book *Arising From Bondage,* which she hoped would soon be published.)

A few months later, I was approached by a Caribbean Examinations Council representative for permission to quote from my first novel *Rama's Voyage*. I granted this and so *Rama's Voyage* was elevated to become one of the few novels to be included in the Caribbean Examinations Council's *Workbook for English A Students*. The author of this important book is Dr Patrick Quan Kep, Former Assistant Chief Examiner of the 'Examinations Council' in 'English A.'

On page 46 of the Workbook, under the heading 'READING COMPREHENSION' the Examiner wrote: 'The following extract is taken from the novel *Rama's Voyage* by Ron Ramdin. Read it carefully and answer the questions which follow.

"Earlier that day, in Port of Spain, the island's capital city, he had seen two tall black men sweeping the quayside and on the way south he saw a black woman and three children who had stopped work on their plot of land to gaze at him and his companions. He had never seen the like of these people before; and judging from their looks, neither did they see the like of him. The Indian cart-

driver noticed Rama's curious look and said, 'Dese people from Africa. Dey come here before we. Now slavery abolish, we replace dem. Now we live in de barracks.'
Rama's Voyage, p.278."'
Such recognition of *Rama's Voyage* was a mark of its distinction in the sphere of Caribbean literature.

'YOU COULD HEAR A PIN DROP ': SPEAKING AT THE VICTORIA & ALBERT MUSEUM

For the rest of the year, I concentrated on the meticulous editing of my autobiography. But after an uninterrupted period, I had to put this work aside because of a special speaking engagement at the Victoria and Albert Museum. An indication of the importance of this 'Talk' was the fact that it was preceded by the publication of an article entitled 'A Tale of Indenture: What's the Story?' in *The Voice* newspaper. This publicity proved effective in getting the word around. I addressed a 'full house,' rare for such an event at the 'V&A,' I was told by the Organiser. Thus, this platform was a good opportunity for me to inform the uninformed. Of special significance were my opening words:

'*To begin with, here is something to consider: Christopher Columbus travelled westwards in the hope of discovering the wealth of the East. On his first landfall in 1492, he believed he had reached India; and on his second voyage, he introduced the sugar cane plant to the West Indies. Given that his main objective was to acquire wealth for the Spanish Crown, Columbus went to his grave believing he had landed in India! He didn't. But here is another thing to consider: If his original intention was to enslave Indians from India on sugar plantations, ironically 346 years later, Indians were indeed planting and reaping canes not in India, but on the very sugar plantations that Columbus had helped to bring into being. How did this happen?*

As we know only too well, one of the greatest crimes against humanity was the notorious Middle Passage and African Slavery. But when African slaves in the Caribbean were Emancipated, Planters were faced with a major problem. How to produce sugar without slaves? The solution, as the Planters saw it, was the introduction of Indian indentured workers which led to the institution of a new labour system which became known as Indian Indentureship...'

After exploring the institution and practice of Indentureship, its abolition and the settlement of Indians and their descendants in the Caribbean, I concluded thus:

*'I concede that different writers will interpret the Indians' arrival, presence and contribution in the Caribbean in different ways. But after decades of a literary odyssey, spanning six genres, I felt compelled to write the novel Rama's Voyage which deals with the Indians' arrival. In essence, it is the story of an orphan child from the Calcutta streets who makes the long, hazardous journey to the Caribbean. Why did I write it? In part, because prior to the novel's publication there was **no such work of fiction**, but also because the growing number of factual accounts in recent years, namely histories, though valuable, present but only a part of the story. Why "only a part" of the story? you may well ask. Because, history is essentially based on evidence; and there are gaps in the evidence. Where history ends, story begins! Historians tell what happened. The novelist tells us how characters feel: how they think and act.*

In the case of Rama's Voyage, we learn about the Indians' feelings, their motivation to migrate and their experience of the journey from India to the New World. Such elements had been, in large part, missing from literature. And so 159 years later, this story of Indian Arrival, portrayed in a novel was eventually published in 2004. The book's Dedication is 'To the homeless children of Calcutta and the world who seek and hope for a better life.' Why this Dedication? Because apart from man's inhumanity to man and a budding romance, the central theme of the novel is that of a boy's homelessness, his feelings of unbelonging, which is the push factor in his decision to leave India.

The boy's name is Rama. At every step of the way on his terrifying journey, he is enlightened by revelation. Home and belonging were among his highest hopes, as it was for the hundreds of thousands who had made the dangerous journey to the Caribbean.

If Rama's Voyage is a crucial complement to my histories, as I engage in writing its sequel "Fields of Lilac," I am reminded of the importance of a novel.

Here, I reiterated what I'd said about life, art, truth and the novel two years earlier at The Tabernacle: *"...Art does not save us, but in our time, art preserves for us a space in which we can be reminded of the story that is told by human beings in search of their humanity and the truth of their existence. It reminds us that the search is crucial to the love of life and that love of life is crucial to our search for the truth of our existence."*

Then I concluded:

'Through my grandfather, the indentured labourer (whom I had the honour of knowing before he died) and his compatriots and their descendants, I learned a great deal about their quest for betterment. I learned that their arrival was just the beginning of multiple journeys: For example, from being bonded labourers to becoming free people; from being immigrants to acceptance as Caribbean citizens; from being marginal agricultural workers to becoming full contributors in almost every aspect of economic life; from being social outcasts – heathen Hindoos who practised idolatrous religious rites in their villages to receiving national recognition. In answer to the question: "Where is home?" some experts direct our attention to a place in the past full of childhood memories, while others regard HOME as being neither here nor there. For Rama, the homeless Calcutta boy who had made the journey to the West, there was no doubt: he knew there was no ship waiting to take him back from whence he came, for all journeys are final. With this sobering reminder, as I conclude this "Tale of indenture," we would do well to pause for a moment's reflection: For better or worse, the post-Columbus enterprise had brought into existence the African and Indian diasporas and, in today's global village of crossing boundaries, here we all are! Wherever you have come from, in this 175th year of the Indians' arrival in the Caribbean, this Special Event is a fitting occasion for us to celebrate each other!'

A lively Question and Answer session followed my Talk. On hand was film-maker Sunara Begum who filmed the entire performance. Afterwards, many people expressed interest in my books and several photographs were taken with people from the audience, a few of them well-known. While conversing with Ms Begum, a young African man approached me. 'You could hear a pin drop!' he said, 'while you were speaking.' These words, I thought, encapsulated

what was an extraordinary, deeply satisfying Event and evening in
the jam-packed room. As Ms Begum put it: 'You have planted a
seed.' This was my third public appearance at the world renowned
Victoria and Albert Museum and I regarded it as no less memorable
than the first two.

Irma's illness and death had led to more frequent calls and
correspondence between myself and Ronnie. Before the end of
2012, I flew to New Zealand to be with him, Melissa, Georgia,
Joshua, Moira and David and the rest of the Slater family. I arrived
in Auckland on the last day of the year and had 24 glorious days
of sunshine. Generally it was quality time spent with my son and
grandchildren Georgia and Josh who had grown very tall for their
ages: sixteen and fourteen, respectively.

For both my son and myself, this was a timely, crucial visit. I met
many of his closest friends and their families at his lovely beach
house on the Coromandel. Unfortunately, this very pleasant time of
catching up with the Slaters was interrupted when Melissa's father
David suffered a heart attack and was rushed to hospital where he
had emergency surgery. Fortunately, he was in good spirits and on
the mend during my last days in Auckland. All things considered,
I returned to England chastened by the experience, but the better
for having made this very important journey.

A few months later, although David had recovered reasonably
quickly from his operation, his wife Moira, who had been in very
poor health for some time, sadly passed away. In my 'Thoughts'
on Moira, which was read out by Ronnie at her funeral, I expressed
my great respect and appreciation for her as a *Very Special* human
being. Moira's death was an added blow for the Slater family,
Ronnie and myself. These were trying times.

Irma's passing, however, had an interesting outcome. As the De
Freitas family rallied round, having not seen her brother Reynold
and his family: wife Pat, Kim, Ann and Janet for almost thirty
years, on their Fiftieth Wedding Anniversary Dinner, Reynold and
Pat kindly, generously invited me to be their Guest of Honour.
This was an opportunity for me to be reacquainted with the family,
including Mike (Kim's husband), John (Ann's husband), as well as

my first meeting with Andy, (Janet's husband) and their children. It was a wonderful coming together.

After congratulating Reynold and Pat and saying a few heartfelt words, one of the things that I presented to them that evening was a framed photograph of Reynold and Irma on the day of my wedding outside the Church in Islington.

News of Irma's demise had also led to contact being made with her sister Veda, husband Charles Huggins and their daughter Sheila.

So in death, Irma had not only brought about a reunion and celebration, but also a reconnection with members of the wider family.

THE HOUSE OF LORDS, AGAIN!

A few weeks after attending the 'All Party Parliamentary Group' AGM in the House of Lords, I was invited back for a meeting with Baroness Benjamin. The purpose was to discuss the possibility of a television film in relation to my novel *The Griot's Tale*. Unlike my previous visit, I arrived much earlier and was even more impressed than before to be in this huge and grand building, the honourable seat of the 'Mother of Parliaments'. At once, I could not help relating its significance to that time when as a barefoot, scantily-clad boy in Trinidad, I'd seen the iconic pictures at school and had heard Pa and his learned friends in the gallery speaking about West Indian political leaders going to London to attend 'Constitutional Talks' in deference to the 'Westminster model' of Government. Being in Westminster Hall and the Palace of Westminster for the second time in eighteen months, Pa's house and the other wooden habitations on the Sand Road and elsewhere in Trinidad seemed so very small. More consciously now I realised my presence here was not as a 'Black MP' (as trade unionist John Sheldon had once suggested) but as a direct result of decades of hard work, an evolving quest and philosophy of venturing to the highest reaches; an ambition, arising from my humbling experiences, hard-won education, unbounded imagination and crucially, my respect for the power of the written word. In short, it was my unwavering literary odyssey that had, in essence brought me to this Palace.

As Historian, my books are full of references to Parliament and its highly-gifted Orators, whose words and decisions: namely the imposition and enactment of laws had profoundly affected millions of people's lives, nationally and globally. Having climbed the steps at the end of Westminster Hall I was no less fascinated by the magnificence of the place than before; and walking further towards the lobby, occasionally I stopped to take a closer look at the images of famous names: Peel, Pitt, Fox, Wilberforce, Gladstone, Disraeli, Palmerston, Brougham, Castlereagh and Lord John Russell. Transported by my historical sense and understanding of some of the momentous things that these characters had said and done in Parliament, I stood as if spellbound. Then, as I sat on a seat watching MPs and others hurrying between the House of Commons and the House of Lords, thoughts of the journeys of my Indian grandfather and my own, played on my mind. Suddenly history was not in the past, but in the present. My thoughts were on the double migrations of Ratnam and myself which, through a tortuous path, had led me to sit in astonishment before William Gladstone's imposing statue. Ironically it was this Prime Minister's father John Gladstone who, as owner of sugar plantations in British Guiana, had first introduced indentured Indians to labour in the Caribbean. Now, amidst the toing and froing of important men and women, it crossed my mind: what is a descendant of the indentured 'helots of the Empire,' a perceived 'Coolie' from The Sand Road doing here? Not bothering to answer myself, I was quickly on my feet and striding no less purposefully than anyone elsein the lobby to the place of my meeting.

When I met Baroness Benjamin, she and her husband kindly invited me to take tea with them in the House of Lords 'Tea Room,' where we discussed the matters in hand. Before our meeting, the Baroness had pointed out various historical paintings relating to both Houses. Afterwards she guided me into the Debating Chamber of the House of Lords where I sat for about fifteen minutes listening to various speakers during a 'Boundaries Commission' debate. On both sides of the House, there were the familiar faces of politicians. Amidst talk about 'Boundaries,' I thought of my own life of crossing boundaries. Then, as I listened some more, I recalled reading Hansard and imagined Lord Eccles in 1972 speaking on behalf of The British Library Bill, hoping very much that it would pass and become The British Library Act. How extraordinary, I thought, that 41 years later, after I'd been elected and had served as the first British Library Staff Side Secretary, I should now be sitting in this very House!

When I parted company with the Baroness at the top of the stairs, once more, I walked through Westminster Hall where President Obama had addressed both Houses of Parliament on an earlier visit to Britain.

On leaving the corridors of power, I crossed Westminster Bridge Road and headed towards the Underground Station on my way home. *'England is a pleasant place for them that's rich and high, but England is a cruel place for such poor folk as I.'* Pa's words following my decision to come to England, came to me with renewed power. He had died a few weeks before my first Westminster Palace visit; now I wondered what he might have said if he'd known of my participation on the 'Parliamentary Committee' and presence in the House of Lords. Coupled with this thought, I was mindful of Euripides's words: *'You have sailed with a furious soul far from your father's house, beyond the double rocks of the sea, and you live in a foreign land.'* With another Parlimentary AGM to come, there was no doubt about the distance, both physical and intellectual that I'd travelled: from what was the little ramshacle dwelling on the Sand Road to meetings in the House of Lords. Still driven, considering the journey that lay ahead, as I walked further away from the awesome splendour of the Palace of Westminster, more than ever, I was mindful of the unfathomable global reach of its historical and contemporary governance.

In the last years of his life, though Pa loved poetry and reciting, he was clearly not a bookish bloke. Indeed, with time, his words and behaviour had become increasingly erratic and contradictory. Nonetheless in spite of his 'Commonsense before book' comment, he was impressed by President Robinson's attendance at my Book Launch at the Hilton Hotel; and after I'd published my second novel, he'd said: 'You will win the Nobel Prize one day.' If at the time, I had given this prediction little attention, now I reconsider those words all the more. Why? Because he was not given to such extravagance of appreciation for his own children's achievements.

In relation to us his children, following Pa's death, I took a break and travelled to Canada for a much-valued reunion with my brothers Kenrick, Joel and David, as well enjoying the welcoming warmth of Benigma. And having not seen Sandy for a very long while, it was a real joy spending some time in her company. We were all older and thanks to the hospitality and generosity of Joel, Benigma and Kenrick, it was as good a time as I could have expected. I also enjoyed the company of Joe and Freida.

On my return to England, I visited my friends Ian and Pat for Ian's surprise Sixtieth Birthday Party. The next morning, Ian suggested that I accompany him to the adjoining country house, where he guided me to the desk of the celebrated poet Lord Alfred Tennyson. I was stunned. As a lover of literature, sitting at that desk was a marvellous moment: Did Tennyson really write *In Memorium* and *The Charge of the Light Brigade* there? I questioned.

Thoughts of Ma, Pa and Lydia's deaths resurfaced on hearing that my brother Jimmy was terminally ill. When his troubled life ended, I travelled to Trinidad for the funeral. After delivering the Eulogy, while standing outside the Church in Marabella, my preoccupation with **time** was powerfully foregrounded: I recalled all the Eulogies that I'd given; and now with the open casket before me, I watched as family members (including Jimmy's wife Patsy and daughters Victoria and Nancy) placed fresh red roses on his remains. Then, as the Undertakers closed the casket, I was overwhelmed by this thought: *If our destiny is death, what is the destiny of death?* This life-affirming question had its genesis some months before while I was writing at my regular desk, Seat 60, in the British Library's Rare Books Reading Room.

Having had the honour of working in three of the world's greatest libraries, what wonderful things I've learned about the world of books and literature. Indeed I am reminded of Folio Society editor Sue Bradbury's closing remarks during a lecture on books and their importance in the multimedia age in relation to libraries and words: 'I have touched on only some of the many ways in which the book has shown itself to be a great deal more than we give it credit. If I had to put this in a single sentence I would say that the difference between the book and the rest of the media was the difference between a love affair and an orgy…we all know that it's the love affair that counts. That's why libraries are so seductive.'

Looking back, from the libraries that I'd known, intertwined with my daily activities of undeviating research and writings spread over fifty questing, tempestuous years, I have produced an unrivalled body of literature that has crossed boundaries.

POSTSCRIPT

Having cheated death at the age of two, increasingly throughout my life, ever conscious of time, I have been deeply concerned with two main themes: 'Home and Belonging' and 'respect for difference.' As I live each day, the essential over-arching themes of Home and Belonging in Britain are no less significant than they had been in decades past. Why? Because historically everyone here has had an ancestor who was not indigenous to the place to which they had come. In other words, the forebears of today's British citizens (and those past) have all stepped on these shores as immigrants. Those who came and settled can be traced back for centuries. Thus Home and Belonging are integral to citizenship and the questions of Being and Beingness are fundamental to Where and What is home?

Twinned with this search for 'Home' on my journey through life is the second and related theme arising from the question Who am I? in relation to the essential value and importance of difference and how we humans organise and have our being and Beingness in societies and communities. As social beings, social relations are, of course, vital. Historically, many social systems have been tried, including Capitalism, Socialism and other isms; and most notably philosophers of great renown have not been silent regarding their views on social relations: the social compact (or Contract). How should society be structured? How should it function? And for whose benefit? Plato, Aristotle and Nietsche have written in defence of slavery. Plato has expounded on 'Philosopher Kings' and their right to Rule over all, while Nietsche declared that 'Every culture needs an exploitable working class, a "slave class." ' He adds: 'There is nothing more dreadful than a barbaric slave class that has learned to regard its existence as an injustice and sets about taking revenge not only for itself but for all generations.' These philosophers were against social mobility of the classes (the masses) which, in effect, meant slavery. While I strongly disagree with the views of Plato, Aristotle and Nietsche on slavery and oppression, others like Karl

Marx have made forthright statements about 'freedom' and 'human rights' in the social system that he had advocated. But as all these 'systems' show, the aggregations of the various 'isms' (ideologies) and consequent groupings, have had an innate totalising effect which stymies, instead of allowing freedom. This tends to diminish and enslave individuals.

Democratic rights, as I see it, can therefore be *meaningful* only when *each person* in society is allowed to exercise his or her 'human right' in accord with an *inclusive* social system. The aggregations of race, colour, gender and religion are therefore basically problematic. Why? Because they inhibit people rather than help to free them: For example, people of one 'race,' 'colour' or 'gender' (or any other aggregation) do not always agree (why should they?) and should therefore be free of being *stereotyped*, thus enabling expression of the multiplicity of views within their social ambit.

Difference, I believe (as I've said) is the DNA of social relations; an idea that has preoccupied me all my life and which I have, in different ways, applied to my writings. Through its exploration I have developed an ever-deepening social sense, arising from my 'individuality' (in conjunction with society) that has evolved through a long process of self-discovery. This atomic realisation helped me to become increasingly inventive which, in turn, has led to certain creations: for example, the putting in place of literature that hitherto did not exist. If in the late Seventies, I was described by some as a 'pioneer,' today my oeuvre, spans six genres: history, novels, biography, travel, a play and autobiography. This literary output, forged amidst austerity, had been enriched by great ambition.

As I have argued, ***respect for difference*** is the key to unlocking the door to real social progress. Without it, 'freedom' and 'human rights' are meaningless. All the more so, because as the Griot declares in *The Griot's Tale*, ultimately, LOVE is denied and devalued without respect for difference and thus for the Other! 'Agreements' and everything else taken on trust between human beings, either as individuals or between groups and communities, cannot be one-offs. Such 'agreements' must be reviewed, revised and renegotiated **regularly** if they are to be meaningful.

Citizenship and belonging would continue to be valueless social and political slogans unless we acknowledge and practice respect for difference.

Though a lover of the theatre, I never did become a professional actor; but when my Drama Teacher had warned that there were few parts for Black actors, I vowed to *write* my own words. In the maelstrom that is the drama of human affairs, through the Comedies and Tragedies, the highs and prolonged lows experienced thus far, I have gained a greater understanding of human behaviour. Intolerant of injustice, and passionately concerned to see fair-play, as a former 'Bloomsbury radical,' I continue to take every opportunity to participate in debates relating to local, national and international affairs. Through this engagement, my awareness of the contradictoriness, as well as the connectedness of things, has deepened, especially now when there is so little compassion as the gap between the Haves and Have-Nots widens alarmingly in Britain and elsewhere in the world.

As I write, it is Remembrance Sunday. After several wet, cold, dull and miserable mornings, the sunshine has broken through while thousands of people gather at the Cenotaph in London to remember the fallen not only in the First and Second World Wars, but also those of recent conflicts in Iraq and Afghanistan. Watching the Cenotaph Commemoration on television, in the silences of Remembrance, I was drawn towards the collective meditation, lest we forget, on the horrors of those bloody acts of man's inhumanity to man. And in the continuing ferment of conflict in Palestine (indeed war-talk and simultaneous violence in the Middle and Far East, Eastern Europe, Africa and elsewhere) the insistent quest for peace on earth remains elusive, but it must never become a hopeless cause!

Through the decades of flux and the world's turmoil, this book has emerged, inextricably linked with great upheavals, reflected in the evolving genres and presentations of my writings. Indeed it was the boyhood desire to learn, observe and importantly to write that had held me spellbound. On this journey, I have never deviated. Why? Because WRITING is at the core of what has been empowering and indispensable in the story of Humankind. Without WRITING, the accumulation of knowledge, civilization and space exploration would have been impossible. Thus, as a consequence of writing, science and technology have developed. WRITING is the DNA of civilization, the means through which we have communicated, understood and passed on knowledge. Indeed through language we have developed and freed our imagination. Thus my passion, through the quest of writing, has always been to go further. And if, as I believe, art is a symbolization of the experience of being, then this Self-Portrait has been an act of creation and re-creation; a continuous bringing into being.

Having survived so many dramatic years, during which I have played many parts, ever hopeful of a better tomorrow, from the margins of possibility in the no man's land of creativity, I improvise, challenged by ideas and artforms, notably the art of literature through symbols and the use of language. From the outset of my literary odyssey, I have been fascinated by, and respectful of, the power and *democratic essence* of words that fill blank spaces with light, shadow and nuanced meanings, infusing colour and vibrancy to character and circumstance; words that, in turn, become sentences, paragraphs and pages as I compose the next chapter of my homecoming...

ACKNOWLEDGEMENTS

First of all I am grateful to my son Ronnie; and to my brothers Kenrick, Joel, David, sister Annette and 'sister' Carlo.

My thanks to David Skilton, Ariella Atzmon, Chris Hughes, Sue Bradbury, Zac Macaulay, Marisa, Margarita and Nacho, Elizabeth Mor, Richard Cullern, David Blake, Michael Woods, Rey Bowen, Paul Rowe, Nigel Cawthorne, Gillian Brown, Julia Warrener, Jamie Parr and Phillip Sargeant. John Fothergill had kindly volunteered and read part of a draft of the book for which I am thankful. Over the years, as an employee and reader, I have had the privilege and honour of accessing the unrivalled and invaluable archives and collections in the British Library. I am especially thankful to Archivist Lyn Young and the many other members of British Library staff, both past and present, who have always been willing to help.

Ron Ramdin,
The British Library,
St Pancras, London,
15 February 2015